Frommer's®

Nicaragua &
El Salvador

2nd Edition

by Charlie O'Malley

WILEY

John Wiley & Sons, Inc.

PUBLISHED BY:

JOHN WILEY & SONS CANADA, LTD.

6045 Freemont Blvd.
Mississauga, ON L5R 4J3

ISBN 978-1-118-07333-9 (paper); ISBN 978-1-118-09470-9 (ePub); ISBN 978-1-118-09468-6 (eMobi); ISBN 978-1-118-09469-3 (ePDF)

Editor: Gene Shannon
Developmental Editor: Melissa Klurman
Production Editor: Lindsay Humphreys
Editorial Assistants: Katie Wolsley & Jeremy Hanson-Finger
Project Coordinator: Kristie Rees
Cartographer: Lohnes + Wright
Production by Wiley Indianapolis Composition Services

Front Cover Photo: Children playing at Lake Nicaragua, Concepcion Volcano. ©SIME / eStock
Back Cover Photo: Tourists at large waterfall on Ruta de las Siete Cascadas, El Salvador. ©Paul Kennedy / Lonely Planet Images

For reseller information, including discounts and premium sales, please call our sales department: Tel. 416-646-7992. For press review copies, author interviews, or other publicity information, please contact our publicity department: Tel. 416-646-4582; Fax: 416-236-4448.

Wiley also publishes its books in a variety of electronic formats. Some content that appears in print may not be available in electronic formats.

Manufactured in the United States

1 2 3 4 5 RRD 16 15 14 13 12

CONTENTS

LIST OF MAPS

ABOUT THE AUTHOR

Charlie O'Malley first became fascinated with Latin America when he watched salsa dancers on a Colombian beach over a decade ago. He has since wrestled with anaconda in Venezuela, rescued turtles in Nicaragua, and been chased by bulls in Ecuador. Based in the Andean Argentine city of Mendoza, he keeps his desire for more adventure in check with lots of good local wine and work on a tourist magazine called *Wine Republic*. With driving skills almost as bad as the locals and an undying penchant for long siestas, he does not think he can ever possibly live in his native Ireland again. He has worked on Frommer's guides to Argentina and South America and contributed to *Frommer's 500 Adventures for Adrenaline Lovers*.

ACKNOWLEDGMENTS

The list of helpful and accommodating people I met along the way is too long to chronicle. Thanks to everyone, but in particular Garry and Deirdre Lesesne, Mark McKnight, Jim Peterson, Larry Johnson, Peter Curtin, Silvia Lorena Villafuerte, Robert Broz and Pascal Lebailly. A big thanks to my editors Gene Shannon and Melissa Klurman for their encouragement and patience and to my fellow Frommer's writer Patrick Gilsenan. A special thanks goes to my wife Ana and son Finbarr.

HOW TO CONTACT US

In researching this book, we discovered many wonderful places—hotels, restaurants, shops, and more. We're sure you'll find others. Please tell us about them, so we can share the information with your fellow travelers in upcoming editions. If you were disappointed with a recommendation, we'd love to know that, too. Please write to:

Frommer's Nicaragua & El Salvador, 2nd Edition
John Wiley & Sons Canada, Ltd. • 6045 Freemont Blvd. • Mississauga, ON L5R 4J3

ADVISORY & DISCLAIMER

The inclusion of a company, organization or Website in this guide as a service provider and/or potential source of further information does not mean that we endorse them or the information they provide. Be aware that information provided through some Websites may be unreliable and can change without notice. Neither the publisher or author shall be liable for any damages arising herefrom.

FROMMER'S STAR RATINGS, ICONS & ABBREVIATIONS

Every hotel, restaurant, and attraction listing in this guide has been ranked for quality, value, service, amenities, and special features using a **star-rating system.** In country, state, and regional guides, we also rate towns and regions to help you narrow down your choices and budget your time accordingly. Hotels and restaurants are rated on a scale of zero (recommended) to three stars (exceptional). Attractions, shopping, nightlife, towns, and regions are rated according to the following scale: zero stars (recommended), one star (highly recommended), two stars (very highly recommended), and three stars (must-see).

In addition to the star-rating system, we also use **seven feature icons** that point you to the great deals, in-the-know advice, and unique experiences that separate travelers from tourists. Throughout the book, look for:

🎁   Special finds—those places only insiders know about

💬   Fun facts—details that make travelers more informed and their trips more fun

😊   Best bets for kids and advice for the whole family

📷   Special moments—those experiences that memories are made of

✋   Places or experiences not worth your time or money

✎   Insider tips—great ways to save time and money

🏷   Great values—where to get the best deals

The following **abbreviations** are used for credit cards:

AE	American Express	**DISC**	Discover	**V**	Visa
DC	Diners Club	**MC**	MasterCard		

TRAVEL RESOURCES AT FROMMERS.COM

Frommer's travel resources don't end with this guide. **Frommers.com** has travel information on more than 4,000 destinations. We update features regularly, giving you access to the most current trip-planning information and the best airfare, lodging, and car-rental bargains. You can also listen to podcasts, connect with other Frommers.com members through our active-reader forums, share your travel photos, read blogs from guidebook editors and fellow travelers, and much more.

THE BEST OF NICARAGUA & EL SALVADOR

N icaragua and El Salvador are still being discovered. Intrepid visitors are retracing the steps of conquistadors and pirates, finding modern day treasure in the form of golden sunsets, silver beaches, and skilled handicrafts.

Whatever you're looking for, Nicaragua and El Salvador have it all—bustling cities and isolated villages, luxury hotels and rustic ecolodges, dense rainforest and wide-open beaches. You can swing from a hammock or zip over a forest, sail around islands, or surf down a volcano. Below are some of my favorite discoveries, just to get you started.

THE best TRAVEL EXPERIENCES

o **Diving in the Corn Islands** (Nicaragua): Spotted tiger rays, blacktip sharks, stingrays, spider crabs, parrot fish, angel fish, barracuda, and triggerfish; they are all out there in the pristine waters, waiting for you to drop in and say hello. The Corn Islands have all the glorious turquoise waters and coral reefs you associate with the Caribbean, but without the crowds. Better still, you don't need an oxygen tank on your back, as the luminous, shallow bays are perfect for snorkeling. See chapter 11.

o **Exploring Isla de Ometepe** (Nicaragua): Catch the boat across to the serene twin peaks of the Concepción and Maderas volcanoes that rise out of Lago de Nicaragua, forming a muddy jungle island. Fireflies dance beneath banana trees as people on old buses, bikes, horses, and even oxen negotiate the rutted roads and countless trails. Rocks carved into zoomorphic figures and pre-Columbian petroglyphs dot the landscape of tropical forest and patchwork fields. Volcán Concepción is still very much alive, hurling rocks and spewing lava four times in the last century. The island is an idyllic adventure spot, a rural retreat, and a hiker's paradise. See chapter 9.

o **Sailing Down the Río San Juan** (Nicaragua): Float down a broad, majestic expanse of fresh water that pours slowly out of Lake Nicaragua towards the Atlantic Ocean 210km (130 miles) away. It passes rainforests and cattle ranches, stilted shacks on the water, quiet river lodges, treacherous rapids, and a 300-year-old Spanish fort called El Castillo. The shoreline teems with wildlife, especially at the mammoth Indo-Maíz Biological Reserve on the Nicaraguan side. See chapter 10.

o **Touring Coffee Farms** (Northern Nicaragua): See the "golden grain" processing facilities of historic plantations set amidst the verdant slopes of Matagalpa. Fincas such as Esperanza Verde and Selva Negra have some lovely trails to hike and wildlife to spy upon, as well as some excellent accommodations. See chapter 12.

o **Exploring the Winding Mountain Roads and Villages of the Ruta de las Flores** (El Salvador): If you're tight on time, this 35km (22-mile) route is an excellent sampling of what El Salvador has to offer. The route is known primarily for its small towns, each offering something different, from the furniture craftsmen of Nahuizalco, to Juayua's weekend food and craft festival, to the artsy vibe and cool restaurants of Ataco. The route also offers amazing views of thousands of flowering coffee plants and one of the country's highest and longest zip-line canopy tours. See chapter 19.

o **Seeing Suchitoto** (El Salvador): This is one of El Salvador's most beautiful and unique towns and is well worth the easy, 1-hour drive north of San Salvador. After a turbulent history during El Salvador's civil war, Suchitoto has reemerged as one of El Salvador's leading international arts and cultural centers, with the country's most luxurious boutique hotels and a famous international arts festival. But despite its international flair, Suchitoto is still very much a distinctly El Salvadoran town, close to the historic town of Cinquera, home to a weekend artisans market, and surrounded by amazing mountain views. See chapter 16.

o **Visiting Volcán Masaya** (Masaya, Nicaragua): The Spanish called this volcano the "Gates of Hell," and you can understand why when you see its boulder-spitting craters and glowing red lava fields. Volcán Masaya is easily one of the most accessible and scariest live volcanoes in the region—it's also one of the most exciting to see up close. Also worth a climb or look are Volcán Maderas and Volcán Concepción. See chapter 7.

o **Turtle-Watching in San Juan del Sur** (San Juan del Sur, Nicaragua): After a spot of sun worshiping on Nicaragua's beaches, come out at night and see one of nature's true wonders—massive turtle hatchings on the very beautiful Playa La Flor. The best time to see turtles nesting is August and September. See chapter 9.

THE best SMALL TOWNS & VILLAGES

o **Catarina,** Nicaragua: The Pueblos Blancos are a string of hilltop villages south of Managua, each specializing in a particular art or craft. Catarina has a spectacular lookout point on the rim of Laguna de Apoyo Crater Lake, with Granada and Masaya at your feet and the twin peaks of Ometepe Island in the distance on Lago de Nicaragua. The town itself is famous for its carved, wooden furniture, bamboo products, basket making, and lush, tropical nurseries. See chapter 7.

o **Alegría,** El Salvador: This lush garden town is surrounded by misty green hills 1,200m (3,937 ft.) above sea level. High up in coffee country, it offers some of the best views in the nation, as well as great hiking trails and a friendly, vibrant community. See chapter 17.

- **Perquín & Mozote,** El Salvador: Exploring the history and tragedy of the towns of Perquín and Mozote should provide unique insight into the troubled history of this complex nation. Perquín is a small town tucked into the high eastern mountains, which formed the base of the people's FMLN organization during the civil war. The nearby village of Mozote was the site of one of Latin America's worst modern wartime atrocities; the square and church now feature the well-known Mozote memorial and the names of the townspeople who were killed. See chapter 17.
- **Ataco,** El Salvador: Whimsical murals set the tone for a town that boasts an artistic style and vibe you won't find elsewhere in the country. Ataco is an unmissable stop while exploring the hilltop villages of the Ruta de las Flores in western El Salvador. See chapter 19.
- **San Juan del Sur,** Nicaragua: This small, colorful fishing village of clapboard houses is slowly morphing into a party town with excellent hotels and restaurants. It sits amid a string of great beaches offering surfing, fishing, sailing, or just glorious idling. See chapter 9.

THE best BEACHES

- **Playa Madera,** Nicaragua: A lovely, dark beach with big waves and some good snorkeling opportunities is 30 minutes north of the seaside town of San Juan del Sur. Popular with surfers and sunset watchers alike, this breezy stretch of sand has some excellent accommodations close by. See chapter 9.
- **Barra de Santiago,** El Salvador: Santiago is a protected reserve and largely undeveloped fishing village along the country's far western coast. The best thing about the place is its isolation and natural beauty; it's surrounded by wide, nearly deserted, sandy beaches and mangrove-filled estuaries where majestic white egrets glide low over the water. And the entire place sits immediately in front of a miles-long line of volcanoes that seem to rise from the palm tree–lined estuary shores. You can fish, swim, surf, paddle, spot sea turtles laying their eggs, or just do nothing and enjoy the view. See chapter 18.
- **Picnic Beach,** Nicaragua: This is the perfect beach: a long white strand lapped by gentle turquoise waters on the unspoiled Caribbean Corn Islands. See chapter 11.
- **Playa El Espino,** El Salvador: A wide, gorgeous beach that is splendidly isolated on weekdays and alive with beachgoers on weekends, Playa El Espino is gaining a reputation as one of El Salvador's best places to throw down a towel and enjoy the sun, sea, and sand. See chapter 18.
- **Playa Maculis,** El Salvador: This is one of El Salvador's hidden gems: a very private 1.5km-long (1 mile) crescent-shaped beach that is dotted with a few houses and a lot of trees. At either end, two rocky points jut out into the sea. This protects the waters from the lateral current that can be so dangerous on the El Salvadoran coast. See chapter 18.

THE best OUTDOOR ADVENTURES

- **Surfing down a Volcano** (Nicaragua): Hurtling down the side of a black volcano at 64kmph (37 mph) on a wooden board brings a whole new perspective to surfing in Nicaragua. The volcano is Cerro Negro, just outside León, in the dusty lowlands northwest of the capital. See chapter #.

o **Trekking in the Parque Nacional Los Volcanes** (El Salvador): Climb the "Lighthouse of the Pacific," a nearly perfect cone known as Volcán de Izalco. It is the park's most visually dramatic volcano and challenging climb, requiring a nearly 3-hour scramble up a steep, rocky, and barren moonscape to the 1,952m (6,404-ft.) summit. Izaco is also one of Central America's youngest volcanoes—it formed in 1770 and erupted almost continuously until 1966. See chapter 20.

o **Canopy Tours Mombacho** (Nicaragua): A spectacular 17-platform canopy system at Hacienda Cutirre on the eastern face of the Mombacho volcano was actually designed by the inventor of the sport, which means you're in for a heart-stopping ride. See chapter 8.

o **Zip-Lining over a Coffee Farm** (El Salvador): Zip on steel cables hundreds of feet off the ground, over lush forests and coffee plantations near the town of Apaneca, on the Ruta de las Flores circuit in El Salvador. Thousands of white coffee flowers cover the fields below, and you can see all the way to Guatemala's active Volcán Pacaya. Conclude the adventure with a steaming cup of locally grown brew. See chapter 19.

o **Hiking & Swimming in Parque Nacional El Imposible** (El Salvador): Parque El Imposible is one of El Salvador's largest, most lush, and richest-in-wildlife national parks, and it's dotted with streams, waterfalls, and natural swimming holes that are perfect for swimming. Tacuba, the small town just outside the park, serves as a great base camp for hiking trips. See chapter 19.

o **Bird-Watching in the Bahía de Jiquilisco** (El Salvador): In between Isla de Montecristo and the beaches to its east is the huge island Bahía de Jiquilisco. Its largely undeveloped inlet offers untouched natural beauty, with dozens of mangrove-lined channels to paddle, islands to explore, great views, and beautiful ocean and bay beaches. The bay is also a major stop for 87 types of migratory birds and a nesting ground for sea turtles. It remains one of El Salvador's most untouched and naturally beautiful areas. See chapter 18.

o **Kayaking Around Isla Juan Venado** (Nicaragua): Pelicans and herons step over crocodiles, iguanas, and caimans as you paddle through a labyrinth of channels and waterways in this protected mangrove swamp on the Pacific coast close to León. See chapter 13.

o **Hiking through Miraflor Nature Reserve** (Nicaragua): Miraflor is a slice of Eden in the northern highlands of Nicaragua. Orchids bloom amid begonias and moss-draped oak trees, while toucans and parakeets hide among the foliage. Hike La Chorrera trail as far as a 60m-high (197-ft.) waterfall, going past ancient caves and prehistoric mounds. See chapter 12.

o **Surfing the Balsamo Coast** (El Salvador): Bodysurfers bob in the water waiting for their turn to ride the waves. The Balsamo Coast is a stretch of bays and inlets famous for its surf. Tourists and El Salvadorans alike flock here on weekends to enjoy the waves, black-sand beaches, laid-back vibe, tasty seafood restaurants, and new and unique hotels. See chapter 18.

THE best HISTORICAL SITES

o **Coyotepe Fort** (Masaya, Nicaragua): Whitewashed battlements and squat, yellow-domed towers overlook Masaya town and lake, and afford a pleasant visit that belies this structure's dark history of revolution and resistance. See p. 94.

- **Archipiélago Zapatera** (Lake Nicaragua): Famous for its pre-Columbian stone carvings, this archipelago off the coast of Granada boasts lots of wildlife, a crater lake, and more than 20 archaeological sites that date back as far as 500 B.C. The vast range of zoomorphic statues reveals that the islands were once important religious sites. Isla el Muerto, in particular, has some of the most spectacular rock drawings in the country, all laid out on a huge slab of stone measuring 100×25m (328×82 ft.) on the island's summit. See p. 122.
- **Joya de Cerén** (outside of San Salvador, El Salvador): Joya de Cerén isn't El Salvador's most visually stunning ruin, but it offers one of Central America's most accurate glimpses into the lives of the region's Maya ancestors in the form of the remains of a Maya village, frozen in time 1,400 years ago when the village was buried beneath the ash of a violent volcanic eruption. Still standing and preserved are the local shaman's house, a community sauna, and private sleeping rooms. See p. 252.
- **Huellas de Acahualinca** (Managua, Nicaragua): Six thousand–year-old footprints of men, women, and children beg the question: Were they fleeing a volcanic eruption or just going for a swim? One thing is for sure, the footprints on display here are some of the oldest pieces of evidence of human activity in Central America. This intriguing site can be visited in a northern suburb of Managua. See p. 84.
- **León** (Nicaragua): This cradle of the revolution has been bombed, besieged, and washed away by hurricanes. Every street corner tells a story, and it's highly recommended that you take a city tour of this fascinating university town with its vibrant murals, tiny plazas, and the biggest cathedral in Central America. Nearby is León Viejo, the original, abandoned colonial city at the feet of its destroyer—Volcán Momotombo. See p. 201.
- **El Castillo** (Río San Juan, Nicaragua): The dark-stained stone remains of the Spanish fort are relics of just how important the San Juan River was. Built to deter marauding pirates bent on raiding prosperous Granada, El Castillo had 32 cannons and a well-stocked armory of 11,000 weapons. Cannon balls and old rum bottles add color to the story. See p. 162.
- **Tazumal** (Santa Ana, El Salvador): El Salvador's most visually interesting and fully excavated set of Maya ruins has a temple pyramid, ball court, and other structures considered to be classic examples of Maya architecture. Though it's much smaller than better-known ruins in Guatemala or Honduras, Tazumal's exemplary Maya architecture makes it worth the drive. See p. 328.

THE best MUSEUMS & CHURCHES

- **León Cathedral** (León, Nicaragua): The biggest church in Central America is a must-see when visiting the historical university city of León. The cathedral is home to some masterpieces of Spanish colonial art, and a statue of a black Christ still bears the hack wounds of a pirate's sword. Here, you'll find the Tomb of Rubén Darío, guarded by a weeping lion. At the cathedral's center is a beautiful, Spanish-style courtyard known as the Patio de Príncipes. The cathedral's domed roof holds the bell La Libertad that announced to the world the independence of Central America, and its Gothic roof is a terrace of lichen-stained cupolas and buttresses with a commanding view of the surrounding city and countryside. See p. 202.

o **Centro de Arte Fundación Ortiz-Gurdián** (León, Nicaragua): This extensive gallery has easily the best art collection in Nicaragua. Two beautifully restored town houses hold a dazzling selection of paintings and sculptures ranging from 16th-century Cuzco School portraits to modern Nicaraguan installations. You'll also find some out-of-place surprises such as works by Rembrandt, Picasso, and Miro. See p. 205.

o **Granada Cathedral** (Granada, Nicaragua): The luminous, ochre-colored facade of this simple church dominates the skyline of this beautiful colonial city, setting the tone for an enchanting stay in what is undoubtedly Nicaragua's most beautiful town. See p. 107.

o **Military Museum** (San Salvador, El Salvador): The museum is home to an astounding, giant relief map of the entire country that conveys just what a strange, vertical, volcanic land you're visiting. Black-topped volcanoes tower over a blue, topographical coastline, all right at your toes in an open-air setting. See p. 250.

o **Museo de Arte** (San Salvador, El Salvador): This museum of rotating and permanent exhibits offers visitors an insightful, visual glimpse into the character of the country. Exceptionally interesting is the art of the country's civil war period. The museum also features the famous towering stone mosaic "Monument to the Revolution," which depicts a naked man whose outstretched arms are thought to symbolize freedom and liberty. See p. 251.

o **Museo de la Revolución Salvadoreña** (Perquín, El Salvador): Rocket launchers, large chunks of a downed army helicopter, and the preserved studio of revolutionary Radio Venceremos are just some of the displays that bring to life the tumultuous events of the 1980s in the revolutionary stronghold of Perquín in the northeastern hills of El Salvador. See p. 279.

o **Museo Nacional** (Managua, Nicaragua): Located in the deserted and dilapidated city center, the Museo Nacional is a hidden gem with high colonial features, a giant courtyard, and an inner gallery. Besides the usual pre-Colombian collections of flint and ceramic urns, there are some very enlightening display boards with a wealth of information about Nicaraguan food, drink, folklore, and music. See p. 83.

o **Antiguo Convento San Francisco** (Granada, Nicaragua): Though the Antiguo Convento San Francisco has a remarkable collection of pre-Columbian statues, it's not the only attraction in this beautiful city. One great way to see all the sites, including the Antiguo Convento, is to take a horse-and-carriage ride through Granada's charming cobbled streets. See p. 107.

o **El Teatro Nacional de Santa Ana** (Santa Ana, El Salvador): This stately 1910 theater features a grand exterior balcony; an ornate, old-world lobby; and a three-story theater, complete with elaborate molding, sweeping staircases, and ceiling portraits of long-dead artists. It now hosts performances and exhibits year-round. See p. 326.

o **Museo Nacional de Antropología Dr. David J. Guzman** (San Salvador, El Salvador): The ancient tools, weapons, pottery, and ceramic artifacts on exhibit here offer an intriguing glimpse into the lives of El Salvador's indigenous communities and explain the evolution of agriculture and early trade in the country. See p. 248.

o **Iglesia El Rosario** (San Salvador, El Salvador): El Rosario's concrete, half-moon, bunker-like appearance is a bit bizarre and un-churchlike from the outside, but inside, visitors are greeted by colored light streaming in from abstract stained glass running up the height of its two curved walls. Abstract metalworks form the altar and run the length of a third wall. This is one of the most visually interesting churches in El Salvador. See p. 250.

o **Tin Marín Museo de los Niños** (San Salvador, El Salvador): At this children's museum that's fun for the whole family, kids can fantasize about being a pilot in the cockpit of a Boeing 727 or lose their bearings in a crooked house known as the *Casa de Graveded* (Gravity House). Little ones can also dress up like doctors in a pretend operating room, put on plays in the theater, or walk inside a huge volcano (complete with lava and smoke). See p. 251.

THE best SMALL & MODERATELY PRICED HOTELS

o **Hotel Anáhuac** (Juayua, Ruta de Flores, El Salvador; © 503/2469-2401; www. hotelanahuac.com): This charming little corner house has the casual vibe of a well-run hostel with an upscale, artistic feel. Beautiful pieces of art and murals adorn each room; the overall design feels like a cool boutique hotel. All this and friendly English-speaking owners, a colorful town in the garden setting of El Salvador's countryside, and great value rates, to boot. See p. 309.

o **Hotel Los Piños** (Zona Rosa, Managua; © 505/2270-0761; www.hotelospinos. info): One of the more tasteful and elegant small hotels in Managua has lots of space, light, and beautiful interiors. Inside are large windows, tall ceilings, dark-wood floors, and lovely art, while outside there is a good-size garden with a generous pool, all just a stone's throw from all the action in the Zona Rosa. See p. 76.

o **Hotel Sábalos** (Río San Juan, Nicaragua; © 505/8894-9377; www.hotelsabalos. com.ni): Hotel Sábalos has a beautiful location right over the water, with sweeping views of the river. The low wooden structure of varnished wood has a wraparound veranda, and you can literally fish from the balcony or just watch the locals passing in their impossibly flimsy canoes while fishermen throw nets into the water. See p. 164.

o **Casa Canada** (Corn Islands, Nicaragua; © 505/2644-0925; www.casa-canada. com): This ocean-side paradise is easily the most beautiful and well-appointed hotel on the Caribbean Corn Islands. A row of cottage-style rooms faces a tiled pool and long rock shore of palm trees and small patches of lawn. Rooms are large, with every type of modern amenity, and line a beachfront garden. See p. 175.

o **Casa Iguana** (Little Corn Island, Nicaragua; no phone; www.casaiguana.net): Palm trees line sandy paths, and colorful cabanas sit close to the shoreline at this charming ecoresort. The complex is run in a sustainable manner, with solar- and wind-powered energy, a recycling program, and fruit and vegetables from an on-site garden. Yoga and massage therapies are available, and some fantastic snorkeling reefs are within paddling distance. See p. 179.

o **Los Almendros de San Lorenzo** (Suchitoto, El Salvador; © 503/2335-1200; www.hotelsalvador.com): This six-room Suchitoto hotel is a rare taste of luxury in a rural mountain village. French owner Pascal Lebailly applied his eye for fashion to create an interior design that's magazine-ready, with a gorgeously lit stone pool, glass-enclosed French restaurant, and walls filled with some of El Salvador's best art. You won't find a more romantic or casually elegant hotel in the country. See p. 265.

o **Hotel Los Arcos** (Estelí, Nicaragua © 505/2713-3830; www.familiasunidas.org/
arcos/presentacion.htm): A large mansion-style house just a half-block from the
laid-back plaza is the setting for this modern hotel in the rural town of Estelí. The
hotel is set amidst arched galleries that overlook a gorgeous garden courtyard with
a fountain and palm trees. See p. 187.

o **La Posada Azul** (San Juan del Sur, Nicaragua; © 505/2568-2524; www.laposada
azul.com): This delightful boutique hotel will make you feel like you've stepped
into a García Márquez novel—its old-school charm is that authentic. High ceilings
grace neat wooden interiors and an Old World living room, and a veranda runs the
length of the house to a lovely flower garden with a fountain and small pool. See
p. 134.

o **Santa Leticia Mountain Resort** (Apaneca, El Salvador; © 503/2433-0357;
www.hotelsantaleticia.com): This luxurious hotel is set amidst a 93-hectare (230-
acre) coffee plantation. Spacious, colorful rooms open out onto a charming gallery.
Two solar-powered pools are center stage, while the cozy restaurant boasts all glass
walls and a stone fireplace. You can do a coffee tour of the nearby farm and view
the 2,000-year-old stone sculptures that dot the property. See p. 312.

o **Quinta El Carmen Bed & Breakfast** (Ataco, El Salvador; © 503/2243-0304;
www.elcarmenestate.com): This low, red-brick villa surrounded by lush gardens
has an adjacent coffee farm and a charming restaurant. Large rattan armchairs sit
on a tiled patio that leads to well-appointed rooms with white walls and dark
wooden rafters. See p. 315.

o **Hotel La Joya del Golfo** (Golfo de Fonseca, El Salvador; © 503/2648-0072;
www.hotellajoyadelgolfo.com): A three-story hacienda-style house sits on the
shoreline of a gorgeous bay with postcard-picture islands; fishing villages; and dark,
volcanic beaches. The rooms are large and well appointed, and each has a private
balcony with panoramic views of the lush surroundings. See p. 303.

o **Hotel y Restaurante Tekuaní Kal** (Balsamo Coast, El Salvador; © 503/2389-
6388): Maya-inspired cement sculptures are scattered around this gardenlike
property, which includes a small infinity pool and waterfall, and overlooks the
beach. See p. 290.

THE best LUXURY HOTELS & ECOLODGES

o **Casa II Bongustaio Boutique Hotel** (San Salvador, El Salvador; © 503/2528-
4200; www.casailb.com: San Salvador's most stylish boutique hotel is a chic collection of dazzling white rooms and installation art located in a peaceful
atmosphere a short stroll from the bustling Zona Rosa. See p. 237.

o **Crowne Plaza Hotel Managua** (Managua; © 505/2228-3530; www.ichotels
group.com): Managua's most famous hotel is shaped like a giant white pyramid.
You'll find luxurious rooms with lots of light and color, and spacious bathrooms, as
well as one of the best outdoor pools in the city. See p. 78.

o **Hotel Contempo** (Managua, Nicaragua; © 505/2264-9160; www.contempohb.
com): Managua's first designer, boutique hotel is slick and contemporary, with a
cool, relaxing vibe. Its 18 rooms are elegant, with minimalist interiors that make for
a contrasting, welcome break from the shambles of Nicaragua's capital. See p. 79.

- **La Gran Francia** (Granada, Nicaragua; ℗ **505/2552-6000;** www.lagranfrancia. com): A beautiful, well-located, colonial mansion has been exquisitely restored, down to the original ironwork faucets that hang over hand-painted washbasins displaying old-fashioned street scenes. A handsome inner gallery with Spanish tiles and a mosaic pool give this hotel an aristocratic, palatial vibe. See p. 114.

- **Palermo Hotel and Resort** (San Juan del Sur, Nicaragua; ℗ **505/8672-0859;** www.palermohotelandresort.com): This five-star resort has manicured lawns, handsome villas, and spacious rooms decked out in hardwood furnishings and local art. The clubhouse is an elegant mix of marble floors, modern sofas, and classical-style tables contrasting with its palm-thatched roof outside. Big windows, all-glass doors, and tall ceilings allow for lots of light. See p. 134.

- **Morgan's Rock Hacienda and Eco Lodge** (San Juan del Sur, Nicaragua; ℗ **505/ 8670-7676;** www.morgansrock.com): A cluster of 15 luxury bungalows is accessed by a 100m (328-ft.) suspension bridge over a tropical gorge. Architecturally stunning and with superb attention to detail, this ecolodge has no phones, Internet, or air-conditioning, but who needs them when you have an exquisite infinity pool and a beautiful, deserted beach? The large property also includes a private nature reserve, shrimp farm, and sugar-processing plant that produces its own rum. See p. 137.

- **Two Brothers Surf Resort** (Rivas, Nicaragua; ℗ **505/8877-7501;** www.two brotherssurf.com): The cottages here are set in an 11-hectare (27-acre) private estate. The interior design is sumptuous and eclectic, with artifacts from around the world, such as Indonesian carved doors and mosaics. Gorgeous Spanish-style floor tiles grace stylish rooms with red curtains and wall arches. See p. 144.

- **Río Indio Lodge** (Río San Juan, Nicaragua; ℗ **506/2296-0095;** www.rioindio lodge.com): This lodge provides the ultimate jungle experience, along with all the creature comforts. A suspended walkway links the wooden cottages, and handsome hardwood interiors grace polished ceramic tiles that lead to chunky wooden balconies outside. The hotel offers tour excursions and birding expeditions, and is regarded as one of the best jungle lodges in Central America. See p. 164.

- **Hotel Plaza Colón** (Granada, Nicaragua; ℗ **505/2552-8489;** www.hotelplaza colon.com): This hotel hits just the right balance between exuding colonial authenticity and matching the modern traveler's expectations. A wide, polished balcony overlooks the boisterous plaza, and exquisite tiled floors lead to a majestic inner balcony that runs around a glorious courtyard and blue mosaic pool. Everything is luxurious and elegant, and the service is prompt and reliable. See p. 114.

- **La Perla** (León, Nicaragua; ℗ **505/2311-3125;** www.laperlaleon.com): La Perla sets a new standard for accommodations in Nicaragua, with impeccable rooms and a palatial interior boasting high ceilings, a spectacular central courtyard, and contemporary Nicaraguan art. See p. 208.

- **Suites Las Palmas** (San Salvador, El Salvador; ℗ **503/2250-0800;** www.hotel suiteslaspalmas.com.sv): This hip city hotel is within walking distance of San Salvador's best restaurants and shops and offers big, modern suites with unusual designs. The pool, Jacuzzi, and sleek Asian-fusion restaurant are all set on the rooftop and feature amazing views, as does the exercise room, which includes a wall of glass overlooking the city. See p. 241.

- **La Cocotera** (Barra de Santiago, El Salvador; ℗ **503/2245-3691;** www.lacocotera resort.com): This is one of the finest ecolodges in all of Central America. La Cocotera offers a rare taste of international style in a remote and beautiful part of the country. This six-room, semi–all-inclusive ecoresort features three modern cabins, each with two huge, luxurious rooms and Asian-inspired bathrooms. The hotel property stretches from the bay to the beach, meaning you have water on both sides. La Cocotera features solar-powered hot water and brown-water recycling, and it even incubates turtle eggs. See p. 295.

THE best DINING EXPERIENCES

o **Il Bongustaio** (San Salvador, El Salvador; ℰ **503 2528-4200**; www.casailb.com): Part of the small, luxury hotel of the same name, this Italian restaurant is an alluring combination of top-notch pasta dishes and luxury surroundings. Arty interiors and lush lawns go well with the best tagliatelle in town. See p. 244.

o **Citron** (San Salvador, El Salvador; ℰ **503/2208-4000;** www.restaurantecitron. com): This exciting, gourmet restaurant offers seasonal, local ingredients with an adventurous, international twist. The result is dishes made from wild mushrooms and raspberries grown on volcano slopes combined with fresh seafood in eye-pleasing arrangements that go perfectly with the restaurant's stylish art-studio ambience. See p. 243.

o **Don Candido** (Managua, Nicaragua; ℰ **505/2277-2485;** www.restaurantedon candido.com): Carnivores in Nicaragua don't have to go far to try some of Central America's best beef. Twenty five different cuts are served in huge portions at this very agreeable, modern restaurant with wines from all over the world. See p. 80.

o **El Botón** (Ataco, Ruta de los Flores, El Salvador; ℰ **503/2450-5066**): This whimsical little French restaurant serving quiche and crêpes perfectly complements the colorful charm of Ataco, a small hamlet on the Ruta de Las Flores. See p. 315.

o **Entre Nubes** (Ataco, Ruta de los Flores, El Salvador; ℰ 503/2452-9643): This garden restaurant offers typical Salvadoran fare in a spectacular roadside setting, with coffee plants and flowers draping each nook and cranny, and a small wooded enclave to explore between courses. See p. 313.

o **Santa Lucía Culinary Institute** (Managua; ℰ **505/2276-2651**): Nicaragua's very own celebrity chef, Nelson Porta, runs this excellent restaurant that doubles as a culinary school. Smoked salmon carpaccio, tortilla soup, and lobster cooked in lemon and wine are all served in stylish and modern surroundings See p. 82.

o **Rotonda Bello Horizonte** (Managua, Nicaragua): Do what the locals do and hang out at this busy roundabout, surrounded by late-night fast food restaurants, *fritangas,* and cheap eateries. Baritone mariachis and wandering troubadours serenade you while you munch on pizza, *vigorón* (yucca and cabbage), or *quesillos* (burritos with cheese). See p. 86.

o **Alo Nuestro** (San Salvador, El Salvador; ℰ **503/2223-5116**): San Salvador is packed with excellent restaurants offering cuisines from around the world. But even in that crowded market, Alo Nuestro stands out for its simply delicious food. The frequently changing menu is a fusion of San Salvador's many ethnic restaurants, with an emphasis on local ingredients. The service is top-notch, and the ambience is formal but comfortable. See p. 244.

o **Mocha Nana Cafe** (Estelí, Nicaragua; ℰ **505/2713-3164**): This simple but elegant cafe offers the best coffee from the northern highlands. Handsome wooden seats and dark-stained tables with polished wood and light-filled decor lead to a little patio out back with simple garden. See p. 188.

o **El Colibrí** (San Juan del Sur, Nicaragua; ✆ **505/8863-8612**): Set within a funky clapboard house with a large veranda overlooking a lovely garden, this enchanting restaurant is a piece of art put together from recycled materials. Mosaic-framed mirrors hang between stained-glass lamps and African face masks, while small colored stones hold down your place mats, lest the sea breeze carry them away. The international, mostly organic fare is a work of art, too. See p. 138.

o **La Casita** (Estelí, Nicaragua; ✆ **505/2713-4917**): At this part–farmhouse restaurant and part-coffeehouse, you can enjoy great local coffee, fresh bread, cheeses, and yogurt in a garden by a beautiful stream with relaxing music in the background. Also on sale are local crafts and herbal medicines. See p. 189.

o **La Perrera Restaurant** (Jinotega, Nicaragua; ✆ **505/8432-7423**): The road between Matagalpa and Jinotega is one of the most beautiful rides in Nicaragua. Enjoy the view from this hacienda-style restaurant that sits on the side of the mountain road. The menu includes beef, chicken, and seafood, and between courses, you can wander through the outside patio and up into the garden nursery. See p. 199.

o **Restaurante La Perla** (León, Nicaragua; ✆ **505/2311-3125;** www.laperlaleon. com): This restaurant's elegant white facade and tall, enchanting ceilings are enough to give you an appetite for Nicaraguan and international cuisine. Paintings by some of the country's greatest artists hang on the walls, and the large salon is framed by handsome mahogany doors. On the menu are Caesar salad, filet mignon, and fresh crab caught the same day from the nearby Poneloya beach. Finish the evening with a coffee from beans grown by the owners on the side of a volcano or a cocktail in the adjoining Canal Bar. See p. 211.

o **Restaurante Barde La Rioja** (Lago de Coatepeque, El Salvador; ✆ **503/2441-6037**): Tasty cream of crab soup and lake fish stuffed with shrimp are just some of the choices at this handsome restaurant on a two-story pier sitting high off the water, with great views and afternoon breezes, overlooking the Hotel Torremolinos' grounds and lake. See p. 332.

o **Señor Tenedor** (San Salvador; ✆ **503/2211-8326**): Señor Tenedor is all modern lines and sensual colors. Booths sit beneath sweeping, translucent silk tied with deep red satin. Live violin music accompanies modern Italian cooking and a nice selection of international wines.

o **Los Patios** (Ruta de las Flores, El Salvador; ✆ **503/2401-8590**): This upscale, modern hacienda-style eatery has a mountain-view patio overlooking thousands of coffee beans laid out to dry. See p. 308.

THE best MARKETS & SHOPS

o **Mercado Nacional de Artesanías** (San Salvador; ✆ **503/2224-0747**): Long rows of vendors sell unique hammocks, textiles, ceramics, and decorative crafts from artisans around El Salvador. The quality of the art and crafts is high, and the prices aren't bad in what is the capital's best handicrafts market. See p. 93.

o **Diconte Artisans' Shop** (Ataco, El Salvador): This five-room shop in the town of Ataco, along the Ruta de las Flores, offers unique whimsical paintings, woodcarvings, and crafts in the surrealistic style of Ataco's two main artists, as well as a room full of colorful textiles made on-site by artisans working five old-style looms.

You can also watch the artisans work from the shade of a small garden-side coffee and dessert cafe here. See p. 312.

o **Mercado Central** (San Salvador, El Salvador): Mercado Central near San Salvador's central plaza is the antimercado. It's a sprawling, seemingly chaotic warren of shouting vendors, blaring horns, and old women in traditional clothes chopping vegetables in the street. Its biggest attraction is that it's *not* an attraction. Instead, it's the place to visit if you want to see a slice of unfiltered El Salvadoran life. See p. 254.

o **Mercado Viejo** (Massaya, Nicaragua): The Gothic, palm-lined walls of Masaya's block-size Old Market offer an endless array of tempting souvenirs, such as intricate pottery, handsome woodcarvings, sturdy leather ware, and beautiful hand-woven hammocks, all made in the surrounding city and hilltop villages known as Pueblos Blancos. See p. 93.

o **El Arbol de Dios** (Av. Masferrer, Colonia Escalon, San Salvador, El Salvador; © **503/2263-9206**): El Salvador's most famous artist has moved to more expansive premises, where he can now display his distinctive naïve art and how he makes it. See p. 219.

NICARAGUA & EL SALVADOR IN DEPTH

Central America's two least-visited countries may not share a border, but they do have a common tumultuous history of war, poverty, crime, and corruption. Devastating earthquakes, hurricanes, and volcanic eruptions, as well as two bitter civil wars that brought both countries to the brink, have plagued both nations.

So, why visit this unlucky duo? A cloud-topped volcano that towers above a pristine lake is one reason. A fabulous Pacific coastline is another. Then there are the sun-kissed Caribbean islands and lush cloud forests. Throw in the rich native-Indian heritage, mixed with a history of ostentatious Spanish colonialism, and you have just some of the reasons why travelers are discovering Nicaragua and El Salvador. Both countries have vibrant music and art scenes that frequently spill out onto the streets in the form of festivals and parades. First-rate ecolodges and mountain refuges have opened up. There are volcanoes to climb, rainforests to hike, Maya ruins to visit, and waves to surf. As you sail down a jungle river or learn Spanish with a local family, you may realize that both countries have finally achieved the better world they fought so hard for.

Both nations may share a love for murals and martyrs, but it's also worth noting what makes them different. El Salvador is the most densely populated country in Central America, a potential economic powerhouse with good infrastructure and a strong work ethic. The downsides are a widening wealth gap, rampant deforestation, and a runaway crime rate. Nicaragua, on the other hand, is the region's least populated country, with a dormant economy overly reliant on agriculture. It's the poorest country in Central America, but also the safest, and its under-population translates to a realistic ambition of converting 20% of its surface area into lush national parks and protected reserves.

NICARAGUA
Nicaragua Today

"This house is not for sale," proclaims a sign on a colonial townhouse in the tourist boomtown of Granada. Its exasperated owner seeks to ward off speculators and swindlers seeking to make a quick buck out of the real estate boom that has come and gone and returned somewhat to Central

America's hottest tourist attraction. Visitors are flocking to a country that hopefully, someday soon, will lose its well worn moniker as the second poorest in the Western Hemisphere. Despite President Daniel Ortega's anti-U.S. rhetoric and pro-Chavez leanings, he's declared the country open for business, attracting tax-shy retirees, beachfront-property hunters, and adventure-loving sun seekers enticed by multiple seasons of television's *Survivor* made on Nicaraguan shores.

It's hard to avoid Ortega's smiling face when traveling the country. Posters proclaiming his loyalty to the people are stationed on government buildings and roadside monuments. The ex–bank robber and veteran Sandinista leader has once again renamed Managua airport after the legendary general Augusto C. Sandino; it had been changed by the right-wing president Arnoldo Alemán when he was in power (originally, the airport was named after Somoza, the unpopular dictator). Ortega has also refused to occupy the Casa Presidencial, calling it a symbol of the opulence of the previous administration. His sincerity is proven somewhat shallow by the cynical pacts he's made with his corrupt rival Alemán that guarantee both men stay in power and push out the smaller parties. A subversion of the country's Supreme Court saw it declare Ortega legally fit to stand for reelection, despite a constitutional ban—a move, along with some electoral fraud in 2008, that saw the U.S. and European Union suspend all aid to the country. The legions of disillusioned Sandinistas are increasing, including the legendary rebel priest and ex-minister Ernesto Cardenal and the folk singer Carlos Mejía Godoy, who has forbidden the FSLN from using his famous anthems.

Nicaragua's real hope lies in its people, and despite the wickedness of everyday politics, it is safe to say that democracy is here to stay, as is the relative freedom of speech that it entails. Now, the only foreign intervention is the increasing groups of visitors, many of whom are deciding to stay. Towns like Granada and San Juan del Sur have an international flavor, with investors, retirees, Peace Corps volunteers, and the simply curious all hoping that this country's future shines brighter than its dark past.

Nicaragua: A Look at the Past

IN THE BEGINNING

People have been traversing Nicaragua since before 18,000 B.C., when the first Asian tribes crossed the Bering Strait and ventured south. Evidence of human life on the isthmus dates back 8,000 years, in the form of shells collected by a tribe called Los Concheros on the Caribbean coast. Ten-thousand-year-old footprints can be viewed at the Museo Las Huellas de Acahualinca in Managua, and there are ceramic remnants from as far back as 4000 B.C. The Maribio tribe traveled from California and settled in northwestern Nicaragua, while the Miskito and Rama peoples settled on the Caribbean side. In the 13th century, the Corotega and Nicarao tribes also settled in the country when they fled south from Aztec Mexico and found refuge around the country's two great lakes. Here, they prospered, building sophisticated societies that benefited from being at the crossroads of two giant continents. These same people gave the Spanish a taste of their fighting spirit when the Europeans first landed in 1519. The tribal leaders Nicaroa and Diriangén engaged the conquistador González

> **Impressions**
>
> "Poetry will exist as long as there is a problem of life and death."
>
> —Rubén Darío

Dávila in a brief battle in 1523, after which the Spanish retreated.

The Spanish explorer Francisco Hernández de Córdoba returned a year later with a well-outfitted army. The tribes were defeated and, despite the occasional rebellion over the next century or so, were eventually subdued and subjugated by the Europeans. Córdoba established a permanent colonial foothold in the country and founded the cities of Granada and León in 1524. Merciless strongman Pedrarias Dávila was installed as the first governor, and Nicaragua became the domain of the Spanish Empire for the next 300 years.

A PROVINCE OF SPAIN

The conquest almost wiped out the local population. When the gold ran out, the invaders traded in slaves, shipping the people south to work in Panama and Peru. Despite Spain outlawing slavery in 1542 and granting the Indians equal rights, the reality on the ground was one of cruel exploitation. Eventually, cattle were introduced to the area, and agriculture became the main activity. A brisk trade in beef, leather, and indigo began, and Granada became a major merchant city because of its access to the Atlantic. León gained in importance as the administrative and religious center of the country. As in other parts of the region, Nicaragua's prosperity led to frequent raids from British, French, and Dutch pirates sailing up the Río San Juan in search of loot and fortune, using the Atlantic coast as their base, where the Spanish had little or no presence.

Nicaragua won independence from Spain in 1821, along with the rest of Central America. It was not a hard-fought war, but more a gradual assertion of power by the *criollos* (Spanish descendants born in Nicaragua who, despite being only 5% of the population, owned everything) bristling against the monopoly economics of the Empire and taking advantage of a Spain in turmoil after the invasion of the French in 1808. Independence did, however, create a power vacuum and unleashed a period of anarchy and civil war in the region as different interests jostled for power. Nicaragua was briefly a province of Mexico before becoming a part of the short-lived Central America Federation. Political infighting and regional rivalries meant it eventually emerged as an independent nation in 1838. The English still retained their presence in the Caribbean, however, controlling the San Juan estuary from the port of Greytown until 1860. In that year, the British signed a treaty surrendering the Caribbean territory to Nicaragua, though in fact, the region remained largely autonomous until 1893.

GRANADA VS. LEON

In addition to growing American influence, the 19th century was dominated by a vicious rivalry centered in the cities of Granada and León that continues, in some way, to this day. During this period, Granada emerged as the establishment capital, favored by landowners and merchants who had little desire to reform the feudal system that existed. León became the center for liberal bourgeoisie who were inspired by the Enlightenment and the American and French revolutions. Both cities declared themselves capitals in 1824, and civil war erupted in 1827. A new constitution was written in 1828, and the general chaos continued, exacerbated by Managua's declaring itself the true center of government. The country was rocked by a civil war that went on intermittently throughout the rest of the century. In 1854, the Granada-based general Fruto Chamorro introduced another constitution, and the León liberals decided to hire some outside help to remedy the situation.

WILLIAM WALKER & THE NATIONAL WAR

The country's political landscape was transformed when mercenary William Walker was hired by the León liberals to help in their latest skirmish with Granada. His private army of 300 roughnecks won the battle but had no intention of going home. Walker declared himself president in 1855 (with the support of the U.S. government) and soon instituted policies such as reestablishing slavery and declaring English the official language with the idea of colonizing the entire isthmus and transforming the whole region into a de facto territory of the United States, with Mexico squeezed in the middle. These policies did not go down well with the locals, and the Leoneses soon united with the conservatives and forces from Costa Rica to defeat Walker at the battle of San Jacinto in 1856. (See the box on p. 108 for more info.) It was the one true case of national unity ever achieved in the country, and even the local indigenous people were engaged in the fight to repel Walker. He retreated to Granada, which he burned to the ground before abandoning the country entirely. The Hondurans captured him 4 years later and promptly executed him. The battle of San Jacinto is celebrated as a national holiday every September 14, and the Guerra Nacional holds more patriotic importance to the Nicaraguans than its somewhat messy independence from Spain.

AMERICAN INTERVENTION

The United States of America has influenced Nicaraguan history from the late 1800s on, with the country being of particular interest to the U.S. because it seemed like a good candidate for building a water channel between the Atlantic and Pacific. Plans for such a canal are still being considered to this day. When the steamship magnate Cornelius Vanderbilt pioneered a land, river, and sea route that saw thousands of North Americans passing up the Río San Juan as part of the California Gold Rush in the 1850s, the country gained even more importance in the eyes of America.

After the debacle of William Walker, the disgraced liberal class surrendered to 36 years of mediocre conservative rule. The fishing village of Managua was declared the country's capital as a compromise. A nationalist general, José Santos Zelaya, took power in 1893 and marched his troops to the Atlantic coast to finally lay claim to what until then was Nicaragua's on paper only. The liberal-leaning Zelaya did much to improve the rule of law in Nicaragua and introduced a new constitution in 1893 that abolished the death penalty, separated church and state, recognized private property, and introduced universal education. He also improved the country's infrastructure with new roads, ports, a postal system, and a limited electric grid. However, he antagonized the Americans by insisting on national control of any waterway and threatening to rival the planned Panama Canal with a foreign-financed project of his own. He was ousted with the aid of American marines in 1909. Three years later, a rebellion led by Benjamín Zeledón was crushed by an invasion of American marines that basically took over the country. For the next 12 years, there were 10 such uprisings against American-backed, conservative governments. After U.S. interests acquired some of Nicaragua's main businesses, Nicaragua soon found itself in hock to the United States and locked into an agreement where no other country could finance a canal that would interfere with Washington's plans in Panama.

A glimmer of hope came in 1924, when the liberals and conservatives finally agreed to a form of power sharing, and the Americans withdrew their military presence. But the pact collapsed when conservative Emilio Chamorro staged a coup d'état and the Constitutional War broke out. Fearing a liberal victory, the U.S. again stepped in and negotiated a settlement that was opposed by liberal general Augusto C. Sandino. He held out in the northern highlands despite an American offensive that included the first recorded bombing of a civilian town, Ocotal. American influence continued throughout the 20th century, including propping up the Somoza dictatorship and Reagan's support for the Contras.

AUGUSTO C. SANDINO & THE RISE OF SOMOZA

Sandino proved a more-than-capable adversary to the Americans, and he pinned the marines down in the northern highlands with successful guerrilla tactics. In 1927, the American-trained National Guard was formed with the idea of creating a neutral military force that would prevent any further civil conflicts. However, the new army was led by an ambitious general, Anastasio Somoza García, who had other plans for the new force. The Americans withdrew, handing power to Juan Bautista Sacasa. Sandino, noting that foreign intervention had abated, accepted the government's invitation to negotiate and signed a peace agreement. Caught off guard, he was kidnapped and assassinated by the National Guard in 1934 in Managua. The murder was followed by a vicious clampdown by Somoza, who eventually took complete control in 1937.

What followed were 42 years of iron rule by a family dynasty that in the end owned everything worth owning in Nicaragua. The Somoza family became fabulously wealthy and all-powerful, with 50% of all productive lands and 65% of the GDP in their hands. They installed the occasional puppet president for appearance's sake and, with the help of the National Guard, rigged elections and repressed any dissent. A revolt by the conservatives in 1954 was quickly quelled, and street protests—such as a student protest in 1959—were met with bullets. When Anastasio Somoza García was assassinated by the poet Rigoberto López Pérez in 1956, he was swiftly replaced by his son Luís "Tacho" Somoza Debayle, and the regime continued as usual. The only good things to come out of such ravenous, profit-driven rule were huge public works such as the Carretera Panamericana (Pan-American Highway) and the Lake Apanás hydroelectric plant. There were several attempts on Somoza's life, including a Cuban-style insurrection in 1959 that petered out after 2 weeks.

The Somoza regime showed its gratitude for American patronage in 1961 by allowing its Atlantic coast to be used as the launching pad for the disastrous Bay of Pigs operation. Tacho lost an election in 1963 and retired from politics. The new president, Renée Schick, was soon ousted by Anastasio "Tachito" Somoza in 1967. This younger brother of Tacho proved to be the cruelest and greediest of all the Somozas. Somoza's support, even by the elite, was seriously undermined when he plundered reconstruction funds for the 1972 earthquake disaster that destroyed Managua. He then arranged the murder of newspaper editor and critic of the regime, Pedro Joaquin Chamorro, in 1978. The stage was set for a revolution and an end to one of Central America's longest and most brutal dictatorships.

THE SANDINISTA REVOLUTION

In 1963, a new organization called the Frente Sandinista de Liberación Nacional (FSLN) made its presence known by staging a thwarted uprising in the north. Led by the Marxist Carlos Fonseca Amador, the Sandinistas were to prove a thorn in the side of an increasingly repressive regime. They robbed banks and staged minor rural attacks throughout the '60s. An ambush by the National Guard in Matagalpa in 1967 wiped out much of the FSLN leadership, and the rebels found themselves on the back foot with many of their leaders either dead or in prison. In 1970, Carlos Fonseca and Humberto Ortega were sprung from prison by a daring airplane hijacking. In 1974, the movement collected a $6-million ransom and the release of Daniel Ortega when it held hostage a group of politicians in Managua. Fonseca was killed in an ambush in 1976, and the leadership of the movement fell into the pragmatic but authoritarian hands of the Ortega brothers, a position they retain to this day.

The assassination of popular conservative leader and newspaper editor Pedro Joaquín Chamorro in 1978 ignited the country. A national strike was accompanied by days of rioting, with protesters targeting the many businesses owned by the Somoza family. Simultaneous uprisings occurred in Rivas, Nuevo Segovia, Monimbo, and Diriamba, often with little help or encouragement from the FSLN. The revolution had gained its own momentum, and ordinary people without any direct links to the rebels were engaging the National Guard, who fought back with increasing brutality. FSLN commandos staged a spectacular coup by taking over the national congress by force and held legislators hostage until the prisoners were released and a ransom paid. Attacks in Masaya, León, Chinandega, and Estelí were met by indiscriminate bombing by the authorities. The rebel forces swelled with new recruits, and the U.S. was compelled to persuade a stubborn Somoza to resign. Total insurrection continued into 1979, with thousands of casualties. Footage of ABC reporter Bill Stewart being executed by the National Guard was aired in the United States, and by the end of July, the rebels were in control of Masaya, eastern Managua, Masatepe, and Sebaco. León was liberated on July 9, and Somoza fled to Miami. The National Guard disintegrated, with many hijacking boats in San Juan del Sur to sail away from a war they had lost. Somoza had a short-lived asylum in Paraguay, where he was blown up by a rocket attack in September 1980.

THE SANDINISTAS IN POWER & THE CONTRA WAR

The Sandinista revolution created a Sandinista government that had little room for non-party factions, such as the conservatives, lead by Chamorro's widow Violetta Barrios de Chamorro. The Sandinistas were intent on building a newer and fairer society from the bottom up, and this meant radical land reform, interventionist economics, and party control of the army, police, and unions. These were policies that made the rich elite flee to Miami, taking their money with them. They also disaffected popular non-Marxist guerrilla leaders such as Edén Pastora and others who presumed democratic elections would take place after the revolution. While the economy collapsed, the poor became educated in a hugely popular and successful literacy drive that proved to be the Sandinistas' one lasting positive legacy.

Meanwhile, trouble brewed in the north, and a new stage in U.S. intervention began. The new Reagan administration watched with dread at what it perceived as a new front in the Cold War. Aid was halted in 1981, and an economic embargo was imposed in 1985, putting the economy into free-fall. A new insurgency appeared.

A Young Country
Forty-five percent of Nicaragua's population is under 15 years of age.

Its roots lay in the controversial death of one the FSLN's most capable non-Marxist commanders, Germán Pomares, who was killed just days before the end of the 1979 uprising by "friendly" fire. One year after Somoza's

---

Hyper Inflation

In 1989, inflation reached a dizzying 2,000% in Nicaragua, and large wads of córdoba bills were required just to buy a soda. Now, inflation is at a much more manageable 7%.

---

defeat, his troops turned on their old comrades and attacked a base in Nueva Segovia. The counter-revolution had begun. The Contras, as they became known, were a well-armed band of ex-Sandinistas and former National Guard members financed and trained by the CIA and led from Honduras. Edén Pastora opened a second front on the Costa Rican border. The Sandinista government had to divert badly needed money toward this new war, as well as impose unpopular policies such as a draft and rationing. It proved a dirty war, with both sides accused of atrocities, but the Contras in particular gained a reputation for slaughtering unarmed civilians and sabotaging the country's already weakened infrastructure.

By the end of the 1980s, both sides of this battle were exhausted. The Iran-Contra scandal had dried up support for the counterinsurgents, and the collapse of the Soviet Union was a serious blow to the revolution. Nicaragua's Central American neighbors proposed a peace accord (though opposed by the U.S.), and the Sandinistas accepted. Elections were held in 1990, and to the surprise of many, the government lost. An unpopular war, a failed agricultural program, and a general lack of freedom of speech meant many Nicaraguans were tired and ready for a change. A further surprise was a peaceful handover of power, with the Sandinistas relinquishing control, but not before a shameful last grab of property and assets that became known as *la piñata* (after the candy-stuffed party package beaten by children to reach its contents).

PEACE, RECONCILIATION & CORRUPTION

Violeta Barrios de Chamorro became the president of this new Nicaragua. The widow of the slain editor and leader of a loose coalition known as UNO, Doña Violeta introduced policies aimed at ending the war, reconciling all sides, and kick-starting the economy, with limited success. With two sons on opposing sides of the war, she had firsthand experience of the divisive nature of Nicaraguan politics and the need for reconciliation. Doña Violeta reduced the army to 18,000 and put it under civilian rule. Freedom of speech blossomed, and foreign investment returned, as did some of the exiles who fled the war. Her tenure was a rocky one, with many protests, failed uprisings, and accusations of corruption. She finished her tenure with low popularity ratings but with hindsight is now regarded as a great woman who miraculously united the country and put it on the path to recovery.

Meanwhile, the Sandinistas embraced democracy and became the main opposition party, led by Daniel Ortega. Despite strong support, Ortega lost the 1996 election to a corrupt, right-wing politician, Arnoldo Alemán, leader of the Partido Liberal Constitucionalista (PLC). Alemán's tenure was rocked by endless kickback scandals and further tarnished by a disgraceful political pact with Ortega that basically divided power, pushed smaller parties out, and guaranteed immunity from prosecution for both leaders.

When Hurricane Mitch struck in 1998, wreaking havoc across the country and killing thousands, Alemán's appallingly slow reaction (he was more concerned with his upcoming wedding) sealed his fate as a one-term president. His vice president, Enrique Geyer Bolaños, came to power in 2002, trouncing Ortega with 56% of the vote. Once in office, Bolaños, acting on his anticorruption campaign pledges, turned on his own party, stripped Alemán of immunity, and had him jailed for 20 years for embezzlement and money laundering. Such justice is a rare thing in Central American politics, and Bolaños paid for his crusade by being virtually paralyzed in a congress made up of disaffected and begrudging colleagues in the pocket of Alemán, who retaliated by trying to convict Bolaños in turn for illegal funding.

In the 2006 election, the Sandinistas were able to capitalize on this infighting and a general downturn in the economy; Ortega won the election with 37% of the popular vote. The initial reaction was a sudden dip in foreign investment, as people feared the country would return to the 1980s-style economy of hyperinflation and debt default. An infamous pact with the convicted Alemán meant the corrupt liberal leader could serve his sentence from his luxury ranch while both parties sewed up the power structure to exclude any smaller parties. Ortega softened his Marxist image and declared himself to be market friendly. Nevertheless, his popularity is low, due to a stalled economy and rising food prices. Both sides of the political spectrum are currently disaffected, with members on the right saying that Ortega has become a crony of Hugo Chávez and members on the left accusing him of selling out. The next elections are due in November 2011, but Ortega has his work cut out for him if he wants to remain in power.

EL SALVADOR

El Salvador Today

When President Barack Obama visited El Salvador in March 2011, he found a country struggling socially and economically, and highly dependent on its rich northern neighbor to muddle through. One third of El Salvador's population lives illegally in the United States and sends approximately US$3.5 billion home in remittances. The downturn in the US economy has affected El Salvador deeply, and its economy is stagnant, with little foreign investment, little growth in tourism, and a widening trade deficit. A highly polarized political scene and a rampant crime rate are two more reasons the country is suffering. This makes it all the more surprising that President Mauricio Funes enjoys a 79% approval rating, making him the most popular president in Central America.

Funes is a youthful ex–TV journalist who was elected in June 2009 on a platform promising change. And his very election is a compelling reason to say that El Salvador has already started changing. The moderate 49-year-old was elected on the ex-rebel FMLN ticket, and he is the country's first leftist president. A peaceful transition of power from the right-wing ARENA party, which held power for 18 years, is in itself a miracle, as it was not so long ago that opposing sides were murdering each other in the streets. Politics still have a polarizing effect on Salvadoran society, as can be seen in the territorial markings of either party painted on poles, curbs, and bridges across the country, but the fact that democracy seems to have taken a hold must surely be seen as a sign of better times to come. Funes has proved to be a moderate, taking the center line on many issues, much to the chagrin of his leftist backers. However this pragmatic approach, along with some well placed social programs for the country's poor, means he's gaining support from a public that wants stability above all else.

Looking Back at Nicaragua & El Salvador

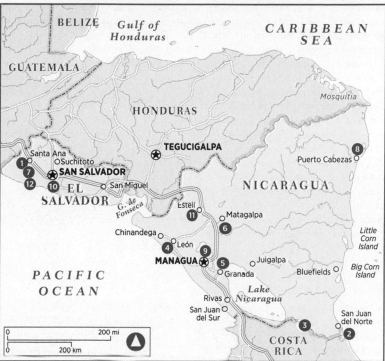

1 900 AD: The Toltec pyramid is constructed at the Maya city of Tazumal.

2 1502: Christopher Columbus sails past the mouth of the Rio San Juan in a vain attempt to find a water passage to the Pacific.

3 1762: The teenage heroine Rafaela Herrera successfully leads the defence of the Spanish river fort El Castillo against British attackers who coveted the Rio San Juan and the riches that lay in Granada.

4 September 15, 1821: The bells of León's imposing cathedral rang out in celebration of Central American independence from the Spanish Empire.

5 1856: The American filibusterer William Walker burns down the prosperous colonial city of Granada, leaving a sign proclaiming "Here was Granada".

6 January 18, 1867: The father of modern Spanish poetry, Rubén Dario, is born in Metapa, close to Matagalpa.

7 1932: The Ruta de los Flores was the scene of a coffee peasant uprising known as La Matanza. 30,000 people were killed in the brutal government repression that followed.

8 April 17, 1961: Eight disguised US air force B-26 bombers leave from Nicaragua's Caribbean coast to attack Cuba in the opening round of the disastrous Bay of Pigs invasion.

9 July 17, 1979: A triumphant Sandinista rebel army enter Managua after overthrowing the dictator Somoza in a long and bitter struggle that costs thousands of lives.

10 March 30, 1980: 250,000 people attend the funeral of slain Archbishop Oscar Romero at San Salvador's national cathedral. The crowd is attacked by bombs and sniper fire and 40 people die.

11 October 29, 1998: Hurricane Mitch sweeps through the region, dropping 6 feet of water and killing 11,000 people.

12 October 1, 2005: Volcán Santa Ana erupts suddenly, killing two people and causing widespread damage.

El Salvador: A Look at the Past

IN THE BEGINNING

El Salvador's earliest residents were the Paleo-Indians, whose history in the country is thought to stretch back 10,000 years and is evidenced by indigenous paintings found near the village of Morazán. The next residents to arrive were the more advanced Olmecs, Mesoamericans who moved into the region around 2000 B.C. The Olmecs held power until roughly 400 B.C., when they were largely replaced by the Maya. The Maya dynasty is responsible for the country's classic pyramid ruins, such as Tazumal and Casa Blanca—these show evidence not only of contact with other Maya from around what is now Central America, but also point to how El Salvador acted as a vital trading center in the Maya world.

Around the 11th century, the Maya dynasty was replaced by the Nahuat-speaking Pipil, who were part of the nomadic Mexican Nahua tribe, and dominated the western part of the country. At the same time, the Lenca tribe, with their own Aztec-based language, settled into and controlled the eastern region of the country, where their descendants remain today. Both the Maya and the Lenca dynasties held power until the arrival of the Spanish in 1524, and both waged ultimately futile efforts to stop the invading conquistadors.

A SPANISH COLONY & INDEPENDENCE

When Spaniard Pedro de Alvarado attempted to claim this territory for Spain in 1524, his army was thwarted by Pipil fighters. Alvarado tried again the following year, however, and was able to bring the region under the Spanish flag. Alvarado then named the region El Salvador or "The Savior." For roughly the next 3 centuries, El Salvador remained under Spanish control. Agriculture became the main source of wealth, with the Spanish planting cotton, balsam, and indigo, the last of which became El Salvador's main export. The vast majority of the population lived as indentured peasants working for a landowning oligarchy known as "the 14 families."

In 1821, El Salvador, along with four other Central American countries, declared its independence from Spain. The first couple of years of freedom, however, weren't easy. In 1822, El Salvador decided against joining Mexico and other provinces in a Central American union and had to fight off troops sent to bring the country in line. The country went so far as to request statehood from the United States government. Ultimately, however, El Salvador was able to expel the troops and joined a more equitable union of Central American states, known as the Central American Federation, in 1823.

Things remained relatively calm until 1832, when El Salvador's poor staged the first of what would be numerous uprisings to protest unfair land distribution. Like later uprisings, the 1832 effort resulted in little change. In 1838, the Central American Federation dissolved, and El Salvador became a fully independent country.

During the 19th century, El Salvador's land-based elite flourished as the coffee industry grew. During that time, the country's much-amended constitution was again restructured to give the majority of its 72 legislative seats to landowners. The head of each department was also appointed by the president. The system allowed wealthy

---

Impressions

"If I die, I will rise in the Salvadorean people."
—Archbishop Monseñor Oscar Romero before he was slain by right-wing assassins in 1980

coffee-plantation owners simply to incorporate much of the country's deedless common land into their coffee farms and to maintain a stranglehold on the landless masses.

20TH-CENTURY UNREST

Coffee became the dominate industry, and at the turn of the 20th century, it accounted for 95% of the country's export earnings, controlled by 2% of the population. The landowners paid no taxes, employed the locals at slave wages, and expropriated indigenous common lands. This obviously didn't sit well with the landless masses, who rose up numerous times to try to force change but were largely powerless against the wealthy elite and their military bidders. The collapse of coffee prices in 1929 meant mass unemployment that further impoverished the locals. An uprising, later named "La Matanaza" (The Massacre), took place in 1932, led by Farabundo Martí, for whom the people's FMLN organization was later named. It was a failed uprising, which resulted in brutal consequences: the death, imprisonment, or deportation of 30,000 indigenous people and government opponents.

Over the next nearly 5 decades, El Salvador's poor suffered under successive repressive governments that occasionally offered token land reforms, allowing for large-scale armed conflict to be largely avoided. The country did engage, however, in a short 5-day war with Honduras from July 14 to July 18, 1969, over immigration issues, known as the Soccer War. More than 300,000 undocumented El Salvadorans were believed to be living in Honduras at the time, and the Honduran government and private groups increasingly sought to blame them for the country's economic woes. During a World Cup preliminary match in Tegucigalpa, a disturbance broke out between fans on both sides, followed by a more intense incident during the next game in San Salvador. El Salvadorans living in Honduras began to be harassed and even killed, leading to a mass exodus from the country. On June 27, 1969, Honduras broke off diplomatic relations with El Salvador, and on July 14, the El Salvadoran Air Force began an assault on Honduras and took control of the city of Nueva Ocotepeque. Though the war lasted only 5 days and ended in a stalemate of sorts, in the end, between 60,000 and 130,000 El Salvadorans were expelled or fled from Honduras, and more than 2,000 people, mostly Hondurans, were killed. While a peace treaty was signed between the two countries in 1980, to this day, relations between them remain strained.

Though the Soccer War quickly became a memory, the anger of El Salvador's poor farmers did not, and by the 1970s, sporadic and violent insurgencies against the government began. The government responded with a largely useless land reform bill in 1976 that did little to improve lives or ease the anger of the *campesinos* (peasant farmers). Some held out hope for improvements when a slightly more moderate group took control in 1979, but that group quickly dissolved under its own political strife and targeting by the military death squads. Many say the final straw came in 1980, with the government's assassination of beloved human rights champion Monseñor Oscar Romero, who was gunned down in the middle of Mass. After four of the country's leading guerilla groups merged into the cohesive and organized Farabundo Martí National Liberation Front, or FMLN, later in 1980, the stage was set for war.

THE CIVIL WAR

The FMLN staged its first large-scale military offensive on January 10, 1981, in which it gained control over the areas around Chalatenango and Morazán. All ages, including children and the elderly, and both sexes joined in the guerilla movement. The El Salvadoran government's response was brutal, particularly at the 2-day,

Scorched Earth

"You must drain the ocean to catch the fish." The Salvadoran military's brutal tactics towards dissent summed up by one of its most notorious officers, Colonel Domingo Monterroso.

December 1981 Mozote Massacre, when military soldiers executed more than 1,000 men, women, and children in the eastern mountain village of Mozote. The war raged on and off over the next 11 years, with international powers viewing the battle as an ideological struggle between democracy and communism. Cuba supported the guerillas, and the United States—to a total of $7 billion—supported the El Salvadoran military government. More than 70,000 people were killed during the war's brutal run, including many who were executed and mutilated by government troops, who then dumped the bodies near town squares in order to warn against terrorism. More than 25% of the country's population was displaced by the war by its end.

The FMLN responded by blowing up roads and bridges, destroying farms, and attacking power lines with the intention of paralyzing the economy. A glimmer of hope came in 1989 when the rebels offered to take part in the elections. The right-wing establishment rejected their overtures, and the fighting intensified. A rebel attack on the capital was countered by a government-sponsored manhunt that killed 4,000 people, including six Jesuit priests, their housekeeper, and her daughter at the Universidad Centroamérica in San Salvador.

By 1991, both sides had had enough of the long stalemate, and a spirit of compromise emerged. In 1992, a truce was declared and a peace deal signed. A new constitution was drafted that enacted a number of land reforms and did away with the military death squads in favor of a national civil police; in addition, the FMLN became a legal political party that remains active today. Amnesty for war crimes, of which there were many, was declared in 1993.

PEACE, CRIME & NATURAL DISASTERS

El Salvador continues to struggle. The plight of its *campesinos* and civil war deaths have been replaced by one of Latin America's highest homicide rates, due mainly to the presence of the notorious street gang Mara Salvatrucha or MS-13. Though MS-13 began on the streets of Los Angeles in the 1980s, heavy deportation of U.S.-based gang members has steadily increased the gang's influence in El Salvador. Continuing government efforts known as Mano Dura (Hard Hand) attempt to break up the gang. Such initiatives have had small, sporadic impacts, but they have raised human rights concerns. Crime remains a central issue of El Salvadoran life and the main preoccupation of its people.

Goodbye Colón

In 2001, El Salvador abandoned its currency, the colón, and adopted the U.S. dollar, joining Ecuador and Panama as Latin American countries attempting to curb inflation with the U.S. currency.

In 1998, El Salvador was hit by catastrophic Hurricane Mitch, which killed 374 people, left 55,000 homeless, and stalled the economy. Mitch was followed in 2001 and 2005 by massive earthquakes that killed over a thousand people, left thousands more homeless, and severely damaged thousands of buildings—many of which

MAYA history

Before the arrival of the first Europeans, Mesoamerica was the land of the ancient Maya. Here, mathematicians came up with the concept of zero, astronomers developed a solar calendar accurate to a single day every 6,000 days, and scribes invented an 850-word hiero-glyphic vocabulary that scholars con-sider the world's first advanced writing system. Some of this civilization's prac-tices were less than civil: The Maya built extensive ball courts to play a game called "pok a tok," where the losing team could be executed.

Evidence of human presence in the Maya region dates as far back as the 10th millennium B.C. Maya history is often divided into several distinct peri-ods: Archaic (10,000–2000 B.C.), Pre-Classic (2000 B.C.–A.D. 250), Classic (A.D. 250–900), and Post-Classic (900–1540). Within this timeline, the Classic period itself is often divided into Early, Middle, Late, and Terminal stages. At the height of development, as many as 10 million Maya may have inhabited what are now Guatemala, Belize, Mexico's Yucatán Peninsula, and parts of Honduras and El Salvador. No one knows for sure what led to the decline of the Classic Maya, but somewhere around A.D. 900, their society entered a severe and rapid decline. Famine, warfare, deforestation, and religious prophecy have all been cited as possible causes. (Try Jared Dia-mond's bestseller *Collapse* [Penguin, 2005] for information and speculation.)

Unlike the Incas of Peru, the Maya had no centralized ruler. Instead, the civiliza-tion consisted of a series of independent city-states, usually ruled by hereditary kings, often at war with one another. The most famous Maya ruin in El Salvador is at Tazumal and includes a temple pyra-mid, ball court, and other structures con-sidered to be classic examples of Maya architecture and similar to those found in other parts of Central America.

According to the Popol Vuh, the sacred Maya book of creation myths and predictions, the world as we know it will end on December 21, 2012. While some New Age analysts have dire predictions for the date, more optimistic prognosti-cators foresee a day of positive human evolution.

remain under repair today, including San Salvador's majestic National Theater. If this was not enough, Hurricane Stan descended on the country in October 2005, leaving 69 dead and countless homeless in its wake.

The war is over, however. Since 1992, the country's new constitution and coopera-tion of the two main political parties have allowed El Salvador to remain politically peaceful. The FMLN has made a successful switchover to party politics, and it won significant congressional elections in 2000 and 2003. The presidency proved more elusive to the former rebels. In 2006, former TV sports presenter Tony Saca became president of El Salvador under the conservative ARENA party. His presidency wit-nessed an underperforming economy with high inflation and 6% unemployment. Remittances from relatives in the U.S. remain an important source of income for the country and make up a whopping 15% of its GDP.

Despite rising inflation and other problems, El Salvador's economy has grown steadily in the last decade—the percentage of El Salvadorans living in poverty has been reduced from 66% in 1991 to just over 30% in 2006. Still, many El Salvadorans think the Central America Free Trade Agreement, which the country joined in 2006, is causing economic woes. As a result, the FMLN party found itself on the upswing and finally won the 2009 presidential elections with its candidate Mauricio Funes, a popular and respected TV journalist. He has toned down his party's left-wing rhetoric, promising to stick with dollarization and keep a friendly distance from Hugo Chávez. He beat the ARENA party with 51% of the vote, making him El Salvador's first leftist president.

2 NICARAGUA & EL SALVADOR IN POPULAR CULTURE

Books

The written word is all-important in Nicaragua. The country is famous throughout the Spanish-speaking world for being a country of great poets and writers. (Despite this, many poor people have only recently achieved literacy, and most Nicaraguans cannot afford a book.) It is a source of great national pride that one of the finest poets in Spanish literature, Rubén Darío, hailed from León. *Songs of Life and Hope* (Duke University Press Books) is an excellent collection by Darío. The anthology *Ruben's Orphans* (Painted Rooster Press), translated into English by Marco Morelli, is a collection of contemporary Nicaraguan poetry.

The Country Under My Skin: A Memoir of Love and War (Anchor) is by one of Nicaragua's best-known writers and poets, Giaconda Belli, and covers her experience as a woman and Sandinista during the revolution. *The Jaguar Smile* (Random House), by Salman Rushdie, gives a poetic and humorous account of a trip he made to Nicaragua in 1986 to experience the revolution firsthand. *Blood of Brothers* (Putnam), by *New York Times* journalist Stephen Kinser, is generally regarded as the best and most evenhanded chronicle of modern Nicaragua.

Perhaps the most famous work of literature that hails from El Salvador is *La Diáspora* (Clasicos Roxsil), an award-winning novel by one of El Salvador's leading contemporary writers, Horacio Castellanos Moya. It chronicles the struggles of exiles from El Salvador's civil war.

Film

Most films that are available in English about Nicaragua inevitably dwell on the recent wars. *Under Fire* stars Nick Nolte as a photojournalist covering the Sandinista revolution, uttering the immortal words, "I don't take sides; I take pictures." *Carla's Song* is a gritty and realistic movie about a Glaswegian bus driver taking a Nicaraguan refugee home to her country. *Walker—A True Story* has Ed Harris playing the American despot. *The World Is Watching* is an acclaimed documentary about the media coverage of the Contra war, and *The World Stopped Watching* is a just-as-fascinating sequel.

Arguably, El Salvador's most heralded film is the 2004 film *Voces Inocentes,* which tells the story of the El Salvadoran civil war through the eyes of an 11-year-old child and is based on the childhood of El Salvadoran filmmaker Oscar Torres, who fled El Salvador for the United States in the midst of the war.

Music

Poetic folk music is very popular in Nicaragua, and the Mejia brothers are perhaps the country's most famous troubadours. They use the guitar and accordion to sing of love and revolution. Over on the Caribbean coast (where Kenny Rogers is phenomenally popular), old-fashioned country-and-western music rules. Finally, you'll find it hard to avoid the cheerful rhythms of marimba (a wooden xylophone), which play on almost every city plaza.

Native indigenous music in El Salvador, using instruments like the marimba, flute, and drums, was repressed in the early 20th century, but has miraculously survived and can be heard today through performers such as Paquito Palaviccini. El Salvador also has its very own take on Colombian cumbia, and the country dances to popular musical forms such as salsa, reggaeton, and hip-hop. There is even a form of hybrid El Salvadoran rock called *guanarock*.

EATING & DRINKING IN CENTRAL AMERICA

Typical Meals

Rice and beans are the bases of most meals—all three of them. At breakfast, they're called *gallo pinto* and come with everything from eggs to steak to seafood. At lunch or dinner, rice and beans are an integral part of a *casado* (which translates as "married" and is the name for the local version of a blue-plate special). A *casado* usually consists of cabbage-and-tomato salad; fried plantains (a starchy, banana-like fruit); and a chicken, fish, or meat dish of some sort. On the Caribbean coast, rice and beans are called rice 'n' beans, and are cooked in coconut milk. A seafood and coconut stew is called rundown.

Pupusa is king in El Salvador and hard to avoid, especially if you are on a budget. The stuffed tortilla comes with *queso* (cheese), frijoles (beans), and *chicharrón* (pork rinds), amongst other fillings.

However, you don't have to look too far to see that the region boasts an abundant variety of other local dishes to sample, which incorporate unique vegetables, fruits, and grains. Though rice and beans will be on almost all menus, in coastal areas, you'll also come across an incredible amount of seafood, especially lobster and shrimp. There is a growing controversy around eating lobster, due to overfishing and the extreme danger lobster pickers are put in for very little money. Avoid eating *huevos de paslama* (turtle eggs), since turtles are an endangered species.

In the highlands, you'll find more beef on the menu in the form of *caldos* (stews) served with yucca (manioc root or cassava in English), along with chicken dishes—just don't be too surprised if your chicken comes with the feet still attached. Everywhere you will find corn-based treats like *tamales* (stuffed cornmeal patties wrapped and steamed inside banana leaves), along with *patacones* (fried green plantain chips), often served streetside. *Nacatamales* are banana leaves stuffed with cornmeal, pork, potato, and onion. *Guirilas* are fried corn pancakes topped with cheese and are popular in Nicaragua's northern highlands.

On the whole, you'll find vegetables surprisingly lacking in the meals you're served throughout Nicaragua and El Salvador—usually nothing more than a little pile of shredded cabbage topped with a slice or two of tomato. Topped with pork skins, this is a popular dish in Nicaragua known as *vigorón*.

The most common fruits are mango, papaya, pineapple, melon, and banana. Other fruits include *marañón*, which is the fruit of the cashew tree and has orange or yellow glossy skin; *granadilla* or *maracuyá* (passion fruit); *mamón chino*, which Asian travelers will recognize as rambutan; and *carambola* (star fruit).

Fruit is often served as dessert in both countries, but there are some other options for sweets, as well. *Queque seco,* literally "dry cake," is the same as pound cake. Quesadilla is a cheesecake popular in El Salvador. Flan is a typical custard dessert. It often comes as either *flan de caramelo* (caramel) or *flan de coco* (coconut). Numerous other sweets are available, many of which are made with condensed milk and raw sugar. *Cajetas* are popular handmade candies, made from sugar and various mixes of evaporated, condensed, and powdered milk. They are sold in differing-size bits and chunks at most *pulperías* (general stores) and streetside food stands. *Rosquillas* are corn biscuit rings topped with cinnamon and are popular in Nicaragua.

Beverages

Nicaragua produces some of the best rum in the world, the most famous brand of which is called Flor de Caña. The whole region is known for *chicha,* a sweet, fermented corn beverage, and an even stronger variation known as *chicha brava. La cususa,* a crude cane liquor that's often combined with a soft drink or tonic, is popular in Nicaragua; its counterpart in El Salvador is called Tic Tac or Torito.

You can find imported wines at reasonable prices in the better restaurants throughout the region. You can usually save money by ordering a Chilean wine over a Californian or European one. *Cerveza* (beer) can be found everywhere, and each country has its most popular native brands, with Victoria and Toña the most common in Nicaragua and Pilsener and Suprema the best known in El Salvador.

Popular nonalcoholic drinks include *pinol,* which is toasted, ground corn with water; and *tiste,* a variation made with cocoa beans and corn. Soda in the form of *gaseosa* is everywhere, as are vendors selling small bags of ice-cold mineral water—much more environmentally friendly than bottles. Look out for excellent fruit juices called *liquadas* or *batidas* that can be served with milk or water. Among the more common fruits used in these shakes are mango, papaya, blackberries, and pineapple. Order *un fresco con leche sin hielo* (a *fresco* with milk but without ice) if you're avoiding untreated water.

If you're a coffee drinker, you might be disappointed here. Most of the best coffee has traditionally been targeted for export, and the locals tend to prefer theirs weak and sugary. Better hotels and restaurants are starting to cater to American and European tastes and are serving superior blends. If you want black coffee, ask for *café negro;* if you want it with milk, order *café con leche.* For something different, ask for *agua dulce,* a warm drink made from melted sugar cane and served with either milk or lemon, or straight.

Although water in parts of the region is safe to drink, bottled water is readily available and is a good option if you're worried about an upset stomach. If you like your water without bubbles, request *aqua mineral sin gas* or *agua en botella.*

Dining Customs

The capital cities have the best choices regarding restaurants, with everything from Italian, Brazilian, and Chinese eateries to chains like T.G.I. Friday's. For cheap meals, buffet-style restaurants are very popular, as are street grills on the side of the road. Informal types of restaurants are known as *pupuserías* and *comedores.*

Outside the major tourist destinations, your options get very limited very fast. In fact, many beach destinations are so remote that you have no choice but to eat in the hotel's dining room. Even on the more accessible beaches, the only choices aside from the hotel dining rooms are often cheap local places or overpriced tourist traps serving indifferent meals. At remote jungle lodges, the food is usually served buffet or family style and can range from bland to inspired, depending on who's doing the cooking, and turnover is high.

People sit down to eat lunch at midday and dinner at 7pm. Some downtown restaurants in big cities are open 24 hours; however, expensive restaurants tend to be open for lunch between 11am and 3pm and for dinner between 6 and 11pm. At even the more expensive restaurants in the region, it's hard to spend more than $50 per person unless you really splurge on drinks.

THE LAY OF THE LAND

El Salvador is the only country in Central America with no Atlantic coast, tucked as it is beneath Guatemala and Honduras. At 21,000 sq. km (8,108 sq. miles), it is also the smallest country in the region, roughly the size of New Jersey and is somewhat dwarfed by its neighbors. Mountains run along its northern border, and the country's lush northern highlands hold its highest mountain, El Pital, at 2,730m (8,957 ft.), and from here, the landscape descends dramatically onto a broad, brown-colored coastal plain towards the coast. Several rivers run from these mountains, the most significant of which is the Río Lempa, which is also the source of the dam Embalse Cerrón Grande.

The hot, coastal plains are pockmarked with more than a dozen volcanoes, many of which hold deep blue crater lakes, the largest of which are Lago Llopango and Lago Coatepeque. The rich soil means much of the country has been deforested, with only two significant patches of protected natural forest left at Parque Nacional El Imposible and Parque Nacional Montecristo.

The coastal plains and protruding conical volcanoes continue southeast into Honduras and Nicaragua and as far as Costa Rica. Here, tectonic plates crunch together, and frequent eruptions and earthquakes make the entire area a geological hot spot. The dark Pacific pounds black volcanic beaches up and down the coast. An island-dotted tropical bay known as the Golfo de Fonseca lies between El Salvador and Nicaragua, denying both countries a land border. The Marabios mountain range rises in the northern lowlands of Nicaragua and holds belching volcanoes such as Mombacho and Momotombo, among many others. Central America's two largest lakes have formed on the Nicaraguan lowlands: Lake Managua and Lake Nicaragua. The latter is the largest freshwater lake in Central America and the 20th-largest in the world; it is a third the size of El Salvador. The volcanic island Isla de Ometepe rises from the lake and is the biggest island of its kind in the world (located as it is in a freshwater lake). The lake also has several archipelagoes, including the Solentiname islands in its southeastern corner. Here, the lake drains eastward, skirting the central highlands, and into the Atlantic via the broad, majestic Río San Juan.

The northeastern landmass, the highlands, and the Atlantic lowlands together make Nicaragua the largest country in Central America, approximately the size of Greece at 130,000 sq. km (50,193 sq. miles). Coffee plantations and cloud forests cover the north-central highlands before they descend into dense rainforest, muddy swamp, marsh, and a myriad of deltas along the Atlantic coast. A narrow shelf of limestone rock extends several miles out into the Caribbean Sea, culminating in the twin paradise known as the Corn Islands, complete with a coral reef. High temperatures, humidity, and poor access mean Nicaragua's eastern Atlantic region is very much undeveloped. Because of this, Nicaragua can boast that one-fifth of its landmass is unexploited, with almost 809,371 hectares (2 million acres) of rainforest, which makes it the most significant tropical nature zone north of the Amazon. The region's longest river, the Río Coco, runs along the Honduran border, while the Río San Juan in the south partially forms the border with Costa Rica.

Central America's Ecosystems

Nicaragua's **lowland rainforests** are true tropical jungles. Some are deluged with more than 508cm (200 in.) of rainfall per year, and their climate is hot and humid. Trees grow tall and fast, fighting for sunlight in the upper reaches. In fact, life and foliage on the forest floor are surprisingly sparse. The action is typically 30m (98 ft.) up, in the canopy, where long vines stream down, lianas climb up, and bromeliads grow on the branches and trunks of towering hardwood trees. A classic example of lowland rainforests is the **Laguna de Perlas** in Nicaragua.

At higher altitudes, you'll find the famed **cloud forests.** Here, the steady flow of moist air meets the mountains and creates a nearly constant mist. Epiphytes—resourceful plants that live cooperatively on the branches and trunks of trees—grow abundantly in the cloud forests, where they must extract moisture and nutrients from the air. Because cloud forests are found in generally steep, mountainous terrain, the canopy here is lower and less uniform than in lowland rainforests, providing better chances for viewing elusive fauna. Some of the most spectacular cloud forests can be experienced at **Parque Nacional Montecristo** on El Salvador's northern border or **Reserva Natural Miraflor** in Nicaragua's north-central highlands.

On the Pacific side of the highlands, you'll still find examples of the otherwise vanishing **tropical dry forest.** During the long and pronounced dry season (late Nov–late Apr), no rain falls to relieve the unabated heat. To conserve much-needed water, the trees drop their leaves but bloom in a riot of color: purple jacaranda, scarlet *poró*, and brilliant-orange flame-of-the-forest are just a few examples. Then, during the rainy season, this deciduous forest is transformed into a lush and verdant landscape. Because the foliage is not that dense, the dry forests are excellent places to view a variety of wildlife, especially howler monkeys and *pizotes* (coati). One of the best examples of dry forest is found at **Chacocente Wildlife Refuge** in Nicaragua.

Along the coasts, primarily where river mouths meet the ocean, you will find extensive **mangrove forests** and **swamps.** Around these seemingly monotonous tangles of roots exists one of the most diverse and rich ecosystems in the region. Birdlife includes pelicans, storks, and pink flamingos, and reptiles such as crocodiles and caimans also thrive in this environment.

In any one spot in both El Salvador and Nicaragua, temperatures remain relatively constant year-round. However, they vary dramatically according to altitude, from tropically hot and steamy along the coasts to below freezing at the highest elevations.

Flora & Fauna

For millennia, the land bridge between North and South America served as a migratory thoroughfare and mating ground for species native to the once-separate continents. Perhaps its unique location between both continents explains why the region comprises only .05% of the earth's landmass, yet it is home to 7% of the planet's biodiversity. More than 15,000 identified species of plants; 900 species of birds; 9,000 species of butterflies and moths; and 500 species of mammals, reptiles, and amphibians are found here. Unfortunately, because of overpopulation and deforestation, El Salvador shares very little of this bounty and has only approximately

800 species. Nicaragua, however, has retained much of its natural diversity and holds some 30,000 species. And that is just what has been cataloged.

All sorts of fish and crustaceans live in the brackish tidal waters off the coast, primarily in the Caribbean, but also in parts of the Pacific. Caimans and crocodiles cruise the maze of rivers and unmarked canals. There are many snakes, but very few are poisonous. Watch out for the tiny coral snake and the bigger *barba amarilla*. Another creature worth avoiding is the poisonous arrow frog.

Hundreds of herons, ibises, egrets, and other marsh birds nest and feed along both countries' silted banks, as well. Mangrove swamps are often havens for water birds like cormorants, frigate birds, pelicans, and herons. Farther out, both coastal waters are alive with marine life that includes turtles, barracudas, stingrays, marlins, dolphins, and red snappers. Nicaragua boasts the only freshwater shark in the world on Lago de Nicaragua, while the Río San Juan that joins it to the Caribbean is famous for a giant silver fish called a tarpon.

The jungle teems with wildlife, particularly birds. Macaws, parrots, hummingbirds, and toucans are just some of the many reasons why both countries are excellent for bird-watching. The larger birds tend to nest up high in the rainforest canopy, while the smaller ones nestle in the underbrush. Count yourself lucky if you catch sight of the beautiful quetzal, or one of the region's elusive big cats, including jaguars, puma, and ocelots. A little easier to spot are howler monkeys and their simian brethren, the spider and squirrel monkeys. Other mammals to look out for on the jungle floor include anteaters, deer, and sloths.

Plant life in this region is very much determined by altitude and climate. The Pacific dry forest is home to hardy species of thorny shrubs that lose their leaves in the high season and burst into flower in April and May. Higher up, the landscape is dominated by pines, oaks, and evergreens. Above 1,600m (5,249 ft.), the flora becomes more lush, with orchids, mosses, and ferns all growing abundantly on giant trees.

Searching for Wildlife

Forest animals are predominantly nocturnal. When they are active in the daytime, they are usually elusive and on the watch for predators. Birds are easier to spot in clearings or secondary forests than they are in primary forests. Unless you have lots of experience in the tropics, your best hope for enjoying a walk through the jungle lies in employing a trained and knowledgeable guide.

Tips to keep in mind include **listening carefully and keeping quiet**—you're most likely to hear an animal before seeing one. Also, it helps to **bring binoculars and dress appropriately.** You'll have a hard time focusing your binoculars if you're busy swatting mosquitoes. Light, long pants and long-sleeved shirts are your best bet. Comfortable hiking boots are a real boon, except where heavy rubber boots are necessary (a real possibility, if it's been raining). Avoid loud colors; the better you blend in with your surroundings, the better your chances are of spotting wildlife. Finally, **be patient.** The jungle isn't on a schedule. However, your best shots at seeing forest fauna are in the very early-morning and late-afternoon hours.

Environmental Threats

The one thing that makes El Salvador different from Nicaragua is that it has lost much of its wildlife and their natural habitat. The jaguar and giant red macaw are now extinct, and less than 5% of the country retains its original forest. This has led to chronic soil erosion and devastating mudslides. Poverty means protected species such as the Ridley turtle often end up on the dinner plate.

The picture is somewhat better in Nicaragua, but only by default. Poor access and infrastructure in the country's Atlantic region means Nicaragua still has an area the size of El Salvador that is untouched and preserved. However, logging, poaching, and squatting mean many of Nicaragua's 76 protected areas are so in name only, and deforestation is an increasing worry. The problem is exacerbated by natural disasters, corrupt politics, and never-ending land disputes. The western lowlands have a poor record environmentally. It is no accident that the tiny crater lake Tiscapa in the center of Managua is known locally as "the toilet." Lake Managua to the north is heavily polluted, and the magnificent Lake Nicaragua is in danger of going the same way. It has almost lost all of its famous freshwater bull sharks.

Unfortunately, environmental issues often fall toward the bottom of the list of priorities when your main worry is where the next meal is coming from. Nevertheless, both countries are waking up to the idea that caring for the environment is increasingly important. Anti-litter campaigns have had some success, and environmental awareness is now on the school curriculum. Suchitoto in El Salvador has instigated a new waste-water management scheme and banned all political graffiti from sidewalks, walls, and telegraph poles—a giant step in a country overrun with ugly political scribblings in both urban and rural areas. Sea turtle schemes encourage locals to protect rather than hunt, and the benefits can be seen in the busloads of curious tourists who come to view the famous reptiles nesting. Yet tourism is not the panacea some proclaim and can be just as destructive, as was revealed by the hotel resort in Nicaragua that was trucking out raw sewage and dumping it near an unsuspecting village. There are some green shoots of optimism, however. Preservation is taking hold in cities such as Granada, which has banned a certain American fast food chain from setting up shop in the center. As well as the official national parks, there are ever-increasing collections of private initiatives and wildlife refuges that are doing their bit to hold onto what is left.

THE ACTIVE NICARAGUA & EL SALVADOR VACATION PLANNER

Biking, hiking, fishing, birding: These are just a few of the choices when planning activities in Nicaragua and El Salvador. Adrenaline lovers can zip over jungles or surf the best breaks in the Americas. Those of a gentler disposition will get a kick out of the fantastic opportunities to see pristine nature and peer into volcanic craters.

There are an infinite number of ways to plan an active vacation in Nicaragua and El Salvador. One major consideration is the availability of outfitters. Mountain biking and kayaking, for example, should be huge here, but unfortunately, there are not many operators offering such tours—not yet, anyway. This chapter lays out your options, from tour operators who run multi-activity package tours that often include stays at ecolodges, to the best places to pursue active endeavors, to an overview of both countries' national parks and bioreserves.

THE BEST NATIONAL PARKS & NATURE RESERVES

Nicaragua

Getting back to nature comes easily in Nicaragua, and wherever you stay, you are almost guaranteed a jungle full of howler monkeys or a smoldering volcanic abyss nearby. There are almost 80 protected areas in the country, encompassing 2 million hectares (nearly 4.9 million acres). They come in the form of national parks, reserves, and privately owned wildlife refuges. Many are protected in name only, as the government's park-management body, MARENA (www.marena.gob.ni), is woefully underfunded. Below are some of the best and most interesting places.

Greenfields Nature Reserve   A private wildlife refuge near the Caribbean port of Bluefields and tantalizingly close to the Pearl Lagoon and the enchanting desert islands known as the Pearl Cays. The reserve can be toured on a day trip from the city, or you can stay at the reserve's lodge. See p. 171.

Isla Juan Venado Wildlife Reserve   A wetland park on the Pacific coast, west of León, where crocodiles and waterfowl occupy a strip of beach and the myriad waterways of mangrove swamp host turtle nesting sites. The reserve is accessible from Las Peñitas beach and is an excellent 1-day excursion from León. See p. 213.

Playa La Flor Nature Reserve ★★★   A beautiful Pacific beach just south of San Juan del Sur, this is also where you should head for a great nighttime excursion to see spectacular turtle nesting. See p. 130.

Miraflor Nature Reserve ★   This lush 6,000-hectare (14,826-acre) mountain retreat features abundant wildlife and small farms conducting sustainable agriculture. It is easily reached from the highland city of Estelí. See p. 184.

Parque Nacional Archipiélago Zapatera   A collection of islands famous for its pre-Columbian stone carvings, this park is 2 hours away from Granada on Lake Nicaragua. See p. 122.

Reserva Charco Verde ★   A black volcanic beach and bay with a green lagoon that offer excellent opportunities for bird-watching. The tiny reserve is located on the twin volcano island Isla de Ometepe in the southwest of the country. See p. 147.

Refugio de Vida Silvestre Los Guatuzos ★★   This 440-sq.-km (170-sq.-mile) park of lush wetland is located on the southern shores of Lago Nicaragua, close to the grimy town of San Carlos. Lizards dash across the water on their hind legs while caimans, turtles, and iguanas bathe in the sun. See p. 159.

Refugio de Vida Silvestre Río Escalante Chacocente ★   This reserve has a long stretch of sand bordered by a tropical dry forest that's teeming with wildlife that includes white-tailed deer, giant iguanas, and nesting turtles. Note, however, that facilities are very basic, and access is difficult at this destination, located north of San Juan del Sur. See p. 142.

Reserva Biológica Indio-Maíz   Located along the banks of the broad Río San Juan that drains from Lago Nicaragua to the Atlantic, this mega park holds 300 species of reptiles and amphibians. It is the second-biggest reserve and one of the largest primary rainforests in Central America. See p. 163.

Reserva de Biosfera Bosawás   The largest piece of pristine rainforest north of the Amazon, this is also the most remote and hardest to reach, located in the northeastern Atlantic region. See p. 198.

Reserva Tisey   Situated in the northern highlands, the reserve offers one of the best views in Nicaragua, as well as an ecolodge and hiking trails. Nearby is the 15m-high (49-ft.) Salto Estanzuela. Both make a great day trip from Estelí. See p. 186.

Volcán Masaya National Park ★★   There's an access road that leads right up to the gaping crater hole here, and the surrounding 5,000-hectare (12,355-acre) park has lava fields, bat caves, and a variety of wildlife that includes sulfur-immune parakeets that live in the crater walls. It's possible to visit the park on a day trip from Masaya, Managua, or Granada. The visitor's center has an interesting museum and offers guided tours. See p. 94.

Volcán Mombacho Nature Reserve The reserve has some beautiful hiking trails and incredible biodiversity, including a cloud forest with orchids and abundant wildlife. There is a biological station that provides lodging, and the park is easily accessible from Granada. See p. 123.

El Salvador

There are only four national parks in El Salvador, and the country is easily dwarfed by Nicaragua when it comes to opportunities to see raw nature. Nevertheless, there are plenty of places here that will thrill and please. The country may lack the larger mammal species of its neighbors, but it has a surprisingly rich range of birds and butterflies.

Barra de Santiago ★★★ This is a protected reserve and tiny fishing village tucked into the southwest corner of the country. It has miles of deserted, pristine beaches that sit a few hundred yards from a mangrove-filled estuary teeming with birds. See p. 293.

Isla de Montecristo ★★ A gorgeous, largely undeveloped 2.5-sq.-km (1-sq.-mile) island is situated where the large Río Lempa empties into the Pacific. The tiny island is home to acres of fruit trees, a few farming communities, and hundreds of nesting birds. See p. 300.

Lago Suchitlán ★★ This manmade dam near the pretty town of Suchitoto is a stopping-off point for thousands of migrating birds and a huge draw for birding enthusiasts. See p. 263.

Parque Ecológio de Cinquera ★★ A 3,921-hectare (9,689-acre) preserve and forest 1 hour from Suchitoto, the park has a small waterfall and a few trails that lead to the historic village of Cinquera. See p. 263.

Parque Imposible ★★ This is one of El Salvador's most verdant and diverse forests and should be a definite stop for nature lovers. The 3,278-hectare (8,100-acre) park derives its name from its challenging terrain, and the park is home to more than 400 types of trees, 275 species of birds, hundreds of species of butterflies, and 100 types of mammals. See p. 319.

Parque Nacional de Montecristo A 1,972-hectare (4,873-acre) protected reserve tucked high into El Salvador's mountains that border Honduras and Guatemala, it features some of the country's most lush forests and most diverse flora and fauna, including dozens of orchid species and numerous rare birds such as toucans, quetzals, and striped owls. See p. 335.

Parque Nacional Los Volcanes ★★ The park comprises 4,500 hectares (11,120 acres) of private and public lands. It is home to the steep and barren Volcán Izalco, the highest volcano in El Salvador, the recently active Volcán de Santa Ana, and the green hills of Cerro Verde. See p. 333.

ACTIVITIES A TO Z
Archeological Sites

If you are looking for Maya splendor, visit the ruins at **Tazumal** in western El Salvador (p. 328). Another interesting Maya site in El Salvador, though not as visually stunning, is the abandoned village known as **Joya de Cerén** (p. 252).

The Maya did not make it to Nicaragua, but that does not mean the country lacks fascinating pre-Columbian heritage. The islands of **Zapatera** (p. 122) and **Ometepe** (p. 144) have large zoomorphic basalt statues, a collection of which can be seen at the **Museo Antiguo Convento de San Francisco** (p. 107). in Granada **León Viejo** is an abandoned colonial city now a UNESCO World Heritage Site (p. 212). **Museo Las Huellas de Acahualinca** (p. 84) in Managua holds a set of footprints that date back to 4000 B.C.

Biking

Challenging roads and rugged landscape make both countries perfect for mountain biking, though rental bikes are limited to a handful of areas, and there are few specialist outfitters or tour agencies. If you are on a long-distance cycle trip, bring spare equipment, as bike stores are few and far between. **San Juan del Sur** has several hostels and restaurants that rent mountain bikes for use on the dirt roads that stretch up and down the coast. **Isla de Ometepe** provides an excellent 35km (22-mile) circuit around Volcán Maderas. You can rent bikes on the island at **Hotel Finca Playa Venecia** and **Hotel Finca Santo Domingo** (p. 150). Another good route in Nicaragua is through the mountain towns of **Los Pueblos Blancos,** close to Masaya (p. 98).

The **Ruta de las Flores** in El Salvador is a rugged arrangement of villages and hills, and you can pick a bike up in the town of Juayúa (p. 308). **Tacuba,** close the El Imposible National Park, is another excellent opportunity for pedaling over some rough terrain. You can hire a bike and guide at **Imposible Tours** at the Hostal Mamá y Papá (p. 321). Colonial **Suchitoto,** north of San Salvador, has some scenic routes in the surrounding mountains and around the lake. Inquire at **Las Puertas de Suchitoto** for bike rentals (p. 264).

Bird-Watching

Nicaragua's eastern region, particularly along the Río San Juan, is becoming a bird-watcher's mecca. Tennessee warblers, kingfishers, red macaw, and the yellow-chested oropendola are just some of the colorful residents you can spot while touring the area. The birdlife of the **Solentiname Islands** has inspired artists and a completely new primitivist art form (p. 155), while the **Refugio de Vida Silvestre Los Guatuzos** on the southern shores of Lago Nicaragua lets you view tropical birdlife undisturbed while you float down a jungle river (p. 159). The beautiful quetzal can be seen in much of the country, including **Miraflor Nature Reserve** in the northern highlands (p. 184). **Isla Juan Venado Wildlife Reserve** west of León has abundant waterfowl (p. 213), and **Reserva Charco Verde** on Isla de Ometepe provides an excellent opportunity to see hummingbirds and scarlet tanagers (p. 147).

El Salvador's bird life is surprisingly rich, considering its lack of forest. **Parque Nacional Los Volcanes** is home to emerald toucanets, woodpeckers, and motmots (p. 333). **Montecristo** and **El Imposible** national parks (p. 335 and 317) have abundant birdlife, and **Barra de Santiago** in the west of the country has yellow-naped parrots and white-fronted parrots nesting in its estuary and mangrove swamps (p. 293). To catch flocks of migratory birds, take a boat trip around **Lago de Suchitlán** near Suchitoto (p. 263).

Canopy/Zip-Line Tours

Canopy tours have taken off (literally) in Nicaragua, and no wonder, as they offer a unique and exhilarating way to experience the forest. By bringing you to the treetops, they allow you to see the place most of the wildlife lives—although most animals are frightened off by gringos flying through the air on a regular basis.

Most of the tours consist of strapping yourself into a climbing harness and walking to a platform approximately 30m (98 ft.) above the forest floor. Usually 10 to 20 platforms connected by metal cables form a course. You, with the help of a guide, will attach your harness to the cable and jump, flying through the air to the next platform, where another guide will be waiting. There's little regulation of the tours, so be sure you feel confident in the course and the safety standards before setting off.

There is no jungle in the capital Managua, but a small crater lake known as **Loma de Tiscapa** provides a three-platform canopy run (just be sure not to fall into the heavily polluted water; p. 84). **Volcán Mombacho,** close to Granada, has two excellent canopy runs, including a 17-platform zip route designed by the inventor of the sport (p. 123). Another great run is **Da Flying Frog** just outside San Juan del Sur, which has lovely views of the ocean as you zip along (p. 129).

El Salvador has less to offer regarding canopy tours, but this should change as the activity catches on. There is one company on the Ruta de las Flores called **Apaneca Canopy Tours** (p. 311) and another called **Reserva Ecológica El Limo** (p. 338) in Metapan that has cables running over 14 hectares (35 acres) of lush, rolling hills traversed by rivers, weirs, and waterfalls.

Diving & Snorkeling

Without doubt, the best diving and snorkeling area for both countries is in the **Corn Islands,** 80km (50 miles) east of the Atlantic coast in Nicaragua. Here, you'll find coral reefs and caves comparable to the best in Honduras and Belize without the crowds (p. 171). The Pacific coast is much more limited. Diving is possible in **San Juan del Sur,** but there are currently no dive shops. **Los Cobanos** on El Salvador's Balsamo Coast is another possible dive area, but poor visibility and no reefs mean it is a poor option compared to the sapphire waters of the Caribbean (p. 292). For something different, try diving in a deep, blue crater lake. **Ilopango,** which reaches a depth of 250m (820 ft.) is a popular diving spot in El Salvador.

Fishing

Nicaragua has the best spots for dropping a hook. **San Juan del Sur** has deep-sea fishing, with sailfish and dorado the catch of the day. Jacks, roosterfish, and snapper are other species fished out of the inshore waters. Sport fishing also turns up some huge and colorful specimens in the gorgeous waters of the **Corn Islands.** Kingfish, red snapper, and barracuda are in abundance, and bonefishing from the shore is also possible. **Lake Nicaragua** provides the best opportunity for freshwater fishing, with huge tarpon and *guapote* often ending up on restaurant dinner plates.

Golf

Las Veraneras Resort on the western Pacific coast (© **503/2420-5000;** www.veranerasresort.com) is the best place to practice your swing in El Salvador. The luxury resort has a 7,000-yard, 18-hole course close to Playa los Cobanos. The best golf course in Nicaragua is the 18-hole **Nejapa Country Club** near Sabana Grande (© **504/2266-9652**).

Hiking

You will never be at a loss for a hiking trail in either country, and somewhere close to your hotel, there is most likely a dirt track with a waterfall at the end of it. **Juayúa,** on El Salvador's Ruta de las Flores, is one such place, with lovely walks over the hills, around lakes, and through coffee plantations (p. 308). **Parque Nacional El Imposible** is *imposible* to miss and easily the most accessible primary forest in the country (p. 317). The popular **Parque Nacional Los Volcanes** has volcanoes to climb, including the dark, barren cone known as Volcán Izalco (p. 333), while the eastern town of **Perquín** has trails that were originally created by guerrillas during the war years (p. 278).

Matagalpa in the Nicaraguan highlands has a dizzying array of hikes (p. 190), as does **Reserva Natural Miraflor** near Estelí (p. 184). However, what makes Nicaragua special is the range of volcanoes begging to be climbed there, including the twin peaks of **Isla de Ometepe** (p. 144). Be sure to hire a guide to show you the way around these often-smoking, active peaks.

Horseback Riding

Although you may see some of the locals getting around in the rural areas by horse, there is a lack of operators offering organized tours. Your best bet is to stay at a hotel or lodge that conducts its own four-legged excursions. **Montecristo River Lodge** on the Río San Juan in southeastern Nicaragua (p. 164) is one good option. Another good place for some time in the saddle is the **Tisey Reserve,** close to Estelí (p. 186).

In El Salvador, tour operators in Suchitoto offer excellent horseback tours around **Volcán Guazapa** and **Parque Ecológico de Cinquera** (p. 263). The upscale **Entre Pinos Resort** in La Palma has private horseback excursions in the surrounding mountains (p. 272). Apaneca and the surrounding area in western El Salvador also offer some beautiful circuits.

Kayaking and Boating

Nicaragua should be the king of kayaking; it has so many rivers, estuaries, and inlets. Indeed, by dugout canoe is how many of the locals get around, especially in areas such as **Las Isletas** in Granada (p. 122), the Río Istián on **Ometepe Island** (p. 144), the **Solentiname Islands,** and the countless mangrove estuaries and islands along the Atlantic coast such as the **Pearl Cays.** Unfortunately, there are few outfitters, and most are based around Granada. Next to asking a local for the loan of a boat (which is entirely normal and possible), your best bet is to stay at a lodge that has its own kayaks and boats, such as the hostels on **Laguna de Apoyo** (p. 124) and the **Hospedaje Charco Verde** on Ometepe Island. (p. 150). **Montecristo River Lodge** will also help get you up the Río San Juan with a paddle (p. 164). **Reserva Natural Isla Juan Venado** near León also conducts kayak tours (p. 213). For laid-back booze cruises, there are several operators in **San Juan del Sur** (p. 127). True hardcore kayak adventurers will find the 700km (435-mile) **Río Coco** along the Honduran border to be the ultimate boating experience. You'll have to bring your own kayak, however, as this area is isolated, with little or no tourist infrastructure.

El Salvador might not have the variety and quantity of options of its southern neighbor, but there are still plenty of opportunities to kayak and boat. The best option is to find a hotel that offers boat excursions, such as **La Cocotera** in the beautiful

HEALTH, SAFETY & etiquette
IN THE WILDERNESS

While most tours and adventure activities are relatively safe, serious risks may be involved for careless participants. However, a little common sense is all you need. Risks most often occur when people try to extend their efforts beyond their physical capabilities. Know your limits. The sometimes-extreme heat and wild temperature shifts found in Nicaragua and El Salvador can take their toll on a body rather quickly. Heavy downpours can occur at any time, thus dropping the temperatures and making rainforest paths beyond slippery. Rain gear is essential in this environment, as is sunscreen. Have dry clothes ready, too, for the end of your excursion.

When hiking through the jungle—there's real, genuine, wild jungle here—and the backcountry, there are general precautions to take. Chances are you will not see many snakes, if any, but if you do, don't encourage one to bite you. Stay calm, don't make any sudden movements, and don't touch it. If you swim in lagoons and near mangrove forests, just remember that healthy populations of critters—from otters to caimans—inhabit most of them. Ask locals where it is safe to swim. Also, avoid swimming in major rivers unless a guide or local operator can vouch for their safety. Be careful with ocean currents, as well, especially along the Pacific coast.

Bugs and bug bites will probably be your greatest health concern in the wet and humid wilderness, and even they aren't as big of a problem as you might expect. Even on the Atlantic coast, there aren't that many mosquitoes. Mostly, bugs are an inconvenience, although mosquitoes can carry malaria or dengue. Strong repellent and proper clothing minimize both the danger and the inconvenience; you might also want to bring along some cortisone or Benadryl cream to soothe itching. At some beaches, you'll probably be bitten by *pirujas* (sand fleas or no-see-ums). These nearly invisible insects leave an irritating welt. Try not to scratch because this can lead to open sores and infections. *Pirujas* are most active at sunrise and sunset, so you might want to cover up or avoid the beaches at these times.

The slogan "Leave nothing but footprints; take nothing but memories" certainly applies here, though if you can avoid leaving footprints, even better. Much of the Nicaraguan wilderness holds an array of rare and little-known flora and fauna, and some of it is highly endangered and endemic to the specific mountain or tract of forest. Do not cut or uproot plants or flowers. Pack out everything you pack in, and please do not litter. Take photos and nothing else.

Barra de Santiago (p. 293). Or go with a tour operator, such as **Mango y Mar** (www.mangoymar.com), who will arrange kayak tours around the **Isla Montecristo, Bahía de Jiquilisco** (p. 301), or the deep blue volcanic lake **Coatepeque** (p. 330). Boating trips are available from several hotels along the **Balsamo Coast,** in particular **Royal Decameron Salinatas** resort at **Playa Los Cóbanas** (p. 292). You can also arrange for an operator to take you out on boat on **Lago de Suchitlán,** near Suchitoto (p. 263).

Spa & Yoga Retreats

Besides the spas you'll find in the capitals' high-end hotels and several exclusive seaside resorts, wellness retreats are a little thin on the ground in both countries. There are, however, some notable places beginning to appear, and it is only a matter of time before the health and pampering scene in Nicaragua and El Salvador will rival that of Costa Rica, especially considering the amount of undeveloped hot springs that dot both countries.

Nica Yoga (© **505/8400-0255;** www.nicayoga.com) is Nicaragua's first yoga community, located 3km (1¾ miles) outside San Juan del Sur. This is an all-inclusive yoga retreat, with accommodations and surfing excursions provided, starting at $700 per person per week (p. 133).

Surfing

You can surf all year round in Nicaragua and El Salvador, with waves as big as 4m (13 ft.) crashing into the coast in the months of March and April. The dry season, from November to February, has smaller waves of 2m (6½ ft.) or less, but the weather is better and the surf ideal for beginners. Water temperatures average around 77°F (25°C). Boards can be bought or rented in La Libertad or San Juan del Sur, but hardcore surfers often bring their own, especially if they intend to go to less developed spots.

El Salvador has arguably the best surf in Central America, mostly based along the western Pacific **Balsamo Coast.** There are plenty of surf shops and hotels here catering to surfers who are taking advantage of rides that can be as long as 150m (492 ft.) or even 200m (656 ft.). Most breaks come from the left, with the exception of surf close to the unattractive town of **La Libertad** (p. 286). **Punta Roca** is the most famous surfing spot, but other appealing runs in this area include **Playa El Zonte, Playa El Tunco,** and **Playa San Blas.** The eastern Pacific is less developed and the terrain broader and straighter than the many coves and inlets of the western shore. Here **Playa El Cuco** and **Playa Las Flores** are drawing the most interest (p. 302).

The southwestern Pacific shores of Nicaragua are where the best surfing takes place, particularly around **San Juan del Sur** and the string of beaches that stretches north and south (p. 128). Here, you'll find cheap beach-bum hostels and luxury surf camps. Beach access is becoming a problem as the area becomes more developed, and many of the best breaks can be reached only by boat. Yet there are plenty of options for all budgets. **Popoyo** is fast becoming the most popular place to surf, and other well-regarded beaches include **Playa Pie de Gigante** and **Playa Madera.** Surfing is also possible on the beaches west of León, such as **Poneloya** and **Las Peñitas** (p. 213). There is little or no surfing along the Atlantic coast.

Swimming

There aren't many places in the world that offer you the opportunity to take a dip in deep blue volcanic lakes. Many lakeside hotels and hostels have piers to dive off, particularly those around **Lago de Coatepeque** in El Salvador (p. 330) and **Laguna de Apoyo** in Nicaragua (p. 124). The Pacific attracts plenty of swimmers too, but beware of strong undercurrents in some areas and remember that lifeguards are non-existent. The beaches are, of course, the best place to top off your tan, but women should note that going topless is not an option anywhere. Several reserves and parks have excellent spring pools, and there is a bounty of waterfalls in El Salvador along the **Ruta de las Flores** (p. 305) and near **Suchitoto** (p. 258).

ECOLODGES

Nicaragua and El Salvador are not immune to the boom in ecotourism, with the former especially well positioned to take advantage of the vast amount of untamed nature it possesses. Lodges vary greatly in luxury and amenities: Be sure to choose a lodge that meets your expectations. Also, take into consideration that many by their very "nature" are in isolated areas.

NICARAGUA

San Simian Eco Resort (© 505/8813-6866; www.sansimian.com; p. 126) is a cluster of ecohuts on the shore of Laguna de Apoyo, just outside Granada.

Mariposa Eco Hotel & Spanish School (© 505/8418-4638; www.mariposaspanishschool.com; p. 92) is situated in the hills between Masaya and Managua and offers a farmhouse-style atmosphere and Spanish classes.

Finca Magdalena (© 505/8880-2041; www.fincamagdalena.com; p. 150) is an old coffee plantation with a simple farmyard lifestyle on the enchanting Isla de Ometepe.

Montecristo River Lodge (© 505/2583-0197 or 505/8649-9012; www.montecristoriverlodge.com; p. 164) is set on the Río San Juan on the way to the old fort of El Castillo. It practices sustainable tourism, with a wildlife refuge and hiking trails.

Greenfields Nature Reserve (© 505/2268-1897; www.greenfields.com.ni; p. 171), near Bluefields, offers excellent jungle excursions and canoeing trips in pristine wilderness.

Selva Negra Mountain Resort (© 505/8612-3883; www.selvanegra.com; p. 197) is a working coffee farm and cloud-forest retreat in the northern highlands.

Finca Esperanza Verde (© 505/2772-5003; www.fincaesperanzaverde.org; p. 194) is a pioneer in responsible tourism and sustainable agriculture, with organic coffee plantations, cloud forest, waterfalls, and a butterfly farm.

Posada La Soñada (© 505/2713-6333; p. 184) is a well-established lodge in the beautiful Miraflor Nature Reserve, close to the northern town of Estelí.

Morgan's Rock Hacienda and Eco Lodge (© 505/8670-7676; www.morgansrock.com; p. 137) combines both luxury and environmentally friendly accommodations. It is located north of San Juan del Sur.

Jicaro Island Lodge (© 505/8403-1236; www.jicarolodge.com; p. 118) is an island paradise located on freshwater Lake Nicaragua, a 10-minute boat ride from Granada.

EL SALVADOR

Perquín Lenca Hotel de Montaña (© 503/2680-4046; www.perkinlenca.com; p. 280) is a mountainside, cabin-style hotel in the rugged hinterland of Perquín, in eastern El Salvador.

La Cocotera (© 503/2245-3691; www.lacocoteraresort.com; p. 295) is a gorgeous property tucked between an estuary and the beach, and surrounded by a coconut plantation on the isolated Barra de Santiago. Stylish rooms with an environmental conscience make this an unforgettable stay.

El Imposible Eco Lodge (© 503/2411-5484; www.elimposible-ecolodge.com; p. 322) is located at the entrance to Parque Nacional El Imposible. A-frame wooden huts with private verandas overlook a small, rock-lined pool here with natural spring water.

Volcano Surfing

Nicaragua's most idiosyncratic extreme sport takes place close to the city of **León** in the northwest of the country, where the black slopes of **Cerro Negro** are attracting legions of adventure seekers intent on doing something different at 64kmph (40 mph; p. 207). If you think that trekking up the side of an active volcano and then shooting down its side sounds like a good time, be sure to check out this unique activity, which has even made it to the pages of *The New York Times*.

ORGANIZED ADVENTURE TRIPS

Tour Agencies

While more and more international tour operators run trips to Nicaragua and El Salvador, they are almost always contracted out through local operators, such as those mentioned here. Booking directly will save you a bundle. A bundle! Most are based in the capitals or the main tourist towns, such as Granada and León. Many hotels and lodges will also help you organize a tour in their particular areas.

EL SALVADOR

Akwaterra (Zona Rosa, San Salvador; ℰ **503/2245-2614;** www.akwaterra.com) arranges surfing, kayaking, and fishing trips, as well as a stay at their Lodge La Escondida in the coffee plantation El Portezuelo on the Ruta de las Flores.

Eco Mayan Tours (Paseo General Escalón 3658, Colonia Escalón, San Salvador; ℰ **503/2298-2844;** www.ecomayantours.com) organizes tours all around the country, including a city tour of the capital and an excursion to Parque Nacional de Las Volcanes.

Eva Tours (3a Calle Poniente 3737, Colonia Escalón, San Salvador; ℰ **503/2209-8888;** www.evatours.com.sv) is a large, catch-all agency that runs tours in every region, including the coast and Morazán. It also has a branch in the Sheraton Hotel.

Imposible Tours (Av. Cuscatlán near Calle 10, Tacuba; ℰ **503/2417-4268;** www.imposibletours.com) arranges 6- to 8-hour day and night tours of El Imposible, as well as an 8-hour waterfall hike.

Sophia Tours (Plaza Via del Mar, Local 3, Puerta de La Libertad; ℰ **503/2242-7841;** www.sophiatours.com.sv) is another conventional agency that runs tours under themes such as archaeological, artisanal, colonial, and ecological.

Tropic El Salvador (Av. Olimpica 3597, Colonia Escalón, San Salvador; ℰ **503/2279-3236;** www.tropicelsalvador.com) has some imaginative tours such as surfing on the Río Lempa and a Maya route that crosses into Guatemala and Honduras.

Eco Tourism La Mora (Suchitoto; ℰ **503/2323-6874;** www.ecoturismolamora.es.tl) offers Spanish-only hiking and horseback tours around Suchitoto and nearby Volcán Guazapa.

Gringo Tours (Calle Francisco Morazan #27, Suchitoto; ℰ **503/7327-2351**) is run by the wise and knowledgeable American expat Robert Broz and offers fascinating tours that specialize in the archaeological heritage and civil war history of the area surrounding Suchitoto.

NICARAGUA

Tours Nicaragua (El Sol #110, Colonial Los Robles, Managua; ℰ 505/2252-4035; www.toursnicaragua.com) specializes in private tours with highly qualified guides.

Itineraries are custom designed and can include nature trips to the Solentiname Archipelago, adventure tours on Ometepe Island, or beach holidays on the Pacific coast.

Nicaragua Adventures (on the corner beside the Spanish Consulate, Granada; © 505/8883-7161; www.nica-adventures.com) runs 1- to 5-day package tours, including one called "3 Seas" that whisks you from the Caribbean Corn Islands to Lago de Nicaragua to the Pacific coast.

Va Pues Tours (on the northern side of Iglesia El Laborio, León; © 505/8606-2276; www.vapues.com) is a more conventional tour company that organizes a variety of group excursions, including day tours to Volcán Mombacho and city tours of León and Managua.

Explore Nicaragua Tours (30m/98 ft. west of Iglesia Las Palmas, Managua; © 505/2250-1534) is a clearinghouse for tours all over the country, including to coffee farms in Matagalapa. They also arrange flights, car rentals, and hotel reservations.

Luz y Luna (1 block north, behind cathedral, Estelí; © **505/8441-8466;** www. cafeluzyluna.com) is owned by English expat Juanita, who is the go-to-person in Estelí for tours and info on the area. Tours include a circuit of the town's murals and visits to the thriving cigar factories.

Matagalpa Tours (½ block east of Banpro, Matagalpa; © **505/2772-0108;** www.matagalpatours.com) is the trekking expert for the area and the best-organized tour company in town. They conduct tours of the coffee farms and arrange overnight stays in nearby ecolodges.

Dale Dagger's Surf Nicaragua (1 block inland from the Mercado Municipal, San Juan del Sur; © **505/2568-2492;** www.nicasurf.com) is one of the better established surfing outfitters, offering excursions and weeklong packages in the San Juan del Sur area.

Solentiname Tours (Apartado Postal 1388, Managua; © **505/2270-9981;** www. solentinametours.com) offers countrywide tours, including several days on the Solentiname Islands and down the Río San Juan.

Zapatera Tours (Calle Palmira and La Cancha, Granada © **505/8842-2587;** www.zapateratours.com) offers 1-day tours to the little-visited Zapatera archipelago, off the shore of Granada.

U.S. & International Adventure Tour Operators

These agencies and operators specialize in well-organized and coordinated tours that cover your entire stay. Many travelers prefer to have everything arranged and confirmed before arriving in Nicaragua or El Salvador, and this is a good idea for first-timers and during the high season. Most of these operators, however, are not cheap, with 10-day tours generally costing in the neighborhood of $1,800 to $3,000 per person, not including airfare.

G.A.P. Adventures (© 800/708-7761; www.gapadventures.com) has adventure and leisure tours in more than 100 countries, including Nicaragua and El Salvador.

Journeys Latin America (© 020/8747-8315; www.journeylatinamerica.co.uk) is a specialty travel agency focusing on all Latin American destinations.

Mesoamerican Ecotourism Alliance/MEA (© 800/682-0584; www.travel withmea.org) offers a handful of very specific, all-inclusive, multiday tours in Nicaragua and El Salvador that explore many of the top and most remote national parks in the country.

Mountain Travel Sobek (② 888/831-7526; www.mtsobek.com), an off-the-beaten-track adventure travel operator that is no stranger to luxury, has 7- to 9-day trips in Nicaragua that take in volcanoes, lakes, and rainforests.

Overseas Adventure Travel (② 800/493-6824; www.oattravel.com) offers good-value natural history and "soft adventure" itineraries with optional add-on excursions. Tours are limited to 16 people and are guided by naturalists. All accommodations are in small hotels, lodges, or tent camps. Their Nicaragua and El Salvador itineraries are usually part of larger Central America tours that take in several countries over several weeks.

SUGGESTED ITINERARIES

They may appear small, but Nicaragua & El Salvador have lots to see and do. If you have less than 2 weeks to spend here, you'll have to make some difficult choices about how to spend your time, but the suggestions below will help you plan. Of course, at many of these stops, you'll be tempted to spend much, much longer.

THE BEST OF NICARAGUA & EL SALVADOR IN 1 WEEK

Money rich but time poor? You have to be both if you wish to see both countries in 1 week. My advice is to avoid the capitals and choose either tour companies or taxis to whisk you around on what will be a whistle-stop tour of each country's highlights. Thankfully, the colonial gems of Suchitoto and Granada have well-developed tourist facilities that will allow you to use both as bases of operations. Their short distances from other attractions mean you can see a lot on day trips. However, you'll have to abandon thoughts of visiting such jungle paradises as the Barra de Santiago and the Río San Juan, as these are multiday destinations in themselves. Below is a 1-week fleeting taste of both countries that will surely have you begging to come back and see more.

Days 1 & 2: Arrive in San Salvador & Transfer to Suchitoto ★★★

Arrange for your hotel to pick you up and transfer you to the pretty village of **Suchitoto,** 1 hour north. Take a stroll around its radiant, cobbled streets and browse through its art galleries and handicraft stalls before jumping on a boat to tour the bird-filled waters of **Lago de Suchitlán.** Stay at the glorious colonial hotel **Los Almendros de San Lorenzo** (p. 265) and dine in the restaurant/gallery/war museum known as **Villa Balanza.** The next day, explore the surrounding countryside with a tour company, visiting the unusual **Los Tercios** waterfall, bullet-scarred villages, and abandoned rebel camps.

Day 3: Ruta de las Flores ★★

The Ruta de las Flores is a collection of beautiful little towns along a 35km (22-mile) stretch of winding mountain road, located about

Nicaragua & El Salvador in 1 Week

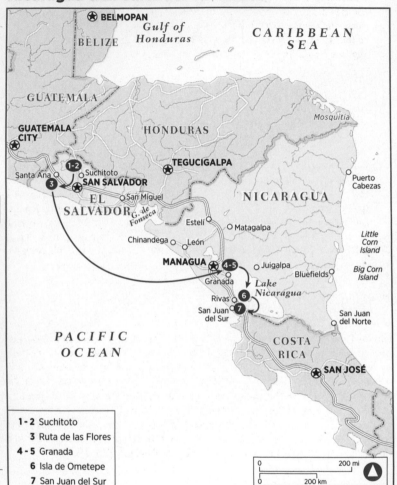

1 – 2 Suchitoto
3 Ruta de las Flores
4 – 5 Granada
6 Isla de Ometepe
7 San Juan del Sur

2 hours west of Suchitoto. You can do the route on a 1-day tour with either a tour company, rented car, or a taxi. Stop in **Nahuizalco** (p. 306) to check out the handcrafted furniture, **Juayúa** (p. 308) to see the black Christ, and **Ataco** ★★★ (p. 312) to experience some cool art you won't find elsewhere in El Salvador. Stop for lunch at the lovely garden restaurant **Entre Nubes** (p. 313). End the day back in Suchitoto to prepare for your flight out the next day.

Days 4 & 5: Arrive in Managua & Head to Granada ★★★

After flying into Managua, don't hang around the capital too long. It has its hidden charms, but more beautiful places beckon, like the radiant colonial city of

Granada, 2 hours south. Head there immediately and settle into the **Hotel Plaza Colón** ★★★ (p. 114) to relax and perhaps sip a rum on the rocks from the gigantic balcony overlooking the colorful plaza. The next morning, catch a horse-and-carriage ride through the city's enchanting cobbled streets and down to the lakeshore, where you can take a short boat tour of **Las Isletas** archipelago (see p. 122 for tips on how to see the islands in a less touristy manner).

Days 6 & 7: Tour Isla de Ometepe ★★ & Arrive in San Juan del Sur ★

Arrange for a tour company to pick you up at your hotel and take you to the small town of **San Jorge,** where you can catch a boat across to the twin-peak jungle island of **Ometepe.** You won't have time to climb its volcanic peaks, but a 4WD can take you on a coastal tour of this island of howler monkeys, pre-Columbian carved stones, and mud-bathing farm animals.

Arrive back in San Jorge in the early evening to be transferred to the beach town of **San Juan del Sur.** Stay at the lovely villa **La Posada Azul** ★★ (p. 134) and eat in the garden of **El Colibrí** ★★ (p. 138). The following day, catch a water taxi up the coast to some beautiful, secluded beaches, or, depending on the time of year, take a night excursion to watch the spectacular turtle hatching in **Playa La Flor** ★ (p. 130). Return to Managua the following day for your trip home.

THE BEST OF NICARAGUA & EL SALVADOR IN 2 WEEKS

Two weeks are better than one, but you'll still find yourself sacrificing some intriguing destinations because of time constraints. The El Salvador itinerary below does not explore the east of the country simply because the largest number of exemplary villages and natural areas in El Salvador are clustered in the west. But eastern El Salvador does offer some excellent attractions, such as Perquín's Museo de la Revolución (p. 279), the historic Mozote monument (p. 280), and the undeveloped and charming Isla de Montecristo (p. 300). The Nicaragua leg also leaves out some amazing places in the north of the country, such as León city and its beautiful cathedral (p. 202), and the northern highland towns of Estelí (p. 181) and Matagalpa (p. 190).

Day 1: Arrive in San Salvador ★

San Salvador is El Salvador's center of luxury, with the type of high-end, international restaurants, shopping, and hotels you won't find elsewhere in the country. So take some time to soak up its modern amenities before heading out into El Salvador's more rural areas. Try to arrive in the morning so that you can settle into your hotel. The 5-star **Hilton** (p. 237) and the boutique **Casa Il Buon Gustaio** (p. 237) are just two of the many accommodation choices in the city. After checking in, take a taxi over to El Centro, the city center. Spend a couple of hours viewing El Salvador's iconic **Catedral Metropolitana** ★ (p. 247), **Teatro Nacional** ★ (p. 248), and huge street market **Mercado Central** ★ (a good spot to grab lunch; p. 254). Then bus or cab over to the other side of town to spend the afternoon in the Zona Rosa and Colonia San Benito neighborhoods, where you can visit the **Museo de Arte** ★★★ (p. 247) and **Museo Naciona**█

Nicaragua & El Salvador in 2 Weeks

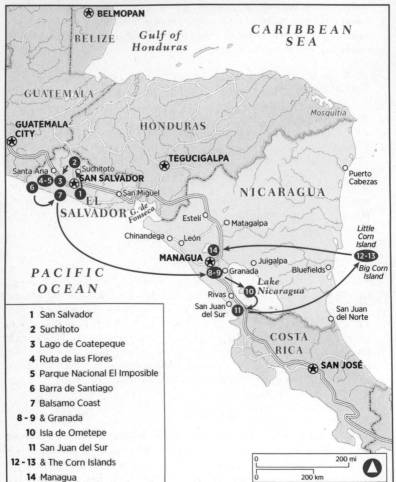

1 San Salvador
2 Suchitoto
3 Lago de Coatepeque
4 Ruta de las Flores
5 Parque Nacional El Imposible
6 Barra de Santiago
7 Balsamo Coast
8 - 9 & Granada
10 Isla de Ometepe
11 San Juan del Sur
12 - 13 & The Corn Islands
14 Managua

de Antropología Dr. David J. Guzman ★★ (p. 248). Afterward, stop by the **Mercado Nacional de Artesanías** ★★ (p. 255) or stroll the shops of the **Boulevard del Hipódromo** (p. 254), where you can enjoy a great dinner in one of the area's ethnic restaurants. If you have the energy, continue on to the night-clubs and lounges of the **Multiplaza Mall** (p. 254), or just head back to the hotel to rest up for a trip to Suchitoto the next day.

Day 2: Suchitoto ★★★

Today, you'll head to Suchitoto by taxi (p. 259), 47km (29 miles) north of San Salvador, and one of El Salvador's most charming towns. A much-disputed territory during the civil war, this town has remade itself into a premier cultural destination, with some of El Salvador's best art galleries and boutique hotels, along with a rich history and abundant natural beauty. You can spend the day simply enjoying the vibe, taking in the weekend artisans' market, or going on a daylong history or nature tour. Stay at the colonial-style **Puertas de Suchitoto** (p. 264), overlooking the town plaza and church.

Day 3: Lago de Coatepeque ★★

Get up early for the 2½-hour trip due west through Santa Ana or San Salvador to Lago de Coatepeque (p. 330). I suggest you rent a car for this part of the journey; the roads are good, and there's a scenic route if you go west from Suchitoto and through the town of Aguilar and continue west to Santa Ana. Coatepeque offers 23 sq. km (9 sq. miles) of pristine, recreational waters in a nearly perfectly round crater lake 740m (2,428 ft.) above sea level. The nation's rich and famous have their mansions along its shores. Each night, a spectacular sun sets behind the lush walls of the crater rim, and visitors can spend the day swimming, fishing, riding watercrafts, or soaking in the views. Stay at the laidback, family-run **Hostal Amacuilco** (p. 332) and dine on the bamboo-style pier at **Restaurante Las Palmeras** (p. 333).

Day 4: Ruta de las Flores ★★

The rural mountain circuit known as Ruta de las Flores is located about 2 hours west of Suchitoto. Appealing hilltop villages stretch for 35km (22 miles) along a winding road with lots to offer, including roadside restaurants and coffee estates. You can see the route on a 1-day tour with either a tour company or taxi, but a rental car allows you to stop at the many roadside attractions and go at your own pace. Stop first in **Nahuizalco** (p. 306) to check out the locally made furniture and then head to **Juayúa** (p. 308) to see the black Christ. Finish up in **Ataco** ★★★ (p. 312) to take in the excellent array of El Salvadoran art. Spend the night at the lovely coffee farm B&B **Quinta El Carmen** (p. 315).

Days 5: Parque Nacional El Imposible ★★ & Barra de Santiago ★★★

Start the next day in Tacuba, the base for various daylong adventures to **Parque Imposible** (p. 317)—a huge, lush national park with one of the country's largest and most diverse wildlife collections and lush, mountainous hiking terrain. To get the most out of your jungle visit, stay at **El Imposible Eco Lodge** (p. 322).

Day 6 & 7: Balsamo Coast to San Salvador

The following day, head 1 hour south to **Barra de Santiago** (p. 293), along El Salvador's Balsamo Coast, and spend 2 nights soaking up the sun and sand at El Salvador's top beach-side retreat **La Cocotera** (p. 295).

Barra de Santiago is a tiny fishing village and protected nature area with a mangrove-filled estuary on one side and the Pacific Ocean on the other. You can fish, swim, and surf its deserted beaches, watch giant sea turtles lay their eggs in season, and bird-watch in the estuary. It's a great place to relax before the second leg of your trip to Nicaragua—San Salvador airport is an easy 2- to 2½ hour drive past the beautiful beaches and small villages of this coast.

Days 8 & 9: Arrive in Managua & Head to Granada ★★★

Fly into Managua and transfer directly by taxi to the picturesque town of Granada. The sprawling capital has its hidden charms but bears no comparison to this elegant, colonial city 2 hours south and located on the shores of Lake Nicaragua. Settle into the **Hotel Plaza Colón ★★★** (p. 114) to relax and enjoy the colorful plaza from the ample balcony that faces the cathedral. The next morning, take a horse-and-carriage ride through the city's enchanting cobbled streets and down to the lake's shore, where you can take a short boat tour of **Las Isletas** archipelago (see p. 122 for tips on how to see the islands by kayak or private boat).

Days 10 & 11: Tour Isla de Ometepe ★★ & Arrive in San Juan del Sur ★

The jungle island of Ometepe is possible to see in a single day if you contact a tour company to pick you up at your hotel and take you to the tiny port town of **San Jorge.** Here, you'll catch a boat across to the serene, twin-peaked island. A 4WD will then meet you at the boat and take you on a coastal tour of this island of howler monkeys, pre-Columbian carved stones, and mud-bathing farm animals. Unfortunately, you won't have time to climb its volcanic peaks, one of which is currently active, during a day trip, but you will get a feel for a place known locally as "the island of peace."

Transfer by taxi or take one of the many local buses (travel time 90 minutes) to the rum-and-sun town of **San Juan del Sur** in the early evening. Stay at the atmospheric boutique hotel known as **La Posada Azul ★★** (p. 134) and eat in the arty surroundings of **El Colibrí ★★** (p. 138). The next day, take a coastal boat to some beautiful, secluded beaches or, depending on the time of year, take a night excursion to watch the spectacular turtle hatching in **Playa La Flor ★** (p. 130).

Days 12 & 13: The Corn Islands ★★

Catch a taxi back to Managua for the midday flight to these Caribbean treasure islands. Soak up the sunset on bleach-white **Picnic Beach ★★★** while sitting in the breezy, canvas covered lounge area of **Arenas Hotel** (p. 175). Or stay at the very comfortable **Casa Canada ★★** (p. 175) and enjoy its gorgeous pool before snorkeling the pink coral beach of **Sally Peaches.**

Day 14: Managua

Head back to Managua, and give the capital a quick look. If you have time to do so before your flight, take a tour of its ghost-downtown, the **Zona Monumental.** Visit the **Teatro Nacional Rubén Darío** and peer into the majestic ruins of the city's old cathedral. Have time for dinner? Enjoy ceviche and a pisco sour at **La Terraza Peruana ★** (p. 81) before trying some bars in the Zona Viva.

TWO WEEKS OF OUTDOOR ADVENTURES

Anxious to get out into the great outdoors? Below is a 2-week itinerary for adrenaline addicts and nature lovers who are shy of cities, museums, and art galleries.

Two Weeks of Outdoor Adventures

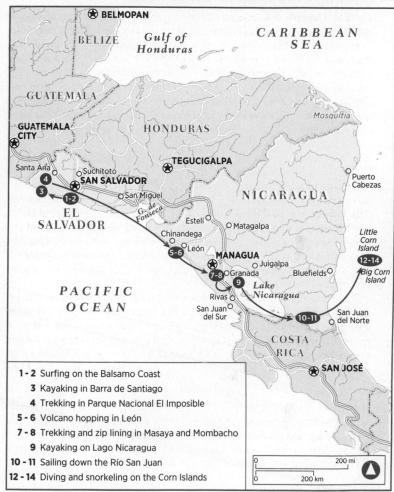

1 - 2 Surfing on the Balsamo Coast
3 Kayaking in Barra de Santiago
4 Trekking in Parque Nacional El Imposible
5 - 6 Volcano hopping in León
7 - 8 Trekking and zip lining in Masaya and Mombacho
9 Kayaking on Lago Nicaragua
10 - 11 Sailing down the Río San Juan
12 - 14 Diving and snorkeling on the Corn Islands

Days 1 & 2: Surfing the Balsamo Coast

Arrive in San Salvador and transfer to the surfers' stretch of coves and inlets known as the Balsamo Coast. Here, you'll find some of the best surf breaks in Central America, including the legendary **Punta Roca.**

Days 3 & 4: Kayaking in Barra de Santiago ★★★

Head up the coast and stay at the amazing ecolodge **La Cocotera** (p. 295) in **Barra de Santiago.** Take a boat tour of the surrounding estuary and mangrove swamps, and release baby turtles into the sea.

Day 4: Trekking in Parque Nacional El Imposible ★★

Take a day trip from La Cocotera to visit the huge, lush **Parque Imposible** (p. 319) on the Guatemalan border, home to some of the country's largest and most diverse wildlife.

Days 5 & 6: Volcano Hopping in León, Nicaragua ★★

A row of dark, volcanic cones sits in the northern lowlands of Nicaragua. Fly into Managua and transfer by taxi directly to the university city of **León,** staying at the sumptuous **Hotel La Perla** (p. 208). You'll appreciate its cool, blue pool after a hot and sweaty day slogging up a smoking mound with astounding views. While there, why not try the latest action thrill sport and surf down the black slopes of a volcano at 60kmph (37 mph)?

Days 7 & 8: Trekking and Zip-Lining Around Masaya and Mombacho

Base yourself at the colonial splendor of **Hotel La Gran Francia** (p. 114) in **Granada** for 2 days while stepping up to the smoking gates of hell at **Masaya Volcano.** Then, take a canopy run along the slopes of **Mombacho Volcano.**

Day 9: Kayaking on Lago Nicaragua ★★

Get up early and kayak the far reaches of the jungle archipelago known as **Las Isletas** or take a boat across to the mysterious islands of **Zapatera** and explore their many ancient petroglyphs and ceremonial stones.

Days 10 & 11: Sailing down the Río San Juan

Sign up with a tour company that flies you out of Managua and into the scruffy river town of **San Carlos** near the Costa Rican border. From here, catch a launch down the wide majestic expanse of the **Río San Juan,** visiting **Los Guatuzos Wildlife Reserve** and the mammoth rainforest known as **Indio-Maíz,** staying at the birder's paradise **Montecristo River Lodge** (p. 164).

Days 12, 13 & 14: Diving & Snorkeling on the Corn Islands ★★

Back in Managua, catch a connecting flight to the Caribbean's best-kept diving secret. **The Corn Islands** offer coral reefs, shipwrecks, and luminous shallows teeming with multicolored sea creatures.

TWO WEEKS OF SHOPPING

You will probably amass a vast array of art, furniture, textiles, ceramics, and clothing if you're a shopper spending time in El Salvador, and Nicaragua may test the patience of even the most understanding airline on your return trip home. Stock up on genuine handcrafted goods at bargain prices, which can be purchased right in the workshops where they come from. Below is a specialized itinerary for those who cannot resist taking home a little piece of each country.

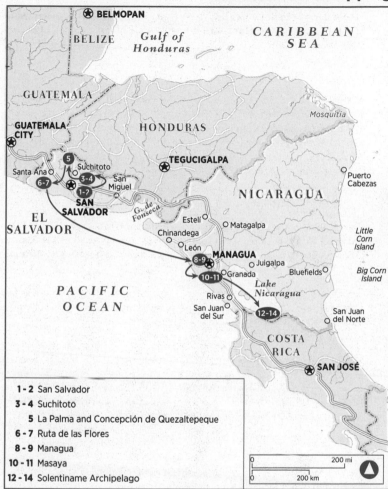

1 - 2 San Salvador

3 - 4 Suchitoto

5 La Palma and Concepción de Quezaltepeque

6 - 7 Ruta de las Flores

8 - 9 Managua

10 - 11 Masaya

12 - 14 Solentiname Archipelago

Days 1 & 2: San Salvador: The City of Malls

The Salvadoran capital has some of the biggest malls in the Americas, complete with faux cobbled streetscapes, designer stores, and cheesy country-themed restaurants and bars. If you are looking for something more genuine, visit the sprawling chaos of the **Mercado Central** (p. 254), which sells everything and anything, including the kitchen sink—literally. For something more subdued, check out the tourist-oriented **Mercados de Artesanías** (p. 255), a good spot to catch all the country's handicrafts in one place. Art lovers should beat a path to **Arbol de Dios** (p. 249), the gallery and workshop of El Salvador's most famous living artist, Fernando Llort. Stay in the **Crown Plaza Hotel** (p. 240) in the upscale neighborhood of Colonia Escalón.

Days 3 & 4: Suchitoto Arts

The weekends-only **This Is My Land Artisans' Market** (p. 264) mixes up crafts and food in a picturesque village increasingly famous for its arts scene. Enjoy an Argentine barbecue at **La Casa del Escultor** (p. 262), where you can pick up a piece of artwork by the owner. Enjoy the pool and lake view at **La Posada de Suchitoto** (p. 264).

Day 5: La Palma and Concepción de Quezaltepeque

Take a day trip north to the hammock heaven known as **Concepción de Quezaltepeque,** a tiny hilltop village north of Lago Suchitlán. Continue towards the Honduran border until you reach the mural-filled mountain town of **La Palma.** Check out the colorful arts and crafts at **Artesanías Kemuel** (p. 272) and **Placita Artesanal La Palma** (p. 272) before returning south to Suchitoto.

Days 6 & 7: Ruta de las Flores

Every town along this picturesque country road has its own specialties. **Nahuizalco's** focus is on furniture and wicker ware, while **Juayúa** focuses on food. **Apaneca** does a thriving line in flowers, and **Ataco** produces premium coffee. All have a grand selection of handicrafts stores displaying art, ceramics, and souvenir knick-knacks. Try staying at the gorgeous villa known as **Quinta El Carmen** (p. 315) in Ataco, where you can also do a coffee tour and horseback riding.

Days 8 & 9: Managua's Art Galleries

The city may not be the prettiest, but its art scene is one of the most vibrant in all of Central America. **Galería Solentiname** (p. 86) has a colorful selection from that colorful archipelago, while **Galería Añil** (p. 86) is more avant-garde and cutting edge. Stay at the famous pyramid-shaped **Crowne Plaza Hotel** (p. 78) and wander the city's many malls in search of top-notch rum and excellent cigars.

Days 10 & 11: Masaya and Los Pueblos Blancos

From the capital, take a 2-day foray into the handicraft mecca of Masaya. You can browse for everything under the sun within the gothic walls of the **Mercado Viejo** (p. 93). Then, venture into the indigenous barrio and arts-and-crafts powerhouse known as Monimbo, where you can visit craftsmen in their back-street workshops.

Days 12, 13 & 14: Solentiname Archipelago

This ground zero in Central American primitivist art is not so easy to reach, and it will require at least 3 days and a tour agency's expertise to get you around this group of jungle islands in the southeastern corner of Lago de Nicaragua. While there, you can visit the artists' community inspired by a priest and see their colorful works in progress in the many workshops and studios. Stay at the **Hotel Mancarrón** (p. 158), located on the island of the same name.

PLANNING YOUR TRIP TO NICARAGUA

Nicaragua is not a ready-made resort designed for your convenience. Tourism is very much in its infancy here, and some pre-planning is highly recommended to avoid any rude surprises. Often, the crumbling infrastructure doesn't match the splendid destinations. Funny money and a strange tongue are just some of the things you'll have to contend with, along with poor roads, a bewildering capital, unmetered taxis, and a chaotic bus system. On the positive side, however, some of the country's best destinations—such as Granada and León—are within easy reach of the airport and capital, the dollar goes far, and the country is safe and peaceful. For unbridled jungle and abundant nature, you'll have to make a special effort and get organized. Below are some pointers to help you get started.

5

WHEN TO GO

In my opinion, December is the best time to visit Nicaragua: It's just after the rainy season, and the Pacific coast is lush, green, and not too hot. As the dry season progresses towards May, it can get uncomfortably hot in this part of the country, and the Pacific basin loses its bloom and becomes dry and leafless. This is the best time for bird-watching in the rainforests and snorkeling in the Caribbean, where the waters are calmer. The rainy season is not as uncomfortable as it sounds, with showers normally occurring in the afternoon and at night.

Christmas, New Year's, and Easter are the big holidays in Nicaragua, when the locals flock to the beaches and hotels are at capacity and charge premium rates. Unless you want to party and spend big, avoid these holiday periods.

CLIMATE Like most of Central America, Nicaragua's climate is tropical, and the year is split between summer (Dec–Apr) and winter (May–Nov), though the temperature is consistent throughout the year, ranging from 54° to 82°F (12°–28°C). The main seasonal difference involves rainfall; the rainy season falls between May and October, with hurricanes buffeting the coast in September and October. Generally speaking, the Caribbean side of the country receives a lot more rainfall than the Pacific side. Altitude is also a factor with the weather—the highlands have a more spring-like climate compared to the hotter and more humid lowlands and coastal areas.

Managua: 1 block south and 1 block west of the Crowne Plaza Hotel (📞 **505/2222-6610**).

Granada: Intur, Calle El Arsenal, 1 block from the cathedral and a half-block behind the Casa de Leones (📞 **505/2552-6858**).

San Juan del Sur: 1½ blocks west of the market (📞 **505/8458-2473**).

León: 2a Av. NO (📞 **505/2311-3682**).

Masaya: Mercado Viejo (📞 **505/2522-7615**).

San Carlos (serving the Solentiname Islands and El Castillo): Malecón, San Carlos (📞 **505/2583-0301** or 505/2583-0363).

Estelí: ½ block south of Parque Central on Av. Central (📞 **505/2713-6799**).

PUBLIC HOLIDAYS Public holidays include New Year's Day (Jan 1); Easter Week (Thurs, Fri, and Sat before Easter Sunday), Labor Day (May 1), and Christmas Day (Dec 25). Liberation Day (July 19) celebrates victory over the Somoza regime, while the Battle of San Jacinto (Sept 14) rejoices the ending of William Walker's tyranny in 1856. Independence Day (Sept 15) is followed by Día de los Muertos (Nov 2), or the Day of the Dead, which is the Latin American version of All Souls' Day. Feast of the Immaculate Conception (Dec 8) is also known as La Purisma.

For an exhaustive list of events beyond those listed here, check http://events. frommers.com, where you'll find a searchable, up-to-the-minute roster of what's happening in cities all over the world.

VISITOR INFORMATION

The **Instituto Nicaragüense de Turismo,** or INTUR, has offices in all the country's main cities, though some are better than others, and only a few have English-speaking staff. The ministry's two websites, **www.intur.gob.ni** and **www. visitanicaragua.com** (or www.visit-nicaragua.com), have very limited information and are written almost entirely in Spanish, but they do contain some gorgeous images.

ENTRY REQUIREMENTS

Citizens of the United States, Canada, Australia and New Zealand, and the European Union require just a passport to enter Nicaragua and may stay for up to 90 days. The passport must be valid for at least 6 months after the date of entry. Visas can be extended at the Office of Immigration in Managua for $12 a month. The office, called the **Dirección General de Migración y Extranjería** (📞 **505/2244-3989**), is located 2½ blocks north of the Tenderí stoplights.

Nicaragua is part of a 2006 border control agreement with Honduras, Guatemala, and El Salvador, allowing travel among the four countries under one tourist card. The number of days of your tourist card is determined at the first of the four countries entered.

When leaving Nicaragua, you must pay a C700 airport tax, which must be paid in cash in either U.S. dollars or Nicaraguan córdobas. (This is sometimes included in the price of your airline ticket.) There is also a tourist entry fee of C100 that must be paid upon arrival into the country.

Nicaraguan Embassy-Consulate Locations

For countries not listed below, consult www.ni.embassyinformation.com.

In the U.S. and Canada: 1627 New Hampshire Ave., NW, Washington, DC 20009 (© **202/939-6531;** fax 202/939-6532).

In the U.K.: 36 Upper Brooke St., London W1Y 1PE (© **171/409-2593;** fax 171/409-2536; www.nicaragua.embassyhomepage.com).

In New Zealand: 50 Clonbern Rd., Remuera (© **64/9373-7599;** fax 64/9373-7646; c.tremewan@auckland.ac.nz).

Customs

There is a C100 entrance fee for all tourists. In theory, you may also be asked for an onward ticket and proof of sufficient funds, but this rarely happens. There is a tax on all electronic, alcohol, and other luxury goods that are not obviously personal objects (things still in their original packaging, for example).

GETTING THERE & GETTING AROUND

Getting to Nicaragua

BY PLANE

Augusto C Sandino International Airport (MGA; © **505/2233-1624;** www. eaai.com.ni) is 11km (6¾ miles) east of Managua and is the country's main airport. Here, you'll find direct flights from Miami, Houston, Dallas, Mexico City, San Salvador, Panama City, and San José. **American Airlines** (© **800/433-7300** or 505/2255-9090; www.aa.com) flies twice a day from Miami. **Continental Airlines** (© **505/2278-7033**; www.continental.com) operates one evening flight from Houston. **Delta** (© **505/2254-8130**; www.delta.com) has a daily flight to Atlanta **Spirit Airlines** (© **505/2233-2884**; www.spiritair.com) operates a daily flight to Fort Lauderdale.

Copa (© **505/2267-0045**; www.copaair.com) has connections all over Central America, particularly to cities in Guatemala and Panama and to San José and San Salvador. **Aeroméxico** (© **800/237-6639** or 505/2266-6997; www.aeromexico. com) flies four times a week to Mexico City from Managua. **TACA** (© **505/2266-3136**; www.taca.com) operates flights from Miami, Panama City, and San Salvador. **Iberia** (© **800/2772-4642;** www.iberia.com) flies once a day to Miami with onward connections to Europe.

BY BUS

There are a handful of established international bus companies that trundle up and down the Central American isthmus. All have separate stations and offices in Barrio Martha Quezada in Managua, and some have offices in León, Rivas, and Granada where you can also alight. **Tica Bus,** 2 blocks east of the Antiguo Cine Dorado (© **505/2222-6094** or 505/2222-3031; www.ticabus.com), is the best-known operator, with intercity routes going as far as Mexico City. The bus from Honduras leaves Tegucigalpa daily at 9:15 a.m., takes hours to reach Managua, and costs C440 one way. The bus from San José in Costa Rica leaves daily at 3 a.m., takes 7 hours, and costs C572. They also operate a route from San Salvador, leaving from the Hotel San Carlos at 3 a.m. and arriving in Managua 6½ hours later. The cost is C660.

King Quality/Cruceros del Golfo, opposite Tica Bus (© **505/2228-1454;** www.king-qualityca.com) has a reputation for being more comfortable and provides meals. Their service from Honduras leaves at 6 a.m and 2 p.m. and costs C1,562. The Costa Rica service leaves San José at 3 p.m., takes 8 hours, and costs C968. The bus from San Salvador leaves at 3:30, 5:30, and 11:30 a.m.. It takes 6½ hours and costs C1,694.

Trans Nica, 300m (984 ft.) north of Rotonda Metrocentro and 50m (164 ft.) east (© **505/2277-2104** or 505/2270-3133; www.nuevo.transnica.com), services El Salvador, Costa Rica, and Honduras. Their bus from Costa Rica departs from San Juan at 4:30, 5:30, and 9 a.m. It takes 9 hours and costs C577. **Central Line,** (© **505/254-5431**), next to King Quality goes south to San José in Costa Rica. The service leaves Costa Rica at 4:30 a.m. and takes 9 hours. The cost is C580. For departure times from Managua, see "Getting There," in chapter 6.

For those who are on a strict budget, are in no hurry, and don't mind the discomfort of jumping off and changing buses at the border, getting around by a chicken bus (see "Getting Around Nicaragua," below, for info), is another option. The two main crossings on the Honduran border are Guasale and El Espino. These buses arrive and depart in Managua at **Mercado Israel Lewites,** also known as **Boer** (© **505/2265-2152**) and **Mercado Mayoreo** (© **505/2233-4729**). The main crossing into Costa Rica is Peñas Blancas. Buses arrive and depart from **Mercado Roberto Huembes** (no phone). It is very important that you get two stamps—an exit and entrance stamp—from the corresponding immigration office on either side, or you may have problems entering or leaving at the border.

BY CRUISE SHIP/FERRY

San Juan del Sur is now a well-established stop-off for luxury cruise liners plying the Caribbean and Pacific coasts via the Panama Canal. Two reputable companies that make this trip are Miami-based **Seabourn Cruise Line** (www.seabourn.com) and California-based **Princess Cruises** (www.princess.com).

Getting Around Nicaragua

Getting around the country is often very taxing, especially if you want to use public transportation. Decrepit roads and a chaotic bus system mean you may have to ante up for an expensive taxi or shuttle ride between cities if you don't fancy taking a chicken bus. Fortunately, everything is relatively close, and the only real epic journeys are if you want to explore the interior highlands or get to the Caribbean by land and sea.

BY PLANE

At the end of Managua's airport terminal, there is a tiny departure lounge that accommodates Nicaragua's domestic airline operator **La Costeña** (© **505/2263-2142**; www.lacostena.com.ni) which provides "puddle jumper" propeller planes that carry people and packages to Puerto Cabezas, San Carlos, Bluefields, and the Corn Islands.

BY BUS

Have you ever wondered where those old yellow school buses go after being decommissioned from carrying North American children? They go south. The potholed roads of Nicaragua are full of trundling **"chicken buses"** or old school buses, which riders (some of whom *do* carry livestock) can hop onto and off of at multiple destinations, making for a very slow ride.

air NICARAGUA

You can relive the romance (and fear) of early aviation on Nicaragua's La Costeña airline. You realize that this is going to be a flight with a difference when you are physically weighed along with your luggage as part of the check-in process. Your boarding pass is a big, plastic, reusable card and the plane itself some-thing you might see in an Indiana Jones movie. You sit so close to the pilots you can hear them chat about their round of golf, since some planes have no cockpit partitions. Yet, these daredevil puddle jumpers do get you there, and the ride on a clear day turns into a glorious aerial tour of the country.

The country also has small express vans that are faster than chicken buses, but—since they still allow as many folks as possible to pile on along the way—they can get very crowded and uncomfortable on long journeys.

Some better-quality bus companies do exist, but in general, traveling by bus is a colorful, yet exhausting and sometimes intimidating, business. The main problem is not the actual buses but the chaotic market bus stations you must negotiate upon departure and arrival. For exact transit points in each city, and for the names of bus companies, check "Getting There" and "Getting Around" info in destination chapters throughout this book.

BY TAXI & SHUTTLE BUS

Taking taxis or shuttle buses is an increasingly popular way of getting around the country. Small, private companies usually connected to a travel agency or hotel will pick you up at your airport or hotel and transfer you to your next destination. It is particularly popular for those traveling among the main tourist destinations of Granada, San Juan del Sur, Managua, and León. The price depends on whether you are lucky enough to have somebody else sharing the ride, but will never be less than C600 between destinations. Two reputable companies are **Tierra Tour** (© 505/2315-4278; www.tierratour.com) and **Paxeos** (© 505/2552-8291; www.paxeos.com). See "By Taxi," in chapter 6, for info on taking taxis within the city.

BY CAR

Nicaragua used to be described as a country of oxen and Mercedes Benzes, but now it is more like a country of old school buses and SUVs. In general, the roads are very bad, and you will be doing yourself a big favor if you spring for a four-wheel-drive. One good thing about driving here is that there is very little traffic. The northern highlands are the most beautiful area for touring by car.

Car rentals are generally cheap, but it is wise to shop around. Make sure you get unlimited mileage or are aware of the charge per kilometer if you go over. A car costs C600 to C2,000 per day, more if you require a 4WD. The best-known company is **Hertz** (© 505/2266-8400 in the Intercontinental Hotel or 505/2222-2320 in the airport; www.hertz.com). **Lugo Rent-a-Car** (© 505/2266-4477) and **Dorado Rent-a-Car** (© 505/2278-1825) are both located at Rotonda El Dorado in Managua. **Alamo** has a desk in the international airport (© 505/2277-4477; www.alamonicaragua.com) and offices in Granada and San Juan del Sur. **Budget,** 1 block south of Estatua Montaya (© 505/2255-9000; www.budget.com.ni) and **Avis,** ½ block south of Estatua Montaya (© 505/2268-1838; www.avis.com.ni) are two other good options. Note that many towns (such as Masaya) lack rental-car outlets, so if you are intent on touring the country by car, it is probably best that you do so from Managua or Granada.

MONEY & COSTS

The official Nicaraguan currency is the **córdoba** (it is sometimes referred to as a peso). It is made up of 100 **centavos.** Money is denominated in notes of 10, 20, 50, 100, and 500 córdobas. Coins are made of 1 and 5 córdobas and 50 centavos. At press time, the exchange rate was 22 córdobas to the American dollar and 36 to the British pound. It's often difficult to find change for 100-córdoba notes and next to impossible to change the princely sum that is a 500-córdoba note (a bank is your best bet for doing so).

Traffic Cops

An on-the-spot "fine" for a missing fire extinguisher is a common trick for a roadside shakedown by unscrupulous traffic police. Check with your car-rental company that your car possesses all the legal requirements.

Córdobas are virtually useless outside Nicaragua and should be changed before you leave. Prices in this guide are quoted in córdobas with the symbol "C" and American dollars with the symbol "$." Because of high inflation and volatile exchange rates, prices quoted here may vary greatly in accuracy.

Sales tax in Nicaragua is known as IGV (Impuesto General de Valor) and allows for an extra charge of 15% on all goods. Always check menus and price lists to see if it's included in the quoted price.

CURRENCY EXCHANGE U.S. dollars are widely accepted in Nicaragua and can be used to pay taxis, hotels, restaurants, and stores. However, do keep some córdobas on hand, since you may run into spots where you'll need them. You can convert your currency in hotels, at *casas de cambio* (money-exchange houses), at some banks, and at Managua International Airport. It is difficult to change traveler's checks outside the capital; see p. 75 for locations of currency-exchange houses there.

ATMS ATMs are becoming increasingly available, even in far-flung places like the Corn Islands. There are plenty in the main cities, such as Managua, Granada, León, and Rivas (try gas stations and shopping malls). Don't bet on finding any off the beaten path. Typically, ATMs are connected to **Cirrus** (*Ⓒ* **800/424-7787**) or **PLUS** (*Ⓒ* **800/843-7587**) networks. Many ATMs also accept Visa and Master-Card.

CREDIT CARDS If you choose to use plastic, Visa, American Express, Master-Card, and Diners Club are the commonly accepted cards. Credit cards are accepted at most hotels and restaurants except the very cheapest ones. You cannot use credit cards in taxis or at most attractions (museums, parks, and so on).

HEALTH CONCERNS

Contaminated water and food, as well as mosquitoes, are the usual sources of discomfort in Nicaragua (and El Salvador). Always be careful about what you eat and insist on bottled water. As for those pesky mosquitoes, a good repellent with DEET should be enough to keep off bugs that bear unwanted gifts such as dengue fever and malaria. Go to www.cdc.gov for more specific info on malaria hot spots (usually rural areas). Vaccinations in general are not required, unless you are traveling from a yellow-fever zone. Nevertheless, you should always have up-to-date jabs for diphtheria, measles, tetanus, mumps, rubella, and polio. The CDC also advises travelers to vaccinate against Hepatitis A and B.

Before You Go

It can be hard to find a doctor you can trust when you're in an unfamiliar place. Try to take proper precautions the week before you depart to avoid falling ill while you're away from home. Amid the last-minute frenzy that often precedes a vacation, make an extra effort to eat and sleep well.

Pack prescription medications in their original labeled containers in your carry-on luggage. Also, bring along copies of your prescriptions in case you lose your pills or run out. Carry written prescriptions in generic form, in case a local pharmacist is unfamiliar with the brand name. If you wear contact lenses, pack an extra pair or your glasses.

If you worry about getting sick away from home, you may want to consider **medical travel insurance** (see "Travel Insurance," in chapter 21)

If you suffer from a chronic illness, consult your doctor before your departure. For conditions such as epilepsy, diabetes, or heart problems, wear a **MedicAlert identification tag** (© 888/633-4298; www.medicalert.org), which will immediately alert doctors to your condition and give them access to your records through MedicAlert's 24-hour hot line.

Contact the **International Association for Medical Assistance to Travelers** (**IAMAT;** © 716/754-4883, or 416/652-0137 in Canada; www.iamat.org) for tips on travel and health concerns in the countries you're visiting, and lists of local, English-speaking doctors.

GENERAL AVAILABILITY OF HEALTHCARE

Not surprisingly, most of Nicaragua's and El Salvador's best hospitals and healthcare centers are in the capitals, but service varies widely. If you do get sick, it's best to contact your home country's consulate or embassy. They all have health departments with staff who can recommend the best English-speaking doctors and hospitals in the area.

COMMON DISEASES & AILMENTS

DIETARY DISTRESS   It's unfortunate, but many travelers to Central America do suffer from some sort of food or waterborne illness. Most of this is just due to tender northern stomachs coming into contact with slightly more aggressive Latin American intestinal flora. Symptoms vary widely—from minor cases of diarrhea to debilitating flulike illnesses. To minimize your chances of getting sick, be sure to always drink bottled or boiled water and avoid ice. In high altitudes, you will need to boil water for several minutes longer before it is safe to drink. If you don't have access to bottled water, you can treat it with iodine or chlorine, with iodine being more effective. You can buy water purification tablets at pharmacies and sporting-goods stores. You should also be careful to avoid raw food, especially meats, fruits, and vegetables. If you peel the fruit yourself, you should be fine.

If you do suffer from diarrhea, it's important to keep yourself hydrated. Many pharmacies sell Pedialyte, which is a mild rehydrating solution. Drinking fruit juices or soft drinks (preferably without caffeine) and eating salted crackers are also good remedies. In extreme cases of diarrhea or intestinal discomfort, it's worth taking a stool sample to a lab for analysis. The results will usually pinpoint the amoebic or parasitic culprit, which can then be readily treated with available over-the-counter medicines.

Typhoid fever is a food- or waterborne illness that occurs throughout Central America and is caused by salmonella. Long-term travelers should seriously consider getting a typhoid-fever vaccine before setting off, as the malaria-like symptoms are very unpleasant.

Hepatitis A is another viral infection acquired through water and food (it can also be picked up from infected people), this time attacking the liver. Usually the symptoms of fever, jaundice, and nausea will pass, but it can in some cases cause liver damage. There is an effective vaccine that you can take before the trip.

TROPICAL ILLNESSES   **Yellow fever** is no longer a problem in Central America. However, if you are traveling from yellow-fever zones in South America or Africa you will require a vaccination certificate to enter Nicaragua and El Salvador.

Malaria does exist in Nicaragua and El Salvador, especially in rural areas. To protect yourself, use mosquito repellent with DEET, wear long-sleeved shirts and pants, and use mosquito nets. You can also take anti-malarial drugs before you go; consult your doctor about the pros and cons of such medications. Be sure to ask whether a recommended drug will cause you to be hypersensitive to the sun; it would be a shame to come down here for the beaches and then have to hide under an umbrella the whole time. Because malaria-carrying mosquitoes usually come out at night, you should do as much as possible to avoid being bitten after dark. Also, be aware that symptoms such as high fever, chills, and body aches can appear months after your vacation.

Dengue fever, transmitted by an aggressive daytime mosquito, is a risk in tropical environments and densely populated urban areas. As with malaria, the best prevention is to avoid mosquito bites; there is no vaccine available. Dengue is also known as "bone-break fever" because it is usually accompanied by severe body aches. The first infection with dengue fever will make you very sick but should cause no serious damage. However, a second infection with a different strain of the dengue virus can lead to internal hemorrhaging and could be life-threatening. If you are unfortunate enough to get it, take some paracetamol and lots of fluids.

BEES, BUGS & BITES   **Snakes, scorpions,** and **spiders** rarely bite without provocation. Keep your eyes open and never walk barefoot. If you're in the jungle or rainforest, be sure to shake your clothes and check your shoes before putting them on. Africanized bees (the notorious "killer bees" of fact and fable) are common in this region, but there is no real danger of being attacked unless you do something silly like stick your hand into a hive. Other than mosquitoes, the most prevalent and annoying biting insect you are likely to encounter, especially along the coast, is sand flies. These tiny biting bugs leave a raised and itchy welt, but otherwise are of no significant danger. They tend to be most active around sunrise and sunset, or on overcast days. Your best protection is to wear light long-sleeved shirts and long pants.

The chances of contracting **rabies** while traveling in Nicaragua and El Salvador are low, but it's not completely impossible. Most infected animals live in rural areas. If you are bitten by an infected dog or bat, wash the wound and get yourself to a hospital as quickly as possible. There is a pre-vacation vaccine that requires three injections, but you should only get it if you are planning a high-risk activity such as cave exploring. Treatment is effective but must be given promptly.

RIPTIDES   Many of the Pacific coast beaches have riptides, strong currents that can drag swimmers out to sea. A riptide occurs when water that has been moved toward the shore by strong waves forms a channel back out to open water. These channels have strong currents. If you get caught in a riptide, you can't escape the current by swimming toward shore; it's like trying to swim upstream in a river. To break free of the current, swim parallel to shore and use the energy of the waves to help you get back to the beach. **Note:** Lifeguards are a rarity both here and in El Salvador.

SUNSTROKE   Do not be a mad dog, nor an Englishman, for that matter. Do as the locals do and stay out of the midday sun. Your proximity to the equator means you burn much faster, and it's no accident that everybody escapes indoors between 10 a.m. and 2 p.m.. Hats and a SPF 30 (or higher) sunscreen are wise accessories, and if you do manage overdo it on the beach, drink lots of water and treat burns with aloe vera.

SAFETY

Nicaragua is the safest country in Central America and has somehow avoided the chronic gang violence so prevalent in Honduras and El Salvador. Nevertheless, there are some dangerous neighborhoods to avoid, especially in Managua and if you choose to get around on public buses; in frequently crowded places such as markets, watch your stuff, as pickpockets and bag snatchers might be tempted.

Staying safe is generally a case of common sense. Stay alert and be aware of your surroundings; don't walk down dark, deserted streets; and always keep an eye on your personal belongings. Keep your passport and credit cards on your person (but not stuffed in your back pocket). It's a good idea to keep separate money amounts, so if you are unlucky, you do not lose everything. Theft at airports and bus stations is not unheard of, so be sure to put a lock on your luggage.

Always report crime to the nearest police station or call ✆ **118.** It may take up some precious time, but your insurance claim will be useless without an official police report. The police are, in general, honest but poorly paid, so you may be solicited for some sort of *multa* (fine) or even just a simple contribution to pay for their gas. Taxis are the way to go at night, especially in Managua. However, single women travelers should avoid getting into cabs that have multiple passengers.

TIPS ON ACCOMMODATIONS, DINING & SHOPPING

Accommodations

Hotels in Nicaragua are improving all the time, but you'll need to lower your expectations a bit the farther you get from the capital or tourist centers like Granada and San Juan del Sur. Even in increasingly popular destinations like the Corn Islands and Isla de Ometepe, luxury hotels are still in short supply. In general, though, the country does offer great variety in terms of accommodations, from all-inclusive resorts on the Pacific coast to authentic Spanish colonial houses in Granada. The northern highlands and the lake islands offer rustic working farms with lots of personality but little in modern amenities. Most prices for hotels in this book are quoted in U.S. dollars only, since most don't quote their rates in córdobas.

Dining

Nicaragua isn't exactly a culinary destination, but Managua has the best restaurant choices, with Granada coming a distant second. León and San Juan del Sur are beginning to get some very good high-end eateries, as well. In general, buffet-style restaurants, called *comedores,* are very popular, as are street grills (*fritangas*) on the side of the road. Every town has a Mercado Municipal, with ultra-cheap food stalls. Corn, rice, and beans dominate most menus, but you'll also come across an incredible amount of seafood, especially lobster and shrimp.

In Nicaragua, prices on menus in most restaurants exclude a 15% tax and a 10% service charge. These are automatically added to your bill at the end.

Shopping

Nicaragua is handicraft heaven. Masaya, 29km (18 miles) south of Managua, is the center of the handicraft scene in the country. Here, you'll find everything, including cotton hammocks, woodcarvings, rocking chairs, textile arts, leatherwork, and ceramics. The Monimbó neighborhood in Masaya is famous for leatherwork, woodwork, embroidery, and toys. Every town and city has a central market where you will find similar goods, as well. The Solentiname Islands are famous for primitive art, and Managua has many art galleries that display such work.

[FastFACTS] NICARAGUA

American Express **American Express** is located at the Viajes Atlántida office (1 block east of Rotonda El Güegüense, Managua; ☏ 505/266-4050). It is open Monday to Friday from 9am to 5pm.

Business Hours Banks are generally open weekdays from 8:30am to 4pm, and some are open on Saturday mornings. Shopping hours are weekdays from 8am to noon and 2 to 5pm, and Saturday 8am to noon. Shopping centers are open daily from 10am to 8pm.

Embassies All embassies are in Managua, as follows: **United States,** Carr Sur Km 4.5 (☏ **505/2266-6012,** or 505/2266-6038 after hours); **Canada,** De los Pipitos, Calle Nogal #25, Bolonia (☏ **505/2268-0433** or 505/268-3323); and the **United Kingdom,** Carretera Masaya, Los

Robles (☏ **505/2278-0014** or 505/2278-0887). **Australia** and **New Zealand** do not have an embassy or consulate in Nicaragua.

Emergencies The following emergency numbers are valid throughout Nicaragua. For an ambulance, call ☏ **128;** in case of fire, call ☏ **115;** for police assistance, call ☏ **118.**

Hospitals The best hospital in Managua is the **Hospital Bautista,** 1km (½ mile) east of the Intercontinental Hotel (☏ **505/2249-7070** or 505/2249-7277; www.hospitalbautistanicaragua.com); some staff members are English-speaking.

Internet & Wifi Access is generally free at most hotels, with the notable exception of larger chain hotels, which generally charge between US$3 and US$8 per day. See individual chapters for information on Internet cafes.

Language Nicaragua's official language is Spanish, but a form of creole English is also frequently used along the Caribbean coast and the Corn Islands.

Maps It is difficult to produce reliable maps of towns and cities that have no street names, but Intur makes a good effort at it. *Guía Mananic* is one good country map that can be purchased at most bookstores in the country.

Newspapers & Magazines Major local papers are *El Nuevo Diario* (center-left) and *La Prensa* (conservative). *La Tribuna* is the country's main business paper, and *El Mercurio* is the most popular tabloid.

Post Offices & Mail Post offices are generally open Monday through Friday from 8am to 6pm and Saturday from 8am to 1pm. Airmail postage for a letter weighing

198g (7 oz.) or less from Nicaragua to North America is 60¢ and $1 to Europe. Mail takes on average between 7 and 10 days to get to the U.S. and Europe.

Safety In the more populated southern parts and poorer areas of Managua, crime is reportedly on the increase, but it's by no means as bad as in other Central American countries. Travelers should be especially alert to pickpockets and purse snatching on the streets and on buses. Always keep your belongings in sight while dining or drinking, and expect street kids to ask for money or food. A different safety concern, but worth noting, is the strong Pacific currents and lack of lifeguards.

Be aware of this while enjoying the beach.

Taxes Nicaragua's value-added tax (IGV) is 15% and is generally added on after the bill, especially when eating in the finer restaurants. If you're ever unsure about a price, ask if the bill includes *el impuesto* (the tax). See "Entry Requirements," earlier in this chapter, for info on the airport departure tax.

Telephone & Fax Public phones take either phone cards (sold at kiosks on the street) or coins. Local calls cost 20 centavos to start and more the longer you talk. ENITEL is the name of the biggest phone company, though it is still often referred to as

TELCOR. You will find an ENITEL office in all major cities and towns. There are telephone booths on many corners, but you may have difficulty finding one that accepts change (it's easier to find ones that work with calling cards). See "Staying Connected," below, for more information.

Tipping A 10% tip is expected at cafes and restaurants. This is often added to the bill automatically, even though the waiter/waitress may never see it. If you are worried your tip is not getting into the right hands, give a little extra to the waiter directly. You are not obliged to pay the automatic tip if the service was bad.

SPECIALIZED TRAVEL RESOURCES

Travelers with Disabilities

Badly maintained sidewalks, complete with death-trap manholes, mean that Nicaragua's cities and towns are going to be a struggle for anybody with mobility issues. There is little in the way of wheel ramps, and disability-friendly transportation is nonexistent. Mud roads and river access in the countryside are no help, either. Yet those who are determined will find a way.

If you are interested in volunteering in this particular field, check out **Los Pipitos** (www.lospipitos.org), a nationwide group that helps Nicaraguan children with disabilities and their families.

Gay & Lesbian Travelers

For such a Catholic and conservative country, Nicaragua is a fairly tolerant place regarding homosexuality. Gay bars exist not just in the capital, but in some of the regional cities, as well. Nevertheless, this is not San Francisco, and discretion is the name of the game—gay sex was only decriminalized in 2008, after all. For listings on gay-friendly bars and hotels, go to www.gaynicaragua.net.

Family Travel

The only inconvenience you might find in Nicaragua regarding traveling with kids is the high price of disposable diapers. Otherwise, traveling with children will actually open doors and make the friendly locals even friendlier. Of course, you'll need to make commonsense accommodations choices, like paying the premium for the all-inclusive resort, rather than staying at the hippy surfer hostel. Also, bus travel might be just too much to handle if you have a trail of toddlers or teenagers behind you. Locations like Granada and San Juan del Sur are the most child-friendly, and the Corn Islands will give any 12-year-old pirate lots of room to roam. Look out for the "Kids" icon throughout this book.

Single Travelers

Like everywhere else, you will pay a premium for that hotel room if you are traveling alone in Nicaragua, and most tour prices are based on groups of two to four people.

Sustainable Tourism

Sustainable tourism is not just about staying in an overpriced ecolodge. How you conduct yourself on your vacation can have a positive or negative effect on the places you visit. Nicaragua's unique attractions and strong community-level organizations provide ample opportunities for you to have a holiday that also benefits the community. For example, when choosing a language school, choose one of the small local schools affiliated with a women's group, rather than a capital-based money maker. When buying souvenirs, choose locally made products, rather than Taiwanese-produced trinkets from a Managua shopping mall. Think twice about handing cash to panhandling kids when you could easily drop into the orphanage around the corner and make a donation. Avoid buying souvenirs made from captured wildlife and don't be tempted by the turtle eggs on the menu. One tenet of sustainable tourism is to spend your money in locally owned establishments, but Nicaragua turns this principle on its head, as often the most community-spirited operations are owned by foreigners.

The most garlanded ecolodges are often the most expensive, such as **Morgan's Rock** in San Juan del Sur (p. 137), but you don't have to pay a king's ransom if you want a truly sustainable holiday. **Finca Esperanza Verde** in Matagalpa (p. 194) is, in my opinion, the best ecolodge in Nicaragua. The rooms may be basic, but the surroundings are beautiful, and the management's environmental policies are spot-on, which is all you really need. As for conventional hotels that are not exactly green but go out of their way to help the community, a few to try include **Hotel Los Arcos** in Estelí (p. 187) and **La Perla** in León (p. 208).

STAYING CONNECTED

The country code for Nicaragua is 505, which you use only when dialing from outside the country. Telephone numbers in this book include it because most businesses' published phone numbers include the prefix.

- **To place a call from your home country to Nicaragua:** Dial the international access code (011 in the U.S., 0011 in Australia, 0170 in New Zealand, 00 in the U.K.) plus the country code (505), the city or region's area code, and the local number.
- **To make long-distance calls within Nicaragua:** Dial a 0 before the seven-digit number.
- **To place an international call from Nicaragua:** Add 00 before the country code.

In 2009, all Nicaraguan telephone numbers increased from seven to eight digits with the addition of the number "2" before all fixed lines (numbers that previously began with 2, 3, 5, and 7) and the number "8" before all cellphone numbers (numbers that previously began with 4, 6, 8, or 9). Telephone numbers have been updated in this guide, but you may come across the old seven-digit system in flyers and brochures when you travel around the country.

- **To call an operator**: Dial © 113 for **directory assistance.** Dial © 110 for **long-distance assistance.** Dial © 116 to make **collect calls** to the U.S., U.K., Australia, and Canada.
- **To make an emergency call:** Dial © 118 for **police** help, dial © 115-06-120 to report a fire, and © 128 for the Red Cross.

ENITEL (www.claro.com.ni), the national telephone company in Nicaragua, was privatized in 2011 and is now owned by Claro. It has call centers dotted around the country in every major town. There are also ENITEL and PUBLITEL phone booths, operated by phone cards that can be bought at most corner stores and service stations.

Cellphones

The cellphone networks are Movistar and Claro. Claro is reputed to have the best overall reception. You will need to buy a new chip on arrival if you wish to bring your own phone; or better and more reliable, but more expensive, is to arrange a roaming facility with your phone company before your trip. The roaming service can cost anywhere between $1 and $4 a minute, while a new chip costs $35. Whichever you decide, consult with your provider beforehand, as many a traveler has found his phone still useless with a new chip; it has something to do with different bands in different countries and not all phones being compatible.

Pay-as-you-go phones can be purchased in the airport or any high street, the cheapest of which cost $60. Make sure to ask if the phone can take international calls and how much this costs, as packages vary and can be restrictively expensive. It's also important to ask how long your credit is valid for; this can vary from 15 to 60 days. Usually, the more credit you buy, the longer the validity. Local calls vary from 10¢ to 50¢ a minute. Look out for promotions such as free incoming calls and cheap international calls for 10¢ a minute with certain networks.

Voice over Internet Protocol (VoIP)

Your best, cheapest bet for making international calls is to head to an Internet cafe. The vast majority have an international calling system called Voice over Internet Protocol (VoIP), which most of us know as Skype. These cafes are easily spotted because they have headphones attached to each computer (and often a loud foreigner shouting down a microphone). International calls made this way can range anywhere from free to $1 per minute—much cheaper than making direct international calls or using a phone card. If you have your own Skype or similar account, you just need to find one of the many Internet cafes in Nicaragua and El Salvador that provide the

5

PLANNING YOUR TRIP | Staying Connected

service. To open an account is easy—just go to www.skype.com and follow the instructions. If you are calling another Skype user, the call is free.

Internet & E-mail

WITH YOUR OWN COMPUTER

Wi-Fi is pretty much in every establishment that deals with tourists in Nicaragua. Hotels, cafes, and retailers are signing on as "hot spots," meaning you can access the Internet from your own wireless-enabled laptop. Most places don't charge, though it is best to check with your hotel. Wireless Internet in Spanish is known as *internet inalámbrico*. Mac owners have their own networking technology: Apple AirPort. iPass providers (www.ipass.com) also give you access to a few hundred wireless hotel lobby setups. To locate other hot spots that provide **free wireless networks** in cities around the world, go to www.personaltelco.net/index.cgi/WirelessCommunities or www.jiwire.com, which holds the world's largest directory of public wireless hotspots.

For dial-up access, most business-class hotels throughout Central America offer dataports for laptop modems.

Wherever you go, bring a **connection kit** of the right power and phone adapters, a spare phone cord, and a spare Ethernet network cable—or find out whether your hotel supplies them to guests.

WITHOUT YOUR OWN COMPUTER

Every self-respecting hotel or youth hostel nowadays has at least one computer you can access the Internet on, and many provide at least 15 minutes free. There are also plenty of cybercafes in every Nicaraguan town and city center. When entering an Internet cafe, ask for *una máquina* and the assistant will direct you to an available computer. Charges vary between C30 and C40 an hour.

If you need to access files on your office computer while you're on the road, look into **GoToMyPC** (www.gotomypc.com). The service provides a Web-based interface for you to access and manipulate a distant PC from anywhere—even a cybercafe—provided your "target" PC is on and has an always-on connection to the Internet (such as with Road Runner cable). The service offers top-quality security, but if you're worried about hackers, use your own laptop rather than a cybercafe's computer to access the GoToMyPC system.

MANAGUA

Y ou must approach Managua city with rose-tinted glasses perched firmly on your nose. Ignore the scrappy, vacant-lot city center; the forbidding poor neighborhoods; the characterless, literally nameless, streets; and the chaotic markets and tacky malls. It is a frustrating, bewildering place and easily the least accessible, hardest to negotiate, toughest to discover capital city in Central America.

If the city seems like one big accident, that is precisely because it is. Originally, it was just a proud little indigenous fishing village on the shores of Lago Xolotlán—proud enough to beat off the somewhat surprised and vengeful Spanish. But the small village suddenly found itself the country's capital when León and Granada reached a compromise to end their vicious 19th-century rivalry and chose Managua. With hindsight, they might have chosen differently. A devastating earthquake in 1931 caused havoc, as did a fire several years later. The city experienced a brief boom in the 1950s and 1960s, and for a while was one of the region's most advanced metropolises. That all changed on December 23, 1972, when another earthquake hit, and 8 sq. km (3 sq. miles) were flattened and 10,000 people killed. It completely destroyed the city center, and planners decided it was pointless to rebuild on such a shifting tectonic nightmare again. Revolution followed, and the city was bombed by its own leaders. The rich elite fled to Miami, and the city stagnated under the Sandinistas. It is only in recent years that Managua has finally begun to emerge from the rubble, and it still has a long way to go before establishing itself as an attractive Central American capital.

Today, Managua is a city of sprawling markets, chaotic bus terminals, tacky theme bars, and boisterous dance clubs. Urban sprawl has seen it stretch southwards with giant malls and upscale residential zones, but the center is sadly neglected. Once you figure out how to negotiate and get around this strange city of 1.5 million souls, you'll see it has a lot to offer. It is, after all, the cultural, political, economic, and academic engine of the country. You also can't avoid Managua, as all international flights land here. Stay long enough, and you can dance on volcanic rims, eat in tropical courtyards, listen to poetic folklore, experience a vibrant art scene, peek into crumbling cathedrals, and ultimately understand Nicaragua all the more.

ESSENTIALS
Getting There & Departing
BY PLANE

The small, modern **Augusto C Sandino International Airport** (**MGA;** *©* **505/ 2233-1624;** www.eaai.com.ni), is 11km (6¾ miles) east of Managua. A taxi from the airport to the city center costs C400, though you can save some money by walking across the roadway in front and hailing an ordinary city cab, which should cost C200. Always negotiate before jumping in. Laden with luggage and in the midday sun, it is easier and safer to pay the premium for the official airport taxis. Frequent city-bound buses pass in front of the airport, but again, you must cross the busy street to hail one, as none enter the airport grounds. (See "Getting There," on p. 57, for more info on arriving into the country by plane.)

BY INTERNATIONAL BUS

Managua has no central bus station, and each international bus company has its own departure points in Barrio Martha Quezada. **Tica Bus,** 2 blocks east of the Antiguo Cine Dorado (*©* **505/2222-6094** or 505/2222-3031; www.ticabus.com), has the most intercity routes and goes as far as Mexico City. For routes and fares see "Getting to Nicaragua" in chapter 5 on p. 57.

King Quality/Cruceros del Golfo, opposite Tica Bus (*©* **505/2228-1454;** www.kingqualityca.com), has a reputation for being more comfortable and also provides meals. For routes and fares see "Getting to Nicaragua" in chapter 5 on p. 57. **Trans Nica,** 300m (984 ft.) north of Rotonda Metrocentro (*©* **505/2277-2104;** www.transnica.com), services El Salvador and Costa Rica. **Central Line,** (*©* **505/ 2254-5431**) next to King Quality goes south to San José in Costa Rica. For more information go to "Getting to Nicaragua" in chapter 5 on p. 57.

BY DOMESTIC BUS

To travel from Managua to other Nicaraguan cities, you must first get your head around the multiple stations, markets, and meeting points that dot each city, each serving as a transport hub for a particular direction.

Mercado Roberto Huembes (no phone) serves the south, primarily Masaya, Granada, Rivas, San Juan del Sur, and the Cost Rican border. It is in the southeast of the city, on Pista Portezuelo, halfway between Rotonda Centroamérica and Semáforos de Rubenia. A taxi to this terminal from the Metrocentro should not cost more than C120. Huembes is the biggest and busiest terminal in the city. Make sure you get off at the bus-stop side of the market, known as *parada de los buses*. Be aware that you will be swamped by touts as soon as you get out of your taxi, and it is normal for them to grab your stuff and run to whatever bus they want to put you on. Always check that the one you get put on truly is the next one leaving or the *expreso* (an express service with fewer stops) by asking around.

Buses to the north and east depart from **Mercado Mayoreo** (*©* **505/2233- 4729**) in the far eastern fringes of the city, on Avenida de Circunvalación Mercado Mayor. Here, you can get buses to Estelí, Matagalpa, Jinotega, and San Carlos. A taxi to the market should not cost more than C160 from the city center, or you can take the urban bus Ruta 102 from Barrio Martha Quezada. **Expresos del Norte** (*©* **505/2233-4729**) is one of the better bus companies, with a punctual schedule and good-condition *expreso* buses that service the northern part of the country.

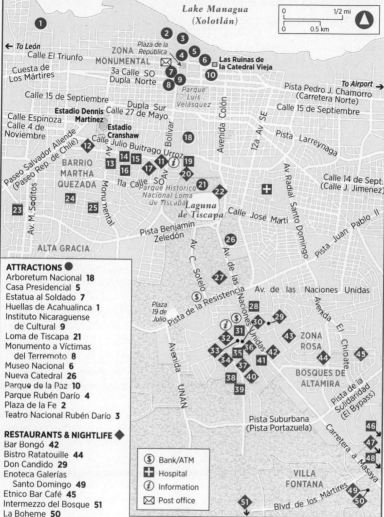

Lake Managua (Xolotlán)

← To León
Calle El Triunfo
Cuesta de Los Mártires
Calle 15 de Septiembre
Calle Espinoza
Calle 4 de Noviembre

ZONA MONUMENTAL
Plaza de la República
3a Calle SO
Dupla Norte
Dupla Sur
Calle 27 de Mayo

Las Ruinas de la Catedral Vieja

To Airport →
Pista Pedro J. Chamorro (Carretera Norte)
Calle 15 de Septiembre

Parque Luis Velásquez

Estadio Dennis Martínez
Estadio Cranshaw
Calle Julio Buitrago Urroz

Paseo Salvador Allende (Paseo Rep. de Chile)
BARRIO MARTHA QUEZADA
11a Calle SO
Parque Histórico Nacional Loma de Tiscapa
Laguna de Tiscapa
Calle José Martí

Avenida Colón
Bolívar
12a Av SE
Pista Larreynaga
Calle 14 de Sept. (Calle J. Jimenez)

Av. Radial Santo Domingo
Pista Juan Pablo II

ALTA GRACIA
Pista Benjamín Zeledón

Pista de la Resistencia
Plaza 19 de Julio
Avenida UNAN

Av. de las Naciones Unidas
Av. de las Naciones Unidas
ZONA ROSA
BOSQUES DE ALTAMIRA

Av. El Chidate
Pista de la Solidaridad (El Bypass)

Pista Suburbana (Pista Portazuela)
VILLA FONTANA
Blvd. de los Mártires

Carretera a Masaya

ATTRACTIONS ●
Arboretum Nacional **18**
Casa Presidencial **5**
Estatua al Soldado **7**
Huellas de Acahualinca **1**
Instituto Nicaraguense de Cultural **9**
Loma de Tiscapa **21**
Monumento a Víctimas del Terremoto **8**
Museo Nacional **6**
Nueva Catedral **26**
Parque de la Paz **10**
Parque Rubén Darío **4**
Plaza de la Fe **2**
Teatro Nacional Rubén Darío **3**

RESTAURANTS & NIGHTLIFE ◆
Bar Bongó **42**
Bistro Ratatouille **44**
Don Candido **29**
Enoteca Galerías Santo Domingo **49**
Etnico Bar Café **45**
Intermezzo del Bosque **51**
La Boheme **50**
La Casa de los Mejía Godoy **11**
La Casa de los Nogueras **37**
La Curva **20**
La Marseillaise **34**
La Terraza Peruana **40**
Marea Alta **30**
Mirador Tiscapa **22**
Piratas **33**
Restaurante Salata **32**
Ruta Maya **12**
Santa Lucia Culinary Institute **47**

Taska Kiko **43**
Tonalli Panadería y Cafetín **17**
Woody's **36**
Z Bar **27**

HOTELS ■
Casa Gabrinma **16**
Crowne Plaza Hotel Managua **19**
Guesthouse Santos **14**
Hilton Princess **31**
Hospedaje Jardin de Italia **15**

Hotel Boutique Villa Maya **46**
Hotel Casa Naranja **41**
Hotel Contempo **48**
Hotel D´Lido **23**
Hotel Europeo **25**
Hotel Intercontinental **28**
Hotel Los Felipe **13**
Hotel Los Piños **39**
Hotel Los Robles **35**
Hotel Montserrat **24**
La Pyramide **38**

$ Bank/ATM
✚ Hospital
ⓘ Information
✉ Post office

0 ——— 1/2 mi
0 ——— 0.5 km

Mercado Israel Lewites (© 505/2265-2152), sometimes referred to as El Boer, takes you west and northwest to León, Chinandega, and the Honduran border. This chaotic place is located in the western outskirts of the city on Avenida Heroes de Batahola, 1km (½ mile) south of the American embassy. A taxi to the market should not cost more than C100 from the city center.

The **UCA** is the city's biggest university and also a convenient spot to jump on an express minibus or microbus to Masaya and Granada. It is located 1 block from the Rotonda Metro Centro. Microbuses depart when full (every 20 minutes or so), from 6 am to 9pm.

Orientation

Managua is less a city and more a collection of bland neighborhoods bundled together, separated occasionally by strips of marsh and wasteland. Be prepared to get lost and confused. No matter where you choose to stay in Managua, you will have to jump in a taxi to properly see the highlights as it is so spread out.

The former downtown area hugs the southern shore of Lago Xolotlán and is now known as the **Zona Monumental.** It sits beside the lakefront in the northwest quadrant of the city. Directly south is the city's hilltop Laguna Tiscapa, and between it and the Zona Monumental is the area with the famous pyramid-shaped Crowne Plaza hotel and the Plaza Shopping Mall. To the east is the budget hotel neighborhood known as **Barrio Martha Quezada.** South of Laguna Tiscapa, the area becomes more upscale and modern. Here begins the **Microcentro,** with its five-star hotels and nightlife district—known as the **Zona Rosa.** Managua's best and safest market, Mercado Roberto Huembes, lies 2km (1¼ miles) east of the Microcentro. The city's more upscale neighborhoods are known as **Los Robles, Altamira, Bolonia,** and **San Juan.** Farther south, you'll find the upscale mall **Galerías Santo Domingo** and the restaurant zone known as **Zona Viva.**

Carretera Panamericana (the Pan-American Highway) crosses Managua in a horseshoe shape and is known as Carretera Masaya on its southeast approach and Carretera Norte in the northeast. The cloud-billowing Masaya volcano appears on the right as you drive south out of the city.

STREET MAPS   If you plan on hanging around Managua, you're going to need a good map. The government organization **INETER** (© 505/2249-2746; www.ineter.gob.ni) produces the best street map of Managua (it's the best city map of any for Nicaragua, for that matter). Maps can be purchased at their main office opposite the Hospital Metrópoli Xolotlán and cost C80. The tourism board **Intur** (© 505/2222-6610; www.visit nicaragua.com) also provides free maps, but these seem to feature only the establishments that are advertised; see "Visitor Information," below, for locations. The main office is located 1 block south and 1 block west of the Crowne Plaza Hotel.

Getting Around

BY BUS   Though Managua's *urbano* bus system is cheap and frequent, it has a woeful reputation for pickpockets and robberies, and well-dressed foreigners are said to be especially targeted. In general, if you stick to the city center and take buses during daylight hours, you should be okay. The buses can also be very overcrowded during rush hour, as they are the only form of public city transportation. Buses come along every 10 minutes and charge a fare of C7.

You can get on the bus only at designated bus stops. Following are the most convenient routes: **Urbano 109** travels from Plaza de la República to Mercado Roberto

Where the Streets Have No Name: Getting Around in Managua

Managua is a city that has no street names or numbers, that uses as reference points landmarks that don't exist anymore, and that insists on using a unit of measurement (the *vara*) not recognized anywhere else. The city also doesn't use the fundamental cardinal points north, east, or west (south is okay, though). To make it worse, some places have two names. It is a wonder people get anywhere!

And yet somehow, they do. Once you master the old indigenous-colonial positioning system, you can appreciate its convoluted logic. Here are some tips on how to "address" the problem.

Landmarks are all-important, whether one exists or not. Most addresses start with a well-known building, roundabout, or monument,

followed by how many blocks or *varas* in whatever direction. (A *vara* is an old Spanish unit of measurement that equals .8m/2½ ft.)

North is *al lago* (toward the lake). East is *arriba* (referring to the rising sun). West is *abajo* (referring to the setting sun). And the South is *al sur*. A typical example of an address using these terms looks like this: *Donde fue la Vicky, 4 cuadras al lago, 30 vrs arriba.* This translates as "from where Vicky was, 4 blocks north and 20 *varas* east." (Incidentally, Vicky used to be a bar now long closed.)

Other important words to remember are *cuadra* (block), *al frente* (in front of), and *contiguo a* (beside). *Casa esquinera* means the corner house.

Huembes, passing by Plaza Inter. **Urbano 110** goes from Mercado Israel Lewites (Boer) to Mercado Mayoreo, passing La UCA, Metrocentro, Rotonda de Centroamérica, Mercado Huembes, and Mercado Iván Montenegro. **Urbano 116** starts at the Montoya statue and passes Plaza Inter and Mercado Oriental before ending at Rotonda Bello Horizonte. **Urbano 118** goes from Parque Las Piedrecitas to Mercado Mayoreo, passing Mercado Israel Lewites (Boer), Rotonda El Güegüense, Plaza Inter, and Mercado Oriental. **Urbano 119** travels from Lindavista to Mercado Huembes, passing Rotonda El Güegüense and La UCA.

BY TAXI Don't worry—cabs will honk at you before you even see them. Even occupancy won't stop them from stopping, and strangers often share taxis (this is a dangerous practice at night). Offer the taxi driver extra cash if you want to travel alone. Taxis are not metered, so it is imperative that you agree on a price before boarding and make sure you determine whether the amount quoted is per person or for the group. Fares go up 50% after dark. Because of Managua's puzzling address system, you will find yourself over-dependent on drivers to get you around. Always try to have the address of your hotel in Spanish. Most hotels will recommend their own favored taxi companies, but many may charge a premium rate. Hotel taxis generally do not pick up strangers on the way to your destination. If you do find a good, reliable taxi driver (and there are many), take his telephone number. Many will gladly show you around the city for a flat day rate of approximately C1,000.

BY CAR Driving in Managua is like getting lost in a huge bowl of noodle soup—the streets are that messy and intertwined. That said, traffic is pretty light, and the roads in the city center are in fairly good condition. Just be warned, even the most advanced

GPS system will still get you lost. You should get a car in this city only if you intend to live here or plan a tour of the country. See p. 59 for car-rental agency info.

ON FOOT   Unless you are a marathon walker, do not mind the heat, and are in absolutely no rush, don't plan on getting around Managua on foot. This city is frustrating for walkers as it is so spread out; in addition, the streets lack charm and, even worse, names. What may hurt the most are the frequent missing manhole covers. If you do insist on getting by on foot, keep your eyes peeled, or you might risk serious injury.

Visitor Information

Intur has its main city office 1 block south and 1 block west of the **Crowne Plaza Hotel** (© 505/2222-6610; www.visit-nicaragua.com). It is open daily from 8 a.m. to 1 p.m. There's also an office at the airport (© 505/2263-3176), which is open Monday to Friday 8 a.m. to 9 p.m., and Saturday and Sunday 8 a.m. to 5 p.m.

[FastFACTS] MANAGUA

ATMs   ATMs are located outside most banks, in malls and service stations, and at the airport. Most banks will also change dollars to córdobas. There are bank branches all over the city, in particular, around Plaza España (also known as Rotonda El Güegüense), along with casual street changers (known as coyotes) who actually give better rates and a faster service with no passport required. **Banpro** (Edificio Malaga, Plaza España; © 505/2266-0069) and **Bancentro,** 1 block south of Rotonda El Güegüense (© 505/2268-5013), are two conveniently located banks.

Drugstores   Farmacia 24 Horas, 150m (492 ft.) east of Rotonda Bello Horizonte (© 505/2240-06233), is good for any late-night pharmacy emergencies. **Farmacia 5 Estrellas,** 3½ blocks north of Semáforo El Colonial (© 505/2248-8026), is an option closer to the center.

Emergencies   The main headquarters of the **Policía Nacional** (© 505/2277-4130) are situated in the Edificio Faustino Ruiz, Plaza del Sol. For **emergencies,** dial © **118.**

Hospitals   Hospital Metropolitano Vivian Pellas (Carretera Masaya Km 9.7; © 505/2255-6900; www.metropolitano.com.ni) is the city's most modern (it was built in 2004) and best-equipped hospital. **Hospital Bautista,** 2 blocks south of Casa RMA (Barrio Largaespada; © 505/2249-7070), also has a good reputation.

Internet   Internet cafes are dotted all around the city, but if you have trouble locating one, just head to any of the malls that dot the city. **iMac Center,** 1 block east and ½ block south of the Semáforo UCA (© 505/2270-5918), offers cheap internet for C30 an hour. It is open daily from 8am to 8pm. **Cyber City,** in front of UCA (© 505/2604-7416), is another good place, as is

the modern and comfortable **Cyber,** on the ground floor of Plaza Inter. They both charge C40 an hour and are open daily 10am to 10pm.

Laundry   Most hotels and hostels will arrange laundry service for a price. **Dryclean USA** (© 505/2270-1107) has branches all over the city. One is close to Plaza Bolonia, behind Santa Fe Steakhouse. Another is at Carretera Masaya Km 3.5.

Post Office   The grandly titled main post office, **Palacio de Correos** (© 505/2222-2048), is 2 blocks west of the Plaza de la República in the former Enitel building. Here, you'll also find an excellent philatelist store.

Restrooms   There are no public restrooms except in malls. Restaurants should allow you to use their bathrooms if you ask nicely. If you find yourself needing a restroom while in the Zona Monumental, head to the

Centro Cultural Managua. There are public bathrooms on the second floor.

Traveler's Checks Exchange all traveler's checks in Managua if you can, as there are very few places outside the city that will change these checks. There's an **American Express** 1 block east of Rotonda El Güegüense (€ 505/2266-4050). **Multicambios,** ½ block east of Rotonda El Güegüense (€ 505/2266-8407), also changes traveler's checks.

WHERE TO STAY

Lodgings of varying quality are spread all over the city, and what zone you choose to stay in will have a big effect on your first and lasting impressions of Managua. The Microcentro is a concrete jungle, but it's where the best accommodations can be found. On the opposite end of the scale, Barrio Martha Quezada is where all the budget hotels and hostels are clustered. With its handful of Internet cafes and bars, the whole zone has earned the name Gringolandia, but I find it to be rather abandoned and uninviting, in general, especially at night. It is relatively safe, though the barrio to the east has a reputation for being dangerous; if you are careful, you will be fine. The central district is where all the backpackers and budget travelers go. Here, you'll find a cluster of hostels and *hospedajes* where quality varies wildly, with the Crowne Plaza an upscale exception. One advantage of Barrio Martha Quezada is that the international bus companies, such as Tica Bus, pass through here.

Ultra budgeters should try **Casa Gabrinma** (€ 505/2222-6650), 1 block south and ½ block east of Tica Bus. Though it might not look like much from the outside, once you get inside, it improves with a nice inner courtyard and five basic, clean rooms. Rates start at $10 per person. **Hospedaje Jardín de Italia** (€ 505/2222-7967), 1 block north of Shannon Pub, is another good budget choice, with clean rooms and private bathrooms. Rates start at $20 for a double.

It must be said, though, that if you really want to enjoy Managua, you should spend a bit more and stay in one of the more upscale districts such as Bolonia and Los Robles. This is where you'll find some of the nicest hotels and restaurants. Hotel rates are quoted in U.S. dollars throughout this guide, as this is how prices are commonly quotes by Nicaraguan hotels.

The Microcentro

Hilton Princess A short, sun-blasted stroll from the Intercontinental, the Hilton Princess is a smaller version of its more expansive neighbor and is popular with a business and diplomatic clientele. The style could best be described as mock classical, with its wood paneling and marble floors somewhat betrayed by low ceilings, garish carpets, and piped-in elevator music. However, rooms are big, gorgeous, and very comfortable with lots of light, a huge bed, a small business desk in dark polished wood, a handy coffeemaker, and an ironing board tucked into the closet. The bathrooms come in that ubiquitous cream color that many hotels seem to prefer, with a sink that's separate from the small bathtub and shower. The hotel's restaurant is open to the public, as is a small gentleman's-style club bar called the Clancy. Staff members are very efficient and quick to resolve the occasional mishap.

2 blocks from Intercontinental Hotel on Carretera Masaya, Microcentro. www.managua.hilton.com. € **505/2255-5777.** Fax 505/2270-5710. 107 units. From $129–$176 double. AE, DC, MC, V. **Amenities:** Bistro; bar; concierge; fitness room; pool; room service. *In room:* A/C, TV, hair dryer, Internet, minibar.

Hotel Casa Naranja ★ 🎁 Casa Naranja has character *and* comfort. This boutique hotel is hidden behind lots of greenery on a quiet residential street close to the commercial district. The decor is warm, inviting, and very tropical. Attractive terra-cotta tiles complement the genuine antique furniture set around a gorgeous colorful garden. The rooms are a good size, with feather-stuffed mattresses and lots of light. There are rooms for the allergy prone, and some are even wheelchair accessible—a novelty in Nicaragua. All in all, you can't do much better if chain hotels are not your style but you still like your luxuries.

Km 4.5 Carretera Masaya, Microcentro. www.hotelcasanaranja.com. © **305/396-2214** in the U.S. or 505/2277-3403. 9 units. From $90 double; from $105 suite. Rates include breakfast. AE, DC, MC, V. **Amenities:** Bar; airport transfers; concierge; room service. *In room:* A/C, TV, hair dryer, Wi-Fi (free).

Hotel Intercontinental ★★ If you want five-star convenience in the center of the city, the Intercontinental is hard to beat. The hotel's lobby, a large attractive space with brick domed ceilings, cream-colored pillars, and fine art on the wide corridor walls, makes a good first impression. The decor throughout is equally muted and modern. Rooms are expansive and soundproof, with king-size beds, flat-screen TVs, wide and accommodating safes, and an all-important in-room coffeemaker. The moderate-size bathrooms have good shower heads and mirrored wardrobes. The mostly business clientele enjoy the on-site international restaurant and the conveniently located mall across the street. It's one of the few places you can buy the export-only El Padrón cigars; ask at the back bar. My only complaint is that the hotel charges a high commission for any currency exchange transactions.

S of Metrocentro Mall on Carretera Masaya, Microcentro. www.ichotelsgroup.com. © **800/444-0022** in the U.S. or 505/2278-4545. Fax 505/278-6300. 164 units. From $161 double; from $345 suite. AE, DC, MC, V. **Amenities:** Restaurant; cocktail lounge; airport transfers (C100 one-way); concierge; health & fitness center; outdoor pool; room service. *In room:* A/C, TV, hair dryer, minibar.

Los Robles and San Juan

Hotel Los Piños ★ This is one of the more tasteful and elegant small hotels I've found in Managua, with lots of space, and light and beautiful interiors. From the outside, it looks like a modern, yellow-and-brown building located on a leafy suburban street close to the Zona Rosa. Inside, you'll find grand windows, tall ceilings, dark wood floors, and lovely art. Black leather seating contrasts with wicker rocking chairs in the many communal spaces upstairs and down. The family photos on the mantelpiece add a personal touch. Rooms are big, with white tile floors and elegant matching furniture that includes wood and wrought-iron headboards. One of its best features is the good-size garden with a generous pool surrounded by hammocks and foliage.

Calle San Juan 314, 1 block S & ½ block E of Gimnasio Hercules, Reparto San Juan. www.hotellospinos. info. © **505/2270-0761.** 15 units. From $65 double. Rates include breakfast. AE, DC, MC, V. **Amenities:** Pool; Internet (free) .*In room:* TV.

Hotel Los Robles ★ Though Casa Naranja pays a little bit more attention to detail, Los Robles comes a close second in the expensive boutique-hotel category. Attractive ironwork and heavy, dark-wood antiques adorn this colonial house with a hacienda-style front. All of this leads to a beautiful leafy garden with splashes of bright flowers and a trickling fountain. The rooms are big and airy, with hand-crocheted bedspreads. The bathrooms are more than adequate and have all-important high-pressure hot showers. Lago Managua is several blocks away, and it's a short stroll to some of Managua's best restaurants and bars. All in all, staying in Los Robles feels like staying in the house of a rich aunt who happens to also do a great breakfast buffet.

30m (98 ft.) S of Restaurante La Marseillaise, Los Robles. www.hotellosrobles.com. ℂ **505/2267-3008.** Fax 505/2270-1074. 14 units. From $95 double. Rates include breakfast. AE, DC, MC, V. **Amenities:** Breakfast room; concierge; room service;. *In room:* TV, hair dryer, Wi-Fi (free).

La Pyramide Managua seems to have a monopoly on pyramid-shaped hotels, and La Pyramide, located in a residential area that is close to shops and bars, is a smaller, more downscale rival to the triangular Crowne Plaza. This particular pyramid-shaped boutique building is decked out in a dated orange color scheme and blue window frames, and was built with the idea of creating "a home on the road." Every suite is named after a Pharaoh. The German owner is very much focused on the comfort of mind, body, and spirit, and is trying to add a New Age design. Rooms feature comfortable queen-size beds, tile floors, and slanted walls. The restaurant is perfect for the diet conscious, with an emphasis on health food and an extensive vegetarian menu.

1 block S, 1 block E & a further 2½ blocks S of Gimnasio Hércules, San Juan. www.lapyramidehotel.com. ℂ **505/2278-0687.** 10 units. From $48 double; from $75 suite. AE, DC, MC, V. Amenities: Restaurant; Internet (free), airport transfers ($20. *In room:* TV, minibar.

Alta Gracia and Bolonia

Hotel D'Lido ✦ Located on a quiet residential street, Hotel D'Lido doesn't particularly stand out from the other suburban homes in this quiet neighborhood. Its rooms are simple but spacious, though the furniture could do with a revamp, and the bedspreads are a little too bright for my taste. Nevertheless, D'Lido is a reliable hotel that has been operating since the 1970s. It's also a good budget option, especially when you consider the inviting pool out back, along with the thatch-roofed veranda and courtyard. It's a 15-minute drive from the center of town.

Km 3 Carretera Sur (2½ blocks S of Centro Toyota Autonica), Altagracia. www.hoteldlido.com. ℂ **505/2266-8965.** 32 units. From $40 double; from $52 triple; from $62 quadruple. Rates include breakfast. AE, DC, MC, V. **Amenities:** Airport transfers ($20); pool. *In room:* TV, Internet (free and onlyin some rooms).

Hotel Europeo ✦ ☺ This is a pleasant, good-value hotel set on a suburban street a 5-minute taxi ride from the Microcenter. Tidy, elegant rooms overlook a tropical courtyard with a nice pool and open-air restaurant serving delicious lobster. Bathrooms are small, with an enclosed shower and somewhat noisy air vents. Despite nice touches such as the art hanging on the walls and attractive wooden ceilings, the decor could stand a little sprucing up. Still, it makes for a relaxing stay and serves as a great escape when you tire of touring the city. The pool area is especially popular spot for kids and their parents to cool off in the hot afternoon sun.

60m (197 ft.) W of Canal 2, Bolonia. www.hoteleuropeo.com.ni. ℂ **505/2268-2130.** Fax 505/2268-5999. 35 units. From $69 double; from $89 triple. Rates include breakfast. AE, MC, V. **Amenities:** Bar & grill; pool. Internet.(free) *In room:* A/C, TV,

Hotel Montserrat "Contemporary meets colonial, with a Nicaraguan twist" is how to best describe the Hotel Montserrat. Open since 1990, it's family run and very much retains a homey feel, with pastel walls and local crafts scattered around. There are times things don't go as smoothly as they should—on my last visit, there was no hot water sporadically, for example—but in general, this is a comfortable hotel in a nice residential zone close to the city center. There's a relaxing restaurant serving an eclectic mix of Thai, Middle Eastern, and Nicaraguan food here, too.

1 block W & ½ block N of Optica Vision, Bolonia. www.hotelmontserrat.com. © **866/978-6260** in the U.S. or 505/2266-5060. 15 units. From $55 double; from $70 triple. Rates include breakfast. AE, MC, V. **Amenities:** Restaurant/bar; airport transfers ($20). *In room:* A/C, TV, fridge, Wi-Fi (free).

Barrio Martha Quezada

Crowne Plaza Hotel Managua ★★   The Crowne Plaza is Managua's most famous hotel and a prominent city landmark; it's shaped like a giant white pyramid. Howard Hughes turned it into his home in the 1970s, when he had plans to transform the Corn Islands into the new Las Vegas. The earthquake soon put a stop to that, and his plane was the first one out of Managua after disaster struck. Formerly known as the Intercontinental, the Crowne Plaza has had an extreme makeover and is very different from the basic hotel that journalists used to hunker down in to cover the war. Today, you'll find luxurious rooms with lots of light and color, and spacious bathrooms. The large outdoor pool is one of the best in the city. This is an excellent stopover if you have little time; its city-center location, in front of La Casa de Los Mejia Godoy and Tiscapa, is very convenient.

Octavo Calle Suroeste 101, Barrio Martha Quezada. www.ichotelsgroup.com. © **505/2228-3530.** 60 units. From $104 double; from $148 suite. AE, DC, MC, V. **Amenities:** Restaurant; airport transfers ($20); concierge; health club; outdoor pool; spa. *In room:* TV, Internet, minibar.

Guesthouse Santos   This is the *mochileros'* (backpackers') favorite place to bunk down for a couple of days and exchange war stories. A large funky courtyard is surrounded by multicolored rooms, some of which have private bathrooms. Try to get a mattress upstairs, as there is more of a breeze up there. Though everything could use a good scrub, the many folks who stay here don't seem to care; this is the best place in town to meet others traveling around Central America.

1 block N & 1½ blocks W of Tica Bus, Barrio Martha Quezada. © **505/2222-3713.** 12 units, 2 w/private bathroom. From $6 dorm bed; from $14–$17 double; from $24 triple. AE, DC, MC, V. **Amenities:** Bar; Internet (free); restaurant. *In room:* Fan, no phone.

Hotel Los Felipe   This is the best budget hotel in the Martha Quezada area. The small rooms have low beds and garish bedcovers, but are quiet, bright, and simply furnished. Some have tiny private bathrooms. There is a swimming pool set in a leafy courtyard with a palm-thatched dining area. The restaurant offers good Nicaraguan fare. Some rooms are quite crammed with bunk beds that hold four people; others are less crowded. All have a psychedelic color scheme that extends out onto the white-railed street entrance, which sports a blue wall and funky wooden sign.

1½ blocks W of Tica Bus, Barrio Martha Quezada. www.hotellosfelipe.com.ni. © **505/2222-6501.** 28 units, 5 w/private bathroom. From $20 double w/no A/C but fan; $30 double w/A/C. AE, MC, V. **Amenities:** Internet ; minigym; pool. *In room:* A/C (in some), fan, TV.

Near the Airport

Best Western Las Mercedes   Technically, you can walk across the street from the airport to this hotel, though you might kill yourself in the process; it's a very busy road. The chalet-style rooms are somewhat simple but perfectly adequate. The hotel's main attraction is a nice pool surrounded by a tropical garden of palm trees and plants. Because of its location, the Best Western makes a good stop-over if you don't plan on hanging around Managua or a good stop if you want to rest and freshen up before you venture farther into the city. Despite its conventional feel, the hotel has made forward-thinking efforts regarding renewable energy, such as using solar panels to heat water. That said, that hot water can be a little unreliable, and in general, the hotel could be a little cleaner. There is a rather soulless restaurant here that's convenient if you find yourself delayed in the airport.

In front of Aeropuerto Internacional de Managua, Km 10.5 Carretera Norte. www.lasmercedes.com.ni. ℭ 800/2528-1234 in the U.S. or 505/2255-9910. 174 units. $90 double. AE, DC, MC, V. **Amenities:** Restaurant; bar; free airport transfers; health club; 2 swimming pools; room service;. *In room:* A/C, TV, hair dryer. Wi-Fi (free)

Outskirts of Managua

Hotel Boutique Villa Maya ★   You'll feel less like you're at a hotel here and more like you happen to know the owners of a gorgeous estate who are letting you stay at their mansion, complete with beautiful grounds laid out with lawns, shrubs, and flower borders that surround a spectacular pool. The building itself is a tasteful mix of Spanish, French, and Italian architecture with elegant, classical furniture and tall windows. A charming set of galleries overlook the outdoor foliage and create a very peaceful and romantic retreat. The rooms themselves are nothing special, unless you spring for the suite with a balcony. The bathrooms are clean but small, with charmless shower curtain rails, but that's a minor criticism in what is a very beautiful, upscale B&B-style property.

Calle los Laureles 105, Las Colinas. ℭ 505/2276-2175. 8 units. From $87 double. Rates include breakfast. AE, DC, MC, V. **Amenities:** Breakfast room; concierge; pool; room service; *In room:* TV, hair dryer, Wi-Fi. (free).

Hotel Contempo ★★ 🎁   The Managua hotel scene will never be quite the same since the debut of this ultra-chic and super-sleek designer hotel in 2009. Cathedral-high ceilings, airport-sized windows, stark black and white decor, and elegant rooms make this a perfect, Zen-like escape for those who like unique properties with five-star comforts. Each room has a different style and theme, such as "lago," "volcan," and "mango," but all have an underlying contemporary sophistication where tack is replaced with tact and grace. Private courtyards, an infinity pools, and an über-minimalist piano lounge are just some of the highlights. The on-premise, glass-enclosed restaurant Azul is run by an award-winning French chef. Its location, 11km (7 miles) from Managua city center may not suit everyone, but it's only 5 minutes from the Santo Domingo mall.

Km 11 Carretera a Masaya. www.contempohb.com. ℭ 505/2264-9160. 18 units. From $84 double. Rates include breakfast. AE, DC, MC, V. **Amenities:** Restaurant; wine bar; breakfast room; concierge; pool; room service; *In room:* TV, hair dryer. Wi-Fi. (free)

WHERE TO EAT

Don't let the city's shabby appearance fool you. When it comes to food, Managua offers everything. If you're finally beginning to tire of *gallo pinto,* the capital offers much more than just rice and beans. You'll find Asian, French, and Italian eateries dotted around the city, but mostly in the better-off neighborhoods or the shopping malls. This is the only place in the country where you can order fondue, Peruvian food, or sushi. For the budget conscious, there's no shortage of street outlets and roadside grills (*fritangas*), especially in the Martha Quezada area and the Rotonda Bello Horizonte. Trendy restaurants open and close all the time or just change addresses, so don't be afraid to ask a local where to find the latest gourmet spots.

Los Robles

La Casa de los Nogueras ★ MEDITERRANEAN   This restaurant's name kept popping up when I asked locals for recommendations, and I wasn't disappointed when I ate here. La Casa de los Nogueras exudes sophistication, and the Mediterranean-style food matches the decor in exquisite taste and presentation. The restaurant is set in an authentic colonial-style villa on a residential street and is decorated with ornate religious paintings hanging beneath high ceilings and set amidst antique furniture with a beautiful garden. Try the delicious breaded veal cutlets on a bed of corn purée with mint sauce. Popular with the business elite, it can be a little formal.

Av. Principal No. 17, Los Robles. © **505/2278-2506.** Main courses around C550. AE, DC, MC, V. Daily noon–3pm & 7–10pm.

La Marseillaise FRENCH   La Marseillaise has been a culinary institution in Managua since before the war; it was one of the first restaurants to offer gourmet cuisine. The building itself is a work of art, with a beautifully manicured lawn and sculpted hedge leading to an arched door and villa-style house. Inside, fine art adorns the walls, and Nicaragua's beautiful people dine on delicious fish and meat dishes napped in rich sauces. The desserts alone are worth a visit. The restaurant is on a suburban street in Los Robles—just look for all the sparkling SUVs parked outside, and you'll know you have arrived.

Calle Principal, #4 (4 blocks N of Enitel Villa Fontana), Los Robles. © **505/2227-0224.** Main courses C500. AE, DC, MC, V. Daily noon–3pm & 6–10pm.

Taska Kiko SPANISH   You might find yourself rubbing elbows with ambassadors and ex-guerrillas at this tapas house, a favorite for power lunches between the country's great and good. The food is great and good, too, with enough platters of octopus, crab, and goat cheese to fuel a run for the presidency. Spanish-owned, it's not surprising that you'll also find some of the best paella in town here. The building itself is large and open air, with a dry frond roof sitting on a wooden framework.

1 block E of Monte de los Olivos, Los Robles. No phone. Main courses C170. AE, DC, MC, V. Mon–Sat 11:30am–10pm.

The Zona Viva

La Boheme MEDITERRANEAN   This restaurant is located in the upscale mall known as Galerías Santo Domingo. Its decor, however, is very much old-world, with granite walls and arched galleries. Everything is beautifully lit by wall candles and back lights, lending a romantic vibe. There is a large circular alcove in the corner and more conventional seating up front. Some dishes are works of art that border on kitsch, such as the chicken and potato purée in the shape of a chick (it is delicious, though). The wine list is particularly good, with labels from all over the world, including France and Italy.

Galerías Santo Domingo, Módulo 3B, Zona Viva. © **505/2276-5288.** Main courses C440. AE, DC, MC, V. Daily noon–midnight.

The Microcentro

Don Candido STEAKHOUSE   Located 2 blocks from the Intercontinental, in Managua's Metrocentro (adjacent to Los Robles), is this upscale steakhouse on an unassuming residential street. The modern interior is unfussy and subdued, with bare brick walls, dark leather seating, black tablecloths, and elegant spotlighting illuminating modern Nicaraguan art. The menu is beef heavy, with 25 different cuts, including entrecote and T-bone steak. Starters include asparagus topped with melted cheese and a chorizo platter with roasted vegetables. Waiters in white shirts and ties hint at this restaurant's up-market sensibilities, which are also reflected in the prices, with some of the main dishes coming in at a whopping $30. Don Candido is therefore not a casual stopover, but more a romantic night out or a business lunch set up to impress.

1 block E & 1 block S of the Intercontinental, Los Robles. www.restaurantedoncandido.com. ✆ **505/2277-2485.** Main courses C500. AE, DC, MC, V. Daily 5–11pm.

La Terraza Peruana ★ ⫯ PERUVIAN   If you want real ceviche washed down with a real pisco sour, La Terraza is the place to go. This is a laid-back restaurant with a great ambience, too, with small stone picnic tables sitting within a tropical veranda covered in terra-cotta tiles and around a trickling fountain. The staff is prompt and serves with a smile. In addition to ceviche, the menu has kabobs, beef stew, pasta, and fish. Try the olive oil—it was the best I had in Nicaragua.

80m (262 ft.) N of the Pasteleria Sampson, Microcentro. ✆ **505/2278-0031.** Main courses C150. AE, DC, MC, V. Daily noon–11pm.

The Zona Rosa

Marea Alta SEAFOOD   One of the best seafood joints in town is also the infamous location of a kidnapping. The U.S. ambassador was taken from here at the height of the revolution. Now, it appears as a rather nondescript corner restaurant with blue walls and a front patio lined with palm trees. Thankfully, kidnappings are a thing of the past, and the restaurant still attracts an upscale clientele. The fish motif hints at the marvelous prawns and paella cooking in the kitchen.

1 block S of Hotel Seminole. ✆ **505/2270-2459.** Main courses C250. AE, DC, MC, V. Daily noon–midnight.

Restaurante Salata MIDDLE EASTERN   Falafel, *shawarma,* and kebabs are what this restaurant does best, and it is one of the most genuine Middle Eastern eateries in town, with a great location close to the Zona Rosa. The decor is modern and minimal, with white walls and hardwood seating. You cannot miss the huge brown canopy outside. Worth a visit for something different.

S corner of Hotel Seminole. ✆ **505/2270-2542.** Main courses C250. AE, DC, MC, V. Mon–Sat 11:30am–10pm.

Barrio Quezada

Tonalli Panadería y Cafetín ⫯ BAKERY   The bright mural outside this bakery, which displays the female gender symbol intertwined with pre-Columbian motifs, gives away that Tonalli is something more than just a shop dispensing delicious bread and pastry. In addition to being a great place to stop for a hearty breakfast or strong afternoon coffee, Tonalli is also a woman's cooperative and is active in promoting health and social issues. The cafe is set in a simple orange cottage with terra-cotta tiling and has a lovely garden courtyard with seating.

2½ blocks from Cine Cabrera, Barrio Martha Quezada. ✆ **505/2222-2678.** Snacks) start at C150. AE, DC, MC, V. Mon–Fri 7am–7pm; Sat 7am–3pm.

Altamira

Bistro Ratatouille ⫯ FRENCH BAKERY   This is the best-kept secret in town and a slice of French charm in the sweltering tropics. Bistro Ratatouille is an unassuming little cafe sitting amidst a row of stores, but the food is excellent, with homemade quiche and crème brûlée topping the list. Owner Laurence specializes in sweets such as apple and cranberry fruit pies, and she even produces her own ice cream. The multicolored furniture only adds to the charm. The Bistro Ratatouille makes a welcome retreat for a mid-morning treat.

In front of Iglesia San Agustín, Altamira. ✆ **505/2270-9865.** Snacks start at C150. AE, DC, MC, V. Mon–Fri 10am–3:30pm.

City Outskirts

Intermezzo del Bosque NICARAGUAN   The location could not be better, on a forested hillside overlooking the city and lake. Wrought-iron furniture sits on a circular platform with a breathtaking view. Behind this platform is a large wooden dome-shaped dining area that calls to mind an indigenous village hall. The menu comprises well-presented seafood and grilled meat dishes. The lobster, served on a bed of pasta in a white sauce, is particularly good. There is live music, with traditional costume and dance performances on weekends. It might get a little too touristy, but you won't care when you take in the view—this place manages to make Managua look beautiful, which is no small achievement.

5km (3 miles) S of Colegio Centroamérica. www.intermezzodelbosque.com. ✆ **505/2271-1428.** Main courses C340. AE, DC, MC, V. Tues–Fri 5–11pm; Sat & Sun 12:30–11pm.

Santa Lucia Culinary Institute ★★★ NICARAGUAN/INTERNATIONAL There aren't many restaurants that can boast five different kitchens, a grill house, a coffee bar, a cocktail bar, and an in-house bakery. Run by Nicaragua's very own celebrity chef Nelson Porta, this excellent eatery doubles as a culinary school and has one of the best wine lists in the country. The dining area includes a spacious patio with white canvas covering a wooden-framed roof. Combined with the red walls and stylish furniture, this gives the venue a classy and modern style. On the menu, you'll find a great variety of international and local dishes, such as smoked salmon carpaccio, tortilla soup, and lobster cooked in lemon and wine The international fare is served with aplomb, and the owner is a gregarious host who speaks perfect English. You can catch his show most mornings on channel 8.

At the entrance to the Las Colinas neighborhood. ✆ **505/2276-2651.** Main courses C240. AE, DC, MC, V. Daily noon–3pm & 6–11pm.

WHAT TO SEE & DO

Downtown

Even the most ramshackle cities usually have a dynamic downtown area. Not, however, Managua. Unfortunately, the city's center (**Zona Monumental**) was destroyed by a powerful earthquake in 1972, and the whole area has been left largely untouched and put aside, as its name implies, for monuments of the past and the occasional government building. It is a dilapidated, decrepit zone with many poor squatters and empty buildings. Yet, it is worth an early-morning stroll around to see what remains and to learn the stories behind each building. At night, it is best avoided. Its center is the **Plaza de la Revolución,** otherwise known as the Plaza de la República, depending on your political point of view. The most interesting thing to see here is **Las Ruinas de la Catedral Vieja,** ½ block east of the plaza—it's a poetic testament to the tragic history of Nicaragua. Completed in 1929, this cathedral survived several earthquakes until the big one in 1972 made it too dangerous to enter. Much of it still stands, and you can peer into its shell-like structure and spy beautiful frescoes and statues.

Palacio Nacional de la Cultura is just south of the old cathedral and was once the National Congress. It was here that Sandinista rebels instigated a hostage siege in 1978 that ended with the release of political prisoners. Now, it is the beautifully restored site of the **Museo Nacional** (© **505/2222-2905**). The museum has an extensive collection of pre-Columbian pottery and statues, and is situated in the same building as the National Library. There is a marvelous revolutionary mural above the main staircase that leads up to the library, plus a set of illustrated displays that explain in detail the many different dishes of indigenous cuisine, and also classic examples of handicrafts from each town and province. The museum is open from 9am to 4pm daily. Admission is C80.

The **Casa Presidencial** sits opposite the Palacio Nacional. Completed in 1999, this president's office created a controversy as loud as its colors because of its exorbitant cost of roughly $10 million dollars. The current Sandinista president Ortega refuses to work from such an opulent building and has threatened to turn it into a giant children's kindergarten. Just south of the plaza is the **Instituto Nicaraguense de Cultural** (© **505/2222-5291**). This used to be Managua's main hotel, the Gran Hotel, until the 1972 earthquake literally toppled the top floors. Now, all that remains are two stories of exhibition rooms and concert halls. It's open from 9am to 4:30pm Monday to Saturday, with later closing times for shows. Murals decorate the entire building, but it is very scruffy and in sore need of a makeover. The building is free to enter, though there may be an admission price for any special exhibitions and performances.

On the lakeside of the Plaza de la República, in **Parque Rubén Darío,** you'll find a stark white statue dedicated to Nicaragua's greatest poet, Rubén Darío. Continue your literary-themed walk by next strolling through **Plaza de la Cultura República de Guatemala.** This is dedicated to the Guatemalan writer and 1967 Nobel winner Miguel Angel Asturias Rosales. His book *El Señor Presidente* (Catedra) is one of Latin America's greatest portraits of a tyrant.

The **Teatro Nacional Rubén Darío** ★ (© **505/2266-3630;** www.tnruben dario.gob.ni) was built in 1969 and is one of the few buildings to survive the 1972 earthquake. It's a beautiful structure and the cultural heart of Managua. The 1,200-person auditorium hosts plays, dance performances, and even the occasional fashion show. There is also an exhibition space upstairs in what is known as the Chandelier Room (after a set of chandeliers donated by the Spanish government). Performances can be sporadic, but its open weekdays from 10am to 6pm and weekends from 10am to 3pm. It's where Nicaragua's great come to rub elbows, but don't let that turn you off. Tickets are very affordable. The theater is 1 block north of the Plaza de la República, in front of the **Malecón,** Managua's lakeside promenade, which features food stalls and great views of the breezy Lago Xolotlán in the distance. (Note that the water is unsuitable for bathing.)

Just west of the theater is **Plaza de la Fe (Faith Plaza),** ex-president Alemán's concrete homage to Pope John Paul II. That president was later discovered to have stolen from the state's coffers, but perhaps he thought his papal extravagance might buy him a place in heaven anyway.

Three blocks south on Avenida Bolívar is the **Estatua al Soldado,** otherwise known as *El Guerrillero sin Nombre* (the Unknown Guerrilla). This is a large, muscular paramilitary statue, with a pickax in one hand and an AK-47 in another. It is an important city landmark, but 3 blocks east, you'll find something a little more conciliatory and bipartisan. The **Parque de la Paz** ★ is a lighthouse growing out of a buried mound of weapons and tanks—a symbolic proclamation by ex-president

Violeta Chamorro that the Contra war was over. The nearby shantytown and general poverty are reminders that this country has some problems to solve yet.

One final, poignant statue to see downtown is the **Monumento a Víctimas del Terremoto,** a memorial to those who died in the earthquake of 1972. It is located in front of the **Cancilleria,** where the Iglesia de San Antonio used to stand. If you want a simple explanation about why this city is so fragmented and just plain ugly, see this portrait of a man standing amid the wreckage of his home, and read its moving poem by Pedro Rafael Gutierrez called "Requiem for a Dead City."

Sights Outside Zona Monumental

Arboretum Nacional ☺ In this small, sunny forest, you'll find a collection of 200 of Nicaragua's native flora. More popular with visiting schoolchildren than tourists, the arboretum is worth a visit for anyone craving greenery in this ungreen city. Still, it must be said, some plants look better than others. It's especially worth visiting in March when Nicaragua's national flower, the sacuanjoche, comes into fragrant bloom. The red flower of the national tree, the malinche, blossoms here May through August.

Av. Bolivar, Barrio Martha Quezada. ℂ **505/2222-2558.** C5 adults. Mon–Fri 8am–5pm.

Huellas de Acahualinca ★ Located 2km (1¼ miles) north of the Telcor building on the way to the lake, this remarkable site displays 6,000-year-old footprints of men, women, and children forming a line along what is suspected to have been a riverbed. The question is: Were they fleeing a volcanic eruption or just going for a swim? One thing is for sure; it is perhaps one of the oldest pieces of evidence of human activity in Central America. The site now has a simple museum showcasing the footprints.

It is best to catch a taxi here and ask the driver to wait to take you home, as the area is a rundown ghetto and a little dangerous. A two-way taxi ride should not cost more than C200 from the Metrocentro. The more adventurous can dress down and catch bus no. 112 in front of Plaza de la República or 102 on Calle Colon in Barrio Martha Quezada. The helpful staff will escort you to a taxi or bus for the trip back.

Acahualinca, El Cauce. ℂ **505/2266-5774.** C88 adults; C110 adults w/camera. Daily 9am–4pm.

Loma de Tiscapa A silhouette-style statue of Sandino stands on this high point behind the Crowne Plaza Hotel (p. 78). Also known as Parque Histórico, the Loma de Tiscapa was once the site of Somoza's presidential palace before it was destroyed by the 1972 earthquake. It now offers a blustery view of the city and the Tilcapa volcanic lagoon. The lake itself is now polluted, but you can do a canopy tour across it to the crater if you are feeling really courageous. The zip-line platform is open Tuesday to Sunday from 8am to 4:30pm and costs C330. Other historical sites in the area include Las Masmorras, a notorious Somoza jail now closed to the public, and the old site of the American Embassy, destroyed in the 1972 earthquake. Underneath the monument site, there is a small pictorial museum devoted to Sandino.

W end of Calle José Martí, 1km (½ mile) N of Nueva Catedral. No phone. C22 adults.

Nueva Catedral From the outside, this church looks like it was designed by a vengeful atheist architect. Inside, the atmosphere is a little more serene and Zen-like, but it's still hard to figure out whether you are in a Soviet nuclear reactor or Islamic prison. Commissioned by Catholic philanthropist and Domino's Pizza founder Tom Monaghan, the building's one abiding characteristic is the onion-shaped domes that make up the roof. Described by one visitor as "the worst church in the world," it has a disquieting feel, not improved by its isolated location alongside squatter shacks and a barbed-wire perimeter fence. The end effect is so bad, it's almost good.

S of Tiscapa, on the Carretera Masaya. ⓒ**505/2278-4232.** Free admission. Mass Tues–Sat at noon & 6pm, Sun 11am & 6pm.

SHOPPING
Markets
Mercado Roberto Huembes ★, both a market and a significant transit stop for the city's chicken buses and intercity expresses, is chaotic, colorful, and overwhelming. It is also the most tourist-friendly and accessible of all the big markets in Managua. You'll find everything, from fruit to hubcaps, here. Its arts-and-crafts stalls are just as good as anything you'll get in Masaya, and it's also a great place to find local music CDs. The market is open daily from 7:30am to 5pm, and is located 4km (2½ miles) southeast of the Zona Monumental on Pista Portezuelo.

There are other major markets dotted around the city's suburbs, most notably **Israel Lewites** (also known as Boer), where you can catch an express bus to Rivas and San Juan del Sur. It is 3km (1¾ miles) southwest of the Zona Monumental on Avenida Héroes de Batahola and sells everything from cheap toys to fresh fruit. It is open daily from roughly dawn to dusk. One market to avoid is the sprawling **Mercado Oriental,** 2km (1¼ miles) east of Plaza de la Revolución. It's part flea market and crime black spot; you should only go to this sprawling hive of commerce and thievery if you are looking for trouble.

Much more civilized is **Mama Delfina,** 1 block north of Enitel Villa Fontana (ⓒ **505/2267-8288**). Here, you'll find a pleasant minimarket of gorgeous handicrafts from all over the country and a coffee shop upstairs where you can cool off and rest. It is open daily from 8am to 7pm.

Malls
Okay, perhaps visiting a shopping mall is not an authentic Latin American experience; but believe it or not, the mall is here to stay, and Nicas have taken to the indoor, air-conditioned experience as heartily as the world in general has. Some of Managua's best restaurants are situated in or beside a mall, and many of the city's malls differ in size, quality, and authenticity. So allow yourself the guilty pleasure if you need to, and run those last-minute errands under one roof. Just be careful which mall you choose. **Metrocentro,** in front of Rotonda Rubén Darío (ⓒ **505/2271-9450;** www.gruporoble.com), is the usual gamut of designer labels and screaming babies, and is best avoided unless you have a penchant for giving your money to rich multinationals while in a poor country that needs it more.

Plaza Inter, in front of Hotel Crowne Plaza (ⓒ **505/2222-2613;** www.plazaintermall.com.ni), is a little more down-to-earth, but still filled with lots of foreign stores and goods. The **Centro Comercial de Managua** (Colonia Centroamérica, in front of Colegio Salvador Mendieta; ⓒ **505/2277-3762**), is an open selection of fashion stores, bookshops, banks, Internet cafes, and one post office. It is 1 block north of the National Cathedral. My favorite mall, however, is **Galerías Santo Domingo** (ⓒ **505/2276-5080**), an up-market collection of stores and open-air restaurants, which is a 10-minute taxi ride southeast of the city center.

Art Galleries
Managua has an exciting art scene, with a forte for producing colorful primitivist paintings that the whole country is famed for. Many of the city's galleries act as

meeting points and venues for the city's musicians, artists, writers, and intellectuals. One such place is **Códice ★**, 1 block south and 2 blocks east of the Hotel Colón (*℃* **505/2267-2635**), with a relaxing patio cafe next to a courtyard and gallery rooms exhibiting paintings and sculptures. It is open Monday to Saturday from 9am to 7pm. **Galería Solentiname,** 60m (197 ft.) south of the UNAN in Barrio Edgard Munguía Transfer, is operated by artist Doña Elena Pineda and specializes in art from the colorful archipelago. Part of a family of artists, Elena can help set you up with trips to the islands. The gallery is open Monday to Saturday from 9am to 5pm.

Galería Casa de los Tres Mundos ★ (2½ blocks north of the restaurant La Marseillaise, Los Robles; *℃* **505/2552-4176**) is the Managua base of poet, sculptor, and priest Ernesto Cardenal and showcases work from the Solentiname Islands. It is also the headquarters of Nicaragua's writers' association and holds a library and bookstore. It's open weekdays from 10:30am to 1:30pm. **Galería Praxis** (1 block west and 1 block north of the Optica Nicaragüense, Colonia; *℃* **505/2266-3563**) exhibits paintings, sculptures, and sketches, and has a pleasant cafe. **Galería Añil** (1 block west and 8m (26 ft.) south of Canal 2 TV, Bolonia; *℃* **505/2266-5445**) features avant-garde work by Nicaraguan and Latin American artists. It's open weekdays from 2 until 7pm.

El Aguila (Km 6 Carretera Sur, in front of Farm 22–24; *℃* **505/2265-0524**) is the house and workshop of one of Nicaragua's most famous artists, Hugo Palma. It's open Monday to Saturday from 9am to 5:30pm, but call ahead to ask about visiting. **Galería Epikentro,** 7 blocks north and 2½ blocks west of Rotunda El Güegüense, holds frequent book readings and shows a mix of contemporary and primitivist art. It's open weekdays from 9am to 6pm. **Galería Pléyades** (Centro BAC, 2nd floor, Km 4 Carretera Masaya; *℃* **505/2274-4114**) exhibits a broad range of Nicaraguan art. It's open weekdays from 9am to 6pm.

MANAGUA AFTER DARK

The capital is undoubtedly the best place in the country if you're a night owl, want to catch some live music, or like to show off your dancing skills. You'll find drinking holes all over the city, but it is best to stick to certain areas that are safer. **Zona Rosa** is the disco strip. It stretches along the Carretera Masaya from the new cathedral to the Rotunda Centroamérica and beyond. Here, you'll find an ever-changing string of pubs, clubs, and restaurants that come and go with alarming frequency. You'll also find a cluster of bars in front of the Hotel Crown Plaza. Another popular nightlife spot is the **Zona Viva,** around the Galerías Santo Domingo shopping mall. For up-to-date listings on what's going on around town, check *Esta Semana,* an entertainment listings supplement in the newspaper *El Nuevo Diario,* or go to the website www.bacanalnica.com.

Live Music

Look hard enough, and you'll find live music performances all over the city. I've listed the best and most established venues below, but if mariachis light your fire, you should also go for a stroll around the **Rotonda Bello Horizonte.** This busy roundabout, surrounded by fast-food restaurants and cheap eateries, is very much a local hangout and is the favored circuit for groups of baritone mariachis and wandering troubadours doing their thing *con gusto.* Bars like the **Shannon Pub** (see below) also stage the occasional live mariachi performance.

La Casa de los Mejía Godoy ★★ 📷   There's no better way to immerse yourself in the heart of Nicaraguan culture than by taking a seat at the Casa de los Mejía Godoy, the city's most famous live music venue. Here, you'll find the renowned musical brothers Enrique and Carlos Mejía Godoy performing what has become the soundtrack to the country's revolution and the heartbeat of a culture that revels in songs and storytelling. Both brothers hail from the country's misty northern hills, but it's Carlos who brings the *campesinos'* take on waltz, polka, and mazurka, using his accordion, guitar, and lyrics to create songs fueled by love, gossip, and nature. His famous song *Nicaragua Nicaraguita* is the country's national anthem in all but name.

Carlos' brother Luis Enrique provides the flip side of Nicaraguan music, the energizing Latin beats of salsa and merengue that blare from every bar and car. Yet he too is an important chronicler of Nicaraguan everyday life. Both brothers have been active Sandinistas from the very beginning—not that politics ever gets in the way of their performances. Both are accomplished, charismatic showmen who move the crowd to tears and laughter with famous songs interspersed with anecdotes and jokes. Carlos often performs on Thursday and Saturday, and his brother on Friday. Reservations are recommended, and tickets cost approximately C285. There is a music and book store, and a restaurant on the premises, so it's very much worth stopping by here, even if you can't make a performance. In front of Crowne Plaza Hotel, Octavo Calle Suroeste, Barrio Martha Quezada. www.losmejiagodoy.com. ℂ **505/2222-6110.** Tickets C100–C285. Main courses C150. 11:30am–11pm.

Mirador Tiscapa   There are not many music venues in the world perched atop a volcano rim. Mirador Tiscapa is an open-air restaurant overlooking the Tiscapa Crater Lake with a large dance floor offering live performances of salsa, merengue, and rumba on Saturday nights. Out back is a smaller dance floor with disco beats for a younger crowd. Bo Largaespada Paseo Tiscapa. ℂ **505/2222-3452.** Cover C160.

Ruta Maya ★   Here, you'll find an open-air courtyard with a marquee that comes alive with crowds dancing to live performances. The music is eclectic, with everything from reggae to salsa and acoustic shows being played. Ruta Maya is a melting pot for all that is happening in Managua regarding music and culture, and generally draws an older, more discerning clientele. 150m (492 ft.) E of Estatua de Montoya. ℂ **505/2268-0698.** Cover C200.

The Bar Scene

Bar Bongó (ℂ **505/2277-4375**) is one of the livelier spots in the Zona Rosa district, with Cuban food and live music on weekends. It is 3 blocks south of the Metrocenter. **Enoteca Galerías Santo Domingo** (ℂ **505/2276-5113**) is a busy wine bar in the shopping mall of the same name that attracts a well-polished clientele, especially on weekends. **Etnico Bar Café** (Planes de Altamira; ℂ **505/2270-6164**) is a moodily lit bar with some world music going on in the background. **Woody's,** 40m (131 ft.) south of Hotel Seminole (ℂ **505/2278-2751**), is a popular "after office" drinks place with a pavement terrace. They specialize in chicken wings and *chichilados* (a spicy beer version of a bloody mary). **Z-Bar** (Antiguo Rest Los Gauchos; ℂ **505/2278-1735**) has an open-air bar with a dance floor churning out good old-fashioned rock 'n' roll. **La Curva** (no phone) is on a corner behind the pyramid-shaped Crowne Plaza. This beach-style bar with bamboo walls and a frond roof looks somewhat out of place amidst the downtown traffic and nighttime corner hookers. It is heaving, however, on Friday nights with crowds dancing to salsa, merengue, and cumbia. Saturdays are a little more sedate with '70s and '80s rock and pop. Its open plan with no walls also means it's a good spot for some early evening people-watching. It is open Monday through Saturday from 5pm to midnight. **Piratas,** 1 block south of Hotel Seminole (② **505/2278-3817**), is a funky theme bar in the heart of the Zona Rosa and a slick establishment of dark woods, pirate murals, anarchic graffiti, and black leather furniture. The wraparound veranda lets you ogle the passing traffic while enjoying pub grub and cocktails. It can get noisy, however, and service is slow.

Nightclubs

El Chamán in the Metrocentro Mall (② **505/2278-6111**) is a young and popular dance club with a most ridiculous American Indian–themed decor. Yet it has been around for quite a while now and keeps packing visitors and locals into its smoke-filled corridors to listen to rock and techno. The cover charge is C200. **El Quetzal** ★ (Rotonda Centroamérica, in front of Registros Públicos; ② **505/2277-0890**) is an old-school salsa and cumbia dance hall. You'll be the only tourist there, but that's fine, just shimmy like the rest of the mixed, raucous crowd. The cover charge is C200.

XS (Zona Rosa; ② **505/2277-3086**) is your typical glittery nightclub with mirrors to admire yourself (and others) and punch the air to techno. The cover charge is C200. It is located in front of T.G.I. Friday's on Carretera Masaya. **Hipa Hipa** ★ (Plaza Coconut Grove; ② **505/2278-2812**) attracts a wealthy and trendy college-age crowd that take to its three boisterous dance floors to groove to salsa, merengue, and techno. It's famed for attracting *fresas*, or strawberries, as Managua's "It girls" are affectionately known. The cover charge is C200. The doormen are notoriously selective, so dress up and pout. At **O.M.** (Carretera Masaya, across from T.G.I. Friday's; no phone), you can be treated like a rock star and charged accordingly. The cover charge is C200.

Island Taste ★★ (2 blocks east of Siemens, Km 6 Carretera Norte; no phone) is a lot more down-to-earth and a famous hangout for Caribbean exiles in the capital. The friendly crowd gets down to proper roots-style Caribbean tunes. **Moods** (Zona Viva, Galerías Santo Domingo; ② **505/2276-5276**) plays disco, house, and electro in a somewhat sterile but boisterous disco-bar. The cover charge is C200. **Club Hollywood** (Zona Rosa, Edificio Delta; ② **505/2267-0263**) is arguably Managua's most exclusive nightclub, so dress sharp. The cover charge is C200.

A SIDE TRIP TO POCHOMIL BEACH

Pochomil is a pleasant Pacific beach that is a 90-minute drive from the city and popular with weekenders. The sand is dark with seashells, and the sea waves are large and relentless. The lone fishermen standing in the water casting nets add to the local, laid-back feel. The beach's "center" is a basic, down-at-the-heel strip of anonymous restaurants selling seafood, soda, and beer. Accommodations options are somewhat limited, and the beach is virtually deserted on weekdays, except during Easter celebrations. It's the most convenient escape from the scorching capital.

Where to Stay

Altamar Altamar is a definite downgrade compared to its more luxurious cousin Vistamar farther up the beach (see below). Here, you'll find very basic rooms in a rickety building, which are crudely decorated but homey in a beach-bum kind of way. Wooden parrots hang from a roof of dirty terra-cotta tiles, and stained floors and moldy walls go hand and hand with a pretty patio, which has a great view of the bay and a shaded veranda with a pool table and makeshift bar. This is definitely a back-packer-class spot, but with lots of character, some lovely staff, and plenty of space. Its location could not be better (or worse) amid all the weekend action.

Pochomil Beach. © **505/2407-9975** or 505/8601-2727. 12 units. From $40 double. No credit cards. **Amenities:** Restaurant; bar; pool. *In room:* A/C, TV.

Vistamar ★ 🖻 ☺   This hotel has the best and most luxurious accommodations on the beach. Pink clapboard chalets are surrounded by a circle of palm trees and a white picket fence; at the center are two inviting, kidney-shaped pools and a small bar thatched with palm fronds and adorned with flowers. The bungalows are split into two good-size rooms with large fans overhead and tiled floors leading to a floor-length window facing the beach. This opens out onto a sunset veranda with rocking chairs and hammocks. The overall mood is light and beach-like, with delightful shell-inlaid tile work in the smallish bathrooms. The hotel is close to the main beach, but you may be happy to stay put and simply enjoy the decent but somewhat expensive restaurant or the small spa. It can get a little noisy on Saturday nights when the pool bar hosts a party.

Pochomil Beach. www.vistamarhotel.com. © **505/2265-0431.** Fax 505/2265-8099. 43 units. From $85 double. AE, DC, MC, V. **Amenities:** Restaurant; bar; babysitting; kids' club; Internet (free); pool. *In room:* A/C, TV.

MASAYA & LOS PUEBLOS BLANCOS

Smoldering volcanoes, raucous street parties, frantic shopping opportunities; Masaya and the Pueblos Blancos have lots to offer every type of visitor. Most travelers experience Masaya as a one-day shopping trip from the capital or Granada, and many never venture beyond the Gothic, palm-lined walls of Masaya's block-size Mercado Viejo (Old Market). That's a pity, as the region has more to offer than what you can stuff in your suitcase. In addition to its beautiful waterfront promenade and an old fort, the nearby Volcán Masaya is the most accessible active crater in the country and the most terrifying and exciting to visit. In the surrounding tabletop mountains are a string of villages known as the Pueblos Blancos, each with its own niche in hand-honed craftsmanship. Masaya is also famous for throwing street parties, with festivals running throughout the year, featuring such colorful participants as 12-foot tall women on stilts, costumed dogs, and "headless" priests. Arrive at the right time, in fact, and you may never want to leave the party.

MASAYA

9km (5½ miles) from Granada

Welcome to Masaya—Nicaragua's capital of shopping. In a country that is a treasure-trove of quality handicrafts, Masaya is the industrious nucleus, churning out an endless array of tempting souvenirs such as intricate pottery, handsome woodcarvings, sturdy leather goods, and beautiful hand-woven hammocks. This restless city of 100,000 creative souls is spread along a hot plain and up a gentle slope to the Masaya Crater Lake, with the smoldering Volcán Masaya in the distance. Though it was first explored by the Spanish in the 16th century, the city was not founded until 1819. It has a fiery history of rebellion and resistance to whoever tried to impose their will, be it a volcano, filibusterer, American Marine, or dictator. What was left of the city's colonial heritage was shattered by a series of earthquakes in 2000, yet it retains a colorful and vibrant character.

Essentials

GETTING THERE

BY BUS From Managua, take any southbound bus from the Mercado Huembes. You'll be dropped off at Masaya's **Mercado Municipal,** on the western side of the city. The journey takes 1 hour and costs C20. Another departure point in Managua is the **UCA** (p. 72), from where microbuses leave every 20 minutes, dropping passengers off at **Parque San Miguel,** 1 block east of the Mercado Viejo. The ride takes 45 minutes and costs C20.

From Granada, take any Managua-bound bus from **COGRAN,** 1½ blocks southwest of the plaza, or one of the Masaya *expresos* that leave from behind the **Palé Supermarket.** The journey takes 45 minutes and costs C20. The Managua bus drops you off at the Esso station close to the town entrance, from which the town plaza is a 20 minute walk. The Masaya *expreso* lets passengers off at Masaya's Mercado Municipal. The Mercado is also the main departure point when you are leaving Masaya.

Spanish Classes near Masaya

Mariposa Eco Hotel & Spanish School (☏ 505/8418-4638; www.mariposa spanishschool.com) is situated in the hills between Masaya and Managua, and offers a farmhouse-like atmosphere with plain, comfortable rooms and Spanish classes. Efficiently run by its English owner Paulette, the program offers a unique mix of wholesome country living and language classes.

Most everything about this place is ecofriendly. The restaurant serves organic food, there's an organic garden, and even the private bathrooms have organic shampoo and soap. The lodge is quite difficult to find, so be sure to arrange a transfer from either Masaya or Managua.

BY TAXI/SHUTTLE **Paxeos,** beside the cathedral in Granada (☏ 505/2552-8291; www.paxeos.com), can organize private and shared transfers to and from Masaya. The trip to Granada costs between C570 and C860, depending on group size.

GETTING AROUND

A car is not necessary in the city but definitely worthwhile if you want to explore the surrounding area. **Budget** (☏ 505/2278-9504; www.budget.com.ni) has an office at Km 28 Carretera Masaya, Managua. **Hotel Ivania's** (p. 97) is the only place in town that rents cars. Alternatively, you might hire a taxi for the day so you can sit back, relax, and not get lost. A car and driver for the day in this area should cost approximately C1,500.

VISITOR INFORMATION

Intur (☏ 505/2522-7615) is inside the Mercado Viejo and offers good maps and information regarding workshops in the surrounding area. It is open Monday to Friday from 8am to 12:30pm and 1:30 to 5pm, and on Saturday from 8am to 12:30pm. The website **www.conozcamasaya.com** is entirely in Spanish but has lots of photos that catch the color and creativity of the town's heritage.

[Fast FACTS] MASAYA

ATMs and Banks
There are plenty of ATMs conveniently located within the Mercado Viejo (Old Market). **Banpro** (☏ 505/2522-7366) is on the southwestern corner of the market, as is **Bancentro** (☏ 505/2522-4337). **Banco de América Central** changes traveler's checks and is located 1 block north of the market. You will also find many street money-changers in this area.

Emergencies Dial ☏ 118 for all emergencies. The city's **police station** (☏ 505/2522-4222) is a half-block north of the Old Market.

Hospital The main **hospital** (☏ 505/2522-2778) is on the main road to Granada.

Internet There are several Internet cafes on the south side of the park. **Cablenet Café** (no phone) is opposite the Hotel Regis and is open daily from 8am to 10pm, except Sunday, when it closes at 3pm.

Post Office A post office is inside the Mercado Viejo, as is a DHL counter.

What to See & Do

Catedral de la Asunción   Newly restored and looking quite magnificent, Masaya's main church is certainly worth a visit and a makes for a quiet break from the frantic shopping. Damaged by the 2000 earthquake, it dates back to 1750 but was modified in the early 19th century. It has a more restrained interior design than the more baroque churches elsewhere in the country, and is all the more interesting for it. Precious woods and intricate tiling go with the simple forms and elegant lines.

Main plaza. No phone. Free admission. Daily 7am–4pm.

El Malecón ★   This is a breezy city promenade 6 blocks west of the central plaza. It sits high above the waterline but affords great views and has several cafes to take a break in. This waterfront comes alive with people whenever there is a game at the nearby baseball stadium and is a favorite spot for canoodling teenagers. It's a great place to visit while atop one of the many horse-and-carriages that traverse the city streets. The lake used to be the town's water supply, carried by a never-ending procession of women with ceramic vases on their heads. Unfortunately, the water is not fit for even swimming at the moment, though there is talk of cleaning it up. The adventurous can make an arduous trek to the water level 300m (984 ft.) below down a steep wall, where they can see some petroglyphs on the way. It is advisable to do this with a local guide.

El Malecón, 6 blocks W of the central plaza, next to Roberto Clemente Baseball Stadium.

Iglesia de San Jerónimo   Though plainer than the cathedral, the San Jerónimo is just as important and affords a great view of the city from its bell tower; likewise, its dome can be seen for miles around. This is the place where most of Masaya's legendary street festivals kick off or end, especially the Fiesta Patronal that runs from September to December, making it one of the longest parties in Central America. Unfortunately, the church was damaged by the 2000 earthquake and is currently propped up by external buttresses while it awaits restoration.

5 blocks N of the central plaza. No phone. C10 adults. Daily 7am–6pm.

Mercado Nacional de Artesanía ★★   Also known as the Mercado Viejo, this is the biggest attraction in town. This entire block is a hive of stalls and cultural activity, and is easily the showcase market for the country's thriving handicrafts industry. Built in 1891, it was originally a university of philosophy and law, but today, it is more a faculty of craftsmanship and haggling. Destroyed by a fire in 1966 and torched by Somoza's troops during the revolution, it was abandoned for 2 decades and used as the town dump. Now, it has been beautifully restored and holds 80 stalls (or *modulos*, as they are known locally) and two cafes. It is easy to stay several hours within its gothic stone walls and browse the many stalls selling everything from cotton hammocks to colorful art. **Grupo Raíces** (Modulo H-6; ℂ **505/2522-4198**) specializes in ceramics and soapstone sculptures, the best of which come from the northern town of San Juan de Limay. **Don Marenco** (Modulo C-2; ℂ **505/8617-7691**) makes and sells *"cabuya"* rope wall hangings with designs of women with long flowing hair, birds in fantastic trees, or other natural scenes. **Duarte** (Modulo I-6) makes shoes, belts, and bags from leather and the skins of iguanas and crocodiles.

You'll also find conventional stores, cafes, ATMs, and even a tourist office in the market. There are live folkloric performances every Thursday at 7pm, accompanied by the ubiquitous tropical sounds of marimba music.

1 block E of the central plaza, also known as Parque 17 de Octubre. Daily 8am–7pm.

> ## 📎 Shipping Home
>
> It's easy to go over your airline weight limit whilst visiting Masaya. DHL (Modulo B3; ✆ 505/2251-2500) has an office within the market to help you with any excess. It is open weekdays 8am to 5:45pm and Saturday 8am to noon. A 5kg (11-lb.) package costs approximately $140 to send to the States and takes about 2 days.

Museo y Galería Héroes y Mártires   Masaya played a crucial role in the Sandinista revolution with an indigenous uprising in Monimbo in 1978. Rebels then used the town as a regrouping place before the final victorious assault on Managua. The small museum here is dedicated to those who fought the Somoza regime. Among its exhibits of photos and guns is an unexploded napalm bomb.

Town hall, Alcaldía, 1½ blocks N of the central park. No phone. Free admission (donations welcome). Weekdays 8am–5pm.

ATTRACTIONS OUTSIDE MASAYA

Coyotepe Fort 📷   The fort has a dark past: It once held political prisoners and was used by the National Guard to mortar-bomb the city during the 1980s revolution. It was also the location of the heroic last stand by national hero Benjamín Zeledón against U.S. Marines in 1912. Now, it is a quieter place, with helpful boy scouts conducting visits of the facility and its unwelcoming dungeons. Whitewashed battlements and squat, yellow-domed towers overlook the city and lakes, and afford a pleasant visit that belies this structure's dark history. The fort is a 1km (½-mile) hike north of the old train station, but I recommend taking a taxi (fare C20), as it is a fairly hard stroll.

Carretera Masaya Km 1. No phone. C22 adults. Daily 9am–6pm.

Volcán Masaya National Park ★★★   Volcán Masaya is not a normal cone-shaped volcano but rather a low, gaping wound of six smoking craters and a constantly glowing lava field. The whole effect is so frightening that the Spanish took to calling this volcano the "gates of hell" and the local Chorotegas tribe christened it the "mountain that burns" and made human sacrifices there in the hope that doing so might avert more eruptions. In colonial times, the crater was home to an old woman the Indians valued as a fortune teller and the Spanish regarded as a witch, not the least because she advised the Indians to go to war with them. A cross can still be seen today where a Franciscan friar attempted an exorcism with the idea of keeping the gates of hell closed and the mountain quiet—to little avail. Another friar was convinced the lava was molten gold and organized an expedition to retrieve some—to no avail. It is easily the most accessible live volcano in Nicaragua because a road leads directly to its chasm, a mere 30 minutes from Managua city center (note that the red-hot lava is not so easy to see anymore, as the west side has been closed because of unstable ground). This park is also an unforgettable experience. It is at once intriguing and terrifying, especially when you learn that in 2000, it hurled a large, flaming boulder that destroyed a nearby car in the parking lot. In the same lot today, the attendants advise you to park facing downhill so as to make a quick getaway—very reassuring.

The park consists of several volcanoes and craters and is easy to explore, with a 20km (12-mile) system of hiking trails, many of which can be done independently.

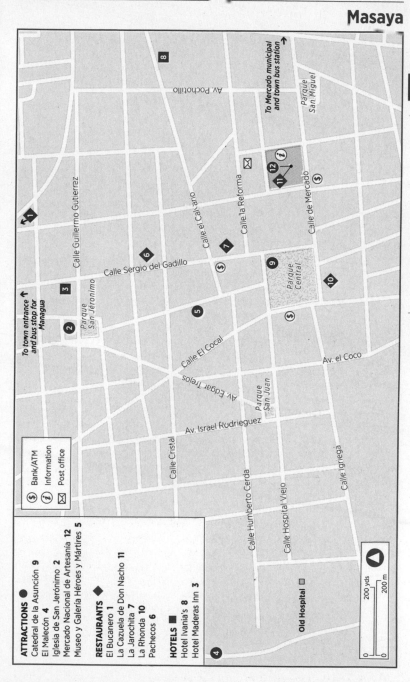

Masaya

ATTRACTIONS ●
Catedral de la Asunción **9**
El Malecón **4**
Iglesia de San Jerónimo **2**
Mercado Nacional de Artesania **12**
Museo y Galería Héroes y Mártires **5**

RESTAURANTS ◆
El Bucanero **1**
La Cazuela de Don Nacho **11**
La Jarochita **7**
La Rhonda **10**
Pachecos **6**

HOTELS ■
Hotel Ivania's **8**
Hotel Maderas Inn **3**

($) Bank/ATM
(i) Information
⊠ Post office

To town entrance and bus stop for Managua

To Mercado municipal and town bus station

Av. Pochotillo
Calle Guillermo Gutierraz
Parque San Jerónimo
Calle Sergio del Gadillo
Calle El Calvario
Calle la Reforma
Calle de Mercado
Parque San Miguel
Parque Central
Calle El Cocal
Av. Edgar Trejos
Parque San Juan
Av. el Coco
Av. Israel Rodriguez
Calle Cristal
Calle Humberto Cerda
Calle Hospital Viejo
Calle Igriega
Old Hospital

200 yds
200 m

The self-guided trail **Sendero los Coyotes** is a 6km (3.7-mile) walk from the visitor center and runs through lava pits to a lake. The terrain is a surreal mixture of moon-scape and shrubbery, including orchids and sacuanjoche flowers. Lizards; raccoons; deer; and, as the trail name implies, coyote are some of the wildlife that can be seen. The **Santiago Crater** is home to a curious species of parakeets that seem immune to the pit's noxious fumes; the crater is best viewed from the parking lot at the edge, and in the afternoon, you can see these amazing birds known locally as *chocoyos* flying happily amidst the noxious gases and entering their tiny nest burrows in the internal rock face. These burrows are some 3m long (9¾ ft.) and lead to a chamber where the bird lays its eggs. Elsewhere, **El Comalito** is a small, smoking hillock and **Tzinan-canostoc** a series of lava tunnels famous for its resident bats. Both can be visited only with a guide along the Coyote trek. On some treks, you may have to change direction because of the fumes, and you'll need to get a gas mask to see the lava holes up close. Your best chance of seeing red-hot lava is by taking a night tour. Most travel operators offer 1-day excursions to the park from Managua, Granada, or Masaya. To get there independently, you must travel 6km (3¾ miles) north of Masaya on the main highway. There are plenty of buses that will drop you off at the entrance, but be warned, it is a hot, shade-less walk to the cliff edge.

A visitor center, where you can get a good map and brochure of the site, and nature museum are 2km (1¼ miles) from the main entrance. Make sure to buy your tour tickets at the visitor center before you rendezvous with your guide at the crater.

Carretera Masaya Km 6. (✆ **505/2552-5415.** C88 adults; night tour C220. Daily 9am–4:45pm. Night tours depart daily 5pm (if there is a group of 5 or more).

Shopping in Masaya

Any shopping excursion in Masaya should include a stop at the Mercado Viejo (see "What to See & Do," above), but there are other shopping outlets around the city that cry out for your attention, too. **Mercado Municipal Ernesto Fernández** is a bigger, more chaotic, and somewhat crammed market with cheap restaurants and butcher stalls, as well as a good selection of handicrafts and leather ware. Goods are also slightly cheaper than at the Mercado Viejo. The market is adjacent to the main bus terminal and a few blocks from the Mercado Viejo. It is open daily from 8am to 7pm.

You'll find hammocks everywhere in Masaya, but if you'd prefer to see their place of origin, check out the *fábricas de hamacas* (hammock workshops) located in Barrio San Juan, 2 blocks east of the Malecón and 1 block north of the Old Hospital. One good stand-alone hammock shop to try is **Los Tapices de Luis,** a store special-izing in hammocks and wall hangings.

Guitarras Zepeda ★, 200m (656 ft.) west of the Unión Fenosa (✆ **505/8883-0260;** www.guitarraszepeda.com), is one of the most respected guitar workshops in the country. The owner, Sergio, will show you how they craft beautiful mahogany and pearl inlaid instruments. Note that he has very few guitars for sale off-the-shelf; you must order most guitars 2 weeks in advance. Prices range from C3,000 to C6,000.

Comunidad Indígena de Monimbo   Don't be so sure that Panama hat you bought in Panama is actually from Panama. It might have the country's name embla-zoned on the head band, but most likely it was made here in what is the handicrafts headquarters of Central America, the indigenous barrio of Monimbo, 1km (½ mile) south of Masaya's central plaza. Here, you'll find a thriving cottage industry of shoe-makers, basket weavers, saddle makers, and woodcarvers churning out a dazzling array of goods with neighboring countries as their market destination and their corresponding names on the product. Most of the workshops are located between Iglesia Magdalena and the cemetery, but it is advisable to go with a guide to get the most from your shopping spree. Ask in the central tourist office for information or just knock on some doors when you get there (but only if you intend to spend some money).

Monimbo has a fiery history of Indian resistance and staged its own uprising in 1978 that surprised even the Sandinistas in its success and ferocity. The natives held off the National Guard for a week with homemade bombs and weapons. A Council of Elders still exists to administer the district, and the locals are fiercely proud of their heritage.

7 blocks S of central plaza on Calle Monimbo.

Where to Stay in Masaya

Considering its many attractions and exhaustive shopping possibilities, Masaya should have more and better hotels. Unfortunately, the town is very much a 1-day excursion on most people's itineraries, with people preferring to stay in Granada or Managua instead. Thus, there's a dearth of decent inns.

Hotel Ivania's   One of the town's better establishments, this hotel has an unusually helpful, attentive staff (a rare thing in Nicaragua), as well as a convenient town-center location and a restaurant. The decor is dated and slightly idiosyncratic—the hotel's facade is an attractive pink color with stone-carved window frames, but inside, it gets rather dark and garish. The rooms are small and the bathrooms smaller, but the hotel does have an all-important backup generator.

3½ blocks from the Iglesia El Calvario. www.hotelivanias.com. © **505/2522-7632.** 17 units. From $65 double. Rates include breakfast. AE, DC, MC, V. Free parking. **Amenities:** Restaurant; room service; Wi-Fi (free). *In room:* A/C, TV, minibar.

Hotel Maderas Inn   This is a small family-run property that's tucked inside a modern yellow house. It has a good location and a friendly staff. The decor is plain, except for the hammocks on the roof terrace—they're a great place to relax.

½ block E of Iglesia San Jerónimo. www.hotelmaderasinn.com. © **505/2522-5825.** 15 units. From $21 double. Rates include breakfast. AE, DC, MC, V. Free parking. **Amenities:** Small health club. *In room:* A/C, TV, Wi-Fi (free).

Where to Eat in Masaya

Nicaraguan comfort food (known as *comida típica*) is the order of the day in the many casual restaurants that dot the town. For people-watching, go to a restaurant close to the central plaza or, better still, within the Mercado Viejo. **La Cazuela de Don Nacho** (northeast of the stage, artisan market; © **505/2522-7731**) has a great atmosphere, as it is located inside the main market and is a perfect place to sit and enjoy the crowd, especially when there is a live performance on Thursday evening. The food is typical Nicaraguan, with beef, chicken, and shrimp. **La Jarochita,** 60m (197 ft.) north of the cathedral (© **505/2522-4831**), is famous for its *sopa de tortilla* and chimichangas. **El Bucanero** (Km 26.5; no phone) has got great views of the lake and a lively clientele at night. If it's a drink you're after, go to Masaya's most popular bar, **La Rhonda,** on the south side of Parque Central (© **505/2522-3310**), which has lots of room in a large, open-plan building. A more modern, moody place for a late drink or snack is **Pachecos**, ½ block north of Curacao (© **505/2522-7628**).

A Masaya Shopping List

Hammocks: Pretend you are an expert by stretching a cotton hammock in your hands to examine the weave; the denser the better. Masaya's hammocks are arguably the best in the world. The actual workshops can be visited and are located close to the baseball stadium and the old hospital. However, you should not go to a workshop if you have no intention of buying.

Traditional clothing: President Ortega is fond of the *guayabera* shirt, otherwise known as a Mexican wedding shirt. The *huiple* is a simple white shirt embroidered with a rainbow of colors. White dresses are popular, as are novelty T-shirts and vests that depict typical Nicaraguan culture.

Fiber wall hangings: Handmade *cabuya* rope wall hangings use fiber as paint in a style that comes from the town of Boaco.

Paintings: Nicaragua is famous for its primitivist paintings that originally came from the Solentiname Islands but are now produced by local artists throughout the country.

Wooden furniture: Furniture ranges from antique-style pedestals to massive mahogany desks to small, delicate boxes in either plain wood or painted in wonderful natural scenes. Handmade rocking chairs are also popular. Vendors will dismantle the chairs so they're easier to carry back on the plane. Another specialty to the region is rattan chairs.

Ceramics: The best come from San Juan de Oriente. Pre-Columbian motifs and shapes are given a modern twist with bas-relief designs and painted slip work. Common are charming bowl-like candleholders, which create a small village scene with holes that simulate a starscape. Designs include contemporary, plants and animals, and pre-Columbian styles.

Soapstone sculptures: The best stone carvings come from San Juan del Limay near Estelí in the northern highlands.

Hats: Chontales is the hat capital of Nicaragua.

Leather goods: Shoes, belts, and bags made from leather are everywhere. *Obando* leather is a local specialty, as are the skins of iguanas and crocodiles sourced from farms along the Río San Juan and the Atlantic Coast.

Knickknacks: The majority are made from local woods, handmade with a typically rural Nicaraguan setting. There is a bewildering array of objects, including goblets, chalices, cups, bowls, dishes, keepsake boxes, teapots, shakers, and puzzle boxes.

LOS PUEBLOS BLANCOS

A scattering of isolated "white villages," or Pueblos Blancos, sits in the hills south of Masaya. The area is a perfect 1-day excursion by car or bus from Masaya, as well as from Managua or Granada. These villages got their name from their simple Spanish-style churches and occasional white *casitas* with colorful doors and windows. Also known as Los Pueblos de la Meseta, they sit at 500m (1,640 ft.) above sea level, meaning they are cooler and greener than the towns and cities below. Each individual town is known for producing a signature handicraft, be it ceramic wind chimes or bamboo furniture, so shopping is the main draw here.

Besides being the youthful stomping ground of General Augusto C. Sandino, the area has a fascinating history as the center of the Chorotega Empire that stretched from Honduras to Costa Rica. This mini-empire was made up of 28 states, each governed by a chief who met with his counterparts in the village of Diriá every 7 years to elect a new leader. One such leader was Diriangen, who put up fierce opposition to the invading Spanish. Their language and tribal dress has now disappeared, but the community is still very aware and proud of its origins.

Getting There

Though it's easiest to see the pueblos by rental car, frequent buses do shuttle around the region, albeit at a slow pace and not passing through every town. Buses leave daily from Mercado Municipal in Masaya, Mercado Huembes in Managua, and 1 block south of Granada's market. *Expreso* buses pass through the Pueblos Blancos every 40 minutes Monday through Friday, but less frequently on weekends. The Intur office in Masaya (p. 92) offers good maps of the region.

What to See & Do in Pueblos Blancos

CATARINA

Any trip to the Pueblos Blancos should start with a journey up the **Catarina Mirador,** a spectacular lookout point on the rim of Laguna de Apoyo Crater Lake. Here, you can make believe you can see all of Nicaragua, with Granada and Masaya at your feet and the twin peaks of Ometepe Island in the distance on Lago de Nicaragua. The town itself is famous for its carved wooden furniture; bamboo products; basket making; and lush, tropical nurseries. The *mirador* (Spanish for look-out point) is behind the 18th-century village church and can be easily approached on foot; if you are driving, you'll have to pay an admission of C20. Here, you'll find an array of market stalls and restaurants, all of which get crowded on weekends with day trippers from Managua and Granada. Otherwise, it is quiet during the week. **El Tunel,** on the north side of the *mirador* (© **505/2558-0303**), is a good place to stop for breakfast or lunch. There is a footpath that leads down to the crater, with an arduous trek back up. Catarina is the place to be on New Year's Eve, with a massive party thrown for San Silvestre. The *mirador* was apparently the favored hangout of the military leader Augusto C. Sandino as a youth, where he dreamed about and plotted Nicaragua's liberation.

SAN JUAN DE ORIENTE

Pottery is the specialty here, and if you ask at any store, they should allow you to take a look at their backyard workshops with kilns. In fact, the town's rich heritage in ceramics earned it the moniker of *San Juan de los Platos,* and while they still make plates, they have branched out into pots and urns. Handmade pottery has been made here for over 1000 years from locally sourced clay. Much of the expertise was lost during the colonial period, but the Sandinistas made a concerted effort to revive the industry in the 1980s. A cooperative was formed called **Artesanos Unidos,** and locals were trained in how to use a potter's wheel and apply pre-Columbian design with paint and polish. The initiative has been a resounding success, with the majority of the population working in some aspect of ceramics. Their products now have an international reputation for quality and creativity. You can visit many of the potters in their individual workshops, the most famous of which is **Helio Gutiérrez,** 1 block west of the second entrance and 300m (984 ft.) south (© **505/2558-0338**). Another ceramics artist worth a visit is **Francisco Calero,** a half-block east of Taller Escuela de Cerámica (© **505/2558-0300**). To see a selection of work, try Cooperativa Quetzal-Coatl, 25m (82 ft.) inside first entrance to the town. It is open daily from 8am to 5pm. The village itself is just across the highway from Catarina.

Come on, you pack of drug fiends! . . .
I don't care how many of you there are.
—General Sandino addressing
American Marines

Mystic, bandit, and *anarchist* are just some of the labels you can stick on General Augusto Sandino. However, the most all-encompassing and accurate are *Nicaraguan patriot* and *national hero.* The public's high regard for this 1920s freedom fighter can be seen in the numerous images of him that dot the nation; usually a black silhouette of a skinny guy with a rather large hat.

Sandino was born in 1895, the illegitimate son of a large landowner in the Pueblo Blanco Niquinohomo outside Masaya. His servant mother initially raised him until his father begrudgingly accepted him into the household. Yet he was always treated as more a servant than son, and this instilled a sense of injustice that remained with him for the rest of his life. His father's philosophy of "If I don't exploit, I will be exploited" is something he set about disproving from early on. Then, at the age of 17, he saw the corpse of Nicaraguan rebel General Zeledón being carted away by his killers, American Marines, after a failed uprising, and this introduced a heavy dose of anti-Americanism into his character.

In 1923, he fled to Mexico after attempting to murder a local who had insulted his mother. There, he worked for Standard Oil and drew heavily on the revolutionary zeal that was sweeping his northern neighbor. He was particularly attracted to the concept of *mestizaje*—a newfound pride in indigenous culture that could unite the region. He returned to Nicaragua in 1926 and immediately took up the cause of the liberals in a revolt against an American-installed president. He gathered a ragtag army of miners in the northern mountains of Segovia and continued fighting long after the liberal movement signed a peace treaty. Sandino could see no peace as long as American interference remained in the country. He looked upon them as occupiers who, among other things, blocked the country's right to an inter-oceanic canal. U.S. Marines were sent in to quell his peasant army, and he engaged them in a grinding guerrilla war that became a blueprint for other rebel armies across the continent in the 20th century. Superior American firepower and aerial bombing could not defeat the mountain general, and his capture evaded the Americans.

Eventually, the Americans gave up and withdrew in 1933. They left a newly founded National Guard led by Anastasio Somoza García to keep the peace. Delighted and vindicated by the American retreat, Sandino entered a peace treaty with his liberal counterparts, but was tricked and kidnapped in Managua by Somoza and then murdered. His grave has never been found. Somoza declared himself dictator 2 years later, and with American support, the Somoza family ruled and practically owned Nicaragua for the next 44 years.

"Death is but one little moment of discomfort," Sandino often told his troops, and his martyrdom was the inspiration for other rebel uprisings in the region, including those in Cuba, El Salvador, and Colombia. Anti-Somoza forces eventually gathered in the 1970s, and the Sandinista National Liberation Front borrowed Sandino's name to propel a revolution that eventually ousted the Somoza dynasty. Sandino's image remains untainted, as he was never corrupted by power, and he remains a siren call for anti-imperialist, anti-American sentiment.

DIRIA

Continue south, and you'll reach the twin villages of Diriá and Diriomo, which face each other on the highway. Diriá has an excellent hilltop view, and some trails from here lead down to the shore of Laguna de Apoyo. This was the most important settlement to the Chorotega tribe, and though the town is now somewhat sleepy and laidback, it comes alive for the annual festivals. The *mirador* is located south of the 17th-century church, east of the cemetery. Here, you'll find some bars and snack joints. Incidentally, the bell tower is a considerable distance from the colonial church because of the constant fear of an earthquake (the last one was in 2000 and caused significant damage). The central park has some interesting statues, including one of the Indian chief Diriangén. The best place to eat in town is an open-air establishment called **Cafetería La Plaza** (© 505/2557-0207) at the north side of the church.

DIRIOMO

Across the main road, **Diriomo** is famous for its black magic and *brujas* (witches) who will read your fortune, or at least give you the right directions back to Masaya. Nicaraguans come from far and wide seeking charms and potions for a myriad of problems. Even if your only problem is an insatiable sweet tooth, though, you are in the right place. *Cajetas* are a traditional Nicaraguan sweet and Diriomo is the epicenter of a sugary operation. Sweet houses such as **La Casa de las Cajetas,** opposite the church (© 505/2557-0015), and **Hortensia González,** 2 blocks north of Enitel (no phone), conduct tours as well as tastings of these delicious confections made from sugar, rice, fruit, and milk. Diriomo's church is an interesting mix of neoclassical and Tuscan architecture with handsome interior cedar posts. Unfortunately, it has suffered considerable earthquake damage. In the mood for armadillo? **El Aguacate,** 120m (394 ft.) north of the town entrance on the highway (no phone), is a restaurant famous for this exotic dish known locally as *cuzuco.*

NIQUINOHOMO

Niquinohomo, which is Chorotega for *Valley of the Warriors,* is fittingly the birthplace of Sandino. A grand, bronze statue of the father of the Sandinistas stands in his honor near the town entrance. The town retains its Indo-colonial charm, though it must be said not much happens here. Its most interesting features are a majestic, 17th-century church called **Parroquia Santa Ana** and a handful of stores selling the local craft specialty: bamboo lamps shaped as pineapples. Close to the northwest corner of the town plaza is Sandino's childhood home, now a small, poorly maintained museum and library (no phone; free admission; open weekdays 9am–noon and 2–6pm).

MASATAPE

This sleepy village is the country's rocking-chair capital and is highly regarded for its excellent mahogany and wicker carpentry. There are lots of roadside stores selling beds, dressers, dining tables and chairs, and wicker cots. Your only problem will be getting all this stuff home. The old railway station at the town entrance is now an emporium displaying everything imaginable that can be made from wood. Here, you can also catch a rickshaw taxi tour of the town for C60. Stop for a late lunch at **Mi Teruño Masatepino** ★ (© 505/8887-4949), a charming open-air eatery just south of town on the highway close to Pio XII. Here, you can try the local specialty, tripe soup, known as *sopa de mondongo,* or for the brave-hearted, *sopa de iguana* (no translation required). This excellent restaurant also specializes in local drinks such as *posol* and *tiste,* and brews their own home-grown coffee.

SAN MARCOS

Continue west 8km (5 miles) after Masatepe, and you'll reach the largest of the Pueblos Blancos, San Marcos, a thriving university town and birthplace of Sandino's nemesis Anastasio Somoza García (his family owned a bakery here and a coffee farm in the outskirts). The town is home to one of the oldest pre-Columbian settlements, and recent excavations have unearthed ceramics that date back to 2500 B.C. The plaza is the raucous scene of one of the best regional festivals—*Tope de las Imágenes de San Marcos*—held on April 24. The simple church has an interesting interior with a tropical-themed fresco above the altar and ceiling murals.

DIRIAMBA

Diriamba does not have much to boast about except a famously good-looking and friendly populace and an elegant church with beautiful dome and interior woodwork. The town also throws one of the best street parties in the country on the last week in September to celebrate San Sebastián. Masked dancers reenact a famous colonial-era play known as *El Güegüence* to much hilarity. There is also an interesting little museum, **Museo Ecológico Trópico Seco,** 4 blocks east of Enel (© **505/2534-2129;** www.adeca.org.ni/museo_eco), that explores the area from an environmental point of view. It is open weekdays 8am to noon and 2 to 5pm, and admission is free.

Where to Stay in Los Pueblos Blancos

Note that most people decide to stay in Granada or Managua when touring the area.

Casa Mateo   The next-best hotel in the area, after the Casa Blanca, this is a conventional three-story hotel. The somewhat bare but adequate rooms are in a mock-colonial building located in the nearby town of Jinotepe.

½ blocks E of BDF Bank, Jinotepe. www.hotelcasamateo.com. © **505/2532-3284.** 40 units. $40 double. Rates include breakfast. AE, DC, MC, V. Free parking. **Amenities:** Restaurant; room service; *In room:* A/C or fan, TV, Wi-Fi. (free)

Hotel Casa Blanca   If you are intent on thoroughly exploring the area, San Marcos makes for a delightful stop over. The rooms here are nothing special, but the building itself is a big, interesting corner house with a shady garden and lots of colonial fixtures.

Opposite Baptist church, San Marcos. www.casablancanica.com. © **505/2535-2717.** 15 units. $40 double. Rates include breakfast. AE, DC, MC, V. Free parking. *In room:* A/C or fan, TV.

 Hertylandia

Family getting bored with all this shopping? Take them to Nicaragua's version of Disneyland: **Hertylandia KIDS** (© **505/2532-2155**), 1km (½ mile) outside Jinotepe. It's a small amusement park with some very rudimentary rides, a giant pool, and a garden setting. It is open Wednesday through Sunday from 9am to 6pm. Admission is C90 adults, with an additional C30 per ride.

GRANADA

A luminous cathedral stands in front of one of the country's most vibrant squares, surrounded by pretty cobbled streets, which run down to the dark shores of Lake Cocibocha (also known as Lago de Nicaragua). Granada is a delightful surprise, in contrast to the mediocre shabbiness of Managua; history clings to every chunky terra-cotta tile covering this town's multicolored one-story cottages and town houses. Beguiling church facades and large handsome Spanish doorways make it a living museum to the opulence of the old Spanish Empire, and it's a city that should be top of your list to explore while traveling in Nicaragua.

Granada's perfectly preserved beauty is all the more surprising considering its tumultuous history of violence and plunder. Back in the 16th and 17th centuries, the city was pillaged by pirates and buccaneers, and completely razed by the despot William Walker. The American tyrant went so far as to plant a sign in its smoldering ruins declaring: "Here was Granada." The words, and the man, soon died, but the city lived on. Originally a Chorotega Indian settlement called Xalteva, the city was founded in 1524 by Francisco Fernandez de Córdoba. It is Nicaragua's oldest city and sits at the foot of the broad, tropical Volcán Mombacho. Its access to the Caribbean via the Río San Juan allowed it to become a rich city of Spanish merchants and landowners. British and French pirates raided it several times in the 17th century, most famously Henry Morgan and William Dampier. They looted and burned each time, and yet the city always managed to resurrect itself. Granada now literally blooms with colonial, neoclassical, and Italian architecture. It is, and was, the conservative bastion of Nicaragua and was capital of the country several times as it pursued a sometimes vicious tug-of-war for control with the more liberal Léon in the north.

Today, Granada is a prosperous, conservative city, benefiting greatly from a surge in tourism and property development. Tourists have replaced pirates, and the only rumpus these days is caused by the squawking flock of jackdaws that swarm through the trees in its central plaza. More and more foreigners are deciding to stay, and there is a legitimate fear that the city will be swamped by well-meaning expats who will nevertheless alter its character and push the locals out. Yet, I suspect this beautiful city will never lose its proud Nicaraguan roots and will handle its surge in popularity with the same resilience with which it met previous invaders. It has some of the country's best hotels and restaurants and is an ideal base from which to explore the rest of the country. Nearby is the finger of islands called Las Isletas, the handicrafts center Masaya, and the towns of Pueblos Blancos, as well as outdoorsy excursions to Volcán Mombacho and Laguna de Apoyo.

ESSENTIALS
Getting There & Departing

BY BUS   Buses leave from Managua for Granada from in front of the university campus UCA (2 blocks west of the Metrocenter) daily every 15 minutes, starting at 5:50am and ending at 8pm. The journey takes 1 hour and costs C20. You can also catch a regular Granada-bound bus from Mercado R Huembes in Managua, starting at 5:25am and terminating at 9:30pm. There are several bus terminals in Granada, depending on where you are going or where you are coming from. **COGRAN** (no phone) is 1½ blocks south of the plaza's southwest corner and is used by *expresos* on route to Managua. The trip takes 1 hour and costs C15. Buses leave every 15 minutes, starting at 4am and ending at 7pm. On weekends, the service ends at 6pm. Buses also leave from the Central Plaza every 15 minutes from 5:30am to 7pm and cost C16. **Parque Sandino** is another departure point. It is on the north side of the city, close to the old railway station. All buses pass by the entrance road to Masaya.

The southbound bus to Rivas from Granada leaves from the **Shell Palmira,** on the south side of the city, beside the Palé superstore. The trip takes 2 hours and costs C25. The first departure is at 5:45am and the last at 2:45pm. If you want a direct bus to Masaya, you must go to the bus stop behind **Palé,** although most Managua-bound buses will drop you off close to the town. The journey takes 45 minutes and costs C10.

International bus companies have their own individual drop-off and departure points, all along Avenida Arrellano on the west side of the city. **TicaBus** (ℂ **505/2552-4301;** www.ticabus.com) is a half-block south of the old hospital. The Panama-bound bus leaves at 7am, but it is advisable to get there at 6:15am. It costs $65 one way. **TransNica** (ℂ **505/2552-6619**) is 3 blocks south of the old hospital, on the corner of Calle Xalteva. There are three departures for Costa Rica, at 6:30, 8, and 11am (arrive early to get a seat). The ride takes 7 hours and costs $23.

BY SHUTTLE/TAXI   **Paxeos,** beside the cathedral on the southeast corner of Parque Colón (ℂ **505/2552-8291;** www.paxeos.com), organizes private and shared transfers to and from Managua airport and other locations such as San Jorge (where you catch the ferry to Isla de Ometepe). The trip to Managua costs approximately C400 per person, depending on group size.

BY BOAT   The small port (ℂ **505/2552-2966**) is located at the east end of Calle La Calzada. Boats leave from here on Monday and Thursday for the 4-hour trip (C80) to Alta Gracia on Isla de Ometepe (a faster ferry leaves from nearby San Jorge). The boat continues on to San Carlos, stopping at Morrito and San Miguelito on the northern shore of Lago de Nicaragua. The entire trip takes 14 hours and costs C250, returning on Tuesday and Friday. There are no cabins or sleeping accommodations on the boat, and it can be quite uncomfortable, especially if there are rough seas and many people.

Orientation

Everything revolves around the central plaza (known as Parque Central or Parque Colón), and the sunlit cathedral that overlooks it will be your first and lasting impression of the city. The best hotels are located around this lively tree-lined plaza. Calle La Calzada runs along the northern side of the cathedral in an easterly direction toward the lake and the dock. This street is pedestrianized and is where you'll find many of the city's most touristy restaurants and cafes, along with some hotels. Its vibe

Festival

Every Nicaraguan is a poet until proven otherwise.

—Granada poet José Coronel Urtecho

Nicaragua's taxi drivers, waiters, street vendors, and ex-guerrillas can all spin a line from some of Nicaragua's many famous poets or, indeed, make an attempt at their own. Even President Ortega and his wife are known to scribble a line of their thoughts in rhyme, and the nation's newspapers are full of stanzas celebrating love and country. This is why Granada's annual poetry festival is such a runaway success. Started in 2004, the wordsmith's jamboree has become a significant date on every poet's calendar and is easily the most important literary get-together in Central America. Poets from all over the world (130 attended in 2009) gather in front of the city's flood-lit facades and recite their lines to an avid audience. Words in English, German, Arabic, and Croat float through the city streets, then are translated into Spanish by a local scribe. Flower-decked floats traverse the city with a team of bards, while musicians, dancers, street performers, and 12-foot puppets known as *fantoches* add a heady air of carnival and celebration. What makes Granada's poetry festival all the more unusual is the distinct difference in the audience from what is usually associated with literary events. Granada's festival attracts a colorful melee of workers, businessmen, and intellectuals. Nuns, school children, farm laborers, and city workers all follow the cycle of readings with unparalleled enthusiasm, as well as delighted tourists who find themselves in the city at one of its most vibrant moments. To read more about the nation's love of poetry, see p. 26. Or, better still, find yourself in the city in the third week of February. For exact schedules, check out the festival website at www.festival poesianicaragua.com.

has become a little tacky in recent years, but it's always lively. Calle Atravesada is a narrow, busy, commercial street, running north and south, 1 block west of the plaza. Volcán Mombacho rises to the south, and the easterly lake has a scruffy waterfront and departure point for Las Isletas, known as Complejo Turístico Cocibolca.

Getting Around

You can easily explore central Granada on foot, though you may want to jump on one of the horse-drawn carriages at the main plaza in order to feel like royalty as you trot through the streets. A half-hour ride should cost no more than C95; always agree on a price before getting on board.

BY BICYCLE   Bicycles are for rent at **Bearded Monkey** (Calle 14 de Septiembre; ✆ **505/2552-4028;** www.thebeardedmonkey.com) or at **Nahual Tours,** 1½ blocks east of the cathedral (✆ **505/8988-2461;** www.nahualtours.com). A bike rental for the day should not cost more than C220, including water and a map.

BY CAR   You don't really need a car to explore Granada itself, but having one will help if you're planning excursions in the surrounding area. Car rentals cost approximately C800 a day. **Alamo** (✆ **505/2552-2877;** www.alamonicaragua.com) has an office in the Hotel Colonial, 20m (66 ft.) west of the plaza's northwest corner. **Budget** (✆ **505/2552-1789;** www.budget.com.ni) is located at the Shell Guapinol station on the road to Managua. **Avis** (✆ **505/8467-4780;** www.avis.com.ni) is on Calle La Calzada in the city center.

BY TAXI   **Taxis** can be found on the southern side of the square. Fares start at C30.

Visitor Information

Intur (Calle El Arsenal; ℂ **505/2552-6858**) is 1 block from the cathedral and a half-block behind the Casa de Leones. It is open Monday to Friday from 8am to noon and 2 to 5pm. Here, you will find a good map detailing all the city's historic buildings. The website **www.granada.com.ni** gives an excellent pictorial display of the city, but little else.

TOUR OPERATORS   **Vapues Tours,** in the blue house next to the cathedral (ℂ **505/2552-8291**; www.vapues.com) is one of the city's main agencies, and it organizes everything from transfers to flights to local tours. **Tierra Tour** (Calle La Calzada, 2 blocks east of the cathedral; ℂ **505/2552-8723**; www.tierratour.com) organizes excursions to Masaya and Ometepe Island, as well as kayaking excursions on Lago de Nicaragua and canopy tours. **Nahual Tours**, 1½ blocks east of the cathedral (ℂ **505/8988-2461**; www.nahualtours.com) organizes regular boat tours of Las Isletas that cost approximately C300 and can also arrange transfers. **Oro Travel** (Calle Coral; ℂ **505/2552-8103**; www.orotravel.com) is a multilingual operation that can provide help with just about every excursion in the area. **Zapatera Tours** (Calle Palmira and La Cancha; ℂ **505/8842-2587**; www.zapateratours.com) offers 1-day tours to the seldom-visited Zapatera archipelago. Prices start at C880 per person per day, with an overnight option camping on the islands. The owner, Kevin, who also runs Imagine restaurant, also offers a mountain bike tour around Mombacho and Masaya and volcano climbs.

[Fast FACTS] GRANADA

ATMs   ATM machines are located at **Banpro** (Calle Atravesada, in front of Teatro González; ℂ **505/2552-2723**) and **Bancentro,** farther down Calle Atravesada (ℂ **505/2552-6555**). There are also machines at Esso Garage on the main road and at Lacayo Supermarket on Calle Real Xalteva.

Emergencies   Call ℂ **505/2552-2977** for the police or ℂ **505/2552-2711** for an ambulance.

Internet   Internet access costs approximately C26 per hour, and there are plenty of cybercafes dotted around the city. Try **Café E-mail** on Avenida Guzman near Parque Central (no

phone). They also have a space located in the Casa de los Leones (no phone). Both are open daily from 7am to 10pm. **Inter Café** on Calle la Libertad (no phone), also near Parque Central, is open from 8am to 9pm Monday to Saturday. Granada has embraced wireless technology with enthusiasm, and you'll find Wi-Fi in most of the city's upscale hotels and cafes.

Laundry   **Piscis Laundry Service** (Calle El Martiro and Avenida Libertad; ℂ **505/2552-8239**) will pick up and deliver to your hotel. **Mapache** (Calle La Calzada and El Cisne; ℂ **505/8611-3501**) also

picks up and delivers laundry; they also do tailoring.

Post Office   The main **post office** is on Calle Atravesada, opposite Cine Karawala (no phone), and is open weekdays 8am to noon and 1 to 5pm, and Saturday 8am to noon.

Traveler's Checks & Money Exchange   **Banco de América Central,** on the plaza (ℂ **505/2552-3355**), changes traveler's checks and gives cash advances on Visa and MasterCard with no commission. You will also find many street money-changers in this area who generally give a good rate and are trustworthy.

WHAT TO SEE & DO

In addition to the attractions listed below, be sure to check out the rest of the city's churches, especially the dark and atmospheric **Iglesia Guadalupe** on the eastern side of the city, 4 blocks from the Parque Colón on Calle La Calzada. On the other side of town, you'll find **Iglesia Xalteva**, 5 blocks west of the central plaza on Calle Xalteva. The high, arched walls were built by the Spanish to separate them from the local architecture. Continue west on Xalteva, and you'll reach the town cemetery, an elaborate *necrolandia* with some grandiose tombs, including a fair attempt at a reproduction of the Magdalena de Paris. On the eastern side of the city, at the end of Calle La Calzada, are the gray shores of **Lago Cocibolca.** Here, you'll find Granada's version of a waterfront walk, known as **Complejo Turístico Cocibolca.** Though the lake provides some magnificent panoramic views, the shore is sadly neglected and litter-strewn. You'll pass it on the way to the departure point for tour boats going to Las Isletas.

Antiguo Convento San Francisco ★★★   This should be at the top of your sightseeing list. This navy-blue structure was first built in 1529 and destroyed by pirate Henry Morgan in 1679 and again by William Walker in 1856 during his notorious sacking of the city. It has risen from the ashes several times and acted as a barracks, university, and now a fully restored museum. As well as being a beautiful building in its own right, with countless galleries and courtyards, it houses a remarkable collection of pre-Columbian statues with zoomorphic forms of birds and jaguars found on Zapatera Island.

2 blocks N & 1 block E of the main cathedral. ✆ **505/2552-5535.** C44 adults. Weekdays 8:30am–5:30pm; weekends 9am–4pm.

Casa de los Leones   This historic 1720 building with a neoclassical facade is now a cultural space, housing exhibition rooms, a library, bookshop, cafe, and concert hall. It's open daily 7am to 6pm and is situated on the majestic, pillar-lined walkway that's called **La Plazuela de los Leones**. This walkway runs along the northeastern corner of the city's epicenter—**Parque Colón** (also known as Parque Central). Along the pedestrian street, you'll find mounted cannons, as this was where Henry Morgan based himself when he ransacked the city. It is also the site of William Walker's inauguration as president, a favor he returned by burning it to the ground. It has now been rebuilt and restored, and makes for a fascinating wander through the city's turbulent history.

Calle Guzman & El Arsenal. ✆ **505/2552-6437** or 505/2552-4167. www.c3mundos.org. Free admission. Daily 8am–6pm.

Catedral Nuestra Señora de la Asunción   The city square also holds Granada's main landmark, the magnificent, luminous orange Catedral on Calle Guzman and La Calzada. Despite the stunning exterior with neoclassical and gothic flourishes, the church's interior is quite simple and somewhat disappointing, except for an icon of the Virgin Mary over the altar. A church was originally built here in 1583, but like many of Granada's buildings, it suffered at the hands of pirates and despots and had to be rebuilt several times. It was finally finished in 1915.

Calle Guzman & La Calzada. No phone. Free admission. Daily 7am–8pm.

Fortaleza de la Pólvora   Those pirates sure were a nuisance. So much so that the city decided to build a fort in 1748 to guard munitions; *pólvora* is Spanish for

William Walker: The Loud American

A rampaging yank intent on subjugating the locals, William Walker is a man you'll read and hear about a lot while traveling in Nicaragua. His life seems like an outright exercise in madness and insane ambition. The infamous American *filibustero* invaded Mexico with just 45 men in 1853. He was quickly repelled and then arrested in the U.S. for conducting an illegal war. Freed, he then set his sights on Nicaragua, which was at the time rife with civil conflict and ripe for exploitation by a young intellectual and white supremacist who thought it was the United States' destiny to spread south and bring slavery with it.

Encouraged by the Nicaraguan liberals, he gathered an army of 400 mercenaries and captured Granada, declaring himself president in 1856. English was announced as the official language, slave emancipation revoked, and white settlers encouraged to move south and carve up the territory. His Nicaraguan supporters soon realized their mistake and joined the conservatives and Costa Ricans to push him out in a campaign financed by Cornelius Vanderbilt. Defeat at Rivas, followed by a cholera outbreak and desertion, forced him to flee north to New York, where he wrote a book about his adventure called *War in Nicaragua* (1860). Undeterred, he soon returned to Central America, was caught by the British, and was swiftly executed by a Honduran firing squad. He was 36.

Yet taken in an historical context, Walker's endeavor to establish a U.S. colony in Nicaragua was no folly and could have easily succeeded. A child genius who graduated from university at 14, Walker enjoyed considerable support back home and was greeted to a hero's welcome whenever he returned to the States. In his initial trial for the Mexican affair, he was acquitted in just 8 minutes by a sympathetic jury. A trained doctor, lawyer, and journalist, he had his allies in Washington and the southern states who saw the annexation of Central America as *manifest destiny,* and Nicaragua was particularly attractive, as it offered that coveted Atlantic-Pacific water route. The U.S. officially recognized him as president in 1956. He could easily have become a Central American version of the British colonialist Cecil Rhodes, who established his own fiefdom in Africa. However, Walker's obvious intelligence did not extend to military and political matters. Tactical blunders like alienating Vanderbilt were key to his downfall. Razing Granada did not gain any favors, either. His main legacy is somewhat different from what he planned. He united a fractious region, both liberals and conservatives, Nicaraguans and Costa Ricans, in a successful attempt to oust him, and the wars against Walker are looked upon as a source of national pride.

gunpowder. Its sturdy, medieval structure with thick oak doors and stone walls also came in handy as an army garrison and then a grisly jail during the Somoza dictatorship. It is now a military museum and makes for an interesting visit—you can even climb one of its five small towers for views of the city. It has no fixed open hours, but you should be able to enter if you arrive during daylight hours.

Calle Xalteva, 6 blocks W of Iglesia de La Merced. No phone. Free admission.

Iglesia de La Merced ★★   If you cross the park and walk east on Calle Real Xalteva for 2 blocks, you'll come across the **Iglesia de La Merced** on Real Xalteva and 14 de Septiembre. This is considered Granada's most beautiful church, and its

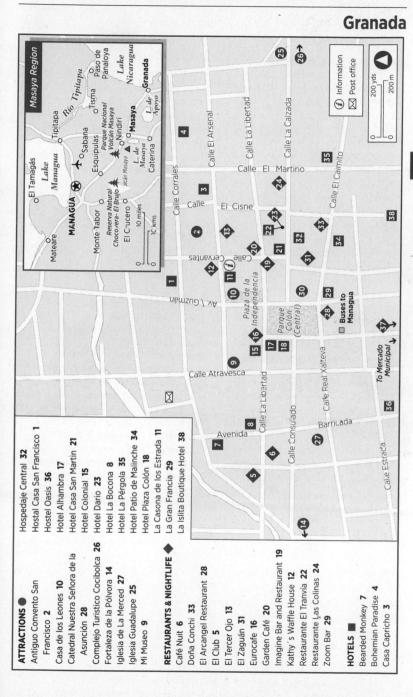

VOLUNTEERING opportunities
IN NICARAGUA

Nicaragua has always attracted an unconventional tourist, starting with the pirates and Californian gold prospectors who came here centuries ago. A new breed of visitor appeared after the Sandinista revolution—thousands of *internacionalistas* intent on joining the great leap forward and helping the country's poor and impoverished (the less than committed were wittily referred to as Sandalistas). Those idealists have now morphed into ordinary people doing amazing things, and Nicaragua is now officially a hot spot for volunteering opportunities in Central America. Below is a list of the more established volunteer organizations offered in the country, but just scratch the surface, and you'll find many more. If you are serious about taking up a good cause, you need to commit considerable time (at least a month) and have basic Spanish skills to get the most from your experience.

GRANADA

Building New Hope (www.buildingnewhope.org) is a Pittsburgh-based nonprofit organization that runs a learning center for underprivileged kids, among many other projects in Granada. The volunteer organizer is Donna Tabor, and she can be contacted through their website. Tax-deductible donations are also welcome.

Hogar Madre Albertina is a girls' orphanage that sorely needs money and volunteers. Desperate to get rid of an old laptop? You can donate yours here, as well as donate your time by teaching a word-processing class. The orphanage (© 505/2552-7661) is located 2 blocks north of Colegio Padre Misieri.

La Esperanza Granada (© 505/2552-7044; www.la-esperanza-granada.org) helps educate locals in rural areas, as well as offers badly needed healthcare. They provide cheap accommodations and can organize homestays if you're looking for total cultural and language immersion. Their office is located in Hospedaje Central, 1½ blocks east of the central plaza.

SAN JUAN DEL SUR

San Juan del Sur Biblioteca Móvil (janem101@aol.com) is sponsored by the Hester J. Hodgdon Libraries for All Program. Teachers and donations are required, as well as Spanish books, which can be sent to the library's U.S. depository at 1716 del Norte Blvd., Loveland, CO 80538, or directly dropped off. The **Newton-San Juan del Sur Sister City Project** (www.newtonsanjuan.org)

baroque facade and intricate interiors have inspired poets for centuries, all the while withstanding a tumultuous history of pirate attacks and civil war skirmishes. First built in 1534, it has been sacked and rebuilt more times than Rome and is all the more beautiful for it. Climb the spiral stairs to the bell tower, where you'll be greeted with great views of the city with the lake and *las Isletas* in the distance and Volcán Mombacho to the south.

Real Xalteva & 14 de Septiembre. No phone. Church free admission; bell tower C20 adults. Daily 10am–6pm.

Mi Museo This is not a bad little museum, considering it's privately owned and admission is free. There aren't many places you'll find thousands of ceramic pieces dating back to 1500 B.C. Indeed, it has the best collection of pre-Columbian art in the country. Started by a Danish collector and philanthropist, the museum is located in a tidy town house with adobe walls and a backroom courtyard. The exhibits are is a Massachusetts-based nonprofit organization that sends teams of doctors, dentists, and builders to San Juan. Visit their website or contact local representative Rosa Elena Bello at rosaebel@ibw.com.ni.

Fundación A. Jean Brugger (www.fundacionajbrugger.org) focuses on children's educational needs, offering uniforms, school supplies, and scholarships to students from poor backgrounds.

MATAGALPA

Habitat for Humanity (✆ 505/2772-6121; www.habitatnicaragua.org.ni) is a Christian organization that builds decent housing for the poor, in an effort to "change Nicaragua house by house." They have projects all over the country, including in León and Bluefields. Their Matagalpa branch is located 2 blocks east of the Deportiva Brigadista.

Centro Girasol (✆ 505/2772-6030) is a community center that can hook you up with different organizations that require volunteers such as indigenous rights campaigners **Movimiento Comunal** and **Comunidad Indígena**. Their offices are located in the yellow building at the bridge, as you enter the city from Managua.

OMETEPE

Nuestros Pequeños Hermanos (www.nph.org) operates an orphanage in San Lázaro that offers volunteer programs on the island and in other parts of Central America.

La Suerte Biological Teaching Station (www.maderasrfc.org) is dedicated to protecting tropical rainforests and wildlife. They offer teaching opportunities to students and professors, and accommodate educational groups with the goal of "Bridging the Americas."

Bainbridge-Ometepe Sisters Island Association (www.bosia.org) does countless good works on the island, including promoting fair-trade coffee and creating schools, scholarships, and water systems.

MANAGUA

Sí a la Vida! (www.asalv.org) works with troubled kids and expands their opportunities through education, sports, and art. They seek volunteers with experience in healthcare, construction, and agriculture. They also operate a retreat on Ometepe Island.

Casa Ben Linder (www.casabenlinder.org) is a meetinghouse and resource center devoted to helping alleviate poverty.

well laid out amidst antique furnishings, each label explaining the origin and period of bowls, pots, or urns that are in remarkably good condition, considering their age. There are guide tours in Spanish.

Calle Atravesada 505, 1 block W of Casa de Los Leones. www.granadacollection.org. ✆ **505/2552-7614.** Free admission. Mon–Sat 8am–5pm.

Nicaragua Butterfly Reserve ☺ A 45-minute hike from the city, you'll find a tiny nature reserve with a wealth of plants, flowers, birds, and butterflies. Two kilometers (1.2 miles) of trails go through gardens, some partially netted to protect a dazzling selection of lepidoptera with huge colorful wings of blue, orange, yellow, and white. Here, a guide can explain the importance of certain plants in attracting the insects to lay eggs and the whole miracle of metamorphosis from caterpillars to winged works of art. The reserve is the perfect spot for photography and brings out the amateur botanist, birder, and biologist in everybody. The reserve is located 2km

(1¼ miles) down a dirt road, right of the cemetery, southwest of the city. The road is too rough for a normal car but can be done in a four-wheel-drive.

Naindame Rd. www.backyardnature.net/nbr. © **505/2895-3012.** C140 adults. Daily 10am–4pm.

Parque Colón ★   The central plaza is a lively central square that's crammed with stalls, food vendors, musicians, and circling horse-and-carriages that carry tourists around the city. Here, you can chew on *vigorón* (a pork and cabbage snack wrapped in banana leaf) while marimba music echoes around the busy meeting place, punctuated by boisterous birds in the trees above. The plaza is surrounded by beautiful architecture, including some of the city's finest hotels. On the southwest corner, there is a yellow colonial building owned by the wealthy Pellas family, owners of Victoria and Toña beers and just about everything else in Nicaragua. Beside the cathedral is a large cross with a 19th-century time capsule buried beneath.

Parque Colon, in front of **Catedral Nuestra Señora de la Asunción**

Outdoor Activities

CANOPY TOURING   The slopes of **Reserva Natural Volcán Mombacho** (www.mombacho.org) offer some spectacular opportunities to glide through the jungle. **Canopy Tours Mombacho** (© **505/2267-8256**) has a 16-platform course that's located close to the park entrance. **Hacienda Cutirre** has a spectacular 17-platform canopy system on the eastern face of the volcano. Trips there can be arranged through **Nahual Tours,** 1½ blocks east of the cathedral (© **505/8988-2461;** www.nahualtours.com). See Reserva Natural Volcán Mombacho, below, for more details.

HIKING   **Reserva Natural Volcán Mombacho** has some of the best-maintained trails in the country. Numerous travel operators offer 1-day excursions here, or you can take a short bus ride to the park entrance. It is possible to hike from the city to the huge crater lake, **Laguna de Apoyo** (p. 124), a popular watering hole holding abundant wildlife within its rim. **Volcán Masaya National Park** (p. 94) offers a jaw-dropping look into the gates of hell and is possible to see in a day excursion from the city.

HORSEBACK RIDING   Blue Mountain (© 505/2552-5323; www.blue mountainnicaragua.com) is a ranch outside the city where you can also lodge and do wildlife excursions. Rates start at C770 for a double.

KAYAKING   Laguna de Apoyo has several launching pads for those who fancy some paddle time. You can rent kayaks from lakeside lodgings **San Simian Eco Resort** (© **505/8813-6866**) or the **Monkey Hut** (© **505/8887-3546**). More interesting to explore are the chain of islands called Las Isletas in Lago de Nicaragua. Here, there are some bird-filled waterways and an interesting island fort called El Fortin. **Nahual Tours**, 1½ blocks east of the cathedral (© **505/8988-2461;** www. nahualtours.com) are the local experts for this.

SHOPPING

The **Mercado Municipal** (open daily 6am–6pm) is a busy, sprawling hive of activity 1 block south of the central plaza. Here, you'll find everything from soap to sombreros, but it is dark and dingy, and slightly claustrophobic. Real shopaholics should take a morning and visit the nearby handicrafts mecca of Masaya (see p. 96). **Galeria Istmo** (Calle Atravesada, in front of Bancentro; © **505/2552-4678**) offers the best in Nicaraguan art and design. **Casa Natal,** 1½ blocks east of Calle El Caimito (no phone), sells handicrafts from all over Nicaragua, including woodcarvings from Solentiname and black ceramics from Jinotega. **Casa de Antiguedades,** 1 block north of Calle Arsenal (© **505/2874-2034;** haroldsandino@hotmail.com), is a treasure-trove of antiques and is great for a morning browse. Fancy a smoke? **Doña Elba Cigar Factory,** 1 block west of Iglesia Xalteva (© **505/8860-6715**), is a small operation producing 3,000 *puros* a day. Located in the family's home, you can learn to roll your own while sitting at an elaborate dining table engraved with a picture of the Last Supper. The factory also produces lovely cedar gift boxes with inset pictures of the Granada cathedral. The factory is open daily from 7am to 7pm. For English- and Spanish-language books and magazines, check out the **Maverick Reading & Smoothie Lounge,** 1 block west of Casa de los Leones on Calle El Arsenal (© **505/2552-4120**).

WHERE TO STAY

Granada has the best selection of colonial-style hotels in all of Nicaragua. Even the most humble *hospedaje* will have an atmospheric courtyard and gallery with rocking chairs beneath arched pillars. That said, the rooms themselves may strike you as small, with tiny bathrooms and dangerously steep stairs, especially if you have had one *cerveza* too many late at night. The high prices (remember, most hotels quote prices without 15% tax) do not often reflect quality or good service, so shop around before you decide.

Expensive

Hotel Dario ★★   Hotel Dario's wedding-cake facade is a little over-the-top, but nevertheless magnificent. The two-story arrangement of white and green classical ornamentation leads to a lobby that is no less impressive, with intricate tiling and handsome wood panels. An elegant inner gallery of slender varnished pillars surrounds a gorgeous courtyard with garden paths and a central fountain. Ornate flowerpots sit on gleaming white walls. The rooms have tall doors, wooden floors, and wrought-iron beds. Some are smallish; the best have balconies with views of Mombacho. There is a small pool and tiny gym, but the best features are the lovely, peaceful communal seating areas with giant fans overhead. The Dario is one of the best quality places in town—reliable and somewhat unforgettable. It's located on the main pedestrian street with lots of restaurants, including its own called the Tranvia. There's also a charming in-house cafe called El Chocolate.

Calle La Calzada. www.hoteldario.com. © **505/2552-3400.** 22 units. From $100 double. AE, DC, MC, V. **Amenities:** Bar; airport transfers ($35); pool. *In room:* A/C, TV, Internet (free).

Hotel La Bocona ★★★ Everything about La Bocona is regal. This beautifully restored colonial complex has six huge rooms surrounding three gorgeous courtyards, one of which has a lovely, turquoise pool. High ceilings and chandeliers hang over giant four-poster beds and elegant period furniture. You cannot help but feel like royalty as you enjoy this palatial property 2 blocks from the main plaza. The Danish owner has remained true to the original architecture with no walls knocked down whilst converting it into a five-star establishment. For this reason, the spacious, modern bathrooms are located across the courtyard, with slippers and robes provided. The street outside can be noisy at night, but there are plenty of fern-adorned nooks and crannies to escape to, including a top-notch spa out back called the Cocoberry. The hotel's name (the *little mouth*) is inspired by a colonial stone post box outside—the first in Granada.

Calle La Libertad, 2 blocks W of Parque Central. www.hotellabocona.com. © **505/2552-2888.** 6 units. $103–$172 double. AE V MC DC. **Amenities:** Airport transfers ($35); pool; spa; *In room:* A/C, Wi-Fi (free).

Hotel Patio de Malinche ✦ This hotel's attractive but humble entrance belies a magnificent colonial complex with two lush courtyards, one with a spectacular pool. A tastefully decorated two-story building of whitewashed walls and arched wooden doorways surrounds the main courtyard. This courtyard leads to large, airy rooms done up in muted tones with the occasional splash of color, such as a scarlet bedspread or hand-woven tablecloth. Rocking chairs and hammocks are placed in strategic locations throughout the hotel, making for an abundance of great places to rest. It might lack the artful details of other historic hotels in the city, but the Patio de Malinche has a bright, welcoming atmosphere that makes up for it.

Calle El Caimito, by Calle El Cisne. www.patiodelmalinche.com. © **505/2552-2235.** 15 units. From $84 double; from $99 triple. Rates include breakfast. AE, DC, MC, V. **Amenities:** Bar; airport transfers ($35); pool. *In room:* A/C, TV, Internet (free).

Hotel Plaza Colón ★★★ 📷 This is a magnificent hotel in every sense. The one abiding memory I have of this beautiful hotel is sipping rum on its wide, polished balcony, while overlooking the boisterous plaza, filled with tourists and vendors working to the rhythm of marimba music. The sumptuous decor hits the right balance between colonial authenticity and the modern traveler's expectations. Rooms have modern amenities such as cable TV, but also come with grand built-in wardrobes and luxurious king-size beds. Exquisite tiled floors lead to a majestic inner balcony that runs around a glorious courtyard and pool. Everything is lustrous and elegant, and the service is prompt and reliable. Make sure to get the staff to adjust the air-conditioning to silent mode, and be prepared for a dawn chorus of jackdaws singing outside.

Calle Consulado, by Parque Colón. www.hotelplazacolon.com. © **505/2552-8489.** Fax 505/2552-8505. 27 units. From $129 double; from $209 suite. Rates include breakfast. AE, DC, MC, V. **Amenities:** Wine bar; Internet (free); pool. *In room:* A/C, TV, minibar.

La Gran Francia ★★ 📷 Staying at La Gran Francia feels like residing in a museum, albeit a beautiful, well-located, and courtly museum. Impeccably done religious paintings hang on the walls, and a wooden monk greets you at the bottom of the stairs. The Spanish-tiled steps lead to an upper gallery surrounding a long courtyard with a small blue pool below. The rooms are grand in every sense. An ample, inviting bed is surrounded by considerable space, punctuated with stout furniture and a small balcony overlooking a busy side street. In the nice-size bathrooms, original ironwork faucets hang over hand-painted washbasins displaying old-fashioned street scenes.

My only criticism of this place is that the staff is very much like the sculptures that grace the hotel's nooks and crannies—wooden and unresponsive. Across the street is the hotel's restaurant, which boasts a mellow, inviting bar where guests can enjoy a free welcome drink after checking in.

SE corner of Parque Central & Calle El Caimito. www.lagranfrancia.com. (*C*) **505/2552-6000.** Fax 505/2552-6001. 21 units. From $90 double; from $103 triple; from $116 suite. Rates include breakfast. AE, MC, V. Amenities: Restaurant; bar; pool; room service. In room: A/C, TV, Internet (free), minibar.

Moderate

Bohemian Paradise ★ 🏷 *Buena, bonita, y barata* (lovely, gorgeous, and cheap) is how you would describe this small, intimate guesthouse. The Bohemian Paradise is in stark contrast to its colonial counterparts in the sense that it's bright, modern, and a little plain. It may not look like much from the outside—a mustard-colored street cottage—but once you enter, there's a pleasant arrangement of comfortable rooms with conventional decor. Sizes vary; the king suite is the largest and most magnificent. It has a Jacuzzi surrounded by tall windows and an open-air shower. There is a lovely private balcony in the king suite with a view of the lake. Out back is a long, narrow garden with a fountain and plants. The co-owner Lucy is English-speaking and friendly, giving the place the feel of a homestay more than a hotel. Pricewise, it beats everybody.

Calle Corrales, 1½ blocks E of Antiguo Convento San Francisco. www.seecentralamerica.com. (*C*) **505/2552-0286.** 5 units. From $40 queen double; $80 king double. AE, DC, MC, V. **Amenities:** Internet (free). In room: A/C, TV.

Casa Capricho Another small town house converted into a guesthouse, Casa Capricho has a funky, eclectic feel. Dark navy walls contrast with fire-engine-red pillars and pastel-colored rooms. The small pool out back is crossed by a blue arch topped with a colorful glass wall. Make sure to book a double room; the singles are somewhat cramped and, frankly, not worth the money. All have wrought-iron beds and open closets instead of wardrobes. The pool area is charming, if a little cluttered, and overall, the price is a little high for what it is. Still, if you want a quirky place with an arty vibe, this should do. The communal kitchen is a big plus for those who like to self-cater.

Calle El Arsenal, 1 block E of Antiguo Convento San Francisco. www.casacapricho.com. (*C*) **505/2552-8422.** 11 units. From $45 double and $30 single. AE, DC, MC, V. **Amenities:** Internet (free). In room: A/C (in most), TV.

Hostal Casa San Francisco Located on a quiet side street, this agreeable little hotel has a sidewalk bar and restaurant out front and a miniature courtyard out back. The main walkway through the property leads to a small pool and, on the right, a picturesque building with delightful, tastefully decorated rooms. Large fans hang over four-poster beds, and the charming bathrooms have a colorful tiled partition separating the shower. The San Francisco is compact, attractive, and well maintained, with lots of character. It makes for a quiet, snug hideaway with a heavy dose of colonial splendor.

207 Calle Corrales, by the Antiguo Convento San Francisco. www.csf-hotel-granada.com. (*C*) **505/2552-8235.** 9 units. From $65 standard double; from $75 king/twin double. Rates include breakfast. 5% discount for cash. AE, DC, MC, V. **Amenities:** Restaurant; small pool; room service. In room: A/C, fan TV, Wi-Fi (free).

Hotel Alhambra   The grand old dame of Granada, the Hotel Alhambra is an example of just how a luxury hotel used to be in the good old days. Here, you'll find a purpose-built hotel with all the creature comforts, as well as a flamboyant nod to Granada's colonial past. The elaborate facade of pillars, arches, cornices, and pink relief leads to an atmospheric lobby with an old-world feel. Marble floors are bordered by intricate Spanish tiles amidst antique furniture and big, old lamps. There's a lush courtyard out back and an ample round pool. The front rooms with balcony are the best appointed, and all have chunky period beds, colorful quilted bedding, and heavy, sagging drapes. Some rooms could do with a little sprucing up, but in general, everything is quite clean and well maintained. Its location right in front of the Central Plaza means you are right in the thick of it.

NW corner of Central Plaza. www.hotelalhambra.com.ni. © **505/2552-4488.** 60 units. From $85 double. AE, DC, MC, V. **Amenities:** Restaurant; Internet cafe; pool; room service. *In room:* A/C, TV, minibar, Wi-Fi.

Hotel Casa San Martín   Quaint, authentic, and reasonably priced, the simple and unassuming exterior of the Casa San Martin gives way to elegant rooms that surround a small courtyard with an inviting gallery of wicker rocking chairs, multicolored tables, and ceramic urns. The decor is simple, with hardwood floors, wrought-iron beds, and vintage lamps. The rooms are large but a little dark. The central location on the main pedestrian street can be a little noisy, and some rooms are too close to the kitchen.

Calle La Calzada, 1 block E of Central Plaza. www.hcasasanmartin.com. © **505/2552-6185.** 8 units. From $55 double. AE, DC, MC, V. *In room:* A/C.

Hotel Colonial ★ 🎁   As you approach this midsize hotel and note its attractive, navy facade and row of international flags, you might think it is just another conventional four-star lodging. Yes, it is conventional, but it's conventional done Granada style. The reception area is a spectacle of green walls and Corinthian pillars holding up an intricate ceiling of classic moldings. Curling balustrades of marble are graced with giant Grecian urns holding potted plants. The courtyard, with a pool and mosaic-covered island bar, is just as lavish a spectacle. The hotel's rainbow colors run into the rooms themselves, which are big with beautiful four-poster beds and polished floors. The suites have giant corner Jacuzzis tucked beneath green tiled archways. It's rather over-the-top, but refreshingly different for anyone used to the muted gray and beige tones of modern chain hotels. This hotel has character, as well as a friendly, professional, bilingual staff.

Calle La Libertad, 25m (82 ft.) W of Parque Central. www.hotelcolonialgranada.com. © **505/2552-7581.** Fax 505/552-7299. 37 units. From $75 double. AE, DC, MC, V. **Amenities:** Restaurant; pool. *In room:* A/C, TV, Wi-Fi (free).

Hotel La Pérgola 🎁   La Pérgola gets its name from a breezy roof terrace with a view of the cathedral and Mombacho. It is not a bad place to end an evening and plan your itinerary while gazing over the rooftops. Cream-colored walls are fringed with colorful tiles and shaded by heavy eaves and simple arches. Rose bushes and swinging chairs adorn a spacious gallery that leads to large, simple rooms. This is the best-value colonial-style lodging I could find, though I must warn you, there are problems with the hot water.

Calle El Caimito, 3 blocks E of Central Plaza. www.lapergola.com.ni. © **505/2552-4221.** 11 units. From $46 double. AE, DC, MC, V. **Amenities:** Bar; room service. *In room:* A/C, Wi-Fi (free).

La Casona de los Estrada ★   A stay at this boutique property ensures that you'll have a classic Granada experience. You'll feel like you are one of the old aristocrats as you walk through its wide entrance hall graced with a huge gilded mirror, and into the large open courtyard filled with plants and flowers. The handsome rooms have high wooden ceilings and tiled floors. Some are much bigger than others—ask what's available at check-in. The bathrooms are smallish but spotless, and everything is well maintained. This place manages to make you feel like you're staying at an enormous palace when actually there are only six rooms, some of which overlook the garden and one of which has a private courtyard. La Casona has the added advantage of a friendly, attentive staff.

Calle El Arsenal, by the Antiguo Convento San Francisco. www.casonalosestrada.com. ℂ **505/2552-7393.** 6 units. From $50 double. Rates include breakfast. AE, DC, MC, V. **Amenities:** Bar; airport transfers ($35); room service. *In room:* A/C, TV.

La Islita Boutique Hotel ★   Tucked away in a small cul-de-sac several blocks from the plaza, La Islita offers Granada's signature colonial architecture with a colorful modern flair, all wrapped up in contemporary Nicaraguan culture. From the outside, it looks like a well-to-do suburban home. Its orange facade contrasts with blue Spanish tile work inside, adjacent to a small tropical garden with gurgling fountain. High cane ceilings and arched doorways lead to an ample lobby with wicker furniture and abundant flowers. The rooms are large and come in different styles; two have private balconies, and there is a small communal rooftop terrace with views of the volcano and cathedral. La Islita is located in a typical Granada neighborhood that can be lively at times, especially during holidays. The sound of fireworks, roosters, dogs, and parakeets can be vibrant and authentic to some or just plain noisy and bothersome to others; earplugs are available on request.

Calle El Cisne, 2 blocks W from the Alcaldia & 1½ blocks S. www.laislita.com. ℂ **505/2552-7473.** 8 units. $75–$85 double. Rates include breakfast. AE, DC, MC, V. **Amenities:** Airport transfers ($35). *In room:* A/C, TV.

Inexpensive

In addition to the places reviewed below, **Hospedaje Central** (ℂ **505/2552-9500**) is a popular backpacker hangout with over 80 beds and a lively social scene. It is not the prettiest property in town, nor the cleanest, but it offers bargain bunk beds for less than $6 a head and also has a cafe. Private rooms are also available. Its large, rambling building is located 1½ blocks east of the central plaza, on Calle La Calzada.

Bearded Monkey   The Bearded Monkey has positioned itself as the most popular and funky *mochilero* (backpacker) hangout in Granada. With its huge bulletin board, free movie screenings, book exchange, music library, and copious number of hammocks, it's a backpacker paradise. The cafe-bar acts as good meeting point, with a dartboard to help break the ice and bikes to rent if you wish to explore more than just the hostel's large courtyard of palm trees. The old colonial building holds both dorms and private rooms, some of which have no windows and all of which have shared bathrooms. A mosquito net will definitely come in handy here, as will bug spray. The owners also operate the Monkey Hut in Laguna de Apoyo (p. 126).

Av. 14 de Septiembre & Costado. www.thebeardedmonkey.com. ℂ **505/2552-4028.** 10 units. From $6 dorm bed; $14–$17 double; from $24 triple; $22–$36 suite. AE, DC, MC, V. **Amenities:** Restaurant; bar; Internet (free). *In room:* No phone.

Hostel Oasis ★★ 🏷 This hostel has nary a multicolored barn door nor a funky mosaic-tiled bathroom in sight. The Oasis breaks the mold by instead offering the sort of stylish facilities you'd expect in a more expensive bed-and-breakfast, except here, guests sleep in dorms and can use the kitchen. Its main asset is its great pool, which is in a back courtyard surrounded by stone-clad columns holding up a gallery of balconies and doorways. There is also a very pleasant garden courtyard with lounge chairs. The dorms are basic but not too claustrophobic, though the bunk beds might be too short for some lankier readers. The private rooms are quite small but functional, all the furniture matches, the TV works, and everything is immaculate. Some have private bathrooms.

Calle Estrada & Av. Barricada. www.nicaraguahostel.com. ✆ **505/2552-8006**. 21 units. From $9 dorm bed; from $20 double. AE, DC, MC, V. **Amenities:** Cafe; Internet (free); pool. *In room:* A/C (extra charge $11), fans, some with TV .

Where to Stay Outside Granada

Jicaro Island Lodge ★★ This is an island-paradise hotel with a difference. Instead of a beach, it has a yoga deck. In place of a rolling turquoise sea, it has a lapping freshwater lake. Yes, there are palm trees and thatched roofs in abundance, but the nine individual cottages are designer-chic installations made from recycled hardwood. The slatted walls frame huge windows bringing in sunset silhouettes of Mombacho volcano. Ample space allows for king beds reached by wide minimalist stairways. Private balconies and soft, earth-colored upholsteries all add to the feeling that this is a carefully planned, thoughtfully designed lodge where both nature and luxury get equal footing. What should be a mundane water tower is transformed into a walk-up observation point with 360-degree views of the lake and the .4-hectare (1-acre) island that is your own private getaway. Excursions such as kayak trips to the nearby islands are available, or you just may choose to wallow in the infinity pool after a relaxing massage. Simple but varied food made from local products includes coconut scones and banana bread, and will satisfy all gourmands, and the ample staff is attentive and helpful. Jicaro Island lodge is a 10-minute boat ride from Granada city and perfect for those who want romance, peace, and nature.

Las Isletas. www.jicarolodge.com. ✆ **505/8403-1236.** 9 units. $380–$540 double. All meals & most activities included. AE, DC, MC, V. **Amenities:** Restaurant; wellness center; pool; kayaks. *In room:* Fan, no phone.

WHERE TO EAT

Granada has its fair share of sidewalk cafes, but be aware that on the more popular streets, you will get harassed by persistent panhandlers if you sit outside. Most restaurants are located on the pedestrian street Calle La Calzada or 2 blocks north of it, close to Antiguo Convento San Francisco. Recent years have seen an explosion of gourmet options, with foreign-owned eateries competing with the locals—and often winning, as they have more variety and are more in line with visitors' tastes. However, if you want a true Granada snack experience, try the delicious *chancho con yuca* (pork served on banana leaf) from a stall on the plaza; served with tropical marimba music in the background, it's at least as good as waffles or smoothies and a mite more genuine.

Expensive

El Arcangel Restaurant ★★ INTERNATIONAL Not everybody can afford to stay at one of Granada's most opulent hotels, La Gran Francia, but most can round up $14 to dine at its elegant restaurant across the road. Decor-wise, it is truly *de Granada,* with the obligatory tropical courtyard, high ceilings, and antique trappings. Anywhere else, this would be amazing, but after several days wandering this city, you begin to take such architectural splendor for granted. What makes Arcangel stand out is its menu. The food is modern, eclectic, and adventurous. Who could resist whiskey-slathered steak or snapper cooked in banana and brown sugar? Treat yourself.

SE corner of Central Plaza. www.lagranfrancia.com. *C* **505/2552-6000.** Main courses C280. AE, DC, MC, V. Daily 11am–9pm.

El Tercer Ojo ★ FUSION   El Tercer Ojo is an exotic haven of Far Eastern delights. The interior is a visual feast, with purple silk cushions and curtains, and a golden Buddha watching from the liquor shelf. A small bar with Parisian prints leads to a pleasant, colorful courtyard adorned with artwork and face masks. The menu is extensive and includes Asian staples such as Thai chicken and shrimp with Vietnamese curry. There are a variety of tapas, shish kabob, and fish dishes such as mussels sautéed in wine. Speaking of wine, this laid-back and intimate restaurant has a pretty good international list, with offerings from Argentina, Italy, Spain, France, and Chile.

Calle El Arsenal, on the corner of Antiquo Convento San Francisco. *C* **505/2552-6451.** Main courses C240. AE, DC, MC, V. Daily 11am–11pm.

Restaurante El Tranvía ★★ INTERNATIONAL/SEAFOOD   This old-fashioned restaurant is tucked inside the roomy Hotel Dario. Its large white salon, with giant doors looking out onto Calle La Calzada and old black-and-white photos on the wall, makes for an elegant and cool (six big fans hum overhead) setting. The menu is very much concentrated on seafood, with lobster from the Corn Islands featured strongly. The shrimp *al Diablo* is a spicy mix of shrimp with pepper, tomatoes, and ginger. Shrimp also come in a curry sauce or a sauce of scotch and mushrooms mixed with coconut milk. The wine list is decent, with average wines hailing from lots of countries. The dining experience here is definitely romantic—you may get serenaded by some wandering musicians during your meal.

Calle La Calzada, 150m (492 ft.) NE from cathedral. www.hoteldario.com. *C* **505/2552-3400.** Main courses C300–C4,000. AE, DC, MC, V. Daily noon–10pm.

Moderate

Doña Conchi SPANISH   This cozy little restaurant is the ideal venue for a romantic dinner, with candles and wind chimes filling an intimate courtyard. The Spanish owner is an attentive host, displaying her artistic creations on the yellow walls and in a tiny store where you can stock up on the vibrant, fish-illustrated wall plates if they strike your fancy. The menu has a distinctive Spanish flair, with steaming plates of paella washed down with jugs of sangria. There is also an abundance of salads and seafood, such as lobster. Live Spanish guitar every evening adds to the Iberian atmosphere.

Calle Caimito, 2 blocks E of cathedral. *C* **505/2552-7376.** Main courses C160. No credit cards. Wed-Mon noon–10pm.

El Zaguán STEAK   This is undoubtedly the best place in town for steak. The redbrick bar and walls are split by a curved wicker partition, and the tablecloths come with a tartan design. However, it's the open-flame grill that will attract your attention, draped as it is with slabs of beef. Some dishes come complete with a mini grill that sits beside you on the table, sizzling with sausage and ribs. The service is excellent, and the experience is often accompanied by serenading mariachis.

Av. La Sirena, behind cathedral. ℰ**505/2552-2522.** Main courses C225. AE, DC, MC, V. Daily noon–3pm & 6–11pm.

Eurocafe CAFE   This busy coffeehouse/bookstore is located on the northeastern corner of the central plaza and has a hip, traveler vibe, with a relaxing courtyard out back and a ping pong table in the corner of the garden. The bookstore is small with a limited selection of paperbacks that start at $10. The real attraction here is a mug of steaming Nicaraguan coffee and delicious homemade Italian ice cream and pastries.

Esquina Noreoeste del Parque Central. www.eurocafenica.com. ℰ**505/2552-2146.** Snacks C150. AE, DC, MC, V. Daily 7:30am–9pm.

Garden Café 🛎CAFE   When a Californian and a Nicaraguan met in a Managua university to study international relations, they took their coursework a little too literally and decided to get hitched. The result is one of Granada's coolest cafes with the brightest, healthiest menu. Here, you'll find a leafy respite with a courtyard that could only be described as 19 sq. m (205 sq. ft.) of sumptuous jungle. Excellent smoothies, well-presented salads, and elaborate sandwiches sate both thirst and hunger. Some of the best coffee in town goes well with the muffins and lemon cake. The large hammock often provokes good-humored arguments amongst diners over whose turn it is to take it.

Calle La Libertad, 1 block E of the plaza. ℰ**505/2552-8582.** Snacks C120. Mon–Sat 7am–3pm.

Imagine Bar and Restaurant INTERNATIONAL   This cozy, corner town house offers much the same architecturally as the countless other attractive buildings in this charming city. However, the difference is in the detail, especially a menu that offers warm brie served with roasted garlic or succulent lamb chops served with *chimichurri* sauce. Owner Kevin Cohen takes pride in such adventurous dishes as duck quesadilla and will gladly give you a quick tour of the open kitchen out back with the hottest grill in town, fired up by lava rocks from Masaya volcano. As well as using homegrown veggies, mangos from Cohen's own farm are featured in the popular dessert of mango bread, drenched in ice cream and chocolate syrup. Cohen is also an accomplished guitarist, and he often jams with the live bands that play Tuesday, Thursday, Friday, and Saturday.

Calle La Libertad & Calle Cervantes. www.imaginerestaurantandbar.com. ℰ **505/2552-4672.** Main courses C180. AE, DC, MC, V. Sun–Wed 5–10pm; Thurs–Sat 5pm–1am.

Kathy's Waffle House CAFE   Kathy's seems to be the breakfast spot for foreigners in Granada, though the occasional local or Managuan also drops by to enjoy menu items such as massive Belgian waffles in a variety of delicious syrups. French toast and full egg breakfasts are also on the menu, as well as very decent milkshakes and smoothies. Diners sit on an elevated patio in front of the beautiful Convento San Francisco—it's a perfect spot to start your day and plot out your itinerary.

Calle El Arsenal, ½ block W of the Antiguo Convento San Francisco. ℰ505/552-7583. Snacks C120. AE, MC, V. Daily 7am–2pm.

Restaurante Las Colinas 🛎 NICARAGUAN/SEAFOOD   People travel from Managua just to eat at this humble, shed-like establishment and try what is reputedly the best fish in Nicaragua—a very ugly lake bass known as *Cocibolca Guapote*. It's fished out of the nearby lake and deep fried before being dipped in a tomato and onion sauce, then served up with lemon and lime. Its looks belie its delicious succulence, and it is one of the most distinctive local dishes you'll try in Nicaragua. Try not to ruin your appetite on the scrumptious yucca and fried cheese cubes that come as a starter. The restaurant is located in a southern, down-at-heel neighborhood called Barrio Las Sabanetas and can be quite difficult to find, though any taxi driver worth his salt should have no problem, as this place is increasingly famous.

Barrio Las Sabanetas. ℂ **505/2552-3492.** Main courses C200. No credit cards. Wed–Mon 10am–10pm; Tues 10am–3pm.

GRANADA AFTER DARK

The more-upscale bars and nightclubs in town are located west of the central plaza, while the more down-at-heel local joints can be found on the lakeshore close to the Complejo Turístico. Here, there is a strip of bars and nightclubs, the best of which are **Pantera** (no phone) and **Cesars** (ℂ 505/2552-7241). Be warned, however, wandering this part of town at night is for the young, adventurous, and even foolish. If you do fancy a night on the tiles by the lake, dress down and make sure you get a taxi back, as the walk into the city is through a notoriously crime-ridden spot.

O'Shea´s (ℂ 505/8454 1140) is a small Irish bar located on the pedestrian street La Calzada and is alive with late night revelers enjoying a hearty menu of fish and chips, baked potatoes and chicken curry. The owner is a Dubliner called Tom who runs the long, narrow bar with efficient ease. The pub quiz on Wednesday is very popular. **Kelly´s Bar** (La Sirena and El Caimito; ℂ 505/8825-1078) is another popular bar, sometimes heaving with beer-soaked gringos and locals at three in the afternoon. It's the type of place where the TV sits on beer crates and you have to shout to be heard, but it is certainly a happening spot with live music on weekends.

Café Nuit ★ One of Granada's liveliest nightspots offers a great opportunity to shake off any reservations and swing your hips to live salsa and merengue. A long walkway of palm plants leads to an attractive courtyard adorned with ivy, fountains, and stone circular seating. There is a corner bar at the back dispensing cold beers and cocktails and a kitchen to the side serving tapas and canapés. The band plays every night and often doubles as bouncers if the crowd of locals and foreigners get a little too excited. ½ block W of the Piedra Bocona, Calle La Libertad. ℂ 505/2552-7376. Fri & Sat cover $1.

El Club A well-appointed disco bar up front leads to a designer-style courtyard of pebbled walkways, backlit palm trees, and purposely worn furniture. Over the bar hangs a series of clocks giving global times with a political twist, one for Napoleon, another for Gandhi, and so on. This establishment is young, trendy, and cool and does not get going until really late. There is also an adjoining hotel of the same name for revelers who like their bed to be close to the dance floor. Calle La Libertad & Av. Barricada Granada. www.elclub-nicaragua.com. ℂ 505/2552-4245. **No cover charge**

Zoom Bar If you are a homesick North American who craves football and beer, then join your peers at the Zoom Bar. The big-screen TV and American football memorabilia means there are lots of expats around who want to drop out of the Nica life, however momentarily. It claims to be Granada's only real pub and the best place for burgers, both of which are debatable, yet there's no doubting its popularity. La Calzada, 3 blocks from Parque Colón. ℂ 505/8643-5855.

SIDE TRIPS FROM GRANADA

Las Isletas

Trailing away from Granada's southern waterfront is the 354-island archipelago known as Las Isletas, formed by a volcanic eruption from nearby Mombacho over 10,000 years ago. These tiny jungle islands are literally parts of the mountain blown into the lake during a massive eruption. They are now lush mounds that host mini-monkey sanctuaries, humble *campesino* huts and lavish mansions, and attractions such as an island cemetery and an old Spanish fort called **Fortín San Pablo.** It is a popular 1-day excursion, and boats leave frequently from the southern end of the **Complejo Turístico Cocibolca** (p. 105). You can go there independently by taking a taxi or walking a half-hour south along the shore of the Centro Turístico until you reach a building with small pontoons and boats that leave as soon as they fill up. Or take a tour with any of the travel operators in the city center (p. 106).

I found the conventional tour of the islands to be a huge disappointment. Every rock seemed to be sporting a real-estate sign, and the motorboats scared away all wildlife. The quality of restaurants in the touristy parts of the islands leaves a lot to be desired, too, with limited menus and outhouse restrooms (bring your own toilet paper). The true way to enjoy the islands, and avoid the hordes, is to get up early and go farther out in a kayak or private boat. Aquatic birds such as egrets, herons, and cranes can be spotted in the early morning or evening, as well as kingfishers and cormorants. You soon realize that the islands are each a community onto itself with a school, cemetery, restaurants, and bars on individual mounds of basalt topped with tall *ceiba* trees and mango orchards. Though wealthy weekenders have now started buying up their own private slices of paradise (usually on the north side of the archipelago), the vast majority of the islanders are dirt poor and survive on fishing *guapote* and *mojarra* from the dark waters on the south side. This is by far the most interesting part to see. Conventional agencies offer short, unsatisfactory tours of the islands. For something more thorough and interesting, try agencies such as **Nahual Tours** (© **505/8988-2461;** www.nahualtours.com).

Parque Nacional Archipielago Zapatera

A separate archipelago from Las Isletas, known as **Archipiélago Zapatera,** lies 2 hours away from Granada and is famous for its pre-Columbian stone carvings (a spectacular collection of which can be seen in the Convento San Francisco; see p. 107). There are 11 islands in total, the largest of which is **Isla Zapatera,** a dormant volcano covered in both tropical dry and wet forest. Rising to 625m (2,051 ft.), the island boasts lots of wildlife, a crater lake, and more than 20 archaeological sites that date back as far as 500 B.C. The vast range of zoomorphic statues, many of which have been shipped to the mainland and as far off as the Smithsonian Museum in Washington, D.C., reveal that the island was once an important religious site. There is still plenty left behind to see; indeed, there is much more suspected buried underneath, but the government cannot afford to dig. One of the most interesting places is **Zonzapote,** which seems to have been part of an amphitheater or a temple belonging to the Chorotega tribe. There are some great hiking opportunities on the island, including a trek to **Banderas Hill** and a more arduous climb to the island's highest point, **Cerro Grande,** also known as **Zapatera Hill.** Needless to say, the view is spectacular with Ometepe Island in the distance. There is a small settlement of people in Sonzapote, made up of ex-refugees from the Contra war, amongst whom you can find a guide to take you around.

Isla el Muerto is a small island to the north. Its moniker "Death Island" might deter you from visiting, but a little fearlessness will pay off, as it has some of the most spectacular rock drawings in the country. They are all laid out on a huge slab of stone measuring 100×25m (328×82 ft.) on the island's summit. The location is believed to be a burial site, thus the name.

It is wise to visit the islands with a reputable tour agency such as **Oro Travel** or **Tours Nicaragua** (p. 42), the latter of which provides a National Museum archaeologist as a guide to explain the island's many wonders. **Zapatera Tours** (Calle Palmira and La Cancha; © **505/8842-2587**; www.zapateratours.com) offers 1-day tours to the archipelago. Prices start at $40 per person per day, with an overnight option camping on the islands. Otherwise, the archipelago is 40km (25 miles) south of Granada, and reaching it can take an hour or more by *panga*. There is a public boat service from Puerto Asese (© **505/2552-2269**), or you can hire a private boat for between C1,900 and C2,850 round-trip. If you do decide to visit independently, remember this is a national park, and a ranger may ask you for your permit from MARENA, which you can get only in San Salvador. Also, a guide is obligatory to hike the island, and there are no stores to buy supplies, though there are a few very rough, basic lodges and restaurants.

Reserva Natural Volcan Mombacho ★★

Look south from your hotel balcony, and you'll see a mountain with a wide, blunted summit. Look closer, and you'll realize that the summit is in fact the jagged crater of a huge volcano that blew its top 10,000 years ago. Volcán Mombacho is still active, though it has been 500 years since its last significant eruption knocked its side wall out and drained its lake, sweeping away an Indian village called Nandaime in the process. Hidden in its high, dark cloud forest are red-eyed frogs, howler monkeys, orchids, a dazzling array of butterflies, and a species of salamander unique to the mountain. In all, there are 119 types of birds, 60 species of mammals, 10 varieties of amphibians, 28 species of reptiles, and an amazing 30,000 different insects, only 300 of which have been documented and identified. Its lower slopes have given way to coffee plantations and ranches, but its upper reaches are now a protected reserve, with some of the best-maintained nature trails in the country. One such trail is called **Sendero el Crater,** a 2-hour track around the volcano's 1,345m-high (4,413-ft.) rim, during which you'll have ample chances to take in the forest-lined interior and its numerous mammals, birds, and types of flora. During this hike, you will also pass fascinating *fumaroles*—ground vents blasting hot, sulfurous air. More serious hikers should try **Sendero la Puma,** a more arduous trek, as it is twice as long and involves climbing to some lookout points with fantastic views. It takes 3 hours to complete. The volcano actually has five craters, three of which are covered in vegetation. The summits can be quite cloudy but are known to clear in the early afternoon, offering great views of Granada and Las Isletas. To see the most of the abundant wildlife, it is recommended that you stay overnight at the research center and trek in the early morning. Day trippers have to suffice with the abundant flora of the cloud forest, including ferns and bromeliads, as the animals disappear during the day.

The reserve is managed by an NGO called **Fundación Cocibolca** (© **505/2552-5858;** www.mombacho.org) and is open from Tuesday to Sunday, though Tuesday and Wednesday are normally reserved for organized groups. Admission is C200. The most convenient way to visit the reserve is through the numerous travel operators in town that offer 1-day excursions; see p. 106 for info. If you wish to go there independently, jump on a Rivas or Nandaime bus and alight at Empalme el Guanacaste. It is then a half-hour walk uphill to the park entrance. Once you pay the entrance fee, an old army truck leaves every 2 hours to take you up to the foundation's Biological Station 6km (3¾ miles) away. Here, they offer mountain lodge–style accommodations if you wish to spend the night on the side of an active volcano. There is also an interesting model of the volcano explaining its evolution. If you have your own transport (4WD only), there is an extra charge of C300 per vehicle to enter the reserve.

In addition to great hiking, the slopes of Mombacho offer some spectacular canopy runs. **Canopy Tours Mombacho** (© **261/8888-2566**) is located close to the reserve entrance. This 16-platform course is 1,700m (5,577 ft.) long, and many tour operators include it in their 1-day tour of the reserve. Here, you sweep over coffee plantations and tall trees before enjoying a drink on a viewing platform at the end of the ride. The company is not part of the park management, but they pick you up in the same area as the park truck; therefore, you have to enter the park. There is also a spectacular 17-platform canopy system at **Hacienda Cutirre** ★ on the eastern face of the volcano. This is a little more hardcore and challenging, but no less exhilarating. The fact that it was designed by the inventor of the sport means you're in for a heart-stopping ride, including a vertical descent on a rappel line at the end. The site is difficult to access independently and best arranged with travel operators and canopy specialists **Nahual Tours** (© **505/8988-2461**; www.nahualtours.com). A day trip costs C800.

Reserva Silvestre Privada Domitila

Thirty-five kilometers (22 miles) south of Granada, on the lakeshore, there is a private reserve with one of the best examples of rare lowland tropical dry forest in the country. Wild cats and howler monkeys prowl this rustic property, and because it is so small, there is a good chance of catching sight of them. Also ready to pose for any amateur photographers are a vast array of birds, butterflies, and mammals. There is a basic lodge at hand, offering full board and accommodations for a somewhat pricey $65 per person, but it is worth it if you are a nature fanatic. The property can be explored on horseback, and the owners also organize sailing trips to the nearby Zapatera Archipelago, which is just offshore. Day-trippers are charged C110 admission, and it's an additional C220 to C330 for a guide to show you around. The foliage can get a little bare in the summer, so it is best to visit in the rainy season from November to January. The reserve can only be reached by 4WD, and the trip is best arranged with the reserve's agent **Amigo Tours** in the Hotel Colonial (© **261/2552-4080**; www.amigotours.net), or contact the reserve owner María José Mejía directly at Casa Dr. Francisco Barbarena, in Granada (© **261/2552-4548**; www.domitila.org).

Laguna de Apoyo

Directly west of Granada is a huge, pristine volcano lake known as Laguna de Apoyo. This dark blue body of water is 200m (656 ft.) deep and set in a lush, forest-covered circular valley with nature trails, small villages, and the occasional ministerial mansion. The crater is alive with animals, including white-face monkeys, butterflies, toucans, and hummingbirds. The Volcán Apoyo is very much dormant, though it is known to tremor occasionally, and the lake holds some underwater thermal vents.

Standing on the dark, breezy shore of Lago de Nicaragua, you might be forgiven for thinking that this was always just a peaceful backwater. In fact, you're standing on a momentous piece of ground whose formation altered the Americas forever. Five million years ago the earth rose up with volcanic might around and within this body of water, forming an 8,264-sq.-km (3,191-sq.-mile) flood plain. Shifting tectonic plates and molten lava conspired to create what is now the narrow Central American isthmus, splitting the Pacific from the Atlantic and connecting two great continents. This new land bridge allowed wildlife and vegetation, and eventually people (a mere 30,000 years ago), to travel between the two landmasses.

Lago Cocibolca (as it is also known) is the largest lake in Central America and only slightly smaller than Lago Titicaca. It is much lower and shallower than its Bolivian counterpart, averaging 26m (85 ft.) in depth and lying just 32m (105 ft.) above sea level.

The Spanish called it *Mar Dulce* (Sweet Sea), and you can see why, as it is teeming with wildlife of the most unusual kind, including prehistoric garfish, sawfish, and tarpon. Perhaps the most unusual is the freshwater shark that confounded scientists for years. Eventually, they discovered it is a Caribbean bull shark that travels up the rapids of the San Juan River, much the same as salmon jump upriver when migrating. That same river gave Granada the huge historical advantage of being an Atlantic port city despite, somewhat paradoxically, being closer to the Pacific.

With its 450 volcanic islands, some of which were important religious sites for the indigenous tribes who worshiped, sacrificed, and practiced cannibalism on them, the lake is a must-see when traveling through Nicaragua. The least you can do is tour Las Isletas near Granada or the twin volcanoes of Ometepe Island. The truly adventurous make it to the magical monument island of Zapatera or the artistic archipelago of Solentiname.

Alarmingly, the lake's ecosystem is under threat. The sharks are long gone, and there are serious concerns about the pollution from fish farms, raw sewage from settlements, and effluent from factories. Sadly, the sweet sea may not be so sweet for much longer, and Central America will be a lesser place for it.

Because of the lake's isolated habitat, it contains several unique species of fish. There are a handful of restaurants and lodges on the lakeshore, but to truly appreciate the lake's sweeping grandeur, it is best to view it from the rim above, especially from the several *miradores* you come across while touring the Pueblos Blancos (see chapter 7, "Masaya").

GETTING THERE

It's a 20-minute drive from Granada to Laguna de Apoyo, and a C300 taxi ride is the most convenient way of getting there. Alternatively, you can arrange the trip via the hostel **Bearded Monkey** (see earlier in this chapter) or its sister lodge the **Monkey Hut** (see below). Don't think about driving on your own; once you get off the highway from Granada, the road is a beautifully brick-paved lane—an anomaly in a country with such bad roads. But the perfect paving stops after just a few minutes, and the rest of the way makes for very difficult driving.

Another way of getting to the lake is to simply walk from Granada. A dirt road from the city cemetery's northeast corner heads west until you reach a crossroads just below the crater's lip. You must then turn right and cross a field to get a view of the lake. The trek takes approximately 3 hours there and back.

WHERE TO STAY NEAR LAGUNA DE APOYO

There are several hotels and lodges along the lakeshore, many with wooden piers for swimmers and kayakers. Below are the best.

The Monkey Hut The Monkey Hut is the sister lodge to the Bearded Monkey in Granada but has a lot more class. This property's wide, terraced garden, filled with comfy sun loungers, leads down to the shore. Guests stay in a handsome wooden cottage with dorms or a separate cabana. There are also a handful of private rooms to choose from. It makes for a nice, peaceful getaway, with homey qualities like a shared kitchen and basketball court. There is a pier to dive off or set sail from in kayaks or tire tubes that are free to use for guests.

Laguna de Apoyo, 100m (328 ft.) from bottom of hill. www.thebeardedmonkey.com/monkeyhut.htm. © **505/8887-3546.** 15 units. From $10 dorm bed; $23–$25 double; from $45–$70 for la *cabaña* (2-4 persons). AE, DC, MC, V. **Amenities:** Bar; watersports equipment. *In room:* No phone.

San Simian Eco Resort Comprising five ecohuts that descend toward the lake, this resort is perfect for those who want isolation and perhaps a good swim while staying someplace that's sustainable. The accommodations themselves are basic but comfortable. Rooms are situated in palm-roofed cottages and are small with circular, open-air bathrooms (plan on cold showers). There is an herb garden below the restaurant and hammocks around the bar. Though some little annoyances exist, like dragging doors and clasps that don't quite catch, what's more important is that the view is spectacular and there's an abundance of outdoor activities on hand, including kayaks, a small catamaran, and rafts to rent from their minidock.

1km (½ mile) past Norome resort. www.sansimian.com. © **505/8813-6866.** 5 units. From $50 double. AE, MC, V. **Amenities:** Restaurant; bar; watersports equipment. *In room:* Fans.

SAN JUAN DEL SUR & THE SOUTHWEST

T ucked between the Pacific and Lago de Nicaragua is a thin sliver of land that connects two huge continents. The Rivas Isthmus is only 19km (12 miles) wide in some parts and is bordered by Costa Rica to the south. Its western shore is a long string of undeveloped beaches increasingly famous for their surf breaks and deep-sea fishing. Here, you'll find the beach town of San Juan del Sur, which competes with Granada for the foreign dollar, be it from the fun seeker or the property hunter. This once-sleepy fishing village has been transformed into the country's main seaside destination and is a magnet for American retirees. It is also the jumping-off point to explore the many beaches north and south, some with amazing turtle-nesting sites. The dark waves of Lago de Nicaragua lap the eastern shore. In the distance, the majestic island of Ometepe stands in the glittering waters. Its twin volcanic peaks, one of which can explode at any moment, dominate the skyline. This rural backwater offers dark beaches to kayak around, coffee farms to explore, and rock paintings to discover, making it a unique place in a very unique region.

SAN JUAN DEL SUR ★

138km (86 miles) S of Managua; 96km (60 miles) S of Granada; 215km (134 miles) S of Léon .

San Juan del Sur used to be a sleepy little Pacific coast hamlet, until it was discovered by backpackers and surfers as the perfect spot to hang a hammock and enjoy a rum-colored sunset. It is now Nicaragua's top Pacific coast destination for foreign visitors, and its pioneering blond-haired wave riders have gradually given way to silver-haired property seekers. Retirement homes are beginning to dot the surrounding hillsides, and upscale hotels are appearing along the coast. There is now even the occasional cruise ship idling in the bay.

San Juan hasn't completely lost the laid-back charm that attracted travelers here in the first place. And even though, on a weekend night, its tiny bar strip on the northern end of the beach can pound like Ibiza, the town is quiet during the week, and the surrounding area is perfect for beach wandering, leisure sailing, deep-sea fishing, and scuba diving. The town really comes alive for holidays, particularly for its delightful religious flotilla on July 17. The lunar cycles between September and April see a beach party of a different kind—the mass hatching of turtles and their spectacular but treacherous rush to the sea. This takes place just south of the town and has to be one of Nicaragua's most amazing sights.

San Juan del Sur's history is as colorful as its perfect, bay-framed sunset. It was discovered by sailor Andres Niño in 1523 in a vain attempt to find a water passage to the Caribbean. It remained a tiny fishing village until the 1850s, when it became the final staging post for Americans heading west to California via the Caribbean on an overland trip from Lago de Nicaragua. William Walker then used it as a base to invade and eventually flee the region. He was prevented from invading again when the British navy ship the *Vixen* blocked the bay. In the 1970s, the area became the stronghold of legendary rebel Commandant Zero, who beat off Somoza's National Guard and forced them to hastily commandeer fishing boats and flee the port as the Sandinistas advanced from Rivas.

Essentials

GETTING THERE & DEPARTING

BY TAXI/SHUTTLE   The safest, fastest, and most convenient way to get to San Juan del Sur is via a shuttle service that picks you up at your Managua or Granada hotel. **Adelante Express** (© **505/8850-6070;** www.sanjuanvan.com) arranges taxis or vans to and from Managua, with rates that run from C600 to C800, depending on group size.

BY BUS   Buses leave from **Mercado R Huembes** in Managua at 10:30am, 4, and 5:30pm (C75; trip time 3 hr.), but it's a long, bumpy ride with lots of stops. The 4pm is the *expresso* in name only. Buses going to Managua directly leave from the **San Juan del Sur market** (at calles Central and Market) at 5 and 6am daily. There are buses to Rivas every 45 minutes (C30; trip time 1 hr.) between 5am and 5:30pm, where you then catch a connection to Managua and elsewhere. **Central Line S.A.,** half a block west of the market (© **505/2568-2573**), has direct buses to Managua at 10am, going to the Antiguo Cine Cabrera, on Avenida 27 Mayo. The fare is C60.

ORIENTATION & GETTING AROUND

San Juan del Sur is small and easy to explore by foot. Beaches farther north and south can be accessed by boat, taxi, or shuttle bus. **Rana Tours** (© **505/8877-9255**) operates a daily water taxi to Maderas beach at 11am, returning at 5pm. They have a beach kiosk in front of the Hotel Estrella from which the boat departs. A round-trip ticket costs C220. The coastal road to the surrounding beaches is at the moment rough and unpaved, with little to see. It is best traveled in a four-wheel-drive until a very slow paving project is complete. Beaches south of the town can be accessed by a regular bus to the southern town of Ostonial that leaves from the market at 1, 4, and 5pm.

Hostel **Casa Oro,** 1 block west of the plaza (© **505/8458-2415;** www.casaeloro. com), organizes beach shuttles three times a day to Majagual and Maderas beach at 10am, 12:30, and 4pm. The cost is C110 round-trip.

Taxis are easy to catch on any street corner, but always negotiate the price before jumping in.

Alamo (© **505/2277-1117**) has an office in front of the restaurant El Velero in the Hotel Colonial. **Elizabeth's Guesthouse,** 75m (246 ft.) east of Mercado Municipal (© **505/8840-0299**), rents bicycles for C132 per day, as well as double rooms starting at C400.

VISITOR INFORMATION

The tourism office **Centro de Informacion Turistico** (📞 **505/2568-3022**; www. visitanicaragua.com) is located in front of the plaza and is open Monday to Saturday from 8am to 5pm. Although the staff is very helpful, only one person speaks English and works the morning shift. The hostel **Casa Oro**, 1 block west of the plaza (📞 **505/8458-2415**; www. casaeloro.com), does a very good job of keeping people up-to-date with what is going on, what excursions are available, and the ever-changing bus timetable. The website **www.sanjuan delsur.org.ni** gives limited listings; **www.vianica.com** is a more comprehensive site, with information such as hotel addresses and telephone numbers. Two other useful sites are www.sanjuandelsurguide.com and www.sanjuansurf.com.

Fiestas Patronales

The entire town comes alive from June 16 to 24, with fun and frolics such as rodeos, pig chasing, and pole climbing.

[FastFACTS] SAN JUAN DEL SUR

Banks You can exchange money or withdraw cash from ATMs at **Bancentro**, half a block east of El Timón restaurant (📞 **505/2568-2449**), or at **Procredit**, 1 block west of the market (📞 **505/8853-3433**). There is another ATM at BDF a half-block from the Casa de Cultura.

Emergencies Dial 📞 **118** for police, 📞 **115** for fire, and 📞 **128** for an ambulance.

Hospitals The closest hospital is in Rivas, though there is a clinic, **Centro de Salud** (no phone), that will take care of minor ailments. It is 20m (66 ft.) southwest of the Texaco station and is open from 7am to 8pm Monday to Saturday and 8am to noon on Sunday.

Internet You will have no problem finding an Internet cafe, as there is one on every corner, usually providing very slow connections. **Cyber Leo's** (no phone) is one of the better-established internet cafes, a half-block south of El Gato Negro. There is another one at the **Hotel Costa Azul,** 1½ blocks west of the market on Calle Central. The rate per hour is C30.

Laundry **Gaby's,** east of market (📞 **505/8837-7493**), is a laundromat that charges C100 per load. Otherwise, most hotels provide a laundry service.

What to See & Do in San Juan del Sur

San Juan del Sur has little of historical significance to see except the town's old clapboard houses and its simple wooden church, **Parroquia San Juan,** on the main plaza. The **Lighthouse,** a 1-hour trek south of the town, is also worth a visit. You must follow a trail behind the town dock until you turn right. This site has a spectacular view of the sea and coast. Below it, there is a pelican nesting area. On the northern side of town is an excellent **petroglyph** by the river depicting a 1,500-year-old hunting scene. To walk there, take the road to Rivas and turn left after the bridge. Continue walking until you reach a farm where water pipes lead you to the river. Be sure to ask permission, as you must cross private land. Otherwise, contact **Da Fly**

Frog (© 505/8613-4460; tiguacal@cablenet.com.ni), which can include a trek to the petroglyph in their canopy excursion. Farther up the river is a small waterfall.

San Juan del Sur's other main attractions are the beaches and sea, though it must be said, this is not the Caribbean. Contradicting what many property-developer brochures may show you, the water is not turquoise clear, and the beaches here are not dazzling white and lined with endless palm trees. There are lots of water activities to be had, though; see "Outdoor Activities," below, for details.

Refugio de Vida Silvestre La Flor ★★★ Eighteen kilometers (11 miles) south of San Juan del Sur is one of Nicaragua's most fascinating beaches—and that's not because of its breaks or palm trees. Playa La Flor is a 1.6km (1-mile) stretch of wildlife preserve and scene of nighttime *arribades*, or mass turtle hatchings. Twenty thousand olive Ridley turtles nest on the beach every year, and 45 days later, their offspring hatch and break for the water. This happens from July to February, though the best time to see the nesting is in August or September. Always go with a reputable guide and be aware of turtle-watching etiquette, like not using the flash on your camera. Besides turtles, the reserve has an abundance of birds in the estuary and the mangroves at the south end of the beach. To the north, you may see hundreds of hermit crabs scuttling up the beach at sunset. Park rangers give instruction in Spanish, and camping is allowed during the hatching at $25 per night per group. There is a small hut that sells some basic supplies, but it is best to come prepared, especially with insect repellent and a mosquito net. **Hostel Casa Oro,** 1 block west of the plaza (© 505/8458-2415), organizes excellent evening excursions, including a brief pre-tour video explaining the turtle hatching and how to act responsibly while witnessing an unforgettable sight.

Playa El Coco. www.marena.gob.ni. No phone. C220 adults.

THE BEACHES

Surfers put this once-sleepy village on the map, and it's the string of beaches north and south of the town that continues to attract the most visitors. The town's beach is itself slightly disappointing, as the sand is dark and there is no privacy, except sometimes at the northern end. Neither is it suitable for surfing, as there is usually just a gentle swell. If you want big waves and paradise-like isolation, you will have to venture farther up or down the coast. A coastal road is slowly coming together, but for the moment, much of it is a bumpy dirt track. Facilities on these beaches are, in general, limited to a few beach-bum campsites and some high-end lodges. New developments are appearing all the time and in danger of denying land access to the beaches. There is little in the way of stores or bars, so be sure to pack some food and refreshments for the day.

NORTH East of the Texaco station, a road leads to Chocolata. After 7km (4¼ miles), turn left at Chocolata. The road to the right goes to Playa Majagual, and the road to the left goes to Playa Marsella and Playa Madera. Rides are available from any of the surf shops, or catch a water taxi from in front of the Hotel Estrella on the waterfront.

Playa Marsella is one of the beaches closest to town and is popular with day trippers who want to bathe and swim. On weekends, there is a small, casual food stall serving fish and beer. The road comes right up to the beach. **Playa Madera ★** is 30 minutes north by water taxi or car. Here, you'll find a lovely, breezy beach with big ~ves and some good snorkeling opportunities. Popular with surfers and sunset ~hers alike, the beach is accessed by road, and there is room for parking. Some ~-looking surf camps offer cheap bunks and lunches. The more upscale **Buena**

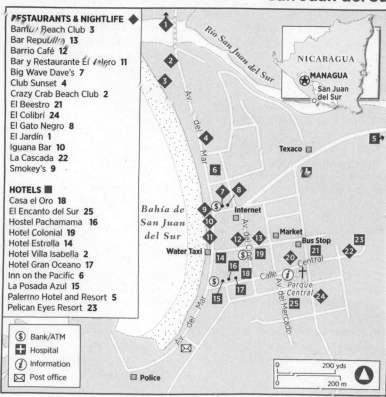

RESTAURANTS & NIGHTLIFE ◆
Barrio Beach Club **3**
Bar Republika **13**
Barrio Café **12**
Bar y Restaurante El Tímpero **11**
Big Wave Dave's **7**
Club Sunset **4**
Crazy Crab Beach Club **2**
El Beestro **21**
El Colibrí **24**
El Gato Negro **8**
El Jardín **1**
Iguana Bar **10**
La Cascada **22**
Smokey's **9**

HOTELS ■
Casa el Oro **18**
El Encanto del Sur **25**
Hostel Pachamama **16**
Hotel Colonial **19**
Hotel Estrella **14**
Hotel Villa Isabella **2**
Hotel Gran Oceano **17**
Inn on the Pacific **6**
La Posada Azul **15**
Palerrno Hotel and Resort **5**
Pelican Eyes Resort **23**

($) Bank/ATM
✚ Hospital
(i) Information
✉ Post office

Vista Surf Club is located on a hilltop overlooking the beach. **Bahía Majagual** is a beautiful cove a little farther to the north, 12km (7½ miles) from San Juan del Sur.

SOUTH A bus service leaves from San Juan del Sur to the southern Pacific town of Ostonial, passing relatively close to many beaches on the way, particularly Playa Yanqui and Playa Coco. The buses depart from the market at 1, 4, and 5pm, returning at 5, 7:30am, and 4pm, and they take 2 to 3 hours to reach Ostonial. Be sure to double-check these times, as they are subject to change.

Playa **Remanso** is the first beach to the south. It has a long shore, which is ideal for exploring and rock hopping. Follow the southern road out of town past the stadium and cemetery. Take the road right at a Y-junction, and you'll find a path to the beach. *Note:* This path has a reputation for robberies, so do not go alone. **Playa Tamarindo** is accessed by walking south for 30 minutes along the rocks. **Playa Hermosa** is a 50-minute walk farther south or a 20-minute stroll from the bus stop at El Carrizal on the main road. **Playa Yanqui** is an expansive beach with powerful waves popular with surfers. It is a 20-minute drive from town. **Playa Coco** ★ 18km (11 miles) south of the town and is the best regarding facilities, with a restaurant, Internet cafe, and several cabins to rent. Close by is the turtle nesting san **La Flor Wildlife Refuge.**

OUTDOOR ACTIVITIES

CANOPY TOURING ★★ Had enough of surf? Fancy tearing across the tree tops at 70kmph (43 mph)? **Da Flying Frog** (© **505/8613-4460**; tiguacal@cablenet.com.ni) specializes in an epic 3.2km (2-mile) canopy ride through the forest that is easily the best in the country. It all takes place on a ranch a small distance from the town on the Chocolata Road. Here, you do a quick tutorial before climbing a hilltop by jeep, where you get a great view of the bay. Sixteen cables connect 17 platforms, the longest of which is 300m (984 ft.). The excursion costs C660, including a pick-up in town. Trekking and horseback riding are also available.

A Beach Bummer

Be aware that some beaches are popular with thieves. Do not leave your belongings unattended, and if you have a car, take advantage of the cheap parking spots on offer by some coastal hostels and restaurants that cost approximately $3.

FISHING ★ The coast offers excellent sea fishing, with marlin, yellow tuna, sail fish, and snapper all available to catch. The best time of the year to fish is April to November. **San Juan Fishing Charter** (© **1-936/522-6723**; www.sanjuanfishingcharter.com) has a boat called the *Aquaholic* that you can rent for a half day or full day for C9,900 or C13,200, respectively.

SAILING ★ San Juan del Sur's surrounding coastland makes the perfect playground for an afternoon on a boat. **Hotel Pelican Eyes** (© **505/2568-2110**) organizes excursions on a 14m (46-ft.) sailboat starting at C760 for a half day and C1,520 for a full day. **Action Tours** (© **505/8843-8157**; www.actiontoursurfnica.com) combines cruising, fishing, and surfing. A full-day trip costs C3,420.

SURFING ★★★ San Juan del Sur has become San Juan del Surf, and you will find many boarders testing the waves on the beaches north and south of what has easily become the surf center of Nicaragua. You can catch good waves all year round but particularly in the rainy season, from March to November, when waves can get as high as 4m (13 ft.). The two big inland lakes ensure there is a constant offshore breeze. The water is warm, averaging 77°F (25°C), but can cool considerably from December to April, when a wetsuit top is a good idea. Beginners are advised to go in the dry season, when the weather is more amenable and the waves average between 1 and 2m (3¼–6½ ft.). Some of the best breaks are accessed by boat only. **Playa Madera** to the north has two left and right breaks and an increasing selection of surf camps. It can get crowded on weekends. **Panga Drops** is a reef break just north of Playa Madera that can be accessed only by boat. **Playa Tamarindo** is probably the best of the beaches south of the town, having a long wave with left and right breaks. Hardcore surfers should go farther north to lose the crowds. Here, a series of beaches are world famous amongst surfers, especially **Popoyo**. Beware of surfing etiquette on each beach, where certain waves are left to the locals to ride and it is considered bad form to hog, especially if you are a beginner. Boards can be hired in town at **Arena Caliente,** beside the market (© **505/8636-1769**; www.arenacaliente.com) for ?20, and lessons are on offer for C700. This outfit can also help you with a lift to ? beach for C95. **Dale Dagger's Surf Nicaragua,** 1 block inland from the ?ado Municipal (© **505/2568-2492**; www.nicasurf.com), is one of the better-established surfing outfitters, offering excursions and weeklong all-inclusive packages for $1,500, including accommodations. It's best to write or call in advance to assure your spot.

OTHER ACTIVITIES

SPANISH CLASSES   Where better to learn the lingo than on the beach? The **Latin American Spanish School,** a half-block east of southwest corner of the central plaza (© **505/8820-2252;** www.nicaspanish.org) offers classes, as well as homestays. The **Spanish School House Rosa Silva,** 50m (164 ft.) west of market (© **505/8682-2938;** www.spanishsilva.com), also offers accommodations and activities.

VOLUNTEER OPPORTUNITIES   San Juan del Sur Biblioteca Móvil (© **505/2568-2338;** www.sjdsbiblioteca.com) was started by the owner of Hotel Villa, Isabella Jane Mirandette, and is supported by the Hester J. Hodgon Libraries for All (www.librariesforall.org). As well as supplying books to the town from a building on the northern corner of the park, it also brings reading material to 27 rural schools in outlying districts. Volunteers can help by teaching English and aiding the mobile library. Books are welcome, as are cash donations.

   Comunidad Connect (© **505/8408-3376;** www.comunidadconnect.org) is a non-profit organization that aims to bring together locals and foreigners to help create sustainable development and poverty alleviation. Projects include a recycling drive, fundraising, and a sports park on the beach. Volunteer programs include homestays and Spanish classes.

YOGA   Nica Yoga (© **505/8400-0255;** www.nicayoga.com) is Nicaragua's first yoga community, located 3km (1¾ miles) north of town on the road to Rivas. Thatched huts surround a hardwood floor communal space. Here, you can take an all-inclusive yoga retreat, with accommodations and surfing excursions provided. Double rooms start at $49 per night, with a minimum stay of 2 nights required.

Shopping in San Juan del Sur

Besides some itinerant boys selling ceramics and some tourist shops selling T-shirts and tat, there is not much to browse in town. **Galeria del Sur Art Gallery** (© **505/2568-2453;** www.galeriadelsur.org) is the only art store in the area, displaying local art, as well as running workshops and art classes. It is located a half-block south of the market and is open weekdays 9am to 7pm, Saturday 9am to 5pm, and Sunday 10am to 3pm.

Holiday Blackouts

If you like creature comforts, make sure to inquire whether your hotel has its own generator; power outages are frequent here, and no electricity often means no water, as well.

Where to Stay in San Juan del Sur

Every rickety town house in San Juan del Sur seems to have a HOSPEDAJE sign, indicating the resident family has some rooms available for budget travelers. The town's more upscale hotels are located on the outskirts or at the northern end of the beach. There are an increasing number of surf camps, beach lodges, gated tourist complexes up and down the coast. Be aware that rates often during Christmas and Easter.

EXPENSIVE

Inn on the Pacific   Its cream-colored, mock-Spanish facade is a touch tacky, but you can't beat this hotel for its beachfront location and comfortable, huge rooms, five of which have large kitchenettes. The lobby is small, dark, and uninviting, but get past that, and you'll find that generally everything is clean and well maintained. Each room has a flat-screen TV and sofa, and the bathrooms are large, if dimly lit. Spacious balconies offer good views of the bay, though they do overlook a busy street that can be noisy.

Av. Costera, 150m (492 ft.) N of Restaurante El Timón. www.innonthepacific.net. © 505/8880-8120. Fax 505/2568-2439. 6 units. From $92 double; from $103 suite; from $126 penthouse; from $126 double suite. Rates include breakfast. AE, DC, MC, V. **Amenities:** Pool. *In room:* A/C, TV, Internet (free), kitchenette (in some).

La Posada Azul ★★   This is the most delightful boutique hotel in town, and it boasts an authentic charm and decor that makes you feel like you've stepped back in time. High ceilings grace neat wooden interiors and an old-world living room. Wicker wardrobes match wicker headboards in the generously sized rooms. The bathrooms are small, but bright and cheerful. The veranda is spectacular; long and wide, it runs the length of the house alongside a lovely flower garden with a fountain and small pool out back. This atmospheric villa was built in 1910 but completely refurbished in December 2007, and everything remains immaculate and top-notch.

Calle Central, 2½ blocks W of Parque Central. www.laposadaazul.com. © 505/2568-2524. 7 units. From $90 double. Rates include breakfast. AE, DC, MC, V. **Amenities:** Pool; *In room:* A/C, Wi-Fi.(free).

Palermo Hotel and Resort ★★ ☺   This is a large, five-star, gated resort with lots of style, comfort, and panoramic views. Manicured lawns surround 50 boxy, condominium-style villas with tiled-roof porches and designer stained walls. The rooms are spacious and immaculate, decked out in hardwood furnishings and local art. Each has an upstairs balcony with beautiful views. The bedrooms have king-size beds and contemporary furnishings spread out across checkered floors that stretch into walk-in closets. The clubhouse is an elegant mix of marble floors, modern sofas, and classical-style tables contrasting with a palm-thatched roof outside. Big windows, glass doors, and tall ceilings allow for lots of light. A fabulous pool and excellent international restaurant complete the equation. Its only fault is its distance from the beaches and town. It's 10 minutes by taxi on the road to La Virgen, but there's a free shuttle service.

Lomas de Palermo. www.villasdepalermo.com. © 505/8672-0859. 50 units. From $350 villa. AE, DC; MC, V. **Amenities:** Restaurant; bar; pool. *In room:* A/C, TV, kitchen.

Pelican Eyes Resort ☝ ☺   This gleaming garden hotel dominates the town's main hillside. Brick steps and white walls rise through the property's gardens and palm trees, and past its large restaurant, La Cascada, before continuing upward to a complex of guest rooms, villa-like cottages, and private homes. The style is big and clunky, with uneven walls and glass tiles adorning open kitchens and expansive bedrooms. These are rooms designed for giants, and they're a bit over-the-top, with a bold, cavernous feel. Farther up, there are a series of pools and the restaurant, all set in lush gardens that are open to the public. The view from the gardens is fantastic. Beware of a 50% cancellation fee if you cancel within 7 days of your stay.

Calle Central, 1½ blocks E of Parque Central. www.pelicaneyesresort.com. © 505/2568-2110. From $270 double; from $270 tp $390 cabins and townhouses.. Rates include breakfast. AE, DC, MC, V. Restaurant; bar; Internet (free); pool. *In room:* A/C, TV, kitchenette.

Don't be fooled by your plush lodge boasting of a private beach. Nicaraguan law is clear when it states that all beaches are open to the public. Unfortunately, some hotels lack a community spirit and deny the public land access to the shore, much to the chagrin of locals who already feel aggrieved at the steep rise in property prices fueled by developers.

MODERATE

El Encanto del Sur   This simple, no-frills hotel is one of the best budget options in town, with a basic no-nonsense decor and a hard-to-beat price. The modern house has a central salon overlooked by an internal balcony with lots of light. The rooms are simple, clean, and appealing, with en suite bathrooms.

2 blocks S of plaza. www.hotelencantodelsur.com. ℂ **505/2568-2222.** 18 units. From $35 double. AE, DC, MC, V. *In room:* A/C, TV.

Hotel Colonial   The large red-brick building belies 12 very small and basic rooms. Brick arches lead to a leafy courtyard and large garden with a wide metal staircase leading to the rooms above. Hammocks and plastic seating dot the property, and the dining room has a colorful, cartoon-style mural of the town. Lack of soap can be irritating, and frequent power cuts seem the norm. The owners are, however, very friendly and will give you a deal if you decide to stay more than 3 nights. Overall, the Colonial is nothing special but an adequate, budget option with a central location.

1 block W & ½ block S of market. www.hotel-nicaragua.com. ℂ **505/2568-2539.** 12 units. From $54 double. Rates include breakfast. AE, DC, MC, V. *In room:* A/C, TV.

Hotel Gran Oceano 🌶   A handsome mansion-style building in the town center, this hotel boasts a huge pool in a landscaped courtyard and an inviting front patio with rocking chairs and beautiful ceramic tile work. However, the standard rooms are not so grand—everything is quite small, including the beds, closets, and bathrooms. Still, rooms are colorful and appealing, and they come at a great price. There are some larger rooms available for more money, as well.

Calle Central, 2½ blocks W of Parque Central. www.hotelgranoceano.com.ni. ℂ **505/2568-2219.** 23 units. From $56 double; from $65 triple. Rates include breakfast. AE, MC, V. **Amenities:** Pool. *In room:* A/C, TV.

Hotel Villa Isabella ★ 💼   This hotel is situated in a handsome house in a leafy area directly behind the town's church. The rooms are generously sized, with two double beds, neat wooden furniture, gleaming white walls, and large ceiling fans; bathrooms are large and pristine. There are apartment-style rooms out back and a medium-size pool. The reception area is large and welcoming, and the adjoining dining room offers great American-style breakfasts (included in the price) that change daily. A generator ensures that there's constant electricity. The American manager Mike is a fount of information regarding the area; he also rents storage space next door.

Calle Central, on the NE corner of Parque Central. www.villaisabellasjds.com. ℂ **505/2568-2568.** 15 units. From $75 double. Rates include breakfast. AE, DC, MC, V. **Amenities:** Pool; Internet (free) *In room:* A/C, TV.

INEXPENSIVE

Casa el Oro ★   Casa el Oro has that colorful, tumbledown feel that's popular with backpacker hostels the world over. This hostel, the best in town, also serves as San Juan del Sur's unofficial tourism office, dispensing info on everything from bus timetables to Spanish classes. You can change traveler's checks, swap books, and organize beach shuttles and turtle-nesting excursions through the proactive owners. They even have a copy of every available restaurant menu for guests to peruse before deciding where to dine. A set of tidy dorms are arranged around a courtyard with an open-air kitchen. There are some private rooms, too, which are small and basic (with shared bathrooms) but comfy.

Calle Central, 1 block W of the plaza. www.casaeloro.com. ✆ **505/2568-2415.** 12 units. $7 dorm bed; from $25 double. AE, DC, MC, V. **Amenities:** Restaurant/bar. *In room:* Fan, no phone.

Hostel Pachamama ★   San Juan del Sur's newest hostel is also the town's party center with a busy, fun loving clientele. The communal areas are modern and spacious, and the two private rooms a bargain, but they require booking well in advance. The American owner Alex is very helpful and will help set up any excursions required. There is a ping pong table up front and lively bar at the back.

Calle Central, 2 blocks W of the plaza. www.hostelpachamama.com. ✆ **505/2568-2043.** 7 units. $8 dorm bed; from $20 double. No credit cards. **Amenities:** Bar. *In room:* Fan, no phone.

Hotel Estrella   This is as ramshackle as you can get. The Estrella is a crumbling corner building facing the beach and claims to be the oldest hotel in San Juan, since it's been in operation since 1929. It's certainly seen better days, but if you're on a tight budget and want to avoid hostels, are looking for a slice of real Nicaragua, and don't mind its derelict decor, this is the place for you. Creaking stairs rise above a small patio out back, leading to some very basic rooms, which have shared bathrooms. Nonetheless, it has character and atmosphere.

Calle Costera, 2 blocks W of the market. hotelestrella1929@hotmail.com. ✆ **505/2568-2210.** 10 units. From $20 double. No credit cards. **Amenities:** Restaurant. *In room:* Fan.

Where to Stay Outside San Juan del Sur

Buena Vista Surf Club ★ 🏕   A hip lodge with a Zen-like vibe, it's set on a hill above Playa Madera, with marvelous views of the beach from an impressive open deck of polished wood. Two tree houses and a suite-style room in the main house are held together by dark, tropical woods and thatched roofs with canopy-style mosquito nets over the beds. The dining area and bar is stylish and impressive, and invites loafing with a chilled-out atmosphere. The food is excellent, with fresh seasonal ingredients. Only nine people can stay at the lodge at any one time, ensuring it remains easy-going, intimate, and laid-back.

Playa Madera. www.buenavistasurfclub.com. ✆ **505/8863-4180.** 5 units. From $95 double. 2-night minimum. No credit cards. **Amenities:** Restaurant; bar; Internet (free); pool. *In room:* A/C.

Empalme a Las Playas ★   This is a jungle lodge with no frills but lots of fronds, bamboo, and wood. Located 6.5km (4 miles) outside of town on the road that leads to Playas Marsella and Maderas, it is set on a hill overlooking the forest. The large, airy cabins sit on stilts and are plain, but attractive and very authentic. Wooden walkways lead to the all-bamboo huts, and wicker chairs go well with solid wooden beds. There are hammocks to roll into and enjoy the jungle sounds of howler monkeys and ds. The English-speaking owners, Roy and Karen, are excellent hosts and an easy introduction into the expat community in the area. They'll encourage you to try your hand at horseshoe throwing. Rustic and basic, the lodge is an enjoyable and very genuine place to stay.

Empalme a las Playas, Chocolata Rd. www.pbase.com/sanjuandelsur/empalme. © **505/8818-3892.** 5 units. From $60 double. Rates include breakfast. No credit cards. **Amenities:** Restaurant; bar.

Mango Rosa ★ 🗲 The Mango Rosa is an upscale resort on the road to Playa Marsella, 7km (4¼ miles) from town. The spacious bungalows are a nice arrangement of white walls, cane ceilings, wicker furniture, and hardwood counters. Lime-green cushions, plants, and pink candles add a sense of style. The bathrooms are long and roomy, with designer stone sinks and tall mirrors. The excellent stepped pool is surrounded by multicolored deck chairs and sand-colored walls. There is a lively bar and grill, and the owner, Greg, will happily set you up with a sunset booze cruise out into the bay. The Mango Rosa is a nice mix of beachside informality and stylish surroundings. The hotel is a 10-minute walk from the beach.

Chocolata Rd. www.mangorosanicaragua.com. © **505/8477-3692.** 6 units. From $95 1-bedroom villa; from $139 2-bedroom villa. AE, DC, MC, V. **Amenities:** Restaurant; bar; pool. *In room:* A/C, TV, Wi-Fi (free).

Morgan's Rock Hacienda and Eco Lodge ★★ Eighteen kilometers (11 miles) north of the town, you'll find a cluster of 15 luxury bungalows, accessed by a 100m (328-ft.) suspension bridge over a tropical gorge. Architecturally stunning with superb attention to detail, the Morgan's Rock combines luxury with environmentally friendly accommodations and has no phones, in-room Internet, or air conditioning. You'll just have to make do with the tremendous infinity pool and the beautiful, deserted Ocotal beach. The bungalows are quite a hike with many steps, but they're delightfully breezy and open. Be sure to request your morning coffee brought to your door in a thermos. The 1,000-hectare (2,471-acre) property includes a private nature reserve, shrimp farm, and sugar processing plant that produces its own rum. Kayaking tours are available, and the farm produces the dairy products, herbs, and vegetables used in the restaurant.

Majagual. www.morgansrock.com. © **505/8670-7676,** or 506/223-26449. 15 units. From $184 double. Rates include breakfast. AE, DC, MC, V. **Amenities:** Restaurant; bar; Internet (free); pool.

Parque Maritimo El Coco The three modern villas here of varying size offer apartments and complete bungalows for rent. The decor is basic and somewhat old-fashioned, with heavy drapes and little ornamentation. However, lots of light and a large veranda ensure a pleasant stay on this beach compound close to Reserva La Flor 18km (11 miles) south of San Juan del Sur. The restaurant Puesta del Sol is also worth a stop if you are in the area (open Wed–Mon 8am–6pm).

Playa El Coco, 18km (11 miles) S of San Juan del Sur. www.playaelcoco.com.ni. © **505/8892-0124.** 9 units. From $152 double. AE, DC, MC, V. **Amenities:** Restaurant/bar; Internet (free); pool. *In room:* A/C, TV, kitchenette.

Where to Eat in San Juan del Sur

In addition to the more formal restaurants reviewed below, you might want to check out one of the many identical thatched-roof restaurants that line the beachfront here. They all serve excellent shrimp and lobster dishes ranging from C300 to C400. Th **Mercado Municipal ★** has a small, cluttered food hall that offers great-val chicken and rice dishes for less than C80 a portion.

The Olive Ridley Comes Out of Its Shell

Foraging dogs, pigs, coyotes, raccoons, and humans are just some of the dangers an Olive Ridley baby turtle faces, and that's before it even hatches. Then, once free of its shell in the sand, it must run to the pounding tide while avoiding vultures, frigate birds, crabs, and dogs. The sea offers cold comfort, as it is awash with preying fish. It's a wonder the harried reptile makes it at all, yet many do triumph and survive, and often swim as far as the Galápagos. The females return a year later to the very same beach to continue the cycle. As many as 20,000 arrive over a couple of days to dig holes with their hind flippers and lay 100 eggs each. A 7-week incubation period follows, during which the sex is determined by the heat; the hotter it is, the more likely the turtles are to be female. Then the eggs hatch again, and the turtles make their precarious nighttime sprint to the sea.

The mass hatchings of the Olive Ridley turtle are a sight to behold, and Nicaragua is one of the best places to see it. **Chacocente** and **La Flor** nature reserves (north and south of San Juan del Sur, respectively) offer the best chance to see this amazing phenomenon. Camping near the nesting areas guarantees a good spectacle, and many lodges and hostels offer nighttime excursions. The best time to see the turtles is from August to October. Caution is advised, as it is a delicate process that can be ruined by a swimming tourist or a flashing camera. Bear in mind that despite being around for 200 million years, the Olive Ridley is now unfortunately an endangered species.

EXPENSIVE

El Beestro ★ INTERNATIONAL   The owner/chef LB runs this gourmet restaurant with the intention of bringing some adventurous, Mediterranean cuisine to the southwestern coast of Nicaragua. This small, modern bistro, opened in 2010, has warm, unfussy design, with bare brick and glass featuring strongly. The menu is full of grill-cooked surprises and includes thin, crusty chorizo pizza, wood-roasted vegetables, and pork flamed with sage. Occasionally, marlin steak is available, as well, in what is always a very agreeable, upscale atmosphere.

½ block W of church. ✆ **505/8369-1935.** Main courses C180–C260. No credit cards. Thurs–Mon 6pm–1am.

El Colibrí ★★ 📷 INTERNATIONAL   This restaurant is as enchanting as its name implies—*el colibrí* is Spanish for hummingbird. Set within a funky-colored clapboard house with a large veranda overlooking a lovely garden, the building itself is a piece of art put together from recycled materials by its Anglo-Irish owner Mary O'Hanlon. Mosaic-framed mirrors hang between stained-glass lamps and African face masks. Elephant woodcuts are illuminated by candelabras, and there are delightful touches like small colored stones that hold down the place mats, lest the sea breeze carry them away. The menu could best be described as adventurous and organic. Hummus dip complements beef kabobs, and the filet mignon comes in a bacon and vodka cream sauce. The homemade pâté is a revelation, made from chicken, bacon, and sherry. Check the chalkboard for the best on offer, as the menu very much seasonal. Laid-back music adds to the overall relaxing atmosphere.

E side of Parque Central, 1 block S of Hotel Villa Isabella. ✆ **505/8863-8612.** Main courses C160. V. Daily 6–11pm.

La Cascada ★ INTERNATIONAL La Cascada is very much like the Pelican Eyes Resort (see earlier in this chapter) it belongs to—it's big, impressive, and somewhat over-the-top. The large, open space is the size of a movie set and doubtless will be used someday in a tropical Hollywood blockbuster. The grandiose thatched roof encompasses a curved bar, spacious dining area, and terrace with a wide-screen view of the bay. There is a pool up front if you fancy a dip between courses. The imaginative menu includes Cajun sausage soup and almond stir-fry, with the usual delicious mix of lobster and shrimp thrown in. The staff is very friendly and speaks English.

Calle Central, 1½ blocks E of Parque Central. www.pelicaneyesresort.com/dining. ✆ **505/2568-2110.** Main courses C180–C280. AE, DC, MC, V. Daily 6:30am–11pm.

MODERATE

Bar y Restaurante El Velero CUBAN/SEAFOOD This Cuban restaurant, situated in a thatched-roof building with an open view of the bay, is typical of the many restaurants that line the beach in town. It is a little down-at-the-heels, but has a nice atmosphere and is the perfect spot for a beer at sunset. Simple lobster and shrimp dishes dominate the menu, and there is a small bar at the back offering beer and rum. The owner José (el Capitán) is often in attendance.

Av. del Mar, 70m (230 ft.) N of the Hotel Estrella. elvelerocontigo@hotmail.com. ✆ **505/2568-2473.** Main courses C130–C200. AE, MC, V. Daily 9am–9pm.

Bambu Beach Club 🖾 MEDITERRANEAN The coolest place in town for a drink and a groove, the Bambu Beach Club is both imaginative restaurant and trendy bar, as well as a hip music venue and occasional cinema. The open-plan lounge overlooks the beach on the northern end of the bay. The Mediterranean-style menu includes open fish sandwiches with pineapple relish and spicy rice salad with mango-orange chutney. Movies are shown twice a week on a white canvas screen hung between palm trees.

N end of bay. www.thebambubeachclub.com. ✆ **505/2568-2101.** Main courses C140–C180. No credit cards. Daily noon–1am.

Barrio Café COFFEEHOUSE Dominating a corner right in the heart of town, this large, busy establishment seems to be where everybody goes for their morning brunch. The noise and bustle spills out from large windows, and there is a back courtyard that makes a nice retreat to nurse a coffee or shake, or indulge in the restaurants specialty, wraps and pastas.

1 block W of Market www.barriocafesanjuan.com. ✆ **505/2568-2294.** Main courses C140–C180. AE, MC, V. Daily 7:30am–10:30pm.

Big Wave Dave's ★ CONTINENTAL The decor at Big Wave Dave's could best be described as "roadhouse meets beach hut"—this rambling but inviting restaurant is inside a yellow wooden shack, with a thatched roof out back. The menu offers comfort food like hamburgers, pasta, and shrimp. There is occasional live music, and the bar comes alive at night, with both expats and locals looking for just what it says on the door: "Cold beer served with a smile." The service is the best in town, and there's even a small book exchange here.

½ block E of Bancentro. ✆ **505/2568-2151.** Main courses C100–C160. No credit cards. Daily 7am–2am.

El Gato Negro ★★ 🏠 CAFE El Gato Negro is the perfect place to while away some hours reading a good book and enjoying great freshly roasted coffee and bagel. This warm, inviting cafe has a long bar, leading to a giant coffee-bean grinder, a attention-getting red walls that are adorned with local photos and paintings. But what really catches your attention here is the extensive book collection, which runs around half the room. Here, you'll find everything from literary novels to airport page-turners to a valuable collection of Nicaraguan history books. *Be warned, however:* Books must be purchased before you can collapse on one of the many sofas and start perusing. There is also a small garden out back if you want to work on your tan while you read. The average paperback costs approximately $15.

1 block E of Timón, next to Big Wave Dave's. © **505/8809-1108.** Main courses C100–C160. AE, DC, MC, V. Daily 7am–3pm.

El Jardín ★ THAI/MEXICAN   This delightful restaurant is located 3km (1¾ miles) north of town, at El Jardín Garden Hotel, but is well worth the trek. The lively Thai-Mexican menu includes Thai beef jerky and cornmeal crêpes. The location itself is delightful, with blue, orange, and yellow walls topped with pink ceilings. If you decide to stay at the hotel, there are 10 medium-size rooms that start at a very reasonable $45. The restaurant is located on Chocolata Road, a dirt road that leads to the northern beaches. After 3km (1¾ miles), a sign indicates El Jardín to the right.

Playa Nacascolo. www.eljardinhotel.com. © **505/8880-4785.** Main courses C160–C280. AE, DC, MC, V. Tues–Sun noon–3pm; Thurs–Sun 5–9pm.

San Juan del Sur After Dark

Like any beach town, San Juan del Sur has its fair share of reveling vacationers enjoying rum and doing extensive research into whether they prefer Victoria or Toña beer. Yet the town's nightlife is pretty sedate and civilized, with just a few bars along the beachfront and two all-night discos. **Iguana Bar** ★, half a block north of El Velero restaurant (© **505/2568-2085**), attracts a lively young crowd of locals and visitors. It is on the beachfront and has a bar upstairs and downstairs. **Bar Republika** (no phone) is a small street bar located a half-block west of the Mercado Municipal. **Club Sunset,** in a green clapboard house on the waterfront (no phone), is open for all-night dancing Friday and Saturday. It has outside seating if the mixture of salsa and reggaeton blaring inside gets to be a little too much. There is a cover charge of C50. **Bambu Beach Club** ★ (© **505/2568-2101**) hosts DJs and bands at its lounge overlooking the beach on the northern end of the bay. At the northern end of restaurant row on the waterfront is a sports bar called **Smokey's** (no phone) that has bamboo walls, a pool table, and some TV screens to watch the latest game. **Crazy Crab Beach Club** (no phone) is a rancho-style disco at the northern end of the beach that packs in both locals and expats every weekend with DJs and occasional live music.

RIVAS

110km (68 miles) S of Managua, 67km (42 miles) S of Granada, 30km (19 miles) N of San Juan del Sur

The bustling yet laid-back market town of Rivas is southern Nicaragua's main city and capital of the province. Though it's not a tourist destination in its own right, this town of 45,000 people serves as a crossroads for travelers from the north who are going south to Costa Rica, west to San Juan del Sur or the beaches close to Tola, or east to the nearby small port of San Jorge, to catch the ferry to Isla de Ometepe. Not many people hang around long enough to savor Rivas' old-world charm, but it is worth taking an afternoon to stroll through its colorful plaza and see the surrounding historic buildings if you connect through it.

This town of mango trees and chattering parakeets has a rich history. It's perhaps best known as the site of William Walker's Waterloo, for the marauding filibusterer was defeated at the Battle of Rivas here in what proved to be the beginning of his end. Some Rivenses, as the locals are known, actually claim to be direct descendants of Walker. Rivas is also the birthplace of Violeta Chamorro, the 1990s-era president who did much to reunite the war-torn country. And Rivas was a major stop on Cornelius Vanderbilt's stagecoach express to the Pacific during the California gold rush. In addition to serving as a key transportation hub, it is now the center of a thriving agricultural hinterland producing corn, rice, beans, sugar cane, and tobacco.

Essentials

GETTING THERE & GETTING AROUND   Buses to Rivas from San Juan del Sur leave every 30 minutes from the bus stop next to the municipal market. Rivas' **bus terminal** (① 505/8453-4333) is 10 blocks west of the Pan-American Highway, next to the market. Buses leave for San Juan del Sur every 45 minutes. The journey time is 1 hour and costs C30. The first bus leaves at 6am and the last at 6pm.

Buses depart for Managua every 25 minutes from 4:30am to 6pm. The ride from Rivas to Managua takes 3 hours and costs C50. Buses leave for Granada every 45 minutes; the trip takes 2 hours and costs C40.

You can catch a taxi to San Juan del Sur from the town center of Rivas. It should not cost more than C160 per person. Shared taxis also go to San Juan del Sur during the day and cost approximately C40 per person.

VISITOR INFORMATION   Exchange money or withdraw cash at **Bancentro,** a half-block east of Iglesia San Francisco (① **505/2563-0001**), or at **Banpro,** in front of Parque Central (① **505/2563-3323**).

The **post office,** northwest of the park (① **505/2563-3600**), also provides a fax service, as does **ENITEL,** 1 block west of the park (① **505/2563-0003**); it's open daily from 7am to 9:40pm. There are a cluster of Internet cafes northwest and west of the park.

Farmacia Rivas, 2 blocks east of park (① **505/2563-4292**), is a well-stocked drugstore, as is **Clínica María Inmaculada,** north side of Parque Central (① **505/2563-3555**). Both are open Monday to Friday from 8am to 4:30pm and Saturday from 8am to noon.

What to See & Do in Rivas

Iglesia Parroquial de San Pedro, 1 block east of the central plaza, is a beautiful but worn-down cathedral with dark stains over its white walls and gilded ledges, along with two very impressive bell towers. It was built in the 18th century and has an interesting mix of architecture styles, with a colonial facade up front and a dome at the rear bearing a colorful fresco that depicts Catholicism conducting a sea battle with secularism and communism and, of course, triumphing. Mass is held here every evening at 6pm. Open hours are daily 7 to 11am and 5 to 8pm. Admission is free. Another interesting church to see is the **Iglesia de San Francisco,** 4 blocks west of Parque Central. Beneath it is a secret tunnel that runs to the city's plaza. The church is open daily from 7 to 11:30am and 5:30 to 8pm. Admission is free.

The town's museum, the **Museo de Historia y Antropología** (3 blocks north of the Iglesia de San Francisco; ① **505/2563-3708**) has an interesting collection of

Crossing the Border into Costa Rica

On Foot or by Bus Peñas Blancas is the main crossing into Costa Rica, and its size and modernity reflect the huge numbers that cross back and forth. Avoid crossing just before major holidays, as crowds of returning Nicaraguans who live in Costa Rica create lengthy delays. Make sure to get stamped on both sides to avoid problems later on. If traveling with an international bus company, an attendant often collects the passports and fees on the bus and does the process for you, though you do have to disembark with your bags to be searched at Customs. A C80 fee is charged when leaving Nicaragua, and a C180 fee is assessed when entering, though these fluctuate slightly if you attempt to cross early in the morning or late at night, when the charges are higher. Be aware of an extra C20 mayor's tax as you enter the Customs area. The border crossing is open from 6am to 10pm every day except Sunday, when it closes at 8pm. Make sure to sell all your córdobas as you leave Nicaragua, as you will not be able to change them farther south.

Buses and taxis are available on both sides if you're not traveling on an express bus.

By Car Rental cars are not allowed to cross the border. To cross with your own car is a little complicated but not impossible. Those going south must pay an exit tax and get an exit stamp. These details are then used to cancel the vehicle papers in the *aduana* (Customs). Without this stamp, you will not be allowed to leave the country, so double-check you have everything in order. If traveling north, go to the *Vehículo Entrando* window, where a permit is issued and a vehicle stamp put in your passport. Title papers, license, passport and insurance are all required to get the permit, which costs C200. Be careful not to lose this document, as its loss incurs a fine of C2,000. Again, double-check that everything is in order, as a zealous official down the road may force you to turn around. Expect your car to get a good dousing in chemicals (for which you'll be charged C10–C20) before being allowed to enter either country.

pre-Columbian artifacts. The building itself is beautiful, with a low, tiled roof and a grassy courtyard. It is a former plantation house that played an important role during the Battle of Rivas, during which William Walker briefly took hold of it. It also has an early published poem by the poet Rubén Darío. The museum is open daily 9am to noon and 2 until 5pm. Admission is C22 adults, C11 children under 16.

Biblioteca Pública de Rivas is the local library and the town's oldest building, with the bullet wounds to prove it. It is open Monday to Friday from 9am to 1pm and 3 to 7pm. **Rivas Cemetery** is a great place to catch a sunset and wander among some ornate graves of important national figures. It's a pleasant stroll southeast of the town.

Refugio de Vida Silvestre Río Escalante Chacocente ★

Nicaragua's southern Pacific coast is a favorite for nesting turtles, and Chacocente Reserve is one of the most important nesting sites. A long stretch of sand is bordered by a tropical dry forest that is teeming with wildlife that includes white-tailed deer and giant iguanas. Facilities are very basic, and it is important that you bring your own supplies if you intend to camp. Very simple bungalows are available to rent at the visitor center. Access is also difficult, as there is only one bus a day from Diriamba and a four-wheel-drive is required in the rainy season. (**Note:** The refuge can be approached from the Pan-American Highway just south of the Río Ochomogo or on the dirt track from Rivas to El Astillero, which takes approximately 90 min.)

El Astillero, Santa Teresa. (𝒞 **505/2532-3293**. $4 adults.

Where to Stay in Rivas

Rivas is not exactly on the "best hotels in the world" circuit, which is not surprising considering that most people opt to base themselves in one of the beachfront paradise hotels in San Juan del Sur or farther up the coast near Tola. Nevertheless, if you do find yourself looking for an inn in town, you could do worse than stay at the **Hotel Nicarao Inn** (𝒞 505/2563-3234; nicaraoinn@turbonett.com.ni). Located 1 block west of the park, it's a modern hotel with comfortable rooms. Doubles start at $70 and include TV and air-conditioning.

Where to Eat in Rivas

Hotel Nicarao Inn (𝒞 505/2563-3234) has the best restaurant in town. The only other decent options are **Chop Suey** (𝒞 505/2563-3235) on the southwest corner of the park and **Pizza Hot** opposite the Iglesia San Pedro. **Café Estilo Libre** is situated north of the Texaco station and has a pleasant outdoor area.

Pacific Beaches Outside Rivas

Farther north of San Juan del Sur and accessed by the road west from Rivas is a long stretch of beaches increasingly famous among surfers. Though much of the coastal road is a dirt track, it is steadily improving, and new hotels and developments are making the area less secluded than it used to be. **Playa Gigante** is the most popular beach with regular weekenders from Rivas an hour away. There are some casual surf camps along the crescent-shaped shoreline, and it gets especially crowded during holidays. Take the Las Salinas bus from Rivas and get off at El Tambor. From there, the beach is a 3km (1¾-mile) walk. **Playa Popoyo** is renowned amongst surfers as having the perfect wave and is considered by many to be the ultimate surf experience in Nicaragua. It can be accessed from a dirt track at Limon or down a paved road from the fishing town of **Las Salinas de Nagualapa,** via the huge, expansive **Playa Guasacate.** Buses leave from Rivas or directly from Managua for El Astillero via Ochomogo.

WHERE TO STAY ON THE PACIFIC COAST

Giant's Foot Surf Lodge   This surf lodge is a large, modern building with a slanted roof and white walls. The rooms are simple in style, holding both single and queen-size beds. A wooden porch with wicker chairs leads to a sandy yard with hammocks and a fire pit for some post-surf bonfires. Accommodations are sold only in packages: A 6-night all-inclusive stay (excluding flights) costs $1,400 per person, including a transfer from Rivas.

Playa Gigante, 17km (11 miles) W of Rivas on the coast N of San Juan del Sur. www.giantsfoot.com. (𝒞 **505/8606-9071.** 6 units. Rates vary w/package. AE, DC, MC, V. **Amenities:** Restaurant; bar. *In room:* A/C, fan.

Punta Teonoste Nature Lodges and Beach Spa ★★   A sister establishment to Managua's Hotel Los Robles, Punta Teonoste raises the bar for beachside accommodations on this stretch of coast. The private bungalows here are situated within a grassy knoll and tropical gardens right on the edge of the beach and the Pacific Ocean. The African-style thatched roofs hide sumptuous duplex villas with bamboo furniture, stone walls, and local artisan-crafted details. The restaurant lounge is a stunning construction of curved wood and soaring thatch held up by a gallery of white pillars. There's a gorgeous pool, as well as a gym and spa, and activities on offer range from fishing to kayaking to surfing to beachfront yoga. Note that it can get windy here. The complex is 30km (19 miles) west of Rivas, close to Salina de Nagualapa.

El Astillero, Tola. www.puntateonoste.com. © 505/2563-9001. 16 units. From $230 double. AE, DC, MC, V. **Amenities:** Bar; restaurant; health club; Internet (in lobby); pool; spa. In room: A/C, TV, kitchenette.

Two Brothers Surf Resort ★★★   The resort comprises a series of neat little cottages with curved walls and rounded eaves and windows set in an 11-hectare (27-acre) private estate. The interior design is sumptuous and eclectic, with artifacts from around the world, such as Indonesian carved doors and mosaics. Gorgeous Spanish-style floor tiles grace stylish rooms with red curtains and wall arches. The bendy veranda pillars frame a perfect view, and the white picket fences open up to a minizoo and stables on the estate. Two Brothers may have been designed for surfers, but it is so gorgeous it suits fishermen, naturalists, ecotourists, and loafers alike.

Las Salinas de Nagualapa, 30km (19 miles) W of Rivas on the coast N of San Juan del Sur. www.two brotherssurf.com. © 505/8877-7501. 4 units. $100–$200 villa. No credit cards. **Amenities:** Restaurant; pool. In room: A/C, fan, kitchenette.

ISLA DE OMETEPE

The twin peaks of the Concepción and Maderas volcanoes rise out of Lago de Nicaragua, forming a muddy jungle island that sustains 35,000 people, countless birdlife, cattle, and howler monkeys. Fireflies dance beneath banana trees as people on old buses, bikes, horses, and even oxen negotiate the rutted roads and countless trails. Rocks carved into zoomorphic figures and pre-Columbian petroglyphs dot the landscape of tropical forest and patchwork fields. The rich, volcanic soil provides abundant bananas, maize, coffee, avocados, and beef, most of which is crammed on the boats that ply the waterway between the island and the mainland port of San Jorge, 1 hour to the west.

The island here, known as Isla de Ometepe, is sacred ground. Legend has it that the Nahuatl tribe fled the Aztecs and went southward in search of a mythical region with two mountains in a lake. There is reason to believe, through the countless artifacts that litter the island, that Nicaragua's pre-Columbian heritage began on the island. In many ways, the islanders remain a people apart from the rest of the country. The turmoil and violence that wracked the mainland for centuries in general bypassed the island, famously referred to by folk singer Luis Enrique Mejia Godoy as "an oasis of peace." The only real drama on the island occurs beneath the ground. In fact, Ometepe used to be two islands before eruptions and lava flow formed the isthmus Istián that now connects both volcanoes. Volcán Concepción is still very much alive, hurling rocks and spewing lava four times in the last century. The last thunderous occasion was in 1957, when the islanders showed their fierce independence and resolutely refused to leave after they were ordered by the government to evacuate.

Their reluctance to leave is understandable. The island is an idyllic adventure spot, a rural retreat, and a hiker's paradise. For many visitors, the peaks beckon to be climbed, but be warned: It is a hard slog and can only be done with a guide. Others prefer just to wander the volcanoes' lower reaches, bathe on the island's dark beaches, cool off in some spring-water pools and waterfalls, or explore the island's many coves and lagoons by foot or kayak.

Essentials
GETTING THERE
BY BOAT **San Jorge** port, 6km (3¾ miles) east of Rivas, is the main departure point to reach the island. The car/passenger *Ferry Ometepe* (© **505/2278-8190;** www.ferryometepenicaragua.com) departs at 7:45 and 10:30am, and at 2:30 and 5:30pm. The fare is C120 per person and C730 per vehicle round-trip, and the crossing takes approximately an hour. Vehicle owners should always call well in advance to book (at least 3 days) and again the day before. Try to get to the dockside office an hour before departure to get your tickets and ensure a spot. The ferry often leaves as soon as it fills up and before the appointed hour. The ferry returns to the mainland from Moyogalpa at 6 and 9am, and at 12:30 and 4pm.

A handful of other boats cross to Moyogalpa, leaving at 9, 9:30, and 11:30am, and at 1:30, 3:30, and 4:30pm. The fare is C30 and, as on the ferry, the passengers are a colorful mix of locals toting cattle, fruit, and whatever else they can get on board. The water can be choppy; it's best to go early in the morning or late in the evening for the smoothest sailing. The smaller boats return to San Jorge from Moyogalpa at 5:30, 6:30, 7, and 11:30am, and at 1:30pm.

You can also get to Ometepe from Granada on a 4-hour voyage that leaves twice a week. The *Mozorola* leaves every Wednesday and Saturday at 11am and docks at Altagracia on the island. It returns every Tuesday and Friday at 11am. The fare is C80. A ferry called the *EPN* leaves Granada every Monday and Thursday at 3pm, stopping in Altagracia before continuing south to San Miguelito and San Carlos. It returns through Altagracia every Tuesday and Friday at 11pm. Be aware, however, that if the sea is rough, the ferry may skip its stop at Altagracia altogether.

GETTING AROUND
ON FOOT The island is a hiker's paradise, with numerous trails, but beware that some of the paths can be rough going, and it is very easy to get lost. You will certainly need a guide for any treks up to the volcanoes.

BY CAR/TAXI If you want to travel around the island independently, you'll have to get a 4WD. **Hotel Ometepetl** rents old Toyotas and Suzukis for approximately C880 for 12 hours. Taxis are plentiful, and drivers will swarm you as soon as you step off the boat, as will touts selling rooms and tours.

A pickup taxi from the port to Santo Domingo beach should cost approximately C360.

BY BUS Old-school buses lumber around the island at hourly intervals between Moyogalpa and Altagracia, and they usually travel in a counterclockwise direction. The fare for these buses is C6. All buses leave directly from the Moyogalpa dock. The journey between the two towns takes 1 hour, and from Altagracia to Balgue, it takes another hour. There are less frequent services to outlying towns like San Ramón and Merida. The bus service on Sunday is much reduced and even sometimes nonexistent. Be warned, these bus journeys can be slow and uncomfortable, and if you are traveling across the isthmus, they can seem to take forever.

VISITOR INFORMATION
There is an **Intur** (no phone) office in the plaza of Altagracia. It is open weekdays from 9am to 1pm and 3 to 5pm. Most of the hotels listed below are good sources of

local information, too. A very good tourist website with lots of information on the history of the island, as well as where to sleep and eat, is **www.visitaometepe.com**.

[FastFACTS] ISLA DE OMETEPE

Banks and ATMs
There are no banks on the island. There is a small credit union in Moyogalpa with an ATM, but it is temperamental and does not accept credit cards or debit cards that are linked to the Maestro program. Across from the credit union there is a *"tienda"* that allows you to take money out on a credit card (MasterCard and Visa), but they charge an extremely large fee. It is better to stuff your wallet in Rivas before boarding the boat.

Hospital **Hospital Moyogalpa** (⌀ **505/2569-4247**) is 3 blocks east of the plaza. Altagracia also has a small **Centro de Salud** (⌀ **505/2552-6089**) on the southeast corner of the town plaza.

Internet For Internet access in Moyogalpa, go to **Arcia Cyber Café** on the main street (no phone). It is open daily from 8am to 9pm. In Altagracia, the **Casa Rural,** on the south side of the plaza (no phone), has Internet service, as does the craft store

Tienda Fashion, 1 block south of the park (no phone).

Post Office There is a **post office** in Altagracia, on the corner of the plaza beside the Museo Ometepe (no phone).

Telephone For phone service, head to **ENITEL** in Moyogalpa, which is 1½ blocks east of the principal street (⌀ **505/2569-4100**), or the **Altagracia** office, which is in front of the plaza beside Museo Ometepe (no phone).

Tour Operators

Ometepe Tours ★, in front of the ferry dock in San Jorge (⌀ **505/2563-4779** in San Jorge or **505/2569-4242** in Moyogalpa), runs an excellent 1-day tour of the island, which leaves San Jorge at 9:30am and arrives back on the mainland by 4:30pm. They also arrange multiday package stays with hotels and transport included. A 1-day tour with a car and driver from San Jorge costs C1,540 for one to four people.

If you decide to trek to the volcanoes, make sure you get a reputable guide (known as a *baqueano*) outfitted with a radio and first-aid kit. Guide quality and prices can vary, so ask around before you decide. **Union Guias de Ometepe** (⌀ **505/8827-7714;** www.ugometepe.com) is a syndicate of 30 local guides that offer full-day and half-day tours of the Island.

What to See & Do on Ometepe

Moyogalpa, on the western side of the island, is a small, quiet town with a sloping main street. The town fountain is a model of the island—it's designed to have water spout from its "volcanoes"—though it has not worked for years. Moyogalpa is the main port that services the island and is a hive of activity when boats arrive. Its pretty, hilltop church is at the top of the main street. It has a white facade and attractive wooden doorways and affords a beautiful view from the bell tower. The town museum **Sala Arqueológica,** 1 block west of the plaza (⌀ **505/2569-4225;** C44 adults), functions half as an artifact display and half as a handicraft store—it sells local crafts

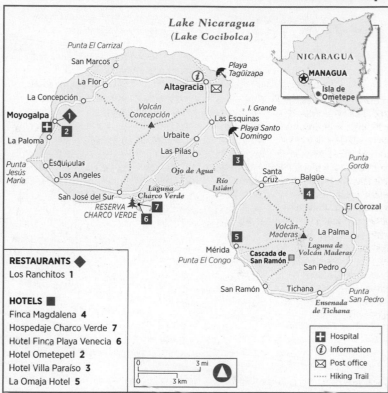

RESTAURANTS ◆
Los Ranchitos **1**

HOTELS ■
Finca Magdalena **4**
Hospedaje Charco Verde **7**
Hotel Finca Playa Venecia **6**
Hotel Ometepetl **2**
Hotel Villa Paraíso **3**
La Omaja Hotel **5**

Hospital
Information
Post office
Hiking Trail

and displays pre-Columbian pieces found by the owner. Both the museum and the shop are open weekdays from 8am to 8pm.

Altagracia is the second-biggest town on the island and a prettier place than Moyogalpa. Its central plaza, known as Parque Central, is a large patch of grass with a shop and playground. The area is famous for its vampire bats, but don't worry, they target only chickens and other small animals. This is where the boats from Granada dock, at a port 3km (1¾ miles) north of the town. **El Museo Ometepe** (1 block from the park; no phone) has some interesting ceramic artifacts found on the island. It is open daily from 9am to noon and 2 to 5pm. Admission is C40. **Playa Taguizapa** is a pleasant beach that's a 30-minute walk east of the plaza.

Five kilometers (3 miles) south of Moyogalpa is the long, sandy peninsula of **Punta Jesús María,** a tranquil beach that offers the opportunity of beer with a sunset. A cab from Moyogalpa should not cost more than C240 each way. Ten kilometers (6¼ miles) east on the islands' underbelly is **Reserva Charco Verde ★**. Here, the jungle rolls down on a black volcanic beach and monkeys howl from the treetops. It is excellent for some bird-watching or for kayaking around the bay or through its green lagoon. Be prepared to get your feet wet, as the wooden walkway has collapsed. Some nearby *hospedajes* offer boat trips and horse-riding excursions.

You don't often get the opportunity to stand beside a lake within a volcano, but you can do so in Isla de Ometepe. However, such bragging rights don't come easy. **Volcán Maderas** may be the smaller of the two volcanoes here, at 1,394m (4,573 ft.), and the most frequently hiked, but it is not easy going. Getting there involves an all-day hike up a steep incline, passing coffee plantations and the occasional pre-Columbian carved stone along the way, and down into its inner rim. This last part requires ropes, so it is imperative that you go with a reputable, fully equipped guide. People who attempt the volcanoes alone can end up lost, injured, or dead. There are two ways of approaching the peak, either through the grounds of Finca Magdalena near Balgue (p. 150; they charge a small fee if you are not a guest) or from the other side at Merida.

Volcán Concepción is the big one—a perfectly formed cone 1,610m (5,282 ft.) high. It's a long and arduous 10 hours up and down, and a different experience from Maderas in the sense that you're walking on a live volcano that could erupt at any time. The last time it rattled its bowels was in 1957, and it has done so four times in the past 100 years. Do the math: It is due for another eruption soon. A thick jungle forest of monkeys and birds gives way to rocks and shale the higher you go here. A stiff wind helps or hinders you along until suddenly the hot sulfurous belch blasts upward from the crater as you reach the rim. This is what forms the almost permanent cloud that clings to the peak. If you're lucky and come on a clear day, you'll be rewarded with the sight of the volcano's chilling stony interior and spectacular views of the island—you'll want to linger and take in its otherworldly atmosphere. La Sabana is the best place to start your climb to Concepción. You can also approach the volcano from a trail behind Altagracia. You must go with a guide, even if you just want to explore the lower reaches, as it's very easy to get lost.

There's a suggested admission fee of C22. From the reserve, you can hike through to an isolated cove called **El Tesoro del Pirata ★**. The two volcanoes stand on either side of this serene and peaceful beach.

However, if it is a real beach you want, you must go to **Playa Santo Domingo.** This 4km (2½-mile) stretch of dark sand, with a green jungle backdrop, connects both islands along the Isthmus Istián. The beach can appear a little tatty in parts but, in general, is very nice and one of the few in the world that can boast a volcano at either end. It's also where the island's best accommodations are located and a great spot for bathing in the shallow waters—the gray-green waters are choppy yet warm and inviting, and there are thatched parasols if the heat gets to be too much. A 30-minute walk up a dirt track beside Villa Paraiso is a bathing complex called **Ojo del Agua ★ (© 505/8664-2788;** www.ojodeaguaometepe.com), a series of rock-lined pools fed by a natural spring and surrounded by tall trees. It can get a little crowded, but it's great fun dangling from the swing ropes and watching suicidal divers jump from crazy heights here. The entrance fee is C44.

Cascada San Ramón is a spectacular 50m (164-ft.) waterfall on the southern slopes of Volcán Madera. To get there, you must go to the small town of San Ramón, 4km (2½ miles) south of Merida. It's a 3-hour hike from there to the falls, but well worth it.

Outdoor Activities

BIKING Volcanic mountains in the area equal lots of slopes, so the island offers some thrilling rides—it is perfect for mountain biking. You can rent bikes from many of the *hospedajes* on the island. **Comercial Arcia,** 2 blocks south of Moyogalpa Church (no phone), also rents bikes, at a rate of C20 an hour.

The east coast of Maderas makes for a particularly good and challenging spin, and along the way, you can stop to see the cave paintings in Tichana and petroglyphs near Corazal. Make sure to get a good bike, as it is tough terrain.

HIKING ★ Besides notching a volcanic peak or two into your belt (see "Climbing Ometepe's Volcanoes," above), the island provides ample opportunities to go for a wander, happen upon ancient pre-Columbian relics, and admire the stunning sunsets. Just pick a path, but remember that much of what you walk upon is private property and, though the islanders in general have no problem with you traipsing across their lands, you should always ask for permission first. Most hotels and lodges have their own set of circuits and interesting things to see close by, one example being the petroglyphs of Finca Magdalena (p. 150).

HORSEBACK RIDING In many ways, horseback riding is the best way to get around this muddy, steep terrain. Indeed, I'm surprised no independent operator is offering rides yet. Ask at your hotel for what they offer regarding saddleback riding.

KAYAKING ★ Reserva Charco Verde is a good spot for paddling. You can rent kayaks to take out there at the nearby **Hospedaje Charcoe Verde** (𝄞 **505/8887-9302**) at hourly rates of C100 for a single and C150 for a double. Another great splash is along the coast north of Merida and up the **Istián River.** It can be tough going if you have the wind against you, but once you get on the river, it makes it all worthwhile. Another less-challenging kayak trip is to **Isla el Congo** south of Merida. Ask at your hotel about kayak rentals for the river Istián and Isla el Congo.

Where to Stay on Ometepe

There are no true luxury hotels on the island. What you get instead are charming, down-to-earth, rustic lodges with slow but friendly service. Moyogalpa has the best concentration of budget options, but my advice is to get out of that town and stay on the island, where there are plenty more places at reasonable rates.

MODERATE

Hotel Villa Paraíso ★ You might have to line up behind a herd of cows on the muddy dirt track leading up to this quite isolated hotel, but the view from your patio hammock will make it all worthwhile. Often cited as the best hotel on the island, the Paraíso offers attractive stone-and-wood cabins perched on a cliff with Volcán Maderas to the right. The rooms are good sized, though the two beds are small and low, and surface areas could be cleaner. Each room comes with a private, rustic bathroom. The restaurant is a mite tacky, with wine barrels set into a concrete bar and a stone mosaic overhead, and service is slow. Still, it offers delicious fresh fish platters, among other dishes.

Playa Santo Domingo. www.villaparaiso.com.ni. 𝄞 **505/2563-4675.** 25 units. From $29 double; from $73 suite; from $73 quadruple. AE, DC, MC, V. **Amenities:** Restaurant; Internet (free); pool. *In room:* A/C, TV.

La Omaja Hotel ☺   On a steep hill with great views of Concepción, La Omaja offers somewhat spartan cabins set amid a lush garden of green lawn, shrubs, and palm trees. The rooms are nice and big, accommodating two good-size double beds. The decor could stand a bit of sprucing up, and the furniture is merely functional, with deck chairs serving as sitting chairs. Only the deluxe and family cabins have private bathrooms. There are no screens on any of the windows, so bring bug repellent.

Merida. www.laomaja.com. ✆ **505/8885-1124.** 6 units. $5 shared cabin bed; from $45 deluxe cabin; from $35 family cabin. AE, DC, MC, V. **Amenities:** Restaurant; Internet (free). *In room:* A/C, fan (in shared cabin), TV.

INEXPENSIVE

Finca Magdalena 👜 ☺   What Finca Magdalena lacks in luxury it makes up for in community spirit and pure heart. It's actually the confiscated property of rich landowners who found themselves on the wrong side during the revolution. It is now a coffee cooperative of 24 families who offer dorm-style accommodations in a huge barnlike hacienda, along with some cottages for those who'd like a little more privacy. There are some closet-size double rooms in the main building. Be prepared for cold showers and communal meals, but also lots of character and a chance to sample a simple farming lifestyle. There's easy access to sites like the Volcán Madera and petroglyphs scattered around the wild garden grounds; but the Finca is quite a long haul from Moyogalpa, 2 hours on the bus followed by a 2km (1¼-mile) walk uphill. Though it lacks the creature comforts of a family resort, it is an idyllic place for kids to roam free. (*Note:* The plantation's coffee and honey are available for purchase.)

Balgue. www.fincamagdalena.com. ✆ **505/8880-2041.** 21 units. $6 dorm bed; $11 double; from $40 cabin. No credit cards. **Amenities:** Restaurant. *In room:* Fan, no phone.

Hospedaje Charco Verde   This hotel is conveniently located right beside the lagoon reserve and offers handsome wooden cabins with lots of light and space. It has a more rural setting than Hotel Ometepetl and is accordingly more rustic. The beds are big and the furniture comfortable, with a nice veranda and hammock. The owners have a farm nearby, and they also rent out kayaks and horses. From here, you can arrange short boat trips to Isla de Quiste or just along the shoreline. There is also a restaurant and bar on the premises that is open to the public.

Charco Verde. www.charcoverde.com.ni. ✆ **505/8887-9302.** 8 units. From $45–$65 double. AE, MC, V. **Amenities:** Restaurant; bike rental. *In room:* A/C or fan.

Hotel Finca Playa Venecia ★ 🍴   This large, hacienda-style property has simple cabins with an excellent location close to the green lagoon of Charco Verde. There is a nice lounge area with hammocks, set in what can best be described as a pastoral paradise. The restaurant is decent, and the owner rents out bikes and horses to explore the area further. Prices range from $15 per person in a triple room with fan, to $25 for a double room with fan, through to $57 for a triple cabin with air-conditioning.

San José del Sur, btw. Moyogalpa & Altagracia. www.fincavenecia.com. ✆ **505/8887-0191.** 8 units. From $15 bed in triple; $25 double; $57 cabana. No credit cards. **Amenities:** Restaurant; bar; bike rental. *In room:* A/C or fan.

Hotel Ometepetl   This hotel is one of the better-established on the island, with a convenient location in the center of Moyogalpa. It has an attractive courtyard, with an effusion of plant life, a large pool, and nice lounging areas with giant hammocks. Chunky wooden furniture sits on tiled floors that lead to pleasant-size rooms with private bathrooms. The open-air restaurant has lots of light and white tablecloths on the tables. Service can be mixed, however, and the air-conditioning problematic. The hotel also offers jeep rentals and is the only place on the island that accepts traveler's checks.

Moyogalpa, 50m (164 ft.) uphill from port. © **505/2569-4276.** 12 units. From $254 double; from $34 triple; from $52 quadruple. AE, DC, MC, V. **Amenities:** Pool. *In room:* A/C or fan.

Where to Eat on Ometepe

All the better hotels in town have restaurants, so you should not have to wander too far for a meal. **Restaurant Villa Paraiso,** in the Hotel Villa Paraiso (© **505/2563-4675**), is one of the best hotel restaurants. It serves international fare and is open daily from 7am to 9pm, serving breakfast, lunch, and dinner. Main courses start at C200. **Restaurante Charco Verde ★**, in the Hospedaje Charco Verde (© **505/8887-9302**), is another pleasant hotel restaurant offering a wide variety of food, such as pasta, steak, and giant filet of fish. The dining area is set under a large wooden roof with open walls. It is open daily from 7am to 8pm. Meals start at C190. Finally, you may want to try **Restaurante Ometepetl** (© **505/2569-4132**) in the hotel of the same name. It has a pleasant open-front dining area and serves Nicaraguan staples. It's open daily from 6am to 10pm. Meals start at C160.

Los Ranchitos NICARAGUAN   For a non-hotel restaurant, try this spot in Moyogalpa, which offers inexpensive fare in an open-air setting. It's popular with both locals and visitors, and the menu includes everything from pizza to fish served in huge portions. The restaurant also offers a taxi service if you've gorged on too many fried plantains and can't walk home.

4 blocks uphill from the dock & ½ block S, Moyogalpa. © **505/2569-4112.** Main courses from C120. No credit cards. Daily 7am–9pm.

SOLENTINAME ISLANDS AND THE RIO SAN JUAN

10

Imagine a rainforest that has more species of flora and fauna in several square kilometers than the whole of Europe; a river that carries more fresh water in 1 day than is needed by Central America in an entire year; a nature reserve crisscrossed by rivers that make the jungle a floating gallery of exotic birds and animals; and an archipelago of islands completely peopled by artists inspired by a rebel priest. You don't have to imagine; just go to southeastern Nicaragua.

The Río San Juan floats through a mini-Amazon that is the heart and lungs of Central America. Guarded jealously by the Spanish, attacked by the British, plundered by pirates, and coveted by the Costa Ricans, this area is as rich in history as it is in nature. The psychedelic colors of the jungle are captured in the naïve paintings that emanate from the Solentiname Islands on Lago de Nicaragua, a huge draw for artists, as well as bird-watchers and nature lovers. Nature reserves such as Indio-Maíz and Los Guatazos offer the opportunity to experience a genuine rainforest up close in all its jaw-dropping glory.

Tourists to this area used to be as rare as the jaguar that prowls its vine-draped interior. Now the word is out, and this isolated region is beginning to attract adventurous nature lovers. Lodges are springing up around the river fort of El Castillo, and tour companies offer bird-watching, fishing, and jungle excursions along the river. However, constant rain, muddy paths, and primitive transportation in single-propeller planes and long canoes mean there is no danger of this becoming another Costa Rica. At least, not yet.

SAN CARLOS

San Carlos is the embarkation point for boats to the splendor of the Solentiname Islands, Los Guatuzos Wildlife Reserve, and the majestic Río San Juan. However, San Carlos itself is not a place in which you want to spend any time. Make sure you arrive early in the day so you have time to make

your connection and get out of town; there's not much to see here, and the choice of hotels is limited to two-bit flea joints.

When you arrive, you'll first see filthy, tin-topped shacks that run down the side of hill to a pleasant waterfront which overlooks the "Sweet Sea" (Lake Nicaragua) flowing into the grand Rio San Juan. San Carlos used to be one of Nicaragua's ugliest human settlements until it got something of a facelift along its waterfront, the *malecon*, in 2010. Relighting and repaving can do only so much, however, and sleazy hotels and rowdy bars still line its rougher streets, playing host to the multitude of transients that pass through on their way to somewhere else. Migrant workers, soldiers, ranchers, fishermen, and renegades all converge on what is the sultry, isolated capital of a sultry and isolated region. They are here because this ramshackle river town of 6,000 people is a major transportation hub, the gateway to the jungle of the east and Costa Rica to the south. It's also the end of the line for all buses that travel the grueling 9-hour trip from Managua on wet, rutted roads that would challenge a tank, never mind an ancient school bus with KENNEDY HIGH in faded lettering on the side.

San Carlos's superb location at the mouth of the Río San Juan that flows from Lago de Nicaragua to the Caribbean means it controls a waterway that almost connects two vast oceans. As Hernán Cortés told the Spanish king in 1524, "He who possesses the

Río San Juan, possesses the world." San Carlos was thus founded in 1526, and a fort was built to guard the waterway and support the larger fort of El Castillo further downriver. Increased trade and its use as a changeover stop for Vanderbilt's gold-rush service meant the town took on the resemblance of 19th-century prosperity, with paved streets and colonial mansions. Trouble was never far off, however, be it from marauding pirates, William Walker's mercenaries, or bloody skirmishes with the local Guatuzo tribe, who were aggrieved that rubber tappers were encroaching on their land. Eventually, the settlers massacred the Indians or illegally traded them as slaves. The steamboat trade disappeared, the rubber price collapsed, and San Carlos' boom was over. Intermittent fighting between Somoza's National Guard and the Sandinistas in the 1970s was followed by a river war between the Sandinistas and the Contras in the 1980s.

Today, the only trouble is the occasional robbery or bar brawl, and diplomatic tiffs with Costa Rica to the south, which has always coveted the Río San Juan.

Essentials

GETTING THERE

BY PLANE   The fastest and most sensible way to get to San Carlos is to catch a small plane from Managua. **La Costeña** (✆ **505/2263-1228** in Managua or 505/2583-0271 in San Carlos; www.lacostena.com.ni) operates two daily "puddle jumper" flights that land at the town's scruffy airport's dirt-track runway. The flights leave Managua at 9am and 1pm Monday to Friday, 9am on Saturday, and 1:30pm on Sunday. They depart from San Carlos at 9:25am and 2:25pm Monday to Friday, 9:25am on Saturday, and 2:25pm on Sunday. *Note:* These schedules frequently change; always double-check the day before your flight. The journey takes 1 hour and costs approximately $126 round-trip. On a clear day, the flight is spectacular, with breathtaking views of Volcán Masaya, Granada, Las Isletas, and Solentiname. Flights should be booked well in advance and reconfirmed the day before. It is wise to turn up early, as overbooking is common and seats are limited. The airport is a 30-minute walk from the town center or C20 by rattling taxi over a pockmarked road.

BY BOAT   A ferry called the *EPN* ((✆ **505/2552-2966**; www.epn.com.ni) leaves Granada every Monday and Thursday at 2pm, stopping in Altagracia on Isla de Ometepe before continuing south to San Miguelito and San Carlos. It arrives in San Carlos at 5am the next day. It is wise to get to the ticket office 2 hours before departure. First-class seats cost C190 one-way and are on the upstairs deck, which is air-conditioned. Second class is on the lower deck, without air-conditioning, and costs C80 one-way. The ferry returns through Altagracia every Tuesday and Friday at 3pm. Be aware, however, that if the sea is rough, it may skip its stop at Altagracia altogether. There are also three boats a day that leave from the Costa Rican town of Los Chiles. Departure times are 7am, and 1 and 3pm, but these are liable to frequent changes. The 2-hour trip costs C160.

BY BUS The bus trip from Managua to San Carlos is a 300km (186-mile) epic journey and a supreme test of endurance. The road is in a terrible condition for much of the way, and the bus ride is a bone-shaking one and travels at a snail's pace. This is purely for people on a strict budget with lots of time on their hands. Buses leave from Managua's Mayoreo Market at 8 and 11:45am. The fare is C200. During bad weather, the road closes completely. San Carlos' bus station is close to the town center by the main dock. It is actually easier to reach San Carlos from Costa Rica. The 3½-hour bus journey from San José to Los Chiles costs C152. From there, you can catch a boat for a 2-hour trip upriver to San Carlos, for which the fare is C220.

GETTING AROUND

The town itself is easily walked. Taxis cost C20. River boats, known as *pangas,* ferry people between the islands and riverside settlements. They are cheap but infrequent. The private boats are much more expensive, but convenient. A 1-hour trip to the Solentiname Islands costs C2,400, a 1½ hour trip downriver to El Castillo costs C3,600. The more passengers there are, the cheaper it is per person.

VISITOR INFORMATION

The **San Carlos Intur office,** Malecón (*©* **505/2583-0301** or 505/2583-0363), has Spanish-speaking staff and brochures, and can help arrange transport to the archipelago or El Castillo. It's open Monday to Friday from 8am to noon and 2 to 5pm. There is also a tourist info kiosk on the waterfront (no phone) that is open daily from 10am to 6pm. Another excellent source of information is **Doña María Amelia Gross** (*©* **505/2583-0271**), who runs the La Costeña office in San Carlos. For updated boat schedules, go to the ticket office at the entrance to the dock.

What to See and Do in San Carlos

If you do find yourself with some time to kill between boats and planes, go to the **Spanish Fort.** Renovated in 2005, it has a library, museum, and cultural center that lay out in detail the town's tumultuous history. Mark Twain passed through here in 1866, referring to the town as Fort San Carlos, implying there was nothing else here. It is open from 9am to noon and 2 to 5pm. The **Mirador,** 1½ blocks south of the church (*©* **505/2583-0377**), is a cannon-adorned lookout point and restaurant with commanding views of the lake that go all the way to Solentiname. It is easily the best restaurant in town and serves chicken, fish, and beef. It is open daily from 7am to 8pm.

Where to Stay in San Carlos

If you find yourself trapped in this grubby little place, the two best hotels are **Hotel Carelys,** ½ block south of the church (*©* **505/2583-0389**), and **Cabinas Leyko,** 2 blocks east of the police station (*©* **505/2583-0354**). Very basic rooms range from $20 to $50.

THE SOLENTINAME ARCHIPELAGO

The Solentiname Archipelago is a scattering of 36 islands in the southern corner of Lago de Nicaragua. Geographically, it is an isolated, tropical backwater, but historically and culturally, it is the nucleus of Nicaragua's world-famous primitive art movement and a hotbed of liberation theology. That's due mainly to poet and priest Ernesto

Cardenal, who came here in the late 1960s and encouraged ordinary islanders to pick up a paint brush and paint what they saw. The result was astounding—vibrant renditions in oil and balsa wood of the islands' nature and people. Complete families became artists, and by the early 1970s TV crews were coming to make documentaries about the phenomenon. Only 750 people live on the islands today, but they act as hosts to hundreds of tourists every year who come to paint, observe, or study the region's rich natural wonders.

Cash Economy

There is only one ATM in San Carlos, located on the refurbished waterfront, and most places do not accept credit cards. Be sure to have cash on hand for expenses.

There are no roads, electricity, telephones, or running water. The islands may be just 2 hours away from the modern squalor of San Carlos, but they might as well be another world, abundant with pristine beauty and simple, primitive living. Dry shrub land runs into dense rainforest, punctuated by open meadows and avocado farms. There is ample wildlife with excellent fishing and bird-watching, as well as trekking and boating.

Essentials
GETTING THERE
BY BOAT   Getting to Solentiname is not easy and is particularly grueling if you are on a budget. The fastest, but most expensive way, is to catch a plane from Managua to San Carlos, and then take the 2-hour boat ride to the dock in Mancarrón. The scheduled boat from San Carlos leaves on Tuesdays and Fridays at 12:30pm, returning on the same days at 4:30pm. It stops at Isla Donald Guevara (also known as Isla la Venada), Isla Elvis Chavarría (also known as Isla San Fernando), and Isla Mancarrón. The cost is C100. Private boats can be arranged, but expect to pay C2,400 each way. You can arrange this directly with a dockside boat owner (*panguero*) or book in advance through **Intur** Malecón, San Carlos (© **505/2583-0301**), or through **Armando Ortiz's Viajes Turísticos,** by the Western Union (© **505/2583-0039**).

GETTING AROUND
Only 2 of the 36 islands have tourist facilities. They are **Isla Mancarrón** and **Isla Elvis Chavarría** (also known as Isla San Fernando). **Isla Mancarroncito** and **Isla Donald Guevara** (also known as Isla la Venada) are the only two other populated islands. Getting around between islands is a major problem. Cheap *colectivo* water taxis that cost C60 run twice a week between these islands; this means you have a minimum stay of 3 days if you're dependent on public transport. You can, of course, charter your own *panga,* at a price—in general, gas is much more expensive in this part of the country. There is a definite advantage to organizing a package trip with a tour company, including transportation, accommodations, and a guide. Independent travelers will need to allot lots of time and adopt a flexible attitude about getting around. Private boats are also twice as fast as the public launches. By the end of your trip, you'll be used to sitting on 6m (20-ft.) canoes in the rain, with a motor engine going full throttle and drowning out any conversation.

VISITOR INFORMATION
There is no tourist information office on the islands, but lodge owners such as María Guevara at **Albergue Celentiname** (© **505/8893-1977**) are more than happy to

help with any queries. Another source of info is **Doña María Amelia Gross** (© 505/2583-0271), who runs the La Costeña office in San Carlos. The **San Carlos Intur office** (Malecón; © 505/2583-0301 or 505/2583-0363; www. solentiname.org), can help arrange transport to the archipelago. It's open weekdays from 8am to noon and 2 to 5pm.

TOUR OPERATORS & TRAVEL AGENCIES

MUSAS (El Museo Archipiélago de Solentiname), organizes 4-day tours of the archipelago, including accommodations and transportation from San Carlos. They can be contacted through their San Carlos office (© 505/2583-0095) or ACRA in Managua (© 505/2249-6176). Prices depend on group size, but expect to pay at least C6,000 for a 4-day tour.

    Solentiname Tours (Apartado Postal 1388, Managua; © 505/2270-9981; www.solentinametours.com) offers countrywide tours, including several days on the islands and down the Río San Juan. **Tours Nicaragua** (Centro Richardson, next to the Nicaraguan central Bank, Managua; © 505w www.toursnicaragua.com) also offers packages on the islands.

What to See & Do in the Solentiname Islands

Visiting the Solentiname Islands requires you to switch frequencies and slow right down. There are zero facilities on these islands except glorious Mother Nature in all her splendor.

ISLA MANCARRON

Mancarrón is the main island. Only 200 people live on its 20 sq. km (7¾ sq. miles) of lush green vegetation, with the 260m-high (853-ft.) Cerro Las Cuevas dominating the waterline. Close to the dock there is a collection of houses and the interesting **Iglesia Solentiname** ★ designed by Ernesto Cardenal. This tiny adobe building is probably the most colorful and quirky church you'll see in Nicaragua, with playful images set on its white walls and a simple altar with pre-Columbian patterns. It was here that Ernesto Cardenal began his project in the 1960s to bring art to the islands, and it displays the first oil painting made on Solentiname, an aerial view of the island. Outside, there is a Sandinista monument and the tomb of the rebel leader Alejandro Guevara. Close by is the **APDS** complex. This is the local development association, and here they have a display room holding books, art, and artifacts about the islands, including info on their artists and Ernesto Cardenal. The village has two small stores that sell snacks and refreshments, and there are several artists' studios you can visit. Ask for a guide to take you to the island's *mirador,* which has commanding views of the archipelago. There is an abundance of birdlife, including parrots and a yellow-tailed blackbird called *Montezuma oropendulas* that lives in long nests that hang from tree branches. The island is famous for a type of palm tree that produces sweet palm wine; thus the local name for palm tree is *mancarrón.*

LA ISLA ELVIS CHAVARRIA

La Isla Elvis Chavarría is named after a young martyr killed during the revolution. Also known as San Fernando, it is the archipelago's second-biggest island and has a sizeable community with a school and a health clinic. **El Museo Archipiélago de Solentiname,** or MUSA (© 505/2583-0095), is a museum, art gallery, library, information point, medicine garden, and arboretum. Just follow the butterflies and hummingbirds up the garden path behind the village, and you'll find it. The museum is open daily from 7am to noon and 2 to 5pm. Admission is C40. It has a great view of the islands and is a good spot to catch the sunset.

LA ISLA DONALD GUEVARA

Also known as La Venada, this long, narrow island is home to **La Cueva del Duende,** an underwater cave of mythological importance to the islanders, primarily the Guatuzu tribe. They believed that it was the path to the other side, and marked on the walls are representations of the dead. It is located on the northern side of the island and is only accessible by boat and in the dry season (Mar and Apr).

The Arellano family lives on the southwestern side of the island and opens their home to guests. You can purchase their work and rent a bed here for the night for C200. You will need a guide to find the house.

OTHER ISLANDS

Mancarroncito is one of the archipelago's wilder, untouched islands with a 100m-high (328-ft.) peak shrouded in thick green jungle. This is a good place for hiking, but it is advisable to go with a guide. **Zapote** is a bird sanctuary with a colony of 20,000 birds—it gets noisy here, especially during the dry season. Species include herons, egrets, spoonbills, and storks. **El Padre** is just as noisy because of its boisterous howler monkey community. A pair was introduced here in the early 1980s, and they found the tree-covered island perfect to reproduce. It is now home to some 50 monkeys. East of El Padre, **Isla la Atravesada** has done much the same with crocodiles. North of Mancarrón, a small island inlet holds the wreck of a 19th-century steamship. All that's left is the chimney poking above the waterline and covered in vegetation.

> ### The Fishing Bat
>
> One of the most arresting nature sights on the islands is the fishing bat. It glides above the water at night with its claws dragging through the water hoping to snag an unsuspecting fish.

Where to Stay in the Solentiname Islands

There are many families on both **Isla Mancarrón** and **Isla Elvis Chavarría** that open their doors to strangers and rent rooms in a homestay fashion. Look around for signs posted outside these houses. Bear in mind that wherever you choose to stay will also be where you will eat, as the islands have no dining scene. **El Buen Amigo,** located in the community center on Isla Mancarrón (**©** **505/8869-6619**), offers basic rooms for $12 per person. **Villa Esperanza,** next to the community center on Isla Mancarrón (**©** **505/2583-9020**), is a step up in comfort and offers rooms for $25 per person.

MODERATE

Hotel Mancarrón   These are by far the plushest accommodations you'll get on the archipelago. The property, made up of homes with red roof tiles and white adobe walls, sits up in a 3-hectare (7½-acre) site that is bordered by forest and lakes. Rooms are simple, spacious, and overlook the dock. A large dining room with a bar is on-site. All water is heated by solar energy, though there is also a backup generator. The hotel organizes excursions to local artists' workshops and will arrange art lessons for those who want to capture the island's colors.

Isla Elvis Chavarría. hmancarrun@ibw.com.ni. ✆ **505/2583-9015** or 505/2583-0083. 12 units. From $35 double; from $45 triple; $50 quadruple. No credit cards. **Amenities:** Restaurant/bar. *In room:* Fan, no phone.

INEXPENSIVE

Albergue Celentiname   Located on the western edge of La Elvis, this family-run lodge has been in operation since 1984 and provides rustic cabins with shared bathrooms. It has a waterfront setting and great views of the islands, volcanoes, and the Costa Rican border. The cabins are basic and a little dark, but are clean and come with an all-important hammock and small porch. There's an attractive restaurant on the grounds. The hospitality of the hosts is what really makes this place memorable; Doña María Guevara and her family are all painters and are enthusiastic in sharing the delights of the island. You also can't beat the lodge when it comes to providing an ultimate jungle experience—you'll be surrounded by a cacophony of wildlife sounds at most times.

Isla San Fernando. ✆ **505/2276-1910.** 8 units. $60 double w/shared bathroom. No credit cards. **Amenities:** Restaurant. *In room:* Fan, no phone.

REFUGIO DE VIDA SILVESTRE LOS GUATUZOS ★★

Suddenly, the discomfort of your journey is completely forgotten. You are standing in one of the most beautiful and abundant wildlife parks in Central America. Or more like floating, as much of this 440-sq.-km (170-sq.-mile) park is lush wetland, fed by 13 rivers, with the **Río Papaturro** the most densely packed with jungle wildlife. The wildlife of Los Guatuzos Refuge is simply spectacular and more visible than in other parks because those many rivers act as the perfect viewing galleries to float down and penetrate the jungle without disturbing the dazzling population as they go about their business. Howler monkeys are the most obvious, and the noisiest, occupants, but white-faced and spider monkeys can also be spotted. Jesus Christ lizards dash across the water on their hind legs while caimans, turtles, and iguanas bathe in the sun. Sloths sleep in the trees while jaguars lurk in the foliage. Birds include spoonbills, storks, laughing falcons, egrets, and herons. There are six species of parrots and five species of kingfishers. In the water prowls a Jurassic-era fish called the *gaspar*, complete with armored scales and fangs. It floats on the water like a log and attacks crabs and turtles.

Situated on a strip of land that lies between the shore of Lago de Nicaragua and the Costa Rican border, the park's history is tragic and its existence accidental. Fifteen-hundred people live here in 11 small communities. They are originally from the Guatuzo tribe, so called by the Spanish because they painted their faces red like the color of a tropical rodent known as a *guatuza*. They called themselves *Maleku*. Nineteenth-century migrant rubber cutters almost wiped them out when they traded them as slaves for 60 pesos a head to the mines in Chontales. The rubber market collapsed and put an end to that business. Cacao farmers and loggers were a 20th-century threat, but the war paralyzed everything, and the natives fled to Costa Rica. When they returned in the 1990s, they found a pristine jungle. Thankfully, somebody had the sense to declare it a protected site, and it now survives with sustainable fishing, farming, and tourism.

Getting There

A boat leaves from the western dock in San Carlos at 7am every Monday, Tuesday, and Thursday, stopping at Papaturro settlement. It takes 4 hours and costs C70. A private boat holding up to 10 people costs C2,400 and takes 1½ hours.

Where to Stay in Refugio de Vida Silvestre los Guatuzos

Centro Ecológico de los Guatuzos 🎁 This research center and guesthouse is located on the Río Papaturro, 4 hours from San Juan. There are two eight-bed dorms in a basic but attractive wooden chalet. The *centro* offers guided tours of the refuge, including bird-watching, kayaking, fishing, boat excursions, and night tours. There is an orchid farm with more than 100 species, including the smallest orchid in the world, as well as a somewhat dilapidated butterfly farm, a turtle nursery, and a caiman breeding center. Above, there is a system of platforms linked by shaky canopy bridges that allow you to view the upper reaches of the rainforest and avoid the persistent mosquitoes below. The manager, Armando, is an excellent guide with extensive knowledge of the area. English-language tours must be arranged in advance or through an agency, as there is normally no English-speaking guide at the center. Tours cost C220 per person, and meals can be arranged in the nearby village for C80. Private transport from San Carlos can also be arranged.

Río Papaturro. www.losguatuzos.com. 📞 **505/2270-3561** in Managua. 2 units. $11 dorm bed. No credit cards.

Esperanza Verde A 280-hectare (692-acre) private reserve that sits on the eastern fringe of Los Guatuzos refuge, 15 minutes by boat from San Carlos. There are six basic rooms with 20 single beds and shared bathrooms. Located in an open clearing along the Río Frío, the rainforest is a 40-minute walk from the lodge, with three hiking trails to explore. Boat excursions can also be arranged. For more information and bookings, drop into the **Fundeverde** office at the **Hotel Cabinas Leyko,** 2 blocks east of the police station in San Carlos (📞 **505/2583-0127;** www.fundeverde.org). To get to Esperanza Verde independently, take the Los Chiles boat down the Río Frío that leaves everyday at 10am, noon, and 3pm.

Río Frío, 4km (2½ miles) from San Carlos. www.fundeverde.org. 📞 **505/2583-0354,** or 505/2277-3482 in Managua. 6 units. $30 dorm bed. Rates include full board & transfer. No credit cards. *In room:* Fan.

THE RIO SAN JUAN ★★

This is a mighty river, a broad, majestic, expanse of fresh water that pours slowly out of Lago de Nicaragua towards the Atlantic Ocean 210km (130 miles) away. It passes rainforests and cattle ranches, stilted shacks on the water, and quiet river lodges. It widens in parts to 350m (1,148 ft.), and in other areas, it narrows into treacherous rapids, particularly at the 300-year-old Spanish fort of El Castillo. More than 25 rivers flow into the San Juan from the Nicaraguan and Costa Rican shorelines, and it forms the border between the two countries from El Castillo to the Atlantic estuary. Needless to say, the shoreline teems with wildlife, especially at the mammoth Indio-Maíz Biological Reserve on the Nicaraguan side. The ghost town of Greytown lies at the end, as does its rebranded and relocated sister town San Juan del Norte.

The Rama tribe lived here before the Spanish arrived, and some remain in Indio-Maíz reserve and on a small island in Bluefields Bay. From 16th-century Granada, the Europeans sent down several expeditions, hoping the river may lead to the sea. The rapids at Río Sábalo thwarted several missions, until finally the Caribbean was reached in 1539 by an intrepid soldier named Alonso Calero. It happened on St. John the Baptist's feast day; thus the river's name. The river became the main conduit to carry all of the Spanish Empire's plunder from the Pacific side of its Central American territories. Gold, silver, and indigo were just some of the commodities that sailed east, and Granada became wealthy and prosperous because of its strategic location. It was a prosperity coveted by other nations. The French and English sent constant raiding parties to take the spoils, and the river's history is a fascinating catalogue of pirate raids and colonial sieges. Mark Twain sailed down this "earthly paradise" on his way to New York from San Francisco, a passenger on Vanderbilt's inter-oceanic steamship service. William Walker made a stand at San Carlos, as did the Contras further downriver during the counter-revolution in the 1980s. Nicaragua and Costa Rica have had countless diplomatic spats over who owns the river, most recently in 2010, when Google Maps mistakenly gave Nicaragua an extra 2km (1¼ miles) of turf, an act that raised the hackles of the Costa Ricans and threatened a military confrontation between both countries. With its beauty and natural wealth, you can understand why the Rio San Juan is so coveted. Perhaps the most shocking is the fact that this stretch of paradise was the waterway that came very close to being the Nicaraguan version of the Panama Canal. Imagine: Instead of giant silver tarpon fish, we would have giant, rusty oil tankers with not a howler monkey or parrot in sight. Thank God for no progress.

Getting There

The only regular boat service is to Castillo from San Carlos. To truly explore the river and its tributaries, you need a private boat with guide, possibly arranged in San Carlos, but best arranged with the expert agencies in Managua who will provide English-speaking, qualified guides. Access to many tributaries is restricted, and you must show written permission from MARENA in Managua to get past the many checkpoints and soldiers. Needless to say, pack the strongest bug repellent you can find and wear clothes that easily dry.

What to See & Do Along the Rio San Juan

A BOAT RIDE DOWN THE RIO SAN JUAN ★★

San Carlos is at the mouth of the Río San Juan and the departure point for a breath-taking river journey 70km (43 miles) downriver to the old historical fort town of El Castillo. The truly adventurous can hire a boat to continue another 140km (87 miles) to the lonely Caribbean port town of San Juan del Norte, passing Reserva Biológica Indio Maíz on the way. Birdlife is abundant along the riverbanks, with large flocks of egrets and cormorants swirling overhead or floating down the mirror-like waters on floating clumps of water hyacinth. Look out for the occasional kingfisher and the large silver fish called a tarpon, which slips through the water like a dolphin, known locally as *sábalo*. This river journey is interrupted by several stops to pick up and drop off people at small settlements on the way to the fort. The occasional boat even pulls up alongside the *colectivo* to sell food, drinks, and fresh fish stored in ice boxes.

Boca de Sábalos is a muddy little settlement of 1,200 people with two decent hotels and a 2,000-hectare (4,942-acre) palm-oil farm and factory. As the town's name implies, it is an excellent place for fishing *sábalo* that can be as long as 2.5m (8¼ ft.).

There is also a local version of the snook fish called *róbalo,* which is very popular as a dish.

Beyond El Castillo, the rapids known as Raudal el Diablo are easily negotiated by an experienced boatman, and the location is a popular fishing spot with locals. The wild jungle of Reserva Biológica Indio Maíz contrasts with bare ranchland on the opposite Costa Rican side. A sunken steamship lies in the mouth of the Río Samoso whilst crocodiles and turtles sunbathe on the sandbanks. Tiny waterways lead to dark grottoes. Giant palms and drapes of vines hang from gigantic cedar trees. At the Río Sarapiquí, there is a border checkpoint and small settlement. This was Contra territory in the 1980s. Past several more tributaries, the river turns north as it approaches the sea, then meanders through wetlands and swamp. A broad beach appears, separated by a long sandbar known as La Barra. Bull sharks lie in the estuary and along the shore feeding on the many fish, meaning this is not a good place to swim.

A series of connected waterways and estuaries to the north are known as Bahía de San Juan. An old dredger lies abandoned in the water, a reminder of human plans to turn this river into a canal. The high-end lodge Río Indio is located here, close to a spectacular river of the same name. The blue waters of the waterway are excellent for fishing and exploring.

Greytown lies abandoned at the edge of a waterway. This derelict ghost town was named after a British governor of Jamaica and had a tumultuous history of English invasion, Nicaraguan possession, and U.S. bombing before it became a steamship boomtown and finally a ragged Contra stronghold. The Sandinistas burned it down in 1982, and the only interesting thing to see is its fascinating jungle-covered cemetery. The 19th-century tombs are segregated by race, and the graveyard is now a national monument. A new settlement was recreated upriver, an uninteresting swamp town called San Juan del Norte. Here, you have finally reached the end of the line, with nothing more but the vast rainforest on one side and the Atlantic on the other.

EL CASTILLO 📷

The dark-stained stone remains of the Spanish fort **El Castillo de la Inmaculada Concepción de María** ★ remind one of a Maya temple. It's a relic of just how important the river was as a gateway between Europe and Central America. The Spanish built several forts along the river to deter marauding pirates bent on raiding prosperous Granada. El Castillo was the biggest, and was constructed between 1673 and 1675. It is Nicaragua's oldest Spanish building still in its original state. The fort is situated on a river bend and sits high over a cluster of stilted houses with red tin roofs and has an excellent view downriver.

In its heyday, it was a formidable obstacle, with 32 cannons trained on any strangers with malice coming this way and a well-stocked armory of 11,000 weapons. It was the scene of many skirmishes and sieges, and the British navy tried several times to take it. In 1762, they laid siege to the fort for 5 days. A captain's daughter called Rafaela Herrera became a national hero when she rallied the troops and lead the defense, breaking the British attack by sending burning flotsam downstream towards the enemy ships and thus breaking their formation. The British tried again in 1779 when seven warships carrying 1,000 troops gathered at the river mouth. A young, unknown captain named Horatio Nelson decided to attack the fort from the jungle behind and successfully took it. However, the Spanish then laid siege, and disease and desertion forced the British to abandon their prize.

There is now a well-stocked and interesting **Museo** that explains the fort's swashbuckling heritage (in Spanish). Cannonballs and old rum bottles add color to the

The question here for almost 500 years was whether an inter-oceanic canal could be built through Nicaragua. Nowadays the question is *why* it never was. Geographically, Nicaragua is perfect for such a momentous waterway. It is the lowest point in the entire Americas, and because Lago de Nicaragua runs into the Caribbean via the broad Río San Juan, the Pacific is just a tantalizing 18km (11 miles) from the lakeshore. Thus, a relatively minor bit of excavation would split South America from North America. Such a project would have had a major effect on the country politically, economically, and environmentally. It is fascinating to see how the Gibraltar of the Americas never came to pass.

It was certainly not from lack of interest. King Philip of Spain ordered a feasibility study back in 1567. The British attacked Nicaragua in the 17th century with the intent of "dividing the Spanish Empire in half." Napoleon Bonaparte III formed the Nicaraguan Canal Company in 1869 but was deposed before he could start digging. The Belgians and Dutch sniffed around, as did Cornelius Vanderbilt, who commissioned the first systematic survey in 1852. An American firm called the U.S. Maritime Canal Company sent a dredger to the mouth of the Río San Juan in 1893. The company went bankrupt, and the boat was abandoned in San Juan del Norte, where it can be seen to this day, a rusting relic. In 1901, the U.S. House of Representatives voted in favor of building a canal through Nicaragua, much to the annoyance of Panama. It looked at last like the project was finally getting off the ground. However, a volcano eruption and some clever scare tactics by the Panamanian lobbyists saw the U.S. Senate vote the motion down. The project went to Panama.

In 1914, the U.S. signed a treaty with Nicaragua in which it was given the exclusive rights "in perpetuity" to build a canal. Washington had no intention of ever doing so, but neither did it want the French or Japanese to step in and rival the Panamanian project. The canal dream was over.

Since then, there has been a revival in interest in building a canal; the treaty was revoked in 1970. A $2-billion "dry canal" was proposed in the 1990s, linking the oceans by a cargo railway line. Other project ideas include a $20-billion Panama-style canal and a $50-million shallow barge waterway known as an Ecocanal. So far, such schemes have remained on the drawing board, and as you survey the splendor of the Río San Juan, you cannot help hoping they stay that way.

story. It is open daily from 8am to noon and 1 to 5pm. There is a single entrance fee of C40. **Centro de Interpretación de la Naturaleza** is another museum behind the fort that showcases the area's flora and fauna. It is open daily from 10am to 4pm.

RESERVA BIOLOGICA INDIO-MAIZ

A rainforest needs a lot of rain. Five meters (197 in.) fall on this reserve a year, making it one of the wettest places on Earth. Not that you'd notice. The 50m-high (164-ft.) trees support an intricate canopy of vines and creepers that crawl up towards the sun, creating a dense canopy umbrella. The abundance of water gives the canopy that lush greenness and provides humidity for fungi to thrive and frogs to flourish. There are 300 species of reptiles and amphibians in this mega park, the second-biggest reserve and largest primary rainforest in Central America. The dark slopes of several volcanoes make this appear as the perfect spot to shoot a King Kong movie. But who needs giant apes when there are 200 species of mammal here, including tapir, deer, and big cats? There are 600 species of birds, including hummingbirds, kingfishers, toucans, flycatchers, and woodpeckers. Indio-Maíz is an ecological blockbuster, but there are zero facilities, and it requires a guide to visit. It is bordered by the Río Bartola in the west and the Caribbean in the east. Check at the Managua MARENA office regarding access or book with a specialist tour agency.

Where to Stay Along the Rio San Juan

Lodges are just beginning to pop up along the river that offer multiday packages. All have generator-provided electricity that is turned off at night, so make sure to pack a flashlight.

Hotel Albergue El Castillo   Undoubtedly the best hotel in town, the Albergue was built by the Spanish government when they restored the fort as part of the 500-year anniversary of the Spanish conquest of the Americas. The large, two-story structure overlooks the river, a short walk from the fort. The rooms are simple but well appointed. A spacious double balcony overlooks the river, and there is an elegant bar and restaurant.

El Castillo. ℭ **505/8892-0195** or 505/8924-5608. 13 units. $30 double. Rates include breakfast. No credit cards. **Amenities:** Restaurant; bar. *In room:* Fan.

Hotel Sábalos 🎁   There aren't many places in the world to stay where caiman quarrel beneath your bed. Hotel Sábalos has a beautiful location right over the water, with sweeping views of the river. The low wooden structure of varnished wood has a wraparound veranda with a line of doors leading to smallish but well-appointed rooms. Narrow single beds sit in the all-wood interior. You can literally fish from the balcony or just watch the locals passing in their impossibly flimsy canoes while fishermen throw nets into the water. The Hotel Sábalos is hard to beat for the quality of its surroundings and its excellent riverside location.

Boca de Sábaloss. www.hotelsabalos.com.ni. ℭ **505/2271-7424** or 505/8659-0252. 10 units. $40 double. Rates include breakfast. AE, DC, MC, V. **Amenities:** Restaurant; bar. *In room:* Fan.

Montecristo River Lodge   Several miles before El Castillo is a rustic resort set on a lush green slope. You can't miss it, as its name, **Montecristo,** is spelled out in huge white letters along the riverbank and a long thatched walkway leads up to its series of huts and apartment cabins. Originally a simple fishing lodge, Montecristo now practices sustainable tourism by offering ecofriendly accommodations set in a wildlife refuge with hiking trails. The hotel also organizes river excursions on their small fleet of boats, including tours of local fish and shrimp farms as well as fishing and birdwatching expeditions. The Mark Twain Bar can get busy on weekends.

Río San Juan. www.montecristoriverlodge.com. ℭ **505/2583-0197** or 505/8649-9012. 24 units. $150 double. Rates include full board & tours. AE, DC, MC, V. **Amenities:** Restaurant; bar; free airport transfers; pool. *In room:* Fan.

Río Indio Lodge ★★   Tired of slumming it in the jungle and desperate to kick off those sweaty gumboots and have a hot bath? Río Indio is by no means the spartan, monastic lodge you might expect in this neck of the woods, but a spare-no-expense, American-style lodge that provides the ultimate jungle experience with all the creature comforts. No need to get your feet dirty, as a suspended walkway links the wooden cottages. Handsome hardwood interiors highlight rooms so ample they accommodate two queen-size beds. Fans whizz over the polished ceramic tiles that lead to chunky wooden balconies outside. The decor is conventional, if a little old-fashioned. Brass chandeliers hang from a jungle roof of bare wood. Reproduction chairs complement quilted bed sheets. Fishing and bird-watching excursions are organized for an extra charge. The restaurant's extensive menu focuses on tropical fruits and fresh, local vegetables highlighted by the river's delicious bounty such as shrimp and *róbalo*.

Indio & San Juan rivers, near San Juan del Norte. www.rioindiolodge.com. ℭ**506/2231-4299** in Costa Rica. 27 units. $192 per person. Minimum stay 5 nights. Rates include full board & tours. AE, DC, MC, V. **Amenities:** Restaurant; bar; free airport transfers; pool. *In room:* Fan.

Sábalos Lodge An attractive collection of bamboo huts with thatched roofs is scattered across a riverside property just downriver from Boca de Sábalos. The rooms are simple but charming, with all-wood interiors and lots of light. Flimsy yellow curtains hang from the windows, and mosquito nets hang over the cot-like beds. The river flows past the veranda, which is adorned with wood lounge chairs and hammocks. The bathrooms are minimalist but immaculate. There is an open-side restaurant and a communal room decorated with fishing tackle and nature books. The lodge has nice open grounds and provides every type of tour on the river and in the forest, including evening caiman excursions.

El Toro Rapids. www.sabaloslodge.com. ℭ**505/8850-7623.** 7 units. $435 per person for 3 days. Rates include full board. AE, DC, MC, V. **Amenities:** Restaurant; bar; free airport transfers; gym. *In room:* Fan.

11

THE CARIBBEAN COAST

D on't let its reputation fool you. Nicaragua's Caribbean coast is not entirely the whirlpool of turquoise post-card images you may have heard about or seen. Most of this steaming 520km (323 miles) of Atlantic coast is a dense and inhospitable plain of tropical forest—impenetrable and very wet. Much of it is unexplored swamps and mangrove estuaries, and towns such as Bilwi and Bluefields have an edgy, lawless feel.

Its spotty weather is one of the reasons La Costa is a world apart from the rest of Nicaragua. The Spanish never actually got around to conquering it. Though Columbus brushed along its shores, the coast's unwelcoming geography and fierce Indian resistance meant the conquistadors did very little conquering, especially when the Miskito tribe killed and ate the first governor in 1545. It was the British who first established a toehold, finding the coves and bays invaluable ports-of-call during the many wars of the period. They also traded with the Miskitos and backed a Miskito king to rule over the neighboring tribes. German Protestant missionaries in the 1800s added to the heady cultural mix, and their legacy can be seen in the stark Moravian churches that dominate each town. In 1894, Nicaraguan president Zelaya marched his army into Bluefields to finally lay claim to the region, but for many years, it was joined in name only with the rest of Nicaragua. American timber and banana companies stepped in, and there was a brisk steamship trade with North America for much of the 20th century. This receded with the advent of the Sandinistas, who tried in vain to strong-arm the region into being ruled from Managua. Eventually, a political settlement in 1987 saw the entire coast gain a limited level of autonomy and self-policing under the name RAAN, the North Atlantic Autonomous Region.

The Caribbean still remains very much isolated from the rest of Nicaragua, and its main town, Bluefields, is accessible only by sea or air. Little tourist infrastructure, be it visitor centers or shopping spots, exists here. Yet there are signs that the coast is opening up, and tropical paradises, such as the Pearl Lagoon outside Bluefields, are attracting more and more visitors. The Corn Islands, 80km (50 miles) off the coast, are particularly becoming more popular, as they do offer a postcard-perfect white-beach paradise. Another great attraction is the region's rich mix of Miskito Indian culture, pirate heritage, English legacy, and African roots. This means its people are more like West Indians than Nicaraguans, and they generally speak a lilting form of English Creole rather than Spanish. They are also the most laid-back population in the country, with a fondness for late-night partying and music. This is all the more evident in the month of May, when cities such as Bluefields rock to the calypso sounds of the Palo de Mayo festival.

BLUEFIELDS

440km (273 miles) SE of Managua; 465km (289 miles) SE of Granada

In Bluefields, a gritty but colorful port town of 50,000, the Caribbean collides with Latin America. The end result is a languid and slightly edgy place, which perhaps is in keeping with the fact that the town was named after a pirate (a Dutch marauder named Blewfeldt) It was a thriving 19th-century town, living off timber, bananas, and God (in the form of Moravian missionaries whose neat little churches dot the region). The 20th century saw a decline in the region's fortunes, compounded by a confrontational attitude by the Managua government.

Today, a heady ethnic mix of Miskito Indian, *mestizo*, Spanish, and West Indian locals call the town home. Bluefields is also an important port with a murky bay and a murkier crime image. This image is somewhat unfounded, though the area is becoming famous for abandoned bales of cocaine rolling up on its coast (known as white lobster) and the social problems such a phenomenon causes. Many people choose to skip the town on their way to the Corn Islands, but if you do decide to linger, you'll find some of the best nightclubs and party spots in Nicaragua, as well as access to incredible coastal wildlife and landscapes such as the Pearl Lagoon and the tropical archipelago known as the Pearl Cays.

Essentials

GETTING THERE

BY PLANE Bluefields Airport (BEF; no phone) is a tiny, modern terminal 3km (1¾ miles) south of the town. There are always taxis outside when a plane arrives. La Costeña (℃ **505/2263-1228** in Managua or 505/2572-2500 in Bluefields; www. lacostena.com.ni) operates daily services between Managua and Bluefields with an onward journey to the Corn Islands. They have small, turbo-powered airplanes that are not for the fainthearted. Flights start at C3,116 round-trip from Managua to the islands.

BY BUS & BOAT Transportes Vargas Peña (℃ **505/2280-4561**) offers a bus-boat package from Managua, leaving Mercado Iván Montenegro at 9pm daily. The journey takes from 12 to 15 hours and is not pleasant, as the road is very bad. Transportes Aguilar (℃ **505/2248-3005**) offers a similar service, leaving from Mayoreo at 9pm. Both trips cost roughly C360 one-way.

The river town of Rama is the boat departure point from the mainland to Bluefields. A large boat leaves every Tuesday, Thursday, Saturday, and Sunday at noon and takes 4½ hours to reach Bluefields. The cost is C50. Faster *panga/lanchas* run daily from 6am until 4pm, which take 2 hours to reach Bluefields. The cost is C100.

GETTING AROUND

Taxis cost less than C20 for most trips within the town, and there are plenty of buses that trundle around. The fare is C5. To go farther afield, you'll need a boat or panga (open motorboat). Jipe (Mercado Municipal; ✆ **505/2572-1871**) is a water-taxi company that provides private excursions to the area's surrounding attractions. Pangas leave for El Bluff and Pearl Lagoon from the town pier and cost between C20 and C60. The last boats return at 4pm.

VISITOR INFORMATION

There is an Intur office half a block south of the park (✆ **505/2572-0221**); it's open Monday to Friday from 9am to 4:30pm. CIDCA (no phone), a research and local history organization, is 50m (164 ft.) north of the police station and offers reliable information on the area. It's open Monday to Friday from 8am to 5:30pm. A good website to check is www.bluefieldspulse.com; it offers events listings and local news.

What to See & Do in Bluefields

Bluefields itself has no bathing beaches. Much of the area was destroyed by Hurricane Joan in 1988, after which the port was moved across the bay to El Bluff. You can reach El Bluff, where giant fishing boats and tankers are docked amid fish-packing factories, on boats that run daily across the bay. It's an ugly but interesting harbor scene. Bluefields' most interesting building is the shore-side Moravian Church. Rebuilt after the hurricane, it was first constructed in 1848, and now sports a red roof and neat wooden paneling reminiscent of Caribbean buildings. It is in front of the Municipal Dock and is open for morning and evening services at 8am and 6pm.

FESTIVALS

Palo de Mayo is the event of the year, when the entire town gets down to some serious Caribbean boogying throughout the month of May. The festival actually has English and Dutch origins, when a maypole was erected in the center of town and the people celebrated the coming of spring by decorating it with ribbons and flowers. The modern version is somewhat racier and erotic, with parades, costumes, and dancing to a soundtrack of tropical calypso music. September 30 is the city's patron saint day, and the locals need little excuse to party, with a repeat festival on October 30 celebrating the region's autonomy. Food, music, and dancing are the order of the day.

Caribbean Creole

Just when you think you are getting a handle on your Spanish, a trip to the Atlantic coast will upset your linguistic compass completely. Nicaraguan Creole is a mutant form of English that is as rapid and incomprehensible as it is endearing and hilarious. Below are some phrases to help you get by, but as a general rule, end every sentence with *mon*.

Alright	Hello
Right here mon	Hello to you
That ain't nothing	Thank you
Me got one good time	I had a lovely time
No feel, no way	Don't worry, it's okay
What time you got?	What time is it?
I no vex	I'm not angry
Ya heard mon	I hear you
She done reach Bluefields	She has arrived at Bluefields
Check you then	Goodbye

Where to Stay in Bluefields

The best places to stay in Bluefields are north of the town pier. I recommend spending a little extra on accommodations here, as some of the budget options are the sort of places that are rented by the hour.

Oasis Hotel Casino ★, 150m (492 ft.) from the bay (✆ **505/2572-2812**;

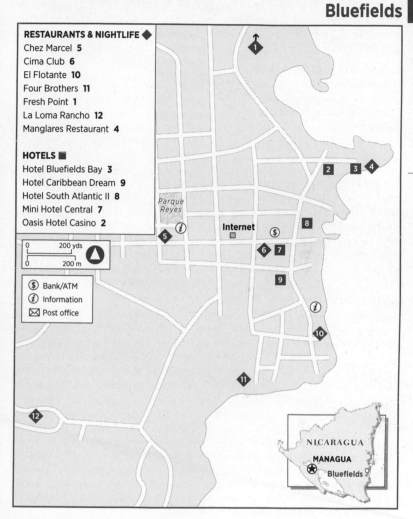

RESTAURANTS & NIGHTLIFE ◆
Chez Marcel **5**
Cima Club **6**
El Flotante **10**
Four Brothers **11**
Fresh Point **1**
La Loma Rancho **12**
Manglares Restaurant **4**

HOTELS ■
Hotel Bluefields Bay **3**
Hotel Caribbean Dream **9**
Hotel South Atlantic II **8**
Mini Hotel Central **7**
Oasis Hotel Casino **2**

0   200 yds
0   200 m

($) Bank/ATM
(i) Information
(✉) Post office

Parque Reyes

Internet

NICARAGUA
MANAGUA
Bluefields

www.oasiscasinohotel.com), is undoubtedly the best hotel in town, with large, reason-ably priced rooms and suites. Beds are big and comfortable, and the rooms come with air-conditioning and cable TV. Doubles start at $55 and include breakfast and an airport shuttle. The Presidential suite is a royal bargain at $165 as it includes an entire floor with two bedrooms, two bathrooms, Jacuzzi, kitchen and two living areas. **Hotel Bluefields Bay** (© 505/2572-0120; www.bluefieldsbay.galeon.com), 2 blocks north of the Municipal Dock, is a well-appointed B&B by the shoreline. Rooms start at $28. **Hotel South Atlantic II,** west of the municipal market (© 505/2572-1022), is another good option. Rooms start at $35 and have air-conditioning and TV.

For slightly less expensive rooms, **Hotel Caribbean Dream,** 20m (66 ft.) south of the Municipal Market (© 505/2572-0107), has a nice blue-and-white veranda facing the main street. Rooms start at $32 and come with air-conditioning and private bathrooms. Alternatively, try **Mini Hotel Central,** dockside by the Municipal Market (© **505/2572-2362**), which is well run and has friendly owners. Rooms start at $25.

Where to Eat in Bluefields

Nicaraguan Country

The popularity of old-fashioned, North American country-and-western music along the Nicaraguan coast is a shock to many visitors. Apparently, the locals' fondness for Kenny Rogers comes from the fact that the only radio station worth listening to during the war years was one out of Houston, Texas.

Fresh seafood is the order of the day here, and shrimp and lobster are featured prominently on every menu. I recommend taking advantage of the relatively cheap prices and trying something more unusual like yellowfin or snapper cooked with vegetables and coconut curry. While in town, you should also try coco bread, a popular puffed loaf of bread, as well as hot coconut buns. Most formal restaurants in town open for lunch and close at 10pm daily.

Manglares Restaurant ★, in the Hotel Bluefields Bay (© **505/2572-0107**), has the best seaside dining in the area, along with a nice location on a dock over the bay. Main courses start at C190. Another seafood restaurant with a great view is **El Flotante,** 4 blocks south of the church (© **505/2572-2988**). Main courses start at C220. **La Loma Rancho** (© **505/572-2875**) is set on a hill overlooking the town and has a pleasant open-air dining area. Main courses start at C190. If you like your meals formal and elegant, go to **Chez Marcel** (© **505/2572-2347**), where they do exquisite lunches and dinners. Main courses start at C260.

The restaurant within the **Hotel South Atlantic II** (© **505/2572-1022**) serves excellent seafood and meat dishes that won't bust your budget. Main courses start at C130. Another good hotel restaurant within the same price range is the **Mini-Hotel Central** (© **505/2572-2362**).

Bluefields After Dark

This so-called "Jamaica of Nicaragua" certainly comes alive at night, and the locals have no inhibitions when it comes to getting down. Bluefields lives and breathes music, and the rough-and-tumble bars and clubs here play an eclectic mix, to say the least. One minute, you might be grinding to Daddy Yankee, and next, weeping into your beer to Tammy Wynette. Whatever you do, dress down and make sure you get a taxi to and from the venues listed below, for safety reasons.

Four Brothers, 6 blocks south of the park in Barrio Puntafria (no phone), is a popular roadhouse disco that gets a good mix of people. It is open Thursday to Sunday, and the party here goes on all night. **Fresh Point** ★ (no phone) is a similar roadhouse disco, but with a slightly livelier scene. It is 2km (1¼ miles) north of the city, northeast of the Municipal Dock, and has a pleasant outdoor area with palm trees and tables overlooking the bay. Saturday night is the best night here. **La Loma Rancho** (© **505/2572-2875;** see "Where to Dine," above), is a restaurant that converts into a happening party spot on Thursday through Sunday, with great views overlooking the city. **Cima Club,** 1 block west of the Moravian Church on Avenida Cabezas (no phone), is a more laid-back joint, with salsa and Latin beats and a little karaoke, as well as open-air seating.

What to See & Do Around Bluefields

GREENFIELDS NATURE RESERVE

Greenfields is a private nature reserve that offers excellent jungle excursions and canoeing trips in the surrounding pristine wilderness. The lush, tropical Swiss-owned property has 25km (16 miles) of hiking trails, lodgings, and ample opportunities to canoe through jungle waterways. There is a botanical garden, bathing pier, and rustic lodge, as well as abundant wildlife such as caimans, otters, and elusive jaguar. The reserve can be seen in a 1-day trip from Bluefields that costs approximately $30 for one or two people, or you can choose to stay the night for $100 (price varies with group size). Contact the owners of the reserve at ℂ **505/2278-0589** or 505/8434-4808, or visit www.greenfields.com.ni for info.

PEARL LAGOON

This small, peaceful village and lake is 1½ hours away from Bluefields by boat and is a lovely, relaxing antidote to the shabbiness of that town. Five jungle rivers pour into this gorgeous estuary, surrounded by rainforest, mangroves, savanna, and pine forests. The town is a neat collection of sandy streets, a lakeside dock, and a beautiful church. The region has a rich mix of Afro-Caribbean and Miskito people. North of the lake is a village called Orinoco, which is the most southern settlement of the Garifuna people, a proud tribe with strong West African roots. November 17 to 19, there is an annual Garifuna festival, celebrating their culture with drumming, dancing, and singing. Pearl Lagoon village has a variety of lodgings and is often used as a base to explore the paradise-like archipelago known as the Pearl Cays ★★. Here, you'll find 18 tiny islands 6km (3¾ miles) east of the coast, each crammed with vegetation and circled by sparkling white beaches. There is little or no tourist infrastructure, so bring lots of water and food. To arrange tours of the Cays (pronounced keys), try the Casa Blanca Hotelito y Restaurante (Barrio May 4; ℂ **505/2572-0508**). These are also the best accommodations in town, with bright, clean rooms and a decent restaurant. Prices range from $10 to $30. Another good, if very basic, lodge is Green Lodge Guesthouse, 1 block south of dock, beside Enitel (ℂ **505/2572-0507**). Here, a tiny room goes for $15, and the owner also arranges tours of the area.

How to Get to Pearl Lagoon

Pangas leave for the lake and village each day regularly (as soon as they fill up), but it is advisable to go to the dock in Bluefields as early as possible (the first leaves at 6am, with another one soon after). There is much less activity on Sundays. The trip itself is beautiful, since it takes you up the Río Escondido and through a maze of streams and waterways filled with wildlife. The fare is C120 one-way.

THE CORN ISLANDS ★★★

"How the Caribbean should be," is how one visitor described Nicaragua's unspoiled island treasures. The Corn Islands, consisting of 6-sq.-km (2¼-sq.-mile) Big Corn and 1.5-sq.-km (½-sq.-mile) Little Corn, are two kernels of Caribbean paradise located 83km (52 miles) east of the Nicaraguan coast and are perhaps my favorite part of Nicaragua. The islands' luminous coastal bays and shores are ideal for diving, snorkeling, fishing, or simply sunning. And how could you not be happy on islands with names like Coconut Point, Sally Peaches, and Jokeman Bank?

Though the islanders, many of whom have surnames like Morgan and Dixon that call to mind the pirates and adventurers who landed here years ago, are traditionally

> **Obeah**
>
> Nicaragua's Creole people practice a form of voodoo called Obeah. Practitioners use herbal infusions, bath salts, and chanting to cure, curse, and heal, and are influential shamans in the Miskito and Afro-Caribbean community.

dependent on fishing and coconut growing for a living, tourism is quickly becoming another prominent economic force here. I sincerely hope that this increasing tourism unfolds in a sustainable manner, for these are two true treasure islands, with some of the best beaches I have ever wandered upon. The laid-back vibe also lends itself to some great parties: During Easter, the otherwise deserted beaches get packed with revelers, as they do for the Crab Soup Festival in late August, a traditional festival celebrating slave emancipation.

There is very little happening here in terms of nightlife, however. Unlike nearby Bluefields, the only thing to do here after dark is stroll along the beach or have a drink in your hotel—so don't come expecting to party.

Big Corn Island

GETTING THERE

BY PLANE Corn Island Airport (RNI; no phone) is served by two small airlines that make connections to Bluefields and Managua. La Costeña (© **505/2575-5131**) and Atlantic Airlines (© **505/2270-5355**) both depart from Managua at 6:30am and 2pm daily and leave the island at 8am and 3pm. The journey takes 1½ hours; arrive at least 30 minutes before departure and always reconfirm your return flight on arrival. Expect to fly in small, antiquated, propeller-powered planes.

The airport is 2km (1¼ miles) from Brig Bay. There are always several taxi drivers waiting at the tiny airport when each plane arrives. The fare is C40 per person no matter where you go, though you may be charged a little extra for luggage.

BY BOAT Three boats depart from Bluefields on different days. A 5-hour express called Río Escondido departs at 9am every Wednesday, returning at 9am on a Tuesday. The cost is C210. A ferry called St. Nikolas (© **505/2695-3344**) leaves on Friday at 9am and takes 7 hours. It returns on Sunday at midday. The cost one-way is C100. The Captain D (© **505/2850-2767**) leaves Rama on Wednesday at noon and goes to El Bluff; from there it departs at 5pm for a 10pm arrival to the Corn Islands. The main return boat departs the Corn Islands at midnight on Saturday for Bluefields. The cost one-way from Rama is C350 and from El Bluff is C250. All boats dock at Brig Bay, Big Corn Island's main port.

GETTING AROUND

A taxi costs C16 per person to travel anywhere on the island and C21 after 10pm or if you have a lot of luggage. There is a small minibus that circles the island at a cost of C5. Perhaps the most fun way to get around is to hire one of the many golf carts that cost C200 per hour. Contact Arenas Beach Hotel (© **505/2456-2220**) to do so.

ORIENTATION

Big Corn (www.bigcornisland.com) has a 12km (7½-mile) ring road that circles the island, frequented by the occasional car, taxi, and golf cart. This is where you'll find the island's main port, Brig Bay, and the only airport. Generally, the best beaches in Big Corn are to the southwest, as it is more sheltered than the eastern side, though the reverse happens in November. The north end has the best spots for snorkeling.

[FastFACTS] CORN ISLANDS

ATMs & Banks **Banpro,** on the road to Hotel Puertas del Sol in Brig Bay (☏ 505/2575-5107), is the only bank on the island. Though the islands' only ATM was installed here in 2008, it's best to bring plenty of cash to the island in case you can't get to the bank. Make sure you are carrying immaculate American dollars, as the locals can be fussy about what they accept. With a Visa credit card, you can take out money at Banpro at the airport. Money transfers can be arranged at the **Western Union** outlet

(☏ 505/2575-5074) beside the Caribbean Depot, close to the dock.

Emergencies For emergencies, dial ☏ **101.** For other police-related matters, call ☏ **505/2575-5201.**

Hospital **Corn Island Hospital** (☏ 505/2575-5236) is behind Nautilus and is open every day, all day. For an English-speaking doctor, call Dr. David Somarriba (☏ 505/2575-5184) or, for a dentist, call ☏ **505/2575-5236.**

Internet Most of the better hotels on the island should have Internet

service. **Cyber Café,** near Nautilus (no phone), charges C40 per hour. The **Western Union** outlet (see above) also provides Internet and fax services.

Pharmacy **Pharmacy Monica** (☏ 505/2575-5251) is in front of the government house in the center of the island. It is open Monday to Saturday from 8am to 6pm and Sunday from 8am to noon. **Pharmacy Guadelupe** (☏ 505/2575-5217) is farther east, close to the baseball stadium, and is open Monday to Saturday from 7am to 9pm.

WHAT TO SEE & DO ON BIG CORN ISLAND

The first thing you should do is head straight for the beaches, the best of which is Picnic Beach ★★★, located in the south bay of Big Corn. This is a long, white, strand beach, with gentle turquoise waters and not a soul in sight (for now, anyway). Another beautiful Big Corn beach is Sally Peaches, on the northeastern side of the island. Here, you have shallow pools and pink coral sand. It is unsuitable for swimming (because of rocks) but makes for great photo opportunities from the hill here, Mount Pleasant, upon which is a small watchtower. The watchtower can be accessed by a path in front of Nicos Bar.

Outdoor Activities

DIVING Spotted tiger rays, blacktip sharks, stingrays, spider crabs, parrot fish, angel fish, barracuda, and triggerfish; they are all out there in the pristine waters, waiting for you to drop in and say hello. Nautilus Dive, north of Brig Bay (☏ 505/2575-5077; www.nautilus-dive-nicaragua.com), is the most-established dive operator on the island. It offers everything from open-water to advanced courses and allows guests to explore the island's three coral reefs or a volcanic pinnacle known as Blowing Rock. Fun dives start at C800, and a 3-day open-water course costs C6,000. Nautilus Dive also offers snorkeling tours and glass-bottom-boat excursions over reefs and shipwrecks for those who don't want to get their feet wet.

FISHING The islands provide excellent sport-fishing opportunities for red snapper, king fish, and barracuda. Blue Runner Charter (Southend; ☏ 505/2847-5745) is run by true-blue local fisherman Alwin Taylor and offers sea tours and fishing trips, which cost between C3,000 and C5,000. Another outfit that offers fishing opportunities

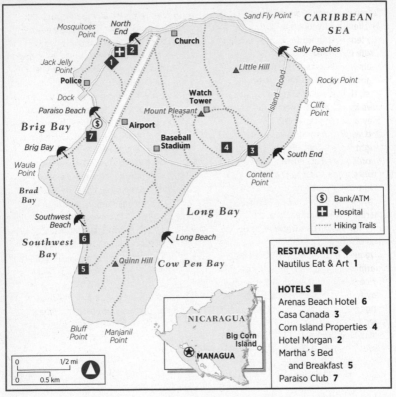

Big Corn Island

Sand Fly Point

CARIBBEAN SEA

Mosquitoes Point

North End

Church

Sally Peaches

Jack Jelly Point

Little Hill

Rocky Point

Police

Island Road

Dock

Watch Tower

Clift Point

Paraiso Beach

Mount Pleasant

Airport

Brig Bay

Baseball Stadium

Brig Bay

South End

Waula Point

Content Point

Brad Bay

Long Bay

Southwest Beach

$ Bank/ATM

✚ Hospital

⋯ Hiking Trails

Southwest Bay

Long Beach

RESTAURANTS ◆

Quinn Hill

Cow Pen Bay

Nautilus Eat & Art **1**

HOTELS ■

NICARAGUA

Arenas Beach Hotel **6**

Casa Canada **3**

Corn Island Properties **4**

Bluff Point

Manjanil Point

Big Corn Island

Hotel Morgan **2**

Martha´s Bed and Breakfast **5**

MANAGUA

Paraiso Club **7**

0   1/2 mi
0   0.5 km

around the islands is Corn Island Flyfishing (✆ **505/8650-6381;** cornislandfly fishing@gmail.com).

SNORKELING   You can pull your goggles on anywhere around the area and go for a fish-filled float. However, one of the best places to snorkel is in the shallow waters around Sandy Fly point. You can rent snorkeling equipment at most hotels for C280 per day.

WHERE TO STAY ON BIG CORN ISLAND

Thankfully, the island has not been overrun with concrete and gated hotels—yet. There are plans to develop conventional resorts here in the next few years, but on a small enough scale for the island's fragile ecosystem to sustain them. Only time will tell if that will happen. For the moment, most of the accommodations options on the island are limited to two-star basics with a few memorable exceptions. It is wise to stay in a hotel that has an adjoining restaurant and to make sure the hotel has its own electric generator. Otherwise, when the lights go out, you'll have to be happy with a hammock and a glass of rum. Since tourism is a relatively new phenomenon in this area, be warned that service can be slow wherever you go. Self-catering is also a new option. Corn Island Properties (✆ **505/8664-5315;** www.cornislandproperties.

Nurse sharks lurk on the ocean floor, docile and shy, despite their 4.3m (14-ft.) length. Diamond-shaped spotted eagle rays glide through the water, their whip-like tails trailing behind. A school of baby barracudas brushes past, their large mouths and powerful jaws indicating the voracious predators they are. They have lots to hunt: red and yellow snapper, blue angelfish with bright yellow fins, damselfish with blue fluorescent spots, striped French grunts, and multicolored parrot fish. Add to this spiny lobsters, crabs, shrimp, sea urchins, octopus, squid, and marine snails, and you can understand why the Corn Islands are regarded as one of the best places in the world to dive and snorkel. Such a cornucopia of marine life is supported by a spectacular coral reef that extends the whole way from Belize, making it the second longest in the world. Unlike Belize, however, the Corn Islands enjoy splendid isolation and have so far avoided the curious, tank-bearing, bubble-emitting herd. You will most likely be alone when floating above the eerie, cerebral mounds of purple and red coral and those antler bushes that look like exotic Christmas trees. The only crowds here wear scales and dorsal fins.

Most diving sites are a 10-minute boat ride from the islands. In addition to the coral, there are some shipwrecks to explore, including a Spanish galleon. There's also a curious rock formation known as Blowing Rock, as well as some intriguing underwater caves. Snorkelers don't have to go far, either. North of the island, near Sand Fly point, are some excellent shallow waters teeming with colorful sea life. Diving certificates can be obtained at any of the three main diving agencies. A PADI Open Water Certificate costs approximately $250 and takes 4 days. Introduction dives cost $75. Because of the relatively few people who come here to dive, beginners get that extra bit of personal attention from an instructor.

com) offers three vacation rentals in South End. Prices range from $230 to $300 for 2 nights in well appointed bungalows and villas with all the modern conveniences and within a stone's throw of the beach.

Expensive

Arenas Beach Hotel ★ ☺   The Arenas is a spacious hotel and cabin complex situated on what must be one of the most spectacular beaches in the world (Picnic Beach). Don't let the exterior colors or decor turn you off. Bright orange and blue walls topped with white lattice arches might not be to everybody's taste, but they hide a collection of spacious rooms with great views and a large veranda. The bungalows have a little more style and character, with their pine walls and stained-glass lamps. The hotel has no pool, but you'll understand why when you step out front onto the amazing white beach—it renders a chlorinated swim obsolete. The hotel also has a very good, if expensive, restaurant and is family-friendly, with a number of rooms that comfortably fit up to six people.

Picnic Beach. www.arenasbeachhotel.com; © **505/2851-8046.** 22 units. From $75 double; from $105 triple; from $120 quadruple. Rates include breakfast. MC, V. **Amenities:** Restaurant; bar; room service. *In room:* A/C, TV, Wi-Fi (free).

Casa Canada ★★   This chunk of ocean-side paradise is easily the most beautiful and well-appointed hotel on the island. The row of cottage-style rooms might look unassuming from the island roadway, but on the other side, they face a nicely tiled pool and long rock shore of palm trees and small patches of lawn. Rooms are large, with every type of modern amenity, including a coffeemaker, small kitchenette, and blessedly silent air conditioner. The beds are big and comfortable, and the bathrooms are medium-size and immaculate. The rooms are lined along a beachfront garden, and the hotel's restaurant provides excellent seafood and hearty breakfasts.

Canadian owner Larry is a perfect, gregarious host, and the staff is equipped to set up many organized tours. Even though the Casa Canada's particular slice of actual sandy beach is very small, since this whole island is one big beach, that shouldn't be a problem. The only possible annoyance is the sound of crashing waves a few feet from your doorway—but I think that's an asset.

South End. www.casa-canada.com; ✆**505/2644-0925.** 21 units. From $137 double. AE, MC, V. **Amenities:** Restaurant; bar; Internet (free); infinity pool. *In room:* A/C, TV/DVD player, minibar.

Paraiso Club This cluster of palm-fringed cabins stands on private grounds a stone's throw from the beach. They look exotic and inviting from the outside but are somewhat disappointing on the inside—cramped, with low ceilings and very basic bathrooms. The beds are also hard, and the decor could do with renovating. The Paraiso Club is a step down from Casa Canada and attracts a younger, hardier clientele. Its main attractions are its two friendly Dutch owners and a lively restaurant bar with excellent food. Access to the hotel is down an unpaved road close to Brig Bay.

Brig Bay. www.paraisoclub.com; ✆ **505/2575-5111.** 15 units. From $51 double; from $92 triple; from $109 quadruple. Rates include breakfast. MC, V. **Amenities:** Restaurant; bar; free airport transfers; room service. *In room:* A/C, TV, Wi-Fi (free).

Moderate

Hotel Morgan This roadside complex of timber–and–pink plaster cottages is a little worn and tired, but a good value. The small, low beds complement the old-fashioned laminated furniture, and the bland bathrooms are smallish and clean. The purple rocking chair out front adds a touch of color to the drab decor, and though rooms don't have views, there is a pretty decent seafood restaurant in the main building, with a good vista of the sea.

North End, beside Victoria beer warehouse. ✆ **505/2575-5052.** 10 units. From $45 double. AE, DC, MC, V. **Amenities:** Restaurant. *In room:* A/C or fan, TV, fridge.

Martha's Bed and Breakfast From a distance, this place appears fantastic. A beach entrance leads to a bridge over a lagoon of inky black water, after which you can follow a flowered pathway through a lawn of palm trees until a plantation-style mansion appears, replete with a veranda and wicker rocking chairs. So far, so good. Up close, though, the property's garish red railings smack of bad taste, and the rooms themselves are a little disappointing. They are average-size, with an overpowering smell of disinfectant; flowered quilts cover low, small beds; and the open wardrobes are oddly placed in the bathrooms. Though it's not perfect, Martha's B&B, owned by

Food for Thought

Never go to a Corn Island restaurant if you're in a hurry or starving. The laid-back, easygoing attitude of the locals is just as predominant in the kitchen as anywhere else on the coast, and you can wait hours for your food. Also, don't take the waitstaff's rude, surly attitude too personally; they're like that with everybody.

the English-speaking Martha (of course), does have an ideal location, right in front of Picnic Beach.

South West Bay. ✆ **505/835-5930.** 8 units. From $58 double; from $64 triple. Rates include breakfast. All-inclusive packages available. No credit cards. **Amenities:** Dining area. *In room:* A/C, TV.

WHERE TO EAT

In addition to the restaurant reviewed below, all hotels listed above have in-house restaurants where you can dine. Lobster and shrimp appear on nearly every menu. The former is causing some controversy, as overfishing and unsafe conditions for poorly paid lobster divers are compelling many people to say it's unethical to eat lobster anymore. What you should definitely try, however, is the popular local dish "run down," a delicious mix of vegetables, coconut milk, and seafood, which is so called because it brings you back to life if you feel a little "run down." Reservations are usually not required.

Nautilus Eat & Art ☺ ECLECTIC   This rickety, old, wooden restaurant is laden with psychedelic artwork that exudes a marine theme. Life buoys, shells, and fishing nets hang as decorations alongside local paintings on the veranda. The food is wholesome and comes in huge portions, with standout items including the delicious callaloo soup, curry, and mounds of steaming shrimp cooked in lemon juice and tequila. Pizza is featured prominently on the menu and is available for delivery—a rarity in the country. There is frequently a live duo of musicians playing country-and-western music, Corn Island style.

Brig Bay. ✆ **505/2451-7216.** Main courses C114–C171. No credit cards. Daily 8am–10pm.

Little Corn Island

Little Corn is as close as you'll get to a deserted island without being left completely forlorn. It's wilder and more untamed than its bigger brother and draws a sturdier traveler who can withstand the 30km (19-mile) boat ride here and the fact that there is no electricity for the entire morning, every morning. There are no cars, and the only concrete path is near the tiny dock; the rest is beach trails and dirt paths. How long it will stay like this remains to be seen, but if you have a primitive streak and enjoy being barefoot and surrounded on all sides by coral reef and mango trees, Little Corn is for you.

GETTING THERE & DEPARTING

A panga leaves daily to Little Corn from the Great Corn Island dock at 10am and 4pm. The journey takes 25 minutes and costs C120 one-way. The boat leaves from Little Corn dock to return to Big Corn at 7am and 2pm daily. There is a charge of C3 to enter the dock. Be warned, it can be a white-knuckle, bone-shaking ride if there's a swell.

WHAT TO SEE & DO IN LITTLE CORN

The Lighthouse is a 30-minute stroll from the waterfront. Follow the sidewalk along the school until you see a footpath that climbs to the island's highest point, with a view of the entire island.

OUTDOOR ACTIVITIES

DIVING   A spectacular reef system with overhangs and caves makes Little Corn an attractive spot for any scuba divers and flipper dippers. Dive Little Corn (Pelican Beach, south of pier; no phone; www.divelittlecorn.com) offers PADI-certified

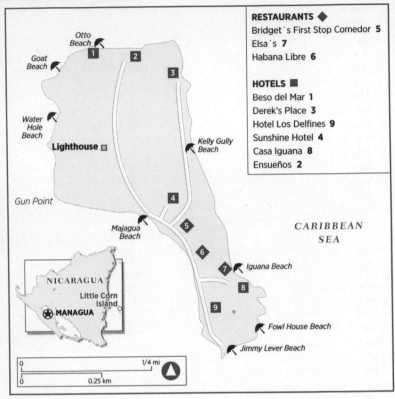

RESTAURANTS ◆
Bridget´s First Stop Comedor **5**
Elsa´s **7**
Habana Libre **6**

HOTELS ■
Beso del Mar **1**
Derek's Place **3**
Hotel Los Delfines **9**
Sunshine Hotel **4**
Casa Iguana **8**
Ensueños **2**

Otto Beach
Goat Beach
Water Hole Beach
Lighthouse
Gun Point
Kelly Gully Beach
Majagua Beach
Iguana Beach
Fowl House Beach
Jimmy Lever Beach

CARIBBEAN SEA

NICARAGUA
Little Corn Island
★ MANAGUA

0   1/4 mi
0   0.25 km

courses, introductory dives, and nighttime excursions. Dolphin Dive (Hotel Los Delfines, north of Jokeman Bank; ✆ **505/2820-2242;** www.hotellosdelfines.com. ni) also operates on the island.

FISHING   Bonefishing is possible from the beach, or both Casa Iguana (south end of Iguana Beach; no phone; www.casaiguana.net) and Hotel Delfines (north of Joke-man Bank; ✆ **505/8820-2242;** www.hotellosdelfines.com.ni) can arrange boat trips for C650.

SNORKELING   There are abundant opportunities all around the island. Just be sure your hotel stocks gear or carry your own.

WHERE TO STAY IN LITTLE CORN

Choose the location of your hotel carefully, as some are at the end of isolated paths that are easy to get lost on when returning at night, yet offer perfect solitude. Most places are located on the lower western shore, but this area can get a little crowded with partying backpackers. Don't forget to pack a flashlight, or candles and water-proof matches, for that matter. Make sure your hotel has snorkel gear if you plan on exploring the reefs. Otherwise, bring your own. In addition to the offerings below, the island will soon have a high-end boutique resort called Beso del Mar, due to open in

January 2012. Located on the gorgeous, white sands of the North Shore, this 16-cabin retreat with pool, yoga platform, and restaurant promises to be one of the best beach hotels on Nicaragua's Atlantic coast. For early bookings, contact garrylesesne@gmail.com.

Casa Iguana ★   This well-run collection of beach houses has a sweeping cliff-top view of a deserted beach on the southern end of the island. Palm trees line sandy paths, and colorful cabanas sit close to the shoreline, surrounding a central common area with lots of books and comfy chairs. Four of the bungalows are rather basic with shared bathrooms, while a further 10 are more upscale, with private bathrooms and verandas. The rooms are simple, with lots of light, double beds, and rainbow-colored furniture, though they could do with some curtains for privacy's sake. Popular with foreign tourists, the complex is run in a sustainable manner with solar- and wind-powered energy, a recycling program, and fruits and vegetables from an on-site garden. Yoga and massage are available, and some fantastic snorkeling reefs are within paddling distance. Overall, Casa Iguana is not a bad place to loaf and soak up the sun, though if you are looking for a more local experience, go somewhere else. Beware: Book early, as it is one of the best accommodations on the island and thus always busy.

S end of Iguana Beach. www.casaiguana.net. No phone. 14 units. $35 double w/shared bathroom; $65 double w/private bathroom. MC, V. **Amenities:** Restaurant; bar; Internet cafe ($3 for 15 min.); snorkel gear & kayaks.

Derek's Place   If Little Corn is not isolated enough for you, stay at Derek's Place. This rustic lodge is a 20-minute forest walk away from the main part of the island, which means you have your own private cove. It offers basic but romantic tree house–style huts on a green lawn overlooking the shore on the northern tip of the island. The rooms are smallish and dark, but sparkling clean, and they have excellent views and a delightful sea breeze. The American-Spanish owners are helpful and cook up family-style dinners in the evening.

Georges Cay. www.dereksplacelittlecorn.com; ✆ **505/2419-0600.** 4 units. $50 double. No credit cards. **Amenities:** Restaurant.

Ensueños   Ensueños takes the description rustic to a whole new level with cabanas that seem to have grown from the ground in a funky, organic form. Palm fronds fringe some tent-like structures that look like tropical squats. One is made from orange clay. Inside you'll find carved wood, twisted trunks, and recycled driftwood. There is not a right angle in sight, nor electricity, for that matter. A shared bathroom sits in the open air, with the rather surreal sight of a white water closet sitting amidst jungle foliage. Ensueños is a unique place you are not likely to forget; however, do not go there if you are not prepared to rough it somewhat. This place puts the "eek" into ecolodge and should be avoided by arachnophobes. Its isolation at the northern end of the island is also a factor to consider.

N end of island, E of Otto Beach. www.ensuenos-littlecornisland.com. No phone. 5 units. $30 double w/shared bathroom; $40 double w/private bathroom. **Amenities:** Restaurant.

Hotel Los Delfines   Caribbean-style bungalows of white wooden pillars and green picket balustrades make this the island's most upscale, conventional hotel. Its location is central, close to where most of the villagers live and the nearby dock. The complex has some beautiful gardens, and the restaurant has a lovely view. However, dodgy electric showerheads, noisy air-conditioning, and a bug problem in some rooms mean it is poor value for the price. An adjacent sports bar with a pool table is popular with locals, but can get a little noisy.

N of Jokeman Bank. www.hotellosdelfines.com.ni; © **505/2820-2242.** 18 units. From $50 double. Children under 11 stay free in parent's room. MC, V. **Amenities:** Restaurant; bar; dive store. *In room:* A/C, TV.

Sunshine Hotel   This bright-yellow establishment with clean and tidy rooms is a 3-minute walk from the pier, where the staff will meet you with a wheelbarrow to carry your luggage. Rooms are small but comfortable. They could, however, be a little cleaner, and the air-conditioner needs upgrading. Another negative is the hotel is not on the beach, but a 2-minute walk away. The owner, Glynis, is famous for her cooking, especially her excellent tea infusions and hearty breakfasts.

50m (164 ft.) N of the Fresh Lobster Company. www.sunshinehotellittlecornisland.com; © **505/2426-5284.** 10 units. $41 double. No credit cards. **Amenities:** Restaurant. *In room:* A/C, TV.

WHERE TO EAT IN LITTLE CORN

Stand-alone restaurants are few and far between in Little Corn. The best places to eat are attached to the hotels listed under "Where to Stay," above, though there are some notable exceptions: Bridget's First Stop Comedor, just north of the dock (no phone), is popular with locals, who come to eat its home-cooked shrimp and lobster, and Elsa's, on the eastern side of the island (no phone), is a beachside restaurant that does hearty grilled dishes. Habana Libre, north of the pier (© 505/8848-5412), is a Cuban-owned bar and restaurant that serves excellent veal and, of course, fresh seafood. The terrace view is delicious, as are the mojitos made from homegrown mint. The bar is popular with both locals and visitors, and has a nice vibe with good music.

NORTH-CENTRAL NICARAGUA

Deep, fertile valleys drift upward into misty skies, hiding humble homesteads, patchy jungle, and tumbling waterfalls. North-central Nicaragua is mysterious, charming, and relatively unknown. It is also very chilly. The lush landscape of the highlands makes for a cool, refreshing climate that will come as a welcome relief if you've just arrived from the hot coast.

Though this is cowboy country today—a land of hardy farmers with easy smiles and humble hospitality—the region hasn't always been so peaceful. This tough, beautiful land was a war zone for much of the 20th century. It was here that the legendary liberal General Sandino battled American marines, part of a war for power with the U.S. in which the mountain town of Ocotal won the honor of being the first city in history to be air-raided in 1931. After an American-backed president came to power in 1937, things were relatively calm here until the rise of the Sandinistas in the 1970s and their march on Managua from the north. Contras in the 1980s then wreaked havoc until a 1990s peace treaty allowed farmers to once again work their fields of tobacco, coffee, and vegetables without a rifle slung over their shoulders. Then, complete disaster struck in the form of Hurricane Mitch in 1998. The devastating storm most affected the north of the country, wiping away entire towns.

Fortunately, this part of Nicaragua is calm again, and the only clouds on the horizon are those real ones that roll down the mountain and envelope you. The north has truly proved itself to be an enduring beauty. Commerce has returned in the form of abundant harvests and swarming street vendors. Ecotourists are attracted by trekking in the pristine jungle. Agrotourism has a great future in the form of coffee farms and tobacco factory tours. Whether it's watching old ladies roll fat cigars in the town of Estelí or exploring isolated rural retreats near Matagalpa, this part of Nicaragua cannot fail to attract and enchant you.

ESTELI

Estelí is sometimes called the "Diamond of the Segovias." Such a sobriquet might be a little exaggerated, but Estelí *is* set on a broad, flat valley, surrounded by peaceful rural villages, and is a glorious sight in the sun. Its elegant cathedral and shady plaza make for very pleasant strolling, and you can easily spend a day or two here taking in its revolutionary murals, shopping for excellent handicrafts, and perhaps visiting one of the cigar factories or coffee farms in the area. Its several universities means it has a youthful, vibrant population, and its location as the last main town before the Honduran border means many travelers stop off here for a taste of the highlands.

A staunch Sandinista stronghold, Estelí was heavily bombed by the Somoza regime during the worst years of the revolution, adding credence to its other, less appealing, nickname—the "River of Blood." Hurricane Mitch left its mark, too—the usually dry Río Estelí became a massive torrent that gorged its way through the city's hinterland, taking people and houses with it. Thankfully, the town has now settled back into a peaceful farming lifestyle. It's currently a city of 110,000 and an important agricultural center for tobacco, wheat, cattle, and cheese. It's also the closest town to the spectacular Miraflor Nature Reserve, the waterfall Salto Estanzuela, and the Tisey Reserve, and it is the biggest Nicaraguan city before the Honduran border.

Essentials

GETTING THERE & DEPARTING

BY BUS   The city's market bus station is known as **COTRAN Sur,** 15 blocks south of Parque Central (© **505/2713-6162**), and it serves major cities such as Managua, León, and Matagalpa. There are hourly buses for the capital that take 3 hours and cost C60. The last bus for Estelí from Managua is at 5:45pm. Matagalpa-bound buses leave from Estelí every 30 minutes, with the last bus leaving at 4:20pm. This trip takes 2 hours and costs C40. There are only two services a day between León and Estelí. These buses leave León at 6:30am and 3pm and Estelí at 6:45am and 3:10pm. The journey takes 3 hours and costs C60.There are also numerous microbuses that serve these routes regularly.

BY CAR   To drive from Managua, you must take the airport road east to Tipitapa, and then go north via Sebaco. The road then forks, with Matagalpa to the northeast and Estelí to the northwest. **Budget Rent a Car** (© **505/2713-2584;** esteli@budeget. com.ni) is located 20m (66 ft.) south of the Monumento Centenario on the Panamericana. **Dollar Rent A Car** (© **505/2713-3060**) is on the Panamericana at Km 1140.

ORIENTATION & GETTING AROUND

The city center is tucked between the Río Estelí and the Pan-American Highway, and is easily explored on foot. The commercial heart is based around the intersecting streets of Calle Transversal and Avenida Principal (also known as Av. Central). There is a street-numbering system based around this axis, but it is typically ignored. Most everything is a few blocks from the Plaza or the Texaco station.

VISITOR INFORMATION

There's a small **Intur,** a half-block south of Parque Central on Avenida Central (© **505/2713-6799**), but it's pretty useless. It is open weekdays from 7am to 2pm. Many of the city's Spanish schools are good sources of information concerning where to go in the area, as well. See "Spanish Language Schools in Estelí," later in this chapter. **Agencia de Viajes Aries** (© **505/2713-3369**) is a conventional agency offering transport bookings and tours of the area. It is located 1 block west and half a block south of the Enitel building on Avenida Principal. **Hospedaje Luna,** (1 block north, behind cathedral; © **505/8441-8466;** www.cafeluzyluna.com) is a great source of local information, and the English owner will even help organize tours such as seeing the towns murals or visiting the thriving cigar factories.

[FastFACTS] ESTELÍ

Banks There are three banks situated on the corner 1 block west and 1 block south of the plaza, including **Bancentro,** 2½ blocks south of the plaza on Avenida Principal (℃ **505/2713-6549**). There is an ATM located at Texaco Starmart, 5 blocks north of the soccer stadium. Money-changers operate along Avenida Principal.

Emergencies In case of emergencies, dial ℃ **101.** For other matters, call the police station at ℃ **505/2713-2615.**

Hospital **El Hospital Regional de Estelí** (℃ **505/2713-6300**) is south of the city on the road to Managua.

Internet A number of Internet cafes are located north of the plaza. All charge approximately C38 an hour and are open all day every day. You might try **@Gnica,** which is 1 block south of the southwest corner of the plaza. The main **Enitel** office is 1 block east of the post office (℃ **505/2713-2222**). It's open Monday to Friday from 8am to 8pm and Saturday 8am to 5pm.

Money Matters Money transfers can be arranged at the **Western Union outlet** (℃ **505/2713-5046**), which is 60m (197 ft.) south of the store Super Las Segovias. **Hotel El Mesón,** 1 block north of the plaza (℃ **505/2713-2655**), is one of the few places in the region that will change traveler's checks.

Pharmacy **Pharmacia Corea,** 1 block north of the market (℃ **505/2713-2609**), offers mail services and money transfers, in addition to stocking pharmaceutical goods.

Post Office The main post office, **Correos de Nicaragua Estelí,** is at the junction with Calle Transversal and Avenida Central (℃ **505/2713-2085**).

Shopping in Estelí

If you're after leather cowboy boots, you need to stop by Estelí. All around Avenida 1a Norte Este and Avenida Central, you'll find stores selling quality leather goods in the form of belts, hats, saddles, and of course, footwear for the discerning *vaquero*. Most shops will carefully measure your feet and rustle up a custom-made pair of boots in less than a week, for around C1,200.

Artesanía La Esquina, 1 block north of the cathedral (℃ **505/2713-2229**), and **Artesanía Nicaraguense,** 1 block south of the cathedral (℃ **505/2713-4456**), have a good selection of local soapstone pieces and Ducualí pottery, as well as general Nicaraguan handicrafts. **Guitarras y Requintas el Arte,** beside INISER (℃ **505/2713-7555**), sells beautifully crafted guitars and mandolins.

What to See & Do in Estelí

In addition to the below attractions, check out the **Museo de Historia y Arqueología** (℃ **505/2713-3753**), which houses a small, mildly interesting collection of pre-Columbian artifacts. It is in the same building as the Casa de Cultura and is open 9am to noon on Monday, Tuesday, Thursday, and Friday.

Iglesia de San Francisco This grand, cream-colored church, with its neoclassical facade and elegant twin bell towers, stands in front of the town's bustling central plaza (Parque Central). The church has been rebuilt several times, each time getting bigger and more sophisticated. It began as a simple adobe structure in 1823 and was revamped with a baroque facade in 1889. Architecturally, it is the most interesting building in the city.

Parque Central. No phone. Free admission. Daily 5–8pm.

Miraflor means "flower view," and the 206-sq.-km (80-sq.-mile) patch of pristine nature that is **Reserva Natural Miraflor** ★★ certainly lives up to its name. It has one of the largest colonies of orchids in the world, with 300 species blooming amid begonias and moss-draped oak trees. Tall pine trees hide toucans and parakeets, while armadillos and skunks scurry across the forest floor. Howler monkeys jump from branch to branch, while sloths just do their thing and hang out. There are more than 200 bird species and numerous butterflies all sharing this diverse habitat of tropical savanna, jet-black marshy swamp, dry bush, and a cloud forest that peaks at 1,484m (4,869 ft.).

Five thousand people are also scattered across the reserve, some of whom offer homestays, where you can sit on a simple, rickety veranda and enjoy the view while sipping home-grown chamomile tea or coffee. You can trek or horseback ride to hilltop lookout points, ancient caves, prehistoric mounds, and pre-Columbian settlements. La Chorrera is one of the more ambitious hikes, the end destination being a spectacular 60m-high (197-ft.) waterfall.

The reserve is very much a local initiative, operated and preserved by the community that lives here with little or no government help. They are pioneers in sustainable farming, organic agriculture, fair-trade produce, and of course, ecotourism. The reserve's facilities are rustic and unassuming. There is little or no electricity, nor piped water. This is no five-star jungle hideaway, but nature in all its raw glory—as such, it's perfect for birders, horseback riders, artists, and orchid lovers. It is possible to visit the reserve in 1 day, but to truly appreciate it, it's wise to stick around, stay with a family for a few days, and explore it further.

UCA, 2 blocks north and 1 block west of the Esso station in Estelí (✆ 505/2713-2971; www.miraflor.org), is one of the main cooperatives that oversee the reserve. They can help with excursions and homestays. The office is open Monday to Friday from 8am to 12:30pm and 2 to 5pm. **Posada La Soñada** (✆ 505/2713-6333) is a well-established lodge that's very basic but comfortable, with a large porch stuffed with hammocks and rocking chairs. The owner, Doña Corina, is famous for her vegetarian cooking. **Finca Lindos Ojos** (www.finca-lindos-ojos.com; ✆ 505/2713-4041) has 14 comfortable rooms that start at $50 for a double. The lodge is an organic coffee farm with solar-powered lighting and is operated by a German couple. They also offer tours in the area.

Miraflor is a 45-minute, bone-shaking ride from Estelí in a colorful school bus. There are four buses a day; the earliest leaves from COTRAN Sur at 6am. The rest leave from COTRAN Norte at noon, 2:15pm, and 3:40pm. The UCA (see above) can also help arrange transportation.

La Casa de Cultura   This is Estelí's cultural nucleus, with activities such as dance performances, art classes, and music instruction taking place every week. The spacious lobby holds regular exhibitions by local artists, and there are live events most weekends. A pleasant open-air cafe is out back, serving vegetarian fare and fresh juices. You can't miss the building, as it is completely covered in colorful murals.

Av. Central & Calle Transversal. No phone. Free admission. Mon–Fri 9am–noon & 2–5pm.

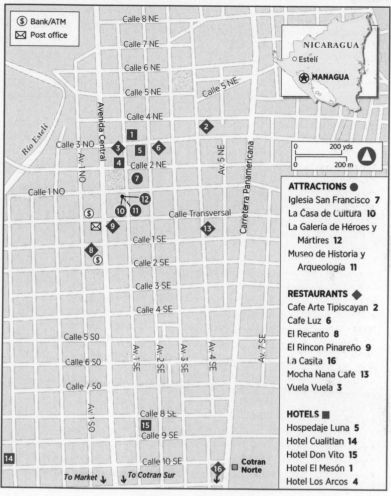

ATTRACTIONS ●

Iglesia San Francisco **7**
La Casa de Cultura **10**
La Galería de Héroes y
  Mártires **12**
Museo de Historia y
  Arqueología **11**

RESTAURANTS ◆

Cafe Arte Tipiscayan **2**
Cafe Luz **6**
El Recanto **8**
El Rincon Pinareño **9**
La Casita **16**
Mocha Nana Cafe **13**
Vuela Vuela **3**

HOTELS ■

Hospedaje Luna **5**
Hotel Cualitlan **14**
Hotel Don Vito **15**
Hotel El Mesón **1**
Hotel Los Arcos **4**

La Galería de Héroes y Mártires   This simple but touching one-room museum is a tribute to the many young men and women who died in Estelí's darkest days—when it was an urban battleground between the Sandinistas and the National Guard. Curated by 300 women who lost their children in the war, the museum exhibits old photos, weaponry, uniforms, and personal items of the fallen. The building itself used to be a Somoza jailhouse, and you'll often find mothers of the martyrs in attendance to give their personal stories of those awful times. You can ask to see other memorabilia that are not on permanent display.

½ block S of the church. ✆ **505/2713-3753.** Free admission. Mon–Sat 9am–4pm.

ATTRACTIONS AROUND ESTELI
Hiking

One of the best area hiking excursions is to the lush, green, and picturesque **Estanzuela Falls,** a 20m (66-ft.) cascade with a pool that's perfect for swimming and cooling off in. You must take the road to the hamlet of Estanzuela just south of the city (turn right after the hospital) to get to the path. It is only an hour-long walk, but bring food and water, as there are no stores after the highway junction. **Reserva Tisey** nature reserve is worth visiting just to climb its hill and enjoy its spectacular view. On a clear day, the Pacific lowlands and a line of volcanic peaks as far away as Lago Managua sweep before you. The reserve itself is made up of organic farms and jungle treks. You can go horseback riding or stay at the **Eco Posada Tisey** (*(C)* **505/2713-6213**), an organic farm that offers simple rooms for $20 and dorm beds for $10. It is 8km (5 miles) southwest of the city, a little beyond Salto Estanzuela on the same road.

Touring the Tobacco Factories

Tobacco will kill you. But in the meantime, why not take advantage of being in the cigar capital of Nicaragua and check out just how they make the world-famous Nicaraguan *puro*. You do not have to be a puffing tycoon to appreciate the rich history and skill that goes into a Churchill or a Cohiba. Estelí's plantations were founded by Cuban exiles in search of the perfect tobacco-growing spot, and their cigars now rival those from that Caribbean island. Cigar tours are still very much a novelty, and visits to the surrounding factories can be hit and miss. Make sure to make an appointment, or better yet, arrange a tour with the friendly staff at Hospedaje Luna (see below).

Nic Cigar Tabacalera Perdomo   The heaps of bicycles outside this industrial building hint at the 500-person workforce inside, sitting at tables hand-rolling 45,000 cigars a day. Cavernous rooms are a hive of activity, with missile-shaped cigars lying wrapped in newspapers with the occasional torpedo hanging from a supervisor's mouth. The factory conducts short 15-minute tours explaining the different stages in the cigar-making process. Traded under the Perdomo label, Nic Cigar exports its wares to Miami, Austria, Mexico, and as far afield as Russia. The leaf is sourced from nearby fields, and the skins are imported from Indonesia and Cameroon to give each brand its own particular color and taste. The factory is located 5 minutes from town on the northern highway, just over the bridge and down a dirt track. There is no formal gift store, but it is possible to buy cigars at the end of the tour.

Barrio el Rosario, Km 150 Carretera Panamericana. *(C)* **505/2713-5486;** www.perdomocigars.com. Free admission. Mon–Fri 8–11:30am & 2–4pm.

Tabacalera Santiago ★   Even the security guard here has a fat cigar in his mouth. Tabacalera Santiago is an attractive cigar factory that offers a very comprehensive tour explaining all the stages that go into making a giant, aromatic stogie. A large, yellow-and-blue warehouse surrounds a courtyard with a fountain and palm trees. Piles of leaves dry under the sun, and hundreds of workers mill around and haul bales from trucks. Each room has a specific purpose, and a worker from each will stop to explain their purpose. There is a fermentation room where piles of leaves sit gathering taste with giant thermometers monitoring their temperature. In the skin room are vapor-soaked leaves imported from all over the world, which will be used as a final wrapper. In the assembly room, hundreds of human rollers sit at tables sprucing five leaves together to form a tight roll in a matter of seconds. The aging room displays giant cigars in a variety of shapes: magnums, Churchills, coronas, and twisters, all of which can be bought at the in-house gift store. *Note:* Call ahead to make an appointment for a tour. Tours are in Spanish. For an English guide, contact Hospedaje Luna (see below).

Km 141 Carretera Panamericana. ℂ **505/2713-2758.** Free admission. Mon–Fri 7–11:30am & 2–4pm.

Where to Stay in and around Estelí

Hospedaje Luna   A clothesline stretches across a plain, central courtyard leading to tall doors that open to two ample dorms and two private rooms. Hospedaje Luna is the backpackers' choice in Estelí, where travelers find a bunk amidst basic decor with local information divulged over free tea and coffee. The helpful owners will set you up with information about what's possible to do here, and there are bikes to help you get around. Across the road is the sister establishment, Cafe Luz.

1 block N behind cathedral. www.cafeluzyluna.com; ℂ **505/8441-8466.** 6 units. $8 dorm bed; $22 double. AE, MC, V. *In room:* Wi-Fi (free).

Hotel Cualitlan   If you ignore the somewhat scuzzy neighborhood and the 4km (2½-mile) distance from town, the Cualitlan is one of the most distinctive hotels in the area. It comprises a set of well-appointed chalets surrounding a lush courtyard teeming with plants and animals. A huge parrot greets you at reception, a bewildering array of cans and pots holds plants and shrubs, and typewriters sit beside ancient radios with the occasional ceramic hen for ornamentation. There are birdhouses, a garden nursery, and an attractive patio restaurant to take it all in. The cabins are handsome and spacious. The beds are a little low, but are surrounded by sturdy rock walls and attractive fittings. The hotel is down an unpaved road, but is perfect for those traveling in their own car and thus free to come and go as they please.

2 blocks S & 4 blocks E of COTRAN Sur. cuallitlan@zonaxp.com; ℂ **505/2713-2446.** 14 units. $35–$50 double. AE, MC, V. **Amenities:** Dining area. *In room:* Fan, TV.

Hotel Don Vito   Estelí's newest hotel (opened in late 2008) is a small, family-run affair with psychedelic colors and lots of mirrors. Orange spiral pillars set the tone as you enter into a small lobby with white floor tiles and blue-and-white ceilings. The rooms are just as colorful but immaculate. There is a balcony upstairs with wicker chairs overlooking the street. Popular with business clientele and the occasional family, the Don Vito makes a welcome mid-range option in a city that lacks good hotels.

½ block E of Jardín Infantil. www.hoteldonvitoesteli.com; ℂ **505/2713-4318.** 26 units. $30 double w/ no A/C, $40 double w/A/C. *In room:* Fan, TV. Wi-Fi.

Hotel El Mesón ♨   One of Estelí's most-established hotels is in fact a rambling, decrepit property with a shabby courtyard and dim, rickety rooms. This low, blue corner building is 1 block from the plaza and holds a cafe and travel agency. An adequate choice if you can't get find anything better or you are watching your córdobas. The hotel also offers a car-rental service and organized tours. It is also one of the few places you can cash traveler's checks in town.

1 block N of cathedral. www.hotelelmesonesteli.com; ℂ **505/2713-2655.** 16 units. $20 double. AE, MC, V. **Amenities:** Dining area. *In room:* Fan, TV.

Hotel Los Arcos ★   Hotel Los Arcos is an excellent nonprofit endeavor that meets the needs of tourists while helping the local community. The large mansion-style house is a half-block from the plaza and has a delightful color scheme of blue and orange set amidst arched galleries that overlook a gorgeous garden courtyard with a fountain and palm trees. The halls are wide and dotted with potted plants. Out

Spanish Language Schools in Estelí

Estelí is a great place to stop and brush up on your Spanish, since it is home to a number of language schools. **Asociación de Madres de Héroes (*(C)* 505/2713-3753; emayorga70@ yahoo.com)** is a good place to start. It is located in the Galería de Héroes y Mártires, listed above. **Cenac Spanish School (*(C)* 505/2713-2025; www. spanishschoolcenac.com)** offers homestays and intensive courses. It is located on the Panamericana, close to Calle 7a SE. **Hijos del Maíz (*(C)* 505/2713-4819; www.hijosdelmaiz. net)** is a community-based initiative that offers homestays in a village called El Lagartillo, 1 hour by bus from Estelí.

back, there is a larger courtyard with a giant mural. The rooms are on the small side but have comfy double beds and big fans. The bathrooms are also a little tight but are delightfully decorated with rainbow-colored tiles. One criticism: The windows look out onto an internal hall or gallery and have no lace curtains, meaning you must pull the heavy curtains and lose the light if you want privacy.

1 block N of cathedral. www.familiasunidas.org/arcos/presentacion.htm; *(C)* **505/2713-3830.** 32 units. From $50 double; from $75 triple or quadruple. AE, MC, V. **Amenities:** Restaurant/bar. *In room:* Fan, TV.

Where to Eat in Estelí

MODERATE

Cafe Arte Tipiscayan NICARAGUAN   Sculptor Freddie Moreno opened this spacious restaurant to display his art and sculptures, and share highland culinary delights such as *puyaso* (grilled meat) and *pinol* (a milky corn drink). Leather-backed chairs surround solid round tables held up with rock sculptures. There is a small garden shrine out back and plans to open a roof terrace, as well as refit the facade with a sculpture of the planet. It's an interesting lunch stop, and if Freddie is around, he'll take you on a tour of his nearby workshop.

200m (656 ft.) north of Shell & 150m west (492 ft.) W. *(C)* **505/2713-7303.** Main courses C120. Tues–Sun noon–10pm.

El Rincon Pinareño NICARAGUAN   Estelí's most formal restaurant is not so formal considering it has pink plastic seating and paper napkins. However, it does have a nice balcony overlooking the street and an extensive, if a little unsurprising, menu. Chicken comes in a dozen varieties, including smoked, roasted, fried, breaded, and in salad. The garlic prawns are delicious, as are the many juices and cocktails. Try the vanilla flan for dessert.

Beside Enacal, Casa 8. *(C)* **505/2713-7303.** Main courses C120. Tues–Sun 11am–10pm.

Mocha Nana Cafe ★ ☺ COFFEEHOUSE   At last a cafe that does *café!* Mocha Nana offers eight coffee varieties, including macchiato and mocha, in a pleasant street bungalow. Inside are chunky wooden seats and dark-stained tables with polished wood place mats, a comfy couch in one corner, and a small bookshop in the other. Overall, the decor is light, elegant, and restrained, and there is a little patio out back with a simple garden with a child's slide. The menu includes hot bagels, cold shakes, and toasted sandwiches.

3½ blocks E of Casa de Cultura. *(C)* **505/2713-3164.** Snacks C80. Mon–Fri 9am–7pm; Sat 11am–9pm.

Vuela Vuela NICARAGUAN   Located in a colorful corner town house a block from the plaza, this is one of Estelí's more inviting restaurants. It has wagon-wheel ceiling lamps and washed-orange walls that lend to the overall laid-back, casual atmosphere. The food is pretty standard and won't be getting any Michelin stars soon. Still, it's a convenient stop for steak, pork, and chicken with a little paella thrown in. The wine list is varied, with 18 labels from Argentina, Chile, Spain, and Italy.

1 block N of cathedral, beside Los Arcos. ☏**505/2713-3830.** Main courses C120. Mon–Sat 8am–11pm.

INEXPENSIVE

Cafe Luz ★ 🎁COFFEEHOUSE/RESTAURANT   This rainbow-colored cafe is more than just a good breakfast stop, it's also a valuable information point run by British proprietor Janie Boyd, known as Juanita to the locals. Tall doorways open onto checkered floor tiles with a small back bar in the corner. Popular with travelers early in the morning or late at night, the kitchen dishes out decent shakes and juices, as well as lasagna and fajitas. The scarlet walls hold a notice board with local events and volunteer opportunities, as well as a tiny gift shelf with cigars and beads. Across the road is the sister establishment, Hospedaje Luna (see above).

1 block N behind cathedral. ☏**505/2713-6100.** Main courses C80. Daily 8am–midnight.

El Recanto COFFEEHOUSE   This popular breakfast stop is a small house with two table-jammed rooms that lead to a small courtyard next to the noisy kitchen. It is packed with locals early in the morning, feasting on generous helpings of *gallo pinto*.

1 block S & ½ block E of post office. ☏**505/2713-2578.** Main courses C40. Mon–Fri 7am–5.30pm; Sat 7am–3pm.

La Casita ★★ 😊COFFEEHOUSE   An inconspicuous little house on the side of the highway is the entrance to a delightful cafe that is also a garden, plant nursery, park, playground, and meeting place. A small wood bridge crosses a flower-trimmed stream, followed by a rock path that leads to a bamboo grove and a cactus garden. School kids sit on the lawn doing their homework while the adults dine on freshly baked bread, cheese, and yogurt. Its Scottish owner, David Thomson, must be commended on creating a charming refuge popular with both locals and visitors. La Casita is a 5-minute taxi ride from the town center.

Beside new hospital, opposite La Barranca. ☏**505/2713-4917.** Main courses C80. Tues–Sun 9am–7pm; Mon 2–7pm.

Estelí After Dark

For such a small town, Estelí has a lively night scene if you know where to look. **Cafe Luz** (see above) is a popular pit stop before venturing further. If you don't know where to go, just follow the crowd.

Ixcoteli   This courtyard bar has a nice vibe, even if it is a little rough at the edges. Two bars border a plant-filled patio with backlit tree trunks. It attracts a mature crowd who come to enjoy good old-fashioned ranchero and romantica music peppered with '80s rock and pop. It makes for a nice lunch stop, too, with average Nicaraguan fare. 1 block S of Petronic. ☏**505/2714-2212.** Daily 10am–midnight.

Las Vegas   This is the only place in town with a carpet, even if it is badly stained and has seen better days. Las Vegas lives up to its name, as its front room is jammed with slot machines. Keep walking through, however, and you'll enter the dark, dingy arena for what is one of Estelí's favorite past times: karaoke. The locals may be shy and reticent in daily life, but hand them a microphone, and they have no shame nor hesitancy to croon and yodel. The somewhat tacky decor (think 1970s peep parlor) with no natural light does not deter the patrons, and it is a popular after-office spot on Thursday and Friday, packed to the rafters until late at night. 100m (328 ft.) S of hospital. No phone. Daily 5pm–midnight.

Semáforo Rancho Bar ★ *Semáforo* means traffic light, and this establishment has two outside, in case you should miss it. They mark the entrance to a gigantic frond-thatched barn with open space and a long bar. A stage to the left hosts live music on the weekends that attracts an older crowd that sits at the red-decked tables tapping their feet to ranchero. Out back, there is another dance floor and patio. Semáforo is located on the highway to Managua with the misnomer "the boulevard." 500m (1,640 ft.) S of hospital. ℂ **505/2813-3814.** Thurs–Sun 5pm–midnight.

MATAGALPA

130km (81 miles) N of Managua; 230km (143 miles) N of León

Enjoy a cup of the finest coffee in the world while admiring this distinctive valley city and its surrounding green hills. The "Pearl of the North" has steep, hilly streets and clean mountain air, and is settled by 80,000 Norteños who occupy themselves mostly with cattle or coffee beans. Though it's not the tidiest of towns, it nevertheless has a rural charm and is comfortably nestled along a narrow, unassuming stream called the Río Grande de Matagalpa—actually Nicaragua's second-longest river, which flows the whole way to the Caribbean.

Matagalpa was first settled by the Nahuatl Indians, and though the Spanish introduced cattle in the 17th century and the Germans introduced coffee in the 19th, they both originally came here looking for gold. While gold wasn't discovered, the city became a coffee boomtown and important economic center for the country. Such fortune has waned a bit since the drop in the price of beans. This town is also the birthplace of the greatest Sandinista, Carlos Fonseca, and the resting place of the much-loved juggling volunteer Benjamin Linder (see box on p. 192). In addition to boasting great shops selling local black ceramics and coffee farms primed for visitors, Matagalpa makes a good base for nearby treks in the beautiful tropical forest; it's also the last stop before the famous Selva Negra Mountain Resort.

Essentials
GETTING THERE
Matagalpa's main bus station, **COTRAN Sur,** 1km (½ mile) west of Parque Darío (ℂ **505/2782-3809**), services routes from Estelí, Jinotega, León, Masaya, and Managua. The Managua buses depart every hour from Mercado Mayoreo in the capital, take 2½ hours to reach Matagalpa, and cost C60.

Small *colectivos* (minivans) also travel every 30 minutes between Matagalpa and Managua, starting at 5am and ending at 6pm. There are two services daily from the León bus station to Matagalpa. They depart at 5am and 3pm, take 3 hours, and cost C50. The reverse service goes to León at 6am and 3pm.

There is a smaller bus station called **COTRAN de Guanaco** (no phone) in the north of the city that serves towns farther in the interior such as San Ramón and Río Blanca. The roads to such places are sometimes impassable in the rainy season, however.

ORIENTATION
The heart of the city stretches along the eastern bank of the river, and its epicenter lies between two plazas, **Parque Morazán** and **Parque Rubén Darío,** the former

of which is alive with people walking, talking, selling, or just admiring the plaza's many trees and birds. Incredibly, there are only two streets with names in the entire city, Avenida José Benito Escobar and Avenida Central Don Bartolomé Martinez.

GETTING AROUND

If your legs are up for it, try to walk everywhere in the city proper—the city's steep streets open up its secret charms. Taxis within the town cost C15, and there are regular city buses that crisscross the town for C5.

The surrounding area has some of the most scenic roads in all of Nicaragua, especially the curving valley road to Jinotega. I recommend renting a car so that you can pull into neighboring coffee plantations and stop to explore beautiful cedar, pine, and hardwood forests. **Budget** (© 505/2772-3041; www.budget.com.ni) has an outlet at La Virgen Shell Station on the southern outskirts of the town. **Autos Económicos de Nicaragua** (© 505/2772-2445) is half a block west of the park on its northern side; **Rent a Car Simo** (© 505/2772-6290) is 1 block west and half a block south of the Banco Mercantil, and **Simo's Rent a Car** (© 505/2772-6260) is on the corner of El Progresso. Rates for all agencies start at C800 per day.

VISITOR INFORMATION

Intur, 1 block north of Parque Rubén Darío (© 505/8612-7060), is open Monday to Friday from 8am to noon and 1:30 to 5pm.

Matagalpa Tours, half a block east of Banpro (© 505/2772-0108; www. matagalpatours.com), is the trekking expert for the area and the best-organized tour company in town. They conduct tours of the coffee farms and arrange overnight stays in nearby ecolodges.

[FastFACTS] MATAGALPA

Banks Most of the city's banks are situated on the southeast corner of Parque Morazán. **Banpro** is 1 block south of Parque Morazán on Avenida Bartolomé Martínez (© 505/2772-2574). There is an ATM at **BAC** (© 505/772-5905), a half-block east of the southeast corner of Parque Morazán. Casual money-changers operate on all corners in this area, as well. Money transfers can be arranged at the **Western Union** (© 505/2778-0069) a half-block north of the Alcaldía.

Emergencies For emergencies, dial © **101.** For other police matters, call © 505/2772-3870.

The fire brigade can be called at
© **505/2772-3167.**

Hospital Matagalpa Hospital (© 505/2772-2081) is north of the city on the road to San Ramón.

Internet Internet outlets are located throughout the city, but **CyberCafé Downtown** (no phone) has the best location, a half-block west of the southwest corner of the Parque Darío. It's open daily from 8:30am to 8pm. All outlets charge approximately C40 an hour.

Telephones Cheap international calls can be made from most Internet cafes. Public phones are in the post office, and a

number of card-based booths are dotted around town. The main **Enitel office** is 1 block east of Parque Morazán (© 505/2772-4600). It's open daily from 7am to 9pm and sells phone cards.

Pharmacy Pharmacy Matagalpa (© 505/2772-7280) is in front of the restaurant Pescamar. It's open Monday to Saturday from 8am to 6pm and Sunday 8am to noon.

Post Office The main post office, **Correos de Nicaragua Matagalpa** (© 505/2772-4317), is 1 block south and 1 block west of Parque Morazán's southeastern corner.

The Life & Times of Benjamin Linder

Benjamin Linder was a young engineering graduate from California who moved to Nicaragua in the early 1980s. An accomplished juggler and unicyclist, Linder was inspired by the 1979 Sandinista revolution and, like hundreds of other *internacionalistas,* wished to contribute toward helping the country's poor. He moved to the northern highlands and helped out in community projects such as vaccination drives. It was there that he put his skills as a juggler to good use. He dressed as a clown and with his unicycle encouraged families to visit the local clinic for measles shots. He also began work on a small hydroelectric dam with the aim of bringing light to the village of San José de Bocay. While working there, the 27-year-old was ambushed and killed by Contra rebels, along with two Nicaraguan companions. His death in 1987 made world headlines, as it came amid an intense debate in the United States over the government's support of counterrevolutionary rebels. Linder's death shone light on a conflict that had killed 30,000 Nicaraguans and it contributed to Congress's finally withdrawing support a year later.

Linder is now revered in Nicaragua and celebrated in countless murals as a juggling ambassador. He is held up by many as an American who made a positive contribution, and his efforts have now been duplicated by countless Americans doing good works in Nicaragua (see the box "Volunteering Opportunities in Nicaragua," on p. 110). Benjamin Linder's grave can be visited in the northern city of Matagalpa (see below).

Shopping in Matagalpa

This area is famous for its black ceramics, and you'll find numerous outlets selling such pottery. **Cerámica Negra,** next to Parque Rubén Darío (© **505/2772-2464**), specializes in this type of ceramics, as does **La Casa de la Carámica Negra,** 2 blocks east of Parque Morazán on the northern side (© **505/2772-3349**). **Centro Girasol,** in the yellow corner building past the first bridge (© **505/2772-6030**), has a crafts store and a food store with local organic produce.

What to See & Do in Matagalpa

Besides the attractions listed below, it's worth a quick stop at two other sites: **La Iglesia de Molaguina,** 2 blocks east and 2 blocks north of Parque Darío (no phone), is a beautiful, simple church. It's popular with locals, although curiously, no one can remember when exactly it was built. East of the city, in the local cemetery, you'll find the final resting place of **Benjamin Linder,** an American volunteer killed during the war (see the box above). His simple gravestone reflects his passion for juggling and unicycling.

Casa Cuna Carlos Fonseca   This tiny adobe building is the birthplace of Carlos Fonseca, founder of the FSLN and martyr of the revolution. As a result, he is Matagalpa's most famous son. The building exhibits artifacts from the *commandant's* life, such as his typewriter, uniforms, and other memorabilia.

1 block E of Parque Darío's S side. © **505/2772-3665.** Free admission. Mon–Fri 8am–noon & 2–5pm.

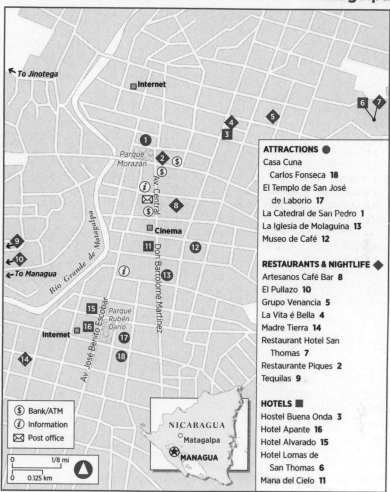

To Jinotega

Internet

Parque Morazán

Av. Central

Cinema

Río Grande de Matagalpa

To Managua

Don Bartolomé Martínez

Parque Rubén Darío

Internet

Av. José Benito Escobar

ATTRACTIONS ●
Casa Cuna
   Carlos Fonseca **18**
El Templo de San José
   de Laborio **17**
La Catedral de San Pedro **1**
La Iglesia de Molaguina **13**
Museo de Café **12**

RESTAURANTS & NIGHTLIFE ◆
Artesanos Café Bar **8**
El Pullazo **10**
Grupo Venancia **5**
La Vita é Bella **4**
Madre Tierra **14**
Restaurant Hotel San
   Thomas **7**
Restaurante Piques **2**
Tequilas **9**

HOTELS ■
Hostel Buena Onda **3**
Hotel Apante **16**
Hotel Alvarado **15**
Hotel Lomas de
   San Thomas **6**
Mana del Cielo **11**

$ Bank/ATM
ⓘ Information
✉ Post office

0   1/8 mi
0   0.125 km

NICARAGUA
Matagalpa
MANAGUA

El Templo de San José de Laborio   One of the earliest church sites in the city, El Templo is historically significant as it was used as base by the indigenous tribes during an uprising in 1881. The current baroque-style church was built in 1917 but rests on the foundations of ruins that date from 1751.

Parque Darío. No phone. Free admission. Daily 5–8pm.

La Catedral de San Pedro   Undoubtedly Matagalpa's most imposing building, the city cathedral seems like many Nicaraguan churches—completely out of proportion to the size and importance of the city. Built in 1874, this is the third-largest church in all of Nicaragua. It has a brilliant white exterior and a huge, cavernous nave guarded by two massive bell towers. It is decorated in a simple baroque style and contains some beautiful woodcarving and paintings inside. Though the church dominates the entire city skyline, it's best viewed from the city's northern hillside.

N side of Parque Morazán. No phone. Free admission. Daily 5–8pm.

Museo de Café More a local history museum than an homage to coffee, this building displays murals and photographs and a small selection of indigenous artifacts. You can buy a bag of local coffee here, and it is good meeting point to hook up with other travelers in the area.

Av. Jose Benito Escobar, 2 blocks E of the mayor's office. ℂ **505/2772-4608.** Free admission. Mon–Fri 8am–noon & 2–5pm.

What to See & Do Around Matagalpa

Cerro Apante is a 1,442m-high (4,731-ft.) hill that dominates the town from its southeastern location. It makes for a good half-day hike and has splendid views at the top. Start at the northeastern corner of Parque Darío and walk southeast down Av. José Benito Escobar . You'll eventually begin to leave the city, walking through the neighborhood of Apante. (If you get lost, just ask for "*el cerro.*") The actual summit is off-limits, but if you follow the ridgeline north, you'll find a footpath that takes you back down to the town another way.

Castillo Cacao ★ This boutique chocolate factory is the real deal and makes "almost organic" chocolate from sacks of beans that go through a roasting machine, then a crusher, and then a grinder, to produce rich, dark chocolate. The Dutch-Chilean owners have set up a nice showroom in a villa-style home, while the factory itself is a dinky little workshop out back designed like a mini-castle. Giggling girls with chocolate-covered hands greet you in the kitchen workshop. Chocolate neophytes, like myself, learn that the cacao beans come from a pod, shaped like an American football, in different varietals, and it is important to know where they are grown regarding quality—in this case, the slopes of Volcán Mombacho. There is only one other chocolate factory in Nicaragua, which makes Castillo Cacao a unique, as well as a charming and instructive, experience. There are no on-site guides, so it is wise to call ahead and arrange a visit or book a tour through your hotel or a local tour operator.

1km (½ mile) E of Esso Las Marías on Carretera La Dalia. ℂ **505/2772-2002;** www.elcastillodelcacao. com. Free admission. Mon–Fri 9am–noon & 2–5pm.

Touring the Coffee Farms Around Matagalpa

While you're in the area, you should definitely try to take a tour of some coffee farms—it's a great opportunity to meet real Nicaraguans in their natural environments, as well as to try some great coffee. However, coffee tourism is very much in its infancy, with very few farms offering set tours in English. It is best to organize a tour through your hotel or lodge.

Finca Esperanza Verde ★★ 🎁 This is one of the better-known coffee-farm lodges, and it's been lauded for its responsible tourism and sustainable practices. It is 30km (19 miles) from Matagalpa, close to the town of San Ramón on the edge of a cloud forest in a very beautiful setting. Here, you can see the bean-processing facilities, admire the verdant slopes of coffee plantations, and hike some lovely trails with fantastic birdlife. The manager, Gifford, is an excellent host and has a wealth of knowledge regarding the art of coffee, explaining the importance of shade-grown plants and the intricacies of fair-trade and organic-labeled coffee. He can also recommend where to go in the surrounding area and will even organize a tour of other nearby coffee estates for guests staying at the lodge. See below regarding accommodations at the *finca*.

Yucul Rd., 18km (11 miles) E of San Ramón. www.fincaesperanzaverde.org; ℂ **505/2772-5003.** C100 adults. Daily 9am–9pm.

Hacienda El Quetzal   Its location is an Edenic series of steep, lush hills dense with tall trees and bordered by the green and red berries of low-lying bushes. Those same bushes are where hundreds of workers in pink plastic aprons, tramping the muddy roads in their gumboots, harvest coffee beans for the Don Paco brand. El Quetzal is a 170-hectare (420-acre) coffee farm that could be regarded as a model for the future. In line with the paternalist tradition, all the workers live on-site in individual homes, and there is also a library and a school. The estate has its own hydroelectric plant, and one of the white clapboard sheds holds a bio-digester churning out methane for re-use. Troughs and pipes mark the harvesting unit where the beans are de-pulped. In the pride of place is a hacienda style house with a large white veranda holding a long line of baseball caps. There are rooms with bunk beds here, and accommodations can be arranged in advance for self-sufficient groups for approximately C400 a bed. Needless to say, the morning coffee in the mountain air is excellent.

El Arenal. www.cafedonpaco.com; ℂ **505/2772-2140.** Daily 8am–4pm. Admission free.

Selva Negra ★★   One of Nicaragua's most famous coffee farms is also a well-known lodge (see below). The 607-hectare (1,500-acre) estate offers day tours of the facilities, and you can also do some excellent forest treks through the sprawling property. The coffee factory itself is a large warehouse in front of the family home. Here, you can see the process where beans are soaked in water pools and de-pulped, surrounded by colorful murals explaining the history of coffee. The owners are making a concerted effort in sustainable agriculture; and because of an extensive recycling program, only one barrel of garbage a week leaves the huge complex, and recycled methane is used for cooking. There is a school, health clinic, and library on the property for the many workers. There is also an interesting little museum within the barn-like restaurant displaying the local history books written by owner and writer Eddie Kuhl. Selva Negra coffee can be bought in the Whole Foods chain in the U.S.

Km 140 Carretera a Matagalpa-Jinotega. www.selvanegra.com; ℂ **505/8612-3883.** C60 adults. Tours daily 9am & 3pm.

Where to Stay in Matagalpa

The choice of hotels is very limited in town, and my advice is try stay in the surrounding countryside to take full advantage of the beautiful nature the area has to offer. Many budget hotels have no hot water, so check beforehand if you dislike cold morning dips. Matagalpa's only hostel, **La Buena Onda,** is a modern, two-story building with courtyard located 1 block north and 2 blocks east of Parque Morazon (ℂ **505/2772-2135;** www.hostelmatagalpa.com). Dorm beds start at $7 and private rooms at $30.

Hotel Alvarado   Somewhat dark and dingy, the Alvarado's main attraction is its great location and super-friendly owners. A dim hallway takes you from the street to a small lobby that could pass for somebody's sitting room. In fact, it *is* somebody's sitting room; you can even admire the family photos while you check in or out. Rooms vary in size and light quality, with the best options at the back, as they are away from the busy street and afford a view of the mountains somewhat interrupted by a water tank. No hot water or breakfast means you might want to try somewhere else first and keep this as a last resort. It helps if you enjoy roughing it amidst '70s furniture.

NW corner of Parque Darío. ℂ **505/2772-2830.** 8 units. From $16 double. No credit cards. **Amenities:** Dining area. *In room:* TV.

Hotel Apante The Apante is much like the Alvarado several doors down, but a little more spruced up and brighter, *and* they have hot water. Checkered floors line a long corridor and a small lobby. The rooms are simple, with open closets and bare walls. The lower-floor rooms have no outside windows and are somewhat darker, with less privacy. The overall feel is rickety and dated, but it's a bargain price, and the hot showers are excellent. Room 5 is a good choice, as it is large and has access to a small communal courtyard.

W side of Parque Darío. ℂ **505/2772-6890.** 18 units. From $11 double. No credit cards. **Amenities:** Dining area. *In room:* TV.

Hotel Lomas de San Thomas ★★ 🗡 ☺ Like its hilltop location, this hotel is way above anything else in town. The mock-colonial style seems rather genuine, with its grand proportions of brick arches resting on thick concrete pillars. A C-shaped gallery runs around a central courtyard with a long pool-like fountain graced with vegetation and a marvelous view. The rooms are so big they could easily accommodate a family of five, with TV, fridge, and walk-in wardrobe. The bathrooms are also rather massive, with blue marble countertops and wooden-board ceilings. Each room has a balcony, with a larger communal balcony at the center. Everything is well maintained and immaculate, with nice touches of Spanish tile and dashes of blue. If it had a pool, it would be perfect. The San Thomas is located several blocks from the town center, up a steep incline that would tax a marathon runner.

Just E of Guanaca school. snthomas2006@yahoo.com; ℂ **505/7272-4201.** 25 units. From $52 double; from $70 triple; from $82 quadruple. AE, DC, MC, V. **Amenities:** Restaurant/bar; Internet (free); room service. *In room:* TV, refrigerator.

Mana del Cielo 🗡 Opened in 2008, the Mana del Cielo is the best option after the San Thomas. Located on a busy street, it is anything but grand, but it is a nicely decorated moderate-size hotel with attractive furnishings and immaculate rooms. The lobby is large and airy, with eye-pleasing stone walls and a blue tiled floor. Rocking chairs sit beneath chintzy curtains, but there is lots of light. The rooms, on the other hand, are a little dark, as their windows face the corridor. The pink walls and flowery bed covers are a little over-the-top, but you may appreciate the cushioned toilet seats, if not the ruffled shower curtains. What's most important is that everything is clean and well maintained, and there are several communal spaces to sit back and read, including an upstairs balcony overlooking the street and church.

1½ blocks S of Banco Uno. www.hotelmanadelcielo.com; ℂ **505/2772-0150.** $20 double. AE, DC, MC, V. **Amenities:** Restaurant/bar; Internet (free); room service. *In room:* TV.

Where to Stay Outside Matagalpa

Finca Esperanza Verde ★★ 🎁 This "farm of green hope" is a pioneer in responsible tourism and sustainable agriculture. Here, you'll find basic, brick cabins and a lodge surrounded by organic coffee plantations, cloud forest, waterfalls, and a butterfly farm. A white picket fence encloses an open, timber-framed dining room. The green-roofed cabins, which can accommodate six, are solar-powered, and the drinking water comes from a natural spring. The simple buildings are constructed from handmade brick and other local materials. The lodge is a leading light on the Ruta del Café, and sets up tours to that route's coffee plantations during harvest time from November to February. The farm itself is a nature reserve, with hundreds of species of birds, butterflies, and orchids. There is also a campsite with a roofed picnic area set amid a coffee and banana grove.

Yucul Rd., 18km (11 miles) E of San Ramón. www.fincaesperanzaverde.org; ✆**505/2772-5003**. 6 units. From $75 cabin. Rates include breakfast. AE, DC, MC, V. **Amenities:** Restaurant. *In room:* Fan, no phone.

Hotel Fuente Pura Don't be surprised if you catch a monkey swinging past the window of your room while watching the beautiful sunset here. This hotel is set at the perimeter of El Arenal Nature Reserve and is surrounded by deep forest and lush coffee plantations. The restaurant is fitted with large windows, so you can take advantage of the stunning panoramic views. The rooms are large, modern, and somewhat low-key, with mismatched furniture and plastic garden chairs. There's lots of light, and everything is sparkling clean.

Km 142 (half-hour drive from Matagalpa on rd. to Jinotega). ✆ **505/8876-5081**. 8 units. From $25 double. Rates include breakfast & dinner. No credit cards. **Amenities:** Dining area. *In room:* TV/DVD player.

Selva Negra Mountain Resort ★★ ☺ An old battle tank marks the entrance to this legendary hotel. The Bavarian-style wood cabins betray its German ownership ("*Selva Negra*" means Black Forest). The cabins are set around a pond in what is a working coffee farm called La Hammonia. You can tour the farm, horseback ride, hike, or simply enjoy the peacefulness of this mountain, cloud-forest retreat. It has excellent wildlife-watching, and there is even a stone chapel for those true romantics who wish to get married amid all this nature. The owners are very friendly and also operate a youth hostel on the grounds. Amazingly, the lodge survived the revolution and war (though guests were required to ration the toilet paper). The wood-frame and brick- and glass-fronted cabins have porches and private bathrooms, and are fairly basic but homey. The farm is also welcomes day visitors. It's a 20-minute drive from Matagalpa on the scenic road to Jinotega.

Km 140 Carretera a Matagalpa-Jinotega. www.selvanegra.com; ✆**505/8612-3883**. 34 units. From $30 dorm bed; $50–$125 bungalow; $100–$150 chalet. AE, DC, MC, V. **Amenities:** Restaurant. *In room:* No phone.

Where to Eat in Matagalpa

Some of the best restaurants are located outside the city. In fact, if you are staying in any of the *finca* lodges listed above, you can experience fresh, organic food right where it is grown. **El Pullazo,** on the highway to Managua (✆ **505/277-4449**), is humble in appearance but big at heart. The menu is genuine Nicaraguan, with great beef dishes, *guirila* pancakes, and *cuajada* cheese. It must be one of the few places with a fish tank in the northern highlands. It is open daily from 10am to 11pm. **Restaurante Piques** (✆ **505/2772-2723**) is a laid-back Mexican restaurant, half a block east of the BAC bank, close to Parque Morazán. It is open daily from 10am to midnight.

La Vita é Bella ★ ITALIAN This is a rare find—a genuine Italian restaurant in the heart of cowboy country. The pasta-filled menu is very vegetarian-friendly, with little chicken Marsala thrown in for die-hard carnivores. They even serve Itali vodka. This pleasant restaurant is open for lunch and dinner, and very popular with locals and expats alike. Located on an alleyway, it can be hard to find, but ask any local as it is well known.

2 blocks E & 2 blocks N of cathedral. © **505/2772-5476.** Main courses C100. No credit cards. Tues–Sun 2–11pm.

Restaurant Hotel San Thomas ★ INTERNATIONAL   You should come here just for the view, and then linger and try one of the eclectic items on the menu, such as the fajitas, steaks, or shrimp dishes. This elegant, spacious restaurant has lots of natural light and a great view over the valley from the all-glass walls. While you're here, stroll down the hallway and check out the in-house chapel. Or stroll through the garden with a glass of the Argentine tempranillo from the excellent wine list.

Just E of Guanaca school. © **505/2772-4201.** Main courses C140. AE, DC, MC, V. Daily 7am–9pm.

Matagalpa After Dark

Grupo Venancia ★, 1½ blocks south of Iglesia de Guadalupe (© **505/2772-3562;** www.grupovenancia.org), is an excellent cultural space that was started by a volunteer women's group with the idea of creating a venue for music, dance, and the arts in general. It has a low-key atmosphere with an open-air bar offering live performances and movie screenings. It attracts a good mix of Matagalpa's well-heeled culture vultures and a bohemian crowd, especially on Saturdays. If you have some time on your hands, they are always looking for volunteers to help out, as they also organize workshops, publish books, and have a radio show.

Parque Darío ★ is the venue for festivals called Noches Matagalpinas every last weekend of the month—expect live music, food stands, and a very festive atmosphere.

In general, locals here are fond of scuffing their cowboy boots to ranchero, merengue, and reggaeton. Saturdays nights are the liveliest, with roadhouse discos like **Tequilas,** 3km (1¾ miles) out on the Managua highway, coming alive with revelers. **Madre Tierra ★** goes all week (except Tues) with an open-air bar offering pub grub and hammocks. It is located 1½ blocks west of Texaco Central.

Considering what else is on offer, **Artesanos Café Bar** (½ block east of Banpro, in front of the Social Club; © **505/2772-2444**) is by far the nicest bar in town, with roomy ambience and a laid-back, hip feel. The building itself is a nicely restored town house, and there's an open-air deck out the back overlooking a small garden. In addition to beer and cocktails, you'll also find smoothies and fruit juices. There's also a short food menu with decent chicken bites and salads. It attracts a healthy mix of old and young, local and foreign. It's open Tuesday through Sunday from 9am to midnight.

A Side Trip to Jinotega ★★★

A 1-hour drive north of Matagalpa is the sprawling mountain town of Jinotega, otherwise known as the "City of Mists." With its low buildings of corrugated roofs and barn doors, it is not the prettiest of cities, but it has a rural authenticity that cannot fail to charm, especially when the mists roll down from the surrounding hills and envelop its cobbled streets. You'll find an **Intur** office (© **505/2713-6799**) 1½ blocks west of Iglesia de los Angeles with limited information on the area. Jinotega is gateway to other mountain towns, such as nearby **San Rafael del Norte,** or to explore the highlands farther north, especially the 20,000-sq.-km (7,722-sq.-mile) forest reserve **Reserva de Biosfera Bosawas.** Access to this park is limited, however, as this really is off the beaten track and requires planning. The main reason to go to Jinotega is to enjoy the view on the way. The road from Matagalpa is one of the most breathtaking in Nicaragua, with mountain views that go as far as Momotombo Volcano in León.

WHERE TO STAY IN JINOTEGA

Hotel Café ★ 🏨   The scrappy little town of Jinotega was the last place I thought I'd find such a beautiful little hotel. Hotel Café is all the more charming because it's been around for years and has an untouched, genuine feel. Its handsome facade of wrought iron and imposing windows hides an old-world restaurant called Borbon, with marble floors, glittering mirrors, and gilded furniture. The food is standard Nicaraguan fare. In the small, central courtyard is a spiral staircase that rises from the foliage. The well-appointed rooms have blue floor tiles, built-in wardrobes, and queen-size beds; the best are nos. 4 and 5. The hotel is located on a main street several blocks from the plaza.

1 block W & ½ block N of Texaco station. www.cafehoteljinotega.com; ✆ **505/2782-2710.** 25 units. Double $65. AE, MC, V. **Amenities:** Restaurant/bar. In room: Fan, TV.

WHERE TO EAT IN JINOTEGA

The down-to-earth **El Disparate de Potter** (✆ **505/621-3420**) makes for a perfect lunch stop while touring the beautiful Matagalpa–Jinotega road. The name refers to a rocky outcrop that was blasted apart by an English landowner while building a road to his coffee farm in the 1920s. The roadside restaurant is popular with locals and serves standard Nicaraguan fare in a space with a great view. (There's even a viewing platform nearby.) The restaurant is open daily from 8:30am to 8pm.

La Perrera Restaurant NICARAGUAN/MEXICAN   This cream-colored, hacienda-style restaurant sits on the side of the mountain road just before Jinotega and affords beautiful views, inside and out. The decor is a warm arrangement of yellows, browns, and oranges, with wicker chairs surrounding brightly colored tabletops. The menu includes beef, chicken, and seafood, and they do a mean Mexican quesadilla.

3.2km (2 miles) S of Jinotega. ✆ **505/8432-7423.** Main courses C100. AE, DC, MC, V. Mon noon–9pm; Wed–Sun 11am–9pm.

LEON & THE VOLCANIC LOWLANDS

13

Granada might have all the style, but León has all the substance. This historic university city may not be as unblemished and beautiful as its southern rival, but its history of rebellion and political radicalism, coupled with a vibrant and enthusiastic populace, means it wears its wounds with pride and makes for a fascinating place to visit. Those wounds come in the form of bullet-scarred buildings and an ancient abandoned colonial city called León Viejo. Its pride comes in the form of countless churches, museums, and the largest cathedral in Central America, along with narrow cobbled streets that lead to tiny parks and provocative murals. León is very much a city with character and a story to tell. Perhaps that's why León is the birthplace of Nicaragua's greatest hero, the poet Rubén Darío, and is the center of an exciting art scene.

Today, it is the dusty, hot capital of the northwest, but León was once the capital of the nation. It lost its title in 1852, but has been at the forefront of Nicaraguan politics ever since and was a focal point during the Sandinista revolution. The Somoza regime met rebellion with bombings and persecution, and at one stage, torched the central market. A failed uprising in 1978 was the beginning of the end for the dictatorship, and the city was liberated soon after. Every sultry corner seems to have a story. If you are going to take only one guided city tour in Nicaragua, you should do so in León.

León is finally opening up to visitors, with new hotels that can match the best in Granada. It is a city you may intend on just passing through but will doubtless end up lingering in longer than you intended. It also makes a great base for seeing the northwest region of the country. Within striking distance are the dark, sandy strands of Poneloya and Las Peñitas beaches, as well as the wildlife reserve of Isla Juan Venado, which offers a mangrove sanctuary for nesting turtles. Ten smoking volcanoes stand in line like sentries from Lago Managua to the Gulf of Fonseca. They stand over the swelteringly hot lowlands, of which historic León, the thriving agro-city Chinandega, and the coastal port Corinto are the most important towns. Those volcanoes may appear ominous, but they provide rich soil—making the area an agricultural powerhouse and the most populated part of the country. Nevertheless, this northwest region is poor and still recovering from the catastrophic consequences of Hurricane Mitch, which washed away every bridge north of Managua. If you come to hike the area's many volcanoes, walk or surf its dark Pacific strands, watch turtles nesting, or simply indulge yourself in León, the cradle of the revolution, you will be helping to play an important part in the burgeoning tourism industry here.

LEON

Getting There & Departing

BY BUS León's bus station (6a Calle NE; © **505/2311-3909**) is 1km (½ mile) northeast of the city center. Managua is 75 minutes away by microbus and costs C40; buses depart from Mercado Isreal Lewites in the capital to León every 30 minutes from 5am to 5pm. They return to Managua every 30 minutes from 5am to 6pm. Estelí is 3½ hours away and costs C81; there are two buses a day at 5am and 3pm. Chinandega is a half-hour away and costs C25. The trip there takes 1½ hours by ordinary bus and 45 minutes by microbus. There are also connections to Corinto (1½ hr.) and Matagalpa (3 hr.), costing C22 and C80, respectively.

BY TAXI-SHUTTLE Tierra Tour, 1½ blocks north of Iglesia La Merced (© **505/2315-4278;** www.tierratour.com), organizes transfers to Managua and farther afield. Their shuttle service leaves daily for Granada at 4pm. Price depends on the size of your group and can vary between C600 and C1,000. Schedules are flexible, and they can drop you off right at your hotel.

Orientation

León's street system is numerical. The junction of Avenida Central and Calle Central Rubén Darío form an axis at the northeast corner of Parque Central. Streets going north or south are called calles and ascend numerically, as do avenidas that go west and east of Avenida Central. Generally speaking, this numbering system is ignored by locals; when giving directions, they will almost always describe a location in terms of landmarks. The main market, called Mercado Central, is situated behind the cathedral. The old indigenous town of Subtiava is now a western suburb.

Getting Around

León is good for strolling around—it's perhaps easiest to discover its many historic buildings on foot. To get to outlying areas, you can take local buses or ruleteros (pickup trucks with canvas covers), which leave from Mercado Central and the bus terminal (see "By Bus," above). Fares cost C6. Note that the roads around the city are in terrible condition, and it is not uncommon to see children filling potholes with dirt in exchange for coins from passing motorists. Taxis are easy to catch on any corner, and fares start at C10.

Visitor Information

The Intur office (2a Av. NO; © **505/2311-3682**) is open Monday through Friday from 8am to 12:30pm and 2 to 5pm. They have an excellent map of the city, and the staff members are very helpful, though they speak little English. Another Intur Tourist Information Office (© **505/2311-3992**) has opened just north of the cathedral, and here, you may be lucky to find some North American volunteers to help you out with maps and directions.

[FastFACTS] LEON

ATMs There are three ATMs 1 block east of the cathedral; banks to try with ATMs are Credomatic (1a Calle NE; ✆ **505/2311-7247;** www.bac.net) and Bancentro, which is 20m (66 ft.) south of Parque La Merced (✆ **505/2311-0911**).

Emergencies The police can be reached at ✆ **505/2311-3137** or the national emergency number, ✆ **118.**

Hospital The area's largest hospital is **Hospital San Vicente** (✆ **505/2311-6990**), past the bus station.

Internet One efficient Internet outlet is **Compuservice,** in front of Policlinica la Fraternidad (no phone). It is fast, reliable, and open Monday to Saturday from 8am to 9:30pm and Sunday from 9am to 6pm. **Club en Conexión,** 3 blocks north and a half-block east of the Cathedral (no phone), offers Internet access, along with air-conditioning, and is open Monday to Friday from 7:30am to 9:30pm and Saturday 7:30am to 7pm. They both charge an hourly rate of C20.

Laundry **Clean Express,** 4 blocks north of the cathedral (✆ **505/8438-8393**), offers 1-hour laundry service. It's open Monday to Saturday from 7am to 7pm.

Pharmacy Go to **Farmacia López** (Calle Rubén Darío; no phone) for any pharmacy needs.

Post Office The main post office, Correos de Nicaragua (✆ **505/2311-2102**), is 3 blocks north of the cathedral. You'll find public phones outside the Enitel office on the northwest corner of the Parque Central.

Tour Operators

Vapues, on the north side of Iglesia El Laborio (✆ **505/2315-4099;** www.vapues. com), is one of the city's main tour operators, organizing everything from flights to hotel reservations. Tierra Tour, 1½ blocks north of Iglesia La Merced (✆ **505/2315-4278;** www.tierratour.com), organizes tours of the area and transfers to Managua and farther afield. Surf Tours Nicaragua (✆ **505/8814-2975;** www.surftoursnicaragua. com) specializes in surfing tours of the north Pacific coast and offers 7-day packages with accommodations included.

Quetzaltrekkers ★, 1½ blocks east of Iglesia La Recollección (✆ **505/2311-6695;** www.quetzaltrekkers.com) is an agency with a difference. It is run by volunteers, and all profits go to helping street kids in León. They conduct volcanic hiking tours to Momotombo and Cerro Negro, among others.

Julio Tours ★, a half-block north of the cathedral (✆ **505/8625-4467;** www. juliotoursnicaragua.com.ni), is operated by Julio Pineda, an excellent English-speaking city guide who specializes in historical and cultural tours of the city.

What to See & Do in León

Catedral de la Asunción ★★★ The Catedral de la Asunción, which took 100 years to build and is easily the biggest church in Central America, is a must-see when visiting the city, and it dominates the town center. Three architectural styles grace its magnificent proportions—colonial, neoclassical, and baroque. Rumors swirl around the question of why such a huge, majestic church was built in such a small city. Some think that the original architectural plans were swapped accidentally for the plans of ima Cathedral. Others believe that the local clergy secretly elaborated on the plans er a much smaller version was approved by Spain. Whatever its origins, it was a

ATTRACTIONS ●

Catedral de la Asunción **14**
Centro de Arte Fundación
  Ortiz-Gurdián **20**
Galería de Heroes y Mártires **13**
La Casa de Cultura **11**
Museo Rubén Darío **19**
Museo de Tradiciones y
  Leyendas **26**
San Juan Bautista de
  Subtiava **18**

RESTAURANTS & NIGHTLIFE ◆

Barbaro **22**
Cocinarte **27**
El Sesteo **12**
La Olla Quemada **9**
Mediterraneo **3**
Restaurante La Perla **7**
Snake Bar **21**
Solera Bar **24**
Teatro Municipal **23**

HOTELS ■

Big Foot **15**
El Convento **10**
Hostal la Casa Leonesa **2**
Hostel Lazy Bones **4**
Hotel Austria **25**
Hotel Los Balcones de León **17**
Hotel Real de León **8**
La Perla **6**
La Posada del Doctor **1**
Posada Doña Blanca **5**
Via Via **16**

huge undertaking. The original bishop who started the project was replaced by seven others before the cathedral finally held its first Mass in 1747.

Underground tunnels once linked the cathedral to the eight most important churches in the city, a cunning plan to thwart pirates. The original building was destroyed by rampaging Englishman William Dampier in 1685, and one statue of a black Christ still bears the hack wounds of a pirate's sword. Those same tunnels were appropriated by the city authorities in the last century and are now part of the city's sewage system.

The cathedral is home to some masterpieces of Spanish colonial art and acts as a kind of pantheon to some of Nicaragua's most famous national figures. Here, you'll find the Tomb of Rubén Darío, guarded by a weeping lion. You will also find ot'

Mad about Poetry: Rubén Darío and Alfonso Cortés

"Words should paint the color of sound, the aroma of a star."

—Rubén Darío

The corner house that is now the **Museo-Archivo Rubén Darío** was home to not just one, but two great poets. It was the childhood home of world-famous father of *Modernismo* Rubén Darío, a child prodigy abandoned by his parents, who left León at 17 and traveled the world. By pure coincidence, it was also the home of the metaphysical poet Alfonso Cortés some years later. Here, Cortés lost his mind 11 years after Darío's death. He ended up chained to the window grill beside Darío's four-poster bed and was eventually committed to a mental hospital, where he spent the next 20 years in rage and despair with moments of poetic lucidity. Cortés' and Darío's lives were very different, but they shared the same city, the same zeal for words, and the same knack for tragedy. Darío is by far the more famous, whereas Cortés, though much loved in Nicaragua, is often referred to as *el poeta loco* (the crazy poet).

It is intriguing to compare the lives of the two poets. Rubén Darío was always famous. Born in 1867, he was a child prodigy who could read by the age of 3 and was published by the age of 13. His most influential collection of poetry, *Azul,* was written at the age of 21, and it changed the face of Spanish poetry, throwing off the old-fashioned baroque pretence of colonial times and making the language alive with searing lyricism and bold metaphors. Darío was a restless character who jumped from country to country acting as diplomat,

journalist, and writer. He lived in Argentina, Chile, Spain, and France and met all the great literary figures of the day. Twentieth-century poets such as Lorca, Neruda, and Paz all cite him as a major influence, and he is Nicaragua's truest national hero—thus his portrait on the 100-córdoba note. Yet his life was plagued by alcoholism and poverty, and a chaotic love life that resulted in four marriages and four children, three of whom died in childhood. He died in his León home at the age of 49.

Cortés was a recluse who never traveled. He wrote his poems in tiny, microscopic scribbles in newspaper margins. After an unremarkable youth as an impoverished poet, he finally lost his mind in 1927 and spent the rest of his life in care. Yet he managed to translate some of the greatest writers, such as Baudelaire and Edgar Allen Poe, and wrote obscure, paradoxical lyrics about space and time that make him one of the few metaphysical poets in Spanish. Now, he has champions such as Nicaragua's priest poet Ernesto Cardenal, and his lines are learned by schoolchildren. He is increasingly famous in the Spanish-speaking world for writing deeply symbolic words about our existence:

"Time, where are we,
you and I, since I live in you
and you do not exist?"

He died in 1969, nursed in his sister's home 2 blocks from Darío's home (this is now a small museum dedicated to Cortés that is unfortunately closed most of the time). He is buried next to Darío in León Cathedral. Of his rival he said: "I am less important than Darío, but more profound."

important figures, such as Alfonso Cortés, Salomón de la Selva, and Miguel Larrey-aga. At the cathedral's center is a beautiful, Spanish-style courtyard known as the io de Príncipes. The cathedral's domed roof holds the bell La Libertad that unced to the world the independence of Central America from the Spanish empire. Be sure to inquire at Intur for a tour of the church's atmospheric, Gothic roof. With its lichen-stained cupolas and buttresses, it's a great photo opportunity, and of course, there is a good view of the surrounding city and countryside from there, too.

Central Plaza. No phone. C40 adults. Mon–Sat 8am–noon & 2–4pm.

Centro de Arte Fundación Ortiz-Gurdián ★★ If you are getting a little tired of fading murals, make your way to this lovely and extensive gallery, easily the best art collection in the country. Two beautifully restored town houses hold a dazzling selection of paintings and sculptures, ranging from 16th-century Cuzco School portraits to modern Nicaraguan installations. You'll also find some out-of-place surprises, such as works by Rembrandt, Picasso, and Miro.

1 block W of Parque Rubén Darío. www.fundacionortizgurdian.org. No phone. Mon–Sat C20 adults; Sun free admission. Tues–Sat 10:30am–6:30pm; Sun 11am–7pm.

Galería de Héroes y Mártires ★★ This is a homegrown photographic exhibition celebrating León's fallen revolutionary figures. It celebrates those who stood and fell against the Somoza regime and is run by the mothers of such martyrs. It is a humble and humbling site, with the faces of Nicaragua's fallen youth in the 1970s and 1980s looking you straight in the eye. There's a small craft shop on-site if you feel like buying a revolutionary souvenir. Ask for the curator Madre Cony to show you around.

1a Calle NE. No phone. C20 adults (suggested). Mon–Fri 8am–5pm; Sat 8am–noon.

La Casa de Cultura ★ This quaint, colonial building with an imposing wooden balcony is a hive of activity regarding culture and education. There is a rotating art exhibition of local and international artists, often with a biting social commentary. You can also take dance, music, and art classes, and there is always a chessboard available to challenge the local Kasparov. See the "Spanish Classes in León" box, below, for information on language classes and homestay immersions here.

1a Calle NE. ✆505/2311-2116. Free admission (varying fees for classes). Mon–Fri 8am–noon & 2–6pm.

Museo Rubén Darío Born in 1867, Darío is Latin America's greatest poet and a pioneer of 19th-century modernism. Here, you can visit his childhood home—a neat and simple adobe-style house. There are copies of the Paris magazine he produced, as well as correspondence from when he was ambassador to Argentina and Spain. You'll also find a collection of original copies of his books filled with the poetry that inspired the Nicaraguan people with words such as "If one's nation is small, one makes it large through dreams."

Calle Central, 3 blocks W of plaza. No phone. Free admission (donations welcome). Tues–Fri 8:30am–noon & 2–5pm; Sat 9am–noon.

Museo de Tradiciones y Leyendas ☺ This is one of León's quirkiest and most interesting museums, housing a collection of handcrafted figurines that celebrates Nicaragua's rich heritage of legends and characters. Its founder,

Spanish Classes in León

León Spanish Language School is located inside **La Casa de Cultura** (Parque de la Merced, 1½ blocks west of Casa de Cultura, Antenor Sandino Hernández; ✆ 505/8865-3579 or 505/311-2116; www.spanishnicaragua leon.net) and offers a variety of Spanish classes and homestays. **Dariana Spanish School,** half a block west of Iglesia El Calvario (✆ 505/8458-4348; www.metropolitana-ss.com), organizes one-on-one classes and immersion courses.

Señora Toruña, has re-created such colorful folk figures as the Pig Witch and the Golden Crab. Kids should particularly enjoy this museum.

2a Calle SO. No phone. C70 adults. Tues–Sun 8am–noon; Tues–Sat 2–5pm.

San Juan Bautista de Subtiava ★ Located 1km (½ mile) west of the central plaza in the old indigenous quarter of Subtavia is León's oldest intact church. Restored in the 1990s, it is remarkable for the gorgeous sun icon that's carved into its ceiling. The clergy placed such an unusual pagan symbol in a Catholic church to attract an initially reluctant local audience. The arched timber roof held up by stout wooden pillars and the intricate filigreed altar is a testament to the amazing skill of the indigenous craftsmen.

13 Av. SO. No phone. Free admission. Mon–Sat 8am–3pm.

OTHER SIGHTS

León has countless churches and plazas to explore, as well as buildings and murals of historical significance. Iglesia de la Recolección (1a Av. NE) is a gorgeous church with carved stone vines around a pillared facade. The baroque construction has a well-preserved and imposing bell tower. Iglesia El Calvario is on a small hill overlooking Calle Central Rubén Darío. Its twin red-brick bell towers guard a neoclassical facade, and inside, you'll find two marvelous statues of the Good Thief and the Bad Thief. Colorful panels depict biblical scenes, while slim wooden columns hold decorative motifs. La Iglesia y Convento de San Francisco, located in front of the Museo Rubén Darío (see above), has two gorgeous altars and a pretty, shaded courtyard to the side.

A block and a half from the city's main cathedral is **Iglesia La Merced.** Constructed in 1762 by the Mercederian order, it's a fine example of baroque and neoclassical design. It faces a small park and has an attractive bell tower, with nice views below. **Iglesia San Juan** (3a Av. SE) is in an old atmospheric part of town amid small adobe houses. This charming church was built in 1625. If you continue farther north, 1 block from its east side, you'll come across León's old abandoned train station.

Every Saturday, the tidy and open **Parque Central ★**, on the northern side of 1 Calle SE, holds a community fiesta called Tertulia Leonesa with live music and lots of food and drink. It starts in the afternoon and goes on until midnight. Many worthwhile attractions radiate from the park. **Colegio La Asunción** (1a Calle SO) was the first theological college in Nicaragua. **Palacio Episcopal** (1a Calle SE) is an attractive colonial building, as is the **Colegio de San Ramón** (1a Calle SE). The **Mausoleo de los Héroes y Mártires** is within a small plaza bordered by a fascinating mural detailing the revolution. **Casa de Obrero** (2a Av. NO) is where poet Rigoberto López Pérez assassinated the dictator Anastasio Somoza García while dressed as a waiter. There is a plaque outside the house celebrating the event as the "beginning of the end." You can take another trip down revolutionary road at the **Old Jail** (4a Calle SO), which was the site of a significant skirmish between rebels and the National Guard. It is now a remembrance garden.

OUTDOOR ACTIVITIES

KAYAKING The nature reserve Isla Juan Venado ★★ is an intriguing stretch of mangrove swamp with abundant wildlife. It makes for a perfect spot of paddling. The reserve is situated 30 minutes west near the beach town of Las Peñitas. Beach hostel Barca de Oro (www.barcadeoro.com; ✆ 505/2317-0275) rents out kayaks and surfboards.

SURFING The nearby coast is not as famous for surfing as farther south, but ere are still plenty of big waves to catch. Surf Tours Nicaragua (✆ **505/8814-2975;**

The **Maribio Volcanoes** are a 60km-long (37-mile) line of black cones and smoldering craters. There are 21 volcanoes in total, and they are within striking distance of León. They afford several 1-day excursions of vigorous mountain climbing rewarded with spectacular views. It is always wise to go with a local guide or tour operator, as some of the slopes can be treacherous and access across private land difficult to negotiate on your own.

Momotombo is one of the most challenging (and can also be visited in 1 day from Managua). Rising 1,280m (4,199 ft.) in a perfect cone shape, it is the country's most famous volcano. Its upper half is made up of loose shale, which makes it hard to conquer. The volcano has erupted 14 times in the past 500 years, and the geothermal plant on its slopes provides a quarter of Nicaragua's electricity. The lower slopes are made up of dry tropical forest and hold wildlife such as iguanas, parrots, and butterflies. It has a lake known as Laguna Monte Escalante. It takes 8 hours up and down, and is best done with a local tour company, though you can get there independently by hiking beyond the ruins of León Viejo and going north along the highway. Here, you enter through the power plant, but access is often denied.

Cerro Negro is a more popular volcano hike and a little easier. That is not to say it is less exciting. This 675m-high (2,215-ft.) volcano may not look as impressive as its sister cones, but it is one of the most active in the country and constantly belches noxious fumes. It takes 3 hours to go up and down, but go early to avoid the midday heat, as there is absolutely no shade. The slopes are increasingly popular for a spot of volcano board surfing (see "Outdoor Activities," below) on the way down,

which is great fun. Any of León's tour operators can arrange this, but make sure you have proper protective gear. To get there independently, you must jump on a bus and go east to the town of Lechecuago. Here, you will find a poorly maintained trail that takes you to the top.

Volcán Telica is one of Nicaragua's most active and is constantly throwing ash over the town of Telica. Active since 1527, the 1,061m-high (3,481-ft.) cone last erupted in January 2007. It holds a 9,000-hectare (22,239-acre) dry forest reserve on its slopes and makes for a good 7-hour round-trip trek. There are two ways to approach it. One is from Telica on the road to a community known as La Quimera. The other is from Santa Clara, the town next to the Hervidores de San Jacinto, where you can pick up a guide to show you the way.

San Cristóbal is the highest and most handsome at 1,745m (5,725 ft.), with an almost perfect symmetrical shape. It is also one of the most active and challenging to climb. Here, you'll definitely need a guide, as the access roads are complicated and ever changing. A guide can be easily found in the town of Chichigalpa, and a horse, too. Hotel Los Balcones offers hiking trips from León that include a stay on a coffee farm on the volcano's slopes. Avoid going from November to March, when the summit can be extremely windy. It is an 8-hour round trip.

Note: None of these volcano hikes are a walk in the park, especially when the wind is up. Bring plenty of water, and be prepared for a workout. It is best to go in the rainy season, as the summer months can be sweltering and uncomfortable, especially when farmers burn their fields from March to May.

www.surftoursnicaragua.com) specializes in surfing tours of the north Pacific coast and offers 7-day packages with accommodations included.

TREKKING The nearby volcanoes Momotombo and Cerro Negro (see the "Volcano-Hopping from León" box, above, for details) are the most popular trekking excursions. Quetzaltrekkers, 1½ blocks east of Iglesia La Recollección (© 505/2311-6695; www.quetzaltrekkers.com), specializes in treks to both places, as does Big Foot Hostel (see above; © 505/8917-8832; www.bigfootnicaragua.com).

VOLCANO SURFING Yes, you read correctly. Hurtling down the side of a live, black volcanic mound has become the latest craze in Nicaragua, and the place to do it is just outside León city, on the 40-degree slope of Cerro Negro. The people at Big Foot Hostel (© 505/8917-8832; www.bigfootnicaragua.com) were the pioneers, and they run daily excursions up to the belching mountain and back for about C400. Tour agency Vapues (© 505/2315-4099; www.vapues.com) also runs daily excursions for the same price. Whomever you go with, make sure you get properly kitted out with jumpsuit, goggles, gloves, and kneepads, as volcano surfing is exactly how it sounds—very exciting and a little dangerous. It takes less than an hour to reach the volcano's base by truck, followed by a 45-minute slog up to the rim.

Shopping in León

León is not a shopping-oriented city, but because of its university, there are many bookstores—with Sandinista-themed books often dominating the shelves. Librería Don Quijote, 2 blocks west of the plaza, is one of the city's better-known book shops. For fruits and vegetables, as well as clothes, go to the central market right behind the cathedral; it opens at 7am and closes at 8pm.

Where to Stay in León

Accommodations in León are improving all the time, and there are plenty of places to choose from in the city center, many with atmospheric courtyards and relaxing hammocks. All hotels listed below are within walking distance of the central plaza and cathedral.

EXPENSIVE

El Convento ★ This luxury hotel certainly lives up to its name—it was actually reconstructed from the ruins of a convent established in 1639. Its low, cream-colored colonial walls are next to a church, so you may feel like you're entering a religious order when you arrive. There is nothing monastic about its interior, however. It has one of the most elaborate courtyards of any hotel in the country—it's immense, with sculpted hedges encircling a beautiful fountain. A blue-pillared gallery surrounds the central patio, leading to sumptuous rooms with polished tile floors, king-size beds, and antique furniture. The ballroom, an immense space with elegant chandeliers, and the art gallery, which boasts an expansive lobby, high-raftered ceilings, and baroque woodcarvings, are both worth peeking into. Overall, this hotel is atmospheric and very seductive, though nearby La Perla trumps it in terms of customer service.

3 Av. NO, by Iglesia San Francisco. www.elconventonicaragua.com; © 505/2311-7053. Fax 505/2311-7067. 32 units. From $114 double; from $152 triple; from $162 suite. Rates include breakfast. AE, DC, MC, V. **Amenities:** Restaurant; coffee shop; room service. *In room:* A/C, TV, Internet.(free)

La Perla ★★ Elegant and spacious, La Perla is a jewel of a property. This large, colonial mansion has been restored with great attention to detail by its two American owners. Its glittering white facade leads to a palatial interior of high ceilings and contemporary Nicaraguan art. In addition to a spectacular central courtyard, there is a smaller courtyard farther back, with a sparkling blue-tiled pool. Rooms vary in size; the presidential suite is the biggest, with sweeping dimensions, a giant, half-poster bed, a grandiose wardrobe with elaborate woodcarvings, and huge double doors that open out onto two small street balconies. The standard rooms are much more compact, but also impeccably decorated, with soft carpets and flat-screen TVs. At the front of the hotel is one of León's best restaurants, the Terrace, while the Canal Bar is a good stop for a drink. The staff is bilingual and super friendly.

1 Av. NO, 1 block N of Iglesia La Merced. www.laperlaleon.com; ℭ **505/2311-3125**. Fax 505/2311-2279. 15 units. From $120 double; from $138 suite; from $178 presidential suite. Rates include breakfast. AE, MC, V. **Amenities:** Restaurant; bar; pool. *In room:* A/C, TV, minibar, Wi-Fi (free).

MODERATE

Hostal la Casa Leonesa   This hostel is slightly more dated and ramshackle than the Hotel Real de León, below, but is the same style of town house, except this one has a central courtyard that holds a small pool. The rooms are average-size with frumpy bedding and old-fashioned furnishings. The main sitting room is very elegant and authentic with dark, polished rocking chairs and intricate tiling. The bathrooms are tiny but immaculate, although everything here could do with sprucing up.

3 blocks N & ½ block E. of cathedral www.casaleonesa.com; ℭ **505/2311-0551**. 10 units. From $55 double. Rates include breakfast. AE, DC, MC, V. **Amenities:** Small pool. *In room:* A/C, TV, Wi-Fi (free).

Hotel Austria ☺   This is a modern, medium-size hotel that lacks somewhat in character but has a good location and decent service. The rooms are large, and some have balconies that overlook an attractive courtyard with a lawn. The decor is modern, with pine and wicker furniture, and loud scarlet and green bedcovers. The rooms could do with a little more light, but the bathrooms are large and well maintained. In general, it is a clean establishment and family-friendly, with triple rooms, a decent restaurant, and an excellent location close to the central plaza.

2 Calle SO, 1 block SW of cathedral. www.hotelaustria.com.ni; ℭ **505/2311-1206**. Fax 505/2311-1368. 35 units. From $61 double; from $73 mini-suite; from $101 suite. AE, MC, V. **Amenities:** Restaurant; Internet (free). *In room:* A/C, TV.

Hotel Los Balcones de León ✦   Los Balcones has a delightful, lived-in, colonial feel. A lush courtyard with lots of flowerpots, plants, and ornaments leads to a handsome wooden stairway and big communal balcony with colorful seating. (Be warned that the balcony can be rather noisy, as it overlooks a busy street.) The rooms vary greatly, but the best are upstairs and have inviting wrought-iron bed frames resting on varnished floorboards. The rooms downstairs are not as nice and lack good light; all rooms come with well-equipped bathrooms.

Corner of 1 Calle NE & 2 Av. NE. www.hotelbalcones.com; ℭ **505/2311-0250**. Fax 505/2311-0233. 20 units. From $59 double; from $71 triple; from $77 quadruple. Rates include breakfast. AE, DC, MC, V. **Amenities:** Restaurant; bar; Internet (free). *In room:* A/C, TV.

Hotel Real de León   A handsome one-story exterior and somewhat bare lobby lead to a lovely inner gallery with rocking chairs and tile floors surrounding a leafy courtyard. The Hotel Real de León is a typical, traditional town house and a fine example of how the locals live amidst shady living rooms and garden chain drains that carry water from the roof. Upstairs, you can take a deck chair on the roof terrace and enjoy the view of the city's rooftops. Rooms are nothing special, but clean and fairly spacious, with a mix of antique and reproduction furniture and open wardrobes.

150m (492 ft.) E of Iglesia la Recolección. www.hotelrealdeleon.net; ℂ **505/2311-2606**. 14 units. From $55 double. Rates include breakfast. AE, DC, MC, V. *In room:* A/C, TV, Wi-Fi. (free)

La Posada del Doctor 🍴 This hotel has struck a nice balance between local charm and modern expectations. The garden patio is spacious and attractive, with fountains gracing a small, verdant lawn. The gallery has an old-world charm; it is so crammed with rocking chairs, antique chests, and art, you may feel like you have stepped into a cozy, sepia photo portrait. A wood-paneled, open-air dining area with steep lean-to roof adds a modern touch, and the colorful assortment of bric-a-brac gives the hotel a playful atmosphere. Smallish rooms surround the courtyard, and they have sunny furnishings and sturdy beds. There is a communal kitchen if you want to self-cater. All in all, a pleasant mix between a modern Leonese home and a B&B.

20m (66 ft.) W of Parque San Martín. www.laposadadeldoctor.com; ℂ **505/2311-4343**. 11 units. From $60 double. Rates include breakfast. AE, DC, MC, V. *In room:* A/C, TV, Wi-Fi.

Posada Doña Blanca This family-run B&B has a friendly staff and a great location just down the street from La Perla (see above). In a roomy old town house with modern touches, it has a large and lush courtyard with a spacious veranda of polished tiles. Rooms (including bathrooms) vary in size from small to super-big, but some are a little dark, with disappointingly low ceilings. Ask for room no. 4; it has much more space and a high ceiling. Everything is immaculate; the furniture is a mix of antiques and replicas.

3 Calle NO, 1 block N of Iglesia La Merced. www.posadadonablanca.com; ℂ **505/2311-2521**. 6 units. From $45 double; from $55 triple. AE, DC, MC, V. **Amenities:** Internet (free). *In room:* A/C, TV.

INEXPENSIVE

Big Foot This hostel has made a name for itself as the expert on volcano surfing (see "Outdoor Activities," above) on the nearby Cerro Negro. This is a fun excursion, but physically exerting, especially if the wind is up. The hostel is located a half-block from the Servicio Gurdián, in front of Via Via hostel (see below). The rooms have little light, and the bathrooms could do with some sprucing up; but it's a friendly, sociable place and a good spot to meet other fellow travelers and to use as a base to sample the city's lively nightlife.

1½ blocks S of Iglesia Recoleccion. www.bigfootnicaragua.com; ℂ **505/8636-7041**. 10 units. From $6 dorm bed; from $26 double w/shared bathroom. AE, DC, MC, V. **Amenities:** Bar; laundry; small pool. *In room:* No phone.

Hostel Lazy Bones This huge open-air hostel strikes a nice balance between privacy and gregariousness, with 11 stable-style private rooms, three of which have their own bathroom, and two big cavernous dorms. These all run the length of a very long courtyard, which functions as part lawn, part bar, part pool, and part pool hall. Decor comes in the form of a big colorful mural overlooking hammocks, sofas, and wicker chairs. The entire building has high ceilings and is partially shaded by a clunky terracotta-tile rooftop. There is free Internet, free coffee, and even free 10-minute phone calls to the folks back home. But for a hostel, it's quite expensive (breakfast is extra and, frankly, not worth it), and it was half empty when I was there—which is maybe not a bad thing.

2 Av. NO, 2½ blocks from Parque de los Poetas. www.lazybonesleon.com; ℂ **505/2311-3472**. 13 units. From $8 dorm bed; from $19 double w/shared bathroom; from $28 double w/private bathroom. AE, DC, MC, V. **Amenities:** Bar; pool. Internet (free) *In room:* No phone.

Via Via Part hostel, part cafe, and part meeting point, Via Via is a backpacker's favorite, with dorms and three private rooms with shared bathrooms facing a lush courtyard. The rooms have recently been decorated and now come with fans and mosquito nets. The courtyard has a lovely atmosphere, particularly in the evenings and on weekends when there's live music. An in-house travel agency provides interesting tours, such as art workshops and cooking classes with locals. The inexpensive restaurant offers hearty meals, including decent vegetarian options. Via Via is part of a global network of hostels and cafes, and a great place to hook up with fellow travelers if you're traveling alone.

2 Av. NE, 50m (164 ft.) S of Servicio Agrícola Gurdián. www.viaviacafe.com; ⓒ **505/2311-6142**. 4 units. 1 dorm w/14 beds & 3 rooms w/shared bath. From $5 dorm bed; from $15 double. AE, MC, V. **Amenities:** Restaurant. *In room:* Fan, no phone.

Where to Eat in León

Down-to-earth León has equally down-to-earth food. Because of its sizeable student population, most restaurants serve comida típica, cheap traditional fare, as well as ubiquitous burgers and pizzas. If you don't mind eating standing up, there are food stalls set up behind the cathedral and outside Colegio La Salle serving chicken topped with cabbage. It might be some time before the city's restaurants earn culinary accolades, yet slowly but surely, gourmet centers are beginning to pop up. Wherever you go, you'll usually get character in the form of high ceilings, tiled floors, and a courtyard.

EXPENSIVE

Restaurante La Perla ★★ INTERNATIONAL/NICARAGUAN Here, you'll find perhaps the finest dining in all of León. Part of La Perla hotel, this restaurant's elegant white facade and tall, enchanting ceilings are enough to give you an appetite. Paintings by some of the country's greatest artists hang on the walls, and the large salon is framed by handsome mahogany doors and large windows overlooking the front courtyard and street. On the menu are Caesar salad, filet mignon, and fresh crab picked on the same day from the nearby Poneloya Beach. The pâté platter is delicious, as is the smoked salmon. The restaurant has one of the finest wine lists in the country. The gracious owners and excellent hosts Mark and Jim are often on hand to share a joke or story. Finish the evening with a coffee from beans grown by the owners on the side of a volcano.

1 Av. NO, 1½ blocks N of Iglesia La Merced. www.laperlaleon.com; ⓒ **505/2311-3125**. Main courses C342–C570. AE, DC, MC, V. Daily noon–3pm & 7–11pm.

MODERATE

Cocinarte VEGETARIAN/CAFE Fancy some falafel? Cocinarte is a handsome little vegetarian eatery with a sister restaurant in Managua. Try their delicious pasta al pesto or just drop by for a steaming cup of organic coffee. The decor is tasteful, and there are themed evenings, such as romantic Fridays and jazzy Sundays.

3 Av. SO, N of Iglesia el Laborío. ⓒ **505/2325-4099**. Main courses C220–C300. No credit cards. Tues–Sun noon–11pm.

Mediterraneo ★ 🍴 INTERNATIONAL This is a colorful, relaxing restaurant with bossa nova humming in the background and well-dressed waiters running between well-heeled diners. Though there's an interior dining area, the courtyard is where the action is. At night, it's an elegant sight with a black-and-white tiled floor, backlit palm fronds, and vibrant artwork on the sunflower-yellow walls. The menu is extensive, offering everything from beef stroganoff to pizza (they even do delivery) to pasta. Delicious complimentary tomato and garlic tapas get the ball rolling. The service could be a little bit more prompt, but it's fast by Nicaraguan standards. There's a nice small bar out front if you fancy an aperitif or want to try a French or Italian wine from the wine list.

2 Av. NO, 1 block N of La Casa de Cultura. ✆ **505/8895-9392.** Main courses C200–C300. No credit cards. Tues–Sun noon–11pm.

INEXPENSIVE

El Sesteo CAFE   This large, airy corner cafe sits on the main plaza with huge doorways looking out onto all the action passing by. Big fans whirl high up in the ceilings, and old photos of León's movers and shakers adorn the walls, while people sit at large wooden tables set on old-fashioned tiles. The establishment oozes history; you can tell that some of the clientele, with faces as worn as the old leather seating, are just bursting to tell a story. The menu is nothing special, offering meat and seafood in hearty portions. It is a good stop for a liquado and a sandwich, though if you fancy something different, try the chancho con yuca (fried pork with yucca and cabbage).

Corner of Av. Central & Parque Central. ✆ **505/2311-5327.** Main courses C160–C200. No credit cards. Daily 7am–10pm.

León After Dark

Needless to say that with all these students in town, the nightlife in León is anything but sleepy, and it goes on all week. Teatro Municipal (2 Calle SO and 2 Av. SO; ✆ 505/2311-1788) is the best venue for live performances of both theater and music. In recent years, a handful of bars and restaurants have sprung up close to the theater south of Parque de Los Poetas. Solera Bar (2 Calle SO and 2 Av. SO; no phone) has a cozy, welcoming decor and attracts a well-to-do clientele, and it has live music Tuesday through to Saturday. It's open from 9am to 2am everyday. Nearby is Snake Bar (Calle José de Marcaleta and 2 Av. SO; ✆ 505/2311-5921), a green corner town house with a roadhouse feel and a long bar popular with students. It is open from 11am to 3am everyday and has live music on Tuesday and Wednesday. Barbaro (Calle José de Marcaleta and 2 Av. SO; ✆ 505/2315-2901) has a touch more class, with whitewashed walls, chunky wooden lintels, and terracotta-tiled floors. There's lots of space and light in this L-shaped salon with Nicaraguan art on the walls and quaint barn doors. It is open everyday from 8am to midnight, closing a little later on weekends. La Olla Quemada (Parque Ruben Dario, 4c O; no phone) has graffiti-scrawled walls and raucous live music shows. A happening underground venue, it catches a lively mix of locals, students, and visitors.

Side Trips Around León
LEÓN VIEJO

León was originally founded in 1524 by Francisco Hernández de Córdoba in the foothills of Volcán Momotombo. The volcano proved to be a volatile neighbor, and after a series of earthquakes and an eventual eruption in 1610, the Spanish were forced to move 30km (19 miles) east and reestablish the city where it now stands. The old city lay lost and covered in ash until it was rediscovered in 1967. Excavations have revealed a fascinating site, including the headless corpse of Hernández de Córdoba beside the remains of his executioner Pedrarias Dávila. The founding Spaniard was punished for insubordination. León Viejo, a neat collection of brick walls and pillar stumps, is now a UNESCO World Heritage Site, with spectacular views from the surrounding hills. It makes for a great 1-day tour and can be organized by most travel agencies in León city. If you would prefer to go there independently, catch a bus to La Paz Centro 3km (1¾ miles) east of the city. There you catch another bus to Puerto Momotombo 15km (9¼ miles) away. Be aware that the last bus returns from the ruins at 3pm. Vapues Tours and Grayline Tours conduct tours of the ruins. On-site, there is a small Visitor Center (no phone), and local English-speaking guides will take you around for a small fee. Admission is C44 adults; C88 if you bring a camera, and C160 if you bring a video recorder. The ruins are open daily from 8am to 5pm.

LOS HERVIDEROS DE SAN JACINTO

Hervidero means "hotbed," and that description is no exaggeration when it comes to this ragged patch of land, 25km (16 miles) north of León. Los Hervideros de San Jacinto is basically a field of boiling mud, with steam rising from thermal vents and hiding the nearby peak of Volcán Telica. The bubbling muck is literally too hot to dip your hand into, though apparently it's very good for your complexion once it has cooled down. There are absolutely no tourist facilities here (though there is talk of the inevitable luxury hotel), and the site itself is not pretty—but it is fascinating. The mud patch is close to the town of San Jacinto and is a good 1-day excursion from the city. Quetzaltrekkers (© **505/2311-6695**, www.quetzaltrekkers.com) and Big Foot (© **505/8636-7041;** www.bigfootnicaragua.com) will help you organize an excursion there, or you can just take a taxi or bus to the town of San Jacinto (take the Estelí or San Isidro service). The entrance has a large arched gateway where there are street vendors and guides.

ISLA JUAN VENADO WILDLIFE RESERVE ★

Have you ever wanted to see a mangrove warbler? Perhaps that's not on everybody's list of things to see, but this small yellow bird can be found only in mangrove swamps, and such a place exists on the Pacific coast west of León, just south of Las Peñitas. Isla Juan Venado is a 21-sq.-km (8-sq.-mile) wetland reserve that you can explore by boat or kayak. Here, you'll find pelicans and herons stepping over crocodiles, iguanas, and caimans in a labyrinth of channels and waterways. This is also an important turtle-nesting site, where thousands of turtles hatch. Tours can be arranged with operators in the city (p. 202), or you can go independently and hire a boat in Las Peñitas village. There is an entrance fee of C40.

PONELOYA & LAS PENITAS BEACHES

20km (12 miles) W of León

A 20-kilometer (12-mile) drive from León, you'll find two beautiful beaches: Poneloya and Las Peñitas. Popular with Leoneses escaping the city heat during the weekend, these dark-sand beaches are deserted on weekdays, though they're growing increasingly popular with surfers. Beware: The dark waves here are big and the currents strong. There is no lifeguard, and drownings are frequent, especially during the high season (around Easter week).

Essentials

Buses leave every half-hour from the Mercadito Subtiava, 12 blocks west of the city center; jump on any of the urban buses that ring the city, and they will eventually pass by the market. Incredibly, the big, old school buses to the beach are sometimes faster than taxis, as the latter drive incredibly slowly in order to avoid the Swiss-cheese–like road's potholes. The last bus returns to the city at 6:40pm and costs C20.

Where to Stay on the Beaches

The best hotels are on the southern strand of Las Peñitas; highlights are listed below.

Barca de Oro   Barca de Oro won't win any architectural awards, but its location is perfect, right on the beach at the northern end of Isla Juan Venado, the mangrove and lagoon reserve famous for its turtle nesting. This hostel, which is set in a simple building held up by red-brick pillars and white concrete trellises, is popular with backpackers and surfers. The decor is basic, with plastic seating and multicolored tablecloths everywhere, but you get a mosquito net with your bed and incredible sunset views. Kayaks and surfboards are available for rent, and the English-speaking owners are proactive when it comes to organizing tours exploring the reserve.

Las Peñitas. www.barcadeoro.com; ✆ **505/2317-0275**. 23 units. $6 dorm bed; $30 double. No credit cards. **Amenities:** Restaurant; bar. *In room:* No phone.

Hotel Suyapa Beach   This three-story, bright-yellow hotel is modern, clean, and family run. There is an open-walled seafood restaurant out front on the beach and a pleasant pool area with sun loungers in the hotel garden. The rooms are simple and medium-size with spotless bathrooms. The small, modern lobby has colorful wicker chairs but is somewhat lacking in ambience and decoration.

Las Peñitas. www.suyapabeach.com; ✆ **505/8885-8345**. 22 units. $63 double. Rates include buffet breakfast. AE, DC, MC, V. **Amenities:** Restaurant; bar; pool. *In room:* A/C, TV, hair dryer, minibar.

PLANNING YOUR TRIP TO EL SALVADOR

Your initial arrival in El Salvador can be a culture shock. The language, the pace, and the heat in the capital, along with its poverty and third-world chaos, can be a little disconcerting, especially if it's your first trip to Central America. However, there are certain factors that make the country an excellent introduction to the region: a familiar currency, relatively good roads and infrastructure, no particular health concerns, and no visa requirements. The food is also excellent, if a little unvaried outside the capital.

Choose your accommodations carefully and think seriously about how you will get around. Below are tips on how to plan your trip, stay safe, and keep in touch with home, as well as more specific information, ensuring you will be prepared for everything, including surprises.

WHEN TO GO

El Salvador's peak seasons are *Semana Santa,* or Holy Week, which precedes Easter Sunday; the month of August; and mid-December through Christmas. Prices during these times can be higher, but not always. Some hotels actually run specials to keep up with the competition; it just depends on how busy the hotel thinks it will be. Either way, you need to book any decent hotel well in advance during these times, or you won't get a room.

December is actually the best time to visit El Salvador, when the rainy season has just ended and the landscape is still green and the air clean and fresh. The rainy season (Mar–Nov) is the best time to surf, though the dry season is still good and more suitable for beginners. Wildlife-watching is best in the dry season, especially since some parks, including Montecristo, are closed during the rainy season. Turtle-watching is the exception: Nesting takes place from May to November.

CLIMATE The country has two distinct seasons in terms of weather. The first is the dry season, which runs from November to April. The second is the rainy season, which runs from May to October. Since there is little temperature variation between these seasons, the question of which season is best for travel is not a simple one. The short answer would be

CORSATUR offices

San Salvador: Edificio Carbonel 1, Colonia Roma, Alameda Dr. Manuel Enrique Araujo and Pasaje Carbonel, San Salvador (✆ **503/2243-7835;** www.elsalvador. travel; Mon–Fri 8am–5pm). The office offers local and national maps and brochures, and tourism official Claudia Argumedo speaks English.

Puerto La Libertad: Malecon, Puerta de La Libertad, La Libertad, El Salvador (✆ **503/2346-1634;** cat.lalibertad@ gmail.com; Mon–Fri 8am–4pm, Sat and Sun 9am–1pm).

Nahuizalco: Km 71 Carretera CA-8, Nauizalco, Departamento de Sonsonate (✆ **503/2453-1082;** cat.rutasdelas flores@gmail.com; Mon–Fri 8am–5pm,

Sat 8am–4pm). No one in this office speaks English, but they do offer some English-speaking hotel and attraction brochures.

Suchitoto: Calle San Martín, Barrio El Centro, Suchitoto, Departamento Custcatlán, El Salvador (✆ **503/2335-1835;** cat.suchitoto@gmail.com; Mon–Fri 8am–5pm, Sat and Sun 8am–4pm). Ask for Manuel Selada.

La Palma: 1a Calle Pte, La Palma, Departamento La Palma, El Salvador (✆ **503/2335-9076;** cat.lapalma@ gmail.com; Mon–Fri 8am–4pm, Sat and Sun 9am–1pm). This small office close to the town square has a friendly staff and lots of literature on the area.

November, when the rains have stopped but the landscape has not yet dried out. However, both seasons have something to recommend them. In the dry season, the country's predominately dirt secondary roads are easier to navigate—some roads are impassible without a four-wheel-drive during the rainy season—and, well, it's not raining. In the rainy season, on the other hand, El Salvador's environment is at its most lush and alive. Rainy season also doesn't necessarily mean all-day downpours: The country's highest elevations do receive daily rain and are often covered in a misty fog, but rainy season in the lower elevations can mean little more than daily afternoon showers.

Temperatures throughout El Salvador vary more according to elevation than season. The beaches and San Salvador can get up into the high 80s°F (low 30s°C) year-round, with even higher heat waves in the summer, while the coldest mountains can fall to near freezing, with averages of 54° to 73°F (12°–23°C) year-round. The coldest month is December, and the hottest month is May.

Public Holidays   Public holidays in El Salvador include New Year's Day (Jan 1); Semana Santa (Holy Thurs–Easter Sun); Labor Day (May 1); the Festival of El Salvador (Aug 1–6, though the rest of Aug remains a busy vacation season); Independence Day (Sept 15); Día de la Raza (Oct 12); All Souls' Day (Nov 2); and Christmas celebrations (Dec 24, 25, and 31).

For an exhaustive list of events beyond those listed here, check http://events.frommers.com, where you'll find a searchable, up-to-the-minute roster of what's happening in cities all over the world.

VISITOR INFORMATION

El Salvador's helpful national tourism organization, **CORSATUR,** has a useful English-language website (**www.elsalvador.travel**), a central office in San Salvador, and offices in Suchitoto in the north, Nahuizalco on the Ruta de las Flores, and Puerto de

Passing by the Turicentro

Don't let the name "Turicentro" or "Tourist Center" fool you. You'll see signs for these outdated parks near towns, lakes, and mountains around El Salvador, but they're nothing special. Though some have pools, and small restaurants or *comedores,* they're usually decades-old parks with cement picnic tables and chairs painted in 1970s colors with a few cinder-block cabins. Turicentros are open daily 8am to 4pm and cost $1 to enter. They are run by the **Instituto Salvadoreño de Turismo (ISTU;** 719 Calle Rubén Darío btw. 9a and 11a Av. Sur; ✆ **503/2222-8000; www.istu.gob.sv).**

La Libertad along the Balsamo Coast; see the box "CORSATUR Offices," below, for specific info. Alternatively, you can always head to the local city hall, called the *alcaldía,* where you'll find the occasional English-speaking employee who can help you out. It's best to do as much research as possible before arriving in El Salvador because most towns don't have tourism offices or English-speaking tourism officials.

If you speak Spanish, some of the country's best sources for local information are the **Casas de la Cultura,** or Houses of Culture. Nearly every town in El Salvador has a Casa de la Cultura, which serves as a small community center, in addition to dishing out tourist-friendly information. They're not designated tourism offices, so the quality of the information is hit-and-miss, but they're by far your best shot at getting local information in the country's smaller villages. Casas de la Cultura addresses and phone numbers are listed in each chapter, where applicable.

Other valuable tourism organizations include the following:

SalvaNatura (33 Av. Sur 640, Colonia Flor Blanca, San Salvador; ✆ **503/2279-1515;** www.salvanatura.org) administers and provides information for Parque Imposible and Parque Nacional Los Volcanes. It's open Monday to Friday from 8am to noon and 2 to 5pm. Staffer Ben Rivera speaks English.

Institute Salvadoreño de Turismo (**ISTU;** 719 Calle Rubén Darío btw. 9a and 11a Av. Sur, San Salvador; ✆ **503/2222-8000;** www.istu.gob.sv) provides information about El Salvador's parks and has a great website. It's open Monday to Friday from 7:30am to 3:30pm.

Ministerio de Medio Ambiente y Recursos Naturales (Km 5.5 Carretera a Santa Tecla, Calle and Colonia Las Mercedes, Building MARN No. 2, San Salvador; ✆ **503/2267-6276;** www.marn.gob.sv) is the organization you have to call to enter Parque Montecristo.

ENTRY REQUIREMENTS

Residents of the United States, Canada, Australia, New Zealand, and the United Kingdom do not need visas and can enter the country at the border with presentation of a valid passport and the purchase of a $10 30-day tourist card. (Visitors can also ask for a 90-day card when entering the country.)

El Salvador is part of a 2006 border control agreement with Honduras, Guatemala, and Nicaragua, allowing travel among the four countries under one tourist card. The number of days of your tourist card is determined at the first of the four countries entered.

EL SALVADORAN EMBASSY LOCATIONS

In the U.S.: 2308 California St., NW, Washington, DC 20008 (© **202/265-9671;** fax 202/232-3763; www.elsalvador.org).

In Canada: 209 Kent St., Ottawa, Ontario, K2P 1Z8 (© **613/238-2939;** fax 613/238-6940).

In the U.K.: Mayfair House, 8 Dorset Sq., Marylebone, London, NWI 6PU (© **0207/224-9800;** fax 0207/224-9878).

In Australia: Consulate only: Level 3, 499 St. Kilda Rd., Melbourne, VIC 3004 (© **03/9867-4400;** fax 03/9867-4455; cherrera@rree.gob.sv).

In New Zealand: Consulate only: 1/644 Manukau Rd., Epsom, Auckland 1023 (© **09/649-625-4770**).

CUSTOMS

Visitors to El Salvador can bring in no more than 200 cigarettes or 50 cigars, 2L (2 qt.) of alcohol, and gifts worth up to $500. Like in most countries, there are heavy restrictions on the import and export of plants, animals, vegetables, and fruit.

GETTING THERE & GETTING AROUND

Getting There

BY PLANE

El Salvador's only international airport is Comalapa International Airport or **Cuscatlán International Airport** (**SAL;** © **503/2339-9455;** www.cepa.gob.sv/aies/index.php), 44km (27 miles) south of San Salvador. It is a major, 17-gate international hub with daily flights from the United States, Canada, Europe, and South America. **Cuscatlán** also serves as the main hub for primary Central and South American carrier Grupo Taca. The airport serves more than 2 million passengers per year and includes numerous rental-car companies, hotel information booths, duty-free shops, and restaurants. All departing international passengers must pay a $32 departure tax, although this may already be included in your flight ticket.

FROM NORTH AMERICA   American, Continental, Delta, and Taca offer flights from the United States. **American** flies out of Miami, Los Angeles, and Dallas/Fort Worth. **Continental** flies to and from Houston and Newark. **Delta Airlines** flies out of Atlanta. **Taca Airlines** stops in Chicago, Dallas/Fort Worth, Houston, Los Angeles, Miami, New York, and Washington, D.C. TACA, Delta, Continental, and **Northwest** offer flights from Canada to San Salvador, too. See chapter 21 for airline info.

FROM THE UNITED KINGDOM, AUSTRALIA & NEW ZEALAND   There are no direct overseas flights from the U.K., Australia, or New Zealand. You'll need to fly first into the United States—many European flights route out of Miami or Houston to San Salvador.

BY BUS

Central America's major luxury bus carrier, **Tica Bus** (© **503/2243-9764;** www.ticabus.com) offers air-conditioned buses to San Salvador from Nicaragua, Honduras, Guatemala, Mexico, Costa Rica, and Panama, with prices ranging from $20 each way to Guatemala to $95 each way to Panama. Tica arrives into San Salvador's **San**

CUT TO THE FRONT OF THE AIRPORT SECURITY LINE AS A registered traveler

In 2003, the **Transportation Security Administration** (**TSA;** www.tsa.gov) approved a pilot program to help ease the time spent in line for airport security screenings when flying from a United States airport. In exchange for information and a fee, persons can be pre-screened as registered travelers, granting them a front-of-the-line position when they fly. The program is run through private firms—the largest and most well-known is Steven Brill's **Clear** (www.clearme.com), and it works like this: Travelers complete an online application providing specific points of personal information, including name, addresses for the previous 5 years, birth date, social security number, driver's license number, and a valid credit card (you're not charged the **$179 fee** until your application is approved). Print out the completed form and take it, along with proper ID, with you to an "enrollment station" (these can be found in over 20 participating airports and in a growing number of American Express offices around the country, for example). It's at this point where it gets seemingly sci-fi. At the enrollment station, a Clear representative will record your biometrics necessary for clearance; in this case, your fingerprints and your irises will be digitally recorded.

Once your application has been screened against no-fly lists, outstanding warrants, and other security measures, you'll be issued a clear plastic card that holds a chip containing your information. Each time you fly through participating airports (and the numbers are steadily growing), go to the Clear Pass station located next to the standard TSA screening line. Here, you'll insert your card into a slot and place your finger on a scanner to read your print—when the information matches up, you're cleared to cut to the front of the security line. You'll still have to follow all the procedures of the day like removing your shoes and walking through the x-ray machine, but Clear promises to cut 30 minutes off your airport wait time.

On a personal note: Each time I've used my Clear Pass, my travel companions are still waiting to go through security while I'm already sitting down, reading the paper and sipping my over-priced smoothie. Granted, a registered traveler programs is not for the infrequent traveler, but for those of us who fly on a regular basis, it's a perk I'm willing to pay for.
—David A. Lytle

Benito Terminal (Blvd. el Hipódromo, Local #301, Colonia San Benito; ✆ 503/2243-9764).

The bus company **King Quality** (✆ 503/2271-1361; www.king-qualityca.com), which also features modern, air-conditioned buses, travels to San Salvador from Guatemalan cities such as Antigua and Guatemala City, as well as San José, Costa Rica. Prices range from $35 to $67. King Quality buses arrive into San Salvador's **Puerto Bus Terminal** (Alameda Juan Pablo II at 19a Av. Norte; ✆ 503/2222-2158).

Finally, the company **Pullmantur** (✆ 503/2243-1300; www.pullmantur.com) offers $35 to $52 trips from Guatemala City to the Hotel Sheraton Presidente in San Salvador (Av. La Revolución, Colonia San Benito; ✆ 800/325-3535).

BY BOAT OR FERRY

Private charters make the trip to La Unión on the eastern Pacific coast of El Salvador from points in Honduras and Nicaragua; visit **www.elsalvador.travel** for details. A ferry cruise journeys about once a month to La Unión from Amapala, Honduras. Check with the navy post in La Unión (☎ **503/2406-0348**) for details.

Getting Around
BY BUS

El Salvador is an easy and fun country to see by bus. There are very few places in this small nation that cannot be reached by one of El Salvador's many decades-old, brightly painted, former-elementary-school buses. Most city buses are 25¢ to 35¢, with few, if any, rides within the country costing more than $2. El Salvador's larger cities have dedicated bus depots, but in smaller villages, the buses often come and go directly from the main square. In small towns and along many slow-moving roads, you can also hail buses like you would a taxi by waving your arm.

Buses in El Salvador are also mobile markets and charities. Be prepared for vendors to hop aboard at each stop to sell fruit, bottled water, and *dulces* (candy). You'll likely encounter brightly dressed clowns who solicit for various charities, as well. Though riding a bus in El Salvador is an excellent way to get to know the country's people and culture, don't detour away from the main tourist routes mentioned in this book and avoid nighttime bus travel, or you'll risk encountering some safety issues.

BY CAR

El Salvador is one of the easiest countries in Central America to see by car, since it boasts newly constructed, well-paved, and well-marked highways running the length of the country from east to west and north to south. Hwy. CA-1, also known as the Pan-American Highway or "Carretera Panamericana," is the nation's main artery traveling from the western Guatemalan border through San Salvador to the eastern Honduran border. Hwy. CA-2 runs the same direction along the coast and is intersected by three major north-south highways running the length of the country. Once you get off the main roads, however, things get a little different. The secondary roads are not usually paved. So, even in the dry season, it's best to rent a truck. In the rainy season, I recommend renting a four-wheel-drive, as some roads are not passable with regular vehicles.

To minimize your risk of robbery, do not drive at night. When visiting larger cities, it's best to leave your car parked in your hotel parking lot and just take buses and cabs;

 Older Is Better

Stick to the older buses in El Salvador. You might be tempted to hop on one of the country's newer, more-modern-looking buses, but these rides rarely have air-conditioning, they cram just as many people on, and because they have bucket rather than bench seats, you'll have even less room than on the older buses. Fortunately, most buses that travel within the country are of the ancient variety. They regularly get fixed up, painted wild colors, decorated with religious symbols, and put back in service. These buses are packed, hot, bumpy, and stop frequently, but they will get you where you need to go, in style and more comfortably.

o "Alto" means stop.

o Many small towns have a one-way system around the central plaza, so keep right as you enter each town.

o Lines of traffic cones will occasionally block your way. These are speed checks, and you just weave through them.

o Make sure you get a "Tarjeta de Circulacion" from your car rental company and double check that it's not out of date. All cars must have this "Circulation Card" to move freely around the country.

o Avoid driving at night in order to minimize your risk of robbery.

o When visiting large cities, leave your car in your hotel parking lot and take buses and cabs, as chaotic traffic and lack of street signs makes city driving difficult.

city streets here are often chaotic, filled with people and vendors, and streets are rarely marked. These are not roads you want to drive while reading a map. You should really keep your eyes peeled while driving anywhere in the country: El Salvador's roads are filled with old jalopies moving at half the posted speed, motorcycles puttering along on the shoulder, farmers walking with carts sticking a few feet into the road, and pedestrians just inches from the lane.

See the individual destination chapters for info on **renting cars** throughout the country.

BY FERRY

There is regular ferry service across Lago Suchitlán to Suchitoto (p. 258), and ferries ply the waters around La Unión, but additional ferry service is nonexistent.

BY TAXI

Taxis are prevalent in the country's bigger cities and are usually easy to catch around each city's main square—they're safe to hail on the street, except at night, when you should have your hotel call you one.

Smaller cities usually don't have taxis, but many feature small moto-taxis (called *tuk -tuks*) which are basically red, canvas-covered, three-wheeled motorcycles. *Tuk tuks* are often much cheaper than regular taxis—sometimes as little as 25¢ for a few blocks—and you get the added bonus of feeling the wind in your hair.

MONEY & COSTS

The unit of currency in El Salvador is the U.S. dollar. The country made the switch from its native colón in 2001, and colónes have been phased out since 2004. Small-town *tiendas* rarely have change for a $20, so get small bills whenever you can. ATMs, known as *cajeros automáticos,* can be found in all major cities but are hard to come by in rural towns. Even when a smaller town has an ATM, it may not accept your card—stock up on cash when you can.

Bank machines accept most major card networks, such as Cirrus, PLUS, Visa, and MasterCard. I've had the best luck with a PLUS card at Scotiabank ATMs. Credit cards are accepted mainly only in the larger hotels, restaurants, and shops. Sometimes, you get lucky in the most unexpected places, but generally, small shops or restaurants in villages are *solo efectivo,* or cash only. Those that accept credit cards usually take American Express, Diners Club, Visa, and MasterCard.

You can just about forget about traveler's checks. Almost no one outside of large San Salvador hotels accepts these anymore. If you feel more comfortable carrying traveler's checks, you can exchange them for currency at most banks or American Express offices (see p. 224 for locations).

The cost of basics in El Salvador varies wildly, depending on where you are. A good general rule of thumb puts San Salvador prices largely on par with those in the United States. You'll spend $6 or more for long cab rides and $5.50 for most fast-food purchases. Outside of San Salvador, however, all costs are considerably lower. A 10- to 15-minute taxi ride in La Palma is $3 and *pupusas* (the national dish) cost 25¢ each in smaller towns. San Salvador's finer restaurants

> **Money Talk**
>
> The widely used local slang for a quarter is a *"cora."*

and hotels—though much more expensive than those in the rest of the country—are also considerably cheaper than comparable places in the United States or the U.K.

HEALTH CONCERNS

The most common travel ailments in El Salvador are diarrhea and food-born stomach upset. To stay healthy, be sure to drink only bottled water and ice you know to be purified, and stick to established restaurants. Dengue fever, known as "broken bones disease," is also on the rise in El Salvador. There is a low risk of malaria in El Salvador, centered mainly in rural areas of high immigration near the Guatemalan border. See "Health Concerns" in chapter 5, "Planning Your Trip to Nicaragua," for more info on how to prevent and treat common ailments.

VACCINATIONS   The only vaccination necessary to enter El Salvador is yellow fever, which is required only for persons 6 months or older coming from high-risk tropical areas. Those traveling from the U.S. and Europe do not need the vaccination, and the World Health Organization does not recommend it. However, it's a good idea to consult your personal physician before leaving home to make sure that all of your regular inoculations are up-to-date, as many diseases that are all but wiped out in other parts of the world still exist in El Salvador. The CDC recommends getting shots for hepatitis A and B, typhoid, measles, rubella, mumps, rabies, and tetanus. It's best to consult a travel clinic 4 weeks prior to travel to check your vaccination history and discuss your itinerary.

SAFETY

El Salvador's reputation for gang violence is warranted. It has the highest homicide rate in the world (excluding Iraq), and the crime wave there has been likened to a low-level war. However, such an image will contrast strongly with your experience of the country's friendly, peace-loving people. The fact is, there are two El Salvadors: the beautiful, fascinating destination that has you reading this book and a darker, hidden society of poor ghettoes and warring tattooed youths. Thankfully, the two never meet. Travelers rarely experience anything worse than being pick-pocketed or distracted in some way and relieved of a backpack (and even this is rare). Gun crime is usually confined to the shantytowns and poor barrios, and rarely affects tourists. In my

TIPS FOR A STRONG stomach

Most travel illnesses start in our delicate North American and European digestive systems, and what you put in your mouth is all-important if you want to stay healthy. Below are some tips on how to avoid a holiday in the restroom:

o Make sure any meat you eat is hot and well cooked.

o Keep your hands clean with frequent washing.

o Make sure any dairy products you try are pasteurized.

o Avoid salads and raw fish.

o Keep flies away from your dish, your glass or bottle, and the table.

o Do not leave food lying around, as this attracts germ-bearing flies.

o Avoid tap water (unless it's been boiled) and ice cubes (unless made from purified or boiled water).

o Eat only fruit that you have peeled yourself.

experience, the more budget-oriented you are, the more vulnerable you are to such theft—a public chicken bus is not as safe as a private shuttle, for example.

Before you depart, check for travel advisories from the **U.S. State Department** (www.travel.state.gov), the **Canadian Department of Foreign Affairs** (www.voyage.gc.ca), the **U.K. Foreign & Commonwealth Office** (www.fco.gov.uk/travel), and the **Australian Department of Foreign Affairs** (www.dfat.gov.au/embassies.html).

Once you're there, keep some common-sense safety advice in mind: Stay alert and be aware of your surroundings; don't walk down dark, deserted streets; and always keep an eye on your personal belongings. Keep your passport and credit cards on your person (but not stuffed in your back pocket). Theft at airports and bus stations is not unheard of, so be sure to put a lock on your luggage. Rental cars generally stick out and are easily spotted by thieves (see "Getting Around: By Car," above, for more info).

Public intercity buses are also frequent targets of stealthy thieves. Never check your bags into the hold of a bus if you can avoid it. If this can't be avoided, when the bus makes a stop, keep your eye on what leaves the hold. If you put your bags in an overhead rack, be sure you can see the bags at all times.

See the individual chapters in this book for more specific safety advice.

TIPS ON ACCOMMODATIONS, DINING & SHOPPING

Accommodations

El Salvador's hotels vary widely in quality, style, and price. San Salvador's larger hotels are mainly multinational chains that follow internationally accepted standards for service and amenities, but most hotels outside the capital are individually owned (which means you'll find some true gems and some real stinkers). There are also a few international and national chain hotels scattered around the country, but generally, most small-town hotels are going to be simple, cinder-block or stucco buildings with medium to smallish rooms, minimal decoration, and old furniture. Most are comfortable, with friendly, helpful on-site owners. Just don't expect everything to be shiny and new.

Rates range from more than $125 for a luxury room in San Salvador to $14 for a simple, comfortable room in a small mountain town. The bigger the town, the higher the price. And an 18% tax, which is included in the prices quoted throughout this guide, is applied to all hotel rooms. Rooms are not necessarily more expensive during Holy Week, Christmas, and early August. Sometimes, they are actually cheaper. But they definitely book solid, so make your reservations for these weeks well in advance.

Dining

Outside of the high-end, international restaurants of San Salvador, El Salvadoran dining can get a bit repetitive, with most small-town restaurants offering roughly the same combo of cooked fish, meat, or chicken with rice and salad. Occasionally a restaurant owner throws in an Argentine sausage or a veggie dish. But for the most part, you'll be offered just plain-ish meat with a starch and greens. There are a few highlights, however. The first is El Salvador's national dish, the *pupusa*. Styles vary, but generally *pupusas* are corn tortillas filled with pork and cheese and grilled warm and brown. They're usually served with a side of hot sauce and a tasty *curtido,* which is like a slightly spicy coleslaw, and sell for 25¢ to $1.50 each. You'll find them everywhere; and two to four make a meal. You'll also want to try El Salvador's *refrescos/ liquados,* which are a combination of fruit, ice, and water or milk. (My favorite's a banana, milk, and honey concoction.)

If you have a strong stomach, you might want to try out one of the country's many *comedores,* which are small, often family-run restaurants, usually with a mom or grandmother in the kitchen serving *pupusas* and a few items based on whatever is available that week. And if you've had your fill of traditional cuisine, a world-class collection of Asian, Brazilian, Italian, Peruvian, and other cuisines is available in San Salvador.

The country's 13% dining tax is normally included in the menu price, with an additional 10% tip automatically added to most bills. Check your tab before tipping.

Shopping

Like dining, there is a world of difference between shopping in San Salvador and shopping in the rest of the country. San Salvador offers nearly everything you could ever want or need, and is filled with high-end malls and expensive designer shops. But the smaller towns often offer only small *tiendas*—one-room food stores with a few necessities—street markets, and small variety stores.

Weekends tend to see town squares turned into markets offering everything from arts and crafts to cheap calculators. Most El Salvadoran markets also sell traditional *artesanías*—a broad term for El Salvador's various textile, wood, and art crafts, which often take the form of wooden crosses, decorative boxes, or natural wood surfaces painted in the unique style of the country's most famous artist, Fernando Llort (p. 255).

[FastFACTS] EL SALVADOR

American Express American Express traveler's checks can be exchanged at most banks, but very few businesses in El Salvador accept them. American Express offices are located in San Salvador (Anna's Travel, 3ra Calle Poniente 3737 btw. 71 and 73 Av. Norte; © **503/2209-8800**; or Servi-Viajes, Paseo General Escalón 3508 #4; © **503/2298-6868**), in San Miguel (Anna's Travel, 8 Calle Poniente 815, Roosevelt Bario San Filipe, San

Miguel; ☎ **503/2661-8282**), and in Santa Ana (Anna's Travel, 2 Calle Poniente and 4 Av. Norte #4, Santa Ana; ☎ **503/2447-1574**).

Business Hours Most banks and Casa de la Cultura community centers are open Monday through Friday 8:30am to 5pm and 8:30am to noon or 1pm on Saturday. Some banks and Casas de la Cultura have extended Saturday hours. Business offices follow a similar schedule, but are closed Saturday and Sunday. Also note that many national tourist sites, such as Tazumal and Joya de Cerén, are open Sunday but closed Monday.

Small-town shops often close for an hour or two around midday, and smaller village restaurants close around 6pm. San Salvador's restaurants close for the night between 8 and 11pm, with nightclubs staying open until the wee hours.

Embassies & Consulates The **U.S. Embassy** in San Salvador is located at Urbanización Santa Elena, Antiguo Cuscatlán (☎ **503/2278-4444**; http://sansalvador.usembassy.gov). The **Canadian Embassy** can be found at Centro Financiero Gigante, Alameda Roosevelt and 63 Av. Sur, lobby 2, location 6 (☎ **503/2279-4655**). **Australia** has no embassy or consulate, but has an agreement allowing the Canadian embassy to assist Australian citizens. The **United Kingdom**

has a consulate at 17 Calle Poniente 320 (☎ **503/2281-5555;** gchippendale@gibson.com.sv). The U.K. embassy in Guatemala City, Guatemala (16 Calle 0-55, Zone 10, Edificio Porre Internacional, level 11; ☎ **502/2367-5425;** www.fco.gov.uk) handles visa and passport issues for residents of the United Kingdom traveling in El Salvador. **New Zealand** does not have a consulate or embassy in El Salvador. Kiwis need to contact the New Zealand embassy in Mexico City (Jamie Balmes 8, 4th floor, Los Morales, Polanco, Mexico, D.F. 11510; ☎ **5255/5283-9460;** jorge.arguelles@nzte.govt.nz) for assistance.

Emergencies Emergencies anywhere in the country can be handled by calling ☎ **911.** Some towns also have local numbers for tourist police, fire, and other agencies. Those numbers are listed in this guide, wherever applicable.

Hospitals The nation's premier private hospital is **Hospital de Diagnóstico y Emergencias Colonia Escalón** (21a Calle Poniente and 2a Diagnol 429, Urbanización, La Esperanza Paseo del General Escalón, San Salvador; ☎ **503/2506-2000**). If you have a serious medical issue but are not ready or willing to leave the country, this is the place you need to go. Public hospitals, which are not recommended, are scattered throughout the country and can get you patched up well enough to get home or

to San Salvador. A complete list of El Salvador's public hospitals with contact information can be found at www.mspas.gob.sv.

Internet & Wifi The hotel listings in this book contain information on what hotels have free internet and WiFi services. Be aware that many high-end hotels charge between $3 and $10 per day for internet use although some will let you log on and print an airline boarding pass free of charge.

Language Spanish is the official language of El Salvador. Few El Salvadorans outside of San Salvador's hotels speak English, so it's a good idea to learn a few words and to bring a Spanish phrasebook with you. (See Chapter 22 for a glossary of Spanish terms and phrases.)

Maps Maps are exceedingly hard to come by in El Salvador. The main CORSATUR office in San Salvador (p. 216) offers large, colorful, tourism-style country and San Salvador maps. But few small towns offer street maps. Most towns are easy to find off the main highways and are walkable once you arrive.

Newspapers & Magazines *El Diario de Hoy* and *La Prensa* are El Salvador's most readily available newspapers. *El Diario* considers itself to be the country's paper, while *La Prensa* seems to have a more international perspective. Both are written in Spanish. The best English-language magazine you'll find in El

2

Salvador is the Guatemala-based *Revue Magazine,* which offers travel, culture, and business features concerning Central America.

Police See "Emergencies".

Post Offices & Mail Most towns in El Salvador have post offices marked by a blue sign reading CORREOS. Offices are open Monday through Friday from 8am to 5pm in larger cities, and 7am to noon and 2 to 5pm in small towns. To mail a standard letter from El Salvador to the United States costs around 65¢ and 85¢ to Europe and Australia. For a list of post office addresses and phone numbers, visit http://www.correos.gob.sv/ and click on "Correos de El Salvador."

Safety See the "Safety" sections in the individual Nicaragua and El Salvador planning chapters.

Taxes All hotels charge an 18% tax. Restaurants charge 13% on the total cost of the bill and often sneak in an automatic 10% for service—check your bill carefully to avoid overtipping. See "By Plane," earlier in this chapter, for info on the country's airport departure tax.

Tipping A 10% tip is automatically added to most restaurant checks, and taxi drivers don't expect a tip. No hard standard exists for bellhops, but $1 per bag will keep you in their good graces. Also, many tour guides work entirely for tips, with a $2 minimum expected for anytime up to an hour. After that, it's up to you to compensate for exceptional service.

SPECIALIZED TRAVEL RESOURCES

Travelers with Disabilities

El Salvador is not well equipped for travelers with disabilities. Where elevators exist, they are often tiny. Many city streets are crowded, narrow, and badly maintained, and public buses so frenetic that even able-bodied people have scarcely time to board before the driver roars off. The nature of the terrain means that climbing in and out of small buses and boats will be challenging.

Yet travelers with disabilities will not feel out of place in El Salvador, as the country has its fair share of people with mobility issues, and able-bodied locals will always be eager to help. **Mobility International USA** (www.miusa.org) is an organization that sets up exchange programs between people with disabilities. There are more resources out there than ever before. Check out **MossRehab** (www.mossresource net.org), which provides a library of accessible-travel resources online; the **Society for Accessible Travel and Hospitality** (SATH; 🕻 212/447-7284; www.sath. org), which offers a wealth of travel resources for all types of disabilities and informed recommendations on destinations, access guides, travel agents, tour operators, vehicle rentals, and companion services; and the **American Foundation for the Blind** (🕻 800/232-5463; www.afb.org), which offers a referral resource for the blind or visually impaired that includes information on traveling with Seeing Eye dogs.

For more on organizations that offer resources to travelers with disabilities, go to Frommers.com.

Gay & Lesbian Travelers

El Salvador is Catholic and conservative. Public displays of same-sex affection are rare and considered somewhat shocking. There are some gay bars in San Salvador, and I even came across a group of late-night transsexuals in tiny Suchitoto, but the scene is well concealed. Gay and lesbian travelers should choose their hotels with care and be discreet in most public areas and situations. For a complete listing of gay-friendly venues, check out www.gayelsalvador.com.

For more gay and lesbian travel resources, visit Frommers.com.

Family Travel

Your kids will have a ball in El Salvador, especially if you choose the kid-friendly accommodations, restaurants, and attractions throughout this guide (look out for the "Kids" icon). All-inclusive resorts on the Balsamo Coast and the Costa del Sol are the obvious choices, but the country throws up some surprise attractions, such as the excellent children's museum in San Salvador. Restaurants and tour operators are child-friendly, though you may have problems on public transportation such as buses, which are uncomfortable for everybody, never mind an energetic 5-year-old.

A handful of hotels give discounts for children 11 and under, or allow children under 3 or 4 years old to stay for free. Discounts and cutoff ages vary according to the hotel, but in general, don't assume that your kids can stay in your room for free. Hotels offering regular, dependable babysitting service are few and far between. If you will need babysitting, make sure your hotel offers it before you make your reservation.

Single Travelers

Like most other destinations, you'll pay a premium if you're traveling alone in El Salvador, and most tour prices are based on groups of two to four people. Many hotels offer single travelers a discounted rate on a double room (known as *tarifa sencilla*).

SUSTAINABLE TOURISM

Sustainable tourism is conscientious travel. It means being careful with the environments you explore and respecting the communities you visit. Two overlapping components of sustainable travel are **ecotourism** and **ethical tourism.** The **International Ecotourism Society** (TIES) defines ecotourism as responsible travel to natural areas that conserves the environment and improves the well-being of local people. TIES suggests that ecotourists follow these principles:

o Minimize environmental impact.
o Build environmental and cultural awareness and respect.
o Provide positive experiences for both visitors and hosts.
o Provide direct financial benefits for conservation and for local people.
o Raise sensitivity to host countries' political, environmental, and social climates.
o Support international human rights and labor agreements.

You can find some ecofriendly travel tips and statistics, as well as touring companies and associations at the **TIES** website, www.ecotourism.org. Also check out **Ecotravel.com**, which lets you search for sustainable touring companies in several categories (water-based, land-based, spiritually oriented, and so on).

While much of the focus of ecotourism is about reducing impacts on the natural environment, ethical tourism concentrates on ways to preserve and enhance local economies and communities, regardless of location. You can embrace ethical tourism by staying at a locally owned hotel or shopping at a store that employs local workers and sells locally produced goods.

IT'S EASY BEING green

Here are a few simple ways you can help conserve fuel and energy when you travel:

- Each time you take a flight or drive a car, greenhouse gases are released into the atmosphere. You can help neutralize this danger to the planet through "carbon offsetting"—paying someone to invest your money in programs that reduce your greenhouse gas emissions by the same amount you've added. Before buying carbon offset credits, just make sure that you're using a reputable company, one with a proven program that invests in renewable energy. Reliable carbon offset companies include **Carbonfund** (www.carbonfund.org), **TerraPass** (www.terrapass.org), and **Carbon Neutral** (www.carbonneutral.org).

- Whenever possible, choose nonstop flights; they generally require less fuel than indirect flights that stop and take off again. Try to fly during the day—some scientists estimate that nighttime flights are twice as harmful to the environment. And pack light—each 15 pounds of luggage on a 5,000-mile flight adds up to 50 pounds of carbon dioxide emitted.

- Where you stay during your travels can have a major environmental impact. To determine the green credentials of a property, ask about trash disposal

and recycling, water conservation, and energy use; also question if sustainable materials were used in the construction of the property. The website **www.greenhotels.com** recommends green-rated member hotels around the world that fulfill the company's stringent environmental requirements. Also consult **www.environmentallyfriendlyhotels.com** for more green accommodations ratings.

- At hotels, request that your sheets and towels not be changed daily. (Many hotels already have programs like this in place.) Turn off the lights and air-conditioner (or heater) when you leave your room.

- Use public transport where possible—trains, buses, and even taxis are more energy-efficient forms of transport than driving. Even better is to walk or cycle; you'll produce zero emissions and stay fit and healthy on your travels.

- If renting a car is necessary, ask the rental agent for a hybrid or rent the most fuel-efficient car available. You'll use less gas and save money at the tank.

- Eat at locally owned and operated restaurants that use produce grown in the area. This contributes to the local economy and cuts down on greenhouse gas emissions by supporting restaurants where the food is not flown or trucked in across long distances.

Responsible Travel (www.responsibletravel.com) is a great source of sustainable travel ideas; the site is run by a spokesperson for ethical tourism in the travel industry. **Sustainable Travel International** (www.sustainabletravelinternational.org) promotes ethical tourism practices and manages an extensive directory of sustainable properties and tour operators around the world.

In the U.K., **Tourism Concern** (www.tourismconcern.org.uk) works to reduce social and environmental problems connected to tourism. The **Association of Independent Tour Operators (AITO;** www.aito.co.uk) is a group of specialist operators leading the field in making holidays sustainable.

Volunteer travel has become increasingly popular among those who want to venture beyond the standard group-tour experience to learn languages, interact with locals, and make a positive difference while on vacation. Volunteer travel usually doesn't require special skills—just a willingness to work hard—and programs vary in length from a few days to a number of weeks. Some programs provide free housing and food, but many require volunteers to pay for travel expenses, which can add up quickly.

For general info on volunteer travel, visit **www.volunteerabroad.org** and **www. idealist.org**. Specific volunteer options in El Salvador are listed on p. 270.

Before you commit to a volunteer program, it's important to make sure any money you're giving is truly going back to the local community and that the work you'll be doing will be a good fit for you. **Volunteer International** (www.volunteerinternational.org) has a helpful list of questions to ask to determine the intentions and the nature of a volunteer program.

Sustainable Tourism in El Salvador

Numerous plush and not-so-plush establishments around the world have adopted the ecolodge label to attract well-meaning visitors when in reality their environmental efforts are cosmetic only. El Salvador is not immune to such greenwashing. One notable exception, however, is the delightful **La Cocotera** in Barra Santiago (p. 295). This luxury lodge has genuine green credentials with solar-powered water, a turtle incubation project, and a concerted effort to train locals in the hospitality industry. Less luxurious but just as green is **Imposible Eco Lodge,** close to the national park of the same name (p. 322).

Where you stay will determine greatly the mark you leave behind. The greenest way to stay in El Salvador is to choose a homestay with a family, but this is not an option if you are on a quick holiday and want some privacy and creature comforts. If you do choose a homestay, try to book directly through a local organization and not a foreign-based agency that collects a whopping commission. The same must be said when signing up for a volunteer program. There are a multitude of Web-based clearinghouses that gouge commissions from your hefty fee while very little of your money reaches the actual community. See text box "Volunteer Opportunities in El Salvador," on p. 270, for reputable organizations.

STAYING CONNECTED

Telephones

The country code for El Salvador is 503, which you use only when dialing from outside the country. Telephone numbers in this guide include this prefix because most businesses' published phone numbers include the prefix.

To place a call from your home country to El Salvador, dial the international access code (011 in the U.S. and Canada, 0011 in Australia, 0170 in New Zealand, 00 in the U.K.), plus the country code (503), plus the eight-digit phone number.

To place a call within El Salvador, simply dial the eight-digit number beginning with 2 for landlines and 7 for cellphones.

To place a direct international call from El Salvador, dial 00 for international access, plus the country code to the nation you are calling, followed by the area code and local phone number. For directory enquiries, dial © **155,** and to make reverse-charge calls abroad, you must call © **155-120.** However, these are automated services that will sorely test your Spanish.

Claro (© **503/2250-5555;** www.claro.com.sv) is the main telephone company, and call center branches can be found in all the main towns and cities. You can also make calls from public booths located on the street. Cards can be bought at most service stations and corner stores.

Cellphones

Cellphones have taken off in El Salvador, with more than 3 million gadgets in use, the vast majority of which are pay-as-you-go. The main companies are Movistar, Tigo, Digicel, and Claro, with Tigo reputedly giving the best overall reception. You will need to buy a new chip on arrival if you wish to bring your own phone; better, more reliable, and more expensive is to arrange a roaming facility with your phone company before your trip. The roaming service can cost anywhere between $1 and $4 a minute, while a new chip costs $35. Whichever you decide, consult with your provider beforehand, as many a traveler has found his phone still useless with a new chip; it has something to do with different bands in different countries and not all phones being compatible.

Pay-as-you-go phones can be purchased in the airport, the cheapest of which cost $60. Make sure to ask if the phone can take international calls and how much this costs, as packages vary and can be restrictively expensive. For example, partially paying for Mom's call will soon blitz any credit you have. Local calls vary from 10¢ to 50¢ a minute. Look out for promotions such as free incoming calls and cheap international calls for 10¢ a minute with certain networks.

Voice over Internet Protocol (VoIP)

Your best, cheapest bet for making international calls is to head to an Internet cafe. The vast majority have an international calling system called Voice over Internet Protocol (VoIP), which most of us know as Skype. These cafes are easily spotted because they have headsets attached to each computer (and often a loud foreigner shouting down one). International calls made this way can range anywhere from free to $1 per minute—much cheaper than making direct international calls or using a phone card. If you have your own Skype or similar account, you just need to find one of the many Internet cafes in El Salvador that provide the service. To open an account is easy—just go on www.skype.com and follow the instructions. If you are calling another Skype user, the call is free.

 Where Are You @?

The @ symbol is hard to find on a Latin American keyboard. You must keep your finger on the "Alt" key and then press "6" and "4" on the number pad to the right. If you're at an Internet cafe, ask the assistant to help you type an *arroba.*

Internet & E-mail
WITH YOUR OWN COMPUTER

Even the most humble hostel has Wi-Fi coverage in El Salvador. Hotels, cafes, and retailers are signing on as "hot spots," meaning you can access the Internet from your own wireless-enabled laptop. Most places don't charge, though there are some high-end hotels in San Salvador that do. Wireless Internet in Spanish is known as *internet inalámbrico*. Mac owners have their own networking technology: Apple AirPort. iPass providers (www.ipass.com) also give you access to a few hundred wireless hotel lobby setups. To locate other hot spots that provide **free wireless networks** in cities around the world, go to www.personaltelco.net/index.cgi/WirelessCommunities or www.jiwire.com, which holds the world's largest directory of public wireless hotspots.

For dial-up access, most business-class hotels throughout Central America offer dataports for laptop modems.

Wherever you go, bring a **connection kit** of the right power and phone adapters, a spare phone cord, and a spare Ethernet network cable—or find out whether your hotel supplies them.

WITHOUT YOUR OWN COMPUTER

Cybercafes are now a common sight in any urban part of El Salvador, though be warned that in the classier districts of San Salvador, they are markedly absent. That should not matter, however, as any self-respecting hotel or youth hostel nowadays has at least one computer you can get to the Internet on, and many provide at least 15 minutes free. When entering a cybercafe, ask for *una máquina,* and the assistant will direct you to an available computer. Charges vary between $1 and $2 an hour.

SAN SALVADOR

When Mayor-elect Norman Quijano announced in 2010 that he was going to beautify San Salvador, he set himself a hard task. This is a frenetic, modern city that suffers from pollution and heavy traffic, and there is a great divide between the rich and the poor, which means there are unsafe, crime-ridden neighborhoods that contrast wildly with luxurious, expensive mall developments. Earthquake damage has taken its toll on older buildings, and the city—which is Central America's second-most populated, after Guatemala City—lacks any grand vistas. Instead of pretty architecture, San Salvador's center is a clogged up mess of canvas-covered markets and rickety stalls with what seems to be the highest concentration of fast-food restaurants in the world.

Yet slowly but surely, the mayor is beginning to transform the city. The chaotic stalls and markets that blocked the city center are being cleared away, revealing that this sprawling metropolis does have something to show besides a high murder rate and plethora of fast food franchises. The volcanoes and hills that surround the city provide a picturesque backdrop, and the center, once cleared and seen, is both interesting and historic.

Overall, the city offers one of Central America's most diverse collections of international restaurants. You can sample fusion, Italian, Asian, Brazilian, and other cuisines at restaurants with top-notch service and, at least by North American and European standards, reasonable prices. You can also lay your head on the fluffy pillows of high-end, luxury hotels such as Hilton, Sheraton, and Intercontinental without emptying your bank account and shop at an international collection of designer stores in sparkling new malls such as the Multiplaza and Gran Via. In addition, the city boasts some excellent museums, a world-class art gallery, a nearby international airport, and beach resorts within an hour's drive. It's a city with a lot going for it.

Founded in 1525, San Salvador was the capital of the united provinces of Central America from 1834 to 1839, when the short-lived confederacy broke up into separate states. Its turbulent history has seen countless earthquakes and volcanic eruptions, as well as political unrest and outright war. Tremors destroyed the city in 1854 and 1873. Volcán San Salvador erupted in 1917, and two earthquakes in 1986 and 2001 caused considerable damage. The city suffered enormously during the civil war of the 1980s, with countless assassinations and riots. The government bombed its own people in a crude attempt to wipe out FMLN fighters hiding out in the poorer neighborhoods. Normality returned only with the end of the war in 1992, but the city still bears many scars from this dark period in its history.

If you have limited time in El Salvador, it's best to see San Salvador in 1 or 2 days. That will give you enough time to enjoy its international comforts and to see the main highlights, but leave you ample time to explore the country's smaller, more charming, towns. However, if you have more time on your hands and a reasonable budget that can afford one of the better hotels in the better areas, you will experience a vibrant, emerging city with a lot to offer.

ESSENTIALS

Getting There

BY PLANE   El Salvador International Airport, also known as Comalapa or **Cus-catlán International Airport (SAL; ℂ 503/2339-9455;** www.cepa.gob.sv/aies) is 44km (27 miles) and a roughly 45-minute drive from San Salvador. Cuscatlán International is serviced by major North American carriers such as **American, Delta,** and **Continental,** as well as Latin American carriers **Copa** and **Mexicana.** It's also a major hub for Taca airlines, with direct flights to major American cities. See "Appendix: Fast Facts, Toll-Free Numbers & Websites" for airline info.

To get to the capital from the airport, take bus no. 138, which costs $2. Alternatively, you can arrange transportation with your hotel or pay $25 for one of the taxis waiting by the airport exit.

BY BUS   There are three main bus terminals in the city servicing different sectors of the country, plus the small, private terminals of the plusher international bus companies. The public stations are chaotic and busy. Some lines have different categories. *Directo* is a misnomer, as these buses usually stop everywhere, much like the *ordinarios. Especial* generally has A/C, comfy seats, TV, and many fewer stops.

Terminal de Oriente (Final de Av. Peralta and Blvd. del Ejército; ℂ **503/2271-4171**) is 4km (2½ miles) from the city center and serves the east and north of the country. You can catch bus no. 29 or 52 from Boulevard de los Héroes, but the drop-off is at a busy roundabout that you must cross by a pedestrian walkway if you are going into the city. It is much more convenient to catch a taxi. Buses here leave for the Honduran border (3 hr.), as well as San Miguel (2½ hr.) and Suchitoto (1½ hr.).

Terminal de Occidente (Blvd. Venezuela, Colonia Roma; ℂ 503/2223-5609) is located closer to the city center, 1.5km (1 mile) southwest of Parque Cuscatlán. It serves the west of the country, including the southwestern coast and most of the Guatemalan border. Main destinations include Joya de Cerén (1¼ hr.), La Libertad (1 hr.), Lago de Coatepeque (40 min.), Los Cóbanos (2 hr.), Santa Ana (1½ hr.), and Sonsonete (1½ hr.).

Terminal del Sur, also known as Terminal San Marco (Carretera a Aeropuerto; no phone) is 5km (3 miles) south of the city and serves the south and southeast of the country. Bus 26 goes to and fro from the city center. The station's main destinations are Costa del Sol (2½ hr.), Zacatecoluca (1½ hr.), and Usulután (2½ hr.).

You can take **Tica Bus** (ℂ **503/2243-9764;** www.ticabus.com), which is one of Central America's largest and most luxurious carriers, with destinations throughout Central America, from the **San Carlos Terminal** (Calle Concepción #121, at the San Salvador Hotel; ℂ **503/2243-9764**) and **San Benito Terminal** (Blvd. del Hipódromo; ℂ **503/2243-9764**). **King Quality/Comfort Lines** (ℂ 503/2271-3330;** www.kingqualityca.com) has two terminals: **Terminal Puerto Bus** (3a Cal Poniente and Alameda San Juan Pablo II) and **Zona Rosa** (Blvd. de Hipódromo a

Av. La Revolución). **Pullmantur** (© **503/2243-1300;** www.pullmantur.com) operates from the Hotel Sheraton Presidente, Avenida La Revolución, Zona Rosa.

Orientation

San Salvador is Central America's largest city in terms of size, sprawling 570 sq. km (220 sq. miles) east from the base of Volcán San Salvador. The three main tourist zones are **El Centro** in the east, and the **Escalón** neighborhood and Boulevard del Hipódromo in **Zona Rosa** in the west. All three neighborhoods are connected by the city's main east-west highway, known as **Alameda Franklin Delano Roosevelt,** east of the **Plaza de Las Américas** and **Paseo General Escalón** west of the plaza. El Centro includes the city's traditional square, national cathedral, and theater and is a crowded, urban area. It's safe during the day, but best not visited at night. Zona Rosa and Escalón are more upscale residential neighborhoods and offer some of San Salvador's top restaurants, nightclubs, and shops. Adjacent to Zona Rosa to the west, you'll find the Colonia San Benito neighborhood, home to the **Museo Nacional de Antropología Dr. David J. Guzman** and **Museo de Arte.** Just south of the Zona Rosa area, past a rather large and brand new Mormon church, you'll find the Multi-Plaza and La Gran Via shopping malls. It's not a good idea to stray too far from these three areas without local knowledge or a guide.

Though most of your travel in San Salvador will be east-west along Roosevelt/Escalón, the city also has a couple of key north-south routes. The main north-south route through the El Centro section is known as Avenida España north of Plaza Barrios and Avenida Cuscatlán south of the Plaza. Avenida Norte, which becomes the Boulevard de los Héroes, splits the middle of the city; to travel south to the Zona Rosa and Colonia San Benito neighborhoods from the Paseo General Escalón, follow Avenida Manuel E Araujo to Boulevard del Hipódromo.

The city has a street system that seems cryptic when first encountered but makes perfect sense once you understand it. Thoroughfares called *avenida* run north and south, split between *norte* and *sur,* depending on what side of Calle Delgado and Calle Arce they fall on. Odd numbers mean the address is west of avenidas España and Cuscatlán, and even numbers mean it is east of them. Likewise, streets called *calle* run east to west and are called *oriente* (east) or *poniente* (west), depending which direction from avenidas España and Cuscatlán they run from. Even numbers are south of avenidas España and Cuscatlán, and odd numbers are to the north of them. If this isn't confusing enough, there are several diagonal avenues that thankfully have their own names, such as Boulevard de los Héroes and Alameda Araujo.

Getting Around

BY BUS Buses rule the road in San Salvador and are a great way to see the city, since they stop frequently and go just about everywhere. Bus no. 30b is the line you'll most need to remember. The 30b will take you from Metrocentro (Blvd. de los Héreos and Calle Sisimiles) across town to Zona Rosa and within walking distance of the city's two major museums. Most intercity buses can be taken from in front of the Metrocentro mall. To travel across the city from El Centro, take bus no. 101 to the Plaza de Las Américas, where you can hop on no. 30b.

Most buses cost 25¢ to 35¢ and run between 5am to 7:30pm daily, with less frequent service on Sundays. The CORSATUR tourist office (see "Visitor Information," below) can provide additional bus route information.

BY TAXI You might want to consider using a cab instead of the bus, depending on how far you're traveling—it costs only about $4 to take a cab many places in the city. Exact fares vary, depending on your negotiating skills, the driver, and whether or not the cab has a meter. If you speak Spanish, you'll get the best deal by finding a cab without a meter and negotiating a price before getting into the cab. If the taxi has a meter, demand at least an estimate of the cost before agreeing to the trip.

San Salvador has numerous taxicab companies, any of which can be safely hailed on the street during daytime as long as you use a traditional-looking taxi (yellow with a little taxi sign on top).

BY CAR Getting around by rental car is a great way to see El Salvador and a horrible way to see San Salvador. The city's roads are packed and not well marked. A wrong turn can send you into a neighborhood you'd rather not visit or into the midst of a bustling street market. Since taxis are relatively inexpensive and easy to grab, and local buses are cheap and numerous, I recommend leaving your rental at your hotel or renting a car on your way out of the city.

San Salvador offers plenty of local and international rental agencies. **Avis** (© 503/2339-9268), **Budget** (airport office © 503/2339-9942; city office © 503/2264-3888), **Hertz** (© 503/2339-8004), **Thrifty** (© 503/2339-9947), **Alamo** (© 503/2367-8000), and **National** (© 503/2367-8001) all have airport and downtown San Salvador locations. Locally, **Brothers Rent A Car** (Centro Commercial Feria Rosa bldg. H, local 208, in front of Casa Presidencial; © 503/2218-1856) offers the best deals. Rates range from $40 to $150 a day with taxes and insurance.

ON FOOT Both of San Salvador's main tourist centers, El Centro and Zona Rosa, are highly walkable. It's in between those neighborhoods where you'll need transportation. El Centro's attractions are centered around the main square, Plaza Barrios, and most of Zona Rosa's sights are along walkable Boulevard del Hipódromo. The city's major museums in the Colonia San Benito neighborhood are also within walking distance of each other.

Visitor Information

San Salvador's national tourism bureau's (CORSATUR) office is located at Alameda Dr. Manuel Enrique Araujo, Pasaje and Building Carbonel #2, Colonia Roma (© 503/2243-7835), and is open Monday through Friday 8am to noon and 1 to 5pm. The airport also offers a tourism office (© 503/2339-9454) with English-speaking staff that's open Monday through Friday from 7am to 6pm.

[FastFACTS] SAN SALVADOR

Banks, ATMs & Traveler's Checks San Salvador offers a plentiful supply of the nation's major banks, and ATMs here accept most common international cards. The best and safest locations are in the city's many malls. Bank hours generally run from 9am to 4pm Monday to Friday, with a half-day on Saturday from 9am to noon. A **Banco Cuscatlán** (© 503/2212-2000) is in the Galerías Escalón mall along Paseo General Escalón. **Banco de América Central** (© 503/2254-9980) is also located on Paseo General Escalón. On Boulevard de los Héroes, there is a **Banco Cuscatlán** (© 503/2212-2000, ext. 4205) located on the intersection with Avenida Izalco and a **Scotiabank** (© 503/2260-9038) located in the Metro Su mall. In the city center you'll find a **Banco**

Cuscatlán on Avenida Cuscatlán and a **Scotiabank** on 2a Calle Poniente. Most of the above banks will cash traveler's checks.

Drugstores **Farmacia Super Medco** (Av. La Revolución and Blvd. Hipódromo, Zona Rosa; ☎ 503/2243-3599) is open 24 hours with an all-night service window on Boulevard Hipódromo. **Farmacia Rowalt** (Av. Los Sisimiles and Av. Sierra Nevada, close to Blvd. de los Héroes; ☎ 503/2261-0515) also dispenses 24/7 and delivers from 8am to 5pm. Just ring the doorbell if it appears closed. In the city center, try **Farmacia Principal** (Calle Delgado 227; ☎ 503/2222-8093), open daily 8:30am to 8pm.

Emergencies The general emergency number is ☎ 911. Ambulances can be reached directly at ☎ 503/2222-5155 and the fire department at ☎ 503/2555-7300. Police can be contacted at ☎ 503/2261-0630.

Hospitals The best medical care is at the modern **Hospital de**

Diagnóstico Escalón (99 Av. Norte, Plaza Villavicencio; ☎ 503/2264-4422). **Hospital de Diagnóstico** (Calle 21 Poniente and 2a Diagonal, Blvd. de los Héroes; ☎ 503/2226-8878) is a well-respected and good-value private clinic.

Post Office **Correos Central** (15 Calle Poniente and 19 Av. Norte, Centro Gobierno, El Centro; ☎ 503/2555-7600) is the main post office and is open weekdays 7:30am to 5pm and Saturday 8am to noon. There is a another **Correos** outlet located on the second floor of the Metrocentro, open weekdays 8am to 7pm and Saturday 8am to noon. **DHL** (☎ 503/2264-2708) has an office on Avenidas Alberto Masferrer Norte. It is open weekdays 8am to 5pm and Saturday 8am to noon.

Internet There are plenty of Internet cafes in the city center, yet very few in the upscale residential zones like Colonia Escalón. Most offer Internet calls and CD burning. Charges vary

from $1 to $2 an hour. **Cyber Café Genus** (Av. Izalco 102-A, Blvd. de los Héroes; ☎ 503/2226-5221) is open weekdays 9am to 11pm and Saturday 10am to 8pm. **PC Station** (Metro Sur, Blvd. de los Héroes; ☎ 503/2257-5791) is another option in the same area. It is open Monday to Saturday 7am to 10pm and Sunday 9am to 7pm. In the city center, go to **Ciber Shack** (2a Av. Sur and 4a Calle Ote; no phone). It's open Monday to Saturday 7:30am to 6:30pm.

Laundry Most hotels offer laundry service, but beware, some are guilty of price gouging and charge as much as $5 per item instead of $5 per load. **Lavapronto** (Av. Los Sisimiles 2949, Blvd. de los Héroes; ☎ 503/2260-1702) is fast, reliable, and cheap. It is open weekdays 7am to 6pm and Saturday 7am to 5pm.

Restrooms There are no public toilets in the city except in shopping malls. However, ask nicely in any restaurant, and you'll have no problems.

FESTIVALS

The **Festival of El Salvador** in early August marks a nearly countrywide vacation during which everyone who can heads to their vacation spot of choice. Schools and businesses close so that communities throughout the country can host parades, celebrations, and religious processions honoring Jesus Christ ("El Salvador") as the patron saint of the country. The largest celebrations are here in the nation's capital.

WHERE TO STAY

n Salvador is an oasis of international hotel style and service in El Salvador. Most he big international chains are here and live up to the high standards their brands nd. All of the hotels listed below are comfortable and have something—be it price, location, or service—to recommend them. The Zona Rosa neighborhood—which includes the Hilton Princess and Las Palmas hotels—is among the city's safest and most tourist-friendly places to stay. Colonia Escalón is quiet and residential, with little but hairdressers and the occasional restaurant in the neighborhood besides some lovely hotels. There are no mid-range or high-end hotels in the rough-and-dirty claustrophobic center.

Very Expensive

Courtyard Marriot ★ ☺   The Marriot has a fresh, contemporary feel, with a busy lobby decked out in lime green and bright orange. A plethora of computers offering free Internet access are crowned by oval lamps and framed by a small bamboo divide. Rooms, though not overly spacious, are elegant and very comfortable, with modern touches such as the flat-screen TVs and granite-tiled bathrooms. The pool is small but adequate, and the breakfast buffet extensive and delicious (though it costs extra). The hotel's biggest asset is its location within San Salvador's plushest mall, an open street known as La Gran Via, with a wide selection of designer stores, restaurants, and bars. Nearby are a Starbucks and a large multiplex, perfect for the kids. Though very pleasant, staying here seems like being in a bubble with little connection to the rest of the city. It makes the nearby Zona Rosa seem authentic.

Esquina Calle 2 y Calle 3, Centro de Estilo de Vida la Gran Via. www.marriot.com; ✆ 503/2249-3000. Fax 503/2249-3001. 136 units. From $152 double. AE, DC, DISC, MC, V. Free parking. **Amenities:** 2 restaurants; bar; airport transfers ($25); concierge; gym; outdoor pool; internet (free); room service. *In room:* A/C, TV, hair dryer, minibar, Wi-Fi (free).

Hilton Princess ★★   It's a close call, but the Hilton Princess wins the title of San Salvador's most luxurious business hotel. What sets this 11-story spot in the heart of tourist-friendly Zona Rosa apart are its detailed, European castle–style interior and after-work amenities with perks such as a huge Jacuzzi and a larger-than-average exercise room. From the rich leather and dark woods of Churchill's Bar to the hotel's European murals and statuary, the Hilton also exudes old-world charm and luxury. If your visit is primarily business and you enjoy conducting it in complete comfort, this is the place to stay. One criticism is the steep charges to use the Internet, whether it is Wi-Fi in your room or a PC in the business center. You can, however, do check-in for a flight and print a boarding pass at no charge.

Av. Magnolias & Blvd. del Hipódromo, Zona Rosa. www.sansalvador.hilton.com; ✆ 800/321-3232 or 503/2268-4545. Fax 503/2268-4500. 204 units. $169–$179 standard double; $204–$219 executive-level double; from $333 suite. AE, DC, DISC, MC, V. Free parking. **Amenities:** Restaurant; 2 bars; airport transfers ($19); concierge; executive-level rooms; health club; Jacuzzi; outdoor pool; room service; sauna; 2 floors nonsmoking. *In room:* A/C, TV, hair dryer, minibar, Wi-Fi.

Casa II Bongustaio Boutique Hotel ★★   The big luxury chains have some serious competition at last. From the moment you step into the large circular courtyard with imposing white portico and experience the beautiful, intricate marble floors, expansive white arches, majestic antique doors, glistening installation art, and pebble-lined interior courtyards of this boutique hotel, you realize the hotel scene in San Salvador will never be the same again. The five huge rooms would make even Philipe Starck gasp at the blindingly white interiors, interrupted with flashes of fire-engine red and transparent Perspex furniture. Room 2 (its number stretches the height of the door on the corridor wall, which has moody ankle-high lighting) has walk-in wardrobe so large Imelda Marcos couldn't fill it, and the bathrooms alone ◂

San Salvador

RES. ESCALÓN

COL. EL PROGRESO

COL. TOLUCA

Av. Bernal

COL. YUMURI

Prolongación Juan Pablo II

Calle del Mirador

3

Av. Alberto Masferrer

79 Av. Norte

COL. STA. ROSA

Boulevard Constitución

COL. ESCALÓN NORTE

4

7

16

75a. Calle Poniente

COL. LOMAS VERDES

5

8

COL. ESCALÓN

COL. DORDELLY

ESCALÓN

6

75a. Av. Norte

Paseo General Escalón

Calle Poniente

17

Calle Circunvalación

Plaza Alegre

9 **10**

11

Plaza de las Américas

12

COL. CAMPESTRE

URB. MAQUILISHUAT

Quebrada La Mascota

Fuente Beethoven

Av. Olímpica

URB. SANTA MÓNICA

COL. PERALTA

18

Calle La Mascota

Calle La Mascota

COL. ROMA

Calle El Progreso

COL. EL ROSAL

19 **20**

COL. SAN BENITO

26

Calle Loma Linda

27 **28**

URB. LA MASCOTA

Boulevard Venezuela

COM. NUEVA ISRAEL

Boulevard de los Héroes

Boulevard del Hipódromo

21 **24**

29

22

Zona Rosa

25 **30**

COL. LAS PALMAS

Alameda Manuel Enrique Araujo

Av. Megavisión

Calle Amberes

23

Av. La Revolución

Av. Las Amapolas

Av. Jerusalem

EL ESPINO

31

34

Parque Nacional de Beisbol

COL. LAS MERCEDES

33

Plaza Italia

COL. MANUEL JOSÉ ARCE

Boulevard Los Próceres (Autopista Sur)

32

Multiplaza

La Gran Via

Pan American Hwy

Antigua Calle Ferrocarril

RES. GUADALUPE

43

42

Av. Río Amazonas

Av. Albert Einstein

44
↓

RES. JARDINES DE GUADALUPE

Antigua Huizúcar

RESTAURANTS ◆

Alo Nuestro **29**
Citron **28**
El Charrúa **8**
Fiasca Do Brasil Rodizio & Grill **14**
Il Bongustaio **20**
Las Cofradias **4**
La Hola **25**
La Ventana **7**
Hunan **17**
nka Grill **26**

Kalpataru **18**
La Cantata Del Café **42**
Tre Tratelli Pasta Café &
   Restorante **27**

HOTELS ■

Casa Il Bongustaio
   Boutique Hotel **19**
Courtyard Marriot **32**
Crowne Plaza Hotel **3**
Hilton Princess **24**

Hostal Plaza Antigua **10**
Hotel Villa Florencia Zona Rosa **31**
Hotel Villa Serena San Benito **21**
Intercontinental Real **13**
La Posada del Angel **5**
La Posada del Rey Primero **6**
Mariscal Hotel & Suites **11**
Quality Hotel Real Aeropuerto **48**
Sheraton Presidente **23**
Suites Las Palmas **30**
Villa Castagnola Hotel **9**

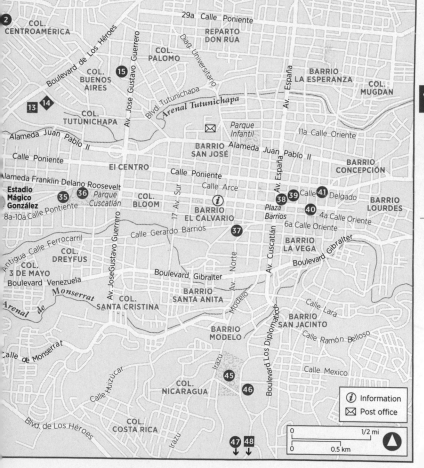

ⓘ Information
✉ Post office

0   1/2 mi
0   0.5 km

as ample as the standard room in an average hotel. The hotel also houses a very fine Italian restaurant and is conveniently located in the Zona Rosa.

Boulevard del Hipódromo 605, Colonia San Benito, San Salvador. www.casailb.co; ℰ **503/2528-4200**. 5 units. From $160 double. AE, DC, DISC, MC, V. Free parking. **Amenities:** Restaurant; room service. *In room:* A/C, TV, hair dryer, Wi-Fi.

Intercontinental Real The Intercontinental Real is a high-end, international chain and solid business hotel, but it's a slightly less appealing option overall than the Hilton Princess or the Sheraton. It's located in the city's main commercial district, which though good for business travelers, isn't tourist friendly; the pool and gym are also small and not overly inviting. On the plus side, the Intercontinental is across the street from El Salvador's biggest shopping mall, Metrocentro, and offers the hippest restaurants (p. 243) and lounges of the big three.

Calle Sisimiles & Blvd. de los Héreos, Colonia Miramonte. www.ichotelsgroup.com; ℰ **800/496-7621** or 503/2211-3333. Fax 503/2211-4444. 234 units. From $131 standard double; $167 executive-level double; from $273 suite. Rates include continental breakfast. AE, DC, DISC, MC, V. Free parking. **Amenities:** 3 restaurants; bar; airport transfers ($15); babysitting; concierge; executive-level rooms; heath club; small outdoor pool; room service; sauna; 181 nonsmoking rooms; spa. *In room:* A/C, TV, hair dryer, Internet, minibar.

Crowne Plaza Hotel ★★ Located on the slope of Colonia Escalón, overlooking the city, the Crowne Plaza (formerly a Radisson) is a large, modern six-story building with a bird-filled garden at one end. Its main attraction is a grand patio overlooking a big, no-nonsense pool. The rooms are ample, with cream walls, carpeted floors, and small, marble-top writing desks, and the bathrooms come with all the modern conveniences you'd expect from a five-star hotel. Everything is new, immaculate, and well maintained. Some rooms have marvelous views of the city and volcano. A big, well-equipped gym faces the pool, and a spa is hidden away in the basement. The staff is very gracious, and all your luxury needs are catered to here; I got so comfortable I stayed longer than intended. On the downside, breakfast is expensive, and there are exorbitant charges to use the computers in the business center or Wi-Fi in your room.

89 Av. Norte & 11 Calle Poniente, Colonia Escalón. www.ichotelsgroup.com; ℰ **800/395-7046** or 503/2257-0700. Fax 503/2257-0710. 126 units. From $126 double; $180 junior suite; $207 master suite. AE, DC, MC, V. Free parking. **Amenities:** 2 restaurants; bar; airport transfers ($19); babysitting; concierge; executive-level rooms; heath club; outdoor pool; room service; internet; sauna; spa. *In room:* A/C, TV, hair dryer, WiFi , minibar.

Sheraton Presidente ★★ Sheraton Presidente is an excellent high-end business hotel with all the amenities you'll need to get your work done, and it's also a slightly better place to stay than the Hilton Princess for those combining business and pleasure. That's because the Sheraton also offers a huge pool and is a short walk from the city's two major museums and the shop-filled Boulevard del Hipódromo. The surprisingly large pool includes a small waterfall that drowns out city noise and is next to an outdoor putting green (rare in El Salvador). The interior of this four-story hotel is what you would expect of a high-end chain but nothing more; rooms are of average size with nondescript, corporate decor. The hotel is often near capacity, so book early and request a room on the back side for pool views and less noise.

Av. La Revolución, Zona Rosa. www.sheraton.com/sansalvador; ℰ **800/325-3535** or 503/2283-4000. Fax 503/2283-4070. 225 units. $99 double; $209 executive-level double; from $289 suite. Executive-level and suite rates include buffet breakfast. AE, DC, DISC, MC, V. **Amenities:** 2 restaurants; bar; airport transfers ($14); concierge; health club; huge outdoor pool; room service; sauna; 120 nonsmoking rooms; spa. *In room:* A/C, TV, hair dryer, kitchen or kitchenette (in suites), minibar, Wi-Fi.

Expensive

Quality Hotel Real Aeropuerto ★ ☺ This Quality Hotel is a bit pricey but much nicer than you would expect of an airport hotel—it's a viable option, even if you aren't leaving early in the morning. Just 5 minutes from the Comalapa International Airport and an easy 35-minute drive from downtown, this three-story hotel offers such non-airport touches as an Xbox video game console, a pool with poolside bar and Jacuzzi, and an upscale restaurant. All the necessary business amenities are also available. The rooms are standard chain size and nondescript, but a few offer pool views. If you want the amenities of the posh city hotels, but the peace and quiet of the suburbs, this is your place.

Km 40.5 Carretera al Aeropuerto, La Paz. www.qualityinn.com; ✆ **877/424-6423** or 503/2366-0000. Fax 503/2366-0001. 149 units. From $130 double. Rates include buffet breakfast. AE, DC, DISC, MC, V. **Amenities:** Restaurant; bar; free airport transfers; babysitting; exercise room; Jacuzzi; outdoor pool; room service. *In room:* A/C, TV, fridge (in some), hair dryer, minibar (in some), Wi-Fi.

Suites Las Palmas ★★★ 🎒 Las Palmas is the best and hippest non-business hotel for the money in the city. This modern, seven-story hotel is within walking distance of Zona Rosa's best restaurants and shops, and offers big, modern suites with kitchens for the price of other hotels' basic rooms. It boasts unusual designs and amenities throughout. The pool, Jacuzzi, and sleek Asian-fusion restaurant are all set on the rooftop and have amazing views, as does the exercise room, which includes a wall of glass overlooking the city. The suites are large with king- or queen-size beds, often with kitchens and couches. Suite amenities and prices vary greatly, so pin down what you're getting when making your reservation; request upper-floor rooms, which have balconies and views. Though Las Palmas' name doesn't carry the cachet of the international chains in the city, it's every bit as luxurious and a better deal.

Blvd. del Hipódromo, Zona Rosa. www.hotelsuiteslaspalmas.com.sv; ✆ **503/2250-0800**. Fax 503/2250-0888. 47 units. $69–$90 standard double; $89–$119 deluxe double; $99–$129 presidential suite. Some rates include breakfast. AE, DC, DISC, MC, V. **Amenities:** Restaurant; bar; airport transfers ($15); small exercise room; Jacuzzi; rooftop pool; room service; nonsmoking rooms. *In room:* A/C, TV, kitchens or kitchenettes (in some), Wi-Fi.

Moderate

Hotel Villa Serena San Benito ★★ It's bare bones, but the San Benito is one of the best moderate options in San Salvador. The hotel offers huge, sunny suites and rooms, spotless facilities, and, like the nearby Sheraton Presidente, is within walking distance of the city's two major museums and Boulevard del Hipódromo's shopping and restaurant district. The large, airy suites feature big kitchens with modern appliances and separate lounging areas. The staff is also incredibly friendly. On the downside, the hotel doesn't have a pool or restaurant. San Benito is the best choice for those who prefer a great location and a good deal over amenities.

Calle Cicunvalación #46, Zona Rosa. www.hotelvillaserena.travel; ✆ **503/2237-7979**. 34 units. $62 double. Rates include continental breakfast. AE, DC, DISC, MC, V. **Amenities:** Airport transfers ($25); nonsmoking rooms. *In room:* A/C, TV, full kitchen (in suites), Wi-Fi.

Hotel Villa Florencia Zona Rosa A yellow corner building adorned with flowers hides a small, modern hotel with an excellent location. The furnishings are a mix of old and new, with comfy sofas in the small lobby and a gold gilded balustrade overlooking a stone-tiled patio, which acts as an open breakfast area in the morning. High ceilings and big beds adorn the good-size rooms with TVs and telephones. No. 7 ha the best view. The staff is friendly but doesn't speak English. Price and location make this hotel an excellent choice.

Calle Las Palmas 262, corner w/Av. La Revolución, Zona Rosa. www.hotelvillaflorencia.com; ✆ **503/2257-0236**. 14 units. $65 double. Rates include continental breakfast. AE, DC, MC, V. **Amenities:** Airport transfers ($25). *In room:* A/C, TV, Wi-Fi.

La Posada del Angel   If you want a home away from home, you can't go wrong with this cozy little guesthouse. Two angels hang over the reception area, and two angels act as hosts to meet your every need. Mother and daughter Ana and Racquel are the proud English-speaking owners of a modern, light-filled suburban-style home. Every room is different but well appointed, with carved headboards and wrought-iron lamps. No. 3 is the largest, with an ample bathroom and tiled floors. There is a lush garden out back with a communal gallery and dining area. The owners go out of their way to make you feel at home and are a fountain of information regarding nearby restaurants and things to do in the city.

85a Av. Norte 321, Colonia Escalón. www.hotellaposadadelangel.com; ✆ **503/2237-7171**. 10 units. From $59 double. Rates include continental breakfast. AE, DC, MC, V. Free parking. **Amenities:** Airport transfers ($25). *In room:* A/C, TV, Wi-Fi.

La Posada del Rey Primero   This handsome residential home has an airy, colonial feel with high ceilings, stucco walls, and wrought-iron furniture. Jungle paintings hang on green-and-orange walls in a handsome lobby and dining area. The rooms are big, with modern flourishes such as air-conditioning and TVs. Big, firm beds are complemented by solid, carved furniture. There is a lovely courtyard out back with a small, unfortunately empty pool surrounded by plants and clay urns. Pleasant communal areas with comfy seats and lots of reading material look out over the courtyard. The rooms on the second floor are larger and best for views and light.

Calle Dordelly, #4425, Colonia Escalón. www.posadadelreyprimero.com; ✆ **503/2264-5245**. 12 units. $65 double. Rates include continental breakfast. AE, DC, MC, V. **Amenities:** Airport transfers ($25). *In room:* A/C, TV, kitchen (in suites), Wi-Fi.

Mariscal Hotel & Suites   The Mariscal is pricier than the other two options in Escalón (see below), but is also a bit more upscale. It features 18 big rooms and suites that aren't necessarily any better than the area's other two hotels, but with matching linens and modern furniture sets, it does feel a bit fancier. The one- and two-room suites are large, with couches, dining tables, and well-appointed kitchens. Suites vary in quality, so request a suite with a modern kitchen: Suite no. 1 is the best, with a big bathroom and two televisions. Mariscal is on a heavily trafficked road, so request a room farthest from the street when you book.

Paseo General Escalón, #3658, Colonia Escalón. www.hotelmariscal.com; ✆ **503/2283-0220**. Fax 503/2223-5889. 18 units. From $76 double; $100 suite. Rates include continental breakfast. AE, DC, DISC, MC, V. **Amenities:** Airport transfers ($20); room service; all rooms nonsmoking. *In room:* A/C, TV, hair dryer, kitchen (in suites), Wi-Fi.

Inexpensive

Hostal Plaza Antigua ★ 🗲   Plaza Antigua is an excellent, low-priced option in a great location. It isn't going to blow you away with its decor or amenities, but it's in one of San Salvador's nicest neighborhoods, Escalón, and steps from the swanky Galerías Escalón mall. The two-story hotel is situated around a courtyard with a small pool. Rooms are of average size—all can be viewed on the hotel's website—with ʿcely tiled bathrooms. Request room no. 5, which is the quietest and catches the afternoon breeze. Given Plaza Antigua's location, they could probably charge more if they decorated a bit.

1a Calle Poniente, #3844, Colonia Escalón (behind Galerías Escalón). www.hotelplazaantigua.net; (C) **503/2223-9900**. Fax 503/2224-5952. 15 units. $41–$50 double. Rates include continental breakfast. AE, DC, DISC, MC, V. **Amenities:** Restaurant; airport transfer ($35); small outdoor pool; room service; 3 nonsmoking rooms. *In room:* A/C, TV, no phone, Wi-Fi.

Villa Castagnola Hotel Villa Castagnola is another excellent option for comfortable, affordable accommodations in the Escalón neighborhood, though it's about half the size of the Plaza Antigua. With only six rooms, Castagnola is as quiet a hotel as you will find in San Salvador. On-site husband-and-wife managers, Raul and Tatiana Nunes, offer a high level of personal service and will help you arrange area tours. The rooms are also larger than you would expect, and there's a pleasant, upstairs, open-air seating area with great views of Volcán de San Salvador. The best room is no. 1, which has two separate sleeping areas and a big bathroom.

1a Calle Poniente & 73 Av. Norte, #3807, Colonia Escalón. www.hotelvillacastagnola.com, (C) **503/2275-4314** or 503/2275-4315. Fax 503/2211-6482. 6 units. $45–$65 double. Rates include continental breakfast. AE, DC, DISC, MC, V. **Amenities:** Restaurant; airport transfers ($25); room service. *In room:* A/C, TV, fridge, Wi-Fi.

WHERE TO EAT

San Salvador offers a world-class array of ethnic restaurants, ranging from Asian to Peruvian. And one of the best places to sample those culinary offerings is the Boulevard del Hipódromo in the tourist-friendly Zona Rosa district. This stroll-friendly street on the city's west side offers a cluster of restaurants within just a few blocks. A few trusted Zona Rosa favorites are listed below, but since the city's restaurant scene is growing rapidly, you might want to take a stroll along the Boulevard to find your own favorite spot. Reservations are needed only where noted below.

Expensive

Citron ★★★ INTERNATIONAL You know a chef takes his job seriously when he spends his spare time hunting wild mushrooms on volcano slopes. Young Washingtonian Eduardo Harth opened this slick, modern restaurant in 2006 with the aim of molding Nicaraguan ingredients into contemporary works of art. A crab appetizer appears on a long, slender dish bathed in a spicy vegetable curry sauce, highlighted with fresh asparagus salad. Purple chunks of tuna come with tiny sesame seeds known as *ajonjil*, garnished with papaya and mango. The menu changes frequently, showcasing whatever is in season, and utilizes the restaurant's herb and vegetable garden. Most of what's on the menu is produced in-house, including the bread. Eduardo's architect father has created an airy, light-filled space that's both simple and elegant. This is easily the most exciting, original, and adventurous restaurant in San Salvador and a must visit for all wandering gourmands.

Calle La Reforma, Coloina San Benito. (C) **503/2208-4000**; www.restaurantecitron.com. Main courses $18–$22. AE, DC, MC, V. Mon–Fri noon–3pm; Mon–Sat 7–11pm.

Fiasca Do Brasil Rodizio & Grill ★★ BRAZILIAN It's all about the meat. Fiasca is one of San Salvador's few Rodizio restaurants, which means they keep the *carne* coming. Rodizio is an all-you-can-eat Brazilian style of dining, in which waiters bring huge skewers of meat or fish to your table and slice the cuts onto your plate. Fiasca specializes in the *picaña* or top rump cut, which many Brazilians consider be beef's finest. And at Fiasco, you don't wait long for your second helping, as the restaurant maintains a ratio of 18 servers to a maximum 92 diners. This is the principal restaurant of the luxury Intercontinental Real hotel (see above) and offers a unique, high-end dining experience for a reasonable price. As a result, the place is often packed, and reservations are required. Ask for one of the raised booths along each wall, which are off the busy main dining floor.

Calle Sisimiles & Blvd. de los Héreos. ✆ **503/2211-3333.** Reservations required. Prix fixe $25. AE, DC, DISC, MC, V. Daily 6–10:30am, noon–3pm & 7–11pm.

Hunan ★ CHINESE   Hunan is *the* place to go for Chinese in San Salvador. A bit plain and strip-mall-looking from the outside, Hunan's one-room, 250-person seating area is a lesson in Chinese interior design, with intricately carved wood chairs and embroidered red velvet seats, enormous wall murals, and dozens of porcelain vases with flowers for sale filling up the huge space. But it's Hunan's unique "Pato Peking"–style cuisine, a particularly spicy and hearty variety of Chinese cooking, that keeps diners coming back. Standout dishes include shrimp with tofu in a lobster sauce and duck with black mushrooms and oyster sauce. Hunan's service is also seamless.

Paseo Escalón, #4999, Colonia Escalón. ✆ **503/2263-9911.** Main courses $18–$26. AE, DC, DISC, MC, V. Mon–Sat noon–3pm; Mon–Thurs 6–10pm, Fri & Sat 6–11pm; Sun noon–4pm & 6–9pm.

Il Bongustaio ★ ITALIAN   Relocated in a gleaming white building that was built to impress, Il Bongustaio is part of the über-chic boutique hotel of the same name. Everything about this restaurant is eye candy and a thrill for those who love the latest in art and architecture. Its mock-colonial style is minimalist with little fuss. Simple Asian-style dividers separate an inner space from a large expansive outside dining area, where white arches frame a lush green lawn interspersed with works of art and orange canvas seating. The menu is strictly Italian, and the chef/owner Roberto Sartogo creates a dizzying array of antipastos, *primis*, and *secondis*. The lamb lasagna is particularly delicious, as is the tuna adorned with chick peas. With 17 different gins on offer, any G&T fanatic should be pleased, and the service is impeccable.

Boulevard del Hipódromo 605, Colonia San Benito. ✆ **503/2528-4200.** Main courses $12–$24. AE, DC, DISC, MC, V. Mon–Fri noon–3pm & 6–10pm; Sat 6–11pm; Sun 6–9pm.

Moderate

Alo Nuestro ★★★ FUSION   For more than a decade, this midsize restaurant has built a quiet, word-of-mouth following as one of the best restaurants in the packed Zona Rosa section of town. What draws the crowds is Alo Nuestro's ability to fuse the best of San Salvador's international dining options into a single restaurant that uses local ingredients. The results are seen in standout dishes such as crispy sea bass in a light soy ginger sauce and garlic-spinach stuffed chicken breast with a blue-cheese wine sauce. Unique weekly specials, such as sautéed tilapia over *loroco* crepes with a basil sauce, keep things fresh. The interior is small but feels spacious, with ample space between the tables, and there's a large romantically lit outdoor deck with a view of the nearby mountains. The restaurant is also surprisingly affordable, with most entrees costing less than $20.

Calle La Reforma, #225, Zona Rosa. ✆ **503/2223-5116.** Reservations recommended. Main courses `12–$20. AE, DC, DISC, MC, V. Mon–Fri noon–2:30pm; Mon–Thurs 7–10:30pm, Fri & Sat 7–11pm.

a Grill ★ PERUVIAN   The Inka Grill is a rare taste of the Andes in El Salvador. woods, deep oranges, and interesting Inca-inspired art greet diners as they enter this Peruvian oasis a few blocks off the Zona Rosa dining district. The dishes are pure Peruvian, with plates such as the *chicharrones* (deep-fried pieces of chicken and pork with artichoke hearts, yucca, and sweet potato) or *tamales de choclo* (corn tamales) with an onion salsa. Inka Grill is part of a seven-restaurant chain with locations in Costa Rica, Guatemala, the United States, and a second San Salvador location at the Gran Via mall. This spot near Zona Rosa is the better of the two because it is more secluded and tranquil, and offers a more uniquely Peruvian ambience.

79 Av. Sur & Pasaje A, Zona Rosa (a few blocks off Blvd. del Hipódromo). ✆ **503/2230-6060.** Main courses $9.95–$20. AE, DC, DISC, MC, V. Sun–Wed 2–10pm; Thurs–Sat 2–11pm.

El Charrúa GRILL HOUSE   Located in front of a palm-lined roundabout in a pleasant residential zone, El Charrúa provides every possible option for the confirmed carnivore. Beef, goat, rabbit, suckling pig, and lamb are just some of the many sizzling delights prepared on a grill in front of the bar. Uruguayan *asado* is a marathon barbecue where a procession of meat keeps coming, including sausage, chicken, and every cut of the cow. The restaurant also does a decent ceviche. The decor includes red brick, flower pots, and an Indian mural—a reference to the Charrúa tribe the restaurant is dedicated to.

Plaza Israel, Colonia Escalón. ✆ **503/2263-3188.** Main courses $6–$12. AE, DC, MC, V. Tues–Sun 8am–11pm; Mon 4pm–midnight.

La Hola SUSHI   Japan and El Salvador collide in spectacular fashion at this large street-corner restaurant in the Zona Rosa. La Hola is a big, rickety arrangement of multi-floored dining areas and patios partitioned with bamboo walls and frond-trimmed roofs. Fairy lights and star lanterns clash in a tacky arrangement of nautical decor and tropical flare. You cannot fault the food, however. The menu is as large as the prawns it offers, and the sushi list includes ample platters of sashimi and Japanese-style ceviche. Lobster, crab, paella, and octopus will sate the appetite of any seafood lover, and there is pasta, pizza, and even fondue for those who prefer something down-to-earth. Generous portions of sake will oil the vocal chords for a spot of karaoke later on the big screen in the corner. A strange but filling experience.

Blvd. del Hipódromo 230, Zona Rosa. ✆ **503/2233-6865.** Main courses $8–$12. AE, DC, MC, V. Mon–Sat 11am–2am; Sun 11am–midnight.

La Ventana INTERNATIONAL   This is an inviting, bar-style restaurant with dark tones of wood, brick, and olive-green walls. Modern art sculptures and photo exhibition stands look a little out of place amidst a counter bar dispensing German beers. The menu is global, with everything from curry *wurst* to Hungarian goulash. There are also Mexican, French, and Italian dishes on the extensive menu. Delicious lentil soup followed by vegetable-stuffed crepes proved very filling. The drinks list includes 41 different cocktails and a variety of wines, including *liebfraumilch*. Located on a leafy street in front of a small plaza, it has a small, shady courtyard out back.

85 Av. Norte 510 & 9 Calle Poniente, Plaza Palestina, Colonia Escalón. ✆ **503/2263-3188.** Main courses $8–$12. AE, DC, MC, V. Tues–Sun 8am–11pm; Mon 4pm–midnight.

Tre Tratelli Pasta Café & Restorante ★★ ☺ITALIAN   The alluring aroma of Italian herbs, garlic, and tomatoes envelops you the moment you walk into this casual, mid-priced Italian restaurant in the heart of Zona Rosa's dining district. The ambience is laidback but busy, with a semi-open kitchen. The two main dining areas, minimally decorated with Italian advertising art, give off the feel of a friendly neighborhood Italian joint, so the sophisticated menu, fusing Italian cooking with light

California fare, may surprise you. You'll definitely want to try the *canelone modi de mar*, rolled pasta stuffed with fish, shrimp, salmon, zucchini, and red peppers in a cream sauce with mussels and asparagus, or the Mediterranean-style ceviche with shrimp, calamari, capers, tomato, onions, and garlic. It also makes for a convenient beer or coffee stop, with an open air bar and patio out front.

Blvd. del Hipódromo, #307, Zona Rosa. ℂ **503/2223-0838.** Reservations required for groups larger than 10. Main courses $8–$16. AE, DC, DISC, MC, V. Daily 11am–11pm.

Inexpensive

Kalpataru ★★ 🌶 VEGETARIAN

If you're thinking vegetarian in San Salvador, think Kalpataru. For 22 years, this restaurant and holistic health center has lived up to its printed-on-the-menu mission statement to serve 100% vegetarian in a friendly environment. A few minutes from the city's main restaurant district, Kalpataru is worth the taxi ride for its large selection of $1.30 vegetarian *pupusas*, and tasty and affordable lunch buffet. Kalpataru also offers tamales, soups, and pizza. The casual, two-story restaurant includes a meditation center and a library with books, CDs, and natural healing products. And Kalpataru is just a 5-minute walk from El Arbol de Dios (p. 249), the gallery of El Salvador's national artist Fernando Llort, making it a great place to stop when you need a break from sightseeing.

Calle La Mascota, #928, Urbanización Maquilishuat. ℂ **503/2263-1204.** Lunch buffet $8.80; main courses $1.30–$5.50. AE, DC, DISC, MC, V. Mon–Fri noon–8pm; Sat 7am–8pm.

La Cantata del Café ★★★ 🎒 SALVADORAN

The vibe is great, the food is better, and the prices are ridiculously low. This little seven-table joint on the corner near the entrance to José Simeón Cañas University doesn't look like much from the outside, but don't let that fool you, this might be one of the tastiest meals you'll have in San Salvador. A young, friendly staff presides over the laidback space, which offers local art on the walls, live music, and books to read while sipping one of 30 hot and cold coffee drinks. Delicious sandwiches, salads, pizza, and pastas all hover around $3. A huge portion of penne arrives piping hot, napped with a rich, spicy sauce with big chunks of chicken, along with a side of tasty garlic bread. Add a beer and bottled water, and the bill still barely reaches 5 bucks.

Calle Mediterranio, #26, Colonia Jardínes de Guadalupe (1 block from entrance to José Simeón Central American University). ℂ **503/2243-9425.** Main courses $2.50–$3.25. No credit cards. Mon–Sat 8:30am–8pm.

Las Cofradias SALVADORAN

This is a great introduction to local food and recipes. A corner counter is piled high with black pots holding soups, corn dishes, and juices that the locals serve to themselves before joining their friends at simple picnic tables. Las Cofradias is as traditional as you'll get, with a dazzling array of local *criolla* dishes such as corn tamales, plantains, and sweet tortillas. *Tradición del Campo* is a hearty mixture of beans, yucca, and beef. The excellent buffet is served at night only but offers 60 different Salvadoran dishes. Lunchtime is from the more limited menu. The decor is a little soulless, with plain walls and barred windows, but there is lots of light. It is easy to miss the entrance door and the steps upstairs, but the security guard will point the way. In an adjoining room, there is a small craft store with a limited stock of ceramics and silverware.

85 Av. Norte, #643, Colonia Escalón (1 block from the Crowne Plaza). ℂ **503/2264-6148.** Main courses $2.50–$5; buffet $8.50. No credit cards. Daily noon–3pm; Sun–Thurs 5–10pm, Fri & Sat 5–11pm.

SPANISH classes IN EL SALVADOR

El Salvadorans are famously friendly, patient, and genuinely pleased when visitors attempt to speak their language. But that doesn't mean your high-school Spanish isn't painful to listen to. So if you're going to be spending some time here, you might as well brush up on the native tongue. Luckily, numerous short-term, affordable language programs are available throughout the country.

In San Salvador, you'll find the **Mélida Anaya Montes Spanish School**—part of El Salvador's human justice organization, Centro de Intercambio y Solidaridad (CIS; Av. Bolivar 103, Colonia Libertad, San Salvador; © **503/2226-5362;** www.cis-elsalvador.org)—which offers one- to four-person classes taught by El Salvadoran teachers, homestays with local families, and a strong emphasis on social justice in El Salvador. Students participate in 4-hour-long daily classes and can also participate in a program introducing them to El Salvador's political progressive organizations, communities, and political parties. Classes begin on Monday year-round

and cost $223, plus a $25 registration fee, per week, including food and lodging. Classes on their own are $100 per week.

The lakeside hostel **Amacuilco** (Calle Principal, Lago de Coatepeque, Santa Ana; © **503/7822-4051;** amacuilcohostal@hotmail.com), by beautiful Lago de Coatepeque, offers a 5-day, 20-hour Spanish course, including food, lodging, and kayak rentals, for $120. El Salvador's **SalvaSpan language school** (5a Calle Poniente, btw. 4 and 6 Av. Sur, #15, Santa Ana; © **503/7051-4171** in El Salvador or 413/374-0159 in the U.S.; www.salvaspan.com) offers language classes at a place of your choosing—for instance, if you want to take 2 days of classes in Suchitoto, 2 days in Playa Sunzal, and 2 days in Ataco, the SalvaSpan teachers can accommodate you. Classes are $175 to $200 per week for 5 days of 4 hours per day, one-on-one instruction. Homestays can be arranged in San Salvador and Santa Ana for an additional $125 to $150 per week.

WHAT TO SEE & DO
The Top Attractions

Catedral Metropolitana ★ El Salvador's national cathedral is not as visually stunning as some famous European cathedrals, but it is steeped in El Salvadoran history and offers an example of the nation's adopted artistic style. Historically, the church was the site of deadly massacres prior to the country's civil war and great celebrations after the 1992 peace accords. The church has been damaged and rebuilt three times and is considered a symbol of the nation's rebirth from tragedy. Today, the cathedral features a huge mural by El Salvador's most revered living artist, Fernando Llort. The tomb of Archbishop Oscar Romero is located on the lower floor beneath the nave and is well visited by admirers and pilgrims alike. The pope knelt at the flower-adorned tomb when he visited in 1993. As the aesthetics here are somewhat secondary to the history, read up a bit before you go to know what you are looking at. Av. Cuscatlán & 2a Calle Oriente at Plaza Barrios. No phone. Free admission. Daily 8am–noon & 2–4pm.

Museo de Arte ★★★ The Museo de Arte is one of San Salvador's must-see. The 2,267-sq.-m (24,402-sq.-ft.) museum includes six rooms of rotating exhibits a a permanent collection that helps newcomers get a sense of the country. One of the highlights is the art exhibited from the 1980-to-1992 civil war period, which clearly but subtly demonstrates the desperation of the time. Immediately in front of the museum is the towering stone mosaic Monument to the Revolution, which depicts a naked man whose outstretched arms are thought to symbolize freedom and liberty. You'll need 1 to 3 hours to explore the museum; English-language tours are free for parties of 10 or more and $40 total for parties of 1 to 9. Call or e-mail (educacion@marte.org.sv) 24 hours in advance to schedule an English-language tour. The museum also has an attractive restaurant called Punto Café.

Final Av. La Revolución, Colonia San Benito. ℭ **503/2243-6099;** www.marte.org.sv. $1.50 adults; 50¢ students; free for children 7 & under. Tues–Sun 10am–6pm.

Museo Nacional de Antropología Dr. David J. Guzman ★★   San Salvador's anthropology museum is the city's other must-see, but only if you speak Spanish or can arrange an English tour. The ancient tools, weapons, pottery, and ceramic artifacts on exhibit here offer an intriguing glimpse into the lives of El Salvador's indigenous community and explain the evolution of agriculture and early trade in the country. However, signs are in Spanish only. Since this is only a 10-minute walk from the art museum, it's still worth a quick look if you can't arrange an English tour and are in the area. An English-speaking tour guide is available at the front desk; book in advance by calling the number below.

Av. La Revolucíon. Colonia San Benito. ℭ **503/2243-3927;** www.munaelsalvador.com. $3 adults; $5 w/ camera or video equipment. Tues–Sun 9am–5pm.

Teatro Nacional ★   The 2001 earthquake denied San Salvador its most treasured cultural institute for almost 8 years. Renovated and reopened in 2009, you can now visit its splendid salons on day visits or enjoy weekend performances of theater, opera, and classical music. Built between 1911 and 1917, the Teatro Nacional is considered one of Central America's oldest theaters and one of El Salvador's grandest buildings. The French Renaissance structure has 10 large columns across the front and a grand European interior of high ceilings, large chandeliers, and an opulent, multistory theater.

2 Av. Sur & Calle Delgado, 1 block E of Plaza Barrios. ℭ **503/2222-8760.** $3 adults. Ticket prices vary by performance. Open Wed–Sun 8am–4pm.

Other Attractions

Centro Monseñor Romero ★   This center tells the story and displays the images and personal items of the six Jesuit priests, their housekeeper, and the housekeeper's daughter who were brutally murdered in the university rectory November 16, 1989, in the midst of El Salvador's bloody civil war. The murders made international headlines and demonstrated the war's high level of personal violence, all the more brutal because the massacre took place in a small museum dedicated to the archbishop who was killed 9 years earlier. The serene rose garden in back contrasts with the grisly exhibits inside, including graphic photos of the murder scene. Considering that El Salvador is a country with a complex and occasionally disturbing history, the half-hour you'll need to see this one-room center are worth it to have a broader understanding of the country.

Universidad Centroamericano José Siméon Cañas. ℭ **503/2210-6600,** ext. 422. Free admission. Mon–Fri 8am–noon & 2–6pm; Sat 8–11:30am.

remembering MONSEÑOR ROMERO

Monseñor Oscar Arnulfo Romero, commonly referred to as Monseñor Romero, is arguably El Salvador's most revered native son. Born in 1917, at age 20, he went to Rome to begin his career in the priesthood. He returned to El Salvador 6 year later and spent the next 20 years as a priest in San Miguel. In 1966, he became secretary of the Episcopal Conference and editor of the archdiocese's newspaper, *Orientación*. In 1975, he was appointed archbishop of the Diocese of Santiago de María and was promoted to Archbishop of San Salvador 2 years later. At this point, Romero was not considered to be a revolutionary, and his appointment disappointed some of the country's more progressive religious leaders.

Less than a month after his appointment as archbishop, however, Romero's friend Rutilio Grande, who had been organizing for the nation's poor, was assassinated. Deeply affected by the killing, Romero took up Grande's mantle and became an outspoken critic of government repression, injustice, and El Salvador's death squads. He also criticized Jimmy Carter and Pope John Paul II for their governments' support of the El Salvadoran military.

On March 24, 1980, following a sermon in which he was reported to have called on El Salvador's government soldiers to end their repressive tactics, Romero was shot and killed. His funeral in front of the country's national cathedral drew more than a quarter of a million mourners and was itself the site of gunfire and bomb blasts. The chapel where Romero was shot (Calle Toluca, Colonia Miramonte, beside Hospital la Divina Provedencia; € **503/2260-0520**) remains open today, with a small plaque marking the tragedy. Across the street, Romero's living quarters have been preserved as a museum with his personal effects and photos of the crime scene and funeral.

El Arbol de Dios Arbol de Dios is the gallery, workshop, and nonprofit office of El Salvador's most revered living artist, Fernando Llort (see p. 255 for more info), who founded an art movement in a small mountain town in 1972 by teaching locals to use available materials to express their lives. His colorful style of art, which is filled with natural and religious references, has since swept the country and can be found in hundreds of shops and at the National Cathedral. The gallery includes a gift store, screen-printing workshop, and a ceramic space on the back patio and takes about 40 minutes to explore. If you want to see a few of the original pieces that inspired thousands of copies, this is the place. If you're not that into art or Llort, it may not be worth the trip.

Av. Masferrer Nte. 575, Colonia Escalon. € **503/2263-9206;** elarboldedios@integra.com.sv. Free admission. Mon-Fri 8am-5pm.

Hospital La Divinia Provedencia ★ It was at the altar of this small hospital chapel in the midst of mass on March 24, 1980, that one of El Salvador's most revered citizens, Monseñor Oscar Arnulfo Romero, was gunned down in front of his parishioners. A single shot was fired from the back and hit the priest in the heart, killing him instantly. Today, the church remains a working chapel, with pictures of Romero and a small plaque marking the place where he was killed. Across the street, Monseñor Romero's living quarters are now a museum displaying his personal items including his blood-stained robes. There are also photos of the crime scene and the thousands who flocked to his funeral in front of the national cathedral. If you're at all interested in the details of El Salvador's civil war, this is worth a visit.

Calle Toluca, Colonia Miramonte. ℂ **503/2260-0520.** Free admission. Mon–Sat 9am–noon & 2–4pm.

Iglesia El Rosario ★★ ⛪ This is one of the most visually interesting churches in San Salvador, if not the whole country, and well worth the 5-minute walk off the main square. El Rosario's concrete, half-moon, bunker-like appearance is a bit bizarre and un-churchlike from the outside, but inside, visitors are greeted by lines of colored light streaming in from abstract stained glass running up the height of its two curved walls. Abstract metal works form the altar and run the length of a third wall. The Stations of the Cross are represented by spare concrete and metal art pieces and are showcased in a low-ceilinged area, which is lit by natural light filtered through small squares of colored glass.

4a Calle Oriente & 6a Av. Sur. No phone. Free admission. Daily 6:30am–noon & 2–7pm.

Jardín Botánico La Laguna ✋ Unless you're really into plants and flowers, you shouldn't make the trip here. La Laguna is a beautiful and lush 3-hectare (7½-acre) park inside an extinct volcano crater with winding paths through hundreds of species of plants and flowers from around the world. The park, which you can explore in 30 minutes, offers an open-air cafeteria beside a small pond and numerous secluded nooks and crannies to escape the heat. The only problem is that the garden is located in the midst of a busy factory district, so you'll need to dodge trucks and walk through less-than-savory surroundings to get to the entrance. If La Laguna were in the city center, it would be a real gem, but I can't say it's worth a special trip.

Universidad Centroamericano José Siméon Cañas, Antigua Custcatlán. ℂ **503/2243-2012;** www.jardinbotanico.org. $1 adults. Tues–Sun 9am–5:30pm.

Military Museum El Zapote Barracks El Zapote Barracks is close to the Parque Zoologico and has a somewhat forbidding appearance, with armed guards and a castle-like facade. I must admit, I had my doubts visiting the citadel of an army whose human rights record is less then exemplary. However, once you get past the security barrier, you'll find a tidy complex with some fascinating exhibits, the best of which by far is a meticulously made relief map of the entire country the size of a tennis court. You really get a feel for the vertical, volcanic landscape that is El Salvador as you eye black-topped pinnacles and cones and verdant green mountains. Elsewhere, a line of battle tanks guard the barrack rampart, and inside is an expansive courtyard with a collection of military hardware that ranges from helicopters to artillery guns. Here, the most interesting exhibits are the Pope mobile used to ferry the Holy See around in 1996 and a Browning gun that literally melted from over-use in the war—perhaps unintentionally symbolic.

Cuartel El Zapote, Barrio San Jacinto. ℂ **503/2250-0000.** Free admission. Daily 8am–5pm.

Monumento a la Memoria y la Verdad ★ The Monument to Memory and Truth is an 85m (279-ft.) black granite wall displaying the names of the 25,000 victims of the civil unrest, political repression, and war of the 1970s and 1980s. It is a stern reminder of just how much this country has suffered and is all the more powerful as you realize how recently these horrendous events took place. The long list gives force to the brutal statistics of a dark period.

N side of Parque Cuscatlán. No phone. Free admission. Daily 6am–6pm.

Museo de Arte Popular *Sorpresas* (literally meaning "surprises") are miniature clay models of El Salvadorans as they go about their daily business. Meticulously detailed, they are extremely popular and one of the country's signature handicrafts. This museum celebrates the skill and craftsmanship that goes into each piece with an excellent collection of literally hundreds of pieces. The doctor, the housewife, and the departing emigrant are just some of the characters created with humor and skill. The town of Llobasco is the best-known source of such lovely creations.

Av. San Jose 125, 7 blocks NW of Blvd. de los Héroes. (*C*) **503/2274-5154;** http://artepopular.org. $1 adults. Tues–Fri 10am–5pm; Sat 10am–0pm.

Museo de la Palabra y la Imagen Black-and-white portraits evoke the left-wing upheavals of the 20th century in three exhibition rooms in a museum dedicated to the writers and activists of that era. The studio of an illegal radio station is re-created in homage to the FMLN-backed broadcaster Radio Venceremos. Themes such as famous El Salvadoran feminists and events of the 1930s are put on show, as well as books and documents. TV war footage is available to view in a small cinema. The museum also holds a small bookshop.

27 Av. Norte, 3 blocks E of Blvd. de los Héroes. (*C*) **503/2275-4870;** www.museo.com.sv. $2 adults. Mon–Sat 8am–noon; Mon–Frit 2–5pm.

Parque Zoológico Nacional ☺ This leafy 7-hectare (17-acre) zoo south of the city center is a hugely popular weekend spot for San Salvador families. Here, you'll find winding, shady paths and numerous small lagoons inhabited by roughly 400 animals and 125 species, including such crowd pleasers as lions, elephants, alligators, and a huge selection of birds.

Final Calle Modelo. (*C*) **503/2270-0828.** 60¢ adults. Wed–Sun 9am–4pm.

Plaza de las Americas ✋ Plaza de las Americas is a large, grassy traffic circle in the midst of a busy intersection containing the much-photographed "Monumento al Salvador del Mundo," or Monument to the Savior of the World. The monument includes a tall, four-sided concrete base with crosses on each side topped with a statue of Christ standing on top of the world. It's fine as statues go; but there's no parking, and it's a bit tricky crossing numerous lanes of traffic to reach the circle. So, unless you're a photography buff searching for the perfect shot, you might want to just take in the view from a bus window.

Alameda Franklin Delano Roosevelt. No phone. Free admission. Daily 24 hr.

Tin Marín Museo de los Niños ☺ This great children's museum and learning center brings out the kid in everybody and boasts 24 interactive exhibits giving kids (and adults) fun, hands-on learning in the areas of culture, the environment, health, and technology. You can fantasize about being a pilot in the cockpit of a Boeing 727 or lose your bearings in a crooked house known as the *Casa de Gravedad* (Gravity House). Little ones can dress up like doctors in a pretend operating room, put on plays in the theater, walk inside a huge volcano (complete with lava and smoke), and learn how to make two child-size houses more environmentally friendly.

6 & 10 Calle Poniente, btw. Parque Cuscatlán & Gimnacio Nacional, Colonia Flor Blanca. (*C*) **503/2271-5147;** www.tinmarin.org. $2 adults. Children must be accompanied by adult & vice versa. Tues–F 9am–5pm; Sat & Sun 10am–6pm.

Nearby Attractions

Joya de Cerén ★★ While not as visually grand as the nearby Tazuma (p. 328), Joya de Cerén offers one of Central America's best glimpses into the d

STAYING safe

"But isn't it dangerous there?" Your friends will most likely ask when you tell them of your upcoming trip. The short answer is no, El Salvador is, in fact, a safe country to travel in. However, it does have its issues and dangers, and those should be taken into account.

The street gang Mara Salvatrucha, which has members throughout the country, is considered to be among the most violent in the world, and El Salvador has one of the planet's highest homicide rates–14 a day in 2011. Street and bus robberies in bad neighborhoods are also not uncommon, and petty extortion is endemic. Sadly this is the reality amongst the Salvadoran poor, but it rarely touches visitors. If you follow a few simple rules, you should have a safe and enjoyable trip.

Among the most important things to consider when traveling in El Salvador is not to stray too far off the travelers' path without knowledge of the area or a guide. Neighborhoods can change quickly, and it's often difficult to distinguish between safe and unsafe areas by appearance alone. Some of the leafier, residential neighborhoods immediately outside larger cities are among the most prone to robbery. The main tourist areas of the bigger cities, however, are usually filled with people and are among the most heavily patrolled.

Small-town squares are also usually filled with locals into the evening and are among the safest places you're likely to visit. Don't be spooked by the presence of heavily armed police and private security guarding many of the country's banks, businesses, and tourist areas: El Salvador has a turbulent history, and the presence of armed guards—even in small towns—has become part of the culture. Heavy firepower does not mean an area is particularly dangerous.

Avoid traveling between towns or walking away from main squares at night; if you must venture out, always take a cab at night in bigger cities. It's also a good idea not to hike in rural, isolated areas without a guide.

Don't carry or display items of obvious value, such as jewelry or expensive cameras; if you don't look like you have anything worth stealing, you're less likely to be robbed. Get in the habit of looping an arm or leg through the strap of your bag when you sit in a restaurant or bus depot, and don't leave bags unattended, even for a moment. Simply being aware of what is around you helps: If someplace doesn't feel safe, it probably isn't. Just walk away.

Perhaps the most important safety tip, stressed to me by many El Salvadoran friends and provided as standard advice by government agencies, is to give up your valuables immediately if robbed. El Salvador's criminals are known to turn quickly violent when resisted. So, if you're confronted, don't try to reason and don't bargain for your laptop.

of the region's Maya ancestors. Discovered in 1976, this UNESCO World Heritage Site comprises the remains of a Maya community frozen in time 1,400 years ago, when it was buried beneath the ash of a volcanic eruption. The archaeological park requires about 1 hour to explore and includes a Spanish-language-only museum and the partial remains of the village's buildings, including a shaman's house, a community sauna, and bedrooms with sleeping platforms. Only parts of the buildings remain, so you'll need a little imagination to appreciate what you are seeing. But you won't find ruins anywhere else in the country that are so well preserved, making this worth seeing.

Km 35 Carretera a San Juan Opica. No phone. $3 adults; free for children 4 & under. Tues–Sun 9am–4pm. For English-speaking guide, call ☏**503/2401-5782**. Bus: 108 from San Salvador.

Lago Ilopango ☝ Ilopango is El Salvador's largest and deepest lake and offers a pleasant afternoon break from the city heat. But unless you are on a prearranged scuba-diving trip, Ilopango is overrated as a major attraction. You're better off heading 56km (35 miles) east to Lago de Coatepeque, which has more pristine surroundings, better restaurants, and more activities. But if you just want to get out of the city for a few hours, the 100-sq.-km (39-sq.-mile) Lago Ilopango is an easy 16km (10-mile) drive from the city, and its tourist center, called Parque Acuatico Apulo, offers a handful of inexpensive, gazebo-style restaurants with lake views, a big pool, and $10-per-30-minute boat tours. You can swim in the lake, but the park features only a small, uncomfortable, pebble-filled beach.

Ilopango, which reaches a depth of 250m (820 ft.), is a popular diving spot, and El Salvador's top diving tour company, **El Salvador Divers** (☏ **503/2264-0961**; call in advance to arrange a trip), has a lakeside dive facility with dive equipment, boats, and overnight facilities.

Canton Dalores Apulo, Ilopango. ☏**503/2299-5430**. 80¢ adults. Daily 8am–4pm. Bus: 15.

Los Planes de Renderos ★★ 📷 Heading up to Los Planes de Renderos to watch the lights of San Salvador come alive on a Sunday night is one of the city's most underrated joys. Planes de Renderos is a small community town about a 20-minute bus ride from San Salvador, with a large overlook offering sweeping views of the city and surrounding mountains. The village also features numerous small shops and pupusarias. Though you can venture up to Renderos any night, Sunday is when you'll find El Salvadoran families enjoying a festival-like atmosphere with music, dancers, and street vendors. At dusk, everyone who can fit lines up along Renderos' overlook to watch the lights of San Salvador in the valley below slowly create a sea of lights while the largely unpopulated surrounding mountains fade to black. It's a beautiful sight. A lot of the crowd then heads over to Pupusaria Señor Pico, which is across the street from the overlook and offers tasty snacks and partial views from an upstairs balcony. Bring extra cash, as the last bus back leaves at 7pm & taxis are $8.

To get there catch bus 30 to Planes Los Renderos.

Parque Archeologío San Andrés If you have time for a third ruin, you'll enjoy your visit here. Otherwise, stick to Tazumal and Joya de Cerén. San Andrés is the partially excavated main plaza of a Maya community that was active between A.D. 600 and 900, and ruled over this Valle de Zapotitlán. The site was excavated in 1977 and today consists of a roughly 9m-tall (30-ft.) pyramid—which may have housed royal tombs—and other partially excavated structures. There's also a Spanish-language museum featuring a 1.5×4.5m (5×15-ft.) topographical country map and a large-scale model of the site. San Andrés offers some beautiful long-range views but doesn't stir the imagination like Cerén or offer Tazumal's exemplary architecture. The ruins require less than 30 minutes to explore.

Km 32 Carretera a Santa Ana. ☏**503/2319-3220** or 503/2235-9453. $3 adults. Tues–Sun 9am–4pm. Bus: 201 from San Salvador to San Andrés.

Volcán San Salvador Volcán San Salvador is an iconic part of the capital, since it looms over the landscape west of the city. The main volcano complex, which peaks at 1,960m (6,430 ft.) was formed after an eruption roughly 70,000 years ago, with smaller volcanic activity forming secondary peaks and craters such as Volcán San

Salvador's most visited spot, the Boquerón or "big mouth" crater, which is 500m (1,640 ft.) deep and more than 1km (½ mile) wide. There have been no violent eruptions on Volcán San Salvador in 800 years, but, say experts, even the slightest eruption could have catastrophic effects on the densely populated city. If you decide to explore the complex, don't do so without a guide, as the volcano's proximity to San Salvador makes it a prime robbery area.

Tour companies, such as Eco Mayan Tours (✆ **503/2298-2844**), can arrange transportation & guided tours here, starting at $25 per person.

SHOPPING

San Salvador offers the best upscale shopping in El Salvador, with most high-end shops centered in four large, modern malls (see below). The city's Zona Rosa section along the **Boulevard del Hipódromo** is lined with smaller independent shops and the small **Basilea shopping center** (Blvd. del Hipódromo; ✆ **503/2279-0833**), which features small boutiques and jewelry stores.

San Salvador's largest but least upscale mall is **Metrocentro** (Blvd. de los Héreos and Calle Sisimiles), across the street from the Intercontinental Real Hotel. Metrocentro has a few designer shops, but it's better for basics. More upscale is the **Galerías Escalón** (Paseo General Escalón, #3700; ✆ **503/2245-0800**), which is a large mall with designer shops, chic restaurants, and a multi-screen cinema in the midst of the exclusive Escalón residential neighborhood. And about 20 minutes from Metrocentro are the Multiplaza and Gran Via malls. The **Multiplaza Mall** (Calle El Pedregal and Carretera Panamericana a Santa Ana, Antigua Cuscatlán; ✆ **503/2248-9800**) is the city's most upscale, with designer shops such as Zara clothing, a multi-screen cinema, and an entire wing offering some of the city's best nightclubs and lounges. About a block from Multiplaza is **La Gran Via Mall** (Carretera Panamericana a Santa Ana and Calle Chiltiupan, Antigua Cuscatlán; ✆ **503/2273-8111**), which is smaller than Multiplaza but centered around a large, inviting outdoor courtyard with upscale designer shops, a multi-screen cinema, and restaurants with outdoor seating. If you have time to visit only one of these malls, Gran Via is the best place to eat and people-watch on its central outdoor plaza, Multiplaza has the best nightlife, and Escalón is the place to go for small boutiques.

Markets

Mercado Central (Central Market) ★   Go here if you want to see a decidedly unfiltered and urban El Salvadoran market. This isn't a tourist-centric, hammock-filled pedestrian plaza. The Central Market is a sprawling, seemingly chaotic mercado of blaring horns, shouting vendors, and old women in traditional clothes chopping vegetables in the street and wrangling live chickens. The main attraction at this multi-block indoor and outdoor market is that it is not designed for tourists: It's just *the* place locals go to buy everything from their dinner to electronic gadgets. 6a Calle Oriente, btw. Calle del Cementerio & Av. 29 de Agosto, El Centro (3 blocks W & 2 blocks S of Plaza Barrios). No phone. Daily 7:30am–around 6pm.

Mercado Ex-Cuartel   Though smaller, calmer, and more tourist-friendly than the nearby Mercado Central, the indoor Mercado Ex-Cuartel is filled with tourist kitsch, the same textile bags you'll see in most Central American markets, and lots and lots of unremarkable women's shoes. There is some original art for sale here, along with a small collection of interesting decorative boxes and crosses. But if you want a souvenir

FERNANDO llort: EL SALVADOR'S PREEMINENT ARTIST

Fernando Llort, El Salvador's most internationally famous and nationally revered living artist, was born in San Salvador in 1949. Interestingly, although he displayed an early talent for art and architecture, his signature style only began to emerge in his 20s after he relocated to France to study theology. It was during that trip that Llort began to appreciate and identify with his native country, and this would heavily influence the style of art we see today on everything from crosses to clocks on sale in markets around the country.

Upon his return in 1972, Llort moved from San Salvador to the little northern village of La Palma and started an art workshop—"La Semilla de Dios" or "God's Seed"—from which he taught locals how to convey their lives through art. Initially his style included simple shapes and colorful patterns, along with references to El Salvadoran life, such as small homes with tile roofs, plants, and animals. Later, as El Salvador's war cast a pall over the country, Llort began to include more religious references in his art. His style of art has since become ubiquitous within El Salvador and has been shown in galleries around the world, including the Museum of Modern Art in New York City, the Vatican, and the White House Museum in Washington, D.C. Perhaps his most famous work currently appears on the front of San Salvador's National Cathedral (p. 247).

Llort left La Palma and returned to San Salvador in 1979 as the talk of war began to escalate. There, he founded the gallery and nonprofit "Arbol de Dios," or God's Tree, from which a portion of sales helps foster art appreciation around the country. He remains in San Salvador today with his wife and three children, and continues to produce art, working with ceramics, lithographs, and engravings.

representative of El Salvador and its artisans, you're better off going to Mercado Nacional de Artesanías or buying in one of El Salvador's small village markets. 8a Av. Sur & Calle Delgado, El Centro (1 block N & 3 blocks E of the National Cathedral). No phone. Free admission. Daily 9am–6pm.

Mercado Nacional de Artesanías ★★ The lack of locals, the paved parking lot, and wave after wave of buses stopping directly in front tells you immediately that this is San Salvador's most touristy marketplace. But despite the lack of local flavor, the quality of the art and crafts is high, and the prices aren't bad. The market includes long rows of vendors selling unique hammocks, textiles, ceramics, and decorative crafts from artisans around El Salvador. A midsize textile bag will run you $8, and a large, well-crafted hammock should cost approximately $26. You could wait to buy directly from a craftsman in a village market, but you can also buy here knowing the quality is high and the price is surprisingly fair. Alemeda Dr. Manuel Enrique Araujo, Colonia San Benito. ℃ **503/2224-0747.** Daily 9am–6pm.

SAN SALVADOR AFTER DARK

San Salvador offers an excellent array of high-end lounges, dance clubs, and a few laidback bars. The city's current hot spot is the strip of nightclubs and lounges in the **Multiplaza Mall.** Don't let the word "mall" fool you: On weekends, this two-story nightlife strip is packed with San Salvador's stylish young elites. Multiplaza's offerings are modern and upscale, and you'll need to dress your best. **Boulevard del Hipódromo** is San Salvador's other happening nightlife spot, anchored by a major dance club and numerous smaller bars and lounges. Like Multiplaza, you can take a cab to Boulevard del Hipódromo and then barhop by foot the rest of the night. Clubs get going around 11pm and generally close at 2am. Some San Salvador neighborhoods can be dangerous at night, so unless you're with a local, it's best to stick to the better-known spots. Also avoid the "private" clubs suggested by cab drivers.

Theater, Dance & Classical Music

San Salvador's performance art scene lags a bit behind its nightlife, but national and international performances can be found. The most glamorous spot in the country for the performing arts is the newly renovated **Teatro Nacional** (2 Av. Sur and Calle Delgado, 1 block east of Plaza Barrios; ✆ **503/2222-5689**). The next best place to see art performances in San Salvador is the **Teatro Presidente** (Final Av. La Revolución; ✆ **503/2243-3407**), located beside the Museo de Arte. The city's downtown **Casa de la Cultura** (Primera Calle Poniente, #822; ✆ **503/2221-2016**) also has a small space with year-round performances and art exhibits.

The country's premier dance school, **La Escuela Nacional de Danza** (1 Calle Poniente, #1233; ✆ **503/2221-0972**), performs often in the Teatro Presidente and around the country. You can also find a nationwide arts calendar on the website of El Salvador's main arts organization, **Concultura** (✆ **503/2510-5320;** www.cultura. gob.sv).

Dance Clubs

Envy ★★   This two-level, flat-screen TV–filled dance club in the Multiplaza mall is considered San Salvador's most exclusive spot, with three VIP lounges and expensive annual memberships required for El Salvadorans to enter. Foreigners pay $10 to dance under the stars of a retractable roof and get down to the sounds of an international cadre of DJs. This place has a great vibe, and the dance floor is always packed. Multiplaza mall, Calle El Pedregal & Carretera Panamericana a Santa Ana. ✆ **503/2243-2576.** Cover $10.

Stanza 6 ★   Next door to Envy is the much smaller, slightly more chill Stanza 6 lounge. It also has a $10 cover, DJs, and an exclusive, international club feel. But it's more intimate, with one level and couches for post-dance conversations. Multiplaza mall, Calle El Pedregal & Carretera Panamericana a Santa Ana. ✆ **503/2243-7153.** Cover $10.

Live Music & Bars

Café de la T ★★   This atmospheric, bohemian bar exudes the revolution and left-wing sentiment. Abstract paintings hang on the walls next to Zapatista posters and *campesino* portraits. Its decor is a mismatch of crude murals, sagging sofas, butt-filled ashtrays, and crumbling walls, but it certainly has atmosphere. A small bar sits in the corner of a large L-shaped space with two large fans hovering overhead. The clientele is a healthy mix of locals and expats; they come to watch movies on Wednesday and Thursday evenings (7:30pm) and dance to salsa on Friday nights (cover charge $2). Great coffee is served—*la t* in the title being a play on *latte,* but you'll also find an abundance of rum and beer. It's open Monday through Thursday from 10am to 10pm and Friday and Saturday from 10am until 2am. Calle San Antonio Abad 2233. ✆ **503/2225-2090.** Fri cover $2.

15

San Salvador After Dark

SAN SALVADOR

La Luna Casa de Arte ★★★ 🎁 Located off the Boulevard de los Héreos, about a 10-minute taxi ride from that street's many nightlife spots, La Luna is worth the trip. This popular travelers' spot features live music, ranging from 1980s metal to merengue, and whatever other unique performances it can scrounge up. It's now well known among *extranjeros*, or foreigners; but I've been there a bunch of times, and it still somehow feels like a special find. Calle Berlín, Urbinazacíon Buenos Aires, off the Blvd. de los Héreos. ✆ **503/2260-2921.**

Zanzibar ★ Zanzibar is a big, fun, open-air bar overlooking Boulevard del Hipódromo. This is a great place to warm up your night. It's loud, friendly, and unpretentious. Local promoters also often stage DJ and live music events on the adjacent patio. Blvd. del Hipódromo, Zona Rosa. ✆ **503/2279-0833.**

SUCHITOTO & NORTH CENTRAL EL SALVADOR

N orth Central El Salvador is dominated by Lago de Suchitlán, a serene valley dam that is now the home of more than 200 species of migrating birds. It is overlooked by the pretty village of Suchitoto, undoubtedly the jewel in the crown of El Salvador's many attractions. A short ride from San Salvador, this former rebel town turned arts center is now the preferred base for visitors who wish to explore the surrounding hills and volcanoes, and learn more about the country's wartime history and rich artistic heritage. From the lake, the hills rise dramatically towards the Honduran border and pinnacle at the country's highest peak, Cerro El Pital. Nestled in those hills are laidback villages and handicraft centers such as Concepción de Quezaltepeque and La Palma. Forests, waterfalls, and former rebel camps are just a few of the many attractions that are explored by many as they make their way north to the Honduran border at the laidback frontier towns of Citala and El Poy.

SUCHITOTO

47km (29 miles) N of San Salvador

Guatemala has Antigua, Nicaragua has Granada, and El Salvador has Suchitoto. If the chaotic modernity of San Salvador makes you question your visit to El Salvador, the delightful quaintness of Suchitoto (47km/29 miles north of San Salvador) will confirm you made the right decision. Its laidback, cobbled streets, low colonial town houses, and gorgeous church are only some of the things that make this little town worth a visit. Incredible views of the surrounding countryside, a central location, and a thriving arts scene may coax you into choosing it as a base of operations instead of the nearby capital.

Suchitoto was a volatile and fought-over territory during El Salvador's civil war, and many battles unfolded on the nearby mountain and former guerrilla stronghold of Cerro Guazapa. But it has since recovered and remade itself into one of El Salvador's premier scenic and arts destinations. With a mix of international arts, upscale boutique hotels, natural beauty, and famously friendly people, it's now a place where you might plan on coming for a day but end up staying for a week.

This small, walkable town and surrounding area offer camera-ready mountain views and a charming main square filled on weekends with locals and visitors enjoying the weekly market. The town has also become an international arts center, with the opening of galleries by an array of international owners and the renovation of Suchitoto's Teatro Las Ruinas. Over the last few years, some of El Salvador's finest boutique hotels, including the exquisitely designed Los Almendros and Las Puertas on the main square, have made the town a destination, too.

With all the opportunities for day trips, like boat rides on the country's largest man-made lake, **Lago Suchitlán,** and tours to an historic village called **Cinquera,** it becomes obvious that Suchitoto is one of El Salvador's must-go destinations.

Essentials
GETTING THERE
BY BUS   From San Salvador, take bus no. 129 from **Terminal de Oriente** (Final de Av. Peralta and Blvd. del Ejército, San Salvador; © 503/2271-4171). Buses leave every 15 minutes, cost 80¢, and arrive in Suchitoto in 1 hour and 45 minutes. Buses stop 1½ blocks from the main square.

BY CAR   If you're driving from San Salvador, follow Carretera Panamericana (the Pan-American Highway) past Lago Ilopango until you see the sign for San Martín. Take the San Martín exit and follow it to the Plaza Central, where you will find signs leading you the remaining 28km (17 miles) to Suchitoto.

ORIENTATION & GETTING AROUND
Most of what you'll want to see in Suchitoto is within a 5-minute walk of the central plaza, known as Parque Centenario. The town is small and walkable, and its streets are quiet and largely traffic free. Avenida 15 de Septiembre runs north-south in front of the plaza, and 2a Calle Oriente runs east-west by the plaza, becoming 2a Calle Poniente west of the plaza. Lago Suchitlán is an easy, 30-minute stroll out of town along Avenida 15 de Septiembre but a tough 45-minute climb back.

A ferry also transports cars and people across Lago Suchitlán to the north daily from roughly 7am to 5pm for $7 per car and $2 per person. To get to the launching area, turn left just before the Turístico Puerto San Juan tourist center and follow the dirt road down to the lake.

VISITOR INFORMATION
Visitor information is easy to come by in Suchitoto. For the formal scoop, head to the **tourist office** (Av. Francisco Morazán, 2 blocks off the main square; © 503/2335-1782), which is open daily from 8am to noon and 1 to 4pm. The office has an English-speaking staff that can offer tips on Suchitoto's attractions and hands out town maps. For a local's perspective, sit a spell with a cup of coffee on the porch of **Artex Café** (© 503/2335-1440), on the southeast corner of the square. Eventually, you'll be joined by an assortment of expats, business owners, and other characters who come here to use the Internet, enjoy a pastry, or simply pass the time.

TOUR OPERATORS
Vista Conga Tours (Final Pasaje, Cielito lindo 7, Barrio Concepcion; © 503/2335-1679 or 503/7118-1999; www.vistaconga.com) offers an array of tours that provide an excellent sense of the region's history and natural beauty. Their most popular

outing is a 6-hour trip that involves hiking in the 3,921-hectare (9,689-acre) Parque Ecológico de Cinquera and visiting the historic civil war village of Cinquera. The tour also includes a 1½-hour presentation by Cinquera resident Don Pablo, translated by a guide, who gives a firsthand account of the gruesome realities of the civil war. Other tours include a 3-hour hike to a nearby waterfall, horseback riding, and nighttime animal-watching tours, as well as a 5-hour flat-water canoe-paddling tour. Tours range from $15 to $35.

Eco Tourism La Mora (✆ 503/2323-6874; www.ecoturismolamora.es.tl) offers Spanish-only hiking and horseback tours to nearby Volcán Guazapa, also known as Cerro Guazapa. This 1,435m (4,708-ft.) mountain is home to 200 plant species and 27 types of birds, as well as many types of butterflies and reptiles. Two- to 5-hour tours cost $16 to $40.

Gringo Tours (Calle Francisco Morazán #27; ✆ 503/7327-2351; www.elgringo suchitoto.com) is run by local restaurant owner and American expat Robert Broz. He is more than happy to give you the lowdown on the town, in addition to offering fascinating tours that specialize in the archaeological heritage and civil war history of the area, including a tour of Cinquera. Tours start at $50 for a half day for a group of one to four. Robert can also organize accommodation and custom-built itineraries.

In town, you can take a 2-hour **Historic Building Walking Tour** via the Suchitoto tourist office (Av. Francisco Morazán; ✆ 503/2335-1782). The tour consists of visits to 32 historic Suchitoto buildings, including the former homes of three presidents and a former convent now serving as an arts center. The tour is in English and Spanish; can be booked with 24 hours notice; and costs $10 for 1 to 5 people, $15 for 5 to 20.

[FastFACTS] SUCHITOTO

ATM Suchitoto has two ATMs, one on the southeastern square and the other a half block north on Av. 15 de Septiembre.

Drugstores Farmacia Santa Lucía (✆ 503/2335-1063) is just off the square at Avenida 5 de Noviembre and Francisco Morazán.

Emergencies The Police Station

(✆ 503/2335-1141) is located close to the town square, on Avenida 15 de Septiembre and 4 Calle Pte.

Hospitals For health emergencies, head to **Hospital Nacional de Suchitoto** (Av. José María Pérez Fernández; ✆ 503/2335-1062).

Internet Air-conditioned, $1-per-hour Internet

service is available at the **InfoCentros chain** (Calle Francisco Morazán, on the main square; ✆ 503/2335-1835).

Post Office The **post office** (✆ 503/2304-0104) is on the other side of the square from InfoCentros, near the corner of Avenida 15 de Septiembre and 2a Calle Oriente.

What to See & Do in Suchitoto

Suchitoto is known as much for its mountain scenery and artsy vibe as for its formal attractions. You can easily spend the morning savoring an Argentine feast prepared by a local sculptor and the afternoon listening to the sounds of thousands of migrating birds on the county's largest man-made lake. You can hike waterfalls and learn of the horrible realities of El Salvador's civil war. Or you can just sit and enjoy the charming square and colorful weekend artisans' market. For some more structured options, though, you may want to consider a guided tour (see above).

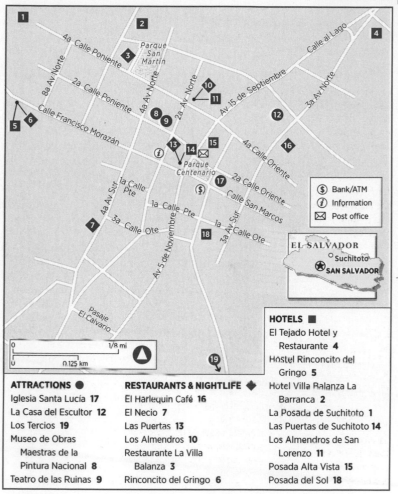

HOTELS ■
El Tejado Hotel y
  Restaurante **4**
Hostel Rinconcito del
  Gringo **5**
Hotel Villa Balanza La
  Barranca **2**
La Posada de Suchitoto **1**
Las Puertas de Suchitoto **14**
Los Almendros de San
  Lorenzo **11**
Posada Alta Vista **15**
Posada del Sol **18**

ATTRACTIONS ●
Iglesia Santa Lucía **17**
La Casa del Escultor **12**
Los Tercios **19**
Museo de Obras
  Maestras de la
  Pintura Nacional **8**
Teatro de las Ruinas **9**

RESTAURANTS & NIGHTLIFE ◆
El Harlequin Café **16**
El Necio **7**
Las Puertas **13**
Los Almendros **10**
Restaurante La Villa
  Balanza **3**
Rinconcito del Gringo **6**

In addition to the below attractions, there's also a small art museum called the **Casa Museo de Alejandro Cotto** (Calle al Lago; ✆ 503/2335-1140) in town, though its hours are so irregular it can't be considered an official tourist site.

Iglesia Santa Lucía ★ Santa Lucía church is one of El Salvador's premier examples of colonial architecture and is currently undergoing a much-anticipated but drawn out restoration. Its brilliant white facade, set against a startling green mountain backdrop, is one of the first things visitors see upon arrival into town, and its dark, rich wood interior packs some serious history. It took 9 years to build and was finally completed in 1853. Above its six-columned atrium is a small clock, topped by a silver plate donated by a grateful bride. The altar is made of elaborately carved wood, and 36 tall wood beams run down the sides of the long, narrow church. Santa Lucía also features numerous life-size statues encased in glass and a small, pen-and-ink drawing of a crying Jesus. It doesn't match the grandeur of Santa Ana's Gothic cathedral (p. 327), but it's one of the country's more beautiful and traditional churches and makes for a peaceful and serene break from the heat.

Parque Centenario, btw. Calle San Marco & 2a Calle Oriente. No phone. Free admission. Daily 8am–noon & 1–6pm.

La Casa del Escultor ★★ The Argentine sculptor Miguel Martino is one of numerous artists who are currently reinventing Suchitoto as an international arts center—but he's the only one who also happens to be a mean cook. In addition to his fine woodworking art, Miguel is well known for his Sunday afternoon Argentine feasts, which take place at his gallery La Casa del Escultor, 2 blocks off the main square. From noon to 4:30pm each Sunday, Miguel prepares huge quantities of Argentine beef and vegetables on a wood-burning grill inside his studio and gallery for the first 30 to 35 people who show up. He then closes the doors, and everyone proceeds to drink Argentine wine and talk art or whatever comes up. Plates include five kinds of meats or five types of veggies. Reservations, though not required, are a good idea. Main course cost between $9 and $15.

2a Av. Sur, #26A. © **503/2335-1836;** www.miguelmartino.com. Free admission; Gallery Sat & Sun 9am–5pm; meals Sun noon–4:30pm.

Los Tercios ★ Even Suchitoto's waterfalls look like art. Los Tercios, a stunning waterfall and small swimming hole located an easy 1.5km (1-mile) stroll out of town, really looks like a piece of modern art, with foot-wide slices of vertical rock jutting out along the face of its 9m (30-ft.) waterfall. The unique shape of the rocks here is thought to have resulted from rapidly cooling ancient magma. Though water only flows over the falls from May to December, Los Tercios is worth a visit year-round, since the unique rock for-

Art & Culture Festival

If you're anywhere near Suchitoto in February, you'll want to stop by the **International Permanent Festival of Art and Culture** ★★. This annual, month-long international performance and art festival was founded by renowned cinematographer and Suchitoto resident Don Alejandro Cotto almost 20 years ago and continues to attract visual and performance artists from around the world.

mations are the main attraction. Be prepared to climb down a few rocks to get a good look. Vendors often come here to sell pupusas and drinks on the weekends, so refreshments should be on-hand after your climb. Though the falls are relatively easy to reach, it is wise to go accompanied by a guide or local, as there have been some reported robberies on the trail. To get there, walk out of town along Av. 5 de Noviembre and turn left onto Calle a Cinquera, just before Noviembre ends; follow Calle a Cinquera to just past the chain-link fence on the left; turn left through the gate btw. the chain link fence and a small building; walk straight and look for a path to your right, which will take you to the falls.

1.5km (1 mile) SE of the main square. Free admission.

Museo de Obras Maestras de la Pintura Nacional The Teatro Las Ruinas (see review below) contains this small gallery of El Salvadoran art, including 31 abstract; Impressionist; and realist, post-1950 paintings, created exclusively by El Salvadoran artists—including Suchitoto's own single-name artist "Chaney," as well as Negra Alvarez and Augusto Crespin. Also included in the gallery is a traditional

Greek-style bust of Suchitoto arts promoter and once-world-famous cinematographer, Alejandro Cotto. You can visit the gallery year-round by calling and making an appointment.

2a Calle Poniente & 4a Av. Norte. © **503/2335-1909.** $1 adults. Tues–Thurs 8am–noon; Fri–Sun 9am–noon & 1–5pm.

Teatro de las Ruinas   As the name implies, this corner theater was a pile of ruins for many years, until a recent renovation led by the filmmaker Alejandro Cotto transformed it into the cultural focal point of a what is now a very cultural town. Grey granite arches lead to exquisite salons with high, coved ceilings and chandeliers. The lobby holds an art gallery with some of the country's best artists on display, including Salvador Llort and Armando Solis. Further inside, you'll find a 300-seat theatre with white-pillared walls and plastic chairs. Here, there are performances of opera, plays, and orchestras, and it is especially alive during the International Permanent Festival of Art and Culture in February and March.

SE corner of Parque San Martín. No phone. Mon–Fri 10am–4pm & during theater performances. Free admission to art gallery; concert tickets $1–$10.

Outdoor Activities

Lago Suchitlán ★★   Just a short bus ride out of town is the 135-sq.-km (52-sq.-mile), man-made Lago Suchitlán, from where you can take a cooling, scenic boat ride to La Isla de los Pájaros (Island of the Birds) and listen to the calls of thousands of migrating birds. Lago Suchitlán was created in 1973 when the government dammed Río Lempa to produce electrical power, and it now serves as a fishing hole for local communities and a stop-off for migrating birds. Surrounding the lake are the **Puerto San Juan** tourist center, a large open-air restaurant, and stands for craft vendors.

Covered tourist boats are just to the left of the tourist center and offer 45-minute to 1-hour $25 lake tours including stops at La Isla de los Pájaros. Also available are $12, 30-minute tours that don't include a stop at the island. At press time, a local operator was setting up an **"Aqua Canopy"** with plans to zip thrill seekers out over the water to an island and back. Ask at the tourist center for more information.

Turicentro, Lago Suchitlán. © **503/2335-1957.** 50¢ adults, 25¢ children 6 & under. Daily 7am–7pm. Take the white minibus w/Suchitoto written on the side from the center of town.

Parque Ecológio de Cinquera and the Village of Cinquera ★★   Parque Ecológio de Cinquera is a 3,921-hectare (9,689-acre) preserve and forest 1 hour from Suchitoto. It's not as grand as Parque Imposible (p. 317) or Montecristo (p. 335), but it has a small waterfall and a few trails, and is worth a walk in the woods when paired with the historic village of Cinquera located a few minutes from the park entrance.

The tiny village of Cinquera was a stronghold of guerrilla resistance during the civil war, and numerous buildings, including the church, have been preserved to show bomb and bullet damage inflicted by government troops. The town square also proudly displays the tail of a downed army helicopter and a mural depicting the history of the war and the image of the brutally executed 15-year-old girl who was the town's first martyr. A separate mural depicts the two ninth-grade boys whose call to arms is said to have sparked the guerrilla resistance in the region. Spanish-language tours of the town are available through **La Asociación de Reconstrucción y Desarrollo Municipal** or ARDM (main square, 1 block from the Alcaldía; © **503/ 2389-5732;** ardmcqr@yahoo.es). Or ask around town for Spanish-speaking Cinquera resident Don Pablo, who can provide a unique firsthand and sadly brutal account of the war.

corn FESTIVAL

Every August, the **Festival de Maiz** celebrates everything there is to do with corn. Church processions, harvest blessings, and food fairs are all part of a celebration that reaches back to pre-Columbian times. There is also a festival king and queen elected to head the festivities. Ask at the tourist office for exact dates.

To get here, take bus no. 482 from Suchitoto, which leaves Suchitoto daily at 9:15am and 1:30pm. It returns from Cinquera only once a day at 1pm. The trip takes 1 hour and costs 80¢. It is a rough road and should not be attempted in an ordinary rental car.

No phone. Park $5 adults. Daily 8am–5pm. Bus: 482.

Shopping in Suchitoto

Galería de Pascal   This small gallery is owned by Pascal Lebailly, a former fashion-convention producer in Paris and owner of the exquisitely decorated Los Almendros Hotel (p. 265). Lebailly has applied that same sense of fashion and design in choosing the El Salvadoran and Central American art on display and for sale at his gallery. The gallery also includes a small gift shop offering El Salvadoran coffee, ceramics, hammocks, and handbags, among other items. It's open weekdays from 10am to 6pm and weekends 9am to 6pm. 4a Calle Poniente, #2B. ℂ **503/2334-1008.**

This is My Land Artisans' Market ★★   It's not the biggest or most diverse mercado in El Salvador, but it's definitely one of the most enjoyable. Each Saturday and Sunday, the Association of Artisans and Artists of Suchitoto sets up shop on the town square with offerings of El Salvadoran crafts and traditional cuisine. Colorful paintings, textiles, and, of course, the Salvadoran food staple, *pupusas*, are in plentiful supply. But the real reason to visit the weekend market is just to enjoy the vibe. There's no better place to watch local families mingle and chat well into the night, listen to local music, and soak in the town's beautiful mountain setting. It's open Friday through Sunday from 8am to 7pm. Parque Centenario. ℂ **503/2335-1782.**

Where to Stay in Suchitoto
EXPENSIVE

La Posada de Suchitoto ★   La Posada is a few blocks further off the square than Suchitoto's other high-end hotels, but the pool, lake view, and slightly lower price are worth the 5-minute walk. The 12-room La Posada offers a traditional hacienda-style atmosphere with an attentive staff decked out in colonial garb and a large, lake-view restaurant with tasty, reasonably priced fare. La Posada is a bit older than the other two pricey hotels, so the rooms and amenities aren't shiny and new. But the colonial character, casual atmosphere, and well-trained staff help balance things out. You'll definitely want to book early to reserve one of the hotel's six lake-view rooms.

Final 4a, Calle Poniente. www.laposada.com.sv; ℂ **503/2335-1064.** Fax 503/2335-1164. 12 units. $73 standard double; $89 lake-view double. Rates include full breakfast. AE, DISC, MC, V. **Amenities:** Restaurant; pool; room service; Wi-Fi (free). *In room:* A/C, fan, TV.

Las Puertas de Suchitoto ★★   Though it's not as luxurious as Los Almendros, you simply can't beat Las Puertas in terms of its view and location. Las Puertas is directly on Suchitoto's charming central plaza, facing the church. Each of its six large upstairs rooms features custom-designed wood furniture and private balconies, which are perfect places to watch the sun rise over the mountains and light up the towers of Iglesia Santa Lucía. All of the rooms are in a single row on the second floor, so no room is better than any other. The hotel also features a large public balcony overlooking Volcán Quazapa and a tasty restaurant.

2a Av. Norte & Av. 15 de Septiembre. www.laspuertassuchitoto.com; ℂ 503/2393-9200. 6 units. From $76–$94 double. Rates include full breakfast. AE, DC, DISC, MC, V. **Amenities:** Restaurant; bar; bike rentals ($6.50/day); room service; 2 nonsmoking rooms. *In room:* A/C, TV, Wi-Fi (free).

Los Almendros de San Lorenzo ★★★   This is by far one of the most luxurious independently owned hotels in El Salvador. Owner and former fashion producer Pascal Lebailly required nearly a year and a half and 30 workers to fully renovate the 200-year-old colonial house that is now his six-room hotel. Each large room is individually decorated in a modern hacienda style with iron bathroom accents and lighting designed specifically for the hotel. A glass-enclosed French restaurant sits above the figure-eight-shaped stone pool, and a small, comfortable bar is located beside a central courtyard with a fountain. But what really makes Los Almendros special is the eye for detail with which Pascal chose the art, furniture, and overall tone. The whole effect is like staying overnight in an interior design show. In 2010, Pascal added two splendid suites where you can stay in utter luxury with lake views as an added bonus.

4a Calle Poniente, #2B. www.hotelsalvador.com; ℂ 503/2335-1200. 8 units. $85–$110 double; $135 suite. Rates include full breakfast. AE, DC, DISC, MC, V. **Amenities:** Restaurant; bar; airport transfers ($80); pool; all rooms nonsmoking. *In room:* A/C, TV.

MODERATE

El Tejado Hotel y Restaurante ★★   This is the best moderately priced option in town. Though El Tejado's view-less rooms are nothing to e-mail home about, they're comfortable and decently sized, with high ceilings and inviting, hacienda-style tiled front patios. What makes Tejado stand out is the price, which is up to $30 less than the three higher-end options in town. Tejado also offers a cool, leafy atmosphere; a large open-air restaurant with great lake views; an excellent location a few blocks off the main square; and a big, inviting pool. If you can't get a room, you can still use the pool for $3.35 a day.

3a Av. Norte, #58. www.eltejadosuchitoto.net; ℂ 503/2335-1769. Fax 503/2335-1970. 9 units. $60–$75 double; $95 suite. Rates include full breakfast. AE, DC, DISC, MC, V. **Amenities:** Restaurant; pool; room service; Wi-Fi (free). *In room:* A/C, TV, no phone.

Posada del Sol   One thing you don't lack here is space. This cream-colored town house holds an ample living room and large courtyard out back that overlooks the town and has nice views of the surrounding mountains. The pool is big, as is the garden, with hammocks and mango and coconut trees. The rooms are clean, if a little old-fashioned, with dark wood furnishings and mirrored wardrobes. Bathrooms are small but immaculate. The hotel is a family-run affair, and though it might do with sprucing up, it is still a great bargain considering the space and amenities.

2a Av. Sur, #39. ℂ 503/2335-1546. 6 units. $35–$60 double. No credit cards. **Amenities:** Restaurant; pool. *In room:* A/C, TV, no phone.

INEXPENSIVE

Hostel Rinconcito del Gringo   A few very bare, basic rooms and one dorm are below a casual restaurant of the same name. This is an extreme budget option, with little in the way of amenities and luxury, though there is a cozy communal area with a TV and sofa. The main advantage of staying here (besides stretching your dollars) is the excellent Nicaraguan and Mexican food at the restaurant upstairs and your

American-Salvadorian host, the gregarious Robert Broz, a fountain of information on the area and an excellent guide who enjoys showing guests the secret delights of the town, including a somewhat eye-opening nightlife tour. The restaurant itself is small, colorful, and casual, with open walls and a sunny atmosphere. It serves great shakes and giant quesadillas.

Calle Francisco Morazán, #27, 1½ blocks W of market & City Hall. www.elgringosuchitoto.com; © **503/2327-2351.** 3 units. $20 double. $10 dorm bed. No credit cards. Free parking. **Amenities:** Restaurant. *In room:* Fan, no phone.

Hotel Villa Balanza La Barranca ★★ 🖉 This is without a doubt the best deal I found in Suchitoto, a charming stand-alone house on the crest of the hill with marvelous views of the lake. The lobby is a sitting room that leads to a little garden with patches of lawn and a wrought-iron gate. Three small rooms lie adjacent, one a small chapel. Upstairs are the two best rooms, with spectacular views and a wrap-around balcony overlooking the lake. However, these two rooms have a shared bathroom, as opposed to the ground-level rooms that have private bathrooms. The rooms are small but immaculate, with carved headboards, tile floors, and tiny wardrobes, and the bathrooms are clean and colorful. Its only drawback is the steep walk into town. **Note:** The hotel should not be confused with the owner's restaurant of the same name located several blocks uphill.

N end of 6a Av. Norte. www.villabalanzarestaurante.com; © **503/2335-1408** or 503/2269-3687. 5 units. $50 double w/shared bathroom; $60 double w/private bathroom. AE, DC, DISC, MC, V. Free parking. **Amenities:** Communal kitchen; Wi-F (free)i. *In room:* Fan, TV.

Posada Alta Vista ★ It's barebones but affordable, modern, and right off the square. Don't look to Alta Vista for much in terms of amenities, but a clean, comfortable, air-conditioned room with a rooftop deck less than 45m (148 ft.) from the main square for roughly $21 per person a night is just about as good a deal as you're going to find. Alta Vista's only downside is that, at press time, the showers were cold-water only. Hotel operators say hot showers are on the way, however. Make sure to request an upstairs front room with a balcony, as those rooms are superior.

Av. 15 de Septiembre, Casa 8, just off Parque Centenario. www.hotelposadaaltavista.com; © **503/2335-1645.** Fax 503/2335-1590. 8 units. $42 double. V. **Amenities:** All rooms nonsmoking. *In room:* A/C, fan, TV, no phone.

Where to Stay Outside Suchitoto

La Bermuda 1525 Located 5km (3 miles) south of the town, La Bermuda 1525 is at the site of El Salvador's first city, established in 1525, before it was moved farther south to where San Salvador is today. All that remains is an *estancia* with some ruins and a low-rise adobe building that is now a guesthouse with vintage tiled floors, raftered ceilings, corner fireplaces, and a small museum. The decor is a little bare and uneven, with mismatched furniture and tacky bric-a-brac. The rooms are ample, with wrought-iron beds and garish bed covers. Local art hangs on the walls, and there is a patio-style restaurant to dine in and a lush garden to explore. La Bermuda is ideal for those who like some rural isolation and are touring by car. Otherwise, you miss the chance to step out and explore Suchitoto town at will.

Km 34.5 Carretera San Martin-Suchitoto, Suchitoto. www.labermuda.com; © **503/2225-5103** or 503/2398-9078. 5 units. $68 double. AE, DC, DISC, MC, V. Free parking. **Amenities:** Restaurant; children's area. *In room:* A/C, fan, TV, no phone.

Where to Eat in Suchitoto

After a long and difficult history, Suchitoto has reinvented itself as a center for good food and art. New restaurants seem to be popping up every year. In addition to the choices below, the main square and side streets also offer many *comedores* and *pupusarias* that are worth checking out. In general, reservations are not necessary.

El Harlequin Café ★★ 🍽️🚻 ☺ SALVADORAN   El Harlequin is the kind of funky little place we all hope to find when traveling. Hidden behind a little sign and a metal door on a quiet street a couple of blocks off the main square, this romantic hideaway is filled with candlelight, jazzy music, interesting art, and tasty food. The menu is simple but offers a lot to choose from, including comfort food such as a delicious chicken and rice, and *cremas,* which are similar to soup but thicker and filled with dinner-size portions of meat; there's even a children's menu. Combine the food with the artsy feel and intimate lighting, and El Harlequin stands out as a great place to pass a quiet evening over a bottle of wine.

3a Av. Norte, #26. ✆ **503/2325-5890.** Main courses $3.50–$8. AE, MC, V, DC. Sun, Mon, Wed & Thurs 10am–10pm; Fri & Sat 10am–midnight.

Las Puertas ★ SALVADORAN   Las Puertas offers a mix of first-class service and delicious food at reasonable prices, with prime people-watching views over the plaza. The service is formal and elegant, the chef is imported from San Salvador, and the kitchen is new and high-tech. The result is delicious dishes such as ravioli with shrimp and vegetables. The restaurant's dining room is an open, upscale space with a soaring ceiling and large windows overlooking the square. Reservations aren't required, but call ahead for outside seating or one of the two window-front tables.

2a Av. Norte & Av. 15 de Septiembre. ✆ **503/2393-9200.** Main courses $12–$15. AE, DC, DISC, MC, V. Daily 7am–9pm.

Los Almendros ★★★ FRENCH   Eat at least one meal here while you're in town. The food is delicious, the setting is elegant, and the price is a lot lower than you would expect. French owner Pascal Lebailly has employed his well-honed eye for design in creating this casual but upscale, glass-enclosed French restaurant that overlooks Los Almendros' romantically lit pool. And with French chef Hérvey Laurent applying his *Cordon Bleu* skills to delicious dishes such as char-grilled salmon with lime and butter, Los Almendros is likely to serve one of your better meals in El Salvador. The restaurant also takes care to use local ingredients and serves only Salvadoran coffee.

4a Calle Poniente, #2B. ✆ **503/2335-1200.** Main courses $8–$16. AE, DC, DISC, MC, V. Daily 7:30am–9pm.

Restaurante La Villa Balanza ★★ SALVADORAN   Here, the decor is as piled high as the food portions. Fishing nets, indigenous sandals, an old radio, clothes irons, and sewing machines make up a local history collection as eclectic as the food. Tacos are piled high with guacamole, mashed beans, and cheese. Corn tortillas accompany excellent salads and fish. There are also more conventional chicken and beef dishes, as well as ceviche and giant prawns. Located in front of the quiet, bushy plaza Parque San Martín, the property is a delightful, rambling arrangement of open patio, picnic tables, chunky roof tiles, plants, and sculptures with old relics from the war on display such as a 340kg (750-lb.) bomb. *La balanza* means scale, with reference to the sculpture of a weighing scale with a pile of tortillas against a bomb.

NW corner of Parque San Martín. ✆ **503/2335-1408.** Main courses $5–$12. AE, DC, DISC, MC, V. Daily 10am–9pm.

Rinconcito del Gringo ★★ 👕 SALVADORAN/MEXICAN   A shake here is a meal in itself, and one portion of quesadillas will feed an army. There are excellent vegetarian options, as well as seafood tacos and burritos. Located in a quiet part of town, the walls are adorned with local art and tables with colorful tablecloths. This is a very relaxed and casual family restaurant with a friendly English-speaking owner. Calle Francisco Morazán, #27, ½ blocks W of market & City Hall. ✆ **503/2327-2351**; www.elgringo suchitoto.com. Main courses $5–$12. No credit cards. Mon–Fri 9am–9:30pm; Sat & Sun 8am–9:30pm.

Suchitoto After Dark

El Necio ★★   Amiable bartenders and posters calling for peace and revolution set the tone for this laidback, lefty dive joint. In fact, the walls are covered with more than enough images of Che, John Lennon, and a virtual history of leftist icons to keep your mind occupied whenever you're not busy listening to the occasional live music or are deep in conversation with one of the friendly locals or travelers who come here to chat over ice-cold pilsners. 4a Av. Sur, by 4a Calle Ote. ✆ **503/2335-1708.** Daily 6pm–midnight (or later). No credit cards.

CONCEPCION DE QUEZALTEPEQUE

30km (19 miles) N of Suchitoto; 77km (48 miles) N of San Salvador

Concepción de Quezaltepeque, known as the City of Hammocks, is a tiny village tucked into El Salvador's northern central mountains, where generations of artisans have devoted their lives to making midday naps more enjoyable. Nearly the entire town is involved in hammock production and sales. Some locals weave intricate tapestries that hang from the sides of the hammocks on sale here; others twist individual threads into thin ropes that are eventually crafted into colorful *hamacas* sold in villages around the country.

Quezaltepeque comprises only a few small streets, on which are gathered a group of hammock shops, surrounding a town square, so don't expect to spend more than a couple of hours here. And since you can buy Quezaltepeque-made hammocks around the country, the shopping is not actually the best part of visiting this town. The most enjoyable thing to do here is to chat up a hammock-shop owner and ask to see where and how their hammocks are made. With a little charm and a good grasp of Spanish, you might convince someone to, quite literally, show you the ropes. Most craftsmen display their work on weekends, but the best time to ask owners for a behind-the-scenes peek is Tuesday and Wednesday, when things aren't so busy.

Essentials

GETTING THERE & GETTING AROUND

From Suchitoto, take bus no. 129; the trip lasts 1½ hours. From San Salvador, take bus no. 126, which takes about 2½ hours. Both trips will cost you less than $2.

From San Salvador, drive north out of the city along Hwy. CA-4, from which you will turn west onto Carretera Longitudinal del Norte toward Chalatenango. Follow this road until you turn north toward Chalatenango and spot signs to Quezaltepeque.

Most of Quezaltepeque's hammock shops and *comedores* are clustered within a few blocks of the square, so the best way to see the town is on foot.

VISITOR INFORMATION

There are no hotels, large restaurants, ATMs, or Internet cafes in town, so there isn't much visitor information to be had. But if you speak Spanish, you can stop by the **Casa de la Cultura** (Barrio El Central, on the main square; ✆ 503/2331-2242) to learn more about the town's history. The nearby city of Chalatenango, which you will pass coming and going to Quezaltepeque, has ATMs, fast-food, and grocery stores.

What to See & Do in Quezaltepeque

The primary activity here is strolling around looking for deals on hammocks crafted by artisans who have dedicated their lives to the art form. But you'll have an even better time if you can get a peek behind the scenes. I can't guarantee it will happen, but if you call Spanish-speaking hammock artisan **Missal Goldames** (✆ 503/2331-2001) in advance, he might just give you a tour around town. You can also stop by his shop along the main road, 1 block short of the square on the right.

If you don't see any hammocks you like along the main street, ask someone for *otras tiendas de hamaca* and, if you're lucky, they will point you to a friend's house where some are for sale.

Where to Stay & Eat in Quezaltepeque

Quezaltepeque has no hotels and requires only a couple of hours to explore, so there isn't a big reason to stay overnight in the area. If you do, your best option is the luxurious Chalate Country Club (see below), 10 minutes outside Quezaltepeque. I don't recommend staying in the nearby city of Chalatenango. It's crowded, unattractive, hard to navigate, and has only three subpar lodging options that rent rooms by the hour.

Food options in Quezaltepeque are limited to a few informal *pupusarias* near the hammock shops. If you want a more substantial meal in town, call the restaurant **Teresa de León** (1 block off the main street; ✆ 503/2331-2381) 1 day in advance, as it's open only upon request. It serves *comidas típicas* (rice and beans with beef and chicken variations), and a main course costs $3.50. You can also head to Chalatenango for fast food or, for the best option in the region, try the restaurant at the Chalate Country Club hotel.

Chalate Country Club ★★ 🛏️😊 Chalate is an oasis of luxury that's worth a visit if you plan to stay in the area for a few days. This 14-room hotel offers large rooms, modern bathrooms, and grassy and tree-filled private grounds to explore, two children's pools, and a playground. Parents can lounge by six adult pools or shoot pool on two tables. And the restaurant is a cut above rural El Salvador's normal roasted-meat-with-rice-and-salad menu. Continental cuisine, such as chicken breast wrapped in bacon, or surf and turf, is $10 to $13. The kids' menu ranges from $3.50 to $4.75. There's no bus to the hotel, so you'll need to take a $7, 15-minute taxi ride from Quezaltepeque or Chalatenango.

Km 63.5 Carretera a Chalatenango, San Rafael, Chalatenango. www.chalatecountryclub.com; ✆ **503/2323-7824.** 14 units. $45 double. AE, DC, MC, V. **Amenities:** Restaurant; 2 children's pools & playground; health club; 6 outdoor adult pools; room service; 2 saunas; tennis courts. *In room:* A/C, TV, WiFi (free).

volunteer **OPPORTUNITIES IN EL SALVADOR**

If you enjoy mixing a little humanitarian work in with your volcano hiking and village visiting, El Salvador offers a plethora of volunteer activities, from building homes and schools to teaching English. Below are the best options.

Habitat for Humanity (Colonia General Arce, Calle Jorge Domingue 4-H; ✆ **503/2298-3290;** www.habitatel salvador.org.sv) began building earthquake-resistant homes here in 1992 almost immediately after the end of the war and now has six offices and ongoing projects throughout the country. By Habitat estimates, El Salvador—in the wake of Hurricane Mitch and the 2001 earthquake—still remains 630,000 homes short of what's needed. Habitat requires a minimum 5-day commitment and a $45 per-day fee for room and board, orientation, and transportation. You'll need to register 3 to 6 months in advance.

If you like working with your hands, you can also check in with **Seeds of Learning** (**SOL;** 585 5th St. W., Sonoma, CA 95476; ✆ **707/939-0471;** www.seeds oflearning.org), which builds schools in rural El Salvador. SOL volunteers work literally side by side with local community members to build schools, so volunteers really get to know the people they are helping. SOL, which has been working in El Salvador since 1999, requires a 10-day commitment, and the program costs $1,200, including lodging at a basic hotel or retreat center, food, transportation, and excursions. Scholarships are available for volunteers under 30 years of age.

English-language skills are also increasingly important to Salvadorans, and the country has numerous English-teaching opportunities. **Global Cross-road** (415 E. Airport Freeway, Ste. 365, Irving, TX 75062; ✆ **866/387-7816;** www.globalcrossroad.com) offers 1- to 12-week teaching programs in San Salvador, Sonsonate, and Santa Ana, beginning at $899 for food, housing, and transportation from the airport upon arrival. Volunteers stay with host families and teach primarily children. Global Crossroad also offers short-term volunteer opportunities teaching computer skills, taking care of orphan children, and helping to maintain communities. Travelers willing to make a longer teaching commitment should check out El Salvador–based **Centro de Intercambio y Solidaridad,** or CIS (Av. Bolivar 103, Colonia Libertad, San Salvador; ✆ **503/ 2226-5362;** www.cis-elsalvador.org). CIS was formed after the signing of the peace accords to help promote solidarity among the Salvadoran people and cultural exchange with other countries. Volunteers pay only a $100 registration fee and $70 per week for room and board with a local family, and volunteers receive half-price ($50) Spanish classes. A 10-week commitment is required, though.

LA PALMA & EL PITAL ★

84km (52 miles) N of San Salvador; 50km (31 miles) W of Chalatenango

La Palma is a thin, rectangular-shaped town wedged along a mountain side. And, at first glance, it seems like any other small, scruffy mountain town high up near the Honduran border. Yet look closer, and you'll see its telegraph poles are painted with bird and flower motifs. The small plaza wall has colorful renditions of armadillos and anteaters, and murals bearing chickens and snakes dot the town. La Palma is in fact the unlikely center of a famous art movement and is the former home of El Salvador's most revered living artist, Fernando Llort. Today, visitors come from around the world to snap photos of the dozens of Llort-style murals decorating the town's walls and browse its many artisans' shops.

Llort moved to La Palma in 1972 and taught the townspeople to create art using available materials to reflect their lives. The resulting works are filled with color, geometric designs, and natural and religious symbols. Llort eventually left La Palma, but the artists he inspired continue to create works on display in the galleries and on the buildings along La Palma's two main roads.

Despite its remote location and small size, La Palma has numerous restaurants and a couple of nice hotels. La Palma is also an excellent jumping-off point for hikes up nearby El Pital mountain, which is the highest point in El Salvador and summits on the border with Honduras.

Essentials

GETTING THERE

BY BUS　From Chalatenango, hop on bus no. 125 and ask the driver to let you off at Amayo, where you can catch bus no. 119 to the center of La Palma. The trip takes about 1 hour and 15 minutes. You can reach Chalatenango in just over 2 hours from San Salvador on bus no. 125.

BY CAR　La Palma is just off Hwy. CA-4, which is the country's main north-south highway. Just drive north a little less than 1 hour from Chaletenango and about 1½ hours from San Salvador, and follow the signs. If you reach the Honduran border, you've gone a few miles too far.

ORIENTATION & GETTING AROUND

Like many of El Salvador's rural towns, La Palma is small enough to walk just about everywhere. There are only two main avenues that you can walk end-to-end in about 10 minutes. But if you're feeling lazy, La Palma offers many three-wheeled moto-taxis that will take you anywhere along those two streets for 25¢. You can also easily catch a $3 moto-taxi that'll take you 10 minutes outside town to the luxurious Entre Pinos Resort or the small village of San Ignacio.

VISITOR INFORMATION

The tourist information office is known as **El Centro Atencion Turistica La Palma** (© 503/2335-9076; cat.lapalma.corsatur@gmail.com) and is located on the north-eastern corner of the central plaza. The staff are very friendly and helpful, but speak limited English. It's open weekdays 8am to 4pm and weekends 9am to1pm. There's a **Banco Cuscatlán** (© 503/2305-8331) with an ATM just off the main square.

What to See & Do in La Palma

The main thing to do in La Palma is view building murals and shop for arts and crafts in the galleries along the town's two main roads. Keep in mind that the galleries here seem to have a lot of the same style of artwork you'll see in every shop in the country. A trained eye would probably be able to tell the difference, but I couldn't. Though you can pick up a small kitschy souvenir for under $10, some of the better, framed pieces can be $40 or more. Since the art is actually fairly expensive, you might just want to bring your camera and take some shots of the beautiful murals—I consider these to be the best art in town.

OUTDOOR ACTIVITIES

La Palma's other attraction is its close proximity to El Salvador's highest point, **El Pital.** El Pital is 30 minutes outside of La Palma, rises 2,730m (8,957 ft.) above sea level, and offers an easy 1½-hour each-way hike to the top up a winding fire road. Only the last 20 minutes get a bit steep, and all along the way are great views. The last stretch to the summit is privately owned, and a family monitors the road. So if two guys come stumbling out of the woods, demanding money, don't sweat it: They own the place. The usual fee is $5 to $8, but you can sometimes get by for half that, depending on your charm and guide.

Just before the summit, ask your guide to show you the four-story-high meteor that hit the mountain long before anyone can remember. Risk takers can climb on top of the meteor by walking across a small tree bridging a 12m (39-ft.) drop. At El Pital's summit, you'll find a small, white monument marking the border with Honduras and a radio tower with a guard and vicious-looking dog behind a fence. Like many remote locations in El Salvador, it's not wise to hike up here alone. Your hotel can arrange a guide. To get here by bus, take a moto-taxi from La Palma for $3 to San Ignacio, where you will catch the no. 509 bus toward Las Pilas. After about 30 minutes, get off at Río Chiquito and have the driver point you in the right direction.

Shopping in La Palma

Artesanías Kemuel ★ This is the best stand-alone shop in town for Llortian-style arts and crafts. The store offers lots of uniquely painted wood crosses that stand out in a town full of painted wood crosses, and it even sells a rare collection of framed Llort-style works on simple white paper. Artesanías's unique collection might be the result of an inside connection, of course—the store's owner and principal artist, Vitelio Jonathan Contreras, is Llort's nephew by marriage The art pieces and larger crosses cost $25 to $75. It's open daily from 8am to 6:30pm. Calle Principal, Barrio El Centro. © **503/2305-8501.**

Mercadito Artesanal This market across from the La Estancia Restaurante is a bit smaller than Placita, with just 10 vendors spread around a small courtyard, and it's a bit heavy on the laminated wood art and wood bracelets you'll see in every other mercado in Latin America. But if you look hard, you can find some genuine pieces of interesting, original, locally created art. The market also has a decent amount of women's clothing with simple Llort-esque designs. Textile bags run around $6, and small, painted decorative chairs run $10 before haggling. The market also has a small *comedor.* It's open daily from 9am to 7pm. Calle Gerardo Varrios, Barrio El Central, in front of La Estancia Restaurante. No phone.

Placita Artesanal La Palma ★ Placita is the best market in town to search for original arts and crafts. It's bigger than Mercadito and seems to offer fewer mass-produced items and more locally produced crafts. I spoke with numerous vendors here, and they were immediately able to give me the actual names and stories of the artists who produced many of the picture frames, wood boxes, and painted crosses on sale. It's open daily from 8am to 6pm. Barrio El Centro, across from La Iglesia Católica. No phone.

Where to Stay in La Palma

In addition to the below hotel options, you might consider the **El Pital Highland Hotel** (www.elpital.com.sv; © 503/2259-0602), which is on the fire road at the start of any hike to El Pital. It offers a restaurant and four-person rooms for $105, two-person rooms for $50, and $150 for a two-story, six-person cabin.

Entre Pinos Resort ★★★ ☺ This upscale, mountain-lodge-style hotel is spread over 45 hectares (110 acres) and offers comfortable, midsize rooms and enough

BORDER crossing

There is no charge to leave El Salvador at El Poy, but there is a $3 tax to enter Honduras. The Salvadoran immigration office is open 24 hours, but its Honduran counterpart closes at night and opens from 4am to 10pm. Bus no. 119 passes through La Palma every half-hour, stopping at 7pm. It takes 30 minutes and costs 50¢. The bus stops 100m (328 ft.) before the border and El Poy immigration office. There are connections to Nueva Coctepeque and Copán Ruinas via La Entrada.

amenities to keep the family busy for days. Guests can hike or horseback-ride 7km (4.3 miles) of private dirt roads and trails, play tennis, swim, soak in the big Jacuzzi, and play soccer on a full-size field. Kids tired of all that outdoor activity should like the video arcade. Though the hotel has a remote location up in the mountains, the English-speaking staff can easily arrange tours to the rest of the country, as well as to the Copán ruins in Honduras and El Pital. Entre Pinos is not exactly on par with the corporate megaresorts you'll find in other countries, but it is among El Salvador's best hotels and serves as a great base for any long El Salvador vacation.

Km 87.5 Carretera Troncal del Norte, San Ignacio. www.entrepinosresortandspa.com; ℂ **503/2335-9312.** Fax 503/2278-2811. 57 units. $75–$94 double; $125 cabin. AE, DC, MC, V. **Amenities:** 3 restaurants; free airport transfers; bikes; health club; Jacuzzi; 2 pools; room service; 10 nonsmoking rooms; spa; tennis courts; Wi-Fi (free). *In room:* A/C, fan, TV, fridge, hair dryer.

Hotel La Palma ★★ 🍴 La Palma is the best affordable hotel choice in town. It's rustic and simple, but offers a cool, gardenlike setting, a range of room options, great service, and a big restaurant with outdoor seating. The proprietor, Salvador, has owned the place for over 30 years and is happy to use the basic English he's picked up to provide information or arrange trips to El Pital. All of the 32 rooms are simply decorated and of average size, but are comfortable. Rooms are spread throughout the large, leafy, hillside property, which winds down to a wide, rocky riverbed. When you book, request room no. 26. It's the newest room and offers the best view. If that's booked, ask for one of the rooms in the new, white building on the hill.

Barrio El Tránsito, La Palma. ℂ **503/2335-9012.** 32 units. $28 double. No credit cards. **Amenities:** Restaurant; babysitting ($6/day); room service. *In room:* No phone, Wi-Fi.

Paso del Pital ☺ This hotel looks like an average motel, with an L-shaped building surrounding a small parking lot right in the center of town. Recent refurbishments, however, actually mean it's a good choice, especially if you get a back room overlooking the huge pool and waterslide. The chalet-style rooms are a little bland, but very clean and quite big, and have lots of light. The bathrooms are faultless, and the back balcony has a great view of the surrounding hills. In general, the decor is a hodge podge of styles and garish colors. Still, it's the pool that makes it, and non-guests can gain day access for a very reasonable $2.

Barrio El Centro, La Palma. ℂ **505/2305-9344.** 9 units. $25 double. No credit cards. **Amenities:** Restaurant; pool; room service. *In room:* TV, no phone, Wi-Fi (free).

Posada de Reyes ★ 🧳 Just a few miles past Entre Pinos and La Palma is the tiny village of San Ignacio. It's a pleasant, typical El Salvadoran village, with a white church beside a small public square. There's no particular reason to visit, except to catch a bus to El Pital and to stay at the unusually comfortable Posada de Reyes Hotel. This 14-room, three-story hotel offers uniquely spectacular views; big rooms; a well-maintained and inviting pool; and a lush, flower-filled landscape. It looks average from the outside but is modern, spacious, and comfortable on the inside. And at around $25, it's about as cheap as Hotel La Palma. Request room no. 15, which has windows on two sides and a balcony. A short moto-taxi ride will get you here from La Palma, or you can take bus no. 119.

1 block N of Alcaldía, Barrio El Centro.. Ⓒ **503/2335-9318.** 15 rooms. $20–$35 double. No credit cards. Pets accepted. **Amenities:** Restaurant; pool; Wi-Fi (in lobby). *In room:* A/C, TV, fridge, no phone.

Where to Eat in La Palma

You'll need some hot coffee while wandering the streets of La Palma. **Café d Café** (Calle Gerarado Barrios 40; Ⓒ **503/2335-9190**) makes the best cup I found and is a bright, pleasant place with pastoral murals adorning the walls. It is on the left as you enter the town from the south at the v-junction just before the plaza. **Soni´s Cake Panaderia y Pasteleria** (2a Av. Sur; Ⓒ **503/258-0125**) has a great selection of pastries, though the decor is a little soulless, with fast-food-style seating.

Del Pueblo Restaurante y Artesanías ★★ 🍴 SALVADORAN   If you want protein, this is the place to come. The scent of spicy, simmering beef is the first thing you'll notice as you enter this simple, two-room restaurant, which features one of the town's most interesting abstract murals on its front wall. The specialty of the house is the 170g (6-oz.) beef-and-sausage combo with salad, rice, cheese, and beans; it's delicious. The other items are variations on the same meat, sausage, and chicken theme. Breakfast is a traditional serving of eggs, beans, cheese, and *plátano*. Wine and beer are also available. Locals consider Del Pueblo to be among La Palma's finest restaurants.

Calle Principal, #70, Barrio El Centro. Ⓒ **503/2305-8504.** Main courses $1.25–$4.95; Main courses $2–$3.25. No credit cards. Daily 7am–8pm.

Restaurante Los Pinares ★★ LATIN AMERICAN/SALVADORAN   Los Pinares, the main restaurant at the Entre Pinos Resort (see above), is definitely worth the few dollars for a moto-taxi ride from La Palma. The restaurant has covered, open-air seating beside an outdoor pool and a large vegetarian, meat, fish, and pasta menu with unique items such as roasted boar and jalapeño steak. But the best choices might be the mixed salad, which is twice the size and features twice the variety of ingredients of the average El Salvadoran restaurant salad, or the creamy spaghetti with chicken, which has just the right amount of spicy kick. Prices here are two to three times that of the restaurants in La Palma, but the food and service match the added cost.

Km 87.5 Carretera Troncal del Norte, San Ignacio. Ⓒ **503/2335-9312.** Main courses $9–$23; breakfast $2–$4.60. AE, DC, MC, V. Mon–Thurs 7am–8pm; Fri–Sun 7am–9pm.

Restaurante y Pupusaria La Palma ★ SALVADORAN   It's cheap and tasty, and the portions are huge—perhaps that's why this is *the* place where locals eat in town. There are no decorations at all here, just one room with bench seating and pictures of the entrees on the wall. The menu is as simple as the decor; highlights include roasted and fried shrimp, and chicken served with rice or fries, tortillas, and a salad. The $1.90 burritos and tacos are a good bet, but the *hamburguesas* are not too tasty.

Calle Central, across the street from Telecom Internet. Ⓒ **503/2334-9063.** Main courses $3.75–$6.50. No credit cards. Daily 8am–8pm.

EASTERN EL SALVADOR

Dark volcanoes jut up through a broad, plain patchwork of sugarcane fields, cotton farms, and cattle
ranches in eastern El Salvador, which, even though
an important economic and agricultural region, still gets
fewer visitors than the attraction-filled west. Yet its rural charm and civil-
war history make this corner of El Salvador well worth the trip. Highlights
include the charming, cool mountainside village of Alegría; the historical
town of Perquín, which has the country's most definitive collection of
FMLN war relics; and the tragic village of Mozote, whose people suffered
one of modern Latin America's worst war-time atrocities. Although this is
also one of the poorest sections of the country, you'll find the residents of
the east to perhaps be the friendliest of your trip.

ALEGRIA ★

49km (30 miles) W of San Miguel

Arguably the flower capital of El Salvador, Alegría is a lush garden hilltop
town surrounded by misty countryside views only 36km (22 miles) from
the capital. Located 1,200m (3,937 ft.) above sea level, high up in coffee
country, it offers some of the best views in the nation, as well as great
hiking trails and a friendly, vibrant community. Late into the evening, the
town's small, recently renovated square teems with multi-generational
families chatting with neighbors, kids playing, and teenagers hanging with
friends—it's no coincidence that alegría means happiness. Situated conveniently between Perquín and San Salvador, Alegría is an easy stop off
the main tourist trail.

Essentials
GETTING THERE & GETTING AROUND
From San Miguel, catch any bus toward San Salvador and tell the driver
to let you off in Triunfo ($1.50). There, you'll catch a minibus to the city
of Santiago de María, where you can take one of a steady stream of buses
the final 4km (2½ miles) to Alegría. Buses also run daily all day between
Alegría and nearby Santiago de María (35¢), where you can make connections to the rest of the country. From San Salvador, catch the bus, route
302, to the town of Usulutan ($1.50), where you then a catch bus, route
348, to Santiago de Maria (35¢).

When driving from San Salvador in the west or San Miguel in the east,
follow CA-1, also known as Carretera Panamericana (the Pan-American

Highway), and get off at the sign for Santiago de María. Follow the signs the remaining 4km (2½ miles) to Alegría.

Alegría is a very walkable town; its tourism office, Internet cafe, restaurants, and hotels are all within a few blocks of its town square.

VISITOR INFORMATION

Tourist information in Spanish is available in a small tourist kiosk just off the main square (© **503/2628-1087;** Tues–Sun 8am–4pm).

FAST FACTS Alegría has no banks, ATMs, or post office, but all of these can be found in nearby Santiago de María. A pharmacy is located 1 block from the square, across from the church. Internet access is available daily from 8am to 9pm for $1 an hour in a cafe just behind the main tourist kiosk; call © **503/2628-1159** for info. Alegría's tourist police can be reached at © **503/2628-1016** and ambulance service is at © **503/2611-1332.**

What to See & Do in Alegría

The small tourism kiosk and the mayor's office (© **503/2628-1087**), both of which are on the main square, can arrange coffee-plantation tours and hikes to a nearby crater lake (admission 25¢), and provide information on the town's more than 150 beautiful flower displays. A half-day hike to the crater costs $15.

Where to Stay in Alegría

Casa de Huespedes La Palma 🦺 This hotel is older and a bit less updated than the Cartagena (see below), but it's comfortable, affordable, and right on the square. The hotel is hidden behind a flower-filled patio, but when you find the front door and ring the bell, you'll be greeted by hotel staff and two very friendly dogs who'll settle you into their comfortable, family-style hotel immediately. The three big rooms here are plain, with almost nothing on the walls. But the rooms are larger than most, and at $10 per person for a room in the center of town, they're a great deal.

Calle Pedro T. Mortiño, on the town square. © **503/2628-1012.** 5 units. $20 double. No credit cards. *In room:* TV.

Cabaña La Estancia de Daniel An orange wall, topped with chunky terracotta tiles and bearing plaques of famous townsfolk, surrounds a lovely, if a little cramped, garden property with five cabin-style accommodations. Tables and hammocks adorn some quiet nooks and crannies inside this family-run property, which is 1 block west of the main plaza. The rooms are smallish but nicely decorated with volcanic flagstones and small shuttered windows. Each cabin sleeps a family of four, and though the property is a little too cluttered, the tropical garden with orchids, coffee bushes, and a fragrant white flower known as galanderias makes up for it. The main drawback is lack of a view, but this is still an excellent budget option with a convenient location.

Calle Manuel Enrique Aruayo & 2a Ave Sur. fredypostecapa@yahoo.com; © **503/2628-1030.** 5 units. $20 double; $25 larger cabin. No credit cards. **Amenities:** *In room:* TV, Wi-Fi (free).

Hostal y Café Entre Piedras ★ 🦺 Located in a stone-walled property on the southeastern corner of the plaza, Entre Piedras may not look like much from the outside, but once you enter, you'll find a spacious, well-built house with lots of white walls and dark wood features. Built by a German immigrant in the 1960s, the structure has stood the test of time and offers handsome, spacious rooms with high cedar-wood rafters and solid furniture and beds. There's also a cafe, and there's a homey feeling here, especially when you sit in the TV salon, which was once the family living room.

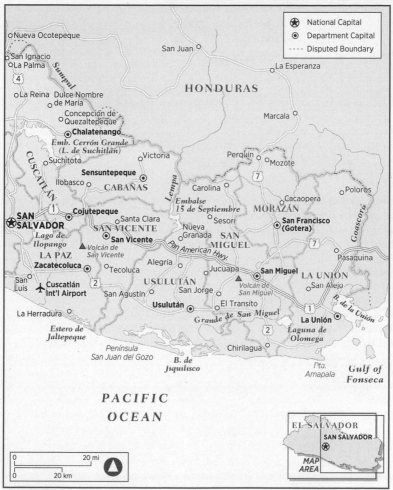

The all-stone courtyard is shaded by orange and mandarin trees, and there's a small private pool out back. This is a great-value place to stay, and its cool tidiness starkly contrasts with the cluttered charm of Casa de Huespedes La Palma across the plaza.

2a Av. Sur & Pje Gimaldi. www.hostalentrepiedras.com; ℭ **503/2313-2812.** 4 units. $10 dorm bed; $16 single; $32 double. No credit cards. **Amenities:** Cafe; bar; pool.

Vivero y Restaurante Cartagena ★ Cartagena isn't the cheapest property in town, but it is Alegría's best hotel. The hotel is a 10-minute walk from the main square, but its flower-filled setting and mountainside views are worth the added trip. The hotel's eight cabins are plain but have inviting front patios and larger-than-average sleeping areas. Cabin nos. 3, 4, and 5 are perched on the edge of the mountain and have amazing views. The cabins fill up in August, December, and around Easter, so reserve well in advance during these times. The hotel also has a restaurant and sells plants and locally produced crafts. The walk to the hotel is all downhill, but it's a tough hike back up; you can ask the hotel to arrange transportation back to the square.

Final Barrio El Calvario. cral1966@hotmail.com; ✆ **503/2628-1131.** 8 units. $50–$80 cabin. No credit cards. **Amenities:** Restaurant. *In room:* No phone.

Where to Eat in Alegría

La Fonda de Alegría ★ SALVADORAN   La Fonda boasts Alegría's largest and most interesting menu. Just down the hill from the square, en route to the Cartagena hotel, this restaurant offers a twist on basic Salvadoran cuisine with items such as steak served with Argentine sausage, avocado, and baby onions, and an Argentine sausage plate with refried beans. The English- and Spanish-language menu also features traditional pupusas, tacos, and hamburgers. La Fonda doesn't offer much in the way of views, but its open-air seating catches the mountain breezes just right.

Av. Gólgata. ✆ **503/2628-1010.** Main courses $4.25–$9. No credit cards. Daily 9am–9pm.

Restaurante El Portal SALVADORAN   Though not as diverse in its offerings as La Fonda, El Portal does offer an ample menu and is right on the square. This 10-table, casual restaurant serves unique items such as Indian-spiced chicken with rice and salad, and more traditional fare such as steak. It also has two big windows, allowing for prime town-square people-watching. But possibly best of all, El Portal has a working cappuccino machine. In a country with thousands of acres of coffee plants, you'd think there would be cappuccino on every corner. It's actually a rarity, so the frothy blends whipped up here are a real find.

Av. Pedro T. Mortiño, on the square. ✆ **503/2628-1144.** Main courses $4.50–$9. No credit cards. Daily 9am–9pm.

PERQUIN ★★

53km (33 miles) N of San Miguel

Perquín is a rugged town with a rugged history. Tucked high in El Salvador's northeast Morazán region, where wooded mountains run to the Guatemalan border, this claustrophobic little town was the headquarters for the FMLN. It thus suffered its fair share of war and suffering. Such pride and resistance can be seen at the fascinating Museo de la Revolución Salvadoreña, which displays artifacts and tells the story of the revolutionary guerrilla movement's efforts during the war. In addition to this must-see museum, Perquín has a tourist-friendly square, a couple of small artisans' shops, and is the gateway to a little explored corner of the country that offers such natural wonders as dense mountain forests and hidden waterfalls.

Essentials

GETTING THERE   From San Miguel, take bus no. 332C roughly 53km (33 miles) to Perquín; the bus stops right in the town square. It costs $1.50 and takes 2½ hours. If you're driving from San Miguel, take highway CA-7 for 53km (33 miles) into Perquín.

ORIENTATION   Perquín is a small, walkable town with a tiny but attractive village square. Most of what you'll want or need is within a few blocks of the center, and the Museo de la Revolución is a 5-minute walk from the center.

GETTING AROUND   Though you can walk to Perquín's attractions, you'll need to arrange a microbus or pickup truck at Perquín's tourist office (Colonia 10 Enero;

Be Careful What You Ask For

Most travelers have some awareness of El Salvador's bloody 12-year civil war, which ended with the signing of peace accords in 1992, and are curious to better understand the war and its aftermath. But be careful with that curiosity. El Salvador's civil war was exceedingly violent, often included torture, and took place in a relatively small area. Because of El Salvador's high population density, very few Salvadorans of a certain age failed to be personally affected by the war. I learned the hard way not to casually ask too many questions about those times. Salvadorans are renowned for their friendly nature and will tell you about the war if asked. But almost inevitably, their stories will include the loss or torture of a wife, a child, or a father. The war is not a taboo subject, but these are horrific memories that should not be casually unearthed. It's better to ask questions of educators or El Salvadorans you know well.

© 503/2680-4086) to take you 8km (5 miles) to Mozote. Also, Perquín's best hotel, the Lenca Montana, is 1.5km (1 mile) south of the square.

VISITOR INFORMATION & FAST FACTS Perquín's tourist information office (Colonia 10 Enero; © 503/2680-4086) is open weekdays from 8am to 5pm and Saturday from 8am to 2pm. There are no banks or ATMs in Perquín. The post office (© 503/2675-1054) is located on the main square, opposite the church. Internet is available for $1 per hour at Servicomputer (Calle Principal; © 503/2680-4353), and a pharmacy is 1 block east of the square, across the street from the church.

What to See & Do in Perquín

El Mirador at Cerro de Perquín Across the street and a 10-minute hike uphill from the Museo de la Revolución (see below) is this lookout point, which is set in an area of the forest that once housed guerrilla camps. There's not much to see here today, since there's nothing obvious remaining from the guerrilla days on the hike. But the Mirador offers a great view and a little exercise.

Av. Los Heroes, Barrio La Paz, across the street from museum. No phone. 50¢ adults. Daily 8am–4pm.

Museo de la Revolución Salvadoreña ★★ This museum is the main reason travelers come to Perquín, and for good reason. The small, four-room museum offers illuminating photos and Spanish-language histories of guerrilla martyrs, including those of the war's many female soldiers, and displays civil-war weaponry and equipment, along with posters of inspirational slogans used during the war. Big rocket launchers, large chunks of a downed army helicopter, and even an old Ford sedan and Peugeot are displayed. One of the more interesting exhibits is the preserved studio of revolutionary Radio Venceremos. Near the station are the remains of a crater from an army bomb that barely missed its mark. Some museum displays include small English-language explanations, and guides are available for a small tip. Don't leave town without visiting this proud piece of the people's history.

Av. Los Heroes, Barrio La Paz, 5-min. walk NW of the square. © **503/7942-3721** or 503/2634-7984. $1.20 adults. Tues–Sun 8:30am–4:30pm.

Where to Stay & Eat in Perquín

Within Perquín's town center, you'll find small comedores offering pupusas and simple roasted chicken or beef. The best are La Cocina de Mama Toya y Mama Juana

(Carretera a Perquín, a few blocks south of the square; © **503/2680-4045**) and La Cocina de La Abuela (Carretera a Perquín, a few blocks south of the square; no phone). Mama Juana is on the left as you enter Perquín and offers the cheapest eats: $2 for a roasted-chicken-and-rice dinner. Mama Juana's also has some not-so-attractive rooms for $6 per night. Across the street from Mama Juana's is La Cocina de La Abuela, or "kitchen of the grandmother," which is open Saturday and Sunday from 7am to 9pm and offers 35¢ pupusas and grilled steak for $4.50 to $7.50.

The best restaurant in the area, however, is 1.5km (1 mile) south of town in the **Hotel de Montaña** (Km 205.5 Carretera a Perquín, Morazán; © **503/2680-4046** or 503/2680-4080). The hotel restaurant has a large, English-language menu with tasty chicken, fish, and meat items from $5.80 to $8.80, including a delicious chicken dish with cheese and mushrooms, rice, and salad for $6. The restaurant also has outdoor seating with great views.

Perquín Lenca Hotel de Montaña ★★ 🎁 Montaña is the best place to stay in the Perquín area. Located 1.5km (1 mile) south of town, this modern, cabin-style hotel sits on a steep mountainside just off the main road and offers modern rooms, a full-service restaurant, and great views. English-speaking hotel owner, informal El Salvador historian, and American native Ronald Brenneman came to the area to assist refugees during the civil war, fell in love with the country, and decided to stay. The hotel's seven cabins were built in 2000, and the 10 rooms were constructed in 2006. The best deals are the rooms, $30 per night for two people, which, although not big, have a modern, rustic feel and are at the top of the mountain with comfortable patios offering high-altitude views. Some of the profits from the hotel are used to fund a grammar school that Brenneman's foundation recently opened in the area.

Km 205.5 Carretera a Perquín. www.perkinlenca.com; © **503/2680-4046** or 503/2680-4080. 17 units. $30–$40 double; $60–$80 quadruple; $50–$110 cabin. Rates include full breakfast. AE, DC, DISC, MC, V. **Amenities:** Restaurant; room service. *In room:* Fan, Wi-Fi (free).

MOZOTE ★★

Mozote is a small village 8km (5 miles) south of Perquín where the El Salvadoran army executed more than 1,000 townspeople on December 11 and 12, 1981. Members of the army rounded up and separated the town's residents into groups of men, women, and children, and then executed each group in and around the square and church. The burning of town buildings followed. The massacre is considered one of the worst in modern Latin American history and drew criticism from around the world. The tragedy was recognized by a United Nations truth commission in 1992 after many of the bodies were excavated at the site. Today, the names of the children killed are inscribed in a shrine in the church garden, and the famous Mozote Memorial—a metal silhouette of a family holding hands—sits in the town square beside squares of wood inscribed with the names of those who died. Stopping in town to view the memorial here is necessary if you want to fully grasp the tragedy of the country's civil war.

To get to Mozote from Perquín, you'll need to arrange a pickup or microbus with Perquín's tourist office (Colonia 10 Enero; © **503/2680-4086**). If you're driving, turn off the main road south of Perquín at the sign BIENVENIDOS A ARAMBALA. Follow the road for 1.5km (1 mile) and veer right at a fork in the road. Follow it for another 1.5km (1 mile) and turn left at the intersection, then go 2 blocks, turn right at the MONUMENTO EL MOZOTE sign, and follow more signs to the town square.

understanding EL SALVADOR'S CIVIL WAR

Exactly how El Salvador's 12-year civil war got started depends on whom you ask. More specifically, it depends on where that person falls on El Salvador's socioeconomic scale. Some on the upper end will tell you the war was caused by senseless terrorism by those who had no right or cause. Some on the lower end of the pay scale see the war as a courageous people's struggle. But, generally speaking, the war began because El Salvador's *campesinos*, or peasant farmers, got tired of living as, well, *campesinos*. By the late 1970s, these *campesinos* had struggled for decades without much forward progress, despite occasional and tepid reforms passed by El Salvador's right-wing military government and land-based oligarchy, and calling for war began to seem like the best way to call for change. Add to the mix yet another failed government reform in 1976, the 1980 government assassination of the beloved human rights leader Monseñor Oscar Romero, and the organization in 1980 of four left-wing people's groups into the formidable **Farabundo Martí National Liberation Front (FMLN),** and the stage for war was set. Some had hoped that war could be avoided when a group of slightly more moderate government agents took control of the government and nationalized some aspects of the economy in 1979 and 1980. But those moderates didn't go far enough and were themselves soon targets of the country's right-wing military death squads.

The FMLN launched its first major offensive against the El Salvadoran military in 1981 and successfully gained control of areas around Chalatenango and Morazán. El Salvador's military's response—with the help of the U.S. government, which spent $7 billion trying to defeat the organization—was fierce and lasting. The war raged on and off for the next 12 years, until both sides had had enough. The atrocities of the right, including individual assassinations and the 1981 **Mozote Massacre** (see p. 23 for info), have been well documented since. A peace deal was signed in 1992, most war crimes were legally forgiven, and the FMLN agreed to halt its military operations and become a political party. This conversion to democracy finally paid dividends when, in 2009, an FMLN-backed candidate, Mauricio Funes, was elected president.

SAN MIGUEL

Chaotic, smog-laced traffic and overcrowded markets are crammed between dirty, modern streets with the occasional colonial gem. San Miguel is eastern El Salvador's main city and a transport hub you shall pass through when traveling in the region. It does not have much to offer, as it lacks the sophistication of big-city San Salvador and the charms of El Salvador's small villages. It's also not the type of place you should wander around at night, as it has a high crime rate. If you're on a tight schedule, you may not want to go out of your way to stop here. But since the town has a large bus terminal with departures around the country, you may very well find yourself at least transferring through here. If you do find yourself in San Miguel with a few hours to kill, rest assured that there are entertaining diversions, including a surprisingly interesting museum, a nearby lagoon, a cathedral, and a national theater to tour.

Essentials

GETTING THERE From San Salvador or stops along Carretera Panamericana (the Pan-American Highway – CA-1), take bus no. 301 approximately 2 hours and 45 minutes west to San Miguel ($2.20).

If driving from San Salvador, head 2½ hours east along Hwy. CA-1, also known as the Pan-American Highway, and follow the signs.

ORIENTATION & GETTING AROUND The church, national theater, and town's largest grocery store are all on or within a short walk of the main square, which is called Parque David J. Guzman. You'll need to take a short $2 taxi ride to the Museo Regional de Oriente. Taxis are readily available on the main square or can be called from the front desk of your hotel. The only bus you'll need around the city is no. 384, which travels to Laguna de Olemega. San Miguel's large bus terminal (6a Calle Oriente; no phone) has departures to Honduras, San Salvador, and other parts of the country daily.

VISITOR INFORMATION & FAST FACTS San Miguel does not have a tourist office. The city's Casa de la Cultura (15 Calle Poniente and 8 Av. Sur; *©* **503/2661-6582**) provides basic information in Spanish.

Scotiabank and Banco Agricultura, which are 1 block from the square, have ATMs. **ZonaWeb Ciber** (2a Calle Poniente; *©* **503/2661-8661;** daily 8am–5pm) is half a block south of the cathedral and offers Internet access for 75¢ per hour. The **post office** (*©* **503/2661-3709**) is just off the square at 4 Av. Sur.

What to See & Do in San Miguel

San Miguel is not a destination city; there simply isn't a whole lot to see and do here. Among the best options in town are the Museo Regional de Oriente (see below) and the Catedral Nuestra Señora de La Paz (4a Av. Norte, on the main square; no phone; free admission; daily 8am–noon and 2–5pm), which features a soaring, four-story ceiling with large, stained-glass windows lining both walls. A striking, two-story, deep-red curtain hangs behind the 7.5m-tall (25-ft.) altar, and crystal chandeliers hang from the ceiling. Just behind the cathedral, at 2a Calle Poniente, is the Teatro Nacional (no phone; free admission; Mon–Sat 8am–4pm). Inside, you'll find a small but traditional two-story European performing arts theater that was built between 1903 and 1909. The theater, which offers occasional art shows and sales in the lobby, was renovated in 2003 but still lacks the grandeur of the Santa Ana Theater. If you do stop here, head upstairs to the right, where you'll find glass doors with great views of the 2,128m-tall (6,982-ft.) Volcán Chaparrastique, also known as the San Miguel Volcano.

Other than the regional museum, San Miguel's most interesting attraction is **Laguna de Olomega.** Olomega is a small lake, just a 30-minute bus ride from San Miguel, from where you can take a boat ride to tiny Los Cerritos Island for $5 or a 2-hour lake tour for $30. You'll need to arrange your trips directly with the local fishermen, so I most recommend this trip for those with Spanish-language skills.

Museo Regional de Oriente ★ 🏛 The Museo Regional de Oriente is one of San Miguel's most fascinating attractions and one of the country's newest and most modern museums. The museum opened in November 2007 and offers a rich history of the region's culture and environment through a collection of ceramic, textile, and photo exhibits. The overall museum is small—only about five rooms—but very well done. The only catch is that the curatorial copy is in Spanish—at least, for the moment.

8a Av. Sur & Calle Oriente. *©* **503/2660-1275.** $1 adults. Mon–Sat 9am–noon & 1–5pm.

Where to Stay in San Miguel

Comfort Inn ★   As boring as chain hotels can be, San Miguel's Comfort Inn happens to be your best option in town. It has a pool, exercise room, Wi-Fi, and small restaurant and bar, and is a short cab ride from the square. It's also across the street from the large, modern Metrocentro Mall. It's a typical, efficient Comfort Inn with typical, efficient Comfort Inn–style rooms, though it does have the feel of a bland, claustrophobic health clinic. You won't find any surprises here, but in a crowded, sometimes-chaotic city like San Miguel, it's nice to have such an oasis of calm efficiency.

Final Alameda Roosevelt & Carratera a La Unión. www.comfortinn.com; ✆ **877/424-6423** or 503/2600-0200. Fax 503/2600-0203. 79 units. $55–$65 double. Rates include full breakfast. AE, MC, DC, V. **Amenities:** Restaurant; bar; small exercise room; pool; room service; nonsmoking rooms. *In room:* A/C, TV, hair dryer, Wi-Fi (free).

Hotel Plaza Floresta   At roughly $10 below the other guys, the 28-room Plaza Floresta is San Miguel's best budget option. It's comfortable, but you get what you pay for in terms of size and amenities: The rooms and bathrooms are small, there's no restaurant, and the interior courtyard's pool is tiny. On the upside, Plaza Floresta does offer Wi-Fi, is a quick $2 taxi ride from the city center, and has a nice open-air seating area. The front-desk staff is also friendly and helpful. If you're looking to save a few bucks and don't mind missing out on frills, you'll be happy here.

Av. Roosevelt Sur #704, Colonia Cuidad Jardín. florestahotel@yahoo.com; ✆ **503/2640-1549.** 28 units. $41–$52 double. AE, DC, DISC, MC, V. **Amenities:** Pool. *In room:* A/C, TV, Wi-Fi.

Tropico Inn   If the Comfort Inn is booked, the Tropico Inn will do. Like the other Tropicos in this national hotel chain, San Miguel's version tries to present itself as a luxury hotel, but doesn't quite get there. You'll be immediately and falsely impressed by the soaring, three-story, recently renovated lobby and the semi-elegant dining area beside the pool. But the luxury stops as soon as you sign on the dotted line. The hallways are dingy, with low ceilings; the rooms are big but dated, with old, tired furniture; and the small pool is crammed in next to a big piece of industrial equipment. Basically, everywhere but the lobby looks like it hasn't been touched since the 1970s. Room no. 1 is the biggest, and room nos. 203 and 239 offer the most quiet; most upstairs rooms have balconies overlooking the hotel's interior courtyard.

Av. Roosevelt Sur #303. info@tropicoinn.net; ✆ 503/2661-1800. 99 units. $47–$104 double. Rates include full breakfast. AE, DC, DISC, MC, V. **Amenities:** Restaurant; pool; room service. *In room:* A/C, TV, Wi-Fi.

Where to Eat in San Miguel

La Pema Restaurante ★ SALVADORAN   If you ask a local where to eat, he'll tell you to head to La Pema's. This 35-year-old San Miguel institution is a $3 taxi ride from the main square and isn't much on ambience. (The restaurant is basic, but it includes a huge, airy front dining room with bench seating and a smaller back room where mariachis regularly wander in and play.) Don't be fooled by the large, florescent menu on the wall, however: This place does not serve fast food. Whatever you order here will be good, quality food, especially the cremas, which are similar to soup but thicker and filled with dinner-size portions of meat, chicken, or fish. Here, they are served with salad and pupusas. La Pema also features a signature $30 grilled lobster, crab, and shrimp plate, as well as a smaller $10 version. On Friday nights it has live music and dancing after 9pm.

Km 142.5 Carretera a Cuco. ✆ **503/2667-6065.** Main courses $8–$15. AE, DC, MC, V. Daily 10am–5pm. Fri 7pm until late.

SAN VICENTE

If you're on your way to or from San Salvador, try to take a short detour into San Vicente to have a look at the town's much-photographed clock tower, damaged by the 2001 earthquake but now restored to its former glory. This laidback, rural town's other big attraction, the Iglesia Pilar cathedral, was also damaged by the quake but has been completely renovated and is also worth a visit.

Essentials

GETTING THERE & GETTING AROUND   From San Salvador, you can take bus no. 116 to the center of town. It takes 1½ hours and costs 80¢. If you're driving, San Vicente is just a few miles off Carretera Panamericana (the Pan-American Highway) and is well marked.

The tower and Iglesia Pilar are on or within walking distance of the square. San Vincent's best hotel, Posada Don Pablito, is about a 10-minute walk from the center.

VISITOR INFORMATION & FAST FACTS   San Vicente has no tourist office, but information in Spanish is available at the city's Casa de la Cultura (Av. Crescencio Miranda #29A, Barrio San Francisco; ☎ **503/2393-1179**). Internet access is also available for 75¢ per hour at the Zona Web Ciber Café (2a Av. Norte #3, Barrio San Francisco; ☎ **503/2393-6729**).

What to See & Do in San Vicente

The five-story white cement tower in the middle of the town square is quite beautiful, with a kind of Dr. Seuss whimsy about it. It is $1 to climb to the top, where you can get some lovely views. Iglesia El Pilar is the city's other main attraction. You can also stop by the Casa de la Cultura for information about trips to Infiernillo, a nearby hot springs, and the nearby crater lake of Laguna de Apastapeque.

Where to Stay & Eat in San Vicente

The best place to stay in town is Posada Don Pablito (Blvd. Jacinto Castellanos #25, Lotificación Vaquerano; ☎ **503/2362-7700**). This 28-room hotel is a fairly typical independently owned property—think basic, but clean and comfortable—but it does have nice-size rooms with air-conditioning and TV, and a restaurant, and is the hotel of choice for organizations such as USAID and Habitat for Humanity. Rooms are $23 to $59 a night. You might also be tempted to stay at the Central Park Hotel on the square. Don't be; it's not very nice.

The most recommended restaurant in town is **Casa Blanca** (2a Calle Oriente, Barrio Santuario; ☎ **503/2393-0549**). Though this place has been around for 20 years and nearly everyone in town will point you straight here, Casa Blanca was a bit of a letdown on my last visit. The ambience is better than the food. Cool sculptures hang on the walls and birds even fly about inside the space, but its handful of meat, chicken, and fish dishes, while fine, don't impress. Main courses are $4 to $12.

THE PACIFIC COAST

El Salvador's western Pacific coast unfolds like the surfing waves for which it's famous. The squalor of the port town La Libertad recedes as the coastal road twists and turns around tiny bays and inlets heading west.

Rocky cliffs overlook jet-black shores. Surfers bob in the water in neat lines, each waiting their turn to ride some of the best waves in Central America. Here, the burgeoning tourism industry is low-key and centered around good surfing and seafood. Tiny lodges sit amidst ramshackle villages with little infrastructure and only the occasional high-class resort. The geography finally flattens out to the west at Los Cobanas, and the beaches become long and desolate, stretching as far as the gorgeous estuary known as Barra de Santiago—one of El Salvador's best-kept secrets.

The eastern coast offers a different vibe as the horseshoe coves of the Balsamo coast gives way to long, expansive beaches. The somewhat tacky, gated resorts of the Costa del Sol contrast with laidback, hidden gems further east, such as Playa El Cuco. These scrappy little beach hamlets come alive on the weekend, or offer splendid isolation on weekdays for those who can extend their vacations just a little bit longer.

THE BALSAMO COAST

25km (16 miles) of coast from Puerto La Libertad to Playa Zonte

The Balsamo Coast, the winding 25km (16 miles) of surf, sand, and cliffside beaches stretching from Puerto La Libertad to just past Playa Zonte, is one of the highlights of El Salvador. Along this strip are some of the country's most beautiful black-sand beaches and traveler-friendly villages. The Balsamo Coast is currently best known, however, for its world-class surfing—the coast is said to be home to the best breaks in all of Central America. The point break in the little village of Playa Sunzal is an excellent place to learn to surf, as the big waves are more than 500m (1,640 ft.) off the beach with smaller, lesson-friendly waves closer to shore. The Balsamo Coast's other famous break, Punta Roca in La Libertad, is an internationally renowned surf spot best left to the experts.

The Balsamo Coast offers plenty for the non-surfer to do, as well; hiking, fishing, swimming, and horseback riding are all within reach, and the coast is just a 1-hour drive from the shops, restaurants, and nightclubs of San Salvador.

Beginning in the port city of La Libertad and traveling west, the main villages of the Balsamo Coast are Playa Tunco, Playa Sunzal, and Playa El Zonte. (And in between these four towns are signs pointing to smaller oceanfront and fishermen's villages that are waiting to be explored.) **Playa Tunco** is the most developed and interesting of the main villages because it has beachfront restaurants, unique hotels, and Internet cafes, along with a coastline that's great for surfers and swimmers. **Playa Sunzal** is a tiny village about .8km (½ mile) farther west, with a famous surf break, a few backpacker surf hostels, and a handful of *pupusarias*. **Playa El Zonte,** the farthest west of the Balsamo Coast's developed villages, is a .8km (½-mile) stretch of hotels and restaurants fronting a beach that's also a good spot for swimmers and surfers. The region's main town, **La Libertad,** is a crowded, hectic oceanfront city best known for its long fisherman's pier and Punta Roca surf break. It also has a reputation for being among the country's most dangerous cities, though it has recently undergone a facelift along the waterfront and is now safe to visit during daylight hours. However, there's no reason to stay overnight in La Libertad considering the better options along the coast.

Essentials

GETTING THERE

BY BUS   From San Salvador, take the frequent bus no. 102 to Puerto La Libertad. The trip costs 55¢ and takes 1 hour. From La Libertad, you'll catch bus no. 192, which travels the length of the Balsamo Coast past Playa El Zonte. It takes 30 minutes and costs 45¢. Bus no. 80 travels between La Libertad and Playa Sunzal, takes 30 minutes, and costs 25¢. Both bus nos. 192 and 80 will stop wherever you request along the main road. Simply tell the driver which town you'd like to visit, and he'll let you off at the right spot. Most towns are a direct 5- to 10-minute walk toward the water from the main road.

BY CAR   From San Salvador, follow Hwy. CA-4 for 45 minutes to 1 hour to La Libertad, where you'll turn right at the ocean and follow coastal Hwy. CA-2 west along the Balsamo Coast. Each town is well marked and a short drive off CA-2.

ORIENTATION

The heart of the Balsamo Coast stretches approximately 25km (16 miles) from La Libertad to just past Playa El Zonte along the winding but well-paved coastal Hwy. CA-2. The region is dotted with small fishing villages, rocky and sandy beaches, and cliff-filled alcoves. La Libertad is the largest city here, with ample grocery stores, ATMs, and a post office. Playa Tunco is the second-most-developed town, with a number of beachfront hotels, restaurants, surf shops, and Internet cafes.

GETTING AROUND

To get around this coast by bus, simply walk to any spot along the main highway CA-2 and hail one of the many no. 192 buses that travel in both directions about every 10 minutes; these will drop you off anywhere along the main road and cost between 25¢ and 45¢, depending on where you are going.

It's easy to drive around this area on your own: The main road linking all towns, coastal Hwy. CA-2, is well maintained, and the entrances to all the coastal towns are well marked.

The Balsamo Coast also has a number of local taxi drivers who can take you from La Libertad to Playa Sunzal for a negotiable $5 and from La Libertad to Playa Zonte

Balsamo Coast & Western Pacific Coast

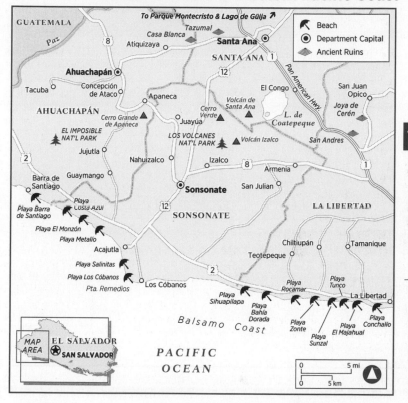

for around $10. Call **Ricardo** (☎ **503/7277-3699**) or **Fausto** (☎ **503/7741-2571**) for a lift.

VISITOR INFORMATION

The region's national tourism office is in Puerto La Libertad (at Km 34.5 Carretera Literal, 90m/295 ft. from the Shell gas station; ☎ **503/2346-1898**). It's open daily from 8am to 5pm.

Most of the Balsamo Coast's banks, ATMs, and pharmacies are in La Libertad, along 2a Calle Poniente, in the center of town. Since La Libertad can be a bit hectic and has a reputation for high crime, it's better to use the ATM and buy your groceries and gas at the large, modern shopping center 1km (½ mile) east of town along the coastal road. The shopping center is a 10-minute walk from the La Libertad pier and includes a grocery store and four ATMs that accept a variety of North America bank cards. A Shell gas station is across the street.

La Libertad's **tourist police** can be reached at ☎ **503/2346-1893, ambulance** service can be called at ☎ **503/2335-3049,** and the **fire department** number is ☎ **503/2243-2054.** La Libertad's **post office** is located along 2a Calle Oriente, directly north of the pier.

La Libertad

Puerto La Libertad is making a valiant attempt at cleaning up its image. This crowded, hardscrabble, oceanfront city 32km (20 miles) south of San Salvador is notorious for drugs and violence, but the local authorities have recently cleaned up its pier and waterfront, and encouraged the opening of cafes and restaurants, as well as a skate park and amphitheater. Despite their efforts, most travelers just stop here briefly to catch buses to the more laidback beach towns and better hotels along the coast, stock up on supplies, or visit the colorful fisherman's pier. Surfers also flock here from around the world to surf the renowned Punta Roca surf break just outside of town.

The long pier and its nearby market are rightly La Libertad's main attractions. The market's prices vary, depending on your negotiating and language skills. Past the market, toward the end of the pier, you can watch as fishermen haul in their morning catch and send it down the pier to market. Just feet from the pier, you can also see local surfers riding the waves and in the distance, the famous surf of the Punta Roca break. The pier is open daily from 6am to 7pm, and nearby, guarded parking is 75¢ a day.

Banks, ATMs, pharmacies, and grocery stores are on the road just north of the oceanfront; a modern shopping center is 1km (½ mile) east along from the pier.

WHERE TO EAT & STAY IN LA LIBERTAD

Note that La Libertad is currently revamping its Malecón (seafront) with a strip of new restaurants that should raise the bar in dining options in the near future. Reservations are not required unless noted.

Hotel Pacific Sunrise Part of a chain of modern, slick, cream-and-orange–colored hotels, the Pacific Sunrise is undoubtedly the best conventional hotel in La Libertad. This plain, 3-story building has nice views of the sea and private access to the beach via a small walkway. The rooms are medium-size with matching dark-wood furniture and checkered bedspreads. There is a decent size pool, though the view of the adjacent car park is not so appealing. Las Olas is a nice, patio-style restaurant located inside the hotel. It dishes out excellent seafood. In general, this is a standard, unremarkable hotel, but when compared to the squalor of the town, it is an oasis of cleanliness and calm.

Calle El Obispo & Carretera Litoral, La Libertad.. ✆ **503/2346-2000.** 30 units. $59 double. DC, MC, V. Free parking. **Amenities:** Restaurant; bar; Internet (free). *In room:* A/C, TV.

La Esquina de Nestor MEXICAN A cheap and cheerful Mexican-style establishment that makes a nice, casual lunch stop. The bright green shop front hides a tiny diner that serves big portions. The shrimp tacos are especially delicious, as are the pork gorditas.

2a Calle Pte & 3a Av. Norte. No phone. Main courses from $4. No credit cards. Daily 10am–10pm.

Punta Roca Surf Resort ★ This famous restaurant (and now hotel) with a panoramic view was established in 1974 by expat surfer Bob Rotterham, who traveled the world in search of the perfect break. He found it on a beach that has now adopted the name of his restaurant; Punta Roca is renowned as one of the best surf spots in Central America. Three generations of surfers have now sprung up in the Rotterham household and, with them, nine comfortable rooms located a short distance away on Playa Cocal and in some well-appointed bungalows with palm-thatched roofs and modern amenities, tall windows, and tidy kitchenettes. Almond trees line a lush

Sink or Swim

You should swim at your own risk all along the western Pacific coast of El Salvador. There are few, if any, public lifeguards, and most beachfront hotels don't provide them. So, if the waves are big, you're not a great swimmer, or it feels like there's too strong a current, you probably shouldn't go in. There are even a number of river mouths meeting the ocean where the current can be particularly overpowering; don't swim in these locations. However, protected Tamarindo area offers the calmest waters in the country, and when the waves are small along Playa Tunco, Playa Sunzal, or Barra de Santiago, you should have no problem. Just keep in mind there is often no one around to save you if you do encounter any issues.

garden, and hammocks rustle in the breeze. The restaurant is still going strong, making some incredible seafood dishes such as filete pizziola, which is just as it sounds, a pizza with fresh fish as a base.

5a Av. Sur & 4a Calle Pte. www.puntaroca.com.sv; ℂ **503/2352-4628.** 9 units. $57 double; from $115 bungalow. Rates include breakfast. AE, DC, MC, V. Free parking. **Amenities:** Restaurant; bar; Internet. *In room:* A/C, TV.

Playa San Diego

This is a long, wide beach 4km (2½ miles) east of La Libertad. It has some private residential houses and a cluster of restaurants at one end where you'll find a river estuary popular with bathers. Two coastal roads run parallel with the beach. On one, you'll find Restaurante Costa Brava (Calle a Playa San Diego; ℂ **503/2345-5698**) 200m (656 ft.) from the beach. The restaurant is nothing special in itself, but it does have a very nice pool, safer than the nearby ocean and certainly cleaner than the estuary. Day-trippers can use the pool for free, as long as they spend more than $5 in the restaurant. Needless to say, it gets packed on weekends. There are also three very basic rooms to rent for $30 each.

Playa San Blas

This private beach offers more seclusion and security than nearby places, without being too exclusive or elitist. Unfortunately, it is not the best for surfing, but its long, dark shore makes for a relaxing day of sunbathing. The gated entrance is located at Km 39.5 on the main coastal road.

Sol Bohemio This small, multicolored establishment has a lovely setting amidst dense foliage, a small pool, and a lush lawn you could play golf on if you had room enough to swing. Blue exterior walls hold up a palm-thatched roof and hide stylish rooms with attractive, traditional tiles, yellow walls, and bright bed covers. Only one room has A/C; the others get a little stuffy, despite having fans. The lodge's main attraction is the hammock-adorned garden and shady communal areas.

Playa San Blas. www.solbohemio.com; ℂ **503/2338-5158.** 3 units. $25 double. AE, DC, MC, V. Free parking. **Amenities:** Restaurant; bar. *In room:* A/C (in one), fan, TV.

Playa Tunco ★

Playa Tunco, 7.5km (4¾ miles) west of La Libertad, is the Balsamo Coast's most tourist-friendly location and a must-stop along this coast. Tourists and El Salvadorans alike flock here on weekends to enjoy the waves, black-sand beaches, laidback vibe, tasty seafood restaurants, and new and unique hotels. Tunco has something to offer most travelers.

Tunco consists of a main road ending on the beach and a side road with beachfront hotels. Numerous small restaurants, hotels, Internet cafes, and a couple of surf shops offering lessons are all tightly packed into this roughly 1km-long (½-mile) area. The beach is long, with black-sand and large rock formations just offshore. The surf at Tunco and nearby Sunzal can get big, but there's usually a small, near-shore break that can accommodate beginner surfers and swimmers.

Opportunities for outdoor tours abound; hiking, kayaking, surfing, horseback riding, and off-road motorcycle tours are offered by some of the hotels and hostels. But my favorite activity here is spending evenings on the second-story, thatched-hut deck of Erika's beachfront restaurant (see below), watching the sun go down behind the surfers. That's paradise.

To get here, take bus no. 192 from La Libertad and get off near Km 42 at the main Tunco entrance, which is marked by a large sign advertising the area's many hotels and restaurants. The town center is a 5-minute walk from there.

WHERE TO STAY IN PLAYA TUNCO

One of the great things about Playa Tunco is that it has accommodations to please everyone. The town offers everything from a $3-a-night campground that's just 44m (144 ft.) from the ocean to a magical retreat with a sweat lodge and cave bar.

Hotel y Restaurante Tekuaní Kal ★★ 🎒 This unusual, artistic, Maya-inspired boutique beachfront hotel is worth every penny of its slightly higher rates. Tekuaní Kal, located a few hundred yards off Tunco's main road, is one of the most unique hotels in the country—it's perhaps best known for its large, whimsical, Maya-inspired cement sculptures that are scattered around the gardenlike property. Rounding out the Maya feel is a newly constructed cave bar and a Maya sweat lodge that hosts weekly traditional purification ceremonies led by a local. The property winds down a rocky cliff to the beach and includes a small infinity pool and waterfall. Rooms are of average size with interesting Maya art; room nos. 1 through 4 have the best ocean views. Service is excellent, with a friendly staff and English-speaking on-site owner.

Km 42 Carretera Literal. www.tekuanikal.com; ℂ **503/2389-6388.** 6 units. $84–$94 double. Rates include breakfast. AE, DC, DISC, MC, V. **Amenities:** Restaurant; small infinity pool & larger swimming pool; room service; sauna. *In room:* A/C, TV, no phone, Wi-Fi (free).

La Guitara Hotel and Bar Tunco has many low-priced lodging options, but what sets La Guitara apart are its modern, efficient, air-conditioned cabins. The hotel has nine attached and semi-attached cabins (adjoining one another) with private bathrooms and patios with hammocks. The large, grassy property is on the beach and offers a big pool, ping-pong and pool tables, and a bar. Papaya's Lodge (see below) is still the best place in town to meet other travelers, but La Guitara is the place to go if you already have travel companions and want a more tranquil experience and nicer rooms.

Km 42 Carretera Literal. info@surfingeltunco.com; ℂ **503/2389-6398.** 9 units. $65 double. No credit cards. **Amenities:** Bar; Internet (free, in lobby); pool. *In room:* A/C (in some), no phone.

Papaya's Lodge 🏄 Papaya's is Tunco's best-known hostel and the best low-cost option. In the middle of the action, on Tunco's main street and just a couple hundred yards from the ocean, Papaya's is a laidback, family-friendly surf hostel with eight basic rooms, including three with private baths. Payapa's also features a fully stocked kitchen open to guests, a breezy upstairs deck, and a gazebo with hammocks over a small river that runs through the area. Since this is a hostel, don't expect a palace, but you'd be hard-pressed to find a more welcoming and well-maintained place to spend a few surf- and hammock-filled days. The hostel is right beside an Internet cafe and surf shop that offers board rentals and bilingual surf lessons.

Km 42 Carretera Literal. www.papayalodge.com; ☏ **503/2389-6231.** 8 units. $15 with shared bathroom–$22 double with private bathroom. No credit cards. **Amenities:** Surfboard rental. *In room:* Fan, no phone.

Roca Sunzal ☺   Roca Sunzal is a good mid-range, beachfront option for those who prefer a hotel over a hostel. Across the street from Papaya's Lodge, the 16-room Roca Sunzal offers an open-air, ocean-view restaurant and a central courtyard with a nice-size pool. Roca Sunzal is also one of Tunco's more family-friendly hotels, so there are often lots of kids running around. The rooms are in a two-story, U-shaped building around the pool, so only a few rooms offer beach views. Room no. 13 is the largest of the ocean-view rooms, with the best view.

Km 42 Carretera Literal. www.rocasunzal.com; ☏ **503/2389-6126.** Fax 503/2389-6190. 21 units. $48–$60 double Mon-Thur; $58–$70 double Fri-Sun; $120–$140 suite. AE, MC, V. **Amenities:** Restaurant; pool; room service ($8–$10); surfboard rental. *In room:* A/C, fan, TV (in some), fridge (in some), kitchen (in some).

Tortuga Surf Club 🧳   This attractive, functional building is located right on the beach with a wood-framed patio and large balcony upstairs leading to four large, bright rooms. Tile floors, tall ceilings, and immaculate fittings look over a small pool and beach deck. Some high stools sit along a counter looking into an open kitchen, and there is a row of surfboards available to guests. There is also a small Internet cafe and gift store, and guides are available with four-wheel-drives to do tours of the area and nearby beaches.

El Tunco Access Rd. www.elsalvadorsurfer.com; ☏ **503/7888-6225** or 503/2298-2986. 4 units. $37 double w/shared bathroom; $45 double w/private bathroom. AE, DC, MC, V. Free parking. **Amenities:** Restaurant; bar; Internet cafe; surf store. *In room:* A/C (in some), fan.

WHERE TO EAT IN PLAYA TUNCO

On the beach at the end of Tunco's main street are two nearly identical restaurants, Restaurante Erika (☏ **503/2389-6054**) and La Bocana Restaurante (☏ **503/2389-6238**). It's easy to confuse the two, as both offer similar two-story deck seating overlooking the ocean and menus with delicious fish entrees ranging from $7 to $16. The distinguishing factor is that Erika's is more of a locals' joint, while La Bocana attracts more tourists. Whichever you choose, aim to grab a seat on one of their decks at sunset, since the views are amazing.

The full-service restaurants at **Tekuaní Kal** (☏ **503/2389-6388**) and **Las Olas** (☏ **503/2411-7553**) also offer great views and fresh seafood entrees, as well as a chance to see these two great hotels without the cost of a room.

PLAYA TUNCO AFTER DARK

Playa Tunco is one of the few small towns in El Salvador to have a nightlife scene, and it's centered around Roots Campground (www.rootscamping.es.tl), right off the town's main road. Each Saturday, Roots sponsors a live music or DJ party on its huge, grassy, beachfront expanse. The cover charge depends on the event, but it's usually a good time.

Playa Sunzal

Playa Sunzal is a tiny community next door to Tunco (and 9km/5½ miles west of La Libertad), which features a couple of surf hostels, a few pupusarias along the main highway, and a rocky point break that's made the village famous among surfers. You can reach Sunzal from the highway or by taking a 10-minute stroll along the beach to the right from Tunco and turning inland at an opening in the retaining wall just before the point break. Follow the path and turn right at your first opportunity. There are several hostels on this path, and the pupusarias are on the highway ahead and to the left. The best of the hostels is Sunzal Point Surf Lodge (✆ 503/7327-9869; www.surfsunzal.com). Rates for private rooms start at $18.

Playa Zonte

Playa Zonte is a beautiful, approximately 1km (½-mile) stretch of sandy and rocky beach a 19km (12-mile) trip west of La Libertad. Many travelers break into Tunco-versus-Zonte camps, with Zonte siders preferring that beach town for its less developed and more laidback vibe. Surfers like its strong beach break, and non-surfers can enjoy its sandier beaches, depending on the tides.

To get to Playa Zonte, follow coastal Hwy. CA-2 west from La Libertad to approximately Km 53 and look for the LA CASA DE FRIDA sign. Turn left there. Coming from the west, look for a sign on your left reading INTERVIDA EL SALVADOR with an image of the Earth. Turn right there. The main road into Zonte has two entrances and is like a giant circular driveway leading to the hotel area. So, you can take either entrance and get to the same place.

WHERE TO STAY & EAT IN PLAYA ZONTE

Playa Zonte offers a small collection of laidback beachfront hostels and restaurants. One of the best places to stay here is the well-known La Casa de Frida (Km 53.5 Carretera Literal #7; www.lacasadefrida.com; ✆ 503/2252-2949). The many portraits of Mexican artist Frida Kahlo hanging by the entrance confirm that you've found your way to this friendly, three-room hostel. Each room has four beds, and it runs $10 per bed or $20 per person to have the room to yourself. The hostel is right on the beach, and its small restaurant is one of the best in town. If Frida's is booked, try the nearby five-room Olas Permanentes Hostal (Km 53 Carretera Literal; www.olaspermanentes.com; ✆ 503/2300-6422). This family- and surfer-friendly hostel offers private rooms with private bathrooms for $25 and surfboard rentals for $12. Horizonte Surf Resort (www.horizontesurfresort.com; ✆ 503/2323-0099) is another oasis of calm amidst what is a ramshackle neighborhood. Some rooms are little more than tarted-up cells, except for a 6-bed suite with large windows, a wooden floor, and split-level layout. What makes the place is its lovely pool and garden area surrounded by lawn and palm trees. Doubles start at $35. Esencia Nativa (www.esencianativa.com; ✆ 503/7737-8879) is a laidback collection of five colorful rooms, a garden, pool, and a communal lounge piled high with books, games, magazines, and hammocks. It's a perfect surfers' hangout with restaurant, surf school, and board rental. Doubles with A/C start at $35.

In addition to the restaurant at La Casa de Frida, the **Costa Brava Restaurante** (Km 53.5 Carretera Literal, a 5-min. walk west from Frida's; ✆ 503/2302-6068) offers a big fish and meat menu for $6 to $12, with ocean-view seating.

Playa Los Cóbanos

Playa Los Cóbanos is a tiny, not very attractive fishing village about an hour's drive west of La Libertad, which lacks any decent hotels and restaurants. The Los Cóbanos area, however, happens to be home to two of the country's best all-inclusive resorts. Decameron and Los Veraneras.

ESSENTIALS

GETTING THERE From Sonsonate, take bus no. 26, which stops directly in Playa Los Cóbanos.

When driving from the east, follow coastal Hwy. CA-2 to Hwy. CA-12, where you will turn south toward the ocean and follow the signs to Los Cóbanos. The road dead-ends in the town center 8km (5 miles) after leaving the highway. From Sonsonate, take Hwy. CA-12 and follow the signs.

ORIENTATION & GETTING AROUND The road off the main highway to Playa Los Cóbanos dead-ends into Cóbanos' 2-block-long, beachfront town center. Both Decameron and Los Veraneras resorts are within a few minutes' drive.

WHERE TO STAY IN PLAYA LOS COBANOS

Las Veraneras Resort ★★ ☺ Veraneras is one of El Salvador's most enjoyable and affordable luxury resorts and is home to one of the country's few public golf courses. The resort's biggest draw is its 7,000-yard, 18-hole rolling but open course, which was completed in December 2007. Veraneras also has plenty for non-golfers to do, such as lounging by one of the pools, taking an ocean swim from the sandy beach club, playing tennis, or letting the kids enjoy the large children's play area. The individual, one-story villas are modern and spare, but comfortable, with separate living rooms, full kitchens, and shady patios. The resort also features some English-speaking staff and can arrange tours around the country. Veraneras more than delivers on its affordable $59, two-adults-with-a-child base rate. Because of all its amenities, Veraneras is a great place to base your El Salvador vacation.

Km 88.5 Carretera a Los Cóbanos. www.veranerasresort.com; © **503/2420-5000** or 503/2247-9191. 60 units. $59–$71 double; $100–$159 villa. AE, DC, DISC, MC, V. **Amenities:** 2 restaurants; 2 snack bars; airport transfers ($30); bikes; children's play area w/pool; exercise room; golf course; 3 pools; room service; Wi-Fi (free). *In room:* A/C, TV, kitchen or kitchenette.

Royal Decameron Salinitas If you like all-inclusives, you won't be disappointed here. Decameron is El Salvador's largest all-inclusive resort and offers all the grandeur and amenities that a large, multinational chain can offer. Four chlorinated pools and a huge saltwater pool stretching into the Pacific are scattered around the sprawling, lush property. Rooms, which are large and colorfully decorated, sleep up to four and are located in four multistory buildings with balconies around the property. A cadre of international, all-you-can-eat-and-drink bars and restaurants keep guests full and happy. The generally bilingual staff organizes on-property activities and can arrange tours for an extra charge to El Salvador's Maya ruins, along with windsurfing, scuba diving, and kayaking trips.

Km 79 Carretera a Acajutla. www.decameron.com; © **503/2429-9000.** 552 units. $118–$178 double. Rates include all food & drink. AE, DC, DISC, MC, V. **Amenities:** 5 restaurants; 4 bars; airport transfers ($23); babysitting; exercise room; Jacuzzi; 5 pools; room service; sauna; spa; free watersports equipment; Wi-Fi (free). *In room:* A/C, TV, fridge.

BARRA DE SANTIAGO ★★★

76km (47 miles) W of La Libertad

A long finger of land packed with coconut trees is lapped by an estuary on one side and the roaring Pacific on the other. Barra de Santiago is, bar none, one of the most beautiful spots in El Salvador. This protected reserve and tiny fishing village, which is tucked into the southwest corner of the country, features miles of deserted, pristine beaches sitting a few hundred yards from a mangrove-filled estuary teeming with birds. And both are set against a backdrop of the lush hills of Parque Imposible and a wall of volcanoes stretching from Guatemala to Volcán de Izalco in El Salvador's Parque Nacional de Los Volcanes. If you love nature and the sea, Barra de Santiago is one of El Salvador's must-sees.

Barra de Santiago is also one of the country's most active turtle-nesting areas, and every August through November, you can witness giant sea turtles laying eggs along the beach and hundreds of hatched baby turtles making the dangerous journey to the water. You can also paddle or arrange guided tours of the lush mangrove forests and narrow, bird-filled channels, take surfing lessons, or just walk for hours, absorbing the isolated natural beauty.

While here, make sure to take the 15-minute walk along the beach from one of Santiago's two main hotels to the tiny thatched hut, Restaurante Julita, which sits just yards from the confluence of the Pacific Ocean and Santiago's estuary. You can munch on fish caught moments before while viewing the waves of the Pacific on one side and, on the other, the calm waters of the estuary reflecting the line of palm trees and miles of volcanoes that seem to rise from its shores.

Barra de Santiago is a 2-hour drive from San Salvador and offers little infrastructure, other than its two beachfront hotels. The town itself is a squalid collection of shacks and huts with Guantanamo-style lodging that is best avoided. You'll need to make advanced reservations for the better-quality hotels farther up the beach. You'll also want to arrange transportation in the area, as it requires a few twists and turns to get to this undeveloped corner of the country.

Essentials

GETTING THERE

La Barra is not easy to find, and access to its two hotels is via the beach. Unless you are determined to travel independently, it is best to arrange a hotel transfer or choose a tour company for a day trip.

BY BUS From San Salvador, take a bus to Sonsonate (see p. 308 for info). Then, catch bus no. 285, which departs Sonsonate for Barra de Santiago daily at 10am and 4:30pm; it leaves Santiago for Sonsonate daily at 4:30am and noon. The trip costs $1 and takes 1¼ hours. The spot where buses arrive and depart is a straight, 5-minute walk from both of Santiago's hotels.

BY CAR You can drive here from most parts of the country by journeying on CA-12, which heads south and then west before turning toward the beach at Km 98.5 (there'll be a sign for Barra de Santiago). From there, it's another 25 to 30 minutes along a bumpy dirt road that dead-ends just before the hotels. It can get a bit tricky; but just stay as close to the beach as possible, and you should find your way. The trip is possible in a regular car, but you cannot take the beach access road to either hotel. You'll need to call your hotel in advance to get info on driving the last few hundred yards along the beach or bay (if you have a 4WD) and also where to park your vehicle when you get there (both hotels have secure parking for regular cars in the village).

ORIENTATION & GETTING AROUND

Santiago's two hotels are side by side on the beach and estuary, so you definitely don't need a car to get around (nor are there local buses). A small, impoverished village with a couple of tiny tiendas is about a 10-minute walk or short drive east along the main road from the hotels.

VISITOR INFORMATION

Both of Santiago's hotels offer small restaurants, but bring everything else you'll need, as the area has no banks, pharmacies, or large stores. There's no official tourist office in town, but the folks at Capricho Beach House or La Cocotera (see below) can arrange tours in the area and provide info, or you can check with guide Julio Caesar Aviles (see below).

What to See & Do in Barra de Santiago

The waves here can occasionally get big, with strong rip currents. But most of the time, the waves are small enough for beginning surfers or those who just want to go for a swim. Santiago's beaches, unlike others on this coast, are wide, sandy, and uncrowded—you won't have to worry about tangling your lines with anyone else when you're fishing, or bumping into anyone else while surfing. Both hotels listed below can arrange surf lessons and board rental.

You can arrange guided tours of the nearby estuary and mangrove forest with local Spanish-speaking guide **Julio Caesar Aviles** (© **503/7783-4765**). A 2-hour tour, including a small hike on the protected Isla de Cahete, where small, covered mounds mark the site of protected indigenous artifacts, is $45 per person. The tour takes you deep into the mangrove channels, where many bird species can be easily spotted. Santiago is also a prime sea turtle–nesting area and has been the subject of numerous turtle conservation projects. Each August through November, giant sea turtles lay their eggs on the beach and the tiny hatchlings stumble their way to the water. Both hotels listed below can arrange turtle-spotting trips.

Where to Stay in Barra de Santiago

Capricho Beach House　Capricho is a five-room hostel right on the beach and steps away from Santiago's protected estuary. It's the more affordable of Santiago's two lodging options, but a definite large step down from the utter luxury next door at La Cocotera. It has four modern, average-size private rooms with shady front patios overlooking the beach. An old cabin with five inexpensive dorm beds and a shared bathroom is also available. But I don't recommend the dorm beds. They're cheap— only $8 per night—but uncomfortable and unattractive. The hotel has a small, slightly overpriced food menu, and guests are allowed to use the full-service kitchen. If you plan to cook, bring everything you'll need, because there are no grocery stores here. The same owners also run a guesthouse in San Salvador.

Final Calle Principal. www.ximenasguesthouse.com; © **503/2260-2481.** 5 units. $8 dorm bed; $70 private room. No credit cards. **Amenities:** Restaurant; airport & San Salvador transfers ($50–$70); surfboard rental ($10/day). *In room:* A/C, no phone.

La Cocotera ★★★ 🎒　This is one of the finest ecolodges in all of Central America and certainly one of the most luxurious hotels in El Salvador. It offers a rare taste of international style in a remote and beautiful part of the country. La Cocotera gets the balance right: utter comfort with a social conscience. It employs locals, uses sustainable energy, promotes nature conservation, and blends right in with its environment. This all-inclusive ecoresort features three modern, two-level cabins, each with two huge rooms, luxurious, Asian-inspired bathrooms, and large flat-screen TVs. The hotel property stretches from the bay to the beach, meaning you have water on both sides. It includes a restaurant, bar, and pool dotted with custom-built furniture. The best rooms are the three upstairs units with soaring ceilings, king-size beds, and water-view balconies. The downstairs rooms have two twin beds with pullouts to sleep four. The hotel also offers mangrove, deep-sea, and estuary fishing tours, as well as water-skiing. As an ecoresort, La Cocotera features solar-powered hot water and brown-water recycling, and it even incubates turtle eggs, gathered from illegal vendors around the country, for release by guests into the sea. The staff is gracious and friendly. Staying here is an unforgettable experience.

Final Calle Principal. www.lacocoteraresort.com; ✆ **503/2245-3691.** 6 units. $93–$141 double downstairs; $118–$184 double upstairs. Rates include airport transfers, meals & nonalcoholic drinks. Package rates vary; see hotel website. AE, DC, MC, V. **Amenities:** Restaurant; bar; free airport transfers; pool; kayaks; water-skiing ($20/hr.); Wi-Fi (free). *In room:* A/C, TV/DVDs player, no phone.

EASTERN PACIFIC COAST

66km (41 miles) SE of San Salvador

In contrast to the west, the eastern Pacific coast is less developed and has no scenic coastal road winding around tiny coves, yet it does have its hidden charms. A flat expanse of desolate beaches is broken up by the occasional fishing village, estuary, and mangrove swamp. Some of those beaches fill up with partying locals on weekends and holidays, especially around the exclusive and elusive strip known as Costa del Sol. The high walls on this long peninsula hide high-end resorts and luxury beach homes. Farther east (known to the locals as the "Wild East"), there are a number of virgin territories to explore, such as Bahia de Jiquilisco, Isla Montecristo, and Isla Meanguera, but little infrastructure. Beach bums and adventurous surfers flock to Playa El Cuco near San Miguel, while sun-worshippers swear by the just-discovered Playa El Espino, all within a 2-hour drive of San Salvador airport. The uninteresting port town of La Union is the country's biggest port and gateway to the rocky, tropical islands of the Golfo de Fonseca, a hot and humid pirate bay shared with Honduras and Nicaragua.

Costa del Sol

Costa del Sol's reputation is better than its reality. This stretch of highway southeast of San Salvador, with the Pacific on one side and a beautiful bay on the other, is known as the beach getaway for El Salvador's wealthy elite. If you're invited to one of the locals' large beach houses, no doubt you'll have a blast. However, for the average traveler, the region is hard to get a handle on. Huge walls block the beach from the region's homes, and Costa del Sol offers no central area of activity. There's no charming cluster of interesting restaurants or shops, and most visitors usually check into their hotel, hang out on their hotel beach, and eat in their hotel restaurant during their stay.

All that said, Costa del Sol can be an excellent beach day trip, as it's only 25 minutes from the airport and 45 minutes from San Salvador, with public beach access at the local tourist center. Costa del Sol's beaches are also bigger, sandier, and, when the waters are calm, better for swimming than the rockier beaches to the west. The area even offers a gorgeous bay with an international cadre of yachts bobbing in its protected waters, where regular folks can rent some watercraft. It's definitely possible to have a great time here, especially if you're looking for a packaged resort experience.

GETTING THERE

BY BUS   From San Salvador, take bus no. 133 toward Zacatecoluca. Ask to be let off at the road to Costa del Sol. From there, wait for bus no. 19, which will drop you off in front of your hotel along Costa del Sol's main road.

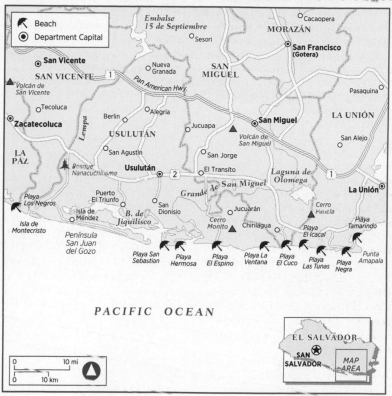

Eastern Pacific Coast

Legend:
- Beach
- ● Department Capital

San Vicente
SAN VICENTE
1
Volcán de San Vicente
Pan American Hwy.
Tecoluca
Zacatecoluca
LA PAZ
Berlin
USULUTÁN
San Agustín
Bosque Nanacuchitiama
Usulután
2
Puerto El Triunfo
Playa Los Negros
Isla de Méndez
Isla de Montecristo
B. de Jiquilisco
San Dionisio
Península San Juan del Gozo
Playa San Sebastián
Playa Hermosa

Embalse 15 de Septiembre
Sesori
Nueva Granada
SAN MIGUEL
Alegría
Jucuapa
San Jorge
El Transito
Grande de San Miguel
Cerro Monito
Playa El Espino
Playa La Ventana

Cacaopera
MORAZÁN
San Francisco (Gotera)
Pasaquina
LA UNIÓN
San Alejo
Volcán de San Miguel
San Miguel
Laguna de Olomega
Jucuarán
Chirilagua
Cerro Pacila
Playa El Icacal
La Unión
Playa Tamarindo
Playa El Cuco
Playa Las Tunas
Playa Negra
Punta Amapala

PACIFIC OCEAN

0   10 mi
0   10 km

EL SALVADOR
SAN SALVADOR
MAP AREA

18

THE PACIFIC COAST | Eastern Pacific Coast

BY CAR From San Salvador, follow Hwy. CA-2 east to Km 43 and look for the detour south toward Costa del Sol. Follow the signs and, as there is no Costa del Sol town center, look for the kilometer markers that match the address of your hotel.

GETTING AROUND

The best way to navigate Costa del Sol is by foot along the beach. You can also catch bus no. 193 anywhere along Costa del Sol's main road, which runs regularly throughout the day. Many of the hotels and homes block access to the non-paying public, though you can find an entrance near the Hotel Haydee Mar at Playa los Blancos (Km 64) or at the end of the peninsula.

VISITOR INFORMATION & FAST FACTS

Costa del Sol doesn't have a tourism office, but some hotels have English-speaking front-desk staffs, and the tourism office in Puerto La Libertad (Km 34.5 Carretera Literal, 90m/295 ft. from the Shell gas station; ✆ **503/2346-1898**) can provide basic information. It's open daily 8am to 5pm.

This entire region is sorely lacking in tourist services—for hospitals, banks, or Internet access, you'll need to journey back to San Salvador or Puerto La Libertad.

WHAT TO SEE & DO IN COSTA DEL SOL

Boating in the bay, and swimming or sunbathing on the beaches are the main attractions here—most people actually just enjoy whatever their hotel has to offer during their visit to the area. But Costa del Sol does have a few places outside of the hotels that are worth checking out, including Aqua Fun (Km 75.5 Blvd. Costa del Sol; ✆ 503/2338-0384; www.aquafundelsol.com), a laidback bar and restaurant on the bay with a big pool, pool table, bay views, and $70-per-hour motorized watercraft rental. They also provide all-day deep-sea fishing trips that start at $699, boat, beer, and captain included. It's a good place to take a break from the beach. If you just want to visit for the day, head to Costa del Sol's Turicentro (Km 63.5 Blvd Costa del Sol.; ✆ 503/2338-2050). This is one of the country's better tourist centers, with beach access, a nice pool, changing rooms, picnic tables, and a restaurant. Admission is 80¢, and the center is open daily from 7am to 4pm.

WHERE TO STAY IN COSTA DEL SOL

Bahía del Sol Hotel 🖐 Bahía del Sol is a reasonably priced and enjoyable-enough place to stay, but it's a bit overhyped. It's developed a megaresort reputation because it is the place to be if you want to dock your yacht, take a $1,200-per-day deep-sea fishing excursion, or play blackjack. Its biggest draws are its small casino and marina. But, for the average traveler, it's just a slightly-above-average resort, albeit one with some ocean- and bay-front rooms and town houses with outdoor Jacuzzis. Most of the rooms, however, are average size, with nondescript decor, and are situated away from the water and the good views.

Km 78 Blvd. Costa del Sol. www.bahiadelsolelsalvador.com; ✆ **503/2337-9999**, or 505/2283-2007 in San Salvador. 115 units. $138–$147 double; $300 suite. Rates include breakfast, lunch & dinner. AE, DC, DISC, MC, V. **Amenities:** 2 restaurants; 2 bars; exercise room; room service; Wi-Fi (in lobby & some common areas). *In room:* A/C, TV, kitchen (in suite).

Bahia Dorado ★★ ☺ The Bahia Dorado might be Costa del Sol's best hotel. This six-story, all-inclusive beachfront hotel was built in 2006, and all the rooms have balconies with beautiful, long-range Pacific views. The grounds include two huge pools—one of which is the largest I've seen in El Salvador—a poolside bar; an open-air restaurant; and a wide, sandy beach. The rooms are at least as large as you'll find in other El Salvador hotels, and the bathrooms are bigger and more modern. Three large suites are also available on the top floor. Room service is a bit slow, and a load of laundry is a ridiculous $13, but the decent room rates compensate for this.

Km 75.5 Blvd. Costa del Sol. www.hoteleselsalvador.com/hotelbahia; ✆ **503/2325-7500**. 63 units. $141 double; $216 suite. Rates include breakfast, lunch & dinner. AE, DC, DISC, MC, V. **Amenities:** Restaurant; bar; 2 pools; room service; nonsmoking rooms available; Wi-Fi (in lobby). *In room:* A/C, TV.

Estero y Mar ★ ☺ Just as the name implies, this mid-size resort is surrounded by "estuary and sea." Shops, bars, restaurants, gardens, and pools are spread across a small peninsula just west of Costa del Sol (note: it is not on the main strip) and only 30 minutes from the San Salvador airport. This is a conventional resort with a jungle feel, as there are mangrove swamps and waterways nearby. Don't expect tranquil nature, however, as guests and local day-trippers take full advantage of the fleet of beach buggies and jet skis available for rent. And don't expect subdued decor, either: The large rooms and suites spread across the property are decked out in psychedelic yellows and blues that might give some people a headache. Such tropical tackiness does not extend to the lovely hardwood balconies with plants and views of the gardens and sea. Facilities are top notch, with excellent pools, a hammock-strewn garden, play courts, and a minizoo. Make sure to ask for a room with reliable hot water, and be aware that access is down a dirt track that runs parallel to the beach, so bring good directions or, better still, arrange for the hotel to pick you up.

Playa El Pimental, San Luis Talpa. www.esteroymar.com; © **503/2270-1172.** 30 units. $88 double. AE, DC, DISC, MC, V. Free parking. **Amenities:** 2 restaurants; 2 bars; 3 pools; Wi-Fi (free). *In room:* A/C, TV.

Hotel Pacific Paradise Pacific Paradise is a pleasant but dated 25-year-old beach-front resort, and it should be your last choice of the larger resorts listed here. Its rooms are a distance from the beach and are not exceptionally attractive—think tired, non-descript decor—and are only average size. The restaurant is also away from the beach in an odd, glass-enclosed structure offering little in the way of ambience or views. The grounds include a pool surrounded by 1970s-like cement tables with plastic chairs. On the plus side, it's on a big sandy beach, has a grassy interior courtyard, and offers a few two-bedroom, pool-view bungalows. When making reservations, either request the presidential suite, one of the bungalows, or at very least, an upstairs room.

Km 75 Blvd. Costa del Sol. www.hotelpacificparadise.com; © **503/2338-0156.** 49 units. $99–$120 double. Rates include breakfast, lunch & dinner. AE, DC, DISC, MC, V. **Amenities:** Restaurant; room service; Wi-Fi. *In room:* A/C, TV, no phone.

Tesoro Beach Hotel This crumbling complex has a faded grandeur. Chandeliers hang in a grandiose lobby with marble floors. Rooms are huge but badly maintained, with peeling walls and outdated decor. They are certainly not worth the price. It is, however, worth a day visit, as a $35 pass allows you to use the two pools and ample grounds, which include an over-the-top Greek-style amphitheatre, and the wide, unkempt beach.

Km 65.5, Blvd Costa del Sol. www.tesorobeachhotel.com; © **503/2337-1447** or 503/2334-0600. 20 units. $200 double. Rates include breakfast, lunch & dinner. AE, DC, DISC, MC, V. **Amenities:** Restaurant; 2 pools; room service; Wi-Fi (free). *In room:* A/C, TV.

WHERE TO EAT IN COSTA DEL SOL

Most visitors stick to their hotel restaurants, but Costa del Sol also has two independent restaurants worth trying. Reservations are not necessary.

Acajutla Seafood Restaurant ★★ SEAFOOD The seafood is delicious, the scenery is beautiful, and the service is excellent. Acajutla, part of a well-reputed 20-year-old seafood chain, is definitely worth leaving your hotel for. Like Mar y Sol, Acajutla is on the bay side of the main road and has great views and bay breezes. But Acajutla surpasses that restaurant with its formal service, its three-page seafood menu, and its exquisitely prepared dishes. Among the best is the grilled lobster and crab with butter and garlic sauce. The sopa de marisco, or fish soup, is quite hearty, and most of Acajutla's entrees are huge by El Salvador standards. Each entree also begins with a tasty appetizer of tortilla chips in a spicy dip sprinkled with cheese.

Km 73.5 Blvd. Costa del Sol. © **503/2338-0397.** Main courses $12–$18. AE, DC, MC, V. Daily 8am–10pm.

Mar y Sol ★ 🍴 SALVADORAN Mar y Sol is a comfortable, laidback, and inexpensive place to have a simple meal and a cold beer, and take in the beautiful view of the bay. The restaurant is located along Costa del Sol's main road and offers a covered, open-air deck with bench seating overlooking the estuary. The one-page, Spanish-only menu is simple, with items like fried or grilled fish, chicken, or steak with rice and salad, and cheap empanadas and pupusas ($4); but it's the scenery you get for the cost that is Mar y Sol's biggest draw.

Km 75.5 Blvd. Costa del Sol. © **503/2301-8250.** Main courses $4–$10. No credit cards. Daily 7:30am–7pm.

Isla de Montecristo ★★

Isla de Montecristo, 80km (50 miles) southeast of San Salvador, is a gorgeous, largely undeveloped 2.5-sq.-km (1-sq.-mile) island, situated where the large Río Lempa empties into the Pacific. The tiny island is home to acres of fruit trees, a few farming communities, and hundreds of nesting birds, such as pelicans and egrets. Most visitors come to the island by dugout canoe or small motorboat to spend a couple of days hiking, fishing, or just swinging in a hammock along the river.

The best way to get to the island is to travel to the nearby community of La Pita and catch a boat there across to the island. This 30-minute $4 canoe journey is half the fun of the trip, since you'll spot birds flying low and fish skimming the surface of the water along the way. It takes a bit of effort, especially by bus, to get to La Pita itself, so it's best to call one of the hostels mentioned below to arrange lodging and transportation.

GETTING THERE

BY BUS   From San Salvador, take bus no. 302 toward Usulután and tell the driver to let you off at San Nicolás Lempa near the Texaco station. Buses leave from there for the 13km (8-mile) trip to La Pita daily at 5am and 2pm, and return at 5:30am and 3pm. The journey takes 40 minutes and costs 70¢.

BY CAR   Follow Hwy. CA-2 to Km 87 and turn at the Texaco station; then follow the unpaved road until it dead-ends in La Pita.

ORIENTATION & GETTING AROUND

Isla de Montecristo is a small, undeveloped island comprising family farms and one tiny town center with two hostels and a restaurant, which serves as the port where visitors arrive and depart. You can walk across the island from the river to the Pacific along unmarked trails in about 30 minutes—there are no buses or taxis on the island.

Avoid Puerto El Triunfo

You must pass through this town to get to Bahia de Jiquilisco, but try not to linger. It has a reputation for high crime and gang violence.

VISITOR INFORMATION & FAST FACTS

For information about the island and accommodations, call Montecristo's two hostels (see below) or the local nonprofit CORDES (℗ **503/2235-8262** or 503/2883-4825; www.cordes.org.sv), which helps local families find work, and can arrange lodging, transportation, and tours.

The island has no shops other than a single *tienda,* so you'll need to head to San Salvador or Puerto La Libertad for things such as banks, hospitals, and Internet access.

WHAT TO SEE & DO IN MONTECRISTO

Isla de Montecristo is home to a wide variety of birds, including majestic white egrets, which, seemingly on cue, pose for near-perfect photos as they glide low over the calm estuary waters here. Locals can take you on tours in dugout canoes to places where you can spot other bird life, along with the area's unique, 15cm-long (6-in.) jumping fish, which skim along the surface near shore. Or you can simply stroll around the island. Note that the currents on the Pacific side can be strong, so swimming in the ocean is not recommended.

Island Wildlife

In between Isla de Montecristo and the beaches to its east is the huge island Bahía de Jiquilisco. This largely undeveloped inlet offers untouched natural beauty with dozens of mangrove-lined channels to paddle, islands to explore, great views, and beautiful ocean and bay beaches. The bay is also a major stop along the way for 87 types of migratory birds and a nesting ground for sea turtles. It remains one of the coast's most untouched and naturally beautiful areas. The only problems are that the easiest way to get here is by passing through the dangerous and seedy port town of Puerto El Triunfo, and there is little tourism infrastructure immediately around the bay. As a result, Jiquilisco is best explored with a tour company, such as Eco Mayan Tours (Paseo General Escalón 3658, Colonia Escalón, San Salvador; ✆ 503/2298-2844; www.ecomayantours.com), which can provide transportation and the equipment necessary to explore the bay.

WHERE TO STAY & EAT IN MONTECRISTO

The island has two thatched-roof hostels with beds and hammocks, and one restaurant that offers fish and pupusas. Cabanas y Rancho Brisas del Mar (✆ **503/2367-2107**; no credit cards) offers two rustic but comfortable two-bed-plus hammock cabins with patios right on the river for $15 a night. Brisas del Mar also has the island's only open-air, riverside restaurant. Round-trip boat transportation is available from La Pita for $20 per person, and there are also 1- to 2-hour estuary tours for $5 to $10 per person. Prices can often be negotiated down.

Back on the mainland in La Pita is **Hostal Lempa Mar** (✆ **503/2310-9901** or 503/7787-5824; no credit cards), which features small but comfortable, three-person, $25-per-night cabins and a riverside restaurant. The hostel will take you to the island for $10 per person each way.

Playa El Espino

A wide, gorgeous beach that is splendidly isolated on weekdays and alive with beachgoers on weekends, Playa El Espino is gaining a reputation as one of El Salvador's best places to throw down a towel and enjoy the sun, sea, and sand. Access was once difficult, but now a newly paved road means you can get there easily by bus or car from the main town of Usulutan. New hotels are popping up all the time, the best of which are listed below.

WHERE TO STAY IN PLAYA EL ESPINO

Hotel Real Oasis Espino 📖 This rather plain, modern building has pink walls and simple lines with little decor or embellishments. A tiled inner stairway leads to rooms upstairs, and out back by the garden, you'll find low yellow buildings with more rooms. Patio doors and large windows ensure lots of light, though the rooms lack character and are a little soulless. Everything, however, is sparkling clean. Its main attraction is the wide-open beachside location and grand-size pool with tiny island and mini-footbridge. There is a thatched, rancho-style dining area with hammocks and deck chairs, and smaller thatched picnic spots you can hire by the day. Look out for all-inclusive packages, such as 2 nights and 3 days for $110 per person.

Playa El Espino. www.realoasisespino.com.sv; ✆ **503/2270-2798** or 503/7856-3445. 15 units. $60 double. AE, DC, DISC, MC, V. Free parking. **Amenities:** Restaurant. *In room:* A/C, TV, no phone.

La Estancia de Don San Luis   This open property sits right on the beach and consists of low, white bungalow rooms, thatched picnic areas, green lawns, and a picket fence. The facilities are modern and basic, with bright, clean rooms and tiny bathrooms. A good pool and friendly owners make for a laidback, casual break.

Calle a Arcos, 1,300m (4,265 ft.) W of school. www.playaespino.com; ℭ **505/2270-1851.** 7 units. $50 double; $110 double w/full board. AE, DC, DISC, MC, V. Free parking. **Amenities:** Restaurant. *In room:* A/C, TV, no phone.

Playa El Cuco

Your first impressions of Playa El Cuco may not be so great when you first arrive and see a ramshackle gathering of food huts and shacks. However, keep going, and it opens up into a vast plain of sand with a distant shore that goes on for miles. El Cuco is a medium-size fishing village that also functions as a popular El Salvadoran beach getaway. Swimmers often share the ocean with small boats heading out for the day (and the occasional jellyfish), and the beach is lined with tables for drying the fishermen's morning catch, as well as thatched-roof-covered restaurants catering to El Salvadorans. If you want to step off the normal tourist path for a couple of days, this is a great place to go. Three kilometers (1¾ miles) west is Playa La Flores, one of the best places to surf in the country and with none of the crowds associated with the Balsamo Coast. To get there, take the bus no. 385 from San Miguel, or drive east along Hwy. CA-2 and follow the signs.

WHERE TO STAY IN PLAYA EL CUCO

Azul Surf Club   This upscale surfing establishment has a genuine Salvadoran authenticity to it, with arch framed verandahs overlooking a tropical garden surrounded by large patios and lots of space. It exercises "give back tourism," with part of the proceeds going into local health and education projects. That is not to say it is frugal with any luxuries, and the fabulous pool with swim-up bar will have you wallowing for hours, when not lazing in the countless hammocks that dot the property. And then, of course, there is the surfing; the hotel boasts some of the best breaks in the country and operates boat trips to nearby islands and beaches.

Playa El Cuco, San Miguel. www.azulsurfclub.com; ℭ **503/2612-6820.** 12 units. $100 double. 5-day all-inclusive packages start at $750 per person. AE, DC, DISC, MC, V. Free parking. **Amenities:** Restaurant; bar; Internet (free); pools. *In room:* A/C, TV.

Las Flores Surf Club   This seven-room, all-inclusive, four-star hotel is a slice of luxury, with the prices to match. You do get what you pay for, however—the grounds are set on a beautiful, and private, beach cove; the rooms are enormous and have a modern, Asian-inspired decor; and the staff is friendly and attentive, and caters to your every need. Huge bathrooms, private decks, and a beautiful pool make Las Flores a notch above your average surf camp. Its biggest asset is its splendid isolation, offering an exclusivity that attracts both surfers and non-surfers.

Playa El Cuco, San Miguel. www.lasfloresresort.com; ℭ **760-494-7392** in the U.S. or 503/2236-0225 in San Salvador. 10 units. $328 per person for 2-night package. Rates include full board. AE, DC, DISC, MC, V. Free parking. **Amenities:** Restaurant; bar; Jacuzzi; 2 pools; spa. *In room:* A/C, TV, Wi-Fi.

La Tortuga Verde 🛏️   Three ocean-side properties sit in a glorious cluster of tall coconut trees, with a centerpiece turquoise pool and sculpture-dotted garden that are delightful and thoughtfully designed by the English-speaking and environment-conscious owner, Tom. Recycled material went into the construction of each beautiful room, bungalow, and house, and each has an unusual screened-in sala that allows you

Conchagua Volcano and Village

Tired of the beach? Take the morning off from sunbathing to visit the 1,243m-high (4,078-ft.) Volcán de Conchagua just south of La Union. Ride to the top in a 4-wheel-drive, and you'll find a mirador with incredible views of the entire Golfo de Fonseca, La Union port, the islands, and the coasts of Honduras and Nicaragua. On its slopes is a pleasant little village of the same name, worth checking out for its 17th-century church, leafy plaza, and laid-back vibe.

to stargaze and turtle-watch at night without any bugs to disturb your reverie. A sanctuary for turtles, La Tortuga Verde is also a peaceful haven for sun-seeking, surf-loving humans, with a yoga temple and the vast, golden sands of Playa Esteron to retreat to and contemplate. It is located 3km (1¾ miles) east of El Cuco.

Calle Pacifica, Playa El Esteron, La Union. www.latortugaverde.com; (C) **503/7774-4855.** 11 units. $20–$30 double; $50–$100 bungalow; $100–$150 casa. AE, DC, DISC, MC, V. Free parking. **Amenities:** Restaurant; bar; Jacuzzi; 2 pools. *In room:* A/C, TV, Wi-Fi.

Other Beaches

Farther east, you'll find the calm waters and uncrowded beaches of Playa Tamarindo. Tamarindo is nestled into a cove near the end of El Salvador's coast, which makes its ocean waters some of the calmest and best for swimming in the country. The area is also known for quality deep-sea fishing and its inhabited islands 1 hour off the coast.

Nearby is one of El Salvador's hidden gems: **Playa Maculis.** This 1.5km (1-mile) crescent-shaped beach is very private, with few houses and lot of trees. At either end, two rocky points jut out into the sea. This protects the waters from the lateral current that can be so dangerous on the Salvadorian coast. In addition, there are no rocks along the shore, so it is perfect for swimming. A few feet away from the tide is **Los Caracoles** (www.hotelsalvador.com; (C) **503/2335-1200**), a breezy four-bedroom house with a lovely round pool surrounded by wooden deck and a bar within arm's reach. Owned by the same proprietor who runs the famous Los Almendros de San Lorenzo in Suchitoto, this lovely little beach house is a little piece of paradise. The house can be rented in its entirety for $220 a night—a bargain, considering it sleeps eight and come with a housekeeper/cook.

Golfo de Fonseca

Now, you have reached the limits, a gorgeous bay with postcard-picture islands; fishing villages; and dark, volcanic beaches. Once a pirate hideout—there is an enduring legend that Sir Francis Drake buried his stolen loot here—the inlet is now shared with Honduras and Nicaragua, and has very little tourist infrastructure. El Salvador has sovereignty over just a handful of islands, the most important of which is Isla Meanguera. Here, there are no roads nor cars, and everybody travels by boat. There is one public boat a day from La Unión, so getting around is very difficult unless you pre-arrange everything with your hotel or go with a tour company such as La Ruta del Zapamiche ((C) **503/2228-1525;** www.larutadelzapamiche.com).

WHERE TO STAY AT GOLFO DE FONESCA

Hotel La Joya del Golfo ★ This three-story hacienda-style house sits on the shoreline, sparkling white amidst mirror-like waters and dense green foliage, with a row of white arches above a handsome wooden deck and private pier. La Joya del Golfo is definitely the best, and fair to say the only true, luxury property in the area. Rooms are large and decorated in muted tones with attractive paintings. They have two queen-size beds; high, coved ceilings; and large patio doors that lead out to a private balcony with panoramic views of the lush surroundings. The honeymoon suite holds an immense four-poster bed. There are fishing and diving excursions, and the catch of the day is served up any way you like it. An American owner means there is little in the way of language barriers. Rates are reasonable, but private boat transfers cost $60 one-way. The communal boat is possible, but leaves at ungodly hours.

Isla Meanguera. www.hotellajoyadelgolfo.com; ℰ **503/2648-0072.** 4 units. $79 double. AE, DC, DISC, MC, V. **Amenities:** Restaurant. *In room:* A/C, TV, no phone.

WESTERN EL SALVADOR

Go west, young man or woman, as that is where most of El Salvador's most interesting sites are to be seen. The west holds the country's most fascinating driving circuit—the Ruta de las Flores—a wonderful 36km (22-mile) drive along a scenic mountain highway winding through thousands of acres of coffee fields and exemplary El Salvadoran villages featuring weekend artisan and food festivals. Here, you can buy handicrafts amidst cobbled streets, or sip the finest coffee in manicured garden cafes, or indeed tour the very coffee farms the rich brew comes from. The Route of Flowers also has some of the country's best rural lodges and restaurants.

When you've had enough of sightseeing and shopping, it is time to get your feet dirty in the country's best national park, the wonderfully named El Imposible. Set in the rolling mountains that skirt the Guatemalan border, this huge national park offers hours of hiking through lush jungles, across streams, and beside picturesque waterfalls. Next to the park is the small village of Tacuba, which serves as a good base camp for park visits and venturing into what is all that is left of the country's original forest.

RUTA DE LAS FLORES ★★★
Hwy. CA-8, Km 72 to Km 107, starts 68km (42 miles) W of San Salvador

Ruta de las Flores, or Route of the Flowers, is a collection of five unique mountain villages along a winding, 35km (22-mile) scenic stretch of Hwy. CA-8 in the heart of El Salvador's coffee country. The route is known for the beauty of its flowering coffee plants and unique arts, crafts, and furniture markets. Highlights include the village of Nahuizalco and its hand-crafted furniture; Salcoatitán, with two of the route's more interesting restaurants; and Juayúa, which features the region's largest food and artisan festival, as well as a renowned black Christ statue. The route also includes the towns of Apaneca, known for its zip-line canopy tour, and Ataco, which is filled with some of the country's most unique art.

The towns along this route are a few kilometers apart, well marked, and only a short distance off the main highway. The highway itself also offers a few interesting hotels and restaurants. Though all five towns can be seen

RUTA DE LAS flores

Make sure you stock up on cash in Juayúa, which is the only town along the Ruta de las Flores with a bank machine. Most vendors and restaurants accept only cash in all five Ruta de las Flores towns. Internet access is available in Juayúa at **Nautilus Cyber** (Calle Merceditas Cáceres and 2a Av. Norte; *C* **503/2452-2343**) and in Ataco at **Cyber Nautica** (2a Calle Poniente, #5, Barrio Santa Lucia; *C* **503/2450-5719**). Small pharmacies are located in Juayúa near the main square.

in one long day or two, you might want to schedule a few days to properly take in the vibe of one of the country's most scenic and culturally unique regions.

Essentials

GETTING THERE

The first stop on the Ruta de las Flores, Nahuizalco, is 5km (3 miles) from Sonsonate and 68km (42 miles) from San Salvador. To get there from San Salvador, take bus no. 205 to Sonsonate followed by bus no. 249, 23, or 53d. Bus nos. 249 and 23 stop about 1km (½ mile) from the center of Nahuizalco but continue into the heart of each of the route's other villages. Bus no. 53d travels only between Sonsonate and Nahuizalco.

Each of the buses mentioned runs daily from roughly 5am to 6pm and costs between 25¢ and $1. The 205 bus from San Salvador runs about every 30 minutes, while the local buses come along about every 10 minutes.

It's easy to drive this route: Each of the towns along the way is just a few minutes off main Hwy. CA-8 and are very well marked.

GETTING AROUND

Bus nos. 249 and 23 will take you from just outside Nahuizalco to each of the route's small towns. Once in each town, you'll be able to walk to whatever you'd like to see, except for the few hotels and restaurants that are scattered along the main highway. Las Rutas does not offer any taxis, but taxi driver Israel Rodriguez (*C* **503/7734-7598**) in Sonsonate can take you from Sonsonate to Las Rutas and from town to town along the route for $15 to $25. Juayúa also offers three-wheeled moto-taxis, which you'll find along the square and which will take you anywhere in Juayúa for less than $1.

VISITOR INFORMATION

A national tourist office branch is located at Km 82, Carretera CA-8, Salcoatitan (*C* **503/2401-8675;** cat.rutasdelasflores@gmail.com). Tourist office staff speak only Spanish but offer some bilingual pamphlets and brochures about the area. Office hours are Monday to Friday from 8am to 4pm and Saturday and Sunday from 9am to 1pm.

Nahuizalco

Nahuizalco is the first stop on the Ruta de las Flores and offers one of the country's best furniture and wood-craft markets. Unlike most El Salvadoran markets, which sell Fernando Llort–inspired arts and crafts (see p. 255 for info), Nahuizalco's market, situated along the town's main road every weekend, is known for its unique wicker and

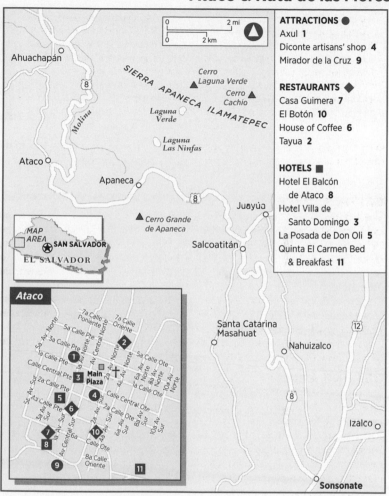

ATTRACTIONS ●
Axul **1**
Diconte artisans' shop **4**
Mirador de la Cruz **9**

RESTAURANTS ◆
Casa Guimera **7**
El Botón **10**
House of Coffee **6**
Tayua **2**

HOTELS ■
Hotel El Balcón
   de Ataco **8**
Hotel Villa de
   Santo Domingo **3**
La Posada de Don Oli **5**
Quinta El Carmen Bed
   & Breakfast **11**

19

WESTERN EL SALVADOR | Ruta de las Flores

wood furniture creations. Many of the wares sold at the weekend market can be found during the week in the shops also lining the main road. One of the best of those shops is Arte y Mueble, or Art and Furniture (© **503/2453-0125**). The shop's furniture is handcrafted by owner José Luis, whose creations are a mix of spare, modern lines and sturdier, dark-wood, nature-inspired designs. The store, which can arrange shipping around the world, is open Tuesday through Sunday from 10am to 5pm. Another shop worth checking out is Artesanías Cassal (© **503/2453-0939**; www.artecassal.com; daily 8am–6pm), which offers interesting wooden masks, jewelry, and art. Finally, about half a block before Nahuizalco's church and square, on the right, is a building with a large, open door, allowing passersby to watch artisans handcraft furniture.

SONSONATE

Sonsonate (65km/40 miles west of San Salvador) is mentioned here only because it is the largest city before the Ruta de las Flores, and you'll likely either bus through or catch a connecting bus from here in order to reach the Ruta de las Flores. Sonsonate is not a city you should visit for fun. It's crowded and just not that attractive. But it can be a good place to stock up on cash at the HSBC Bank or groceries at the large La Dispensa de Don Juan grocery store, both right on the main square.

If you find yourself with a few hours here while you're waiting for a bus, Sonsonate does have one redeeming quality—**Parque Acuatico Atecozol.** This is a huge water park located about 10 minutes (about a $5 taxi ride) out of the city with lots of shady gardenlike places to relax, a pool-side restaurant, a kids' pool, and the biggest public pool with a water slide I've seen in El Salvador. The park is open daily from 8am to 4pm and admission is 80¢.

Nahuizalco is 72km (45 miles) west of San Salvador and is well marked off the main highway. A single main road leads into town and terminates at Nahuizalco's small cathedral and square. The square offers a fountain, a few shady seating spots, and an English-language plaque that lists a short town history. Note that one of Nahuizalco's well-known attractions, the "candlelight market," no longer exists, at least, in its old form. Vendors added electric light bulbs to this market a few years ago and now sell mostly family necessities, so it's been rendered unworthy of a visit.

Salcoatitan

The second town along the Ruta de las Flores is also the route's smallest village. Though Salcoatitán is pleasant enough, there's no compelling reason to stop here; it takes about 30 seconds to drive through town, and Nahuizalco and Juayúa's weekend markets are larger and more interesting. About 2 blocks before Salcoatitán, however, is one of the route's more interesting restaurants, Los Patios.

Los Patios (Calle Principal, 2 blocks east of Salcoatitán; © **503/2401-8590**) is an upscale, modern, hacienda-style eatery. The restaurant's mountain-view patio overlooks thousands of coffee beans laid out to dry and the machinery used to process them. Los Patios is a bit pricier than other area eateries at roughly $12 an entree, but the food and ambience are worth the price. International dishes are given a modern Salvadoran twist. Try the milky *horchata* drink, made with ground *morro* seeds, cinnamon, and sesame seeds. The restaurant's owner is also a local abstract sculptor who displays and sells her work in a space beside the restaurant.

Juayúa

Next up is the Ruta de las Flores' largest, most bustling town, offering the region's longest-running weekend food and artisan festival, as well as mountain and coffee plantation tours. Juayúa is a good place to base your Ruta de las Flores stay, as it is roughly in the middle of the route and has hotels, restaurants, and a bank machine in addition to its attractions.

Each Saturday and Sunday, the large main plaza fills with locals and travelers enjoying daylong live music, dozens of artisan vendors, and a dozen or so food vendors who, for more than a decade, have been frying everything from *pupusas* to chicken tenders. It's a fun, family-friendly atmosphere worth planning your Ruta de las Flores trip around.

Juayúa is perhaps best known for its "Black Christ" statue, which sits above the altar of the **Iglesia de Cristo Negro** cathedral on the main square. Visually, the black Christ looks just like a regular Christ statue painted black. But the concept of the black Christ dates back hundreds of years and is revered throughout Central America via annual black Christ celebrations, including a Juayúa festival each January 6 to January 15. La Iglesia is open daily from 6am to noon and 2 to 6pm, and admission is free.

Guided tours based out of Juayúa take hikers through coffee plantations, past towering waterfalls—including the well-known Los Chorros de la Calera—and up to natural hot springs and geysers. Bring a bathing suit and prepare to get muddy (the mud at the hot springs is supposed to be good for the skin). Tours usually leave early in the morning, range from 5 to 7 hours, and cost $7 to $20. For tour information, visit **Hotel Anáhuac** (1a Calle Poniente and 5a Av. Norte; ℂ **503/2469-2401; www.hotelanahuac.com**).

WHERE TO STAY IN JUAYUA

Casa Mazeta Hostal This yellow and brown corner house acts as both a funky lodge and an atmospheric hostel. It has only four rooms, one of which is a dorm. With its communal kitchen, TV room, big garden, and huge laundry room, Casa Mazeta is geared for the young, independent traveler. High ceilings, dark wood furnishings, traditional tiled floors, and arty fixtures such as pewter relief doors make this place stand out from the average hostel. One small room out the back even has its own powerful fountain. It might not be as spic and span as the Hotel Anáhuac 4 blocks away, but it certainly has character at a great price (there's also laundry service here for just $3). Useful practical touches are the big rucksack-sized lockers in the dorm and the giant garage that can be used for secure parking.

1a Calle Ote, at 2a Av Norte. hostalcasamazeta@gmail.com; ℂ **503/2406-3403.** 4 units. $10 per person. $30 double. No credit cards. Free parking. **Amenities:** Kitchen, lockers, laundry service. *In room:* Fan, Wi-Fi (free) TV.

Hotel Anáhuac ★★ ✔ ⛄ This well-designed little corner house offers a laidback, hostel-style environment with a classy, boutique hotel touch. It has two dorm rooms and four superbly decorated private rooms, plus a communal kitchen. Bright yellow walls and hip, artistic murals set the tone, along with an overgrown garden courtyard highlighted with wood sculptures and hammocks. The rooms are medium size, brightly lit with skylights in the bathrooms, and decorated with excellent local art. (I stayed in the sculpture room and wanted to take several pieces home with me.) All the rooms open out onto the courtyard, and overall, the hotel has a cozy, earthy feel. The young owners Cesar and Janne are warm and welcoming, speak perfect English, can organize tours, and have lots of information about the route and surrounding areas.

1a Calle Poniente & 5a Av. Norte. www.hotelanahuac.com; ℂ **503/2469-2401.** 6 units. $7 dorm bed; $25 double. AE DC MC V. Free parking. **Amenities**: Wi-Fi. *In room:* Fan, no phone.

Hotel y Restaurante El Mirador Rooms here are basic, but comfortable and efficient, with brightly colored walls and private baths. All have tile floors and face out onto a courtyard. Overall, the hotel is clean and comfortable, and it is just off the main square—you can't miss its bright blue and yellow facade. Perhaps Mirador's best features are its friendly staff and its airy, top-floor, glass-enclosed sitting and dining areas, which have incredible views of the surrounding countryside and distant volcanoes.

4a Calle Poniente, on the left as you enter town. www.elmiradorjuayua.com; (© **503/2452-2432.** 19 units. $28 double. AE, DC, DISC, MC, V. Free parking. **Amenities:** Restaurant; Wi-Fi. *In room:* Fan, TV.

Posada El Encanto With its brick and cream-colored walls, this small hotel looks like a well-to-do residential home done in faux colonial style. It certainly has a neat suburban feel, with tile floors and white walls that lead to a tiny garden out back. The rooms are a decent size, with solid dark wood furniture and wardrobes, and not a dreaded white plastic garden chair in sight. All the rooms have private bathrooms, and everything is well done and maintained, but compared to Hotel Anáhuac, it's a decent, if bland, and relatively expensive second choice. The hotel is located 6 blocks east of the main plaza on the road to Santa Ana. Don't confuse it with the same-name establishment on the opposite side of the road; a sprawling restaurant, event venue, and pool area with the same owners, but unfortunately open only weekends (guests, however, have access to the pool).

Colonia La Esmeralda 7677, Juayúa. (© **503/2452-2187.** 8 units. $32 single; $50 double. Rates include breakfast. No credit cards. Free parking. **Amenities:** Pool; Wi-Fi. *In room:* A/C (in some), fan, TV.

WHERE TO EAT IN JUAYA

Among the better places to eat in Juayúa is Restaurante R&R (2 blocks off the main square at Calle Merceditas Cáceres No. 1–2; (© **503/2452-2083**). English-speaking El Salvadoran chef Carlos Cáceres has created a little Louisiana-style steak house in the midst of the El Salvadoran mountains, and the menu features spicy takes on Tequila-, Texas-, and New Orleans–style steaks. The Texas steak is amazing. A veggie plate is also available, and most items are $3.50 to $10. Parque Restaurante La Colina (Km 82 Carretera a Juayúa; (© **503/2452-2916**) is outside the town but worth the visit, as it offers excellent—and hard to find—fajitas, along with other Mexican dishes and a host of grilled fish and meat dishes. Most entrees are $4.50 to $9.50. A lovely little find is Tienda San José (2a Calle Pte.; (© **503/2479-2349**) on the northeastern corner of the main plaza. It looks like a normal shop piled high with toiletries, until you turn left as you enter and find an old world salon with pre-revolution decoration (pick which revolution) and sunflower-themed knickknacks. It's dark, but it has a cluttered charm and, more importantly, an excellent window table overlooking the color and chaos of the plaza outside. Popular with locals, the menu offers ribs, ribs, and more ribs, with some rice and salad added for variety. Main courses range from $3 to $5. El Cadejo (Av. Daniel Cordon Norte and 1a Calle Ote.; (© **503/73527470**) is a funky, garage style bar and restaurant that spills out onto the street Thursday to Sunday from 3pm to late. Live music, theater, and poetry make this colorful little venue the bohemian center of Juayúa. The bar is decorated with local art, but don't criticize too loudly, as the barman is probably one of the painters. He'll serve you snacks and occasionally hard-to-get sushi. If you're here to drink, try the raspberry mojitos.

Apaneca

Continuing down CA-8 to Km 91, you'll find the small village of Apaneca, which is surrounded by hills of flowering coffee plants and has become best known in the last couple of years for its high-wire, zip-line canopy tour. Information about Apaneca can

LA MATANZA

The picturesque landscape of the Ruta de las Flores belies a horrific past and one of the most tragic episodes in El Salvadoran history—a peasant rebellion and its brutal repression known as *La Matanza* or the Slaughter.

In 1932, the indigenous *Pipil* tribe had much to be unhappy about. They had been robbed of their ancestral lands and indentured onto coffee farms as de facto slaves. A military coup by Maximiliano Hernández Martínez and the blatant electoral fraud that followed meant their voices would not be heard by legitimate means. The country was ruled by 30 powerful families who regarded the local tribes with suspicion and outright racism. The collapse of the price in coffee and the mass unemployment that followed only exacerbated the problem, and the situation was ripe for both indigenous and communist agitation. On the night of January 22, 1932, peasant groups took over several towns in the area, including Sonsonate, where the mayor was killed. Initially successful, the rebellion soon petered out, and Martínez sent in heavily armed troops to stamp out the uprising. What followed was a systematic manhunt that can only be described as genocide. Thirty thousand locals were slaughtered, including the Indian leader Feliciano Ama, who was publicly hanged from an olive tree in the town plaza of Izalco, and the communist leader Agustín Farabundo Martí was executed in prison. In some villages, all males over the age of 12 were killed. Neighbors turned on neighbors, and local Catholic priests singled out communist sympathizers to be arrested and killed.

Such horrific events were buried in the nation's official history for nearly 50 years. The trauma and fear the event created virtually wiped out the *Pipil* as a people, and survivors abandoned their style of dress, customs, and rituals so as not to attract attention from the authorities. *La Matanza* silenced political dissent for 50 years, until it exploded once again in the late 1970s in the form of the Farabundo Martí National Liberation Front, a rebel alliance inspired by the slain leader of the Matanza.

be found at the local Casa de la Cultura (Av. 15 de Abril Sur and Calle Francisco Manendez Oriente, Barrio San Pedro; ☏ 503/2433-0163).

Apaneca Canopy Tours (Av. 15 de Abril and Calle Central; ☏ 503/2433-0554), which has an office in the center of town, offers 1-hour and 1½-hour zip-line tours, where you zip on steel cables hundreds of feet off the ground, over lush forests and a nearby coffee plantation. The company offers 13 cables that are roughly 1,800m (5,906 ft.) above sea level; its longest cable stretches 280m (919 ft.), and the highest is 125m (410 ft.) off the ground. During April and May, coffee flowering season, thousands of white coffee flowers cover the fields below the tour; and in January and February, or harvest season, the flowers are replaced by bright, red berries. All year round, tour participants can see all the way to Guatemala's active Pacaya Volcano from the highest perch. Also included in the tour is a half-hour walk through a local coffee plantation, during which an English-speaking guide explains the elements of the coffee plant and the growing process. The canopy tour even includes some locally grown brew to cap off your experience.

Tours are $30 and leave from the tour office Tuesday through Sunday at 9:30 and 11:30am, and 3 and 7pm from June through October and are offered daily from

November through May. It's best to make a reservation in advance, but you can also just show up at the times stated above to see if you can get a spot. Off-road **motorcycle and bicycling tours** can also be arranged through Apaneca Canopy Tours.

WHERE TO STAY IN APANECA

Hotel y Restaurante Las Cabañas   This lovely, 15-cabin hotel is owned by the same artist owner as Salcoatitlán's Los Patios restaurant (see above), and she has applied the same artistic eye for detail here to create a lush, secluded, garden setting dotted with individual cabins with shady front patios. The cabins themselves are simple, without an overarching design theme except bold colors and log wood trimmings. They are slightly larger than average and very comfortable. Las Cabañas is on Hwy. CA-8 and just a few blocks' walk from the Apaneca town center. Its hillside location affords lovely views of the green valley below, and the excellent restaurant has a handsome interior with wide, arched windows. It serves Salvadoran and international food, with the focus on quality imported beef and homegrown vegetables and fruit.

Km 91 Hwy. CA-8, Apaneca. www.cabanasapaneca.com; ✆ **503/2433-0500.** 15 units. $52 double. Rates include breakfast. AE, DC, DISC, MC, V. **Amenities:** Restaurant. *In room:* Fan, TV, no phone.

Santa Leticia Mountain Resort ★   Situated 2km (1¼ miles) south of Apaneca, Santa Leticia Mountain Resort is a luxurious 19-room hotel and a 93-hectare (230-acre) coffee plantation. A large log-cabin facade with chunky wooden porch leads to a large, atmospheric restaurant with funky colored rooms out back and eight stand-alone bungalows. Rooms are spacious and cheerful, with multicolored fabrics; wrought-iron beds; and small, private bathrooms. The rooms open out onto a charming gallery with spindly, tree-trunk pillars and roof rafters. Two solar-powered pools are center stage, and the cozy restaurant boasts all glass walls and a stone fireplace. The bungalows are larger and more private, with shaded porch areas and hammocks. In addition to offering coffee tours of the nearby farm, there is a fascinating collection of pre-Colombian relics, such as 2,000-year-old stone sculptures, throughout the property.

Km 86.5 Hwy. CA-8, just outside Apaneca. www.hotelsantaleticia.com; ✆ **503/2433-0357** or 503/2298-2986. 19 units. $58 double; $68 cabin. AE, DC, DISC, MC, V. **Amenities:** Restaurant; children's playground; two pools. *In room:* Fan, TV.

Ataco ★★★

Ataco is my favorite stop along the Ruta de las Flores—it has an artistic style and vibe you really won't find elsewhere in the country.

The first thing you may notice about Ataco is the unique, fantastical murals of surreal animals with big eyes and wild hair painted on some of the town's buildings. These whimsical murals set the tone for the town and are the work of young married artists Cristina Pineda and Alvaro Orellana. Their designs, also available on wood, ceramic, and traditional canvas in Ataco's shops, are unlike artwork you'll see anywhere else in El Salvador. The couple's main gallery is called **Axul** (1a Calle Poniente and 1a Av. Norte #5; ✆ **503/2450-5030**) and is just off the main square. The shop is marked by a fanciful mural on the outside and offers the couple's signature surreal style in various formats. You can chat with Pineda and Orellana, and watch other artists at work in the back of the shop daily from 9am to 6pm.

Another of Ataco's attractions is the **Diconte artisans' shop** (2 Av. Norte and Calle Central Oriente #8; ✆ **503/2450-5030;** ring the doorbell to enter the shop on weekdays), which is part art shop, part textile mill, and part dessert bistro. Diconte

A garden OF EARTHLY DELIGHTS

Just 4km (2½ miles) before Ataco as you drive north from Apaneca, you will come across a little slice of Eden known as **Entre Nubes** (Km 94; © **503/2452-9643;** www.entrenubescafe.com). This garden restaurant (the name means "amidst the clouds") makes for the perfect coffee stop as you immerse yourself in the glories of Salvadoran nature. The owner's son, Daniel, is a trained agronomist, speaks perfect English, and is happy to give a 20-minute walking tour of the 1.6-hectare (4-acre) hillside property. Paths covered with freshly cut cypress leaves lead you through lines of tall hardwood trees known as *gravileo* that shade coffee plants and big blue explosions of hortensia. You can pick fruit from the orange, lemon, and mandarin trees; see where avocados and plantains come from; and emulate hummingbirds as you sip nectar from a yellow bell-like flower known as *thumbergia*, all the while listening to Daniel's enthusiastic and enlightening explanation of the lifecycle of each plant, animal, and insect around you. At the end of the tour is a homegrown coffee tasting and demonstration. Entre Nubes is open every day from 8am to 6:30pm. Meals cost between $3.50 and $8, and all credit cards are accepted. Tours are free, but call ahead if you are in a large group. The roadside restaurant is located on the right-hand side just after the Autogas station as you go north towards Ataco.

offers five rooms of whimsical woodcarvings, paintings, and other crafts in the unique Ataco style, as well as a room of colorful textiles made on-site by artisans working five old-style looms. Visitors can watch the textile artisans at work from Diconte's garden-style dessert and coffee shop.

If you want to take a break from art shopping, hike up to the town's **Mirador de la Cruz.** The Mirador is a mountain overlook located a 15-minute hike from the main square. To get there, walk 5 blocks south from the church along 2a Avenida Norte, which becomes 2a Avenida Sur after crossing Calle Central. Continue walking until the road bends to the right. At the bend is a Catholic church, behind which are steps to the overlook. At the end of the steps, turn right, walk through an opening in the fence, and follow the trail to the cross that marks the top of the hill. The hike up to the top is steep but paved, and you'll be rewarded with a great view, some benches to relax on, and a small plaque with information (in English) about Ataco.

WHERE TO STAY & EAT IN ATACO

Ataco booms on the weekend with locals coming from the capital and Sonsonante. For this reason, many hotels and restaurants are open on weekends only. Hotel Villa de Santo Domingo (1 Av. Norte, #6 in front of the Casa de la Cultura; © **503/2450-5242**) is a good midrange choice offering an 11-room hacienda-style hotel around a main courtyard with a small restaurant and comfortable $25-to-$35 rooms. On Friday and Saturday only, you can also stay at the well-known, but slightly overrated La Posada de Don Oli (www.la-posada-de-don-oli.blogspot.com; 1a Av. Sur #6; © **503/2450-5155**). This half–private home and half-hotel has a restaurant and three standard rooms ($28 per night) set around a courtyard. Ask for one of the upstairs rooms with a balcony for the best deal.

COFFEE republic

In 1856, 693 bags of coffee were first exported from El Salvador. A century later, it was 3.5 million. No other country in the region became so dependent on the *golden grain* for its income. In 1920, 90% of the country's export earnings came from coffee, earning it the sobriquet *the Coffee Republic*.

Such overdependence on one commodity has its obvious financial dangers, yet the repercussions of El Salvador's chronic coffee habit run deeper than one can imagine and have had a tortuous effect on its destiny. The coffee boom created a small elite of coffee barons who ruled huge tracts of land, the military, and the presidency for most of the 20th century. Coffee laws outlawed and expropriated communal Indian lands and criminalized vagrancy, ensuring an abundant, impoverished, and subsistent labor force. All infrastructure—such as roads, rails, and ports—was planned around the industry. Civil strife, such as *La Matanza* and the FMLN rising, all have roots in a dissatisfied rural workforce, so much so that the rebels often imposed wage controls and war taxes on farm owners to gain local support. Right-wing deaths squads retaliated by undermining attempted land reform in the 1980s and attacking cooperatives and small holders. It got so bad human rights groups campaigned against consuming Salvadoran coffee and labeled it *Death Squad Coffee*. Add to this the fact that El Salvador had a poor reputation for producing low-grade commercial beans, and you wonder how the industry survived at all.

But survive it has, and the green shoots of a coffee renaissance have been sprouting up in recent years. Forty percent of producers are now small holders or cooperatives, and many are producing higher-standard, organic coffees. Incentives such as the Fair Trade coffee mean the farmer may not be as exposed to the ravages of the market as before. Conditions such as soil, altitude, and climate are almost perfect, and highly regarded bean varietals such as *Bourbon* and *Pacamara* are attracting caffeine aficionados from around the world. The war's impediment to modernization has actually proved a good thing, with many plantations remaining as prized shade farms, rather than monocultured fields. As well as making better coffee, such forested plantations provide badly needed habitat for wildlife, and the fact that 15% of El Salvadoran land is coffee plantation somewhat mitigates the disastrous deforestation and soil erosion the country has suffered elsewhere.

Finally, such great beans and beautiful surroundings mean coffee farms are attracting the coffee tourist in search of the perfect cup and a glimpse of nature. Coffee farms are opening up and offering instructive tours of the facilities that finish with a delicious tasting. Many are also providing delightful coffee lodge accommodations. Some of the best such places can be found along the Ruta de las Flores. **Santa Leticia Coffee Estate** (www.hotelsantaleticia.com) is a pioneer in this respect. A large yellow truck takes guests and day-trippers around the property, where they pick the red berries and watch the drying process turn them into golden-brown nuts. **El Carmen Estate** (www.elcarmenestate.com) is another such coffee farm offering tours and a chance to stay in a beautiful country villa. **La Escondida Lodge** (www.akwaterra.com) is another coffee-themed guesthouse, part of Portozuelo coffee farm and a park close to Apaneca.

Hotel y Restaurante El Balcón de Ataco ★ This small, six-room guesthouse is perched on the side of a hill high above town, with room-front balconies offering long-range views of the town and surrounding mountains. The hotel opened in 2007, and the rooms have a modern, though somewhat bare, feel. They are, however, unusually sunny and have in-room Wi-Fi. El Balcón is a decent second choice if El Carmen B&B is full.

8a Calle Oriente & Calle el Naranjito. elbalcondeataco@gmail.com; ✆ **503/2450-5171.** 6 units. $35–$45 double. Rates include full breakfast. AE, DC, DISC, MC, V. **Amenities:** Restaurant. *In room:* TV, no phone, Wi-Fi (free).

Quinta El Carmen Bed & Breakfast ★ This low, red-brick villa surrounded by lush gardens makes for a luxurious and interesting stay, not just because of its delightful design, but also because it has an adjacent coffee farm and charming restaurant. Large rattan armchairs sit on a tiled patio that leads to well-appointed rooms with white walls and dark wooden rafters. An inviting living room is next to an elegant dining room with indigenous handicrafts and textiles hanging on walls and sitting on shelf spaces. The rooms are ample, with lots of light, adjoining bathrooms, and well-equipped kitchenettes. The restaurant serves burgers and pupusas, and of course, excellent coffee. Coffee tours are available. The entrance is on the right as you travel north to Ahuachapan and is a 15 minute walk from the town plaza.

Km 97, Ataco. www.elcarmenestate.com; ✆ **503/2243-0304.** 4 units. $62 double; $93 suite. Rates include breakfast. AE, DC, DISC, MC, V. **Amenities:** Restaurant. *In room:* TV, no phone, Wi-Fi.

WHERE TO EAT IN ATACO

One big reason Ataco is my top Ruta de las Flores pick is its unique restaurants. However, like the hotels here, many restaurants and bars are open only on weekends. Those listed below are open all week.

Casa Guimera ★ ☺ This low, cream-colored building used to be the well-respected Hostal Alepac before the owner fell in love and ran off with a Dutch backpacker. Now, it has reincarnated itself as one of the finest dining experiences in Ataco, a lovely little two-roomed Spanish eatery with hundreds of tiny photos of very satisfied customers lining the walls, while a Spanish galleon sails overhead and a grandfather clock ticks in the corner. Time indeed passes quickly here as you work through delicious 224g (8-oz.) steaks, a variety of tapas, and a selection of wines from the vineyards of faraway La Rioja. Montse, the Spanish owner, speaks decent English, and there's a children's play area here. This cozy place is located next to the gorgeous white-domed chapel Iglesia El Calvara, 3 blocks west from the town entrance.

Secunda Av. Sur Final. ✆ **503/2406-6312;** www.casaguimera.webs.tl. Main courses $7–$10. No credit cards. Tues–Fri 10am–9pm; Sat 8am–10pm; Sun 8am–5pm.

El Botón ★ This utterly charming little French restaurant features a rare-in–El Salvador find of quiche and crêpes, along with empanadas, coffee, and beer. The decor could best be described as whimsical, with a tiny corner counter that also functions as a multi-colored button display. Primary-color furniture and flower-decorated shelves complete the picture. El Botón is certainly one of the most distinctive restaurants in El Salvador and comes alive on Saturday night with live music.

2a Av. Sur No. 19. ✆ **503/2450-5066.** Main courses $7–$10. AE DC MC V. Wed–Mon 10am–8pm; Sat 8am–11pm.

The House of Coffee ★ With its slate-gray walls, arty black-and-white photos, and dark leather seating, the House of Coffee is an island of style in a rugged, rural hamlet. Its moniker is to be taken seriously, with the focus of this hip cafe firmly on just that – café. The Escalon family has been growing coffee since the 1880s, and this store is a showroom for their passion. A glass partition with heaped beans inside overlooks a pleasant courtyard, in the corner of which is a stainless steel coffee roaster that produces 20 varieties of coffee. (Their Café Pacamara recently won the Oscar of coffee awards known as the Cup of Excellence.) In addition to hot coffee, cold coffee, and frozen cappuccinos, there are also waffles, crêpes, brownies, and crème brûlée. Note: There is a sister establishment in San Salvador at Plaza Futuro, in front of the Crowne Plaza.

Av. Central 13. ✆ **503/2450 5353;** thoc@hotmail.el. Snacks $2.50. AE, DC, MC, V. Tues–Sun 9am–7pm.

Tayua   The menu is small but surprising here, with a focus on gourmet sandwiches, salads, and pastas served in a cool Asian-style space. Standout items include the El Democratico sandwich, with mushrooms and Gruyère cheese on a baguette, and the El Variado—perhaps El Salvador's tastiest sandwich—with Black Forest ham, salami, and Gouda on a baguette.

Av. Central Norte No. 31. No phone. Main courses $4–$8. AE, DC, MC, V. Sun–Fri 10am–8pm; Sat 8am–11pm.

WHERE TO STAY OUTSIDE ATACO

Hotel Alicante ☺   Hotel Alicante is unbeatable when it comes to amenities. It offers a big Jacuzzi and sauna, exercise room, and massage service, along with an elaborate outdoor pool, all spread out through a property of lush lawns, trees, and flowerbeds. A series of cabins and larger outhouses feature tin roofs, varnished log walls, and rock pillars. The rooms are plain but cheerful (each has two double beds), and the two cabins on the property have compact kitchens and living areas, as well as private patios. It's excellent for families, with a playground and an elaborate pool with island bridge and waterfall. There is also a rather large, alpine-style restaurant. Though it has nice views, the hotel is close to the highway and lacks a little of the tranquility you'll find in other lodges in the area, such as Santa Leticia.

Km 93.3 Carretera CA-8, btw. Juayúa & Ataco. www.alicanteapaneca.com; ✆ **503/2433-0572.** 28 units. $70 double; $150 cabin. Rates include breakfast. AE, DC, DISC, MC, V. Free parking. **Amenities:** Restaurant; health club; Jacuzzi; sauna. In room: Fan, TV, no phone.

El Jardín de Celeste ★ 🔥   The best value and most beautifully situated stay along the CA-8 highway is this small, 10-cabin hotel and restaurant 4km (2½ miles) east of Ataco. This beautiful complex is part lodge, part plant nursery and is set up like a secret garden, with log-style cabins spread among winding, flower-filled paths. The three- to five-person cabins include front porches with hammocks; barbecue grills; and depending on the cabin, kitchens, dining rooms, and living rooms. All are rather simply furnished, with white walls, tiled floors and the occasional painting or textile. The suite is especially nice, with a fine 4-poster bed draped in lace curtains. Flowers adorn every corner, including a handsome restaurant with carved doors, old elaborate pillars, nice wood furnishings, and an international menu.

Km 94, btw. Apaneca & Ataco. www.eljardindeceleste.com; ✆ **503/2433-0277** or 503/2433-0281. 10 units. $40–$63 cabin. $85 suite. AE, DC, DISC, MC, V. Free parking. **Amenities:** Restaurant. In room: TV, no phone.

Las Flores de Eloisa   Lovely little cabins set amidst lush gardens seem to be the main theme with hotels in the area. It is no surprise, then, when you find out that Las Flores de Eloisa belongs to the same family as El Jardín de Celeste just down the road. Again, you have a plant nursery acting as the grounds, hiding several cabins with simple and attractive furnishings. The bungalows have lots of space, with two separate rooms, bathrooms, and solid beds. The property also operates a little garden cafe serving lunch and dinner.

Km 92.5, btw. Apaneca & Ataco. www.eljardindeceleste.com; ©**503/2433-0415** or 503/2433-0277. 7 units. $39 cabin. $47 bungalow. AE, DC, DISC, MC, V. Free parking. **Amenities:** Restaurant. *In room:* TV, no phone.

Ahuachapan

Like Sonsonate, Ahuachapán (44km/27 miles west of Sonsonate and 16km/10 miles off the route's main CA-8 highway) is technically part of the Ruta de las Flores, but as the busy capital of this department, it is more a place to grab some cash or check your e-mail before heading elsewhere, rather than a destination in its own right. Ahuachapán is, however, known for its high level of geothermal activity, and visitors here can tour nearby Los Ausoles, a multi-acre gathering of gurgling, steaming pits of superheated mud and water, as well as check out the inside of a nearby power plant that transforms that subterranean heat into electricity. Eco Mayan Tours (Paseo General Escalón 3658, Colonia Escalón, San Salvador; © **503/2298-2844;** www.ecomayantours.com) provides tours to the pits—including a chance to roast corn on the cob over them—and a tour of the plant. Tours are $30 from Ahuachapán or $75 to and from San Salvador.

Unlike Sonsonate, there are also some sights to see right in town. **Plaza Concordia** (3a Calle Poniente, btw. Av. Menéndez and 4a Norte) is the more pleasant of the city's two plazas, which are just 5 blocks apart on the main street, Avenida Menéndez. Concordia Plaza is home to Ahuachapán's plain, main cathedral, **Nuestra Señora La Asunción,** which is known for its interesting stained-glass windows (I don't think they're that spectacular, though). The other main church in town, **Iglesia El Calvario,** is 5 blocks down from the Plaza Concordia on Avenida Menéndez and sports a similarly spartan exterior to the Nuestra Señora.

Most buses arrive and depart town from a crowded section of 10a Calle Oriente, a few minutes' moto-taxi ride from Plaza Concordia. A **Scotiabank** is at Avenida Menéndez and 4 Calle Poniente, and there's Internet access at **Ciber Café Cetcomp** (2a Av. Sur, at 1a Calle Poniente; © **503/2413-3753**).

PARQUE NACIONAL EL IMPOSIBLE★★ & TACUBA

If the mists clear, you can see all the way to Guatemala from the lookout points perched above El Salvador's most splendid park with the most wonderful name. Parque Nacional El Imposible has some unbelievable beauty and makes a brave attempt at making up for all the lost nature the rest of the country has suffered. Green, rugged hills hold gurgling streams, fern-lined waterfalls, moss-draped caves, and Maya petroglyphs. Abundant with birdlife and animal life, old coffee farms have become forests again, and fragrant flowers and pink mushrooms border the park's trails and eight rivers. Only 2 hours west of the capital, the park has two official entrances, on its southern and western borders, though you might find it more convenient to enter by the northern back door through the sleepy town of Tacuba, at the extreme end of the Ruta de las Flores circuit.

Tacuba

60km (37 miles) W of Sonsonate; 100km (62 miles) W of San Salvador

Tacuba is a small town in far western El Salvador that hugs the edge of the 3,278-hectare (8,100-acre) Parque Nacional El Imposible and serves as base camp for treks into the park. In addition to boasting great views of the surrounding mountains and volcanoes, and a pretty central plaza, Tacuba has a number of tiendas to keep you stocked up on food and drink, and happy after a long day's hike. Until recently, this area had very few tourists, however, and it's still slowly developing its infrastructure. Currently, there are no banks or ATMs, and only a handful of viable lodging options, so plan your accommodations in advance and bring all the cash you'll need.

GETTING THERE & GETTING AROUND

Buses coming to Tacuba from around El Salvador first feed into nearby Ahuachapán, where you can then catch bus no. 264 or one of the many buses with TACUBA written across the top. The trip takes 40 minutes and costs 60¢. You'll be dropped off near Tacuba's town square. From San Salvador to Ahuachapán, take bus no. 202 ($1.10; 2¼ hr.); from Santa Ana to Ahuachapán, take bus no. 210 (50¢; 1¼ hr.); and from Sonsonate to Ahuachapán, take bus no. 249 ($1; 2 hr.).

From San Salvador, you can drive Carretera Panamericana (the Pan-American Highway) in the north or CA-8 along the Ruta de las Flores in the south to the town of Ahuachapán. In Ahuachapán, look for Parque Concordia and the white church there, where you'll see a sign directing you onto the road for Tacuba. The drive from Ahuachapán takes about 30 minutes.

Tacuba is a very small town, and most everything is within a short walk of the main square.

VISITOR INFORMATION

Tacuba does not have a tourist office, so the best source of information is local English-speaking guide Manolo Gonzales (see below under Tour Operators) If you speak Spanish, information is also available at Tacuba's Casa de la Cultura (1a Calle Oriente and Av. España, 1 block south of the Alcaldía; © **503/2417-4453**).

Tacuba

Tacuba has no banks or ATMs, so bring cash. However, Tacuba's main street, Avenida Cuscatlán Sur, south of the square, offers a few small *tiendas* and shops with signs reading CIBER, where there are a few Internet-access computer stations.

TOUR OPERATORS

Since there is no official northern entrance to the park, it's easiest to go with Tacuba's well-known, English-speaking guide, Manolo Gonzales. Manolo is the owner of Imposible Tours (Av. Cuscatlán near Calle 10, Tacuba; © **503/2417-4268;** www.imposibletours.com) and the son of the owners of Hostal de Mama y Papa (see below). Manolo offers 6- to 8-hour day and night tours into the park for $20 per person, including the entrance fee. His most popular tour is an 8-hour waterfall tour, which involves hiking for hours deep into the jungle and jumping from waterfalls ranging from 2 to 12m (6½–39 ft.) in height. On this tour, you'll have to jump or be lowered down the highest waterfall, in addition to taking part in hours of rigorous hiking. Note: If you're out of shape or afraid of heights, the tour may not be for you.

Manolo offers an easier $20 coffee plantation and hot springs tour in which you witness the entire coffee cultivation process from field to factory, or bean to cup, and then head into the mountains to spend the afternoon soaking in hot springs. There's also a 2-day bicycle tour, where participants are driven to the highest point in the park

Parque Nacional El Imposible

ATTRACTIONS ●
Centro de Visitantes Mixtepe **1**
Park Entrance **2**

HOTELS ■
El Imposible Eco Lodge **3**

and ride bicycles down through the jungle all the way to the Pacific Ocean. The rock-bottom $55 cost includes round-trip transportation from Tacuba, dinner and drinks at the beach, breakfast and lunch, and a kayak tour, along with stops at some towns along the Ruta de las Flores. Other tours include a night animal-watching tour and a tour in which you're driven to the park's highest point before hiking down to a natural swimming pool. Try to call at least 2 days in advance to schedule tours.

Exploring Parque Nacional el Imposible ★★

Parque Imposible is one of El Salvador's most and diverse forests and should be a definite stop for nature lovers. The 3,278-hectare (8,100-acre) park derives its name from its challenging terrain and once-dangerous gorge, which for years claimed the lives of men and mules who traversed the area transporting coffee crops to the south. The animals had to be blindfolded, so terrifying was the crossing, with a narrow ridge and a drop of 3,000m (9,843 ft.) on either side. A bridge was built over the gorge in the 1960s and celebrated with a plaque declaring May 1968—No Longer Impossible. The forest was declared a national park in 1989. Today, the park is home to more than 400 types of trees, 275 species of birds, and hundreds of species of butterflies. Pumas, wild pigs, and some 100 other types of mammals, many on the endangered species list, make their home in the park, along with more than 50 kinds of reptiles and amphibians. In addition to enjoying ample opportunities to spot wildlife, visitors can easily spend days hiking trails through the thick forests, swimming in the natural pools, and jumping off the waterfalls here.

Park admission is $6 per person. All visitors must first register with park administrator **SalvaNatura** (33 Av. Sur, #640, Colonia Flor Blanca, San Salvador; © **503/2279-1515;** www.salvanatura.org) to secure a guide and get permission to enter the park. SalvaNatura also offers $10-per-day Spanish-language guides and $40 day trips from San Salvador including transportation, a Spanish-speaking guide, and entrance fee.

The official park entrance is on the park's south side, near the community of San Benito. To enter from the south, beginning in Sonsonate, catch bus no. 24-HAS to Cara Sucia. In Cara Sucia, you can catch a $1 pickup ride for the remaining 45 minutes to the park. The pickups leave Cara Sucia at 6:30, 8, and 10am, and 12:30 and 2:30pm. They leave the park to return to Cara Sucia at 7, 9, and 11am, noon, and 2pm. You can also make the drive yourself, but the road is very bumpy and requires a four-wheel-drive or truck with good ground clearance. There is a new entrance farther west at San Francisco Menéndez, the turnoff for which is 5km (3 miles) west of Cara Sucia.

Centro de Visitantes Mixtepe   Located 100m (328 ft.) inside the San Benito entrance, this old wooden house has been restored and turned into a simple museum and solar-powered interpretation center. The colorful rooms hold the park's administration office and are where you go to pick up your guide to show you around the park. There are some display cases explaining the park's different facets, as well as a very barebones gift store and bookshop. A lookout post gives you a sense of place, with the Pacific and Guatemala in the distance. It is not necessarily a place you want to hang around in too long, as all the interesting stuff is outside in the forest, though you will be thankful for the restrooms.

San Benito Entrance, Parque Nacional El Imposible. www.salvanatura.org. No phone. Free admission.

TRAILS WITHIN PARQUE IMPOSIBLE

Guides are obligatory and will be assigned to you at the visitor center. The three main trails are not too difficult, and it is possible to switch and combine. A $10 tip per group to the guide is customary, as they receive no salary. The easiest trek is to Mirador El Mulo, a lookout point with lovely views of the Río Guayapa Valley. The 1km (.6-mile) trail is sign-posted with displays explaining the local flora and fauna. You pass a river source and the old coffee plantations now replaced by forest. Farther past Mirador Mulo, there is another viewing point called Mirador Madre Cacao. The trail then drops drastically towards a beautiful river pool called Los Enganches, approximately 3.5km (2.2 miles) from the trail start. Back up the hill on the trail that passed Mirador Madre Cacao, the path continues upriver for 1km (.6 mile) until you reach a waterfall and pool. Here, you'll find a carved stone known as Piedra Sellada, adorned with Mayan script that dates from A.D. 1500. The trail to Cerro El León is the most ambitious, with a steep 4km (2.5-mile) hike to the park's tallest mountain at 1,113m (3,562 ft.). The trail leaves from the visitor's center and descends into a jungle gorge before emerging on the other side through a dense forest to the peak, which, needless to say, has some beautiful panoramic views.

Where to Eat in Tacuba

El Restaurante de Mamá y Papá ★ 🍴 SALVADORAN   This small, laidback joint, half a block or so from the hostel of the same name, has no written menu, but Mamá has the ingredients to fix you up pretty much whatever comfort food you crave. For lunch or dinner, usually she'll prepare a variety of roasted chicken with French fries or tacos, hamburgers, or hot dogs for around $5. For breakfast, she might cook you a big omelet with whatever veggies are available that day, or a large traditional breakfast of eggs, cream, cheese, beans, and fruit for $6. Beer is just $1, and they usually stay open late to accommodate any late-night drinkers.

10a Calle Poniente & Av. Cuscatlán Sur, near the Hostal de Mama y Papa. ⓒ **503/2417-4268.** Main courses $3–$6.. No credit cards. Daily 7am–9pm.

Where to Stay in Tacuba

Hostal de Mamá y Papá ★   This small, well-known hostel lives up to its reputation as the place to stay in Tacuba. The setting is lush and gardenlike, with a few hillside rooms offering patios and views. Numerous animals run around the place, and there's an actual Mamá and Papá tending to the property who will make you feel right at home. (Mamá also runs the hostel's restaurant about 91m/299 ft. down the road.) As with many of the country's small, independently run hotels, don't expect state-of-the-art rooms or fancy decor. The rooms are average size, and the bathrooms are merely functional. But the vibe is friendly, and you'll get to hang out with the English-speaking guide Manolo (see "Exploring Parque Nacional El Imposible," above) who lives here. Note that the guest rooms have no locks, but the owners can secure valuables in the hostel office.

Av. Cuscatlán, near Calle 10. ⓒ **503/2417-4268.** 5 units. $6 dorm bed; $15 per person double. No credit cards. **Amenities:** Restaurant. *In room:* Fan (upon request), no phone.

Hostal y Restaurante Miraflores   A low, red-brick building with green doors and an arched entrance leads to a lush courtyard surrounded by five basic rooms. The rooms are clean, but the shared bathroom could do with a scrub. (Note: There is no hot water.) Small and humble, the Miraflores should be your third choice if the other two hotels listed here do not work out. It does have a pretty good restaurant with a varied menu, including Chinese, Mexican, and Italian.

2a Av. Norte, at 7a Calle Ote. miraflores@hotmail.com; ⓒ **503/2417-4746.** 5 units. $23–$29 double. No credit cards. **Amenities:** Restaurant. *In room:* Fan, no phone.

Las Cabañas de Tacuba Hotel y Restaurante   Las Cabañas is where you should stay if Mamá y Papá's is already booked. It's certainly nice enough, but not as handy as a base camp for trips into Parque Imposible; hotel staff will actually tell you to go to Mamá y Papá's for any info about the park. Though the property consists of just a few rooms contained in pretty nondescript buildings, the grassy grounds of the hotel are pleasant, and there's a big pool (which was being repaired at press time) and open-air restaurant. The newer "cabins" beside the pool are the best value.

1a Calle Poniente, roughly 90m (295 ft.) down the hill from Alcaldía, Barrio San Nicolas. ⓒ **503/2417-4332.** 12 units. $35–$45 double. $52 cabin. Rates include full breakfast. V. **Amenities:** Restaurant; pool. *In room:* Fan, TV.

Where to Stay in Parque El Imposible

In addition to the ecolodge below, Parque Nacional El Imposible offers three camp-sites for $4 per night. Facilities are basic, with no showers, though there is a river close by you can bathe in without using soap or shampoo.

El Imposible Eco Lodge ★★ 🎁 Five six-person cabins are located 800m (2,625 ft.) from the park entrance at San Benito on the southern fringes of the park. Located on the side of a hill, the cabins are basic, A-frame wooden huts, but large and handsome, with all-wood walls and private verandas with easy chairs and ham-mocks. Inside, they are quite spacious, with room for one double bed and four bunks, and they offer lots of privacy. On the top of the hill is a restaurant called Ixcanal, with red-brick walls and wood trimmings, serving simple regional dishes. There's also a small, rock-lined pool here with natural spring water. The lodge also functions as a research center for the NGO SalvaNatura and is solar powered, with an organic compost waste system.

Caserio San Miguelito, San Benito. ✆ **503/2411-5484** or 503/7700-4699. 5 units. $39 double; $55 cabin. No credit cards. **Amenities:** Restaurant; pool. *In room:* Fan, no phone.

SANTA ANA & THE NORTHWEST

D ark volcanic cones, rolling green hills, and tidy coffee farms are what characterize the northwest of El Salvador, the capital of which is the bustling provincial city known as Santa Ana. Without doubt the country's most pleasant large city, Santa Ana has some fine architecture and interesting colonial features, yet it is not a great destination in itself. Instead, it is the gateway to the gorgeous lakeside playground known as Lago de Coatepeque, a deep blue volcanic pool that is the lakeside holiday residence of the country's great and good—thankfully, they left a little of the shore for day trippers. Parque Nacional Los Volcanes is just as its sounds, a cone-dotted park with one summit that became known as the "lighthouse of the Pacific" to passing sailors in the 19th century. And, of course, there is Tazumal, the country's finest Maya ruins, much of which is still unexcavated and undiscovered. Farther north, sharing the border with Guatemala and Honduras, is Parque Nacional Montecristo, a towering cloud forest with excellent hikes and wildlife.

20

SANTA ANA ★

64km (40 miles) W of San Salvador

Though El Salvador's charms aren't normally found in its crowded, hectic cities, Santa Ana's unique Gothic cathedral, ornate theater, and easy access to the country's most significant Maya ruin make it a place worth visiting.

Santa Ana, an easy 40-minute drive west of San Salvador, is the country's second-largest city, with approximately 275,000 residents. Yet it avoids the sprawling nature of San Salvador because most of its attractions are centered around the city's leafy main square, Parque Libertad. The city's main in-town attractions are its large, neo-Gothic cathedral and ornate and brightly painted theater. Both are among the country's more architecturally interesting landmarks. The plaza itself also offers a glimpse into old and new El Salvador, with young, mohawk-sporting skate punks mingling with matriarchs in traditional dress.

Perhaps the best reason to visit Santa Anta is that El Salvador's most important Maya ruin, Tazumal, is only a 13km (8-mile) bus ride away. Santa Ana also offers the modern conveniences of bank machines,

Internet outlets, and a super grocery store. Though it was once the county's most prosperous town, it now has some unsafe neighborhoods. However, the tourist-filled main plaza and its immediate surroundings are safe and well patrolled.

The city's faded glory comes from the coffee boom of the late 19th century, when the town became a major processing center and the coffee barons built haciendas in the surrounding green rolling hills. The collapse in coffee prices in the early 20th century lead to a workers' revolt in 1932 that saw the death of 30,000 *campesinos*. The city's history goes back much farther, however, as it was originally a pre-Columbian settlement of the Pocomante tribe, and then a place the Pipiles called Sihuatehuacán, meaning *place of priestesses*. A Spanish bishop saw fit to rechristen it Santa Ana in 1569. It became known as the *heroic city* in 1569, when it was the center of a successful revolt against the dictator Carlos Ezeta. Though coffee is still an important industry, the city is a major retail and manufacturing center with several foreign-owned factories located in the north.

Essentials

GETTING THERE

BY BUS From San Salvador, take bus no. 201 to Santa Ana's Metrocentro terminal (at 10a Av. Sur; no phone). The trip takes about 1 hour and 30 minutes, and costs $1 to $1.50.

Buses to and from Metapán (p. 335) leave from Santa Ana's Metrocentro terminal. Bus no. 218 to Tazumal leaves from the corner of 4a Avenidas Sur and 9a Calle Poniente. Lago de Coatepeque (p. 330) can be reached via bus no. 209 from either the Metrocentro terminal or in front of La Universidad Catolica de Occidente. All these buses leave approximately every 20 minutes, and fares start at 35¢.

BY CAR Simply follow the signs on your 1-hour drive west from San Salvador along the well-paved and well-marked Pan-American Highway, and you'll reach Santa Ana.

ORIENTATION

Santa Ana is a large city but is easily navigated, as most everything you need is immediately on or near Parque Libertad (the center of the city). The main east-west thoroughfare near the central plaza is Calle Libertad Poniente, which becomes Libertad Oriente east of Parque Libertad. And the main north-south route is Avenida Independencia Sur, which becomes Independencia Norte north of the plaza. The character of the surrounding neighborhoods around Parque Libertad can change quickly, especially after dark, so don't wander too far off the main plaza.

GETTING AROUND

BY BUS The only bus you'll likely take while in Santa Ana will be bus no. 51, which runs daily every 5 minutes from 8am to 10pm from the main square to the Metrocentro mall. Keep in mind that the main terminal at 10a Avenidas Sur is crowded, and the buses there often take awhile to depart. Rates within the city run 25¢.

BY TAXI Taxis are easily found on or near Parque Libertad and cost $4 to $6 to most parts of Santa Ana. Taxis are not easy to hail off the main square, so you'll need to ask your hotel or restaurant to call you a cab in other areas of town; always take a taxi at night, even if it's just for a few blocks.

BY CAR Like San Salvador, it's best to park your car immediately upon arrival. Many of Santa Ana's streets are poorly marked, so it's easy to get lost. And the character of Santa Ana's neighborhoods can change abruptly, so you don't want to take too many wrong turns. Off-street parking is recommended.

DEFINING MS-13

Throughout your trip in El Salvador, you'll likely hear the word "Mara" whispered in conversation, as if Maras are boogeymen. And in a way, they are. "Mara" refers to El Salvador's internationally notorious street gang Mara Salvatrucha or "MS-13." The name has a few meanings, depending on the person telling the story. Some people think the name hails from a combination of the words *"marabunta,"* which is the name of a fighting ant, and *"trucha,"* which means "cleverness." Others believe the name is derived from *"mara,"* meaning gang, and "Salvatrucha," referring to El Salvador's guerrilla fighters.

Whatever the origins of its name may be, MS-13 has transformed itself into one of the world's deadliest gangs, with chapters throughout the United States and Latin America. Mara Salvatrucha was formed in the 1980s in the barrios of Los Angeles by the sons of El Salvadoran immigrants fleeing the country's civil war. The gang is thought to have formed originally as a defense against vicious Los Angeles street gangs already in place. Today, with steady deportations of gang members back to El Salvador, MS-13 maintains a strong presence in the country.

However, the El Salvadoran government is continuing its efforts to decrease MS-13 influence, and the majority of the violence has been confined to rival gang members' territories. Other than hearing the name "Maras" whispered in conversation, then, you're unlikely to be affected by this gang during your travels.

For more information about safety in El Salvador, see p. 63.

ON FOOT   Most everything you'll want to see is right on Parque Libertad or within a couple of blocks of the square. You'll need a taxi to reach a few of the better hotels and restaurants in town, but otherwise, you can easily walk from sight to sight.

VISITOR INFORMATION

Santa Ana does not have a tourist office, so your best source of tourist information will be your hotel staff or an English-language tour guide provided by a company such as Nahua Tours (© 503/7874-8402; www.nahuatours.com). If you speak Spanish, Santa Ana's Casa de la Cultura (2a Calle Poniente; © 503/2447-0084) can also provide information.

[FastFACTS] SANTA ANA

Banks and ATMs   **Scotiabank** is 1 block off the Parque Libertad, behind the Municipal Palace, at the corner of Calle Libertad and 2a Avenida Norte. The bank has two external ATMs. Another option is **Banco Cuscatlán** (Av. Independencia Sur and 3a Calle Ote; © 503/2489-4876). Banks are open weekdays from 8:30am to 5pm and Saturday 8:30am to noon. **MetroCentro Mall** (Final Avenida Independencia Sur; © 503/2440-6277) has several banks and ATMs located inside. It is open daily from 9am to 9pm.

Drugstores   **Farmacias Económicas,** in the Metrocentro Mall (© 503/2440-2877), is open weekdays from 8am to 6pm and Saturday 8am to noon.

Emergencies   Call © **911** for all emergencies.

Hospital   For any health issues go to **Hospital Nacional Regional San Juan de Dios** (Final 13 Av. Sur, #1; © 503/2447-9037).

Internet   Internet access is available at **SGD/Soluciones Gráficas Digitales** (Calle Libertad Poniente; ✆ **503/2447-2750**), which is upstairs in a small shopping center on the
southeast corner of the square, as well as at the national Internet chain **InfoCentros** (1a
Calle Poniente and Av. Jose Matías Delgado; ✆ **503/2447-7750**). Another is **Cibernet** (1a
Calle Ote and 1a Av. Norte; ✆ **503/2447-7746**). Most Internet cafes are closed on Sunday. The going rate is $1.50 per hour.

Post Office   Santa Ana's post office is 4 blocks south of the square at 7a Calle Poniente #30, near the corner of 7a Calle Poniente and Avenida Independencia Sur
(✆ **503/2441-0084**).

SPANISH CLASSES

Escuela Sihuatehuacán (Calle E Polígono N2, Urbanización El Milagro; ✆ 503/2441-
4726; www.salvaspan.com) will do more than just improve your Spanish. The school
organizes day trips to surrounding attractions, activities, and salsa classes. Homestays
are available, as are short or long structured Spanish courses.

FESTIVALS

If you are in Santa Ana in July, you'll want to check out the "Fiestas Julias," or the July
Festival. This month-long celebration involves parades, carnival rides, and music and
is also known as Fiesta Patronal, since it honors the city's patron saint.

What to See & Do in Santa Ana

Santa Ana's main attractions are its Gothic-style cathedral, old-world–style theater,
and the nearby Maya ruins of Tazumal. Many also visit simply to stock up on supplies
at the city's modern grocery store before heading north to the Parque Montecristo
(p. 335). In addition to these major attractions, you may also wish to take a peek at
these notable buildings: The Centro de Arte Occidental (✆ **503/2447-6045**), opposite the Santa Ana theater, once housed an art museum, but now offers arts classes
to local children. You can poke around the mildly interesting building for free if you
ask at the front desk. Also on the square is the Palacio Municipal, which is Santa
Ana's town hall and is usually filled with folks standing in line to do all the things one
does at city hall. Though there's not much to see here overall, the palace's courtyard
is surprisingly inviting and serves as a respite of peace and quiet from Santa Ana's
more hectic main square. You can peek in for free Monday to Saturday from 8am to
noon and 2 to 6pm. The Casino Santaneco is a private club across from the national
theater with a swank, restored interior. Though it's not open to the public, it can be
glimpsed if you manage to convince the guy at the front door to let you in.

El Teatro Nacional de Santa Ana ★   This is not only one of El Salvador's most
attractive buildings, but also very likely its most lime green. The odd, nearly fluorescent exterior color is the first thing you'll notice about this beautiful theater, which
opened in 1910 and features a grand balcony overlooking the square. Inside, you'll
find an ornate, old-world lobby leading to the grand, three-story theater, complete
with elaborate molding, sweeping staircases, and portraits on the ceiling of long-dead
artists. Two rows of balconies line the walls, and an intricate tile floor fronts the stage.
The theater's construction was funded by the coffee trade, and the theater was a
source of local pride in the early years, staging opera and theater performances. It
later became a cinema in the 1930s and fell into disrepair, losing much of its ornamentation and original furniture. In 1979, reconstruction began, and over the course
of 2 decades, it was restored to its former glory, and even enhanced with a high-tech
light and sound system. It now showcases art performances and exhibits held

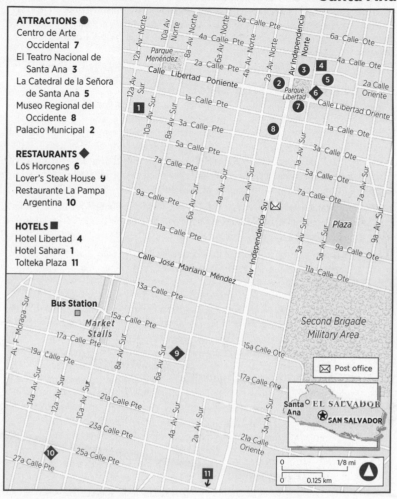

ATTRACTIONS ●
Centro de Arte Occidental **7**
El Teatro Nacional de Santa Ana **3**
La Catedral de la Señora de Santa Ana **5**
Museo Regional del Occidente **8**
Palacio Municipal **2**

RESTAURANTS ◆
Lós Horcones **6**
Lover's Steak House **9**
Restaurante La Pampa Argentina **10**

HOTELS ■
Hotel Libertad **4**
Hotel Sahara **1**
Tolteka Plaza **11**

Second Brigade Military Area

Bus Station
Market Stalls

⊠ Post office

Santa Ana ○ EL SALVADOR
★ SAN SALVADOR

0   1/8 mi
0   0.125 km

year-round. Call the theater for performance dates and times. Shows cost 50¢ to $3, or you can just take a look inside for a 50¢ admission fee.

Parque Libertad. ✆ **503/2447-6268.** 50¢ adults. Mon–Sat 8am–noon; Mon–Fri 2–6pm, Sat 2–5:30pm.

La Catedral de la Señora de Santa Ana   Santa Ana's primary in-town attraction, the cathedral has a more elaborate, European, neo-Gothic style than El Salvador's traditional white, Spanish colonial churches. Built between 1906 and 1913, the cathedral features an exterior with lots of old-world–style nooks, crannies, and arches with bell towers on each side. The interior has grand columns and a beautiful marble altar. You can, of course, visit during services, but it is not good manners to wander around.

1a Av. Norte, Parque Libertad. ✆ **503/2447-7215.** Free admission. Mon–Sat 6:30am–noon, Sun 7am–noon; daily 2–5:30pm.

Museo Regional del Occidente   Located 2 blocks southwest of the square, in the city's old Banco Central de Reserva building, this museum tells you everything there is to know about western El Salvador's historical heritage. There are rotating exhibits covering the natural, social, and economic development of the region, including an archaeological collection. There is also a permanent, in-depth history of the country's currency.

Av. Independencia Sur, #8. © **503/2441-1215.** $1 adults. Tues–Sat 9am–noon & 1–5pm.

ATTRACTIONS OUTSIDE SANTA ANA

Parque Arqueológico Casa Blanca ♨   Casa Blanca is a smaller Maya site worth seeing largely because it's a 5-minute taxi ride from Tazumal. Casa Blanca is basically a leafy park with a Spanish-language museum and a winding, 15-minute trail passing a few grassy mounds; one slightly excavated, two-story mound with exposed stone steps; and the park's main attraction, a roughly 9m-tall (30-ft.), partially excavated Maya pyramid. Casa Blanca isn't worth traveling all the way from Santa Ana to see, but if you're in the area, you might as well stop by.

Km 74.5, on the bypass at the E entrance to Chalchuapa. © **503/2408-4641.** $3 adults. Tues–Sun 9am–4:30pm. Bus: 210 from Santa Ana or 218 from Santa Ana to Tazumal.

Sitio Archeologico Tazumal ★★★   If you had to choose only one ruin to visit in El Salvador, this should be it. Tazumal is the county's most visually interesting and fully excavated set of Maya ruins. Located 13km (8 miles) from Santa Ana, Tazumal, which means "the place where the victims were burned" in the early Quiche language, is the remains of a Maya community that inhabited the area from A.D. 100 to 1200. It's believed that Tazumal functioned as an important trading center and that much of the site still remains unexcavated. Most of the construction here is believed to have taken place from A.D. 400 to 680, and so there are signs of a definite Teotihuacán influence (the Mexican site reached its peak during the same period) in many structures.

On view today are 10 sq. km (3¾ sq. miles) of ruins, including a fully excavated Maya temple pyramid, ball court, and other structures considered to be classic examples of Maya architecture and similar to those found in other parts of Central America. The park also contains numerous other structures that archaeologists are leaving covered until proper funding and care can be ensured; in addition, officials are currently returning the main pyramid to its natural state via the removal of a ridiculous cement shell that was once thought protective, but was later deemed unnecessary. Visitors are no longer allowed to climb any structures here due to damage from the 2001 earthquake.

The site also includes a small museum with a number of artifacts that indicate that this society was in contact with other Central American Maya communities. Though it's much smaller than better-known ruins in Guatemala or Honduras, and requires only about 45 minutes to explore, Tazumal's importance to El Salvador's history and its exemplary Maya architecture make it worth the drive. Most tour companies, such as the local company **Nahua Tours** (© 503/7874-8402; www.nahuatours.com) and the larger **Eco Mayan Tours** (© 503/2298-2844; www.ecomayantours.com), make stops here.

Entrance on Calle Tazumal, Chalchuapa. © **503/2444-0010.** $3 adults; free for children 4 & under. Tues–Sun 9am–4pm. Bus: 218 from Santa Ana stops 547m (1,795 ft.) from the entrance.

Shopping in Santa Ana

The main Mercado Central (8a Av. Sur) is a chaotic, rambling collection of stalls selling everything from chickens to chicles. It is open daily from 7am to 5pm.

For handicrafts, go to Mercado de Artesanías (1a Av. Sur), open Monday through Saturday from 8:30am to 6pm. Though Santa Ana doesn't have any small boutique shops worth mentioning, it does have a large modern shopping mall called Metro-Centro (© **503/2440-6277**) with chain stores, superstores, and a cinema. It's on Final Avenida Independencia Sur and is open daily from 9am to 9pm.

Where to Stay in Santa Ana

Hotel Libertad ★ 🖋 If you don't need anything fancy, stay here. Hotel Libertad is as barebones as it gets. There's no hot water, no Internet, and no restaurant. But it's safe, clean, and just 1 block off Parque Libertad—which means it's mere minutes away from the cathedral, theater, restaurants, and most of what you'll need in Santa Ana. Because Parque Libertad is Santa Ana's tourist center, the area is also safe and well patrolled by police. Yes, the hotel will not exactly grace the pages of interior design magazines, but it's well maintained, and the staff will go out of their way to meet your demands. Ask for room no. 15 or 16, both of which are upstairs and farthest away from the lobby.

4a Calle Oriente #2, 1 block N of square (near the corner of Calle Oriente & 1a Av. Norte). © **503/2441-2358.** 12 units. $12–$20 double. No credit cards. *In room:* Fan, TV, no phone.

Hotel Sahara ★ ✋ Despite its 50-year reputation as Santa Ana's grand hotel, Sahara really isn't that great. Hotel Tolteka Plaza offers more amenities and Hotel Libertad is a lot cheaper. But when you combine location and comfort, Sahara ekes out a victory. It's only 5 blocks from Parque Libertad, offers the convenience of a full-service restaurant and Wi-Fi, and has a pleasant rooftop deck. The rooms are only of average size, and the bathrooms even smaller; request room no. 204, which is the biggest overall, or room no. 215, which offers the most peace and quiet. The area between the hotel and the main square bustles with a street market during the day but is deserted and can be dangerous at night. Always have the front desk call you a cab after dark.

3a Calle Poniente, btw. Av. Sur & Av. José Matías Delgado. hotel_sahara@yahoo.com; © **503/2447-8865.** Fax 503/2447-0456. 30 units. $44–$58 double. Rates include full breakfast. AE, DC, DISC, MC, V. **Amenities:** Restaurant. *In room:* A/C, TV, Wi-Fi free.

Tolteka Plaza ★ Tolteka is Santa Ana's most modern and luxurious hotel option. The rooms are larger than you might expect, and the hotel offers a rare-outside-San-Salvador water-heating system (rather than the usual electronic shower heads). There's also an inviting courtyard pool, Wi-Fi, and a full-service restaurant. The hotel is just a short taxi ride or long walk to the Metrocentro bus terminal, which also means it's about a 10-minute cab ride to Parque Libertad. As part of a national hotel chain, the Tolteka also has a rather corporate feel, with no unique charm and no interesting decor. When booking, try to reserve room no. 101, 106, 201, 219, or 220, as they overlook the pool and are farthest from street noise. The English-speaking staff can arrange tours or a taxi to Parque Libertad.

Av. Independencia Sur. www.hotoleselsalvador.com/hoteltolteka; © **503/2487-1000.** Fax 503/2479-0868. 50 units. $59–$71 double. AE, DC, DISC, MC, V. **Amenities:** Restaurant; bar; pool; room service; nonsmoking rooms; Wi-Fi (in lobby). *In room:* A/C, TV, hair dryer.

Where to Eat in Santa Ana

Los Horcones ★ SALVADORAN   This laidback two-story restaurant and bar is a great place to end the day with a cold beer, comfort food, and a nice view from the

The Guatemalan border is only 1 hour away, and Santa Ana is the last major town on the way. The border crossing is at San Cristóbal and is open 24 hours. Bus no. 236 leaves every 20 minutes from Santa Ana from 5:30am to 9pm and costs 50¢. The *Especial* buses are much more comfortable and go all the way to Guatemala City, taking 4 hours and costing $12.

upstairs deck overlooking Parque Libertad. The reasonably priced menu features the usual grilled steak, chicken, and fish dishes with salad, rice, and tortillas. You can also find tasty sandwiches and tacos for under $5. Though Los Horcones roughly translates as "the pitchforks," the restaurant's downstairs is inexplicably decorated not with farm furnishings, but with decades-old telephones, a 1970s-era Atari game console, a 1.8m-long (6-ft.) stuffed fish, and a nearly antique DVD player.

1a Av. Norte, on Parque Libertad. ℂ **503/2484-7511.** Main courses $5–$11. No credit cards. Daily 10:30am–9pm.

Lover's Steak House ★★ ☺ STEAK　Lover's Steak House is nearly as tasty as its rival La Pampa, but with a more casual, family-friendly atmosphere. Bench seating and beer-brand advertising set the laidback tone of this 16-year-old restaurant. The English and Spanish menu is larger than La Pampa's and includes North American favorites such as chicken wings, hamburgers, and a club sandwich. Portions are also larger, with bigger baked potatoes and lots of vegetables. Since Lover's and La Pampa are about evenly priced and both require a taxi ride, your choice depends on your mood. If you want an upscale, romantic dinner, head to La Pampa. If you have a talkative group or a few kids, or just want a casual vibe, Lover's is the better choice.

4a Av. Sur & 17 Calle Poniente. ℂ **503/2440-5717.** Main courses $9–$22. AE, DC, DISC, MC, V. Sun–Thurs 11am–10pm; Fri & Sat 11am–11pm.

Restaurante La Pampa Argentina ★★★ STEAK/ARGENTINE　La Pampa steakhouse is by far Santa Ana's finest restaurant, and it serves what is likely to be one of the tastiest steaks you'll have in El Salvador. The restaurant is styled after, and shares a menu with, the well-known San Salvador steakhouse of the same name. You'll need a taxi and a few minutes to get here, but it's worth the trip. The modern, hacienda-style interior is elegant but comfortable, with tables far enough apart to allow for quiet conversation. Upstairs seating overlooks the main dining room and includes two small outdoor terraces. The service is outstanding and on par with that at San Salvador's finest restaurants, with Spanish-speaking waiters able to explain the intricacies of the steaks and cuts; but the specialty of the house is the 224g (8-oz.) entraña, or skirt-cut steak. Every large steak platter is served with salad, vegetables, potatoes, and a delicious beef consommé.

25 Calle Poniente, btw. 10a & 12a Av. Sur. ℂ **503/2406-1001.** Reservations recommended. Main courses $10–$25. AE, DC, DISC, MC, V. Mon–Thurs 11am–3pm & 6–10pm; Fri–Sun 11:30am–11:30pm.

LAGO DE COATEPEQUE ★★

18km (11 miles) S of Santa Ana; 56km (35 miles) W of San Salvador

Lago de Coatepeque, an almost perfectly round crater-lake that is 740m (2,428 ft.) above sea level, is one of El Salvador's most beautiful and enjoyable getaways. The deep blue lake is a short drive from Santa Ana, which means it's an easy day trip from that town—but it's really worth staying a couple of days here to enjoy all its attractions; the 23-sq.-km (9-sq.-mile) pristine lake is ideal for swimming, fishing, riding watercraft, and simply soaking in beautiful views.

Lago Coatepeque was formed thousands of years ago by the eruption of the nearby ancient volcano, the Coatepeque Caldera. Today, the lake's rich blue waters and lush, tree-filled crater walls serve as a weekend getaway for El Salvador's rich and famous, whose mansions line the shore. Luckily, those rich and famous folks left a roughly 500m (1,640-ft.) section open to the public, which is now filled with restaurants and hotels offering tours, watercraft rentals, and fishing piers. There's little lake access, other than through these hotels or restaurants, but most allow single-day use of their piers for a small fee. Perhaps the highlight of any visit here, though, is the sunsets: Each evening, visitors line the hotel piers with cameras ready to capture classic and captivating photos of the sun dipping below the crater walls.

Essentials

GETTING THERE

BY BUS   From Santa Ana (p. 323), take bus no. 209 or 220. From San Salvador (p. 232), take bus no. 201. Tell the driver you want to head to Lago Coatepeque, and he'll let you off anywhere you wish along the lake's strip of hotels and restaurants. The ride from Santa Ana takes a little less than 1 hour; the ride takes 1½ hours from San Salvador.

BY CAR   From San Salvador, travel west, and from Santa Ana, travel east, along the well-paved Pan-American Highway, following the well-marked signs to the lake. After reaching the lake area, you'll drive slowly down a winding dirt road along the crater wall to the water. Lago Coatepeque includes only one small section of hotels, so if you get lost, just say, "Los Hoteles?" and locals will point you in the right direction.

ORIENTATION & GETTING AROUND

The majority of Lago Coatepeque's hotels and restaurants are located along a single, approximately 500m (1,640-ft.) stretch of the lake. A dirt road rings the lake and is lined with a nearly unbroken stretch of high cement walls hiding the lake houses of the nation's wealthy.

The best way to get around this area is by foot; the hotels and restaurants are clustered within walking distance of one another, and some great views can be had by taking a long stroll around the lake. If you are driving, keep in mind that the dirt road around the lake is rocky and best navigated by truck or four-wheel-drive.

You'll need to call a taxi, such as the local company **Taxi Leo** (© **503/2502-2495**) in advance to take you to Santa Ana or the region's other attractions, since taxis can't be hailed on the street.

VISITOR INFORMATION

Lago Coatepeque doesn't have a visitor center, so your best source of information will be hotel staff or tour companies, such as Santa Ana–based, bilingual Nahua Tours (© **503/7874-8402;** www.nahuatours.com). The closest national tourist office is along the Ruta de las Flores 1km (½ mile) east of the town of Nahuizalco (Km 71, Nahuizalco; © **503/2453-1082;** Mon–Fri 8am–5pm, Sat and Sun 8am–4pm). You can also call the national tourist office in San Salvador (© **503/2243-7835**) for info.

There are no bank machines, Internet cafes, or large stores in the area.

What to See & Do in Lago de Coatepeque

Lago de Coatepeque is primarily a place to lounge by the water, take a swim, or just enjoy the view. For day-trippers, the best deal is the $2-per-day fee to use the pier and $4-per-hour kayak rental offered at Hostal Amacuilco (see below). Or stop by Restaurante Las Palmeras (see below), which offers $70-per-hour motorized watercraft rental and 30-minute to 3-hour lake tours for $25 to $80.

Where to Stay in Lago de Coatepeque

Lago de Coatepeque can be a great place to base your exploration of this part of the country; the archaeological sites of Tazumal, San Andrés, and Joya de Cerén, as well as the hiking trails and vistas of Parque Nacional Los Volcanes, are all within 1 hour's drive. Below are your best accommodations options.

Hostal Amacuilco ★ 🖊 If you like a laidback hostel vibe, you'll love Amacuilco (also known as Hostal 3er Mundo). Amacuilco offers nearly everything you'll find at Torremolinos, only cheaper and with less formality. This small (there are just five rooms), family-friendly hostel sits right on the water and has a lake-view restaurant, a pool, a pier, and the most gardenlike setting of all the lake's hotels. Its rooms—including two private rooms every bit as pleasant as those at Torremolinos—are spread among leafy grounds and include a dorm room directly over the water with great views. Amacuilco also offers free kayak use and Internet access, as well as a comfortable lounge area with TV. Like most hostels, Amacuilco isn't perfect and could use some paint here and there. But it's cheap, friendly, and offers all the necessities you'll find at the lake's more expensive hotels. A 5-day Spanish course, including food and lodging, is also available for $120.

Calle Principal. amacuilcohostal@hotmail.com; © **503/7822-4051.** 5 units. $4 campsite; $9 dorm bed; $14–$28 double. No credit cards. **Amenities:** Restaurant; Internet (free); room service; free kayak rental. *In room:* A/C (in some), fan.

Hotel Torremolinos Torremolinos is kind of like the resort in the movie Dirty Dancing—it has the look and feel of a grand 1950s-era Catskills hotel. Unfortunately, the '50s were a long time ago, and today, this once grand hotel remains charming but very dated. The rooms seem to have been decorated 20 years ago with whatever mismatching items were lying around, the bathrooms aren't attractive, and there's no Internet. On the plus side, the hotel's lakefront property offers cozy gardens, lounge areas with wrought-iron tables and chairs, two pools, and a two-story pier restaurant over the water with nice breezes and great views.

Calle Principal. www.torremolinoslagocoatepeque.com; © **503/2441-6037.** 16 units. $32–$47 double. Rates include continental breakfast. AE, DC, DISC, MC, V. **Amenities:** Restaurant; bar; laundry service; pool; nonsmoking rooms; canoe, jet ski & kayak rental. *In room:* A/C, fan, TV (in some), fridge (in some).

Where to Eat in Lago de Coatepeque

Restaurante Barde La Rioja ★★ SALVADORAN This spot inside the Hotel Torremolinos (see above) has the best service, food, and ambience on the lake—though the hotel might be a bit dated, its restaurant has definitely kept pace with its grand reputation. Torremolinos offers two large seating areas; choose between the main hall with arched columns overlooking the hotel grounds and lake, or a two-story pier sitting high off the water with great views and afternoon breezes. The specialties of the house are the tasty cream of crab soup and lake fish stuffed with shrimp. As with many fine

Central American restaurants, diners get a tiny sample appetizer to nibble before the main entree. Prices are slightly lower than at the area's other two large restaurants. The main dining room has live music Sunday afternoon from 1 to 5pm.

Calle Principal. ✆ **503/2441-6037.** Main courses $3.50–$12. AE, DC, DISC, MC, V. Daily 8am–9pm.

Restaurante Las Palmeras ☺ SALVADORAN   Palmeras is a great place to hang out during the day and have a snack or cold beer (but when it's time for dinner, head to Restaurante Barde La Rioja, above). This restaurant is the lake's newest and flashiest, featuring dining spaces under a thatched hut and on a bamboo-style pier. You can't go wrong with the chicken sandwich with fries, the garlic shrimp appetizer, or the Caesar salad. Though the dinner menu is extensive, with more than 20 fish, beef, and chicken dishes, and the management maintains a family-friendly atmosphere, the entrees are a bit expensive and not as tasty as those at Barde La Rioja.

Calle Principal. ✆ **503/7248-5727.** Main courses $8–$20. AE, DC, MC, V. Daily 7am–9pm.

Restaurante Rancho Alegre SALVADORAN   Alegre is Palmeras' neighbor—its older and slightly run-down, but less expensive and every bit as tasty neighbor. The two restaurants have nearly identical fish, beef, and chicken dishes, and are both situated on long piers over the water. But Alegre is not as flashy as Palmeras, and its pier has begun to show signs of age. (Renovations were underway at press time.) This appears to be the restaurant of choice for El Salvadorans, though, no doubt because the locals are drawn by the cheap, delicious cuisine. Menu highlights include a delicious $5 Salvadoran breakfast of eggs, beans, cheese, and plátanos. The restaurant offers rooms for rent, as well, but they aren't recommended.

Calle Principal, by Las Palmeras. ✆ **503/2441-6071.** Main courses $6–$15. V. Daily 9am–8pm.

A Side Trip to Parque Nacional Los Volcanes ★★

Parque Nacional Los Volcanes is the informal name given to the 4,500 hectares (11,120 acres) of private and public lands 8km (5 miles) southwest of Lago de Coatepeque, which are home to the steep and barren Volcán Izalco, the highest volcano in El Salvador; the recently active Volcán de Santa Ana; and the green hills of Cerro Verde.

The park, known officially as Parque Nacional Cerro Verde, is centered around a parking lot near the top of Cerro Verde Mountain, from which visitors set off on challenging, 4-hour round-trip hikes to both Volcán Santa Ana and Volcán de Izalco. An easy 35-minute hike near the summit of Cerro Verde also begins and ends at the parking lot. If you love to hike, this park offers some of the most interesting and convenient treks in the country.

Volcán Santa Ana is the third-highest point in the nation and one of its most active volcanoes; in October 2005, an eruption here killed two people, disrupted numerous villages, and spewed huge volcanic boulders up to a mile away. The eruption closed the volcano to hikers for 3 years, but officials reopened the mountain in March 2008. The 4-hour hike to the 2,381m (7,812-ft.) summit is strenuous, but you will be rewarded with stunning views of Lago de Coatepeque. The climb is difficult, and you'll need to be in shape; but it's the easier of the park's two major hikes.

Volcán de Izalco is the park's most visually dramatic volcano and challenging climb, requiring a nearly 3-hour scramble up a steep, rocky, and barren moonscape to the 1,952m (6,404-ft.) summit. Izaco is also one of Central America's youngest volcanoes—it formed in 1770 and erupted almost continuously until 1966. The eruptions were said to be so violent that they could be seen by sailors at sea; hence, the volcano was nicknamed the "Lighthouse of the Pacific." Today, the summit is a nearly perfect cone, and its spare, blackish landscape stands in sharp contrast to the lushness of the surrounding hills.

Climbing Izalco is only for those in good physical shape. And no matter how physically fit you are, you can't do both climbs in 1 day. All hikes in the park must be led by a guide, and guided hikes with a minimum of three people leave the parking lot only once daily at 11am.

ESSENTIALS

GETTING THERE & GETTING AROUND From Santa Ana, take bus no. 248, which stops at the park entrance near the parking lot. Buses leave Santa Ana at 8:30am Tuesday through Thursday and 7:30am Friday through Sunday. They return daily at 3pm. From San Salvador, take a bus directly to Santa Ana (see p. 323 for info) and then follow the directions above, or get off short of Santa Ana in El Congo and ask the driver to direct you to the spot where you can catch the no. 248 bus to the park.

If you're driving from San Salvador, follow Hwy. CA-8 to the exit for El Congo. After exiting, turn right at the gas station. Follow that road until you turn left at the sign for Cerro Verde. The road will dead-end into the Cerro Verde parking lot. From Santa Ana, follow Hwy. CA-1 to the exit for Lake Coatepeque. Almost immediately after exiting, turn left onto Hwy. CA-8. Follow this road until you turn right at the sign for Cerro Verde, after which point, the road will dead-end into the park's lot.

VISITOR INFORMATION Park information is available from park administrator SalvaNatura (33 Av. Sur 640, Colonia Flor Blanca, San Salvador; ✆ **503/2279-1515;** www.salvanatura.org). The park is open daily 8am to 5pm, but you'll need to arrive before 11am to secure a guide to hike one of the volcanoes; groups meet at the small building in the parking lot that says "Caseta de Guías." Admission is $1, and the guides work for tips; plan on giving at least $5 per person. A small comedor serving pupusas, roasted chicken, and rice is located in the far corner of the parking lot.

WHERE TO STAY NEARBY

Lago de Coatepeque and Santa Ana are both less than 30km (19 miles) away, so you can easily base your trip to Parque Nacional Los Volcanes out of one of those two areas. But if you want to stay overnight so that you can hike both volcanoes, the best option is nearby Campo Bello, with great views of Volcán de Izalco. SalvaNatura (see above) also offers cabins and rooms just off Cerro Verde's parking lot.

Cabañas Campo Bello ★★ 📸 Located just 20 minutes from the Parque Nacional Los Volcanes, Campo Bello stands out as the most surreal but stunning accommodations choice in the area—seven small, bright white, cement igloos with different colored, brightly-painted doors dot the property, which is backed by a near eye-level view of Volcán de Izalco's rim. Each spare but comfortable igloo features two small bedrooms and a bathroom. Igloo no. 1 offers the best view of the volcano. One-bedroom cabins and tent campsites are also available, and Campo Bello provides tips-only guided tours of both volcanoes from the hotel property.

To get to Campo Bello, veer right at the Campo Bello sign off the main road toward the Cerro Verde parking lot. You'll then need a four-wheel-drive during rainy season or a high ground–clearance truck the rest of the year to drive the remaining 15 minutes to the hotel. You can also take the no. 248 bus here; simply tell the driver to let you off at the road for Campo Bello.

At the entrance to Parque Nacional Cerro Verde. www.campobello.com.sv; ✆ **503/7729-3712** or 503/2271-0853. Fax 503/2222-1861. 14 units. $25 2-person cabin; $40 4-person cabin. No credit cards. *In room:* No phone.

Lago de Coatepeque

SANTA ANA & THE NORTHWEST

PARQUE MONTECRISTO & LAGO DE GUIJA

Three countries converge at the cloud-forested summit of Cerro Montecristo. This border triumvirate of Guatemala, Honduras, and El Salvador is an isolated and hard-to-reach national park. It is one of the country's few remaining pieces of pristine jungle, excellent for hiking, camping, and bird-watching. The scruffy cowboy town of Metapán is its gateway and also the best jumping-off point to explore the serene Lago de Güija to the southwest. Metapán is also the beginning of a rough and marvelous mountain road that leads to the town of Citala-El Poy on the Honduran border.

Metapán

46km (29 miles) N of Santa Ana

Most travelers view Metapán as nothing more than a scruffy town on the highway to the northwest border with Guatemala. However, take the time to descend into its historical center, and you'll be pleasantly surprised as the main road begins to transform into a quaint set of streets, low-rise colonial buildings, and a picturesque church. A 300-year-old ceiba tree stands in the middle of a fine plaza and the splendidly restored town hall (alcaldia) boasts two giant jaguar statues (symbols of local indigenous strength and resilience), as well as railings made from rifle barrels captured in a 1903 war with Guatemala. The town's most unique feature is a two-story whitewashed building with a gallery running the length of the plaza; nothing unusual there, until you ascend the steps to a restaurant upstairs and discover a full-size soccer pitch with spectator stands out back—apparently the place to be on a Friday night, as the proud locals (known as Metapánecos) contest the national champion title. Besides its authentic small-town appeal, Metapán does not have much in the way of accommodations or restaurants (for the moment). However, it is the gateway to the beautiful Parque Montecristo cloud forest and to the relatively unexplored but gorgeous Lago de Güija.

ESSENTIALS

GETTING THERE & GETTING AROUND Buses to and from Metapán connect at Santa Ana's Metrocentro terminal with onward connections to San Salvador. The town's rudimentary bus depot is located next to the Hotel San José on the main highway and the entrance into the town center, which is a 5-minute walk downhill. Here, you can catch local buses every 30 minutes to the Guatemalan border crossing at Anguiatú or a twice-daily bus to the Honduran border at Citalá, which is a rough-and-tumble 3-hour drive, but with memorable mountain scenery.

The entrance to Parque Montecristo is approximately 16km (10 miles) and a 40-minute drive north of Metapán. Buses don't run to the park, but you can arrange transportation at the bus depot, where you'll find numerous pickup trucks waiting to take you to the park. A 1-day round-trip pickup ride is about $55. **Note:** There is no point attempting this without a park permit acquired in San Salvador. The park's offices are located at the **Ministerio de Medio Ambiente y Recursos Naturales** (Km 5.5 Carretera a Santa Tecla, Calle and Colonia Las Mercedes, Bldg. MARN No. 2, San Salvador; © **503/2267-6276;** www.marn.gob.sv). The process takes an hour and costs $6 for the entrance fee and $1.15 per vehicle.

To get to Lago de Güija from Metapán, take bus no. 235 (25¢), which leaves about every 10 minutes from the bust terminal. Tell the driver "Lago de Güija," and you'll get off about 5 blocks from the lake, beside a small, bright-blue building and a sign reading PLAYA TURISTA with an arrow pointing to a road on the right. Follow that road to the lake.

If you're driving, turn left out of the Hotel San Jose and for about 10 minutes until you see the PLAYA TURISTA sign. Turn right and follow the road to the water. The pickups that take travelers to Parque Monticristo also run the route to the lake for $10 each way.

VISITOR INFORMATION   Metapán Tourism Office (© **503/2402-3123;** metapanturistico@hotmail.com) is located on the southwestern corner of the plaza and is open Tuesday to Saturday 8am to 5pm and Sunday 8am to noon. The staff has limited English, but is very enthusiastic and will help book accommodation and transportation in the surrounding area. There's a Scotiabank (© **503/2402-0039**) at Avenida Ignacio Gómez, with a 24-hour ATM. The Hospital Nacional Metapán Arturo Morales (© **503/2442-0184**) is on Carretera Principal, 400m (1,312 ft.) south of the town's entrance. For Internet access, head to Ciber Café (© **503/2442-4029**) on 2 Av. Sur.

What to See & Do in Parque Nacional de Montecristo

EXPLORING PARQUE MONTECRISTO

Parque Nacional de Montecristo is a 1,972-hectare (4,873-acre) protected reserve tucked high in El Salvador's mountains, bordering Honduras and Guatemala. The park's highest point, known as Punto Trifinio, actually extends into Honduras and Guatemala, and reaches 2,400m (7,874 ft.). It features some of the country's lushest forests and most diverse flora and fauna, including dozens of orchid species and numerous rare birds, such as toucans, quetzals, and striped owls. Wild pigs, spider monkeys, coyotes, and other wildlife also inhabit the park but aren't so easily spotted.

The best time to visit is right after rainy season in December, when the park is at its most lush. Year-round, though, the region's high humidity and low-hanging clouds give the park its mystical cloud-forest feel and maintain its perpetually cool, damp environment, which hovers between 42° and 64°F (6°–18°C). Note, however, that full access to the park is limited from May to November. The thick canopy provided by the towering laurel and oak forests also provides the dark cover necessary for an array of orchids, mosses, lichens, and ferns to thrive here. The garden, De Cien Años, offers Montecristo's best orchid viewing and is an hour's drive (on bumpy, gravel road) from the park entrance. This garden, which is 1,798m (5,899 ft.) above sea level, is open daily from 8am to noon and 1:30 to 3pm. Montecristo also offers an historic hacienda-style house and a museum with an odd collection of objects ranging from a 3.5m-tall (11-ft.) model of a lookout tower to various animal skulls, along with info about the park's fauna. The museum is open daily from 8am to 3pm.

Los Planes and Montecristo's higher-altitude cloud forests are open November 1 through April 30 from 7am to 3pm daily. Those areas are closed May 1 through October 31 to foster breeding. The rest of the park, including the museum, is open year-round. All visitors must receive prior permission to enter the park from Montecristo's administrative offices at the **Ministerio de Medio Ambiente y Recursos Naturales** (Km 5.5 Carretera a Santa Tecla, Calle and Colonia Las Mercedes, Bldg. MARN No. 2, San Salvador; © **503/2267-6276;** www.marn.gob.sv). The entrance fee is $6 per person and $1.15 per vehicle. Hiking without a guide is prohibited

BORDER crossing

The Guatemalan border is a 30-minute ride north of Metapán. Buses leave every 30 minutes to the border crossing at Ahguiatú and cost 50¢. The immigration office is open 24 hours, and it costs nothing to leave El Salvador or enter Guatemala. Here, you can catch a 1-hour bus ride to Chiquimula with onward connections to Guatemala City and Copa Ruinas in Honduras.

If you have the time, and the stomach, you can cross into Honduras via the border town of Citala-El Poy, 3 hours east of Metapán. There are only two buses daily at 5am and noon, and the trip costs $2. The trip is spectacular as you cross the mountains on an unpaved road, driving through dense forests and over high ridges, but it is not for the fainthearted, as the bus is old and rickety and the precipices high and vertigo-inducing. The border crossing is open 24 hours, and there is a charge of $3 to enter Honduras.

beyond the immediate camping and cabin areas, since the trails are not well marked and it's easy to get lost in the haze of the cloud forest.

The park rents cooking burners, gas stoves, and outdoor barbecue grills for $35 per night and camping sites for $3 to $6 per night. Dorm beds in an old colonial house near the park entrance with a big, shady front porch are $10 per night. To reserve a room, call the **Ministerio de Medio Ambiente y Recursos Naturales** (**✆ 503/2267-6276**) or the park's main tour guide, **Carlos Gutierres Mejía** (**✆ 503/7201-7557**). Carlos speaks only Spanish but can reserve sleeping space, lead guided hikes, or arrange transportation from the park entrance to its higher altitudes.

EXPLORING LAGO DE GUIJA

Also near Metapán is the stunningly beautiful Lago de Güija and the marshlands of Lagunas de Metapán. The deep blue Lago de Güija is a 45-sq.-km (17-sq.-mile) lake straddling the El Salvadoran and Guatemalan borders whose shores are lined with largely undeveloped fishing villages and whose waters are dotted with islands where pre-Columbian artifacts were uncovered nearly 85 years ago. The lake's main attractions are its unspoiled beauty and lack of tourist infrastructure. You won't find any info kiosks here. You can just wander the shore until you find a local fisherman who'll take you out on the lake, where you can soak in outstanding views of the surrounding inactive lakeside volcanoes.

If you need to make more concrete plans, call local Spanish-speaking fisherman and tourist boat–owner **Pedro San Doval** (**✆ 503/2483-9949**) in advance to arrange a tour for about $25 per hour. **La Perla** (**✆ 503/2415-6490**) can set up a boat trip across the border for lunch in a small Guatemalan village for about the same cost.

Where to Stay Around Metapán

Hotel San José This is the most convenient place to stay in Metapán if you're heading to Parque Montecristo. It's located across the street from the small bus terminal and the collection of pickup trucks that take you to the park. The cream-and-blue 5-story tower doesn't look too inspiring from the outside and is much the same inside. The decor is dated and a little depressing, and it has little in the way of amenities, but unfortunately, it is the only viable option in town, and it is at least clean and safe, with secure parking. The hotel is within a block of a couple of sandwich shops

reserva ECOLÓGICA EL LIMO

Can't make it to Montecristo National Park because of limited time or lack of permits? **Reserva Ecológica El Limo** makes for an excellent Plan B with 14 hectares (35 acres) of lush, rolling hills traversed by rivers, dams, and waterfalls surrounded by mountains, coffee plantations, and cane fields. It is located 4km (2½ miles) north of Metapán on a rough, mountainous road that requires a sturdy 4×4 and some expert driving. In addition to its rural allure, the private reserve also has three very well appointed cottages for rent and a 1,400m (4,593-ft.) canopy zip-line for those who prefer to fly, rather than hike. The attractive and well-designed cottages are a bargain, as they cost $55, sleep five, and have gorgeous views. A half-day of canopy zip-lining is $30, including transportation to and from Metapán. To book and arrange transfers, contact the owner, Siegfredo ((C) **503/2442-0149**), or pop into the tourist office located on Metapán's main plaza. The owner can provide secure parking in town if you do not wish to brave the mucky road by car.

and next door to the large Supermercado de Todo, where you can stock up on supplies before heading out on any hikes.

Carretera Internaciónal 113. (C) **503/2442-0556.** 34 units. $47 double. AE, DC, DISC, MC, V. Free parking. *In room:* A/C, TV.

Restaurante y Cabanas La Perla ☺ The most enjoyable place to stay in the area is located is right on Lake Güija, about 20 minutes outside Metapán. This small, four-cabin hotel offers gorgeous views of the lake, pedal boats for rent, and a boat that will take you across the lake for lunch in a small Guatemalan village. La Perla features large, modern rooms with two queen-size beds, a big pool with a poolside bar, and a restaurant with Salvadoran classics and American comfort food ranging from $5 to $7.50. The rooms also have rooftop decks overlooking the water. The decor is a little cheesy, but the huge pool and the location are perfect. The hotel provides free round-trip transportation from Metapán with advance reservations. If you don't mind adding 20 minutes to your ride to Montecristo or want to spend a few days on the lake, you should stay here.

Canton Las Piedras, Caserio, Azacualpa. www.laperladeazacualpa.com; (C) **503/2415-6490,** or 310/880-9782 in the U.S. 4 units. $35 double. AE, DC, MC, V. Free parking. **Amenities:** Restaurant; bar; pool. *In room:* A/C, TV.

Where to Eat

Even if you just plan a quick circuit of Metapán plaza before continuing on your way, it's definitely worth your time to stop for a coffee at **Balompie Café** (3ra. Av. Norte, Local 17, second floor; (C) **503/2402-3567;** www.balompiecafe.com), which has a beautiful arched colonial facade on one side and a full-size soccer field on the other. You can literally have one eye on a local game and the other on the pretty plaza while enjoying standard fare such as chicken, pasta, and beef. The restaurant is open from Wednesday to Sunday from 10am to 1pm. The same building runs the length of the plaza and has several casual cafes and pupuserias, but for the moment, the town lacks any choice in fine dining.

At **Parque Acuático Apuzunga** (Km100 Carretera de Santa Ana; (C) **503/2440-5130;** www.apuzunga.com), you can zip over the river, raft the river, fish the river, and then eat the fish from the same river. This is a sprawling garden restaurant, fish farm, rafting outfitter, and pool complex located 12km (7½ miles) south of Metapán. The rancho-style restaurant has a riverside setting and spacious gardens, with open air dining areas interrupted occasionally by thrill-seekers gliding by on a cable. It specializes in a local tilapia, which is farmed on-site and served with salad and rice. The owner Jesus Sanabria Zamora is a gregarious host who will take you on a tour of the property he is very proud of. Look for the entrance signs approximately 12km (7½ miles) south of Metapán, on the left as you travel south. It is open every day from 7am to 6pm. Zip-lining costs $7.50 per person, or $15 including transport from Metapán. Two hours of rafting costs $30 per person, or $35 including transport. Group discounts are available.

FAST FACTS

[FastFACTS] NICARAGUA & EL SALVADOR

American Express See the individual "Planning Your Trip" chapters, chapters 5 and 14, for info.

Area Codes The country code for El Salvador is 503; the country code for Nicaragua is 505. Country codes are not required when making calls within the country.

ATM Networks & Cashpoints See the "Money" sections throughout individual destination chapters for info.

Business Hours In Nicaragua, banks are generally open weekdays from 8:30 a.m. to 4 p.m., and some are open Saturday mornings. Shopping hours are weekdays from 8 a.m. to noon and 2 to 5p.m., and Saturday 8 a.m. to noon. Shopping centers are open daily from 10 a.m. to 8 p.m. In El Salvador, most banks, businesses, and cultural centers are open weekdays 8:30am to 5 p.m., and 8:30 a.m. to noon or 1 p.m. on Saturday. Some banks and attractions have extended Saturday hours. In rural areas, many businesses and banks take afternoon siestas between noon and 2 p.m.

Car Rentals See "Toll-Free Numbers & Websites," p. 343.

Drinking Laws The legal drinking age in both countries is 18, although it is often not enforced. Beer, wine, and liquor are all sold in most supermarkets and small convenience stores from Monday through Saturday. No liquor is sold on Good Friday, Easter Sunday, or election days. If you're caught possessing, using, or trafficking drugs anywhere in the region, expect severe penalties, including long jail sentences and large fines.

Driving Rules The official rules of the road in Nicaragua and El Salvador are very much the same as those in North America. People drive on the right, and standard international signage makes it clear who has the right of way at city junctions. Seat belts are obligatory, and speed limits apply to urban areas.

Not that anybody notices. The standard of driving in both countries is poor and sloppy, with speeding and fender benders very common. Watch out for drivers turning without indicating and chaotic city traffic circles where anything goes. Huge potholes are frequent, especially in rural areas of Nicaragua, where kids make a living by filling these hazardous craters with dirt in exchange for change from drivers.

A valid driver's license is necessary in both countries, and it is recommended that you get an international license before you travel. Police checkpoints are frequent. It is important never to move your car after an accident, even if it is blocking the road. If an accident causes an injury, both drivers are taken into custody until the matter is cleared up, which can take several days.

Also see the "Getting There" and "Getting Around" sections throughout this book.

Electricity Nicaragua and El Salvador run on 110 volts, 60 Hz, the same as the United States and Canada. However, three-prong grounded outlets are not universally available. It's helpful to bring a three-to-two prong adapter. European and Asian travelers should bring adapters with any accompanying appliances. Be prepared for frequent blackouts and bring surge protectors.

Embassies & Consulates   See individual country chapters for information.

Emergencies   Call ☎ **911** for emergencies. See individual city chapters throughout this book for local information.

Holidays   See "When to Go," in the "Planning Your Trip" chapters.

Internet Access   Internet access is easy to find in the region, as even the smallest towns usually have at least one Internet center. Access usually costs $1 to $2 per hour. Nearly every hotel has at least one computer with Internet access; some have dataports or Wi-Fi (usually in the hotel lobby or business center). See "Fast Facts" throughout the country chapters for specific locations.

Insurance

Medical Insurance   For travel overseas, most U.S. health plans (including Medicare and Medicaid) do not provide coverage, and the ones that do often require you to pay for services upfront and reimburse you only after you return home.

As a safety net, you may want to buy travel medical insurance, particularly if you're traveling to a remote or high-risk area where emergency evacuation might be necessary. If you require additional medical insurance, try **MEDEX Assistance** (☎ **410/453-6300;** www.medexassist.com) or **Travel Assistance International** (☎ **800/821-2828;** www.travelassistance.com; for general information on services, call the company's **Worldwide Assistance Services, Inc.,** at ☎ **800/777-8710**).

Canadians should check with their provincial health plan offices or call **Health Canada** (☎ **866/225-0709;** www.hc-sc.gc.ca) to find out the extent of their coverage and what documentation and receipts they must take home in case they are treated overseas.

Travelers from the U.K. should carry their **European Health Insurance Card (EHIC),** which replaced the E111 form as proof of entitlement to free/reduced-cost medical treatment abroad (☎ **0845/606-2030;** www.ehic.org.uk). Note, however, that the EHIC covers only "necessary medical treatment," and for repatriation costs, lost money, baggage, or trip cancellation, travel insurance from a reputable company should always be sought (www.travelinsuranceweb.com).

Travel Insurance   The cost of travel insurance varies widely, depending on the destination, the cost and length of your trip, your age and health, and the type of trip you're taking, but expect to pay between 5% and 8% of the vacation itself. You can get estimates from various providers through **InsureMyTrip.com**. Enter your trip cost and dates, your age, and other information, for prices from more than a dozen companies.

U.K. citizens and their families who make more than one trip abroad per year may find an annual travel insurance policy works out to be cheaper. Check **www.moneysupermarket. com**, which compares prices across a wide range of providers.

Most big travel agents offer their own insurance and will probably try to sell you their package when you book a holiday. Think before you sign. **Britain's Consumers' Association** recommends that you insist on seeing the policy and reading the fine print before buying travel insurance. The **Association of British Insurers** (☎ **020/7600-3333;** www.abi.org.uk) gives advice by phone and publishes *Holiday Insurance,* a free guide to policy provisions and prices. You might also shop around for better deals: Try **Columbus Direct** (☎ **0870/033-9988;** www.columbusdirect.net).

Trip-Cancellation Insurance   Trip-cancellation insurance will help retrieve your money if you have to back out of a trip or depart early, or if your travel supplier goes bankrupt. Trip cancellation traditionally covers such events as sickness, natural disasters, and State Department advisories. The latest news in trip-cancellation insurance is the availability of **expanded hurricane coverage** and the **"any-reason"** cancellation coverage—which costs more but covers cancellations made for any reason. You won't get back 100% of your prepaid trip cost, but you'll be refunded a substantial portion. **TravelSafe** (© **888/885-7233;** www.travelsafe.com) offers both types of coverage. Expedia also offers any-reason cancellation coverage for its air-hotel packages. For details, contact one of the following recommended insurers: **Access America** (© 866/807-3982; www.accessamerica.com); **Travel Guard International** (© 800/826-4919; www.travelguard.com); **Travel Insured International** (© 800/243-3174; www.travelinsured.com); and **Travelex Insurance Services** (© 888/457-4602; www.travelex-insurance.com).

Language   Spanish is by far the dominant language in the region, except on Nicaragua's Atlantic coast, where English is spoken—a lilting creole that has West Indian roots. A number of indigenous languages have survived, most notably Miskito in Nicaragua's eastern autonomous region. It is also advisable to learn some basic Spanish before you travel here; we recommend picking up a copy of *Frommer's Spanish Phrase Finder & Dictionary*.

Lost & Found   Be sure to tell all of your credit card companies the minute you discover your wallet has been lost or stolen, and file a report at the nearest police precinct. See individual city chapters for local police contact information.

If you need emergency cash, you can have money wired to you via **Western Union** (© **800/325-6000;** www.westernunion.com). Their website can direct you to the closest location.

Mail   Both countries have a reliable, albeit slow, mail service (known as *correo*). In general, expect it to take 2 weeks for your letter or postcard to reach home and the cost to vary from 70¢ to $1 for a letter to North America or Europe. If you're sending a parcel, a Customs officer may have to inspect it first. Theft is a common problem. Always try to send mail from a main post office and insist that the envelope be stamped in front of you. It's wise to send things via registered post, though often the letter can be tracked as far as the border and no more. Private courier services are everywhere, but most are expensive. See the individual city chapters throughout this book for post office locations.

Measurements   See the chart on the inside front cover of this book for details on converting metric measurements to non-metric equivalents.

Passports   The websites listed below provide downloadable passport applications, as well as the current fees for processing applications. For an up-to-date, country-by-country listing of passport requirements around the world, go to the "International Travel" tab of the U.S. State Department website at **http://travel.state.gov**.

For Residents of Australia   You can pick up an application from your local post office or any branch of Passports Australia, but you must schedule an interview at the passport office to present your application materials. Call the **Australian Passport Information Service** at © **131-232** or visit the government website at www.passports.gov.au.

For Residents of Canada   Passport applications are available at travel agencies throughout Canada or from the central **Passport Office** (Department of Foreign Affairs and International Trade, Ottawa, ON K1A 0G3; © **800/567-6868;** www.ppt.gc.ca). *Note:* Canadian children who travel must have their own passport. However, if you hold a valid Canadian passport issued before December 11, 2001, that bears the name of your child, the passport remains valid for you and your child until it expires.

For Residents of Ireland   You can apply for a 10-year passport at the **Passport Office** (Setanta Centre, Molesworth Street, Dublin 2; © **01/671-1633;** www.dfa.ie). Those 17 and under, or 66 and older, must apply for a 3-year passport. You can also apply at 1A South Mall, Cork (© **21/494-4700**) or at most main post offices.

For Residents of New Zealand   You can pick up a passport application at any New Zealand Passports Office or download it from their website. Contact the **Passports**

Office at ✆ **0800/225-050** in New Zealand, or 04/474-8100, or log on to www. passports.govt.nz.

For Residents of the United Kingdom   To pick up an application for a standard 10-year passport (5-year passport for children 15 and under), visit your nearest passport office, major post office, or travel agency; contact the **United Kingdom Passport Service** at ✆ **0870/521-0410;** or search its website at www.ukpa.gov.uk.

For Residents of the United States   Whether you're applying in person or by mail, you can download passport applications from the U.S. State Department website at **http://travel.state.gov**. To find your regional passport office, either check the U.S. State Department website or call the **National Passport Information Center**'s toll-free number (✆ **877/487-2778**) for automated information.

Police   Call ✆ **911** for emergencies. See individual city chapters for local contact information.

Smoking   There are no government smoking bans in Nicaragua or El Salvador at the moment. Private companies do not allow smoking in places like cinemas or long-distance buses, however. The better hotels and restaurants have nonsmoking rooms and areas, but in general, you can still puff wherever you want.

Taxes   See chapters 5 and 14.

Telephones   See chapters 5 and 14.

Time   Nicaragua and El Salvador are 6 hours behind Greenwich Mean Time.

Tipping   Ten percent is the general rule for tipping in restaurants, though tips are sometimes included in bills. In hotels, tip **bellhops** at least $1 per bag ($2–$3 if you have a lot of luggage) and tip the **chamber staff** $1 to $2 per day. See individual chapters for more info.

Toilets   These are known as *sanitarios, servicios sanitarios,* or *baños.* They are marked *damas* (women), and *hombres* or *caballeros* (men). Public restrooms are hard to come by in both countries. You will almost never find a public restroom in a city park or downtown area. You can take refuge in the many huge malls that are now springing up in both countries. Otherwise, one must count on the generosity of some hotel or restaurant. Same goes for most beaches. Most restaurants and, to a lesser degree, hotels will let you use their facilities, especially if you buy a soft drink or something. Bus and gas stations often have restrooms, but many of these are pretty grim. Don't flush toilet paper; put it in the trash bin.

Water   The water in the major cities and tourist destinations is ostensibly safe to drink. However, many travelers react adversely to water in foreign countries, and it's probably best to drink bottled water and avoid ice or food washed with tap water throughout your visit to the region. See the "Planning Your Trip" chapters for both countries for more info.

TOLL-FREE NUMBERS & WEBSITES

AIRLINES

Aeroméxico
✆ 800/237-6639 (in the U.S.)
www.aeromexico.com

Air Canada
✆ 888/247-2262 (in the U.S. and Canada)
www.aircanada.com

Air New Zealand
✆ 800/262-1234 (in the U.S.)
✆ 800/663-5494 (in Canada)
✆ 800/028-4149 (in the U.K.)
www.airnewzealand.com

American Airlines
☏ 800/433-7300 (in the U.S. and Canada)
www.aa.com

British Airways
☏ 800/247-9297 (in the U.S. and Canada)
☏ 087/0850-9850 (in the U.K.)
www.british-airways.com

Continental Airlines
☏ 800/523-3273 (in the U.S. and Canada)
☏ 084/5607-6760 (in the U.K.)
www.continental.com

Copa Air
☏ 800/265-2672 (in the U.S. and Canada)
www.copaair.com

Delta Air Lines
☏ 800/221-1212 (in the U.S. and Canada)
☏ 084/5600-0950 (in the U.K.)
www.delta.com

Frontier Airlines
☏ 800/432-1359 (in the U.S. and Canada)
www.frontierairlines.com

Iberia Airlines
☏ 800/722-4642 (in the U.S. and Canada)
☏ 087/0609-0500 (in the U.K.)
www.iberia.com

Lan Airlines
☏ 866/435-9526 (in the U.S.)
☏ 800/977-6100 (in the U.K.)
www.lan.com

Martin Air
☏ 800/627-8462 (in the U.S.)
www.martinair.com

Qantas Airways
☏ 800/227-4500 (in the U.S. and Canada)
☏ 13-13-13 (in Australia)
www.qantas.com

Spirit Airlines
☏ 800/772-7117
www.spiritair.com

TACA
☏ 800/400-8222 (in the U.S. and Canada)
☏ 087/0241-0340 (in the U.K.)
www.taca.com

United Airlines
☏ 800/864-8331 (in the U.S. and Canada)
☏ 084/5844-4777 (in the U.K.)
www.united.com

US Airways
☏ 800/428-4322 (in the U.S. and Canada)
☏ 084/5600-3300 (in the U.K.)
www.usairways.com

Virgin Atlantic Airways
☏ 800/862-8621 (in the U.S. and Canada)
☏ 0844/209-7777 (in the U.K.)
www.virgin-atlantic.com

GLOSSARY OF SPANISH TERMS & PHRASES

Central American Spanish (called castellano by the locals) is a myriad of accents and vocabulary. Dropped syllables, forgotten consonants, combined vowels, and local slang all conspire to throw the average traveler into a linguistic knot. Add to this a strong indigenous influence and marked differences between urban and rural speakers, the educated and uneducated, and males and females, and it's enough to make you throw your phrase book out the bus window. This topic is worthy of a book itself, but following are some limited examples of the differences in dialect in both countries.

- In El Salvador, the form of address *vos* is used instead of *tú*.
- In both countries, the plural of *tu* is *ustedes* as opposed to *vosotros*.
- *B* is used like *v* wherever you go in Central America, but is particularly common in El Salvador and Nicaragua, where *las vidas* becomes *laz bidas*.
- In El Salvador, *j* becomes a weak *h* or disappears altogether. For example, you should say *Meíko* instead of *Méjico* (Mexico).
- Nicaraguans have the habit of dropping the *s* in connecting words—such as *lo do* instead of *los dos*.
- Members of the rural class like to drop the "*g*" from some words, as by pronouncing *agua* as *awa,* while sophisticated urban dwellers are prone to stressing the "*g*," as by saying *gueso* instead of *hueso* (bone). In El Salvador and Nicaragua, the *g* is particularly hard in words such as *guerra*.

It would be helpful to take some Spanish classes before you visit Nicaragua and El Salvador; even a basic vocabulary of 100 words or so can make all the difference when trying to break the ice. You will be especially thankful for a little advance studying if you're stopped by a traffic cop or chatted up by a good looking local. Taking further classes when you get to your destination is a great way of making contact with real people, and you may be surprised how much you can learn in a week with lots of practice.

However, don't get your tongue in a twist over dialects; though Central Americans are fond of laughing at the way their neighbors speak, the truth is they still understand each other and will make allowances for a foreigner with halting Spanish. Most important is not to lisp on the *c* and *z* like they do in parts of Spain (that will definitely provoke laughter), and keep rolling your *rrrrrs*.

BASIC WORDS & PHRASES

English	Spanish	Pronunciation
Hello	Buenos días	**Bweh-nohss dee-ahss**
How are you?	¿Cómo está usted?	**Koh-moh ehss-tah oo-stehd**
Very well	Muy bien	**Mwee byehn**
Thank you	Gracias	**Grah-syahss**
Goodbye	Adiós	**Ad-dyohss**
Please	Por favor	**Pohr fah-vohr**
Yes	Sí	**See**
No	No	**Noh**
Excuse me (to get by someone)	Perdóneme	**Pehr-doh-neh-meh**
Excuse me (to begin a question)	Disculpe	**Dees-kool-peh**
Give me	Deme	**Deh-meh**
Where is . . . ?	¿Dónde está . . . ?	**Dohn-deh ehss-tah**
the station	la estación	**la ehss-tah-syohn**
the bus stop	la parada	**la pah-rah-dah**
a hotel	un hotel	**oon oh-tehl**
a restaurant	un restaurante	**oon res-tow-rahn-teh**
the toilet	el servicio	**el ser-vee-syoh**
To the right	A la derecha	**Ah lah deh-reh-chah**
To the left	A la izquierda	**Ah lah ees-kyehr-dah**
Straight ahead	Adelante	**Ah-deh-lahn-teh**
I would like . . .	Quiero . . .	**Kyeh-roh**
to eat	comer	**ko-mehr**
a room	una habitación	**oo-nah ah-bee-tah-syohn**
How much is it?	¿Cuánto?	**Kwahn-toh**
The check	La cuenta	**La kwen-tah**
When?	¿Cuándo?	**Kwan-doh**
What?	¿Qué?	**Keh**
Yesterday	Ayer	**Ah-yehr**
Today	Hoy	**Oy**
Tomorrow	Mañana	**Mah-nyah-nah**
Breakfast	Desayuno	**Deh-sah-yoo-noh**
Lunch	Almuerzo	**Ahl-mwehr-soh**
Dinner	Cena	**Seh-nah**
Do you speak English?	¿Habla usted inglés?	**Ah-blah oo-stehd een-glehss**
I don't understand Spanish very well.	No entiendo muy bien el español.	**Noh ehn-tyehn-do mwee byehn el ehss-pah-nyohl**

NUMBERS

1	uno (oo-noh)	16	dieciséis (dyeh-see-sayss)
2	dos (dohss)	17	diecisiete (dyeh-see-syeh-teh)
3	tres (trehss)	18	dieciocho (dyeh-see-oh-choh)
4	cuatro (kwah-troh)	19	diecinueve
5	cinco (seen-koh)		(dyeh-see-nweh-beh)
6	seis (sayss)	20	veinte (bayn-teh)
7	siete (syeh-teh)	30	treinta (trayn-tah)
8	ocho (oh-choh)	40	cuarenta (kwah-rehn-tah)
9	nueve (nweh-beh)	50	cincuenta (seen-kwehn-tah)
10	diez (dyehss)	60	sesenta (seh-sehn-tah)
11	once (ohn-seh)	70	setenta (seh-tehn-tah)
12	doce (doh-seh)	80	ochenta (oh-chehn-tah)
13	trece (treh-seh)	90	noventa (noh-behn-tah)
14	catorce (kah-tohr-seh)	100	cien (syehn)
15	quince (keen-seh)	1,000	mil (meel)

DAYS OF THE WEEK

Monday	**lunes**	(*loo*-nehss)
Tuesday	**martes**	(*mahr*-tehss)
Wednesday	**miércoles**	(*myehr*-koh-lehs)
Thursday	**jueves**	(*wheh*-behss)
Friday	**viernes**	(*byehr*-nehss)
Saturday	**sábado**	(*sah*-bah-doh)
Sunday	**domingo**	(doh-*meen*-goh)

MENU TERMS

FISH

almejas clams
atún tuna
bacalao cod
calamares squid
camarones shrimp
cangrejo crab
ceviche marinated seafood salad

dorado dolphin or mahimahi
langosta lobster
lenguado sole
mejillones mussels
ostras oysters
pargo snapper
pulpo octopus
trucha trout

MEATS

albóndigas meatballs
bistec beefsteak
cerdo pork
chicharrones fried pork rinds
cordero lamb
costillas ribs

jamón ham
lengua tongue
pato duck
pavo turkey
pollo chicken
salchichas sausages

VEGETABLES

aceitunas olives
alcachofa artichoke
berenjena eggplant
cebolla onion
elote corn on the cob
ensalada salad
espinacas spinach
frijoles beans

lechuga lettuce
maíz corn
palmito heart of palm
papa potato
pepino cucumber
tomate tomato
yuca yucca, cassava, or manioc
zanahoria carrot

FRUITS

aguacate avocado
banano banana
carambola star fruit
cereza cherry
ciruela plum
durazno peach
frambuesa raspberry
fresa strawberry
granadilla sweet passion fruit
limón lemon or lime
manzana apple

mango mango
maracuyá tart passion fruit
melón melon
mora blackberry
naranja orange
papaya papaya
piña pineapple
plátano plantain
sandía watermelon
toronja grapefruit

BASICS

aceite oil
ajo garlic
arreglado small meat sandwich
azúcar sugar
casado plate of the day
gallo corn tortilla topped with meat or chicken
gallo pinto rice and beans
hielo ice
mantequilla butter
miel honey
mostaza mustard

natilla sour cream
olla de carne meat and vegetable soup
pan bread
patacones fried plantain chips
picadillo chopped vegetable side dish
pimienta pepper
pupusa grilled corn tortilla filled with pork and cheese
queso cheese
sal salt
tamal filled cornmeal pastry
tortilla flat corn pancake

DRINKS

agua con gas sparkling water
agua purificada purified water
agua sin gas plain water
bebida drink
café coffee
café con leche coffee with milk
cerveza beer
chocolate caliente hot chocolate

jugo juice
leche milk
natural fruit juice
natural con leche milkshake
refresco soft drink
ron rum
té tea
trago alcoholic drink

GLOSSARY OF SPANISH TERMS & PHRASES

OTHER RESTAURANT TERMS

al grill grilled
al horno oven-baked
al vapor steamed
asado roasted
caliente hot
cambio or vuelto change
cocido cooked
comida food
congelado frozen
crudo raw
el baño toilet

frío cold
frito fried
grande big
la cuenta the check
medio medium
medio rojo medium rare
muy cocido well-done
pequeño small
poco cocido or rojo rare
tres cuartos medium-well-done

OTHER USEFUL TERMS

HOTEL TERMS

aire-acondicionado air-conditioning
almohada pillow
baño bathroom
baño privado private bathroom
calefacción heating
cama bed
cobija blanket
colchón mattress
cuarto or habitación room
escritorio desk

habitación doble double room
habitación simple/sencilla single room
habitación triple triple room
llave key
mosquitero mosquito net
sábanas sheets
seguro de puerta door lock
telecable cable tv
ventilador fan

TRAVEL TERMS

aduana customs
aeropuerto airport
avenida avenue
avión airplane
aviso warning
bus bus
calle street
cheques viajeros traveler's checks
correo mail, or post office
cuadra city block
dinero or plata money
embajada embassy
embarque boarding
entrada entrance

equipaje luggage
este east
frontera border
lancha or bote boat
norte north
occidente west
oeste west
oriente east
pasaporte passport
puerta de salida or puerta de empbarque boarding gate
salida exit
tarjeta de embarque boarding pass
vuelo flight

EMERGENCY TERMS

ambulancia ambulance
¡auxilio! help!
bomberos fire brigade
clínica clinic or hospital
doctor or médico doctor
emergencia emergency
enfermera nurse
enfermo/enferma sick

farmacia pharmacy
fuego or incendio fire
hospital hospital
ladrón thief
peligroso dangerous
policía police
¡váyase! go away

Index

Accommodations— Nicaragua